PROVENCE & THE FRENCH RIVIERA

Rick Steves & Steve Smith

2011

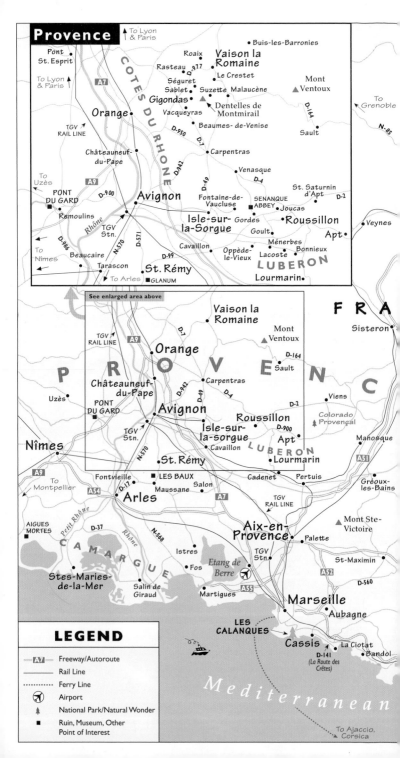

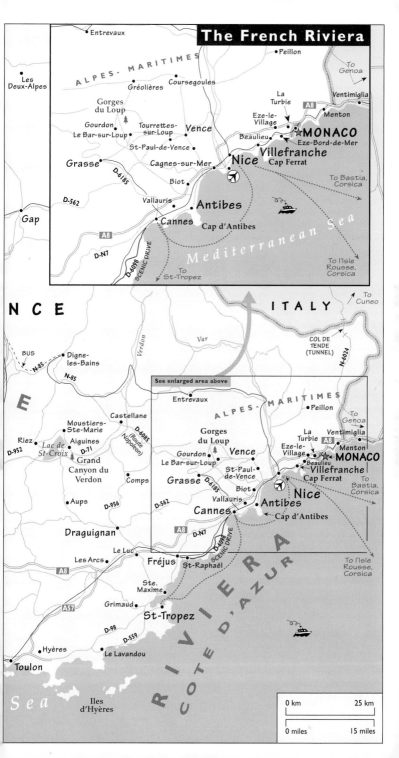

Rick Steves'

PROVENCE &
THE FRENCH RIVIERA

2011

Pont du Gard

Côtes du Rhône

Grand Canyon du Verdon

Avignon

Luberon

Arles

Monaco

Nîmes

Antibes

Camargue

Aix-en-Provence

Nice

Cassis

Marseille

DCH

AVALON
TRAVEL

CONTENTS

Introduction 1

  Planning 6

  Itinerary by Car 8

  Itinerary by Train/Bus 10

  Practicalities.................. 13

  Money 14

  Sightseeing................... 20

  Sleeping 21

  Eating....................... 31

  Traveling as a
    Temporary Local 39

  Back Door Travel
    Philosophy................. 40

Provence 41

▶**Arles** 60

  Sights....................... 65

  Sleeping 78

  Eating....................... 83

▶**Near Arles** 88

  Les Baux 89

  St. Rémy-de-Provence...... 97

  The Camargue............. 104

▶**Avignon** 109

  Sleeping 125

  Eating...................... 130

▶**Near Avignon**............. 135

  Nîmes 137

  Pont du Gard 149

  Uzès....................... 154

▶**Orange and the
Côtes du Rhône** 157

  Orange..................... 160

  Near Orange:
    Châteauneuf-du-Pape.... 165

  Vaison la Romaine......... 167

  The Best of the Côtes
    du Rhône Villages........ 175

  More Côtes
    du Rhône Drives 189

▶**Hill Towns of
the Luberon** 192

  Isle-sur-la-Sorgue......... 194

  The Heart of the Luberon .204

  More Luberon Towns ... 215

▶**Marseille, Cassis,
and Aix-en-Provence**..... 232

  Marseille................... 232

  Cassis 249

  Aix-en-Provence.......... 259

The French Riviera 277

▶ Nice 286
  Sights 297
  Sleeping 307
  Eating 316
▶ Welcome to the Riviera
  Walk 325
▶ Old Nice Walk 330
▶ Chagall Museum Tour 337
▶ Villefranche-sur-Mer,
  Cap Ferrat, and
  Eze-le-Village 346
  Villefranche-sur-Mer 346
  The Three Corniches 358
  Cap Ferrat 359
  Eze-le-Village 367
  La Trophée des Alpes 370
  Riviera Bus Tour from
    Nice to Monaco 372
▶ Monaco 376
  Near Monaco: Menton 390
▶ Antibes, Cannes,
  and St-Tropez 391
  Antibes 391
  Cannes 408
  St-Tropez 414

▶ Inland Riviera 421
  St-Paul-de-Vence 424
  Vence 426
  Grasse 431
  Le Grand Canyon
    du Verdon 435

Traveling with
Children 442

Shopping 447

France:
Past and Present 454

Appendix 463
  Tourist Information 463
  Communicating 464
  Transportation 474
  Resources 491
  Holidays and Festivals 496
  Conversions and Climate 498
  Essential Packing Checklist 501
  Hotel Reservation Form 502
  French Survival Phrases 503

Index 505
Map Index 517

Top Destinations in Provence & the French Riviera

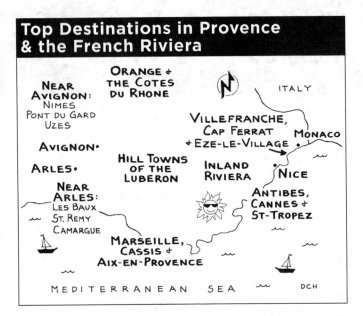

INTRODUCTION

Provence and the French Riviera are an intoxicating bouillabaisse of enjoyable cities, warm stone villages, Roman ruins, contemporary art, and breathtaking coastlines steaming with sunshine and stirred by the wind. There's something about the play of light in this region, where natural and man-made beauty mingle to dazzle the senses and nourish the soul. It all adds up to *une magnifique* vacation.

Provence and the Riviera stretch along France's southeast Mediterranean coast from the Camargue (south of Arles) to Monaco, and ramble north along the Rhône Valley into the Alps. The regions combined are about the same size as Massachusetts—you can take a train or drive from one end to the other in just three hours—yet they contain more sightseeing opportunities and let's-live-here villages than anywhere else in France. Marseille and Nice, the country's second- and fifth-largest cities, provide good transportation and an urban perspective to this otherwise laid-back region, where every day feels like a lazy Sunday.

In Provence, gnarled sycamores line the roads that twist their way through stone towns and between oceans of vineyards. France's Riviera is about the sea and money—it's populated by a yacht-happy crowd wondering where the next "scene" will be. And though Provence feels older and more *español* (with paella on menus and bullfights on Sundays), the Riviera feels downright Italian—with fresh-Parmesan-topped pasta and red-orange, pastel-colored buildings. For every Roman ruin in Provence, there's a modern-art museum in the Riviera. Provence is famous for its wines and wind, while the bikini and ravioli were invented on the Riviera. You can't go wrong.

This book covers the predictable biggies, from jet-setting beach resorts to remote canyons, but it also mixes in a healthy dose of

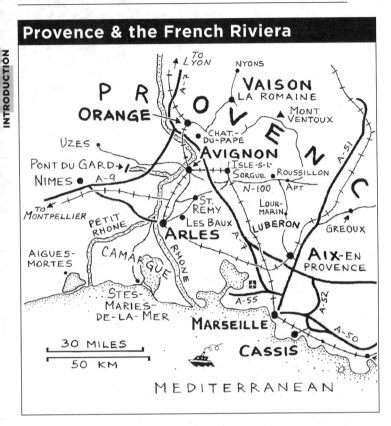

Provence & the French Riviera

Back Door intimacy. Along with Pont du Gard, Nice, and Avignon, we'll introduce you to our favorite villages and scenic walks. You'll sample delicious wineries and find yourself alone at overlooked Roman ruins. You'll marvel at ancient monuments, take a canoe trip down the meandering Sorgue River, and settle into a shaded café on a made-for-movies square. Claim your favorite beach to call home, and at day's end dive headfirst into a southern France sunset. You'll enjoy tasty-yet-affordable wines while feasting on a healthy cuisine heavy on olives, tomatoes, and spices. Just as important, you'll get on a first-name basis with many of our Provençal friends—hoteliers, restaurateurs, vintners, and lots more.

This book is selective, including only the most exciting sights and romantic villages. There are *beaucoup de* Provençal hill towns... but we cover only the most intriguing. And though there are scads of beach towns on the Riviera, we recommend our favorite three.

The best is, of course, only our opinion. But after spending more than half of our adult lives writing and lecturing about travel, guiding tours, and gaining an appreciation for all things

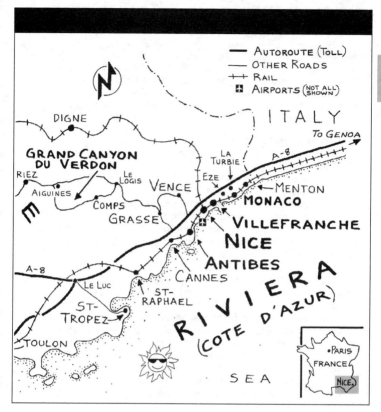

French, we've developed a sixth sense for what touches the traveler's imagination.

About This Book

Rick Steves' Provence & the French Riviera 2011 is a personal tour guide in your pocket. Better yet, it's actually two tour guides in your pocket: The co-author of this book is Steve Smith. Steve lived in France as a child and has been traveling to France—as a guide, a researcher, a homeowner, and a devout Francophile—every year since 1985. He has restored an old farmhouse in Burgundy and today keeps one foot on each side of the Atlantic. Together, Steve and I keep this book up-to-date and accurate (though for simplicity, from this point "we" will shed our respective egos and become "I").

This book consists of two obvious parts: Provence and the Riviera (although almost everything covered in this book is officially considered part of the "Provence–Alpes–Côte d'Azur region" by the French government). The Provence half highlights

INTRODUCTION

Key to This Book

Updates

This book is updated every year—but once you pin down Provence, it wiggles. For the latest, visit www.ricksteves.com /update, and for a valuable list of reports and experiences— good and bad—from fellow travelers, check www.ricksteves .com/feedback.

Abbreviations and Times

I use the following symbols and abbreviations in this book:
Sights are rated:

▲▲▲	Don't miss
▲▲	Try hard to see
▲	Worthwhile if you can make it
No rating	Worth knowing about

Tourist information offices are abbreviated as **TI,** and bathrooms are **WC**s. To categorize accommodations, I use a **Sleep Code** (described on page 25).

Like Europe, this book uses the **24-hour clock.** It's the same through 12:00 noon, then keep going: 13:00, 14:00, and so on. For anything over 12, subtract 12 and add p.m. (14:00 is 2:00 p.m.).

When giving **opening times,** I include both peak season and off-season hours if they differ. So, if a museum is listed as "May–Oct daily 9:00–16:00," it should be open from 9 a.m. until 4 p.m. from the first day of May until the last day of October (but expect exceptions).

For **transit** or **tour departures,** I first list the frequency, then the duration. So a train connection listed as "2/hour, 1.5 hours" departs twice each hour, and the journey lasts an hour and a half.

Arles and Avignon, and their day-trip destinations; the photogenic hill towns of the Côtes du Rhône and Luberon; and the coastal towns of Marseille and Cassis, and nearby Aix-en-Provence. On the high-rolling French Riviera, I cover the waterfront destinations of Nice, Villefranche-sur-Mer, Cap Ferrat, Monaco, Antibes, Cannes, and St-Tropez—plus the best of the inland hill towns and the truly grand Grand Canyon du Verdon.

The introductions to **Provence** and **The French Riviera** acquaint you with the history, cuisine, and wine of the places you'll be visiting, and give practical advice on what to see, how to get around, and lots more. Don't overlook the valuable tips in these chapters.

In the destination chapters, you'll find these sections:

Planning Your Time suggests a schedule, with thoughts on how best to use your limited time in each place.

Orientation includes specifics on public transportation, helpful hints, local tour options, easy-to-read maps, and tourist information.

Sights describes the top attractions and includes their cost and hours.

Self-guided walks help you explore these fascinating towns and places on foot: Avignon, Nîmes, Arles, Aix-en-Provence, Les Baux, Isle-sur-la-Sorgue, Roussillon, Monaco, Antibes, Villefranche-sur-Mer, and Cannes. (A few of the in-depth walks and tours get their own chapters: a stroll along Nice's promenade des Anglais, a walk through Old Nice, and a guided visit to the Chagall Museum.) I also include a few **self-guided driving tours,** allowing you to explore the Côtes du Rhône wine road, the Grand Canyon du Verdon, and inland hill towns of the Riviera with the knowledge of a local.

Sleeping describes my favorite hotels, from good-value deals to cushy splurges.

Eating serves up a range of options, from inexpensive take-out joints to fancier restaurants.

Connections outlines your options for traveling to destinations by train and bus, plus route tips for drivers.

The book also includes detailed chapters on these key topics:

Traveling with Children offers general tips and destination-specific advice, like kid-friendly hotels and restaurants. Both co-authors have kids (from 9 to 23 years old), and we've used our substantial experience traveling with children to improve this book. Our kids have greatly enriched our travels, and we hope the same will be true for you.

Shopping has suggestions for this region's best souvenirs and bargains. My longtime friendships with shopkeepers, local guides, and vintners have contributed greatly to the savvy shopping advice.

France: Past and Present gives you a quick overview of the country.

The **appendix** is a traveler's tool kit, with telephone tips, useful phone numbers, recommended books and films, a festival list, climate chart, handy packing checklist, hotel reservation form, and French survival phrases. I also provide detailed information on transportation for getting around the region by train, bus, or car.

Browse through this book and select your favorite sights. Then have a *fantastique* trip! Traveling like a temporary local, you'll get the absolute most out of every mile, minute, and euro. I'm happy that you'll be visiting the places I know and love, and meeting my favorite French people.

Planning

This section will help you get started on planning your trip—with advice on trip costs, when to go, and what you should know before you take off.

Travel Smart

Your trip to France is like a complex play—easier to follow and really appreciate on a second viewing. While no one does the same trip twice to gain that advantage, reading this book in its entirety before your trip accomplishes much the same thing.

Design an itinerary that enables you to visit museums and festivals (see page 496) on the right days. Note holidays, specifics on sights, and days when sights are closed. If you're using public transportation, read up on the tips for trains and buses (see pages 480 and 482 of the appendix). If you're renting a car, peruse my driving tips and study the examples of road signs (see page 485).

Be sure to mix intense and relaxed periods in your itinerary. To maximize rootedness, minimize one-night stands (I recommend three-night stands, where possible). Every trip—and every traveler—needs at least a few slack days (for picnics, laundry, people-watching, and so on). Pace yourself. Assume you will return.

Reread this book as you travel, and visit local tourist information offices. Upon arrival in a new town, lay the groundwork for a smooth departure; write down the schedule for the train or bus that you'll take when you leave. Use taxis in the big cities, bring a water bottle, and linger in the shade.

Get online at Internet cafés or at your hotel, and buy a phone card or carry a mobile phone. You can get tourist information, learn the latest on sights (special events, English tour schedules, etc.), book tickets and tours, make reservations, reconfirm hotels, research transportation connections, check weather, and keep in touch with your loved ones.

Connect with the culture. Cheer for your favorite bowler at a *pétanque* match, leave no chair unturned in your quest for the best café, find that perfect hill-town view, and make friends with a waiter. Slow down to appreciate the sincerity of your Provençal hosts, and be open to unexpected experiences. Ask questions—most locals are eager to point you in their idea of the right direction. Keep a notepad in your pocket for organizing your thoughts. Wear your money belt, and figure out how to estimate prices in dollars. Those who expect to travel smart, do.

Trip Costs

Five components make up your total trip cost: airfare, surface transportation, room and board, sightseeing and entertainment, and shopping and miscellany.

Airfare: Nice is the handiest airport for Provence and the Riviera (though Marseille is attracting more airlines every year). A basic round-trip flight from the US to Nice or Paris costs $800–1,600 (including taxes and fuel charges), depending on where you fly from and when (cheaper in winter). Smaller budget airlines provide bargain service—often more economical than train travel—from Paris and other European cities to places such as Marseille, Avignon, and Montpellier (see "Cheap Flights" on page 491 for details). If your trip covers a wide area, consider saving time and money in Europe by flying "open jaw" (into one city and out of another—e.g., into Nice and out of Paris).

Surface Transportation: Allow $30 per day per person for public transportation (trains, buses, and taxis), or $50 per day per person for a rental car (based on two people sharing) for rental fees, tolls, parking, gas, and insurance. Car rental and leases are cheapest if arranged from the US. Train passes only make sense if you are traveling to regions beyond Provence and the Riviera, as distances within this region are short, and point-to-point fares are reasonable. Railpasses are normally available only outside of Europe (see "Transportation" on page 474, for more details on car rental, rail trips, and bus travel).

Room and Board: You can thrive in Provence and the Riviera on $135 a day per person for room and board. A $135-a-day budget allows an average of $12 for breakfast, $18 for lunch, $40 for dinner with drinks, and $65 for lodging (based on two people splitting the cost of a $130 double room). That's definitely doable. Students and tightwads do it on $50 a day ($25 per bed, $25 for meals and snacks).

Sightseeing and Entertainment: Allow about $10 per major sight (Arles' Roman Arena-$8, Nice's Chagall Museum-$9, Avignon's Palace of the Popes-$13) around $6 for minor ones (e.g., climbing church towers), $25 for guided walks, and $35 for splurge experiences (e.g., bullfights or concerts). Arles and Avignon each offer a money-saving museum pass (details listed in this book)—and most of Nice's museums are free. An overall average of $20–25 a day for sightseeing and entertainment works for most people. Don't skimp here. After all, this is the driving force behind your trip—you came to sightsee, enjoy, and experience Provence and the French Riviera.

Shopping and Miscellany: Figure $5 per ice-cream cone, coffee, or soft drink. Shopping can vary in cost from nearly nothing to a small fortune (for tips on stretching your euros, see the Shopping chapter). Good budget travelers find that this category has little to do with assembling a trip full of lifelong and wonderful memories.

INTRODUCTION

Best Two-Week Trip of Provence & the French Riviera by Car

Day	Plan
1	Fly into Nice. Settle in at your hotel, then take a walk along the promenade des Anglais up to Castle Hill (see the Welcome to the Riviera Walk chapter). Sleep in or near Nice.
2	Start the morning with my self-guided tour of Old Nice (see the Old Nice Walk chapter). Take time to smell the *fougasse* and sample a *café*. Spend your afternoon at one or more of Nice's fine museums (see the Chagall Museum Tour chapter). Have dinner on the beach. Sleep in or near Nice.
3	Take the train or bus to nearby Villefranche-sur-Mer, explore, and have lunch. Consider my recommended seaside walks in Cap Ferrat, or the one-hour boat cruise from Nice's port. Everyone should spend the afternoon or evening in nearby Monaco. Sleep in or near Nice.
4	First thing in the morning, pick up your rental car in Nice. Drive north to Vence or Grasse (you choose), then continue on to the Gorges du Verdon and sleep in tiny Aiguines or Moustiers-Ste-Marie.
5	Continue west into the Luberon and explore the villages of *La Provence Profonde.* Stay in or near Roussillon.
6	Spend your day sampling hill towns in the Luberon. Taste a village market, then drive over the hills to the valley of the Côtes du Rhône. Sleep in or near Vaison la Romaine (Monday arrival is ideal because market day is Tuesday). If you're here from late June to late July, when the lavender blooms, the drive to Vaison la Romaine via Sault is a must.
7	Explore Vaison la Romaine's upper medieval village and lower Roman city. Set sail along the Côtes du Rhône wine road (following my self-guided driving tour) and visit a winery or wine cooperative. Tour little Le Crestet and take a walk above Gigondas. Sleep in or near Vaison la Romaine.
8	Start your day touring the Roman Theater in Orange and consider a quick stop in Châteauneuf-du-Pape. Continue south and set up in Avignon. In the afternoon, take my self-guided Avignon walks and enjoy dinner on one of the town's many atmospheric squares. Sleep in Avignon.
9	Relax in Avignon this morning, then divide the rest of your

Sightseeing Priorities

Depending on the length of your trip, here are my recommended priorities:

6 days: Arles and day trips to Pont du Gard and Les Baux, a night in a Côtes du Rhône village, and Nice with a day trip to Monaco

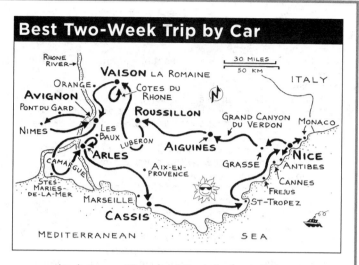

Best Two-Week Trip by Car

day between Nîmes and Pont du Gard. If the weather's good, bring your swimsuit and float on your back below the 2,000-year-old Pont du Gard. Sleep in Avignon.

10 Take a joyride through the Camargue (if it's summer, when flamingos are scarce and mosquitoes aren't, visit Les Baux this morning rather than tomorrow evening) and wind up in Arles (big market day on Saturday). Sleep in Arles.

11 Spend your day in Arles. Drive to Les Baux for dinner. Sleep in Arles.

12 Drive to Cassis and stop for lunch and a midday visit to Aix-en-Provence or Marseille (Marseille is dicier by car). Set up in Cassis and watch the sun set from the old port while you savor a bouillabaisse dinner. Sleep in Cassis.

13 Spend all day in Cassis enjoying *la vie douce.* Take a boat trip to the *calanques,* watch the *pétanque* balls fly, and end your day with a drive up Cap Canaille. Sleep in Cassis.

14 Drive to St-Tropez and spend your morning carousing along its old port (searching for Brigitte Bardot). In the afternoon, drive to Nice via the scenic detour from Fréjus to Cannes. Sleep in Nice.

15 Trip over.

   9 days, add: Avignon and Cassis
12 days, add: Luberon, Grand Canyon du Verdon, and Antibes
14 days, add: Nîmes, Marseille, Aix-en-Provence, and the
                     Camargue

For a day-by-day itinerary of a two-week trip, see this chapter's two recommended routes (by car, and by train and bus).

Best Two-Week Trip of Provence & the French Riviera by Train and Bus

Note that on Sundays, fewer trains run, and bus service often disappears.

Day Plan

1 Fly into Nice. Settle in at your hotel, then take a walk along the promenade des Anglais and up to Castle Hill (see the Welcome to the Riviera Walk chapter). Sleep in or near Nice.

2 Start the morning with my self-guided tour of Old Nice (see the Old Nice Walk chapter). Take time to smell the *fougasse* and sample *un café*. Spend your afternoon at one or more of Nice's fine museums (see the Chagall Museum Tour chapter). Have dinner on the beach. Sleep in or near Nice.

3 Take a train or the bus to nearby Villefranche-sur-Mer, explore, and have lunch. Consider my recommended sea-side walks in Cap Ferrat, or take the one-hour boat cruise from Nice's port. Everyone should spend the afternoon or evening in almost-neighboring Monaco. Sleep in or near Nice.

4 Take a bus north to Vence and St-Paul-de-Vence. Stop for a stroll and visit the Fondation Maeght and/or Matisse's Chapel of the Rosary. Or link Vence with Grasse by bus (skipping St-Paul-de-Vence to save time). Sleep in Vence or back in Nice.

5 Take a train from Nice to Isle-sur-la-Sorgue via Marseille (best to arrive on Sat or Wed and awaken the next morning for market day). Wander and explore the town. Consider a canoe ride down the crystal-clear Sorgue River. Sleep in Isle-sur-la-Sorgue.

6 Enjoy market day this morning, then take a train to Avignon. Take my self-guided Avignon walks this afternoon and enjoy dinner on one of Avignon's many atmospheric squares. Sleep in Avignon.

When to Go

With more than 300 days of sunshine per year, Provence and the Riviera enjoy France's sunniest weather. Spring and fall are best, with generally comfortable weather—though crowds can be a problem if you're not careful, particularly during holiday weekends and major events (May is worst—see the "Major Holidays and Weekends" sidebar on page 27). April can be damp, and any month can be windy.

Summer means festivals, lavender, steamy weather, long hours at sights, and longer lines of cars along the Riviera. Europeans vacation in July and August, jamming the Riviera, the Gorges du Verdon, and Ardèche (worst from mid-July through mid-Aug), but

7 Day-trip to Nîmes and the Pont du Gard aqueduct in the morning. If the weather's good, bring your swimsuit and float on your back below the 2,000-year-old Pont du Gard. Explore Avignon in the afternoon and spend the night there.

8 Take a morning bus to Vaison la Romaine (market day is Tue, so a Mon arrival is ideal). Set up in Vaison la Romaine for two nights. Explore Vaison la Romaine's upper medieval village and lower Roman city this afternoon.

9 Tour the wine villages near Vaison la Romaine. Take a mini-van tour of the wine road (see "Tours of Provence" on page 46), bike to Séguret and Gigondas, or hike to Le Crestet for lunch (taxi back). Check out Vaison la Romaine's wine cooperative. Sleep in Vaison la Romaine.

10 Take a morning bus to Orange, visit the theater, then hop a train to Arles (big market day on Sat) and explore the city this afternoon. Check into Arles for the next two nights.

11 Take a taxi (or, in summer, a bus) to Les Baux and have breakfast with a view. Return to Arles by taxi and spend your afternoon there; or take a taxi from Les Baux to St. Rémy-de-Provence, explore there, then catch a bus back to Arles.

12 Hop the train to Cassis. Take a boat trip to the *calanques,* watch the *pétanque* balls roll, and end your day with a taxi ride up Cap Canaille. Sleep in Cassis.

13 Take a train to Aix-en-Provence. Have lunch and take my self-guided walking tour of the city, then return home to Cassis and watch the sunset from the old port while you savor a bouillabaisse dinner. Sleep in Cassis.

14 Take the short train ride into Marseille (check your bag at the station), explore the city, then take a train back to Nice. Sleep in Nice.

15 Trip over.

leaving the rest of this region relatively calm. Though many French businesses close in August, the traveler hardly notices.

September brings the grape harvest, when small wineries are off-limits to taste-seeking travelers (for information on wine-tasting, see page 55). Late fall delivers beautiful foliage and a return to tranquility.

Although you can find mild, sunny weather in any season, Provence is famous for its bone-chilling temperatures when the wind blows (see page 59). Winter travel is OK in Nice and Avignon, but you'll find smaller cities and villages buttoned up tight. Sights and tourist-information offices keep shorter hours, and some tourist activities (such as English-language castle tours) vanish altogether. To get the latest weather forecast in English, dial 08 99 70 11 11, then press 1. Also see the climate chart in the appendix.

Thanks to Provence's temperate climate, fields of flowers greet the traveler much of the year:

May: Wild red poppies *(coquelicots)* sprout.

June: Lavender begins to bloom in the lower hills of Provence, generally during the last week of the month.

July: Lavender is in full swing in Provence, and sunflowers are awakening. Cities, towns, and villages everywhere overflow with carefully tended flowers.

August–September: Sunflowers flourish.

October: In the latter half of the month, the countryside glistens with fall colors (since most trees are deciduous). Vineyards go for the gold.

Know Before You Go

Your trip will more likely go smoothly if you plan ahead. Check this list of things to arrange while you're still at home.

You need a **passport**—but no visa or shots—to travel in France. You may be denied entry into certain European countries if your passport is due to expire within three to six months of your ticketed date of return. Get it renewed if you'll be cutting it close. It can take up to six weeks to get or renew a passport (for more on passports, see www.travel.state.gov). Pack a photocopy of your passport in your luggage in case the original is lost or stolen.

Check to see whether you'll be visiting France during any **holidays or festivals,** when rooms can cost more and get booked up quickly. (See "Major Holidays and Weekends" sidebar on page 27).

Call your **debit- and credit-card companies** to let them know the countries you'll be visiting, to ask about fees, and more (see page 16).

Do your homework if you want to buy **travel insurance.** Compare the cost of the insurance to the likelihood of your using it and your potential loss if something goes wrong. For more information, see www.ricksteves.com/insurance.

If you're bringing an MP3 player, you can download free information from **Rick Steves Audio Europe,** featuring hours of travel interviews and more (at www.ricksteves.com and on iTunes; for details, see page 492).

If you'll be **traveling with children,** read the list of pre-trip suggestions on page 444.

If you're planning on **renting a car** in France, you'll need your driver's license. An International Driving Permit is recommended (see page 483).

All **high-speed trains** in France require a seat reservation—book as early as possible, as these trains fill fast. If you're using a railpass, it's especially important to reserve early—there's a tight limit on seat reservations for passholders. If you're taking an overnight train (especially to international destinations), and you need a *couchette* (overnight bunk) or sleeper—and you *must* leave on a certain day—consider booking it in advance through a US agent (such as www.raileurope.com), even though it may cost more. (For more on train travel, see the appendix.)

Because **airline carry-on restrictions** are always changing, visit the Transportation Security Administration's website (www .tsa.gov/travelers) for an up-to-date list of what you can bring on the plane with you...and what you have to check.

Practicalities

Emergency and Medical Help: In France, dial 17 for police help or 15 for a medical emergency. If you get sick, do as the French do and go to a pharmacist for advice. Or ask at your hotel for help; they know of the nearest medical and emergency services.

Lost or Stolen Passport: To replace a passport, you'll need to go in person to a US embassy or consulate (see page 471). While not required, having a back-up form of ID—ideally a photocopy of your passport and driver's license—speeds up a replacement. For more info, see www.ricksteves.com/help.

Time Zones: France, like most of continental Europe, is generally six/nine hours ahead of the East/West Coasts of the US. The exceptions are the beginning and end of Daylight Saving Time: Europe "springs forward" the last Sunday in March (two weeks after most of North America) and "falls back" the last Sunday in October (one week before North America). For a handy online time converter, try www.timeanddate.com/worldclock.

Business Hours: You'll find much of rural France closed weekdays from noon to 14:00 (lunch is sacred). On Sunday, most businesses are closed (family is sacred), though some small stores such as *boulangeries* (bakeries) are open until noon, special events and weekly markets pop up, and museums are open all day (but public transportation options are fewer). On Monday, some businesses are closed until 14:00 and sometimes all day. Smaller towns often are quiet and downright boring on Sundays and Mondays, unless it's market day. Saturdays are virtually weekdays (without the rush hour).

Shopping: The Shopping chapter, near the end of this book, offers you tips on how to enjoy Provence's market days. For the nuts-and-bolts details on clothing-size conversions, see page 498 of the appendix. For customs regulations and VAT refunds (the tax refunded on large purchases made by non-EU residents), see page 18.

Watt's Up? Europe's electrical system is different from North America's in two ways: the shape of the plug (two round prongs) and the voltage of the current (220 volts instead of 110 volts). For your North American plug to work in Europe, you'll need an adapter, sold inexpensively at travel stores in the US. As for the voltage, most newer electronics or travel appliances (such as hair dryers, laptops, and battery chargers) automatically convert the voltage—if you see a range of voltages printed on the item or its plug (such as "110–220"), it'll work in Europe. Otherwise, you can buy a converter separately in the US (about $20), though these tend to be heavy and unreliable, and get really hot when in use. For small appliances that don't automatically convert voltage, I suggest going without or buying a cheap replacement in France. You can buy low-cost hair dryers and other small appliances at Darty and Monoprix stores, which you'll find in major cities (ask at your hotel for the closest branch).

Discounts: Discounts are not listed in this book. However, seniors (age 60 and over), youths under 18 or even 26, and students and teachers with proper identification cards (www.isic.org) can get discounts. Always ask. Some discounts are available only for EU citizens. To inquire about a senior discount, ask, *"Réduction troisième âge?"* (ray-dook-see-ohn twah-zee-ehm ahzh).

News: Americans keep in touch by reading the *International Herald Tribune* (published almost daily throughout Europe and online at www.iht.com). Other newsy sites are http://news.bbc.co.uk and www.europeantimes.com. Every Tuesday the European editions of *Time* and *Newsweek* hit the stands with articles of particular interest to travelers in Europe. Sports addicts can get their daily fix online or from *USA Today*. Many hotels have CNN and BBC News television channels.

Money

This section offers advice on how to pay for purchases on your trip (including getting cash from ATMs and paying with plastic), dealing with lost or stolen cards, VAT (sales tax) refunds, and tipping.

What to Bring

Bring both a credit card and a debit card. You'll use the debit card at cash machines (ATMs) to withdraw euros for most purchases, and the credit card to pay for larger items. Some travelers carry a third card as a backup, in case one gets demagnetized or eaten by a temperamental machine.

As an emergency backup, bring cash. One of your co-authors

Exchange Rate

1 euro (€) = about $1.25

To convert prices in euros to dollars, add about 25 percent: €20 = about $25, €50 = around $65. (Check www.oanda.com for the latest exchange rates.) Just like the dollar, the euro is broken down into 100 cents. You'll find coins ranging from 1 cent to 2 euros, and bills from 5 euros to 500 euros.

---

brings a few hundred dollars; the other brings a few hundred euros (in either case, denominations of 20 are best). Dollars are pricey to exchange in France at currency booths (banks won't take them), but euros are pricey to buy in the States. For travelers taking a France-only trip, the best solution could be to bring along a hundred dollars as a backup, and stock up on euros soon after you arrive in France. Regardless, skip traveler's checks—they're a waste of time (long waits at slow banks) and a waste of money in fees.

Cash

Cash is just as desirable in Europe as it is at home. Small European businesses (hotels, restaurants, and shops) prefer that you pay your bills with cash. Some vendors will charge you extra for using a credit card, and some won't take credit cards at all.

Throughout Europe, ATMs are the standard way for travelers to get cash. To withdraw money from an ATM—known as a *retrait* or *distributeur (de billets)*—you'll need a debit card (ideally with a Visa or MasterCard logo for maximum usability), plus a PIN code. Know your PIN code in numbers; there are only numbers—no letters—on European keypads. You could use a credit card for ATM transactions, but it's generally more expensive (because it's considered a "cash advance" rather than a "withdrawal"). For security, it's best to shield the keypad when entering your PIN at the ATM.

When using an ATM, taking out large sums of money can reduce the number of per-transaction bank fees you'll pay. If the machine refuses your request, try again and select a smaller amount (some cash machines limit the amount you can withdraw—don't take it personally). If that doesn't work, try a different machine. If the ATM gives you big bills, try to break them at a bank or larger store, because it's easier to pay for purchases at small businesses using smaller bills. Most ATMs in France are located outside of a bank. Try to use the ATM when the branch is open. If your card is eaten by a machine, you can immediately go inside for help.

To keep your cash safe, use a money belt—a pouch with a strap that you buckle around your waist like a belt and wear under your clothes. Pickpockets target tourists. A money belt provides peace of mind, allowing you to carry lots of cash safely. Don't waste time every few days tracking down a cash machine—withdraw a week's worth of money, stuff it in your money belt, and travel!

Credit and Debit Cards

For purchases, Visa and MasterCard are more commonly accepted than American Express. And though you can use either a credit card or a debit card for most transactions, credit cards offer a greater degree of fraud protection (because debit cards draw funds directly from your account).

Just like at home, credit or debit cards are accepted by larger hotels, restaurants, and shops. I typically use my credit card only in a few specific situations: to book hotel reservations by phone, to make major purchases (such as car rentals, plane tickets, and long hotel stays), and to pay for things near the end of my trip (to avoid another visit to the ATM).

Ask Your Credit- or Debit-Card Company: Before your trip, contact the company that issued your debit or credit cards.

• Confirm your card will work overseas, and alert them that you'll be using it in Europe; otherwise, they may deny transactions if they perceive unusual spending patterns.

• Ask for the specifics on transaction **fees.** When you use your credit or debit card—either for purchases or ATM withdrawals—you'll often be charged additional "international transaction" fees of up to 3 percent (1 percent is normal) plus $5 per transaction. Some banks have agreements with European partners that reduce or eliminate the transaction fee. For example, Bank of America debit-card holders can use French Paribas-BNP ATMs without being charged the transaction fee (but they still pay a 1 percent international fee). If your fees are too high, consider getting a card just for your trip: Capital One (www.capitalone.com) and most credit unions have low-to-no international fees.

• If you plan to withdraw cash from ATMs, confirm your daily **withdrawal limit** (€300 is usually the maximum). Some travelers prefer a high limit that allows them to take out more cash at each ATM stop, while others prefer to set a lower limit in case their card is stolen.

• Ask for your credit card's **PIN** in case you encounter Europe's "chip-and-PIN" system.

Chip and PIN: If your card is declined for a purchase in Europe, it may be because of chip and PIN, which requires card-holders to punch in a PIN instead of signing a receipt. Much of Europe, including France, Great Britain, Ireland, the Netherlands, and Scandinavia, is adopting this system. Chip and PIN is used by some merchants, and also at automated payment machines—such as those at train and subway stations, toll roads, parking garages, luggage lockers, bike-rental kiosks, and self-serve pumps at gas stations. If you're prompted to enter your PIN (but don't know it), ask if the cashier can print a receipt for you to sign instead, or just pay cash. If you're dealing with an automated machine that won't take your card, look for a cashier nearby who can make your card work. The easiest solution is to carry sufficient cash.

Dynamic Currency Conversion: If merchants offer to convert your purchase price into dollars (called dynamic currency conversion, or DCC), refuse this "service." You'll pay even more in fees for the expensive convenience of seeing your charge in dollars.

Damage Control for Lost Cards

If you lose your credit, debit, or ATM card, you can stop people from using it by reporting the loss immediately to the respective global customer-assistance centers. Call these 24-hour US numbers collect: Visa (410/581-9994), MasterCard (636/722-7111), and American Express (623/492-8427). For another option (with the same results), you can call these toll-free numbers in France: Visa (08 00 90 11 79) and MasterCard (08 00 90 13 87). American Express has a Paris office, but the call isn't free (01 47 77 70 00, greeting is in French only, dial 1 to speak with someone in English). Diners Club has offices in the US (303/799-1504, call collect) and Paris (08 10 31 41 59).

At a minimum, you'll need to know the name of the financial institution that issued you the card, along with the type of card (classic, platinum, or whatever). Providing the following information will allow for a quicker cancellation of your missing card: full card number, whether you are the primary or secondary cardholder, the cardholder's name exactly as printed on the card, billing address, home phone number, circumstances of the loss or theft, and identification verification (your birth date, your mother's maiden name, or your Social Security number—memorize this, don't carry a copy). If you are the secondary cardholder, you'll also need to provide the primary cardholder's identification-verification details. You can generally receive a temporary card within two or three business days in Europe.

If you report your card lost or stolen promptly, you typically won't be responsible for any unauthorized transactions on your account, although many banks charge a liability fee of $50.

Tipping

Tipping *(donner un pourboire)* in France isn't as automatic and generous as it is in the US, but for special service, tips are appreciated, if not expected. As in the US, the proper amount depends on your resources, tipping philosophy, and the circumstances, but some general guidelines apply.

Restaurants: At cafés and restaurants, a 12–15 percent service charge is always included in the bill *(service compris)*, and most French never tip (credit-card receipts don't even have space to add a tip). However, if you feel the service was *exceptional*, it's fine to tip up to 5 percent. When you hand your payment plus a tip to your waiter, you can say, *"C'est bon"* (say bohn), meaning, "It's good" (and you don't want any change back). Never feel guilty if you don't leave a tip.

Taxis: To tip the cabbie, round up. For a typical ride, round up to the next euro on the fare (for a €13 fare, give €14); for a long ride, round to the nearest €10 (for a €75 fare, give €80). If the cabbie hauls your bags and zips you to the airport to help you catch your flight, you might want to toss in a little more. But if you feel like you're being driven in circles or otherwise ripped off, skip the tip.

Special Services: It's thoughtful to tip a couple of euros to someone who shows you a special sight and who is paid in no other way. Tour guides at sights sometimes hold out their hands for tips (€1–2) after they give their spiel. If I've already paid for the tour, I don't tip extra, unless they've really impressed me. At hotels, if you let the porter carry your luggage, it's polite to give them a euro for each bag (another reason to pack light). I don't tip the maid, but if you do, you can leave a euro per overnight at the end of your stay.

In general, if someone in the service industry does a super job for you, a small tip (the equivalent of a euro or two) is appropriate, but not required.

When in doubt, ask. If you're not sure whether (or how much) to tip for a service, ask your hotelier or the tourist information office—they'll fill you in on how it's done on their turf.

Getting a VAT Refund

Wrapped into the purchase price of your French souvenirs is a Value-Added Tax (VAT) of about 19.6 percent. You're entitled to get most of that tax back if you purchase more than €175 (about $220) worth of goods at a store that participates in the VAT-refund scheme. Getting your refund is usually straightforward and, if you buy a substantial amount of souvenirs, well worth the hassle. If you're lucky, the merchant will subtract the tax when you make your purchase. (This is more likely to occur if the store ships the goods to your home.) Otherwise, you'll need to:

Get the paperwork. Have the merchant completely fill out the necessary refund document, *Bordereau de Vente a l'Exportation*, also called a "cheque." You'll have to present your passport at the store.

Get your stamp at the border or airport. Process your cheque(s) at your last stop in the EU (e.g., at the airport) with the customs agent who deals with VAT refunds. It's best to keep your purchases in your carry-on for viewing, but if they're too large or dangerous (such as knives) to carry on, track down the proper customs agent to inspect them before you check your bag. You're not supposed to use your purchased goods before you leave. If you show up at customs wearing your chic new French ensemble, officials might look the other way—or deny you a refund.

Collect your refund. You'll need to return your stamped document to the retailer or its representative. Many merchants work with a service, such as Global Refund (www.globalrefund.com) or Premier Tax Free (www.premiertaxfree.com), which have offices at major airports, ports, or border crossings. These services, which extract a 4 percent fee, can refund your money immediately in your currency of choice or credit your card (within two billing cycles). If the retailer handles VAT refunds directly, it's up to you to contact the merchant for your refund. Or you can mail the documents from your point of departure (using a stamped, addressed envelope you've prepared or one that's been provided by the merchant). You'll then have to wait—it can take months.

Customs for American Shoppers

You are allowed to take home $800 worth of items per person duty-free, once every 30 days. The next $1,000 is taxed at a flat 3 percent. After that, you pay the individual item's duty rate. You can also bring in duty-free a liter of alcohol (slightly more than a standard-size bottle of wine; you must be at least 21), 200 cigarettes, and up to 100 non-Cuban cigars.

As for food, you can take home vacuum-packed cheeses; dried herbs, spices, or mushrooms; and canned fruits or vegetables, including jams and vegetable spreads. Baked goods, candy, chocolate, oil, vinegar, mustard, and honey are OK. Fresh fruits or vegetables (even that banana from your airplane breakfast) are not permitted. Meats are generally not allowed, though canned pâtés are permitted if made from geese, duck, or pork. Just because a duty-free shop in an airport sells a food product, that doesn't mean it will automatically pass US customs. Be prepared to lose your investment.

Note that you'll need to carefully pack any bottles of wine, jam, honey, oil, and other liquid-containing items in your checked luggage, due to the three-ounce limit on liquids in carry-on baggage. To check customs rules and duty rates before you go, visit www.cbp.gov, and click on "Travel," then "Know Before You Go."

Sightseeing

Sightseeing can be hard work. Use these tips to make your visits to Provence's and the Riviera's finest sights meaningful, fun, efficient, and painless.

Plan Ahead

Set up an itinerary that allows you to fit in all your must-see sights. For a one-stop look at opening hours in the bigger cities, see the "At a Glance" sidebars for Arles, Avignon, Marseille, Nice, and Monaco. Most sights keep stable hours, but you can easily confirm the latest by checking their website or asking the local TI.

If you'll be visiting during a holiday, find out whether a particular sight will be open by phoning ahead or checking its website. And don't put off visiting a must-see sight—you never know when a place will close unexpectedly for a holiday, strike, or restoration.

When possible, visit major sights in the morning (when your energy is best) and save other activities for the afternoon. Hit a sight's highlights first, then see the rest if you have the stamina and time.

Going at the right time helps avoid crowds and traffic jams. This book offers tips on specific sights. Ideally, visit the following sights on weekdays, and arrive early or late: Les Baux, Pont du Gard, Séguret, Roussillon, Fontaine de Vaucluse, Nice's Chagall and Antibes' Picasso museums, St-Paul-de-Vence, Eze-le-Village, and St-Tropez. The *calanques* near Cassis are best early, but not late.

Read ahead. To get the most out of the self-guided tours and sight descriptions in this book, read them before you visit. Several cities offer sightseeing passes that are worthwhile values for serious sightseers; plan ahead.

At Sights

Here's what you can typically expect:

Some important sights may have metal detectors or conduct bag searches that will slow your entry; others require you to check daypacks and coats. They'll be kept safely. If you have something you can't bear to part with, stash it in a pocket or purse. To avoid checking a small backpack, carry it under your arm like a purse as you enter. From a guard's point of view, a backpack is generally a problem while a purse is not. If you check a bag, the attendant may ask you (in French) if it contains anything of value—camera, phone, money, passport—because these cannot be checked.

Flash photography is banned at most major sights, but taking pictures without a flash is usually OK. Look for signs or ask. Flashes damage oil paintings and distract others in the room.

Even without a flash, a handheld camera will take a decent picture (or you can buy postcards or posters at the museum bookstore). If photos are permitted, video cameras are generally OK, too.

Some museums may have special exhibits in addition to their permanent collection. Some exhibits are included in the entry price; others come at an extra cost (which you may have to pay even if you don't want to see the exhibit).

Many sights rent audioguides, which generally offer useful recorded descriptions in English (about €6, sometimes included with admission). If you bring along your own pair of headphones and a Y-jack, you can sometimes share one audioguide with your travel partner and save money. Guided tours in English are most likely to be offered during peak season (around €8) and range widely in quality. Some sights also run short films featuring their highlights and history. These are generally well worth your time. I make it standard operating procedure to ask when I arrive at a sight if there is a film in English.

Expect changes—artwork can be on tour, on loan, out sick, or shifted at the whim of the curator. To adapt, pick up any available free floor plans as you enter. Ask the museum staff if you can't find a particular painting. Say the title or artist's name, or point to the photograph in this book, and ask for its location by saying, *"Où est?"* (oo ay).

Important sights often have an on-site café or cafeteria (usually a good place to rest and have a snack or light meal). The WCs at many sights are usually free and nearly always clean (it's smart to carry tissues in case a WC runs out).

Many places sell postcards and guidebooks that highlight their attractions. Before you leave, scan the postcards and thumb through the biggest guidebook (or skim its index) to be sure you haven't overlooked something that you'd like to see.

Most sights stop admitting people 30–60 minutes before closing time, and some rooms close early (generally about 45 minutes before the actual closing time). Guards usher people out, so don't save the best for last.

Every sight or museum offers more than what is covered in this book. Use the information in this book as an introduction—not the final word.

Sleeping

Accommodations in Provence and the Riviera are a good value and generally easy to find. Choose from one- to four-star hotels (two stars is my mainstay), bed-and-breakfasts (*chambres d'hôte*, usually cheaper than hotels), hostels, campgrounds, and even homes (*gîtes*, rented by the week). I like hotels and B&Bs that are clean, central, friendly, a good value, run with a respect for French traditions, and small enough to have a hands-on owner and stable staff. Four of these six virtues means it's a keeper.

For tips on making reservations, see page 29.

Types of Accommodations

Hotels

In this book, the price for a double room will range from €40 (very simple, toilet and shower down the hall) to €300-plus (grand lobbies, maximum plumbing, and the works), with most clustering at around €80–110 (with private bathrooms).

The French have a simple hotel rating system based on amenities and rated by stars (indicated in this book by asterisks, from * through ****). One star is modest, two has most of the comforts, and three is generally a two-star with a fancier lobby and more elaborately designed rooms. Four stars offer more luxury than you usually have time to appreciate. Two- and three-star hotels are required to have an English-speaking staff, though virtually all hotels I recommend have someone who speaks English (unless I note otherwise in the listing).

Generally, the number of stars does not usually reflect room size or guarantee quality. Some two-star hotels are better than many three-star hotels. One- and two-star hotels are inexpensive, but some three-star (and even a few four-star hotels) offer good value, justifying the extra cost. Unclassified hotels (no stars) can be bargains or depressing dumps.

Most hotels have lots of doubles and a few singles, triples, and quads. Traveling alone can be expensive, as singles are usually doubles used by one person—so they cost about the same as a double. Room prices vary within each hotel depending on size, and whether the room has a bath or shower, and twin beds or a double bed (tubs and twins cost more than showers and double beds). A triple is often the same as a double room, with a double or queen-size bed plus a sliver-size single. Quad rooms usually have two double beds. Hotels cannot legally allow more in the room than what's shown on their price list. Modern hotels generally have a few family-friendly rooms that open to each other *(chambres communiquantes)*.

Given the economic downturn, hoteliers are willing and eager to make a deal. I'd suggest emailing several hotels to ask for their best price. Comparison-shop and make your choice. As you look over the listings, you'll notice that some hotels promise special prices to my readers who book direct (without using a room-finding service or hotel-booking website, which take a commission). To get these rates, mention this book when you reserve, then show the book upon arrival.

Types of Rooms

Study the price list on the hotel's website or posted at the desk, so you know your options. Receptionists often don't mention the cheaper rooms—they assume you want a private bathroom or a bigger room. Here are the types of rooms and beds:

une chambre sans douche et WC	room without a private shower or toilet (uncommon these days)
une chambre avec cabinet de toilette	room with a toilet but no shower (some hotels charge for down-the-hall showers)
une chambre avec bain et WC	room with private bathtub and toilet
une chambre avec douche et WC	room with private shower and toilet
chambres communiquantes	connecting rooms (ideal for families)
un grand lit	double bed (55 inches wide)
deux petits lits	twin beds (30–36 inches wide)
un lit single	a true single bed
un lit de cent-soixante	queen-size bed (literally 160 centimeters, or 63 inches wide)
le king size	a king-size bed (usually two twins pushed together)
un lit pliant	folding bed
un bérceau	baby crib
un lit d'enfant	child's bed

In general, prices can soften up if you do any of the following: offer to pay cash, stay at least three nights, or mention this book. You can also try asking for a cheaper room or a discount. To save money off-season, consider arriving without a reservation and dropping in at the last minute.

Hotels in France must charge a daily tax *(taxe du séjour)* of about €1–2 per person per day. Some hotels include it in the price list, but most add it to your bill.

You can save as much as €25 by finding the rare room without a private shower or toilet. A room with a bathtub usually costs more than a room with a shower (and generally is larger). Hotels often have more rooms with tubs than showers and are inclined to give you a room with a tub (which the French prefer).

A double bed is usually cheaper than twins, though rooms with twin beds tend to be larger. Many hotels have queen-size beds (a bed that's 63 inches wide—most doubles are 55 inches).

Keep Cool

If you're visiting southern France in the summer, the extra expense of an air-conditioned room can be money well spent. Most hotel rooms with air-conditioners come with a control stick (like a TV remote) that generally has the same symbols and features: fan icon (click to toggle through wind power, from light to gale); louver icon (choose steady airflow or waves); snowflake and sunshine icons (cold air or heat, depending on season); clock ("O" setting: run X hours before turning off; "I" setting: wait X hours to start); and the temperature control (20 or 21 degrees Celsius is comfortable; also see the thermometer diagram on page 499).

To learn if a hotel has queen-size beds, ask, *"Avez-vous des lits de cent-soixante?"* (ah-vay-voo day lee duh sahn-swah-sahnt). Some hotels push two twins together under king-size sheets and blankets to make *le king size*.

If you prefer a double bed (instead of twins) and a shower (instead of a tub), you need to ask for it—and you can save up to €20. If you'll take either twins or a double, ask generically for *une chambre pour deux* (room for two) to avoid being needlessly turned away.

Hotel lobbies, halls, and breakfast rooms are off-limits to smokers, though they can light up in their rooms. Still, I rarely smell any smoke in the hundreds of rooms I check each year. Some hotels have non-smoking rooms or floors—ask about them if this is important to you. If your room smells of smoke, ask for another one.

Most hotels offer some kind of breakfast, but it's rarely included in the room rates. The price of breakfast correlates with the price of the room: The more expensive the room, the more expensive the breakfast. This per-person charge can add up, particularly for families, so beware. While hotels hope that you'll buy their breakfast, it's optional unless otherwise noted (for more on breakfast, see "Eating," later in this chapter).

Some hotels, especially in coastal resort towns, strongly encourage their peak-season guests to take *demi-pension* (half-pension)—that is, breakfast and either lunch or dinner. By law, they can't require you to take half-pension unless you are staying three or more nights, but, in practice, many do during summer. And though the food is usually good, it limits your ability to shop around. I've indicated where I think *demi-pension* is a good value.

Most hotels rooms have a TV and phone, and Internet access (usually Wi-Fi) is increasingly common. To turn on your TV, press

Sleep Code

(€1 = about $1.25, country code: 33)

To help you sort easily through these listings, I've divided the rooms into three categories based on the price for a standard double room with bath:

$$$	**Higher Priced**
$$	**Moderately Priced**
$	**Lower Priced**

I always rate hostels as $, whether or not they have double rooms, because they have the cheapest beds in town.

Prices can change without notice; verify the hotel's current rates online or by email. For other updates, see www .ricksteves.com/update.

To give you maximum information in a minimum of space, I use the following code to describe the accommodations. Prices listed are per room, not per person. When a price range is given for a type of room (such as double rooms listing for €100–130), it means the price fluctuates with the season, size of room, or length of stay.

- **S** = Single room (or price for one person in a double).
- **D** = Double or twin.
- **T** = Triple (generally a double bed with a single).
- **Q** = Quad (usually two double beds).
- **b** = Private bathroom with toilet and shower or tub.
- **s** = Private shower or tub only (the toilet is down the hall).
- ***** = French hotel rating system, ranging from zero to four stars.

According to this code, a couple staying at a "Db-€90" hotel would pay a total of €90 (about $115) for a double room with a private bathroom. You can assume a hotel takes credit cards unless you see "cash only" in the listing. Unless otherwise noted, hotel staff speak basic English, and breakfast is not included (but is usually optional).

If I list "Internet access," there's a public terminal in the lobby for guests to use. If I mention "Wi-Fi", you can generally access it in your room (usually for free), but only if you have your own laptop.

the channel-up or channel-down button on the remote. If it still doesn't work, see if there's a power button on the TV itself, then press the up or down button again.

Towels aren't routinely replaced every day. Hang up your towel to dry. Extra pillows and blankets are often in the closet or available on request. To get a pillow, ask for *"Un oreiller, s'il vous plaît"* (un oh-ray-yay, see voo play).

Hoteliers can be a great help and source of advice. Most know their city well, and can assist you with everything from public transit and airport connections to finding a good restaurant, the nearest Internet café (*café internet,* kah-fay an-ter-net), or a self-service launderette (*laverie automatique,* lah-vay-ree oh-to-mah-teek).

Even at the best hotels, mechanical breakdowns occur: air-conditioning malfunctions, sinks leak, hot water turns cold, and toilets gurgle and smell. Report your concerns clearly and calmly at the front desk. For more complicated problems, don't expect instant results.

If you suspect night noise will be a problem, ask for a quiet room in the back or on an upper floor. To guard against theft in your room, keep valuables out of sight. Some rooms come with a safe, and other hotels have safes at the front desk. Use them if you're concerned.

Checkout can pose problems if surprise charges pop up on your bill. If you settle up your bill the night before you leave, you'll have time to discuss and address any points of contention (before 19:00, when the night shift usually arrives).

Some hoteliers will ask you to sign their *Livre d'Or* (literally "Golden Book," for client comments). They take this seriously and enjoy reading your remarks.

Modern Hotel Chains: France is littered with sterile, ultra-modern hotels, usually located on cheap land just outside of town, providing drivers with low-stress accommodations. The antiseptically clean and cheap Formule 1 and ETAP chains (about €40–50/room for up to three people), the more attractive Ibis hotels (€80–100 for a double), and the cushier Mercure and Novotel hotels (€110–170 for a double) are all run by the same company, Accor (www.accorhotels.com). Though far from quaint, these can be a good value (particularly if you find deals on their website), and some are centrally located. A smaller chain, Kyriad, offers good prices and quality (France tel. 08 25 00 30 03, overseas tel. 33 1 64 62 46 46—push 1 to make a reservation, www.kyriad.com; these telephone numbers also work for eight affiliated chains, including Clarine, Climat de France, and Campanile). For a long listing of various hotels throughout France, see www.france.com.

Bed & Breakfasts

B&Bs (*Chambres d'hôte,* abbreviated "CH") generally are found in smaller towns and rural areas. They're a great deal, offering double the cultural intimacy for much less than most hotel rooms. While you may lose some hotel conveniences—such as lounges, in-room phones, daily bed-sheet changes, and credit-card payments—I happily make the trade-off for the personal touch and lower rates.

Major Holidays and Weekends

Popular places are even busier on weekends...and inundated on three-day weekends. Holiday weekends can make towns, trains, roads, and hotels more crowded than in summer; you'll be competing with locals for seats on planes and trains, or for lanes on the autoroute. Book your accommodations and train trips well in advance if you'll be traveling during busy times.

In 2011, be ready for crowds during these holiday periods: Easter weekend (April 22-25 and the week on either side; Easter Monday is a holiday, too); Ascension weekend (June 2-5); Pentecost weekend (June 10-13; Pentecost Monday is a holiday too); Bastille Day (July 14) and the week during which it falls; and the winter holidays (Dec 17-Jan 2). Note that Christmas week is quieter than the week of New Year's. Two major holidays, Labor Day (May 1) and WWII Victory Day (May 8), fall on Sundays in 2011, which should make them unusually quiet. For more information, check the list of festivals and full list of holidays near the end of the appendix.

You'll find B&Bs in this book and through local tourist offices often listed by the owner's family name. It's always OK to ask to see the room before you commit. And though some CHs post small *Chambres* or *Chambres d'hôte* signs in their front windows, many are found only through the local tourist office.

I recommend reliable CHs that offer a good value and/or unique experience (such as CHs in renovated mills, châteaux, and wine *domaines*). While *chambres d'hôte* have their own star-rating system, it doesn't correspond to the hotels' rating system. So, to avoid confusion, I haven't listed these stars for CHs. But most of my recommended CHs have private in-room bathrooms, and some have common rooms with refrigerators. Doubles with breakfast generally cost €55-75 (breakfast may or may not be included—ask). *Tables d'hôte* are CHs that offer an optional, reasonably priced, home-cooked dinner (usually a fine value, must be requested in advance). And though your hosts may not speak English, they will almost always be enthusiastic and pleasant.

Hostels

You'll pay about €20 per bed to stay at a hostel *(auberge de jeunesse)*. People of any age are welcome if they don't mind dorm-style accommodations or meeting other travelers. Cheap meals are sometimes offered, and kitchen facilities may be available. Expect youth groups in spring, crowds in the summer, snoring, and great variability in quality from one hostel to the next. Family and private rooms may available on request.

There are two basic types of hostels: official and independent. **Official hostels** belong to the same parent organization, Hostelling International. They adhere to various rules (such as a 17:00 check-in, lockout during the day, and a curfew at night). If you plan to spend at least six nights at official HI hostels, buy a membership card before you go ($28/year, www.hihostels.com); nonmembers pay an extra $5 per night.

Independent hostels tend to be more easygoing and colorful, but not as reliably clean or organized as official hostels. Independent hostels don't require membership cards or charge extra for nonmembers, and generally have fewer rules. Various organizations promote independent hostels, including www.hostelworld.com, www.hostelz.com, www.hostelseurope.com, and www.hostels.com.

Camping

In Europe, camping is more of a social than an environmental experience. It's a great way for American travelers to make European friends. Camping costs about €18 per campsite per night, and almost every destination recommended in this book has a campground within a reasonable walk or bus ride from the town center and train station. A tent and sleeping bag are all you need. Many campgrounds have small grocery stores and washing machines, and some even come with cafés and miniature golf. Local TIs have camping information. You'll find more detailed information in the annually updated *Michelin Camping France*, available in the United States and at most French bookstores.

Gîtes and Apartments

Throughout France you can find reasonably priced rental homes, and nowhere are there more options than in Provence and the Riviera. Because this region is so small, you could rent one home in Provence and one in the Riviera, and day-trip to most of the sights described in this book.

Gîtes (pronounced "zheet") are country homes (usually urbanites' second homes) that the government rents out to visitors who want a week in the countryside (the homes are rented for at least a week at a time, from Saturday to Saturday). The objective of the *gîte* program was to save characteristic rural homes from abandonment and to make it easy and affordable for families to enjoy the French countryside. The government offers subsidies to renovate such homes, then coordinates rentals to make it financially feasible for the owner. Today, France has more than 9,000 *gîtes*. One of your co-authors restored a farmhouse a few hours north of Provence, and even though he and his wife are American, they received the same assistance that French owners get.

Gîtes are best for drivers (they're usually rural, with little public-transport access) and ideal for families and small groups (since they can sleep many for the same price). Homes range in comfort from simple cottages and farmhouses to restored châteaux. Most have at least two bedrooms, a kitchen, a living room, and a bathroom or two—but no sheets or linens (though you can usually rent them for extra). Like hotels, all *gîtes* are rated for comfort from one to four (using ears of corn—*épis*—rather than stars). Two or three *épis* are generally sufficient quality, but I'd lean toward three for more comfort. Prices generally range from €400–1,300 per week, depending on house size and amenities such as pools. For more information on *gîtes* in Provence, visit www.provence-guide.com, www.gites-de-france.com/gites, or www.gite.com.

Apartments, less common than *gîtes,* are available in cities and in towns along the Riviera (one-week minimum rentals). Avignon, Aix-en-Provence, Nice, and other Riviera towns have the biggest selection. It's usually more expensive to stay in an apartment than in a *gîte.*

You'll find homes and apartments for rent through TIs and on the Internet. Here are two good independent sources to consider: **France Homestyle** is run by Claudette, a service-oriented French woman from Seattle who handpicks every home and apartment she lists (US tel. 206/325-0132, www.francehomestyle.com, info @francehomestyle.com). Or try **Ville et Village,** which has a bigger selection of higher-end places (US tel. 510/559-8080, www .villeetvillage.com, rentals@villeetvillage.com).

Phoning

To call France from the US or Canada, dial 011-33 and then the local number—without the initial 0. (The 011 is our international access code, and 33 is France's country code.) If calling France from another European country, dial 00-33-local number—without the initial 0. (The 00 is Europe's international access code.) To make calls within France, simply dial the local number. For more tips on calling, see page 465.

Making Reservations

Given the quality of the accommodations I've found for this book, I recommend that you reserve your rooms in advance, particularly if you'll be traveling during peak season. Book several months ahead, or as soon as you've pinned down your travel dates. Note that some national holidays merit your making reservations far in advance (see "Major Holidays and Weekends" sidebar). Just like at home, holidays that fall on a Monday, Thursday, or Friday can turn the weekend into a long holiday, so book the entire weekend well in advance.

Requesting a Reservation: To reserve, contact hotels directly by email, phone, or fax. Email is the clearest, most economical way to make a reservation. Or you can go straight to the hotel website; many have secure online reservation forms and can instantly inform you of availability and any special deals. But be sure you use the hotel's official site and not a booking agency's site—otherwise you may pay higher rates than you should. If you're phoning from the US, be mindful of time zones (see page 13). Most hotels listed are accustomed to guests who speak only English.

The hotelier wants to know these key pieces of information (also included in the sample request form in the appendix:

- number and type of rooms
- number of nights
- date of arrival
- date of departure
- any special needs (e.g., bathroom in the room or down the hall, twin beds vs. double bed, air-conditioning, quiet, view, ground floor, etc.)

When you request a room, use the European style for writing dates: day/month/year. For example, for a two-night stay in July, I would request: "1 double room for 2 nights, arrive 16/07/11, depart 18/07/11." (Consider carefully how long you'll stay; don't just assume you can tack on extra days once you arrive.) Mention any discounts offered (for Rick Steves readers or otherwise) when you make the reservation. If you don't get a reply to your email or fax, it usually means the hotel is already fully booked (but you can try sending the message again, or call to follow up).

Confirming a Reservation: If the hotel's response includes its room availability and rates, it's not a confirmation. You must tell them that you want that room at the given rate. Most hoteliers will request your credit-card number for a one-night deposit to hold the room. While you can email your credit-card information (I do), it's safer to share that personal info by phone call, fax, two successive emails, or secure online reservation form (if the hotel has one on its website).

Canceling a Reservation: If you must cancel your reservation, it's courteous to do so with as much advance notice as possible—at least three days. Simply make a quick phone call or send an email. Family-run hotels and *chambres d'hôte* lose money if they turn away customers while holding a room for someone who doesn't show up. Understandably, many hotels bill no-shows for one night.

Cancellation policies can be strict: Some hotels require seven days' notice, while most want three days; otherwise, you might lose a deposit. Or you might be billed for the entire visit if you leave early. Internet deals may require prepayment, with no refunds for cancellations. If concerned, ask about cancellation policies before you book.

If canceling by email, request confirmation that your cancellation was received to avoid being accidentally billed.

Reconfirm Your Reservation: Always call to reconfirm your room reservation a day or two in advance from the road. Smaller hotels and *chambres d'hôte* appreciate knowing your time of arrival. If you'll be arriving after 17:00, let your hotelier know. On the small chance that a hotel loses track of your reservation, bring along a hard copy of their emailed or faxed confirmation.

Reserving Rooms as You Travel: You can make reservations as you travel, calling hotels or *chambres d'hôte* a few days to a week before your visit. If everything's full, don't despair. Call a day or two in advance and fill in a cancellation. If you'd rather travel without any reservations at all, you'll have greater success snaring rooms if you arrive at your destination early in the day. When you anticipate crowds (weekends are worst), call hotels around 9:00 or 10:00 on the day you plan to arrive, when the hotel clerk knows who'll be checking out and just which rooms will be available. If you encounter a language barrier, ask the fluent receptionist at your current hotel to call for you.

Eating

The French eat long and well—nowhere more so than in the south. Relaxed and tree-shaded lunches with a chilled rosé, three-hour dinners, and endless afternoons at outdoor cafés are the norm. Local cafés, cuisine, and wines should become a highlight of any French adventure. It's sightseeing for your palate. Even if the rest of you is sleeping in cheap hotels, let your taste buds travel first class in France. (They can go coach in England.) You can eat well without going broke—but choose carefully: You're just as likely to blow a small fortune on a mediocre meal as you are to dine wonderfully for €20. For specific suggestions on what to order where, see my cuisine suggestions in the introductions to Provence (page 51) and the Riviera (page 283).

The no-smoking revolution hit France in 2008, when a law mandated that all café and restaurant interiors be smoke-free. Today the only smokers you'll find are at outside tables, which—unfortunately—may be exactly where you want to be.

Waiters probably won't overwhelm you with friendliness (their tip is included in the bill, so there's less schmoozing than we're used to at home). Notice how hard they work. They almost never stop. Cozying up to clients (French or foreign) is probably the last thing on their minds. They have to deal with client overload, too, because the French rarely hire part-time employees, even to help with peak times. To get a waiter's attention, say, "*S'il vous plaît*" (see voo play)—"please."

Breakfast

You'll almost always have the option of breakfast at your hotel, which is usually pleasant and convenient. *Petit déjeuner* (puh-tee day-zhuh-nay) starts with café au lait, hot chocolate, or tea, and a roll with butter and marmalade. Some hotels offer only this classic continental breakfast for about €8, whereas others put out a buffet breakfast for about €10–15 (cereal, yogurt, fruit, cheese, croissants, juice, and the occasional hard-boiled egg)—which I usually spring for.

If all you want is coffee or tea and a croissant, the corner café offers travelers more atmosphere and is cheaper (though you get more coffee at your hotel). Go local at the café and ask for *une tartine* (oon tart-een; baguette slathered with butter or jam) with your café au lait. To keep it really cheap, pick up some fruit at a grocery store and pastries at your favorite *boulangerie* (bakery), and have a picnic breakfast, then savor your coffee at the bar *(comptoir)* while standing, like the locals do. For a less atmospheric alternative, some fast-food places offer very cheap breakfasts.

Picnics and Snacks

Great for lunch or dinner, French picnics can be first-class affairs and adventures in high cuisine. Be daring. Try the smelly cheeses, ugly pâtés, sissy quiches, and minuscule yogurts. Shopkeepers are accustomed to selling small quantities of produce. Get a tasty salad to go, and ask for a plastic fork *(une fourchette en plastique)*. A small container is *une barquette*. A slice is *une tranche*. If you need a knife *(couteau)* or corkscrew *(tire-bouchon)*, ask to borrow one from your hotelier. And though wine is taboo in public places in the US, it's *pas de problème* in France.

Gather supplies early for a picnic lunch; you'll want to visit several small stores to assemble a complete meal, and many close at noon for their lunch break. Or visit open-air markets *(marchés)*, which are fun and photogenic, but shut down around 13:00 (many are listed in this book; local TIs have complete lists). There's much more information about these wonderful Provençal experiences in the Shopping chapter (see "Market Day" on page 449).

Here are some ideas of what to look for, but don't hesitate if something unknown whets your appetite.

At the ***boulangerie*** (bakery), choose some bread. A baguette does the trick, or choose from the many square loaves of bread on display, such as *pain aux céréales* (whole grain with seeds), *pain de campagne* (country bread, made with unbleached bread flour), *pain complet* (wheat bread), or *pain de seigle* (rye bread). To ask to have it

Picnic Vocabulary

English	French	Pronounced
please	*s'il vous plaît*	see voo play
a plastic fork	*une fourchette en plastique*	oon foor-sheht ahn plah-steek
a box	*une barquette*	oon bar-keht
a knife	*un couteau*	uhn koo-toh
corkscrew	*tire-bouchon*	teer-boo-shohn
sliced	*tranché*	trahn-shay
a slice	*une tranche*	oon trahnsh
a small slice	*une petite tranche*	oon puh-teet trahnsh
more	*plus*	ploo
less	*moins*	mwan (rhymes with man)
It's just right.	*C'est bon.*	say bohn
Thank you.	*Merci.*	mehr-see

sliced, say, *"Tranché, s'il vous plaît."*

At the ***pâtisserie*** (pastry shop, usually the same place you bought the bread), choose a dessert that's easy to eat with your hands. My favorites are *éclairs* (*chocolat* or *café* flavored), individual fruit tartes (*framboise* is raspberry, *fraise* is strawberry, *citron* is lemon), and *macarons* (made of flavored cream sandwiched between two meringues, not coconut cookies like in the US).

At the ***crémerie*** or ***fromagerie*** (cheese shop), choose a sampling of cheeses. I usually get one hard cheese (like *Comté, Cantal,* or *Beaufort*), one soft cow's milk (like *Brie* or *Camembert*), one goat's milk cheese (anything that says *chèvre*), and one bleu cheese (*Roquefort* or *Bleu d'Auvergne*). Goat cheese usually comes in individual portions. For all other large cheeses, point to the cheese you want and ask for *une petite tranche* (a small slice). The shopkeeper will place a knife on the cheese indicating the size of the slice they are about to cut, then look at you for approval. If you'd like more, say *plus.* If you'd like less, say *moins.* If it's just right, say *"C'est bon!"*

At the ***charcuterie*** or ***traiteur*** (for deli items, prepared salads, meats, and pâtés), I like a slice of *pâté de campagne* (country pâté made of pork) and *saucissons sec* (dried sausages, some with pepper crust or garlic—you can ask to have it sliced thin like salami). I get a fresh salad, too. Typical choices are *carottes râpées* (shredded carrots in a tangy vinaigrette), *salade de betteraves* (beets in vinaigrette), and *céleri rémoulade* (celery root with a mayonnaise sauce).

At a *supermarché*, *épicerie*, or *magasin d'alimentation* (small grocery store or minimart), you'll find plastic cutlery, paper plates, napkins, drinks, chips, and sometimes a meek display of produce. Local *supermarchés* are less colorful than smaller stores, but cheaper, more efficient, and offer adequate quality. Department stores often have supermarkets in the basement. On the outskirts of cities, you'll find the monster *hypermarchés*. Drop in for a glimpse of hyper-France in action.

In stores, unrefrigerated soft drinks, bottled water, and beer are one-third the price of cold drinks. Bottled water and boxed fruit juice are the cheapest drinks. Avoid buying drinks to go at streetside stands; you'll find them for far less in a shop. Try to keep a water bottle with you. Water quenches your thirst better and cheaper than anything you'll find in a store or café. I drink tap water throughout France, filling my bottle in hotel rooms as I go.

Sandwiches and Other Quick Bites

Everywhere in Provence and the Riviera, you'll find bakeries and small stands selling baguette sandwiches, quiche, and pizza-like items to go for about €4. Usually filling and tasty, they also streamline the picnic process. Here are some sandwiches you'll see:

Fromage (froh-mahzh): Cheese (white on beige)

Jambon beurre (zhahn-bohn bur): Ham and butter (boring for most)

Jambon crudités (zhahn-bohn krew-dee-tay): Ham with tomatoes, lettuce, cucumbers, and mayonnaise

Poulet crudités (poo-lay krew-dee-tay): Chicken with tomatoes, lettuce, maybe cucumbers, and always mayonnaise

Saucisson beurre (saw-see-sohn burr): Thinly sliced sausage and butter

Thon crudités (tohn krew-dee-tay): Tuna with tomatoes, lettuce, and sometimes cucumbers, but definitely mayonnaise

Look also for anything *à la provençale* (ah lah proh-vehn-sahl)—made with marinated peppers, tomatoes, and eggplant—and grilled *panini* sandwiches *à la italienne*.

Typical quiches you'll see at shops and bakeries are *lorraine* (ham and cheese), *fromage* (cheese only), *aux oignons* (with onions), *aux poireaux* (with leeks—my favorite), *aux champignons* (with mushrooms), *au saumon* (salmon), or *au thon* (tuna).

Café Culture

French cafés and brasseries provide user-friendly meals and a refuge from museum and church overload. At either, feel free to order only a bowl of soup or a salad or *plat* (main course) for lunch, dinner, or any time of day.

Cafés and brasseries usually open by 7:00, but closing hours vary. Unlike restaurants, which open only for lunch and dinner and close in between, some cafés and all brasseries serve food throughout the day (though with a more limited menu than at restaurants), making them the best option for a late lunch or an early dinner. (Note that many cafés in smaller towns close their kitchens from about 14:00 until 18:00.)

Cafés are not necessarily less expensive than many restaurants and bistros. Their key advantage is flexibility: they offer longer serving hours, and you're welcome to order just a salad, a sandwich, or a bowl of soup, even for dinner. It's also fine to split starters and desserts, though not main courses.

If you're a novice, it's easier to sit and feel comfortable when you know the system. Check the price list first, which by law must be posted prominently (if you don't see one, go elsewhere). There are two sets of prices: You'll pay more for the same drink if you're seated at a table *(salle)* than if you're seated at the bar or counter *(comptoir)*. For tips on beverages, see next page.

Standard Menu Items: *Croque monsieur* (grilled ham-and-cheese sandwich) and *croque madame* (*croque monsieur* with a fried egg on top) are generally served day and night. Sandwiches are least expensive, but very plain (*boulangeries* serve better ones). To get more than a piece of ham *(jambon)* on a baguette, order a sandwich *crudité,* which means garnished with veggies. Omelets come lonely on a plate with a basket of bread. The daily special—*plat du jour* (plah dew zhoor), or just *plat*—is your fast, hearty, and garnished hot plate for €10–15. At most cafés, feel free to order only *entrées* (which in French means the starter course); many find these lighter and more interesting than a main course. A vegetarian can enjoy a tasty, filling meal by ordering two *entrées.* Regardless of what you order, bread is free; to get more, just hold up your bread basket and ask, *"Encore, s'il vous plaît?"*

Salads: They're typically large—one is perfect for lunch or a light dinner. To get salad dressing on the side, order "*la sauce à côté*" (lah sohs ah co-tay). Classics include:

Salade niçoise (nee-swahz), a specialty from Nice, usually includes green salad topped with green beans, boiled potatoes, tomatoes, anchovies, olives, hard-boiled eggs, and lots of tuna.

Salade au chèvre chaud is a mixed green salad topped with warm goat cheese on small pieces of toast.

Salade composée is "composed" of any number of ingredients, such as *lardons* (bacon), Comté (a Swiss-style cheese), Roquefort (bleu cheese), *œuf* (egg), *noix* (walnuts), and *jambon* (ham, generally thinly sliced).

Salade paysanne usually comes with potatoes *(pommes de terre),* walnuts *(noix),* tomatoes, ham, and egg.

Salade aux gesiers has chicken gizzards (and often slices of duck).

Restaurants

Choose restaurants filled with locals. Consider my suggestions and your hotelier's opinion, but trust your instincts. If a restaurant doesn't post its prices outside, move along. Refer to my restaurant recommendations to get a sense of what a reasonable meal should cost.

Restaurants in the south open for dinner at 19:00 and typically are most crowded about 20:30 (the early bird gets the table). Last seating is usually about 21:00 (22:00 in cities and on the French Riviera, possibly earlier in small villages during the off-season).

If a restaurant serves lunch, it generally begins at 11:30 and goes until 14:00, with last orders taken about 13:30. In contrast, most cafés and brasseries offer a minimal menu (or more) all day (described earlier under "Café Culture").

If you ask for the *menu* (muh-noo) at a restaurant, you won't get a list of dishes; you'll get a fixed-price meal. *Menus,* which usually include two or three courses, are a good value if you're hungry. A three-course *menu* generally lists several options per course for you to choose from. You'll select a starter *(entrée),* a main course with vegetables *(plats principal),* plus a cheese course or a choice of desserts. Two-course *menus* always include the *plat principal* and usually offer you a choice between *entrée* and dessert *(entrée et plat* or *plat et dessert).* Restaurants that offer a *menu* for lunch often charge about €5 more for the same *menu* at dinner. Many restaurants offer a reasonable *menu–enfant* (kid's meal). And if all you want is a salad or soup, go to a café instead.

Ask for *la carte* (lah kart) if you want to see a menu and order à la carte rather than get a fixed-price meal. Request the waiter's help in deciphering the French. Consider his or her recommendations and anything *de la maison* (of the house), as long as it's not an organ meat *(tripes, rognons,* and *andouillette).* Galloping gourmets should bring a menu translator; the *Rick Steves' French Phrase Book,* with a menu decoder, works well for most travelers. Wines are often listed in a separate *carte des vins.*

In the south, I usually order *une entrée* and *un plat* from *la carte* if I'm hungry (often as a fixed-price, two-course *menu* or *formule),* then find an ice-cream or crêpe stand and take a dessert stroll. If that sounds like too much, just order *un plat.* Two people can split an *entrée* or a big salad (since small-size dinner salads are usually not offered á la carte) and then each get a *plat principal.* At better restaurants, it's considered inappropriate for two diners to share one main course.

Coffee and Tea Lingo

By law, the waiter must give you a glass of tap water with your coffee or tea if you request it; ask for *"Un verre d'eau, s'il vous plaît"* (uhn vayr doh, see voo play).

Provence is known for its herbal and fruit teas. Look for *tilleul* (linden), *verveine* (verbena), or interesting blends such as *poire-vanille* (pear-vanilla).

Coffee

French	Pronounced	English
un café allongé (also called *café longue*)	uhn kah-fay ah-lohn-zhay (kah-fay lohn)	closest to an American cup of coffee
un express	uhn ex-press	shot of espresso
une noisette	oon nwah-zeht	espresso with a shot of milk
café au lait	kah-fay oh lay	coffee with lots of steamed milk (closest to an American latte)
un grand crème	uhn grahn krehm	big café au lait
un petit crème	uhn puh-tee krehm	small café au lait
un décaffiné	uhn day-kah-fee-nay	decaf—available for any of the above drinks

Tea

French	Pronounced	English
un thé nature	uhn tay nah-tour	plain tea
un thé au lait	uhn tay oh lay	tea with milk
un thé citron	uhn tay see-trohn	tea with lemon
une infusion	oon an-few-see-yohn	herbal tea

Beverages

Water: The French are willing to pay for bottled water with their meal (*eau minérale;* oh mee-nay-rahl) because they prefer the taste over tap water. Badoit is my favorite carbonated water (*l'eau gazeuse;* loh gah-zuhz). If you prefer a free pitcher of tap water, ask for *une carafe d'eau* (oon kah-rahf doh). Otherwise, you may unwittingly buy bottled water.

Wine and Beer: House wine at the bar is cheap and good in this region (about €3/glass at modestly priced places). At a restaurant, a bottle or carafe of house wine costs €8–18. To get inexpensive wine, order regional table wine (*un vin du pays;* uhn van duh pay) in a pitcher (*un pichet;* uhn pee-shay), rather than a bottle (only

How Was Your Trip?

Were your travels fun, smooth, and meaningful? If you'd like to share your tips, concerns, and discoveries, please fill out the survey at www.ricksteves.com/feedback. I value your feedback. Thanks in advance—it helps a lot.

available when seated and when ordering food). Note, though, that finer restaurants usually offer only bottles of wine.

If all you want is a glass of wine, ask for *un verre de vin rouge* for red wine or *vin blanc* for white wine (uhn vehr duh van roozh/blahn). A half-carafe of wine is *un demi-pichet* (uhn duh-mee pee-shay); a quarter-carafe (ideal for one) is *un quart* (uh kar).

The local beer, which costs about €4 at a restaurant, is cheaper on tap (*une pression;* oon pres-yohn) than in the bottle (*bouteille;* boo-teh-ee). France's best beer is Alsatian; try Kronenbourg or the heavier Pelfort. *Une panaché* (oon pah-nah-shay) is a tasty French shandy (beer and lemon soda).

Regional Specialty Drinks: For a refreshing before-dinner drink, order a *kir* (pronounced "keer")—a thumb's level of *crème de cassis* (black currant liqueur) topped with white wine. In Provence, try sweet wines such as Muscat de Beaumes de Venise or Rasteau (Vin Doux Naturel). Both should be served chilled (from the fridge, never with ice cubes) and can be enjoyed before dinner or with some desserts; they're terrific with foie gras, melons, peaches, or Roquefort cheese. Look also for sparkling wines, usually inexpensive versions of the pricey Champagne.

If you like brandy, try a *marc* (regional brandy) or an Armagnac, cognac's cheaper twin brother. *Pastis,* the standard southern France aperitif, is a sweet anise (licorice) drink that comes on the rocks with a glass of water. Cut it to taste with lots of water.

Soft Drinks: For a fun, bright, nonalcoholic drink of 7-Up with mint syrup, order *un diabolo menthe* (uhn dee-ah-boh-loh mahnt). For 7-Up with fruit syrup, order *un diabolo grenadine* (think Shirley Temple). Kids love the local orange drink, Orangina, a carbonated orange juice with pulp and without caffeine. They also like flavored syrups mixed with bottled water (*sirops à l'eau;* see-roh ah loh). In France *limonade* (lee-moan-ahd) is Sprite or 7-Up.

Ordering: Be very clear when ordering drinks—you can easily pay €8 for an oversized Coke and €12 for a huge beer. When you order a drink, state the size in centiliters (don't say "small," "medium," or "large," because the waiter might bring a bigger drink than you want). For something small, ask for 25 cl (about 8 ounces); for a medium drink, order 33 cl (about 12 ounces—a normal can of soda); a large is 50 cl (about 16 ounces); and a super-size is one liter (about a quart—which is more than I would ever order in France). The ice cubes melted after the last Yankee tour group left.

Traveling as a Temporary Local

We travel all the way to Europe to enjoy differences—to become temporary locals. You'll experience frustrations. Certain truths that we find "God-given" or "self-evident," such as cold beer, ice in drinks, bottomless cups of coffee, hot showers, and bigger being better, are suddenly not so true. One of the benefits of travel is the eye-opening realization that there are logical, civil, and even better alternatives.

With a history rich in human achievement, France is an understandably proud country. To enjoy its people, you need to celebrate the differences. A willingness to go local ensures that you'll enjoy a full dose of French hospitality.

The French generally like Americans. But if there is a negative aspect to the French image of Americans, it's that we are big, loud, aggressive, impolite, rich, and a bit naive.

The French place a high value on speaking quietly in restaurants and on trains. Listen while on the bus or in a restaurant—the place can be packed, but the decibel level is low. Try to adjust your volume accordingly to show respect for their culture.

While the French look bemusedly at some of our Yankee excesses—and worriedly at others—they nearly always afford us individual travelers all the warmth we deserve. Judging from all the happy feedback I receive from travelers who have used this book, it's safe to assume you'll enjoy a great, affordable vacation— with the finesse of an independent, experienced traveler.

Thanks, and *bon voyage!*

Back Door Travel Philosophy

From *Rick Steves' Europe Through the Back Door*

Travel is intensified living—maximum thrills per minute and one of the last great sources of legal adventure. Travel is freedom. It's recess, and we need it.

Experiencing the real Europe requires catching it by surprise, going casual..."Through the Back Door."

Affording travel is a matter of priorities. (Make do with the old car.) You can eat and sleep—simply, safely, and enjoyably—anywhere in Europe for $120 a day plus transportation costs. In many ways, spending more money only builds a thicker wall between you and what you traveled so far to see. Europe is a cultural carnival, and time after time, you'll find that its best acts are free and the best seats are the cheap ones.

A tight budget forces you to travel close to the ground, meeting and communicating with the people. Never sacrifice sleep, nutrition, safety, or cleanliness to save money. Simply enjoy the local-style alternatives to expensive hotels and restaurants.

Connecting with people carbonates your experience. Extroverts have more fun. If your trip is low on magic moments, kick yourself and make things happen. If you don't enjoy a place, maybe you don't know enough about it. Seek the truth. Recognize tourist traps. Give a culture the benefit of your open mind. See things as different, but not better or worse. Any culture has plenty to share.

Of course, travel, like the world, is a series of hills and valleys. Be fanatically positive and militantly optimistic. If something's not to your liking, change your liking.

Travel can make you a happier American, as well as a citizen of the world. Our Earth is home to six and a half billion equally precious people. It's humbling to travel and find that other people don't have the "American Dream"—they have their own dreams. Europeans like us, but with all due respect, they wouldn't trade passports.

Thoughtful travel engages us with the world. In tough economic times, it reminds us what is truly important. By broadening perspectives, travel teaches new ways to measure quality of life.

Globetrotting destroys ethnocentricity, helping us understand and appreciate other cultures. Rather than fear the diversity on this planet, celebrate it. Among your most prized souvenirs will be the strands of different cultures you choose to knit into your own character. The world is a cultural yarn shop, and Back Door travelers are weaving the ultimate tapestry. Join in!

PROVENCE

PROVENCE

"There are treasures to carry away in this land, which has not found a spokesman worthy of the riches it offers."
—Paul Cézanne

This magnificent region is shaped like a giant wedge of quiche. From its sunburned crust, fanning out along the Mediterranean coast from the Camargue to Marseille, it stretches north along the Rhône Valley to Orange. The Romans were here in force and left many ruins—some of the best anywhere. Seven popes, artists such as Vincent van Gogh and Paul Cézanne, and author Peter Mayle all enjoyed their years in Provence. This destination features a splendid recipe of arid climate, oceans of vineyards, dramatic scenery, captivating cities, and adorable hill-capping villages.

Explore the ghost town that is ancient Les Baux, and see France's greatest Roman ruins, the Pont du Gard aqueduct and the theater in Orange. Admire the skill of ball-tossing *boules* players in small squares in every Provençal village and city. Spend a few Van Gogh–inspired starry, starry nights in Arles. Youthful but classy Avignon bustles in the shadow of its brooding Palace of the Popes. Stylish and self-confident Aix-en-Provence lies 30 minutes from the sea and feels more Mediterranean. It's a short hop from Arles or Avignon into the splendid scenery and villages of the Côtes du Rhône and Luberon regions. Should you need an urban fix—and feel the need to really understand southern France—Marseille is a must. If you prefer a Provençal beach fix, find Cassis, just east of Marseille.

Choose a Home Base
With limited time, make Arles or Avignon your sightseeing base—particularly if you have no car. Italophiles prefer smaller

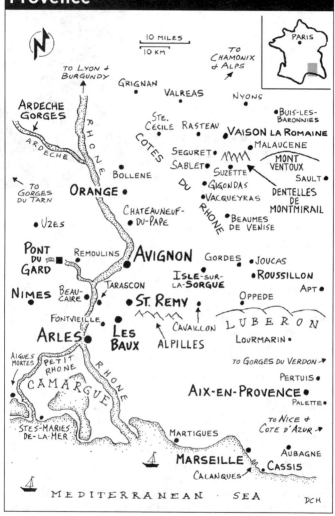

Provence

Arles, while poodles pick urban Avignon. Many enjoy nights in both cities. (With a car, head for St. Rémy or the hill towns.)

Arles has a blue-collar quality; the entire city feels like Van Gogh's bedroom. It also has this region's best-value hotels and is handy to Les Baux, St. Rémy, and the Camargue.

Avignon—double the size of Arles—feels sophisticated, with more nightlife and shopping. Avignon makes a good base for non-drivers thanks to its convenient public-transit options (within an hour, you can reach Pont du Gard, Uzès, and St. Rémy by bus, or

Marseille by train; within a half-hour, you can reach Arles, Nîmes, Isle-sur-la-Sorgue, and Aix-en-Provence by train).

Or, for drivers who prefer a smaller-town base, **St. Rémy** is manageable and centrally located. It offers a nice range of hotels with free and easy parking, good restaurants, and a few sights of its own. Or you can sleep in one of Provence's many hill towns, or out in the countryside; the towns of **Vaison la Romaine** (in the Côtes du Rhône region) and **Roussillon** (in the Luberon) are two good but remote options.

Planning Your Time

The bare minimum you should spend in Provence is three days: one day for sightseeing in Arles and Les Baux (Arles is best on Wed or Sat, when it's market day); a day for Pont du Gard and Nîmes; and a full day for Orange and the Côtes du Rhône villages. Add two more days to explore Avignon; Uzès or St. Rémy; and more Provençal villages. Allow an additional two days in Cassis, using one of them for a day trip to Marseille or Aix-en-Provence (or both). Ideally, see the cities—Arles, Nîmes, Avignon, Aix-en-Provence, and Marseille—by train, then rent a car for the countryside.

To measure the pulse of rural Provence, spend at least a few nights in the smaller towns. (They come to life on market days, but can be quiet on Mondays, when shops are shuttered tight.) I've described many towns in the Côtes du Rhône and Luberon. The Côtes du Rhône is ideal for wine connoisseurs and an easy stop for those heading to or from the north. The Luberon is for hill-town lovers and works well for travelers heading east, toward Aix-en-Provence or the Riviera. Don't day-trip to these very different areas; nights spent in Provençal villages are what books are written about. One or two nights in each area make for a terrific start.

The small port town of Cassis is a wonderful Mediterranean meander between Provence and the Riviera (and more appealing than most Riviera resorts). It has easy day-trip connections to Marseille and Aix-en-Provence.

Depending on the length of your trip, here are my recommended priorities for Provence:

3 days:	Arles and Les Baux; Pont du Gard and Nîmes; and Orange and Côtes du Rhône villages
5 days, add:	Avignon and either St. Rémy or Uzès
7 days, add:	Cassis, Marseille, Aix-en-Provence
9 days, add:	Luberon hill towns, Camargue

Getting Around Provence

By Bus or Train: Public transit is good between cities and decent to some towns, but marginal at best to the villages. Frequent trains link Avignon, Arles, and Nîmes (about 30 minutes between each). Avignon has good train connections with Orange, and decent service to Isle-sur-la-Sorgue. Marseille is well-connected to all cities in Provence, with frequent service to Cassis and Aix-en-Provence (about 30 minutes to each).

Buses connect many smaller towns, though service can be sporadic. From Arles you can catch a bus to Stes-Maries-de-la-Mer (in the Camargue) or St. Rémy. From Avignon, you can bus to Pont du Gard, St. Rémy, Uzès, Isle-sur-la-Sorgue (also by train), and less easily to Vaison la Romaine and some Côtes du Rhône villages. St. Rémy, Isle-sur-la-Sorgue, and Uzès are the most accessible small towns.

While a tour of the villages of the Côtes du Rhône or Luberon is best on your own by car, excellent minivan tours and basic bus excursions are available. (TIs in Arles and Avignon have information on bus excursions to regional sights that are hard to reach *sans* car; see "Tours of Provence," below.)

By Car: The region is made to order for a car. Orange Michelin map #527 (1:275,000 scale) covers this book perfectly. Michelin maps #332 (Luberon and Côtes du Rhône) and #340 (Arles area) are also worth considering. I've described key sights and a variety of full-day drives deep into the countryside. Be wary of thieves: Park only in well-monitored spaces and leave nothing valuable in your car.

Avignon (pop. 100,000) is a headache for drivers. Arles (pop. 52,000) is easier but still urban. Les Baux and St. Rémy work well from Arles or Avignon (or vice versa). Nîmes and Pont du Gard are a short hop west of Avignon and on the way to or from Languedoc. The town of Orange ties in tidily with a trip to the Côtes du Rhône villages and with destinations farther north. If you're heading north from Provence, consider a three-hour detour through the spectacular Ardèche Gorges (see page 191). The Luberon villages are about halfway between Arles or Avignon and Aix-en-Provence (consider basing yourself in little Lourmarin for day trips to Aix-en-Provence). And if you're continuing on to the Riviera, let yourself be lured into the Grand Canyon du Verdon detour (see the Inland Riviera chapter). Most drivers will prefer exploring congested Marseille on foot—leave your car behind and take the train from Cassis or Aix-en-Provence (both towns have parking at their train stations and frequent trains and buses to the center of Marseille).

Tours of Provence

It's possible to take half-day or full-day excursions to most of the sights described in this book (best from Avignon). Most TIs have brochures on excursions and can help you make a reservation. Here

Top 10 Provençal Towns and Villages

1. Roussillon (beautiful hill town sitting atop a huge ochre deposit, giving it a red-rock appeal, popular with American tourists)
2. Uzès (chic town with manicured pedestrian streets, popular with European tourists)
3. Joucas (adorable little village where flowers and stones are lovingly maintained, popular with artists)
4. Brantes (spectacularly situated cliff village with little tourism)
5. Lourmarin (lovely upscale village, busy in the day but quiet at night)
6. Le Crestet (an overlooked village with a sensational hilltop location and one commercial enterprise)
7. Séguret (a linear hillside village with memorable views and many day-trippers, but few overnighters)
8. Gigondas (world-famous wine village with a nice balance of commercial activity and quiet)
9. Vaison la Romaine (a popular midsize town with Roman ruins and lots of activity, spanning both sides of a river)
10. Nyons (an overlooked midsize town with a few pedestrian streets; famous for its olive oil and ideal climate)

are several good options to consider:

Wine Safari—Dutchman Mike Rijken runs a one-man show, taking travelers through the region he adopted more than 20 years ago. Mike came to France to train as a chef, later became a wine steward, and has now found his calling as a driver/guide. His English is fluent, and though his focus is wine and wine villages, Mike knows the region thoroughly and is a good teacher of its history (€55/half-day, €100/day, priced per person, group size varies from 2 to 6; pickups possible in Arles, Avignon, Lyon, Marseille, or Aix-en-Provence; tel. 04 90 35 59 21, mobile 06 19 29 50 81, www.winesafari.net, mikeswinesafari@wanadoo.fr).

Avignon Wine Tour—For a playful, informative, and distinctly French perspective on wines of the Côtes du Rhône region, contact François Marcou, who runs his tours with passion and energy, offering travelers different itineraries every day. Based in Avignon, François can pick you up at your Avignon hotel, the TI, or at either of the city's train stations (€75/person for all-day wine tours that include 4–5 tastings, €350 for private groups, mobile 06 28 05 33 84, www.avignon-wine-tour.com, avignon.wine.tour @modulonet.fr).

Imagine Tours—Unlike most tour operators, this organization runs on a not-for-profit basis, with a focus on cultural excursions. It offers low-key, personalized tours that allow visitors to discover the "true heart of Provence." The itineraries adapt to your interests, and the volunteer guides will meet you at your hotel or the departure point of your choice (€150/half-day, €275/day, prices are for up to 4 people, mobile 06 89 22 19 87, fax 04 90 24 84 26, www .imagine-tours.net, imagine.tours@gmail.com). They also offer free assistance to travelers, should you want advice planning your itinerary, need help booking hotel rooms, or run into problems during your trip.

WineInProvence—This Aix-en-Provence–based outfit runs half-day and full-day wine tours, covering the lesser-known areas of Cassis, Bandol, and Aix-en-Provence (€155/person for half-day, €225/person for all day, mobile 06 33 69 42 95, www.tastesof provence.com, also see listing on page 264).

Wine Uncovered—Passionate Englishman (is that an oxymoron?) Olivier Hickman takes small groups on focused tours of selected wineries in Châteauneuf-du-Pape and in the villages near Vaison la Romaine. Olivier is serious about French wine and knows his subject matter inside and out. His in-depth tastings include three wineries for €55 per person (his minimum half-day fee is €155; full-day is €195). If you need transportation, he can help arrange it (mobile 06 75 10 10 01, www.wine-uncovered.com, olivier.hickman@wine-uncovered.com).

Visit Provence—This company runs trips from Avignon (and a few from Arles) to most destinations covered in this book, and provides introductory commentary to what you'll see (but no guiding at the actual sights). They have eight-seat minivans (about €60/ half-day, €100/day; they'll pick you up at your hotel in Avignon). Ask about their cheaper big-bus excursions, or consider hiring a van and driver for your private use (plan on €210/half-day, €400/ day, tel. 04 90 14 70 00, check website for current destinations, www.provence-reservation.com).

Madeleine's Culinary and Active Adventures—Madeleine Vedel, an effervescent American expat, plans small group tours from Avignon and Arles to visit food artisans and wineries. Madeleine also leads kid-friendly hikes in the countryside (€300/ day, flat rate for 1–5 people, mobile 06 82 15 51 74, www.cuisine provencale.com).

How About Them Romans?

Provence is littered with Roman ruins. Many scholars claim the best-preserved ancient Roman buildings are not in Italy, but in France. These ancient stones will comprise an important part of your sightseeing agenda in this region, so it's worth learning about how they came to be.

Classical Rome endured from about 500 B.C. through A.D. 500—spending about 500 years growing, 200 years peaking, and

Top 10 Roman Sights in Provence

1. Pont du Gard aqueduct and its museum
2. Roman Theater in Orange
3. Ancient History Museum in Arles
4. Maison Carrée in Nîmes
5. Arena in Nîmes
6. Arena in Arles
7. Roman city of Glanum (in St. Rémy)
8. Ruined aqueduct near Fontvieille
9. Roman city of Vaison la Romaine
10. St. Julien Bridge (near Roussillon)

300 years declining. In 49 B.C., Julius Caesar defied the Republic by crossing the Rubicon River in northern Italy, conquering Provence (and ultimately all of France)—and killing about a third of its population in the process. He erected a temple to Jupiter on the future site of Paris' Notre-Dame Cathedral.

The concept of one-man rule lived on with his grandnephew, Octavian (whom he had also adopted as his son). Octavian killed Brutus, eliminated his rivals (Mark Antony and Cleopatra), and united Rome's warring factions. He took the title "Augustus" and became the first in a line of emperors who would control Rome for the next 500 years—ruling like a king, with the backing of the army and the rubber-stamp approval of the Senate. Rome morphed from a Republic into an Empire: a collection of many diverse territories ruled by a single man.

Augustus' reign marked the start of 200 years of peace, prosperity, and expansion known as the *Pax Romana.* At its peak (c. A.D. 117), the Roman empire had 54 million people and stretched from Scotland in the north to Egypt in the south, as far west as Spain and as far east as modern-day Iraq. To the northeast, Rome was bounded by the Rhine and Danube Rivers. On Roman maps, the Mediterranean was labeled *Mare Nostrum* ("Our Sea"). At its peak, "Rome" didn't just refer to the city, but to the entire civilized Western world.

The Romans were successful not only because they were good soldiers, but also because they were smart administrators and businessmen. People in conquered territories knew they had joined the winning team and that political stability would replace barbarian invasions. Trade thrived. Conquered peoples were welcomed into the fold of prosperity, linked by roads, education, common laws and gods, and the Latin language.

Provence, with its strategic location, benefited greatly from

PROVENCE

Rome's global economy and grew to become an important part of its worldwide empire. After Julius Caesar conquered Gaul, Emperor Augustus set out to Romanize it, building and renovating cities in the image of Rome. Most cities had a theater (some had several), baths, and aqueducts; the most important cities had sports arenas.

The Romans also erected an infrastructure of roads, post offices, schools (teaching in Latin), police stations, and water-supply systems.

With a standard language and currency, Roman merchants were able to trade wine, salt, and olive oil for foreign goods. The empire invested heavily in cities that were strategic for trade. For example, the Roman-built city of Arles was a crucial link in the trade route from Italy to Spain, so they built a bridge across the Rhône River and fortified the town.

A typical Roman city (such as Nîmes, Arles, Orange, or Vaison la Romaine) was a garrison town, laid out on a grid plan with two main roads: one running north–south (the *cardus*), the other east–west (the *decumanus*). Approaching the city on your chariot, you'd pass through the cemetery, which was located outside of town for hygienic reasons. You'd enter the main gate and speed past warehouses and apartment houses to the town square (forum). Facing the square were the most important temples, dedicated to the patron gods of the city. Nearby, you'd find bathhouses; like today's fitness clubs, these served the almost sacred dedication to personal vigor. Also close by were businesses that catered to the citizens' needs: the marketplace, bakeries, banks, and brothels.

Aqueducts brought fresh water for drinking, filling the baths, and delighting the citizens with bubbling fountains. Men flocked

to the stadiums in Arles and Nîmes to bet on gladiator games; eager couples attended elaborate plays at theaters in Orange, Arles, and Vaison la Romaine. Marketplaces brimmed with exotic fruits, vegetables, and animals from the far reaches of the empire. Some cities in Provence were more urban 2,000 years ago than they are today. For instance, Roman Arles had a population of 100,000—double today's size.

In these cities, you'll see many rounded arches. These were

constructed by piling two stacks of heavy stone blocks, connecting them with an arch (supported with wooden scaffolding), then inserting an inverted keystone where the stacks met. *Voilà!* The heavy stones were able to support not only themselves, but also a great deal of weight above the arch. The Romans didn't actually invent the rounded arch, but they exploited it far better than their predecessors, stacking arches to build arenas and theaters, stringing them side by side for aqueducts, stretching out their legs to create barrel-vaulted ceilings, and building freestanding "triumphal" arches to celebrate conquering generals.

When it came to construction, the Romans' magic building ingredient was concrete. A mixture of volcanic ash, lime, water, and small rocks, concrete—easier to work than stone, longer-lasting than wood—served as flooring, roofing, filler, glue, and support. Builders would start with a foundation of brick, then fill it in with poured concrete. They would then cover important structures, such as basilicas, in sheets of expensive marble (held on with nails), or decorate floors and walls with mosaics—proving just how talented the Romans were at turning the functional into art.

Provence's Cuisine Scene

Provence has been called France's "garden market," stressing farm-fresh food (vegetables, fruit, and meats) prepared in a simple way, and meant to be savored with family and friends. Grilled foods are typical, as are dishes derived from lengthy simmering—in part a reflection of long days spent in the fields. Colorful and lively, Provençal cuisine hammers the senses with an extravagant use (by French standards) of garlic, olive oil, and herbs. Order anything *à la provençal,* and you'll be rewarded with aromatic food heightened by rich and pungent sauces. Thanks to the proximity of the Riviera, many seafood dishes show up on Provençal menus (see "The Riviera's Cuisine Scene" on page 283).

Unlike other French regional cuisines, the food of Provence is inviting for nibblers. Appetizers (hors d'oeuvres) often consist

of bowls of olives (try the plump, full-flavored black *tanche* or the green, buttery *picholine*), as well as plates of fresh vegetables served with lusty sauces ready for dipping. These same sauces adorn dishes of hard-boiled eggs, fish, or meat. Look for tapenade, a paste of pureed olives, capers, anchovies, herbs, and sometimes tuna. True anchovy-lovers seek out *anchoïade* (a spread of garlic, anchovy, and parsley) or *bagna cauda* (warm sauce of anchovies and melted butter or olive oil).

Aioli—a rich, garlicky mayonnaise spread over vegetables, potatoes, fish, or whatever—is another Provençal favorite. In the summertime, entire village festivals celebrate this sauce. Watch for signs announcing *aioli monstre* ("monster aioli") and, for a few euros, dive into a deeply French eating experience (pass the breath mints, please).

Despite the heat, soup is a favorite in Provence. *Soupe au pistou* is a thin yet flavorful vegetable soup with a sauce (called *pistou*) of basil, garlic, and cheese—pesto minus the pine nuts. Or try *soupe à l'ail* (garlic soup, called *aigo bouido* in the Provençal dialect). For seafood soups, see "The Riviera's Cuisine Scene" on page 283.

Provençal main courses venerate fresh vegetables and meats. (Eat seafood on the Riviera and meat in Provence.) Ratatouille is a mixture of Provençal vegetables (eggplant, zucchini, onions, and peppers are the usual suspects) in a thick, herb-flavored tomato sauce. It's readily found in charcuteries and often served at room temperature, making it the perfect picnic food. Ratatouille veggies also show up on their own, stuffed and served in spicy sauces. Look for *aubergines* (eggplants), *tomates* (tomatoes), *poivrons* (sweet peppers), and *courgettes* (zucchini—especially *fleurs de courgettes,* stuffed and batter-fried zucchini flowers). *Tians* are gratin-like vegetable dishes named for the deep terra-cotta dish in which they are cooked and served. *Artichauts à la barigoule* are stuffed artichokes flavored with garlic, ham, and herbs (*barigoule* is from the Provençal word for thyme, *farigoule*). Also look for *riz de Camargue*—the reddish, chewy, nutty-tasting rice that has taken over the Camargue area, which is otherwise useless for agriculture.

The famous herbs of Provence influence food long before it's cooked. The locally renowned lambs of the *garrigue* (shrub-covered hills), as well as rabbits and other small edible beasts in Provence, dine on wild herbs and spicy shrubs—essentially preseasoning their delicate meat. Regional specialties include lamb (*agneau,* most often leg of lamb, *gigot d'agneau*), grilled and served no-frills, or the delicious *lapin à la provençale*—rabbit served with garlic, mustard, tomatoes, and herbs in white wine. The people here have a curious passion for quail *(caille).* These tiny, bony birds are often grilled and served with any variety of sauces, including those sweetened with Provençal cherries or honey and lavender. *Daube,* named for the traditional cooking vessel *daubière,* is generally beef simmered in wine with spices and herbs—and perhaps a touch of orange zest—until it is spoon-tender; it's then served with noodles or the local rice. *Taureau* (bull's meat), usually raised in the marshy Camargue, melts in your mouth.

By American standards, the French undercook meats: *bleu* (bluh) is virtually raw (just flame-kissed); *saignant* (seh-nyahn) is close to raw; *à point* (ah pwahn)—their version of "medium"—is rare; and *bien cuit* (bee-yehn kwee, "well cooked") is medium. (Because French cows are raised on grass rather than corn, the beef is leaner than in the US, so limiting the cooking time keeps the meat tender.)

There are a few dishes to avoid: *Pieds et paquets* is a scary dish of sheep's feet and tripe (no amount of Provençal sauce can hide the flavor here). *Tourte de blettes* is a confused "pie" made with Swiss chard; both savory and sweet, it can't decide whether it should be a first course or dessert (it shows up as both).

Eat goat cheese *(fromage de chèvre)* in Provence. Look for *banon de banon* or *banon à la feuille* (dipped in *eau-de-vie* to kill bad mold, then wrapped in a chestnut leaf), spicy *picodon* (the name means "spicy" in the old language), or the fresh, creamy *brousse du Rove* (often served mixed with cream and sugar for dessert). On Provençal cheese platters, you'll often find small rounds of bite-size chèvres, each flavored with a different herb or spice—and some even rolled in chopped garlic (more breath mints, please).

Desserts tend to be fairly light and fruit-filled, or tradition-ally French. Treat yourself to fresh tarts made with seasonal fruit, Cavaillon melons (served cut in half with a trickle of the sweet Rhône wine Beaumes de Venise), and ice cream or sorbet sweet-ened with honey and flavored with various herbs such as lavender, thyme, or rosemary.

Wines of Provence

Provence was the first area in France to be planted with grapes, in about 600 B.C., by the Greeks. Romans built on what the Greeks started, realizing even back then that Provence had an ideal climate for producing wine: mild winters and long, warm summers (but not too hot—thanks to the cooling winds). This sun-baked, wine-happy region offers Americans a chance to sample wines blended from several grapes—resulting in flavors unlike anything we get at home (yes, we have good Cabernet Sauvignons, Merlots, and Pinot Noirs, but Rhône wines are new to most of us). Provence's shorts-and-T-shirt climate and abundance of hearty, reasonably priced wines make for an enjoyable experience, particularly if you're willing to learn. See "Provençal Wine-Tasting 101," later in this chapter, for the basics.

In France wine production is strictly controlled by the gov-ernment to preserve the overall quality. This ensures that vintners use specified grapes that grow best in that region and follow cer-tain grape-growing procedures. The *Appellation d'Origine Controlée* (AOC) label found on many bottles is the government's seal of approval indicating that a wine has met a series of requirements. The type and percentages of grapes used, vinification methods, and taste are all controlled and verified.

French Wine Lingo

Here are the steps you should follow when entering any wine-tasting:

   1. Greetings, Sir/Madam: *Bonjour, Monsieur/Madame.*

   2. We would like to taste a few wines: *Nous voudrions déguster quelques vins* (noo voo-dree-ohn day-goo-stay kehl-kuh van).

   3. We want a wine that is _____ and _____: *Nous voudrions un vin _____ et _____.* (noo voo-dree-ohn uhn van _____ ay _____).

   Fill in the blanks with your favorites from this list:

English	French	Pronounced
wine	*vin*	van
red	*rouge*	roozh
white	*blanc*	blahn
rosé	*rosé*	roh-zay
light	*léger*	lay-zhay
full-bodied, heavy	*robuste*	roh-boost
fruity	*fruité*	frwee-tay
sweet*	*doux*	doo
tannic	*tannique*	tah-neek
jammy	*confituré*	koh-fee-tuh-ray
fine	*fin, avec finesse*	fan, ah-vehk fee-nehs
ready to drink (mature)	*prêt à boire*	preh tah bwar
not ready to drink	*fermé*	fair-may
oaky	*goût de la chêne*	goo duh lah sheh-nuh
from old vines	*de vieille vignes*	duh vee-yay-ee veen-yah
sparkling	*pétillant*	pay-tee-yahn

*With the exception of the fortified white Beaumes de Venise (Muscat), few Provençal wines would be considered "sweet."

   Provençal vintners can blend wines using a maximum of 13 different grapes (5 white and 8 red)—unique in France. (In Burgundy and Alsace, only one grape variety is used for each wine—so Pinot Noir, Chardonnay, Riesling, Tokay, and Pinot Gris are each 100 percent from that grape.) Only in Châteauneuf-du-Pape are all 13 grapes used; most vintners blend 4 or 5 grapes. This blending allows Provençal winemakers great range in personalizing their wine. The most prevalent grapes are Grenache, Mourvèdre, Syrah, Carignan, and Cinsault. The white grapes include Grenache-

Blanc, Roussanne, Marsanne, Bourboulenc, and Clairette.

There are three primary growing areas in Provence: Côtes du Rhône, Côtes de Provence, and Côteaux d'Aix-en-Provence. A few wines are also made along the Provençal Mediterranean coast. All regions produce rich, fruity reds and dry, fresh rosés. Only about 5 percent of wine produced here is white (the best of which comes from Cassis). Most Provençal whites are light, tart, with plenty of citrus and minerals, and work best as a pre-dinner drink or in a *kir*.

In Provence, I generally drink rosé instead of white. Don't confuse these rosés with the insipid blush stuff found in the US; French rosé is often crisp and fruity, a perfect match to the hot days and Mediterranean cuisine. Rosé wines are made from red grapes whose juice is clear, until crushed with their skins. The clear juice is left in contact with the dark-red skins just long enough to produce the pinkish color (no more than 24 hours). Rosés from Tavel (20 minutes north and west of Avignon) are the darkest in color and most well-known outside of Provence, but you'll find many good producers at affordable prices in other areas as well. If you're unaccustomed to drinking rosés, try one here.

Provençal Wine-Tasting 101

The American wine-tasting experience (I'm thinking Napa Valley) is generally informal, chatty, and entrepreneurial (logo-adorned baseball caps and golf shirts). Although Provençal vintners are welcoming and more easygoing than in other parts of France, it's still a serious, wine-focused experience. Your hosts are not there to make small talk, and they're likely to be "all business." For some people it can be overwhelming to try to make sense of the vast range of options among Provençal wines, particularly when faced with a no-nonsense winemaker or sommelier. Take a deep breath, do your best to follow my instructions below, and don't linger anywhere you don't feel welcome (I've tried to identify which places are most accepting of wine novices). Visit several private wineries or stop by a *cave coopérative*—an excellent opportunity to taste wines from a number of local vintners in a single, less intimidating setting. You'll have a better experience if you call ahead to let them know you're coming—even if the winery is open all day, it's good form to announce your visit (ask your hotelier for help).

Provençal winemakers are happy to work with you...*if* they can figure out what you want (which they expect you to know). When you enter a winery, it helps to know what you like (drier or sweeter, lighter or full-bodied, fruity or more tannic, and so on). The people serving you may know those words in English, but you'd be wise to learn and use these key words in French (see "French Wine Lingo" sidebar). Avoid visiting places between noon and 14:00—many are closed, and those that aren't would rather be at lunch.

French wines usually have a lower alcohol level than American or Australian wines. Whereas many Americans like a big, full-bodied wine, most French tend to prefer more subtle flavors. They judge a wine by virtue of how well it pairs with a meal—and a big, oaky wine would overwhelm most French cuisine. The French also enjoy sampling younger wines and determining how they will taste in a few years, allowing them to buy bottles at cheaper prices and stash them in their cellars. Americans want it now—for today's picnic.

Remember that the vintner is hoping you'll buy at least a bottle or two. If you don't, you may be asked to pay a minimal fee for the tasting. They know that Americans can't take much wine with them, and they don't expect to make a big sale, but they do hope you'll look for their wines in the US. Some of the places I list will ship your purchase home—ask.

Côtes du Rhône Wines

The Côtes du Rhône, which follows the Rhône River from just south of Lyon to near Avignon, is the king of Provence wines. Our

focus is on the southern, Provençal section, roughly from Vaison la Romaine to Avignon (though wine-lovers should take note of the big, complex reds found in the northern Rhône wines of St. Joseph, Hermitage, and Cornas, as well as the seductive white of Condrieu). The wines of the southern Rhône are consistently good—and sometimes exceptional. The reds are full-bodied, rosés are dry and fruity, and whites are dry and fragrant, often with hints of flowers. Côtes du Rhône whites aren't nearly as good as the reds, though the rosés are refreshing and ideal for lunch on the terrace. For more on this wine region, including a self-guided driving tour of the area's villages and vintners, see the Côtes du Rhône chapter.

Many subareas of the southern Côtes du Rhône are recognized for producing distinctly good wines, and have been awarded their own *appellations* (like Châteauneuf-du-Pape, Gigondas, Beaumes de Venise, Côtes de Ventoux, Tavel, and Côtes du Luberon). Wines often are named for the villages that produce them. The "Côtes du Rhône Villages" is a smaller appellation on the eastern side of the Côtes du Rhône. There are just over 20 villages in this appellation, including Séguret, Sablet, Rasteau, and Cairanne. As it is the top

On the Wine Label

appellation	area in which a wine's grapes are grown
bouchonné	"corked" (spoiled from a bad cork)
bouquet	bouquet (the fragrance when first opened)
cave	cellar (or wine shop)
cépage	grape variety (Syrah, Chardonnay, etc.)
côte, côteaux	hillside or slope
domaine	wine estate
étiquette	label
fût, tonneau	wine barrel
grand vin	excellent wine
millésimé	wine from a given year
mis en bouteille au château/à la domaine	estate-bottled (bottled where it was made)
vin de table	table wine (can be a blend of several wines)
vin du pays	wine from a given area (a step up from *vin de table*)

PROVENCE

wine for vintners in these villages, there are strict guidelines for production.

Here's a summary of what you might find on a Côtes du Rhône *carte des vins* (wine list):

Châteauneuf-du-Pape: Almost all wines from this famous village are reds (often blends; the most dominant grapes are typically Grenache, Mourvèdre, and Syrah). These wines have a velvety quality and can be spicy, with flavors of licorice and prunes. Châteauneuf-du-Pape wines merit lengthy aging. Considered among the best producers are Château de Beaucastel, Le Vieux Télégraphe, Clos des Papes, and Château la Nerthe. You can easily find their wines in North America. It's also worth seeking out lesser-known names and smaller wineries (many of which are listed in this book).

Gigondas: These wines have many of the same qualities as Châteauneuf-du-Pape, but are lesser known and therefore cheaper. Gigondas red wines are spicy, meaty, and can be pretty tannic. Again, aging is necessary to bring out the full qualities of the wine. Look for Domaine du Terme, Château de Montmirail, Domaine de Cassan, or Domaine de Coyeux for good quality.

Beaumes de Venise: While reds from this village are rich and flavorful, Beaumes de Venise is most famous for its Muscat—a sweet, fragrant wine usually served as an apéritif or with dessert. It often has flavors of apricots and peaches, and it should be consumed within two years of bottling. Try Domaine de Coyeux, Domaine de Durban, and Château Redortier.

Rasteau: This village sits across the valley from Gigondas and shares many of its qualities—at lower prices. Rasteau makes fine rosés, robust (at times "rough") and fruity reds, and a naturally sweet wine (Vin Doux Naturel). Their Côtes du Rhône Villages can be excellent. The cooperative in Rasteau is good, as are the wines from Domaine des Girasols.

Sablet: This village lies down in the valley below Gigondas and makes decent, fruity, and inexpensive reds and rosés.

Tavel: The queen of French rosés is 20 minutes north and west of Avignon, close to Pont du Gard. Tavel produces a rosé that is dry, crisp, higher in alcohol, darker, and more full-bodied than other rosés from the region. Look for any rosé from Tavel.

Côtes de Provence Wines

The lesser-known vineyards of the Côtes de Provence run east from Aix-en-Provence almost to St-Tropez. Typical grapes are Cinsault, Mourvèdre, Grenache, Carignan, and a little Cabernet Sauvignon and Syrah. The wines are commonly full-bodied and fruity, and are meant to be drunk when they're young. They cost less than Côtes du Rhônes and have similar characteristics. But the region is most famous for its "big" rosés that can be served with meat and garlic dishes (rosé accounts for 60 percent of production).

For one-stop shopping, make it a point to find the superb **La Maison des Vins Côtes de Provence** on RN-7 in Les Arcs-sur-Argens (a few minutes north of the A-8 autoroute, about halfway between Aix-en-Provence and Nice). This English-speaking wine shop and tasting center represents hundreds of producers, selling bottles at vineyard prices and offering free tastings of up to 16 wines (June–Oct daily 10:00–19:00; Nov–May Mon–Sat 10:00–18:00, closed Sun; tel. 04 94 99 50 20, www.caveaucp.fr).

Côteaux d'Aix-en-Provence Wines

This large wine region, between Les Baux and Aix-en-Provence, produces some interesting reds, whites, and rosés. Commonly used grapes are the same as in Côtes de Provence, though several producers (mainly around Les Baux) use a higher concentration of Cabernet Sauvignon, which helps distinguish their wines. The vintners around Les Baux produce some exceptionally good wines, and many of their vineyards are organic. Try Domaine d'Eole or Domaine Gourgonnier. The tiny wine-producing area of Palette houses only three wineries, all of which make exceptional rosés;

Le Mistral

Provence lives with its vicious mistral winds, which blow 30-60 miles per hour, about 100 days out of the year. Locals say it blows in multiples of threes: three, six, or nine days in a row. The mistral clears people off the streets and turns lively cities into ghost towns. You'll likely spend a few hours or days taking refuge—or searching for cover. The winds are strongest between noon and 15:00.

When the mistral blows, it's everywhere, and you can't escape. Author Peter Mayle said it could blow the ears off a donkey (I'd include the tail). According to the natives, it ruins crops, shutters, and roofs (look for stones holding tiles in place on many homes). They'll also tell you that this pernicious wind has driven many people crazy (including young Vincent van Gogh). A weak version of the wind is called a *mistralet.*

The mistral starts above the Alps and Massif Central mountains and gathers steam as it heads south, gaining momentum as it screams over the Rhône Valley (which acts like a funnel between the Alps and the Cévennes mountains) before exhausting itself when it hits the Mediterranean. And though this wind rattles shutters throughout the Riviera and Provence, it's strongest over the Rhône Valley...so Avignon, Arles, and the Côtes du Rhône villages bear its brunt. While wiping the dust from your eyes, remember the good news: The mistral brings clear skies.

one (Château Simone) also makes a delicious white wine. The Côtes de Provence–Sainte-Victoire wineries, with their beautiful views of Mont Ste-Victoire (famously painted by Cézanne), produce some excellent rosés.

Provençal Mediterranean Wines

Barely east of Marseille, Cassis and Bandol sit side by side, overlooking the Mediterranean. Though very close together, they are designated as separate wine-growing areas because of the distinctive nature of their wines. Cassis is one of France's smallest wine regions and is known for its strong, fresh, and very dry whites (made with the Marsanne grape)—arguably the best white wine in Provence. Bandol is known for its luscious, velvety reds. This wine, aged in old oak and made primarily from the Mourvèdre grape, is my favorite.

ARLES

By helping Julius Caesar defeat Marseille, Arles (pronounced "arl") earned the imperial nod and was made an important port city. With the first bridge over the Rhône River, Arles was a key stop on the Roman road from Italy to Spain, the Via Domitia. After reigning as the seat of an important archbishop and a trading center for centuries, the city became a sleepy backwater of little importance in the 1700s. Vincent van Gogh settled here in the late 1800s, but left only a chunk of his ear (now long gone). American bombers destroyed much of Arles in World War II as the townsfolk hid out in its underground Roman galleries. But today Arles thrives again, with its evocative Roman ruins, an eclectic assortment of museums, made-for-ice-cream pedestrian zones, and squares that play hide-and-seek with visitors.

The city's unpolished streets and squares are not to everyone's taste. This workaday city has not sold out to tourism, so you won't see dolled-up lanes and perfectly preserved buildings. But to me, that's part of its charm.

Orientation to Arles

Arles faces the Mediterranean, turning its back on Paris. And though the town is built along the Rhône, it largely ignores the river. Landmarks hide in Arles' medieval tangle of narrow, winding streets. Virtually everything is close—but first-timers can walk forever to get there. Hotels have good, free city maps, and Arles provides helpful street-corner signs that point you toward sights and hotels. Racing cars enjoy Arles' medieval lanes, turning sidewalks into tightropes and pedestrians into leaping targets.

Tourist Information

The **main TI** is on the ring road boulevard des Lices, at esplanade Charles de Gaulle (April–Sept daily 9:00–18:45; Oct–March
Mon–Sat 9:00–16:45, Sun 10:00–13:00; tel. 04 90 18 41 20, www
.arlestourisme.com). There's also a **train station TI** (Mon–Fri
9:00–13:30 & 14:30–16:45, closed Sat–Sun).

At either TI, pick up the city map, note the bus schedules
(displayed in binders), and get English information on nearby destinations such as the Camargue wildlife area (described in the next
chapter). Ask about "bullgames" (Provence's more humane version
of bullfights—see page 77) and walking tours of Arles. Skip the
useless €1 brochure describing several walks in Arles, including
one that locates Van Gogh's "easels" (better explained on page 72).
Both TIs can help you reserve hotel rooms (credit card required for
deposit).

Arrival in Arles

By Train: The train station is on the river, a 10-minute walk from
the town center. Before heading into town, get what you need at
the train station TI. There's no baggage storage at the station, but
you can walk 10 minutes to stow it at Hôtel Régence (see "Helpful
Hints," later).

To reach the town center, turn left out of the train station
and walk 15 minutes; or wait for the free Starlette bus at the shelter across the street (3/hour, Mon–Sat only). Taxis usually wait in
front of the station, but if you don't see any, call the posted telephone numbers, or dial 04 89 73 36 00. If the train station TI is
open, you can ask them to call. Taxi rates are fixed—allow about
€10 to any of my recommended hotels.

By Bus: The Centre-Ville bus station is a few blocks below
the main TI, located on the ring road at 16–24 boulevard Georges
Clemenceau.

By Car: Most hotels have parking nearby—ask for detailed
directions (€1.50/hour at most meters, free 12:00–14:00 & 19:00–
9:00). For most hotels, first follow signs to *Centre-Ville,* then
Gare SNCF (train station). You'll come to a big roundabout (place
Lamartine) with a Monoprix department store to the right. You
can park along the city wall and find your hotel on foot; the hotels
I list are no more than a 10-minute walk away (best not to park
here overnight due to theft concerns and markets on Wed and Sat).
Fearless drivers can plunge into the narrow streets between the
two stumpy towers via rue de la Calade, and follow signs to their
hotel. Again, theft is a problem—leave nothing in your car, and
trust your hotelier's advice on where to park.

If you can't find parking near your hotel, Parking des Lices

Arles

← Van Gogh Walking Tour
P   Parking
B   Bus Stop
✺   View
⌂   Easel

100 YARDS
100 METERS

Van Gogh Sights

1. The Yellow House (Easel)
2. Starry Night Over the Rhône (Easel)
3. Rue de la Cavalerie
4. Arena (Easel)
5. Fondation Van Gogh
6. Alpilles Mountains View
7. Jardin d'Eté (Easel)
8. To Les Alyscamps Cemetery
9. Place du Forum & Café la Nuit (Easel)
10. Espace Van Gogh (Easel)
11. Trinquetaille Bridge (Easel)

Other

12. Baggage Storage & Bike Rental
13. Launderette
14. To Avis Car Rental
15. Europcar Car Rental
16. Hertz Car Rental
17. Le Petit Train Departure Point
18. Bus #1 (to Ancient History Museum)

TRINQUETAILLE BRIDGE

MARX

QUAI

TRUCHET

DR. FANTON

TO ANCIENT HISTORY MUSEUM

R. JOUVE.   R. LIBERTE

RUE A. FRANCE

ARLATEN FOLK MUSEUM
(CLOSED UNTIL 2013)

RUE GAMBETTA

REPUB-

ESPACE VAN GOGH

10

END

RUE

MOLIERE   R.

18 B

TO ANCIENT HISTORY MUSEUM ←

BLVD.

BUS STN.

DCH

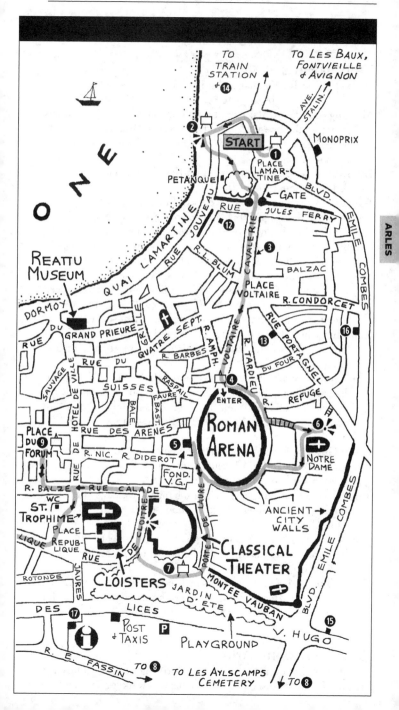

ARLES

(Arles' only parking garage), near the TI on boulevard des Lices, is a good fallback (€3/hour, €8/24 hours).

Helpful Hints

Market Days: The big markets are on Wednesdays and Saturdays. For all the details, see page 77.

Meetings and Festivals: An international photo event jams hotels in early July. The let-'er-rip, twice-yearly Féria draws crowds over Easter and in mid-September (see www.arlestourisme .com for dates).

Internet Access: Internet cafés in Arles change with the wind. Ask your hotelier or at the TI

Baggage Storage and Bike Rental: The recommended Hôtel Régence (see page 79) will store your bags for €3 (daily 7:30–22:00 mid-March–mid-Nov, closed in winter). They also rent bikes (€6/hour, €14/day, one-way rentals within Provence possible, same hours as baggage storage). Ask about their electric bikes—handy on windy days, but with limited power. From Arles you can ride to Les Baux (20 miles round-trip, very steep climb at the end) or into the Camargue (40 miles round-trip, forget it in the wind)—provided you're in great shape.

Laundry: There's a launderette at 12 rue Portagnel (daily 7:00–21:30, you can stay later to finish if you're already inside, English instructions).

Car Rental: Avis is at the train station (tel. 04 90 96 82 42), and **Europcar** and **Hertz** are downtown (Europcar is at 2 bis avenue Victor Hugo, tel. 04 90 93 23 24; Hertz is closer to place Lamartine at 10 boulevard Emile Combes, tel. 04 90 96 75 23).

Local Guide: Charming **Jacqueline Neujean,** an excellent guide, knows Arles and nearby sights intimately and loves her work (€90/2 hours, tel. & fax 04 90 98 47 51).

English Book Exchange: A small exchange is available at the recommended **Soleileis** ice-cream shop (see page 86).

Cooking Courses: Food-lovers enjoy cooking classes and market tours offered by gentle Erick Vedel (tel. 04 90 49 69 20).

Public Pools: Arles has three public pools (indoor and outdoor). Ask at the TI or your hotel.

Boules: The local "bouling alley" is by the river on place Lamartine. After their afternoon naps, the old boys congregate here for a game of pétanque (see page 208 for details on this popular local pastime).

Getting Around Arles

In this flat city, everything's within **walking** distance. Only the Ancient History Museum requires a healthy walk (or you can take a taxi or bus). The elevated riverside promenade provides Rhône views and a direct route to the Ancient History Museum (to the southwest) and the train station (to the northeast). Keep your head up for *Starry Night* memories, but eyes down for decorations by dogs with poorly trained owners.

Arles' **taxis** charge a set fee of about €10, but nothing except the Ancient History Museum is worth a taxi ride. To call a cab, dial 04 89 73 36 00 or 04 90 96 90 03.

The free **Starlette bus** circles the town (3/hour, Mon–Sat only), but is only useful for access to the train station.

Le Petit Train d'Arles provides a helpful orientation to the lay of the land—if you prefer sitting to walking (€6.50, 35 minutes, stops in front of the main TI and at the Arena).

Sights in Arles

Most sights cost €3.50–7, and though any sight warrants a few minutes, many aren't worth their individual admission price. The TI sells three different monument passes (called Passeports). **Le Passeport Avantage** covers almost all of Arles' sights (€13.50, under 18 for €12; Fondation Van Gogh discounted); the €9 **Le Passeport Arelate** covers Arles' four Roman sights and the Ancient History Museum; and the €9 **Le Passeport Liberté** lets you choose any five monuments (one must be a museum). Depending on your interests, one of the €9 Passeports is probably best.

Start at the Ancient History Museum for a helpful overview (drivers should try to do this museum on their way into Arles), then dive into the city-center sights. Remember, many sights stop selling tickets 30–60 minutes before closing (both before lunch and at the end of the day). To make the most of Arles' Roman history, see "How About Them Romans?" on page 48.

▲▲Ancient History Museum
(Musée de l'Arles et de la Provence Antiques)

Begin your town visit here, for Roman Arles 101. Located on the site of the Roman chariot racecourse (the arc of which is built

into the parking lot), this air-conditioned, all-on-one-floor museum is just west of central Arles along the river. Models and original sculptures (with almost no posted English translations but a decent handout) re-create the Roman city, making workaday life and culture easier to imagine.

Arles at a Glance

▲▲▲**Roman Arena** This big amphitheater, once used by gladiators, today hosts summer "bullgames" and occasional bullfights. **Hours:** Daily May–Sept 9:00–19:00, March–April and Oct 9:00–18:00, Nov–Feb 10:00–17:00. See page 71.

▲▲**Ancient History Museum** Filled with models and sculptures, this is Roman Arles 101. **Hours:** Wed–Mon April–Oct 9:00–19:00, Nov–March 10:00–18:00, closed Tue year-round. See page 65.

▲▲**Forum Square** Lively, café-crammed square that was once the Roman forum. **Hours:** Always open. See page 68.

▲▲**St. Trophime Church** Church with exquisite Romanesque entrance. **Hours:** Church open daily April–Sept 9:00–12:00 & 14:00–18:30, Oct–March 9:00–12:00 & 14:00–17:00; cloisters open daily March–Oct 9:00–18:00, Nov–Feb 10:00–17:00. See page 69.

▲**Fondation Van Gogh** Small gallery with works by major contemporary artists paying homage to Van Gogh (but no Vincent originals). **Hours:** April–June daily 10:00–18:00, July–Sept daily 10:00–19:00, Oct–March Tue–Sun 11:00–17:00, closed Mon. See page 71.

▲**Arlaten Folk Museum** Shares the treasures and pleasures of Provençal life from the 18th and 19th centuries—but closed for renovation until 2013.

Classical Theater Ruined Roman theater, recently restored and still used for events. **Hours:** Daily May–Sept 9:00–19:00, March–April and Oct 9:00–12:00 & 14:00–18:00, Nov–Feb 10:00–12:00 & 14:00–17:00. See page 70.

Réattu Museum Decent, mostly modern art collection in a fine 15th-century mansion. **Hours:** Tue–Sun July–Sept 10:00–19:00, Oct–June 10:00–12:30 & 14:00–18:30, closed Mon year-round. See page 72.

Cost and Hours: €6, Wed–Mon April–Oct 9:00–19:00, Nov–March 10:00–18:00, closed Tue year-round, presqu'île du Cirque Romain.

Information: Ask for the English booklet, which provides a helpful if not in-depth background on the collection, and inquire whether there are any free English tours (usually daily July–Sept at 17:00, 1.5 hours). Tel. 04 90 18 88 88, www.arles-antique.cg13.fr.

Getting There: To reach the museum on foot from the city center (a 20-minute **walk**), turn left at the river and take the riverside path to the big, blue, modern building. As you approach the museum, you'll pass the verdant Hortus Garden—designed to recall the Roman circus and chariot racecourse that were located here, and to give residents a place to gather and celebrate civic events. A **taxi** ride costs €10 (museum can call a taxi for your return). **Bus #1** gets you within a few minutes' walk (€0.80, 3/hour Mon–Sat, none Sun). Catch the bus in Arles (clockwise direction on boulevard des Lices), then get off at the Musée de l'Arles Antique stop (before the stop, you'll see the bright-blue museum ahead on the right). Turn left as you step off the bus, and follow the sidewalk. (To return to the center, the bus stop is across the street from where you got off.)

❯ Self-Guided Tour: A huge map of the Roman Arles region greets visitors and shows the key Roman routes accessible to Arles. Find the impressive row of pagan and early-Christian **sarcophagi** (from the second to fifth centuries). These would have lined the Via Aurelia outside the town wall. In the early days of the Church, Jesus was often portrayed beardless and as the good shepherd, with a lamb over his shoulder.

Next you'll see **models** of every Roman structure in (and near) Arles. These are the highlight for me, as they breathe life into

the buildings as they looked 2,000 years ago. Start with the model of Roman Arles, and imagine the city's splendor. Find the Forum—still the center of town today, though only two columns survive. Look at the space Romans devoted to their Arena and huge racecourse—a reminder that an emphasis on sports is not unique to modern civilizations. The model also illustrates how little Arles seems to have changed over two millennia, with its houses still clustered around the city center, and warehouses still located on the opposite side of the river.

Look for individual models of the major buildings shown in the city model: the elaborately elegant forum; the floating bridge that gave Arles a strategic advantage (over the widest, and therefore slowest, part of the river); the theater (with its magnificent stage wall); the Arena (with its movable stadium cover to shelter spectators from sun or rain); and the circus, or chariot racecourse. Part of the original racecourse was just outside the windows, and, though long gone, it must have resembled Rome's Circus Maximus in its day—its obelisk is now the centerpiece of Arles' place de la République.

Finally, check out the **3-D model** of the hydraulic mill of Barbegal, with its 16 waterwheels and eight grain mills cascading down a nearby hillside (well worth a side-trip if you have a car—see page 96).

Other rooms in the museum display pottery, jewelry, metal and glass artifacts, and well-crafted mosaic floors that illustrate how Roman Arles was a city of art and culture. The many **statues** that you see are all original, except for the greatest—the *Venus of Arles*, which Louis XIV took a liking to and had moved to Versailles. It's now in the Louvre—and, as locals say, "When it's in Paris...bye-bye."

In Central Arles

Ideally, visit these sights in the order listed below. I've included some walking directions to connect the dots.

ARLES

▲▲**Forum Square (Place du Forum)**—Named for the Roman forum that once stood here, place du Forum was the political and religious center of Roman Arles. Still lively, this café-crammed square is a local watering hole and popular for a *pastis* (anise-based apéritif). The bistros on the square, though no place for a fine dinner, can put together a good-enough salad or *plat du jour*—and when you sprinkle on the ambience, that's €10 well spent.

At the corner of Grand Hôtel Nord-Pinus (a favorite of Pablo Picasso), a plaque shows how the Romans built a foundation of galleries to make the main square level in order to compensate for Arles' slope down to the river. The two columns are all that survive from the upper story of the entry to the Forum. Steps leading to the entrance are buried—the Roman street level was about 20 feet below you (you can get a glimpse of it by peeking through the street-level openings under the Hôtel d'Arlatan, two blocks below place du Forum on rue Sauvage).

The statue on the square is of **Frédéric Mistral** (1830–1914). This popular poet, who wrote in the local dialect rather than in French, was a champion of Provençal culture. After receiving the Nobel Prize in Literature in 1904, Mistral used his prize money to preserve and display the folk identity of Provence. He founded the regional folk museum (the Arlaten Folk Museum, closed for renovation until 2013) at a time when France was rapidly centralizing. (The local mistral wind—literally "master"—has nothing to do with his name.)

The **bright-yellow café**—called Café la Nuit—was the subject of one of Vincent van Gogh's most famous works in Arles. Although his painting showed the café in a brilliant yellow from the glow of gas lamps, the facade was bare limestone, just like the other cafés on this square. The café's current owners have painted it to match Van Gogh's version...and to cash in on the Vincentcrazed hordes who pay too much to eat or drink here.

• *Walk a block uphill (past Grand Hôtel Nord Pinus) and turn left. Walk through the Hôtel de Ville's vaulted entry (or take the next right if it's closed), and pop out onto the big...*

Republic Square (Place de la République)—This square used to be called "place Royale"...until the French Revolution. The obelisk was the former centerpiece of Arles' Roman Circus. The lions at its base are the symbol of the city, whose slogan is (roughly) "the gentle lion." Find a seat and watch the peasants—pilgrims, locals, and street musicians. There's nothing new about this scene.

• *Near the corner of the square where you entered, look for...*

▲▲St. Trophime Church—Named after a third-century bishop of Arles, this church sports the finest Romanesque main entrance (west portal) I've seen anywhere.

Like a Roman triumphal arch, the church facade trumpets the promise of Judgment Day. The tympanum (the semicircular area above the door) is filled with Christian symbolism. Christ sits in majesty, surrounded by symbols of the four evangelists: Matthew (the winged man), Mark (the winged lion), Luke (the ox), and John (the eagle). The 12 apostles are lined up below Jesus. It's Judgment Day...some are saved and others aren't. Notice the condemned (on the right)—a chain gang doing a sad bunny-hop over the fires of hell. For them, the tune trumpeted by the three angels above Christ is not a happy one. Below the chain gang, St. Stephen is being stoned to death, with his soul leaving through his mouth and instantly being welcomed by angels. Ride the exquisite detail back to a simpler age. In an illiterate medieval world, long before the vivid images of our Technicolor time, this was a neon billboard over the town square.

Enter the church (free, daily April–Sept 9:00–12:00 & 14:00–18:30, Oct–March 9:00–12:00 & 14:00–17:00). Just inside the door on the right, a chart locates the interior highlights and helps explain the carvings you just saw on the tympanum.

Tour the church counterclockwise. The tall 12th-century Romanesque nave is decorated by a set of tapestries showing scenes from the life of Mary (17th century, from the French town of Aubusson). Amble around the Gothic apse. Just to the left of the high altar, check out the relic chapel—with its fine golden boxes that hold long-venerated bones of obscure saints. Farther down is a chapel built on an early-Christian sarcophagus from Roman Arles (dated about A.D. 300). The heads were lopped off during the French Revolution.

This church is a stop on the ancient pilgrimage route to Santiago de Compostela in northwest Spain. For 800 years pilgrims on their way to Santiago have paused here...and they still do today. As you leave, notice the modern-day pilgrimages advertised on the far right near the church's entry.

• *Leaving the church, turn left, then left again through a courtyard to enter the cloisters.*

The adjacent **cloisters** are worth a look only if you have a pass (big cleaning underway, enter at the far end of the courtyard). The many small columns were scavenged from the ancient Roman theater. Enjoy the sculpted capitals, the rounded 12th-century Romanesque arches, and the pointed 14th-century Gothic ones. The pretty vaulted hall exhibits 17th-century tapestries showing scenes from the First Crusade to the Holy Land. On the second floor, you'll walk along an angled rooftop designed to catch rainwater—notice the slanted gutter that channeled the water into a cistern and the heavy roof slabs covering the tapestry hall below (€3.50, daily March–Oct 9:00–18:00, Nov–Feb 10:00–17:00).

• *Turn right out of the cloisters, then take the first right on rue de la Calade to reach the...*

Classical Theater (Théâtre Antique)—This first-century B.C. Roman theater once seated 10,000...just like the theater in Orange.

But unlike Orange, here in Arles there was no hillside to provide support. This theater was an elegant, 3-level structure with 27 arches radiating out to the street level. From the outside, it looked much like a halved version of Arles' Roman Arena. For more on Roman theaters, read about the theater in Orange (see page 161) and spring for the helpful €3 brochure.

Start with the video outside, which provides helpful background information and images that make it easier to put the scattered stones back in place (crouch in front to make out the small English subtitles). Next, walk to a center aisle and pull up a stone seat. To appreciate the theater's original size, look to the upper-left side of the tower and find the protrusion that supported the highest seating level. The structure required 33 rows of seats covering three levels to accommodate demand. During the Middle Ages, the old theater became a convenient town quarry—St. Trophime Church was built from theater rubble. Precious little of the original theater survives—though it still is used for events, with seating for 3,000 spectators.

ARLES

Two lonely Corinthian columns are all that remain of a three-story stage wall that once featured more than 100 columns and statues painted in vibrant colors. The orchestra section is defined by a semicircular pattern in the stone in front of you. Stepping up onto the left side of the stage, look down to the slender channel that allowed the brilliant-red curtain to disappear below, like magic. The stage, which was built of wood, was about 160 feet across and 20 feet deep. Go backstage and browse through the actors' changing rooms, then loop back to the entry behind the grass (€3, daily May–Sept 9:00–19:00, March–April and Oct 9:00–12:00 & 14:00–18:00, Nov–Feb 10:00–12:00 & 14:00–17:00). Budget travelers can peek over the fence from rue du Cloître, and see just about everything for free.

• *A block uphill is the...*

▲▲▲**Roman Arena (Amphithéâtre)**—Nearly 2,000 years ago, gladiators fought wild animals here to the delight of 20,000

screaming fans. Today local daredevils still fight wild animals here—"bullgame" posters around the Arena advertise upcoming spectacles (see page 77). A lengthy restoration process is well underway, giving the amphitheater an almost bleached-teeth whiteness.

In Roman times, games were free (sponsored by city bigwigs), and fans were seated by social class. The many exits allowed for rapid dispersal after the games—fights would break out among frenzied fans if they couldn't leave quickly. Through medieval times and until the early 1800s, the arches were bricked up and the stadium became a fortified town—with 200 humble homes crammed within its circular defenses. Three of the medieval towers survive (the one above the ticket booth is open and rewards those who climb it with terrific views). To see two still-sealed arches—complete with cute medieval window frames—turn right as you leave, walk to the Andaluz restaurant, and look back to the second floor (€6, daily May–Sept 9:00–19:00, March–April and Oct 9:00–18:00, Nov–Feb 10:00–17:00). For more on Roman amphitheaters, see page 139.

• *Turn left out of the Arena and walk uphill to find the...*

▲**Fondation Van Gogh**—A refreshing stop for modern-art-lovers and Van Gogh fans, this two-level gallery shows works by contemporary artists (including **Roy Lichtenstein** and **Robert Rauschenberg**), who pay homage to Vincent through thought-provoking interpretations of his works. The black-and-white photographs (both art and shots of places that Vincent painted)

ARLES

complement the paintings. (But be warned that the collection contains no Van Gogh originals.) Unfortunately, this collection is often on the road July through September, when non–Van Gogh material is displayed (€6, €4 with Le Passeport Avantage; good collection of Van Gogh souvenirs, prints, and postcards for sale in gift shop; April–June daily 10:00–18:00; July–Sept daily 10:00–19:00; Oct–March Tue–Sun 11:00–17:00, closed Mon; facing Arena at 24 bis rond-point des Arènes, tel. 04 90 49 94 04, www.fondationvangogh-arles.org). For more on Vincent, see "Van Gogh Sights in and near Arles," below.

• *The next two attractions are back across town. The Arlaten Folk Museum (closed until 2013) is close to place du Forum, and the Réattu Museum is near the river.*

▲Arlaten Folk Museum (Musée Arlaten/Museon Arlaten)— This museum, which normally explains the ins and outs of daily Provençal life, is closed for renovation until 2013 (www.museon arlaten.fr).

Réattu Museum (Musée Réattu)—Housed in the former Grand Priory of the Knights of Malta, this mildly interesting, mostly modern-art collection includes 57 Picasso drawings (some two-sided and all done in a flurry of creativity—I like the bullfights best), a room of Henri Rousseau's Camargue watercolors, and an unfinished painting by the Neoclassical artist Jacques Réattu... but none with English explanations. Occasional special exhibits show off the museum's impressive permanent collection, which is mostly in storage (€7, Tue–Sun July–Sept 10:00–19:00, Oct–June 10:00–12:30 & 14:00–18:30, closed Mon year-round, last entry 30 minutes before closing for lunch or at end of day, 10 rue du Grand Prieuré, tel. 04 90 96 37 68, www.museereattu.arles.fr).

Van Gogh Sights in and near Arles

In the dead of winter in 1888, 35-year-old Dutch artist Vincent van Gogh left big-city Paris for Provence, hoping to jump-start his floundering career and personal life. He was inspired, and he was lonely. Coming from the gray skies and flat lands of the north, Vincent was bowled over by everything Provençal—the sun, bright colors, rugged landscape, and unspoiled people. For the next two years he painted furiously, cranking out a masterpiece every few days.

None of the 200-plus paintings that Van Gogh did in the south can be found today in the city that so moved him. But you can walk the same streets he knew and see places he painted, marked by about a dozen steel-and-concrete "**easels**," with photos of the final paintings for then-and-now comparisons. The TI has a €1 brochure that locates all the easels (those described in this book are easily found without the brochure—see the map on page 62).

Small stone markers with yellow accents embedded in the pavement lead to the easels.

• *Take a walk in Vincent's footsteps (roughly north to south through Arles' center) and watch his paintings come to life by putting yourself in his shoes. Start at* **place Lamartine** *and find the stone easel across the grass from the Civette Arlesienne bistro.*

Vincent arrived in Arles on February 20, 1888, to a foot of snow. He rented a small house on the north side of place Lamartine. The house was destroyed in 1944 by an errant bridge-seeking bomb, but the four-story building behind it—where you see the Civette Arlesienne—still stands (find it in the painting).

The house had four rooms, including a small studio and the cramped trapezoid-shaped bedroom made famous in paintings. It was painted yellow inside and out, and Vincent named it..."**The Yellow House.**" In the distance, the painting shows the same bridges you see today, as well as a steam train—which was a rather recent invention in France, allowing people like Vincent to travel greater distances and be jarred by new experiences. (Today's Eurail system continues that trend.)

Freezing Arles was buttoned up tight when Vincent arrived, so he was forced to work inside, where he painted still-lifes and self-portraits—anything to keep his brush moving. In late March, spring finally arrived. In those days, a short walk from place Lamartine led to open fields. Donning his straw hat, Vincent set up his easel outdoors and painted quickly, capturing what he saw and felt—the blossoming fruit trees, gnarled olive trees, peasants sowing and reaping, jagged peaks, and windblown fields,

all lit by a brilliant sun that drove him to use ever-brighter paints.

• *Walk to the river, passing a monument in honor of two American pilots killed in action during the liberation of Arles. The monument was erected in 2002 as a post-9/11 sign of solidarity with Americans. Find the easel in the wall where ramps lead down to the river.*

One night, Vincent set up along this river west of place Lamartine and painted the stars boiling above the city skyline— **Starry Night over the Rhône.** Vincent looked to the night sky for the divine and was the first to paint outside after dark, adapting his straw hat to hold candles (which must have blown the minds of locals back then). As his paintings progressed, the stars became larger and more animated (like Vincent himself). The lone couple in the painting pops up again and again in his work. Experts say that Vincent was desperate for a close relationship with another being...someone to stroll the riverbank with under a star-filled sky. (Note: This painting is not the *Starry Night* you're thinking of—that one is described on page 101.)

To his sister Wilhelmina, Van Gogh wrote, "At present I absolutely want to paint a starry sky. It often seems to me that night is still more richly colored than the day; having hues of the most intense violets, blues, and greens. If only you pay attention to it, you will see that certain stars are lemon-yellow, others pink or a green, blue, and forget-me-not brilliance." Vincent painted this scene on his last night in Arles. Come back at night to match his painting with today's scene.

• *Turn around and walk through the small park, then go into town between the stone towers along* **rue de la Cavalerie.**

Van Gogh walked into town the same way, underneath the arch and along this street. Arles' 19th-century red light district was just east of rue de la Cavalerie, and the far-from-home Dutchman spent many lonely nights in its bars and brothels.

• *Pass through place Voltaire, continue walking up rue Voltaire to the* **Arena,** *and then find the easel at the top of the Arena steps, to the right.*

All summer long, fueled by sun and alcohol, Vincent painted the town. He loved the bullfights in the Arena (note the bull in the easel), and sketched the colorful surge of the crowds, spending more time studying the people than watching the bullfights. Vincent had little interest in Arles' antiquity—it was people and nature that fascinated him. (Near the Arena, the Fondation Van Gogh—described on page 71—exhibits paintings by artists inspired by Van Gogh.)

• *Walk clockwise around the Arena, then up the cobbled lane next to Andaluz restaurant. Keep left in the parking lot to find a viewpoint.*

This view to the **Alpilles Mountains** (no easel) pretty much matches what Vincent would have seen (be here late in the day for the best light). Vincent was an avid walker. Imagine him hauling his easel into those fields under intense sun, leaning against a ferocious wind, struggling to keep his hat on. He did this about 50 times during his stay in Arles, just to paint the farm workers. Vincent venerated but did not glorify peasants. Wanting to show their lives and their struggles, he reproached Renoir and Monet for elevating them in their works.

Vincent carried his easel as far as the medieval abbey of **Montmajour,** that bulky structure three miles straight ahead. The

St. Paul Hospital where he was eventually treated in St. Rémy is on the other side of the Alpilles, several miles beyond Montmajour. On a clear day, you can make out the hill town of Les Baux at about 2 o'clock (with Montmajour at high noon).

• *Continue past the upper end of the Arena, turn left before the Classical Theater, and walk out rue de Porte de Laure. At the end of the street, step down into the park and find the easel on the last path before the end of the park to the right.*

Vincent spent many a sunny day painting the leafy **Jardin d'Eté.** In another letter to his sister, Vincent wrote, "I don't know whether you can understand that one may make a poem by arranging colors…. In a similar manner, the bizarre lines, purposely selected and multiplied, meandering all through the picture may not present a literal image of the garden, but they may present it to our minds as if in a dream."

Vincent never made real friends, though he desperately wanted to. The son of disinterested parents, he never found the social skills necessary to sustain close friendships. He palled around with (and painted) his mailman and a Foreign Legionnaire. (The fact that locals pronounced his name "vahn-saw van gog" had nothing to do with his psychological struggles here.)

Packing his paints and a picnic in a rucksack, he day-tripped to the old Roman cemetery of **Les Alyscamps** (a 10-minute detour from this route, across the busy street and to the left).

• *Continue through the gardens and exit at the far-right corner. Work your way past the Classical Theater on rue du Cloître, and take the first left on rue de la Calade. Continue to **place du Forum** and locate an easel one café down from the yellow Café la Nuit.*

In October, lonely Vincent—who dreamed of making Arles a magnet for fellow artists—persuaded his friend Paul Gauguin to come. He decorated Gauguin's room with several humble canvases of sunflowers (now some of the world's priciest paintings), knowing that Gauguin had admired a similar painting he'd done in Paris. Their plan was for Gauguin to be the "dean" of a new art school in Arles, and Vincent its instructor-in-chief. At first, the two got along well. They spent days side by side, rendering the same subject in their two distinct styles. At night they hit the bars and brothels. Van Gogh's well-known *Café at Night* captures the glow of an absinthe buzz at Café la Nuit on place du Forum.

After two months together, the two artists clashed over art and personality differences (Vincent was a slob around the house, whereas Gauguin was meticulous). The night of December 23, they were drinking absinthe at the café when Vincent suddenly went ballistic. He threw his glass at Gauguin. Gauguin left. Walking through place Victor Hugo, Gauguin heard footsteps behind him and turned to see Vincent coming at him, brandishing a razor.

Gauguin quickly fled town. The local paper reported what happened next: "At 11:30 p.m., Vincent Vaugogh [*sic*], painter from Holland, appeared at the brothel at no. 1, asked for Rachel, and gave her his cut-off earlobe, saying, 'Treasure this precious object.' Then he vanished." He woke up the next morning at home with his head wrapped in a bloody towel and his earlobe missing. Was Vincent emulating a successful matador, whose prize is cutting off the bull's ear?

• *From here retrace your steps a bit, then walk through the place de la République, turn right in the far corner, and find the Arlaten Folk Museum. Turn left on rue Président Wilson, and find Espace Van Gogh (on the right). There's an easel in the center of the courtyard.*

ARLES

Vincent was checked into the local hospital—today's **Espace Van Gogh** cultural center (the Espace is free, but only the court-

yard is open to the public). It surrounds a flowery courtyard that the artist loved and painted when he was being treated for blood loss as well as for hallucinations and severe depression that left him bed-ridden for a month. The citizens of Arles circulated a petition demanding that the mad Dutchman be kept under medical supervision. Félix Rey, Vincent's kind doctor, worked out a compromise: The artist could leave during the day so that he could continue painting, but he had to sleep at the hospital at night. Look through the postcards sold in the courtyard and find a painting of Vincent's ward showing nuns attending patients in a gray hall *(Ward of Arles Hospital)*.

In the spring of 1889, the bipolar genius (a modern diagnosis) admitted himself to the **St. Paul Monastery and Hospital in St. Rémy-de-Provence** (see page 100), where he spent a year, thriving in the care of nurturing doctors and nuns. Painting was part of his therapy, so they gave him a studio to work in, and he produced more than 100 paintings. Alcohol-free and institutionalized, he did some of his wildest work. With thick, swirling brushstrokes and surreal

colors, he made his placid surroundings throb with restless energy. Today, at the hospital in St. Rémy, you can see a replica of his room and his studio, plus many scenes he painted *in situ* like these in Arles—the courtyard, the plane trees, the view out the upstairs window of nearby fields, and the rugged Alpilles Mountains.

In the spring of 1890, Vincent left Provence to be cared for by a doctor in Auvers-sur-Oise, north of Paris. On July 27, he wandered into a field and shot himself. He died two days later.

The next easels are less central, but easily located and worth the effort for Van Gogh fans: the **Trinquetaille Bridge,** on the river walkway toward the Ancient History Museum (the current bridge is a 1951 replacement); and the most famous, the **Langlois Drawbridge** (1.5 miles south of town along a Rhône canal—today's bridge is a 1926 duplicate of the original).

Events in Arles

▲▲**Markets**—On Wednesday and Saturday mornings, Arles' ring road erupts into an open-air festival of fish, flowers, produce...and you name it. The main event is on Saturday, with vendors jamming the ring road from boulevard Emile Combes to the east, along boulevard des Lices near the TI (the heart of the market), and continuing down boulevard Georges Clemenceau to the west. Wednesday's market runs only along boulevard Emile Combes, between place Lamartine and bis avenue Victor Hugo; the segment nearest place Lamartine is all about food, and the upper half features clothing, tablecloths, purses, and so on. On the first Wednesday of the month, a flea market doubles the size of the usual Wednesday market along boulevard des Lices near the main TI. Join in: Buy some flowers for your hotelier, try the olives, sample some wine, and swat a pickpocket. Both markets are open until 12:30.

Part of the market has a North African feel, thanks to the Algerians and Moroccans who live in Arles. They came to do the lowly city jobs that locals didn't want, and now they mostly do the region's labor-intensive agricultural jobs (picking olives, harvesting fruit, and working in local greenhouses; see sidebar on page 235).

▲▲**Bullgames (Courses Camarguaises)**—Occupy the same seats that fans have used for nearly 2,000 years, and take in Arles' most memorable experience—the *courses camarguaises* in the ancient Arena. The nonviolent "bullgames" are more sporting than bloody bullfights (though traditional Spanish-style bullfights still take place on occasion). The bulls of Arles

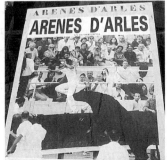

(who, locals stress, "die of old age") are promoted in posters even more boldly than their human foes. In the bullgame, a ribbon *(cocarde)* is laced between the bull's horns. The *razeteur,* with a special hook, has 15 minutes to snare the ribbon. Local businessmen encourage a *razeteur* (dressed in white with a red cummerbund) by shouting out how much money they'll pay for the *cocarde*. If the bull pulls a good stunt, the band plays the famous "Toreador" song from *Carmen*. The following day, newspapers report on the games, including how many *Carmens* the bull earned.

Three classes of bullgames—determined by the experience of the *razeteurs*—are advertised in posters: The *course de protection* is for rookies. The *trophée de l'Avenir* comes with more experience. And the *trophée des As* features top professionals. During Easter and the fall rice-harvest festival *(Féria du Riz),* the Arena hosts traditional Spanish bullfights (look for *corrida*) with outfits, swords, spikes, and the whole gory shebang. Bullgame tickets run €5–15; bullfights are pricier (€14–80). Schedules change every year—ask at the TI or check online at www.arenes-arles.com.

Don't pass on a chance to see *Toro Piscine,* a silly spectacle for warm summer evenings where the bull ends up in a swimming pool (uh-huh...get more details at TI). Nearby villages stage *courses camarguaises* in small wooden bullrings nearly every weekend; TIs have the latest schedule.

Sleeping in Arles

Hotels are a great value here—many are air-conditioned, though few have elevators. The Calendal, Musée, and Régence hotels offer exceptional value.

$$$ Hôtel le Calendal*** is a seductive place located between the Arena and Classical Theater. Enter an expertly run hotel with airy lounges and a lovely palm-shaded courtyard. Enjoy the elaborate €12 buffet breakfast, have lunch in the courtyard or at the inexpensive sandwich bar (daily 12:00–15:00), and take advantage of their four free laptops for guests. You'll also find a Jacuzzi and a "spa" with a Turkish bath, hot pool, and massages at good rates. The comfortable rooms sport Provençal decor and come in all shapes and sizes (standard Db-€100–115, Db with balcony-€135–165, Tb-€120–170, Qb-€140–180, price depends on room size, air-con, Wi-Fi, reserve ahead for parking-€10, just above Arena at 5 rue Porte de Laure, tel. 04 90 96 11 89, fax 04 90 96 05 84, www.lecalendal.com, contact@lecalendal.com).

$$$ Hôtel d'Arlatan***, built on the site of a Roman basilica, is classy in every sense of the word. It has sumptuous public spaces, a tranquil terrace, a designer pool, a turtle pond, and antique-filled rooms, most with high, wood-beamed ceilings and

Sleep Code

(€1 = about $1.25, country code: 33)
S = Single, **D** = Double/Twin, **T** = Triple, **Q** = Quad, **b** = bathroom,
s = shower only, * = French hotel rating system (0-4 stars).
Unless otherwise noted, credit cards are accepted and English
is spoken.

To help you sort easily through these listings, I've divided
the rooms into three categories based on the price for a
standard double room with bath:

$$$ **Higher Priced**—Most rooms €80 or more.
  $$ **Moderately Priced**— Most rooms between €60-80.
   $ **Lower Priced**—Most rooms €60 or less.

Prices can change without notice; verify the hotel's
current rates online or by email. For other updates, see www
.ricksteves.com/update.

stone walls. In the lobby of this 15th-century building, a glass floor looks down into Roman ruins (standard Db-€137, bigger Db-€157, Db/Qb suites-€180, apartments-€200–250, excellent buffet breakfast-€15, air-con, bathrobes, ice machines, elevator, Wi-Fi, parking garage-€14, 1 block below place du Forum at 26 rue Sauvage—tough by car, tel. 04 90 93 56 66, fax 04 90 49 68 45, www.hotel-arlatan.fr, hotel-arlatan@wanadoo.fr).

$$ Hôtel du Musée** is a quiet, affordable manor-home hideaway tucked deep in Arles (tough to find by car). This delightful refuge comes with 28 air-conditioned and wood-floored rooms, a flowery two-tiered courtyard, and comfortable lounges. Lighthearted Claude and English-speaking Laurence, the gracious owners, are eager to help (Sb-€50, Db-€60–70, Tb-€75–90, Qb-€95, Wi-Fi, laptop available for guests, garage-€10, follow signs to *Réattu Museum* to 11 rue du Grand Prieuré, tel. 04 90 93 88 88, fax 04 90 49 98 15, www.hoteldumusee.com, contact @hoteldumusee.com).

$$ Hôtel de la Muette**, with reserved owners Brigitte and Alain, is another good choice. Located in a quiet corner of Arles, this low-key hotel is well-kept, with stone walls, brown tones, and a small terrace in front. You'll pay a bit more for the upgraded rooms, but it's money well-spent (most Db-€66, bigger Db-€75, Tb-€77, Qb-€92, buffet breakfast-€8, air-con, Internet access and Wi-Fi, private garage-€8, 15 rue des Suisses, tel. 04 90 96 15 39, fax 04 90 49 73 16, www.hotel-muette.com, hotel.muette@wanadoo.fr).

$ Hôtel Régence**, a top budget deal, has a riverfront location, immaculate and comfortable Provençal rooms, safe parking,

ARLES

Arles Hotels & Restaurants

← VAN GOGH WALKING TOUR

P PARKING

Ⓑ BUS STOP

↙ VIEW

100 YARDS

100 METERS

① Hôtel/Rest. le Calendal
② Hôtel d'Arlatan
③ Hôtel du Musée
④ Hôtel de la Muette
⑤ Hôtel Acacias
⑥ Hôtel Régence
⑦ Hôtel/Rest. Voltaire
⑧ To La Peiriero & Domaine de Laforest Hôtels
⑨ To Mas du Petit Grava Hôtel
⑩ Le 16, Le Gaboulet & Au Bryn du Thym Restaurants
⑪ Bistrot à Vins Restaurant
⑫ La Guele de Loup Restaurant
⑬ La Cuisine de Comptoir Rest.
⑭ Café de la Major (Coffee/Tea)
⑮ Le Grillon Restaurant
⑯ Le Criquet Restaurant
⑰ Media Luna Restaurant
⑱ L'Atelier & A Côté Restaurants
⑲ Soleileis Ice Cream

TRINQUETAILLE BRIDGE

MARX

QUAI

TRUCHET

RUE A. FRANCE

DR. FANTON

⑬

TO ANCIENT HISTORY MUSEUM

R. JOUVE. R. LIBERTE

ARLATEN FOLK MUSEUM
(CLOSED UNTIL 2013)

RUE GAMBETTA

REPUB.

ESPACE VAN GOGH

RUE

MOLIERE

R.

Ⓑ

TO ANCIENT HISTORY MUSEUM ←

BLVD.

BUS STN.

DCH

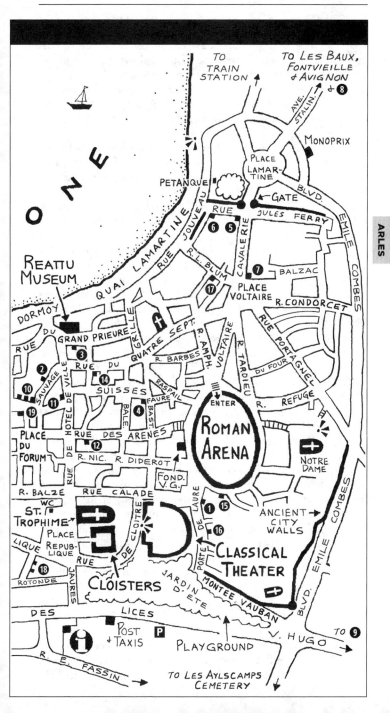

ARLES

TO
TRAIN
STATION

TO LES BAUX,
FONTVIEILLE
& AVIGNON
⚓ ❽

AVE. STALIN

MONOPRIX

R H O N E

PLACE
LAMARTINE

PETANQUE

GATE

BLVD.

RUE
JOUVEAU

QUAI LAMARTINE

RUE

CAVALERIE

JULES FERRY

EMILE COMBES

❻ ❺

REATTU
MUSEUM

R. L. BLUM

❼

BALZAC

PLACE
VOLTAIRE

R. CONDORCET

DORMOY

RUE DU GRAND PRIEURE

QUATRE SEPT.

❶❼

VOLTAIRE

RUE PORTAGNEL

RUE

RUE
DE
VILLE

❸

RUE DU

R. BARBES

R. AMPH.

RUE TARDIEU

DU FOUR

❷

SAUVAGE

SUISSES

❶❹

RASPAIL

FAURE

BAST.

R. REFUGE

❿

HOTEL

❶❶

BALE.

❹

ENTER

ROMAN
ARENA

❶❾

RUE DES ARENES

❶❷

R. NIC.

R. DIDEROT

NOTRE
DAME

PLACE
DU
FORUM

RUE DE

FOND.
V. G.

ANCIENT
CITY
WALLS

R. BALZE

RUE CALADE

DE LAURE

❶ ❶❺

WC

ST.
TROPHIME

PLACE
REPUBLIQUE

DE CLOITRE

❶❻

CLASSICAL
THEATER

LIQUE

❶❽

RUE

JAURES

PORTE DE LAURE

MONTEE VAUBAN

EMILE COMBES

ROTONDE

CLOISTERS

JARDIN
D. ETE

BLVD.

DES

LICES

V. HUGO

TO ❾

R. E. FASSIN

POST
& TAXIS

P

PLAYGROUND

TO LES AYLSCAMPS
CEMETERY

and easy access to the train station (Db-€50–60, Tb-€65–70, Qb-€75–80, good buffet breakfast-€6, choose river view or quieter courtyard rooms, most rooms have showers, air-con, no elevator but only two floors, Internet access and Wi-Fi; from place Lamartine, turn right immediately after passing between towers to reach 5 rue Marius Jouveau; tel. 04 90 96 39 85, fax 04 90 96 67 64, www.hotel-regence.com, contact@hotel-regence.com). The gentle Nouvions speak some English.

$ Hôtel Acacias**, just off place Lamartine and inside the old city walls, is a modern hotel with less personality. The pretty pastel rooms are on the small side, but they're reasonably priced (standard Sb or Db-€53, larger Db-€64–78, extra bed-€15, breakfast-€6, air-con, elevator, Wi-Fi, 2 rue de la Cavalerie, tel. 04 90 96 37 88, fax 04 90 96 32 51, www.hotel-acacias.com, contact@hotel-acacias.com).

$ Hôtel Voltaire* rents 12 small, spartan, and questionably clean rooms with ceiling fans and nifty balconies overlooking a fun square. A block below the Arena, it's good for starving artists. Smiling owner "Mr." Ferran (fur-ran) loves the States, and hopes you'll add to his postcard collection (D-€30, Ds-€35, Db-€40, 1 place Voltaire, tel. 04 90 96 49 18, fax 04 90 96 45 49, levoltaire13@aol.com). They also serve a good-value lunch and dinner in their recommended restaurant.

Near Arles

Many drivers, particularly those with families, prefer staying outside Arles in the peaceful countryside, with easy access to the area's sights. See also "Sleeping in Les Baux" on page 95.

$$$ La Peiriero***, 15 minutes from Arles in the town of Fontvieille, is a pooped parent's dream come true, with a grassy garden, massive pool, table tennis, badminton, massage parlor, indoor children's play area, and even a few miniature golf holes. The spacious family-loft rooms, capable of sleeping up to five, have full bathrooms on both levels. This complete retreat also comes with a terrace café and a well-respected restaurant, and helpful owners, the Levys (streetside Sb or Db-€100, gardenside Db-€120, Db with terrace-€144, loft-€218, dinner *menu*-€31, breakfast and dinner-€38, air-con, Wi-Fi, free parking, just east of Fontvieille on road to Les Baux, 34 avenue des Baux, tel. 04 90 54 76 10, fax 04 90 54 62 60, www.hotel-peiriero.com, info@hotel-peiriero.com). Just a short drive from Arles and Les Baux (and 20 minutes from Avignon), little Fontvieille slumbers in the shadows of its big-city cousins—though it has its share of restaurants and boutiques.

$$$ Mas du Petit Grava is a vintage Provençal farmhouse 15 tree-lined minutes east of Arles. Here California refugees Jim and Ike offer four large and well-cared-for rooms with tubs, tiles, and memories of Vincent (Jim is an expert on Van Gogh's life and art—ask him anything). A lovely garden surrounds a generously sized pool, but what draws most here are Jim and Ike (Db-€110–130, includes a fine breakfast, no air-con, free Wi-Fi, tel. 04 90 98 35 66, www.masdupetitgrava.net, masdupetitgrava@masdupetit grava.net). From Arles, drive east on D-453 toward St. Martin de Crau; 2.5 kilometers (about 1.5 miles) after passing through Raphèle, turn left on Route Saint Hippolite.

$$ Domaine de Laforest is ideally located a few minutes below Fontvieille, near the aqueduct of Barbegal. It's a big 320-acre spread engulfed by vineyards, rice fields, and swaying trees. The sweet owners (Sylvie and mama Mariette) have eight two-bedroom apartments with great weekly rates, though they may be rented for fewer days when available (€310, €400, or €700 per week, air-con, washing machines, Internet and Wi-Fi in all apartments, pool, big lawn, swings, mosquitoes can be a problem, 1000 route de l'Aqueduc Romain, tel. 04 90 54 70 25, fax 04 90 54 60 50, www.domaine-laforest.com, contact@domaine-laforest.com).

Eating in Arles

You can dine well in Arles on a modest budget—in fact, it's hard to blow a lot on dinner here (most of my listings have *menus* for €22 or less). The bad news is that restaurants here change regularly, so double-check my suggestions. Before dinner, go local on place du Forum and enjoy a *pastis*. This anise-based apéritif is served straight in a glass with ice, plus a carafe of water—dilute to taste. Sunday is a dead night for restaurants, though most eateries on place du Forum are open.

For **picnics,** a big, handy Monoprix supermarket/department store is on place Lamartine (Mon–Sat 8:30–19:25, closed Sun).

On or near Place du Forum

Great atmosphere and mediocre food at fair prices await on place du Forum. By all accounts, the garish yellow Café la Nuit is worth avoiding. Most other cafés on the square deliver acceptable quality and terrific ambience. A half-block below the Forum, on rue du Dr. Fanton, you'll find a lineup of more tempting restaurants. The first three are popular, and all have good indoor and outdoor seating.

Le 16 is a warm, affordable place to enjoy a fresh salad (€10)—though it's almost too popular for its own good (€13 *plats*, €21 three-course *menu,* closed Sat–Sun, 16 rue du Dr. Fanton, tel. 04 90 93 77 36).

Le Gaboulet has created a buzz in Arles by blending a cozy interior, classic French cuisine, and service with a smile (thanks to owner Frank). It's the most expensive of the places I list on this street, but it's still jammed every night—book ahead or come early (€27 *menu*, great fries, closed Sun–Mon, 18 rue du Dr. Fanton, tel. 04 90 93 18 11).

Au Bryn du Thym, next door, has long been reliable and specializes in traditional Provençal cuisine at fair prices—the bull steak is delicious. Arrive early for an outdoor table or call ahead, and let hardworking and sincere Monsieur and Madame Colombaud take care of you. Monsieur does *le cooking* while Madame does *le serving* (€19 three-course *menu*, closed Tue, 22 rue du Dr. Fanton, tel. 04 90 49 95 96).

Bistrot à Vins suits wine-lovers who enjoy pairing food and drink, and those in search of a good glass of *vin*. Sit at a convivial counter or at one of five tables while listening to light jazz (book ahead for a table). Affable Ariane speaks enough English and offers a limited selection of simple, tasty dishes. Her savory tartes and fresh green salad make a great meal (€10–16), and the wines— many available by the glass—are well priced (indoor dining only from 18:30 to 22:00, closed Mon–Tue, 2 rue du Dr. Fanton, tel. 04 90 52 00 65).

La Guele de Loup is a small, traditional place with a loyal following (reserve ahead). Its fine blend of Provençal and classic French cuisine is served in an intimate setting under wood beams in an upstairs room (€31 three-course *menu*, closed Wed, 39 rue des Arènes, tel. 04 90 96 96 69).

At **La Cuisine de Comptoir,** a cool little bistro, locals of all ages abandon Provençal decor. Welcoming owners Alexandre and Vincent offer light *tartine* dinners—a delicious cross between pizza and bruschetta, served with soup or salad for just €10 (a swinging deal). Sit at the counter and watch *le chef* at work (closed Sun, indoor dining only, just off place du Forum's lower end at 10 rue de la Liberté, tel. 04 90 96 86 28).

Café de la Major is *the* place to go to recharge with some serious coffee or tea (closed Sun, 7 bis rue Réattu, tel. 04 90 96 14 15).

Near the Roman Arena

For about the same price as on place du Forum, you can enjoy regional cuisine with a point-blank view of the Arena. Because they change regularly, the handful of (mostly) outdoor eateries that overlook the Arena are pretty indistinguishable.

Le Grillon owns the best view above the Arena and serves good-enough salads, crêpes, and *plats du jour* for €9–12 (closed all day Wed and Sun nights, at the top of the Arena on rond-point des Arènes, tel. 04 90 96 70 97).

Le Criquet is a sweet little place serving Provençal classics at good prices two blocks above the Arena (€18 three-course *menu,* closed Mon, indoor dining only, 21 rue Porte de Laure, tel. 04 90 96 80 51).

Hôtel le Calendal serves lunch in its lovely courtyard (€12–18, daily 12:00–15:00) or delicious little sandwiches for €2 each (three make a good meal) at its small café (also listed under "Sleeping in Arles," earlier).

Hôtel Voltaire, well-situated on a pleasing square, serves simple three-course lunches and dinners at honest prices to a loyal clientele (€13 *menus*; hearty *plats* and filling salads for €10—try the *salade fermière, salade Latine,* or the filling *assiette Provençale;* closed Sun evening, a few blocks below the Arena at 1 place Voltaire, tel. 04 90 96 49 18; also listed under "Sleeping in Arles," earlier).

Media Luna, a good choice for vegetarians, uses fresh, organic ingredients in its flavorful dishes. It's open on Sundays (rare in Arles) and welcomes guests with easygoing service (€14–16 *plats,* filling €15 vegetarian dish, organic wines, closed Tue, between the river and place Voltaire at 65 rue Amédée Pichot, tel. 04 90 97 81 89).

A Gastronomic Dining Experience

One of France's most recognized chefs, Jean-Luc Rabanel, has created a sensation with two very different options 50 yards from place de la République (at 7 rue des Carmes). They sit side by side, both offering indoor and terrace seating.

L'Atelier is so intriguing that people travel great distances just for the experience. Diners fork over €90 (at lunch, you'll spoon out €50) and trust the chef to create a memorable meal...which he does. There is no menu, just an onslaught of delicious taste sensations served on artsy dishes. Don't plan on a quick dinner, and don't come for the setting—it's a contemporary, shoebox-shaped dining room, but several outdoor tables are also available. The get-to-know-your-neighbor atmosphere means you can't help but join the party. You'll probably spot the famous chef (hint: he has long brown hair), as he is very hands-on with his waitstaff (closed Mon–Tue, best to book ahead, friendly servers will hold your hand through this palate-widening experience, tel. 04 90 91 07 69, www.rabanel.com).

A Côté saddles up next door, offering a smart wine bar/bistro ambience and top-quality cuisine for far less. Here you can sample the famous chef's talents for as little as €16 (daily *plat*) or as much as €32 (three-course *menu*, smallish servings, reasonably priced wines, open daily, tel. 04 90 47 61 13).

And for Dessert...

Soleileis has Arles' best ice cream, with all-natural ingredients and unusual flavors such as *fadoli*—olive oil mixed with nougatine. There's also a shelf of English books for exchange (open daily 14:00–18:30, across from recommended Le 16 restaurant at 9 rue du Dr. Fanton).

Arles Connections

Some trains in and out of Arles require a reservation. These include connections with Nice to the east and Bordeaux to the west (including intermediary stops). Ask at the station.

From Arles by Train to: Paris (11/day, 2 direct TGVs—4 hours, 9 with transfer in Avignon—5 hours), **Avignon Centre-Ville** (11/day, 20 minutes, less frequent in the afternoon), **Nîmes** (9/day, 30 minutes), **Orange** (4/day direct, 35 minutes, more frequent with transfer in Avignon), **Aix-en-Provence Centre-Ville** (10/day, 2.25 hours, transfer in Marseille, train may separate midway—be sure you're in section going to Aix-en-Provence), **Marseille** (20/day, 1.5 hours), **Cassis** (7/day, 2 hours), **Carcassonne** (8/day, 3.5 hours, most with transfer in Nîmes or Narbonne, direct trains may require reservations), **Beaune** (10/day, 4.5 hours, 9 with transfer in Nîmes or Avignon and Lyon), **Nice** (11/day, 3.75–4.5 hours, most require transfer in Marseille), **Barcelona** (2/day, 6 hours, transfer in Montpellier), **Italy** (3/day, transfer in Marseille and Nice; from Arles, it's 4.5 hours to Ventimiglia on the border, 8 hours to Milan, 9.5 hours to Cinque Terre, 11 hours to Florence, and 13 hours to Venice or Rome).

From Arles Train Station to Avignon TGV Station: If you're connecting from Arles to the TGV in Avignon, it's easiest to take the SNCF bus directly from Arles' train station to Avignon's TGV station (10/day, 1 hour). Another option—which takes the same amount of time, but adds more walking—is to take the regular train from Arles to Avignon's Centre-Ville Station, then catch the *navette* (shuttle bus) to the TGV station from there.

From Arles by Bus to: Nîmes (6/day, 1 hour), **St. Rémy-de-Provence** (bus #54, 3/day Mon–Sat, none on Sun, 50 minutes; bus #57 also goes to St. Rémy—see below), **Fontvieille** (6/day, 10 minutes), **Camargue/Stes-Maries-de-la-Mer** (bus #20, 5/day Mon–Sat, 3/day Sun, 1 hour). The bus station is at 16–24 boulevard Georges Clemenceau (2 blocks below main TI, next to Café le Wilson). Bus info: tel. 04 90 49 38 01 (unlikely to speak English).

From Arles by Bus to Les Baux and St. Rémy: Bus #59/57 connects Arles to **Les Baux** and **St. Rémy** (6/day daily July–Aug, Sat–Sun only in June and Sept; 35 minutes to Les Baux, 50 minutes to St. Rémy). Bus #54 (see above) also goes to St. Rémy but not via Les Baux. For other ways to reach Les Baux and St. Rémy, see page 90.

NEAR ARLES

Les Baux • St. Rémy •
The Camargue

The diverse terrain around Arles harbors many worthwhile and easy day trips. The medieval ghost town of Les Baux haunts the eerie Alpilles Mountains, while chic and compact St. Rémy-de-Provence awaits just over the hills, offering Roman ruins and memories of Vincent van Gogh. For an entirely different experience, the flat Camargue knocks on Arles' southern door with sandy beaches, saltwater lakes, rice paddies, flamingos, wild horses, and wild black bulls.

Planning Your Time

Because public transportation in this area is sparse, these sights are easiest to reach by car, taxi, or minivan tour. For a memo-

rable one-day road trip from Arles or Avignon, spend the morning in Les Baux (before the crowds), have lunch in St. Rémy and explore its sights, then finish at the Roman aqueduct of Barbegal. Non-drivers can do the same day trip (without the aqueduct) by bus and taxi. If you have more time or are a nature or bird-watching buff, head for the Camargue. A good market pops up on Friday mornings in little Eguyières (near Les Baux and St. Rémy).

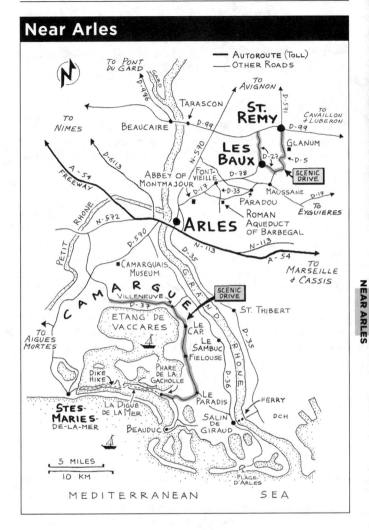

Near Arles

AUTOROUTE (TOLL)
OTHER ROADS

TO PONT DU GARD

TO AVIGNON

TARASCON

BEAUCAIRE

ST. REMY

TO NIMES

TO CAVAILLON & LUBERON

GLANUM

LES BAUX

SCENIC DRIVE

ABBEY OF MONTMAJOUR

FONT-VIEILLE

MAUSSANE

TO EYGUIERES

PARADOU

A-54 FREEWAY

RHONE

ARLES

Roman Aqueduct of Barbegal

TO MARSEILLE & CASSIS

CAMARGUAIS MUSEUM

SCENIC DRIVE

VILLENEUVE

ST. THIBERT

ETANG DE VACCARES

LE CAP.

TO AIGUES MORTES

LE SAMBUC FIELOUSE

PHARE DE LA GACHOLLE

DIKE HIKE

RHONE

LE PARADIS

FERRY

DCH

STES-MARIES-DE-LA-MER

LA DIGUE DE LA MER

SALIN DE GIRAUD

BEAUDUC

5 MILES
10 KM

PLAGE D'ARLES

MEDITERRANEAN   SEA

NEAR ARLES

Les Baux

The hilltop town of Les Baux crowns the rugged Alpilles (ahl-pee) Mountains, evoking a tumultuous medieval history. Here, you can imagine the struggles of a strong community that lived a rough-and-tumble life—thankful more for their top-notch fortifications than for their dramatic views. It's mobbed with tourists most of the day, but Les Baux rewards those who arrive by 9:00 or after 17:30. (Although the hilltop citadel's entry closes at the end of the day, once you're inside, you're welcome to live out your medieval fantasies all night long.) Sunsets are dramatic, the castle is brilliantly illuminated after dark, and nights in Les Baux are pin-drop peaceful. If you like what you see here, but want a more off-the-beaten-path experience, head for the Luberon and find the Fort de Buoux (see page 227).

Getting to Les Baux

By Car: Les Baux is a 20-minute drive from Arles: Follow signs for *Avignon*, then *Les Baux*. Drivers can combine Les Baux with St. Rémy (15 minutes away) and the ruined Roman aqueduct of Barbegal (both described later).

By Bus: From Arles, bus #59/57 runs to Les Baux daily July through August and Saturday–Sunday in June and September (6/day, 35 minutes, via Abbey of Montmajour, Fontvieille, and Paradou).

It's possible to combine Les Baux and St. Rémy into a worthwhile day trip from Arles or Avignon: From either city, take the bus to St. Rémy (50 minutes from Arles, 45 minutes from Avignon, see the "Connections" sections in those chapters for bus frequency). If buses aren't running to Les Baux, taxi there from St. Rémy, then take another one back to St Rémy or to your home base.

By Taxi: Count on €37 for a taxi one-way from Arles to Les Baux (€45 after 19:00), and allow €15 one-way from St. Rémy (mobile 06 80 27 60 92).

By Minivan Tour: The best option for many is a minivan tour, which can be both efficient and economical (easiest from Avignon; see page 46).

Orientation to Les Baux

Les Baux is actually two visits in one: castle ruins perched on an almost lunar landscape, and a medieval town below. Savor the castle, then tour—or blitz—the lower streets on your way out. Whereas the town, which lives entirely off tourism, is packed with shops, cafés, and tourist knickknacks, the castle above stays manageable because crowds are dispersed over a big area. The lower town's polished-stone gauntlet of boutiques is a Provençal dream come true for shoppers.

Tourist Information

The TI is immediately on the left as you enter the village (daily 9:00–17:30, later in summer, tel. 04 90 54 34 39, www.les bauxdeprovence.com). Ask about **combo-ticket** deals, such as the castle ruins and Cathédrale d'Images for €13 (saves €3), and the €15.50 **Les Baux Jours pass,** which covers the castle ruins, the Cathédrale d'Images, and the Yves Brayer Museum (saves €4.50).

You'll also see deals combining Les Baux with other sights in the region (such as the theater in Orange). The TI can also call a cab for you.

Arrival in Les Baux

Drivers must pay €5 to park at the foot of the village, or €3 to park several blocks below (you'll pass the parking on your way in). Pay at the machine just below the town entry (next to telephone, WC, and bakery).

Walk up the cobbled street into town, where you're greeted first by the TI. From here the main drag leads directly to the castle—just keep going uphill (a 10-minute walk).

Sights in Les Baux

▲▲▲The Castle Ruins (The "Dead City")

The sun-bleached ruins of the "dead city" of Les Baux are carved into, out of, and on top of a rock 650 feet above the valley floor.

Many of the ancient walls of this striking castle still stand as a testament to the proud past of this once-feisty village.

Cost and Hours: €8 (ask about family rates), includes excellent audioguide, daily July–Aug 9:00–20:00, Easter–June and Sept–Oct 9:00–19:00, Nov–Easter 9:30–17:00. If you are inside the castle when the entry closes, you can stay as long as you like. From April to October, medieval pageantry, tournaments, or fun-for-kids demonstrations enliven the mountaintop. If you bring your lunch, enjoy the picnic tables.

History: Imagine the importance of this citadel in the Middle Ages, when the Lords of Baux were notorious warriors. (How many feudal lords could trace their lineage back to one of the "three kings" of *Christmas Carol* fame, Balthazar?) In the 11th century, Les Baux was a powerhouse in southern France, controlling about 80 towns. The Lords of Baux fought the counts of Barcelona for control of Provence...and eventually lost. But while in power, these guys were mean. One ruler enjoyed forcing unransomed prisoners to jump off his castle walls.

In 1426, Les Baux was incorporated into Provence and France. Not accustomed to subservience, Les Baux struggled with the French king, who responded by destroying the fortress in 1483. Later, Les Baux regained some importance and emerged as a center of Protestantism. Arguing with Rome was a high-stakes game

NEAR ARLES

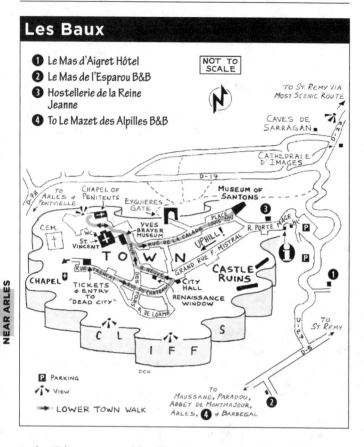

Les Baux

1. Le Mas d'Aigret Hôtel
2. Le Mas de l'Esparou B&B
3. Hostellerie de la Reine Jeanne
4. To Le Mazet des Alpilles B&B

NOT TO SCALE

TO ST REMY VIA MOST SCENIC ROUTE

CAVES DE SARRAGAN

CATHEDRALE D'IMAGES

D-17

TO ARLES & FONTVIELLE

CHAPEL OF PENITENTS

EYGUIERES GATE

MUSEUM OF SANTONS

C.E.M.

ST. VINCENT

YVES BRAYER MUSEUM

WC

PLACE LOUIS JOU

R. PORTE MAGE

WC

P

TOWN

RUE DE LA CALADE

UPHILL!

GRAND RUE F. MISTRAL

i

P

CHAPEL

RUE TRENCAT

RUE NEUVE

CASTLE RUINS

1

TICKETS & ENTRY TO "DEAD CITY"

RUE DES FOURS

RUE DU CHATEAU

CITY HALL

RENAISSANCE WINDOW

TO ST REMY

R. DE LORME

D-5

C L I F F S

PCH

TO ST REMY

D-5

P — PARKING

— VIEW

➡ — LOWER TOWN WALK

TO MAUSSANE, PARADOU, ABBEY DE MONTMAJOUR, ARLES, 4 & BARBEGAL

2

in the 17th century, and Les Baux's association with the Huguenots brought destruction again in 1632 when Cardinal Richelieu (under King Louis XIII) demolished the castle. Louis rubbed salt in the wound by billing Les Baux's residents for his demolition expenses. The once-powerful town of 4,000 was forever crushed.

Touring the Castle: Buy your ticket in the old olive mill, inspect the models of Les Baux before its 17th-century destruction, and then pick up your audioguide after entering the sight. The audioguide follows posted numbers counterclockwise around the rocky spur. Take full advantage of this tool—as you wander around, key in the number for any of the 30 narrated stops that interest you.

As you walk on the windblown spur (*baux* in French), you'll pass kid-thrilling medieval siege weaponry (go ahead, try the battering ram). Good displays in English and images help reconstruct the place. Try to imagine 4,000 people living up here. Notice the water-catchment system (a slanted field that caught rainwater and drained it into cisterns—necessary during a siege) and find the reservoir cut into the rock below the castle's highest point. Look for post holes throughout the stone walls that reveal where beams once supported floors.

For the most sensational views, climb to the blustery top of the citadel. Hang on. The mistral wind just might blow you away.

The St. Blaise chapel across from the entry/exit runs videos with Provençal themes (plays continuously; just images and music, no words).

▲Lower Town

After your castle visit, you can shop and eat your way back through the new town. Or you can escape some of the crowds by following my short tour, below, which covers these minor but worthwhile sights as you descend (all stay open at lunch except the Yves Brayer Museum).

• *On the main drag (grand rue Frédéric Mistral), a few blocks below the castle exit, is the...*

Manville Mansion City Hall—The 15th-century city hall flies the red-and-white flag of Monaco, a reminder that the Grimaldi family (which has long ruled the tiny principality of Monaco) owned Les Baux until the French Revolution (1789). In fact, in 1982, Princess Grace Kelly and her royal husband, Prince Rainier Grimaldi, came to Les Baux to receive the key to the city.

Twenty yards up rue Nueve, the lovely 1571 **Renaissance** window frame, marking the site of a future Calvinist museum, stands as a reminder of this town's Protestant history. This was probably a place of Huguenot worship—the words carved into the lintel, *Post tenebras lux,* were a popular Calvinist slogan: "After the shadow comes the light."

• *At the end of rue Nueve, head right on rue des Fours to get to the...*

Yves Brayer Museum (Musée Yves Brayer)—This enjoyable museum lets you peruse three floors of paintings (Van Gogh–like Expressionism, without the tumult) by Yves Brayer (1907–1990), who spent his final years here in Les Baux. Like Van Gogh, Brayer was inspired by all that surrounded him. Brayer picked up inspiration from his travels through Morocco, Spain, and the rest of the Mediterranean world (€4, daily 10:00–12:30 & 14:00–18:30, tel. 04 90 54 36 99). Pick up the descriptive English sheet at the entry.

• *Next door is...*

St. Vincent Church—This 12th-century Romanesque church was built short and wide to fit the terrain. The center chapel on the right (partially carved out of the rock) houses the town's traditional Provençal processional chariot. Each Christmas Eve, a ram pulled this cart—holding a lamb, symbolizing Jesus, and surrounded by candles—through town to the church.

• *Around the corner (to the left as you leave the church) are public WCs. Directly in front of the church is a vast view, making clear the strategic value of this rocky bluff's natural fortifications. A few steps away is the...*

Chapel of Penitents—Notice the nativity scene painted by Yves Brayer, illustrating the local legend that says Jesus was born in Les Baux. On the opposite wall, find his version of a starry night. Leaving the church, turn left. Wash your shirt in the old-town "laundry"—with a pig-snout faucet and 14th-century stone washing surface designed for short women.

• *Heading downhill at the junction on rue de la Calade, you'll pass cafés with wonderful views, the town's fortified wall, and one of its two gates. After passing a free (and curiously evangelical) "museum of aromas and perfumes," you hit the awe-inspiring...*

Museum of Santons—This free museum displays a collection of *santons* ("little saints"), popular folk figurines that decorate local Christmas mangers. Notice how the nativity scene "proves" once again that Jesus was born in Les Baux. These painted clay dolls show off local dress and traditions (with good English descriptions). Find the old couple leaning heroically into the mistral.

Near Les Baux

A half-mile beyond Les Baux, D-27 (toward Maillane) leads to dramatic views of the hill town. There are pullouts and walking trails at the pass, and two attractions that fill cool, cavernous caves in former limestone quarries dating back to the Middle Ages. (The limestone is easy to cut, but gets hard and nicely polished when exposed to the weather.) Speaking of quarries, in 1821, the rocks and soil of this area were found to contain an important mineral for making aluminum. It was named after the town: bauxite.

Caves de Sarragan—The best views of Les Baux are from this parking lot, occupied by the Sarragan Winery (which invites you in for a taste). While this place looks like it's designed for groups, the friendly, English-speaking staff welcomes individuals (free, daily April–Sept 10:00–12:00 & 14:00–19:00, Oct–March until 18:00, tel. 04 90 54 33 58, www.caves-sarragan.com).

▲▲**Cathédrale d'Images**—This similar cave nearby offers a mesmerizing sound-and-slide show with a different program every year. In 2011, the remarkable life of Leonardo da Vinci will be highlighted. The show, which features 48 projectors flashing countless images set to music on quarry walls, never fails to thrill wandering visitors (€8, March–Dec daily 10:00–18:00, closed Jan–Feb, www.cathedrale-images.com). Dress warmly, since the cave is cool.

D-27 continues to St. Rémy, allowing for a handy loop trip (to complete the loop, return from St. Rémy to Les Baux via D-5).

Sleeping in Les Baux

Many of these accommodations are actually scattered around the countryside surrounding Les Baux. For more accommodations in this area, see page 82.

$$$ Le Mas d'Aigret*, barely east of Les Baux on the road to St. Rémy, is a well-run, lovely refuge that crouches under Les Baux. Lie on your back and stare up at the castle walls rising beyond the swimming pool, or enjoy valley views from the groomed terraces (Db with no view-€115, larger Db with balcony and view-€155, Tb/Qb-€200–240, two cool troglodyte rooms-€200, half-pension option with big breakfast and good dinner for about €40/person more, air-con, rooms have some daytime road noise, tel. 04 90 54 20 00, fax 04 90 54 44 00, www.masdaigret .com, contact@masdaigret.com, Dutch Marieke and French Eric).

$$ Le Mas de l'Esparou *chambre d'hôte,* a few minutes below Les Baux toward Paradou, is welcoming and kid-friendly, with three spacious rooms, a big swimming pool, table tennis, and distant views of Les Baux. Sweet Jacqueline loves her job, and her lack of English only makes her more animated (Db-€68, extra bed-about €16, includes breakfast, cash only, between Les Baux and Maussane les Alpilles on D-5, look for white sign with green lettering, tel. & fax 04 90 54 41 32).

$ Hostellerie de la Reine Jeanne, an exceptional value, is a good place to watch the sun rise and set from Les Baux. Warmly run by Gaelle and Marc, this place offers a handful of sufficiently

---

Sleep Code

(€1 = about $1.25, country code: 33)

S = Single, **D** = Double/Twin, **T** = Triple, **Q** = Quad, **b** = bathroom, **s** = shower only, * = French hotel rating system (0–4 stars). Unless otherwise noted, credit cards are accepted and English is spoken.

To help you easily sort through these listings, I've divided the rooms into three categories, based on the price for a standard double room with bath:

$$$ Higher Priced—Most rooms €80 or more.
  $$ Moderately Priced—Most rooms between €60–80.
    $ Lower Priced—Most rooms €60 or less.

Prices can change without notice; verify the hotel's current rates online or by email. For other updates, see www .ricksteves.com/update.

comfy rooms above a busy (and good-value) restaurant (standard Ds-€52, standard Db-€58, Db with view deck-€62–72, Tb-€70–80, cavernous family suite-€105, air-con in half the rooms, ask for *chambre avec terrasse*, good *menus* from €16, 150 feet to your right after entry to the village of Les Baux, tel. 04 90 54 32 06, fax 04 90 54 32 33, www.la-reinejeanne.com, reine.jeanne@wanadoo.fr).

$ Le Mazet des Alpilles is a small home with three tidy, air-conditioned rooms just outside the unspoiled village of Paradou, five minutes below Les Baux. It may have rooms when others don't (Db-€56–60, ask for largest room, includes breakfast, cash only, air-con, child's bed available, pleasant garden, follow brown signs from D-17, in Paradou look for route de Brunelly, tel. 04 90 54 45 89, www.alpilles.com/mazet.htm, lemazet@wanadoo.fr). Sweet Annick speaks just enough English.

Eating in Les Baux

You'll find quieter cafés with views along my self-guided tour route. The recommended **Hostellerie de la Reine Jeanne** offers friendly service and good-value meals indoors or out (€12 salads, €16 *menus*, try the *salade Estivale*, open daily).

Sights Between Les Baux and Arles

The following stops are easiest for drivers.

Abbey of Montmajour—This brooding hulk of a ruin, just a few minutes' drive from Arles toward Les Baux, was once a thriving abbey and a convenient papal retreat (c. A.D. 950). Today, the vacant abbey church is a massive example of Romanesque architecture and an overpriced sight (€7.50; May–Aug daily 10:00–18:30; Sept–April Tue–Sun 10:00–17:00, closed Mon; tel. 04 90 54 64 17). Film buffs will appreciate this sight as the setting for *The Lion in Winter*, where Eleanor of Aquitaine (played by Katherine Hepburn) battled with her husband, Henry II (Peter O'Toole). For more on abbeys, see sidebar on page 220.

The surrounding fields were a favorite of Van Gogh's, who walked here from Arles to paint his famous wheat fields. Now they're rice fields, which wouldn't have looked nearly as good on canvas.

▲Roman Aqueduct of Barbegal—To be all alone with evocative Roman ruins, drivers can take a quick detour to the crumbled arches of ancient Arles' principal aqueduct.

From the parking area, follow the dirt path through the olive grove and along the aqueduct ruins for 200 yards. Approaching the bluff with the grand view, you'll see that the water canal is split into two troughs: One takes a 90-degree right turn and heads for

Arles; the other goes straight to the bluff and over, where it once sent water cascading down to power eight grinding mills. Romans grew wheat on the vast fields you see from here, then brought it down to the mega-watermill of Barbegal. Historians figure that this mill produced enough flour each day to feed 12,000 hungry Romans. If you saw the model of this eight-tiered mill in Arles' Ancient History Museum (see page 65), the milling is easy to visualize—making a visit here quite an exciting experience.

Returning to your car, find the broken bit of aqueduct—it's positioned like a children's playground slide—and take a look at the waterproofing mortar that lined all Roman aqueducts.

Getting There: Coming from Arles, take D-17 toward Fontvieille; three kilometers (less than two miles) before Fontvieille, look for signs for *L'Aqueduc Romain* on D-82 (it's signed coming from Fontvieille to Arles as well, on the left). In less than three kilometers, park at the dirt pullout (no sign—it's just after the *Los Pozos Blancos* sign, where the ruins of the aqueduct cross the road). Leave no valuables visible in your car; the gravel twinkles with the remains of broken car windows.

NEAR ARLES

St. Rémy-de-Provence

Sophisticated and sassy, St. Rémy (sahn ray-mee) gave birth to Nostradamus and cared for a distraught artist. Today, it caters to

shoppers and Van Gogh fans. A few minutes from the town center, you can visit the once-thriving Roman city called Glanum, the mental ward where Vincent van Gogh was sent after lopping off his lobe, and an art center dedicated to his memory. Best of all is the chance to elbow your way through its raucous Wednesday market (until 12:30). A ring road—which local drivers mistake for a racecourse—hems in a pedestrian-friendly center that's well-stocked with fine foods, pottery boutiques, art galleries, and the latest Provençal fashions.

Getting to St. Rémy

By Car: From Les Baux, St. Rémy is a spectacular 15-minute drive over the hills and through the woods. Roads D-5 and D-27 each provide scenic routes between these towns, making a loop drive between them worthwhile. The most scenic approach is on D-27;

from Les Baux, take the road toward Maillane that passes the Cathédrale d'Images. Take advantage of the many good pullouts and get out of your car for that view. From St. Rémy to Les Baux, follow signs for *Tarascon,* and you'll see the D-27 turnoff to Les Baux in a few miles. Parking in St. Rémy is tricky; it's easiest at the TI lot (€1/3 hours, free Mon–Sat 12:00–14:00 and all day Sun). Parking on place Charles de Gaulle is always free, but farther from the center (leave the ring road on avenue Frédéric Mistral).

By Bus: It's 50 minutes from Arles (bus #54 or bus #59/57, 3–6/day, none on Sunday off-season) and 45 minutes from Avignon (6/day). If arriving at St. Rémy by bus, get off on the ring road at the République stop. The TI is a block up avenue Durand Maillane (to the right).

By Taxi: From Les Baux, allow €15 one-way; from Avignon, count on €35 (mobile 06 80 27 60 92 or 06 09 52 71 54). St. Rémy's four taxis park on place de la République, next to the bus stop.

Orientation to St. Rémy

From St. Rémy's circular center, it's a 15-minute walk along a busy road with no sidewalk to Glanum and the St. Paul Monastery (Van Gogh's mental hospital).

Tourist Information

The TI is two blocks toward Les Baux from the ring road (Mon–Sat 9:00–12:30 & 14:00–18:00, Sun 10:00–12:00—except closed Sun Oct–April; tel. 04 90 92 05 22, www.saintremy-de-provence .com). At the TI, pick up a town map, bus schedules, and a map tracing Van Gogh's favorite painting locations with *in situ* copies of the painted scenes (the *Starry Night* panel is just outside the TI). They can also call a taxi for you. Get information about the English "In the Footsteps of Van Gogh" walking tours (€8, 1.5 hours; departs TI at 10:00 usually on Tue, Thu, Fri, and Sat; also occasional afternoon tours of the town, 6-person minimum, call ahead to confirm).

Sights in St. Rémy

St. Rémy's best attractions are outside the town center: the ruins at Glanum and the Vincent van Gogh sights nearby. This cluster of sights is an unappealing 15-minute walk south of the TI. If you're driving, you can park for free at the St. Paul Monastery (coming from Les Baux, it's the first right after passing Glanum) and walk five minutes to Glanum from there (or pay €2.50 to park at the Glanum site).

St. Rémy Area

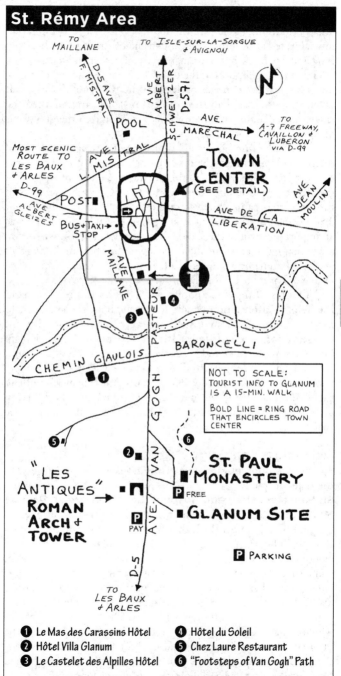

TO MAILLANE

TO ISLE-SUR-LA-SORGUE & AVIGNON

F. MISTRAL AVE
D-5 AVE

AVE ALBERT SCHWEITZER D-571

POOL

AVE. MARECHAL

TO A-7 FREEWAY, CAVAILLON & LUBERON VIA D-99

MOST SCENIC ROUTE TO LES BAUX & ARLES D-99

AVE. L. MISTRAL

TOWN CENTER (SEE DETAIL)

AVE JEAN MOULIN

POST

AVE ALBERT GLEIZES

BUS & TAXI STOP

AVE DE LA LIBERATION

AVE MAILLANE

🛈

AVE PASTEUR

④

③

BARONCELLI

CHEMIN GAULOIS

NOT TO SCALE: TOURIST INFO TO GLANUM IS A 15-MIN. WALK

BOLD LINE = RING ROAD THAT ENCIRCLES TOWN CENTER

❶

❺

AVE. VAN GOGH

❷

⑥

ST. PAUL MONASTERY

P FREE

"LES ANTIQUES" **ROMAN ARCH & TOWER**

P PAY

■ **GLANUM SITE**

P PARKING

D-5

TO LES BAUX & ARLES

❶ Le Mas des Carassins Hôtel
❷ Hôtel Villa Glanum
❸ Le Castelet des Alpilles Hôtel
④ Hôtel du Soleil
❺ Chez Laure Restaurant
⑥ "Footsteps of Van Gogh" Path

NEAR ARLES

▲Glanum Ruins

These crumbling stones are the foundations of a Roman market town, located at the crossroads of two ancient trade routes between Italy and Spain. A heavy Roman arch and tower stand across the road as proud reminders of the town's glory days, and indicate how much larger the town was back then (the Roman city was about seven times bigger than the visible ruins). The arch marked the entry into Glanum, and the tower is a memorial to the grandsons of Emperor Augustus Caesar.

While the ruins are, well...ruined, their setting at the base of the rocky Alpilles is lovely. It's also unshaded, so if it's hot, come early or late. These ruins highlight the range and prosperity of the Roman Empire, and along with other Roman monuments in Provence, they paint a more complete picture of Roman life. About 2,500 people lived in Glanum at its zenith. And though this was an important town, with grand villas, temples, a basilica, a forum, a wooden dam, and aqueducts, it was not important enough to justify an arena or a theater (such as those in Arles, Nîmes, and Orange). For more on Roman history, see page 48.

The free English handout, the exhibits in the entry, and the helpful information panels scattered about the site all help put this picture together. Still, eager Romanophiles will want to spring for the well-done "Itineraries" book (€7). Stroll up Glanum's main street and see remains of a market hall, a forum, thermal baths, reservoirs, and more. The view from the belvedere justifies the effort (€7, under 18 free, daily April–Sept 9:30–18:30, Oct–March 10:30–17:00, parking-€2.50, tel. 04 90 92 23 79). There's a pleasant on-site café with Roman specialties and classic snack fare.

Retracing Van Gogh's Steps

For more on Vincent van Gogh's time in this region, see page 72 in the Arles chapter.

St. Paul Monastery and Hospital (Le Monastère St. Paul de Mausole)—Just below Glanum is the still-functioning mental hospital (Clinique St. Paul) that treated Vincent van Gogh from 1889 to 1890. Here you'll enter Vincent's temporarily peaceful world: a small chapel, intimate cloisters, a re-creation of his room, and a small lavender field with six (of my favorite) paintings copied on large displays. Read the thoughtful English explanations about Vincent's tortured life. Amazingly, he completed 143 paintings and more than 100 drawings in his 53 weeks here—none of which remains anywhere nearby today. The contrast between the utter simplicity of his room (and his life) and the multimillion-dollar value of his paintings today is jarring. The site is managed by Valetudo, a center specializing in art therapy for psychiatric disorders (€4, daily April–Sept 9:15–18:45, Oct–March 10:30–17:30, tel. 04 90 92 77 00).

Around the complex, you'll see panels of Vincent's works—some located right where he painted them. Several are located along the short road into the site (the TI has a map with a list of the reproductions). Stand among flamelike cypress trees, gaze over the distant skyline of St. Rémy, and realize you're in the midst of Van Gogh's most famous work, *The Starry Night*.

Centre d'Art Présence Vincent van Gogh—This center in old St. Rémy is an ongoing tribute to the painter and features a small room of reproductions and worthwhile video presentations (usually with English subtitles). The theme changes each year, though the subject always remains Vincent van Gogh. Upstairs is a rotating exhibit that reflects the enormous influence of Vincent's work on contemporary artists. You'll also find a worthwhile collection of works by Cubist precursor Albert Gleizes (€3.30, Tue–Sun 10:00–12:30 & 14:00–19:00, closed Mon, inside the ring road on rue Estrine, tel. 04 90 92 34 72).

Sleeping in St. Rémy

(€1 = about $1.25, country code: 33)

$$$ Le Mas des Carassins***, a 15-minute walk from the center, is impeccably run by friendly Michel and Pierre. Luxury is affordable here. Your hosts pay careful attention to every detail, from the generously sized pool and gardens to the muted room decor and optional €30 home-cooked dinner. Reservations are smart—its 21 rooms fill fast (standard Db-€129, deluxe Db-€165, deluxe Db with terrace-€185–209, extra bed-€32, includes American breakfast, air-con, Wi-Fi, table tennis, look for signs 200 yards toward Les Baux from TI, 1 Chemin Gaulois, tel. 04 90 92 15 48, fax 04 90 92 63 47, www.masdescarassins.com, info@masdescarassins .com).

$$$ Hôtel Villa Glanum*** is a modern hotel on the main road (some traffic noise) across from the St. Paul Monastery and the Glanum ruins. It's a 15-minute walk from the town center, with tight but well-maintained rooms. The best rooms, which come with higher rates, are in bungalows around the pretty pool and lush gardens (Db-€90–120, Tb-€140, Qb-€150, cheaper off-season, 46 avenue Van Gogh, tel. 04 90 92 03 59, fax 04 90 92 00 08, www.villaglanum.com, contact@villaglanum.com).

$$ Le Castelet des Alpilles*** is way Old World, but the location is good (halfway between St. Rémy's old town and the Roman ruins), the terrace is big, the price is fair, and the rooms are plenty comfortable. Most are big and airy, and the balcony rooms have views of the Alpilles (Db-€75–85, Db with air-con and view

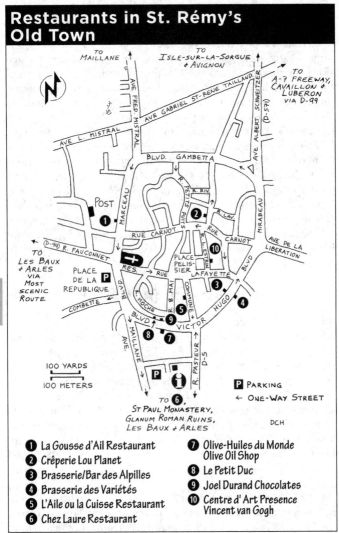

Restaurants in St. Rémy's Old Town

NEAR ARLES

1 La Gousse d'Ail Restaurant
2 Crêperie Lou Planet
3 Brasserie/Bar des Alpilles
4 Brasserie des Variétés
5 L'Aile ou la Cuisse Restaurant
6 Chez Laure Restaurant

7 Olive-Huiles du Monde Olive Oil Shop
8 Le Petit Duc
9 Joel Durand Chocolates
10 Centre d' Art Presence Vincent van Gogh

balcony–€100, Tb–€120, Wi-Fi, 6 place Mireille, tel. 04 90 92 07 21, fax 04 90 92 52 03, www.castelet-alpilles.com, hotel.castel .alpilles@wanadoo.fr).

$$ Hôtel du Soleil**, an easy walk from St. Rémy's center, is a budget traveler's refuge, with simple, air-conditioned, and spotless rooms clustered around a pleasant courtyard and pool. Happy Monsieur Monset is behind the desk (standard Sb/Db–€73, bigger Sb/Db–€85, Tb–€115, 3 rooms have small terraces, 2-room apartment–€100–130, Internet access and Wi-Fi, easy parking, a block

Food-Lovers' Guide to St. Rémy

Wednesday is market day in St. Rémy, but you don't have to fast until then. Foodies will appreciate the three shops gathered on the ring road in St. Rémy, near the turnoff to Les Baux.

Start at **Olive-Huiles du Monde,** where you can sample the best olive oil and vinegar in the area in a wine bar–like setting. The friendly staff speaks English and is happy to spoon up samples of three olive oils and two surprisingly tasty vinegars. Check out the impressive display of other products made from olive oil, and the good truffle display (daily 10:00–12:30 & 15:00–19:00, 16 boulevard Victor Hugo, tel. 04 90 15 02 33).

Le Petit Duc, across the road, offers a remarkable introduction to antique cookies (daily 10:00–13:00 & 15:00–19:00, 7 boulevard Victor Hugo, tel. 04 90 92 08 31).

Just one whiff from **Joel Durand Chocolates** will lure chocoholics inside. Ask for a sample and learn the letter-coded system. The lavender is surprisingly good (daily 9:30–12:30 & 14:30–19:30, a few doors down from Le Petit Duc at 3 boulevard Victor Hugo, tel. 04 90 92 38 25).

above the TI at 35 avenue Pasteur, tel. 04 90 92 00 63, fax 04 90 92 61 07, www.hotelsoleil.com, info@hotelsoleil.com).

Eating in St. Rémy

The town is packed with fine restaurants, each trying to outdo the other. Join the evening strollers and compare.

La Gousse d'Ail is no secret, but even so, it's a reliable, warm place for a mini-splurge (*menus* from €32, closed Thu, on the ring road just after the turnoff to Maillane at 6 boulevard Marceau, tel. 04 90 92 16 87).

Crêperie Lou Planet, on pleasant place Favier, is cheap and peaceful, with outdoor seating in summer, delicious crêpes, and good salads. Owner Jean has been here for more than 25 years and still hasn't changed the menu (daily April–Sept 12:00–22:00, behind Hôtel de Ville).

Brasserie/Bar des Alpilles, which sits on the ring road, offers travelers a great salad selection and good standard café fare, including pasta dishes for €9 (daily lunch and dinner, 21 boulevard Victor Hugo, tel. 04 90 92 0 17).

Brasserie des Variétés has good kids' menus, along with computers and Wi-Fi (daily, #32 on the ring road, tel. 04 90 92 42 61).

L'Aile ou la Cuisse offers a chic, fresh salad bar for €12 and elegant dinner meals (€16–28 *plats*, €40 *menus*). It's a friendly and funky place with delicious cuisine and gorgeous desserts (in front of the Hôtel de Ville at 5 rue de la Commune, tel. 04 32 62 00 25).

Chez Laure is a simple, local, and relaxed outdoor restaurant. It's located a mile from St. Rémy in a park-like setting with toys available for kids (€11 lunch *menu*, €18 dinner *menu*, closed Mon, on route du Lac, tel. 04 90 92 51 99). To find the restaurant, look for signs between the Glanum ruins and the TI.

The Camargue

The Camargue region, occupying the vast delta of the Rhône River, is one of Europe's most important wetlands. This marshy area exists where the Rhône splits into two branches (big and little), just before it flows into the Mediterranean. Over the millennia, a steady flow of sediment has been deposited at the mouth of the rivers—thoroughly land-locking villages that once faced the sea.

Since World War II, farmers have converted large northern tracts of the Camargue to rice fields, making the delta a major producer of France's rice. Salt is the other key industry in the Camargue—you can see vast salt marshes and evaporation beds around the town of Salin de Giraud. Because the salt marshes were long considered useless, the land has remained relatively untouched, leaving it a popular nature destination today.

Today the Camargue Regional Nature Park is a protected and "wild" area, where pink flamingos, wild bulls, nasty boars, nastier mosquitoes (in every season but winter—come prepared), and the famous white horses wander freely through lagoons and tall grass. For more on these animals, see the sidebar.

The Camargue's subtle wetlands beauty makes it a worthwhile joyride for some, but it's a take-it-or-leave-it sight for many (unless it's spring and you've never seen a flamingo in flight). The Everglades-like scenery is a birder's paradise, and occasional bulls and wild horses add to the enjoyment. But for avid city sightseers, this can feel like a big swamp—interesting to drive through, but where's the excitement? Read ahead and decide for yourself (tel. 04 90 97 86 32, www.parc-camargue.fr, info@parc-camargue.fr). The birds are fewest and the mosquitoes are greatest in summer, so I'd

The Wildlife of the Camargue

In this nature reserve, amusing flamingos and countless other bird species flourish—attracting birdwatchers from all over the world. Once an endangered species, the flamingos flock here because of all that salt—which is why they come to the Camargue rather than to, say, the sandy beaches of the Riviera. Ten thousand flamingos leave here each fall, heading to warmer climates, and then return in March to pink up the Camargue (a visit here in the spring reaps big, pink rewards). To see a formation of these long, clumsy-looking birds in flight is an experience you won't soon forget.

The black bulls are raised for bullfights (by local cowboys called *gardians*) and eventually end up on plates in Arles' restaurants (you may have met one already). The *gardians*, who have patrolled the Camargue on local horses for centuries, give the area a Wild West aura. The region's unique small horses—born brown or black, later turning light gray or white—are one of the oldest breeds in the world, and may have existed in the area since prehistoric times.

With the continual loss of wetlands throughout the world, it's critical that places like this remain preserved and that we understand their significance.

NEAR ARLES

pass on the Camargue at that time.

However, if you have children who can't take the city anymore, a picnic on the long sandy beach at plage d'Arles may be just what the doctor ordered. Also called plage de Piemançço, this public beach is 10 kilometers (6 miles) after Salin de Giraud (see map on page 89). Bring everything you might need, as there are no vendors, but the sand is soft and the sea is warm.

Getting to the Camargue

There are several ways beyond a car to experience the Camargue: horseback, mountain bikes, and jeep safaris. All three options are available in Stes-Maries-de-la-Mer, and jeep safaris are also offered from Arles (ask at TI). Hiking is not good in the Camargue, as there are few decent trails (check www.kustgids.nl/camargue-en). The best biking is across the Digue (dike) to Phare de la Gacholle.

By Scenic Drive: There are two primary driving routes from Arles through the Camargue: to Stes-Maries-de-la-Mer, and toward Salin de Giraud.

My favorite route is toward **Salin de Giraud:** Leave Arles on D-570 toward Stes-Maries-de-la-Mer, passing the D-36 turnoff to Salin de Giraud (you'll return along this route). After a stop at the Camarguais Museum, continue along D-570, then turn left on D-37 toward Salin de Giraud and follow it as it skirts the Etang de Vaccarès lagoon. The lagoon itself is off-limits, but this area has views and good opportunities to get out of the car and smell the marshes. Turn right off D-37 onto the tiny road at Villeneuve, following La Capelière and La Fiélouse.

Make time for a stop at **La Capelière** (headquarters for Camargue sightseers), where you can pick up an excellent map, ask the eager staff questions, and enjoy a small exhibit and one-mile walking trail with some English information on the Camargue (modest trail fee). Birders can look at the register to see what birds have been spotted recently (observations in English are in red).

The best part of the Camargue (particularly in spring) awaits at **La Digue de la Mer,** about 10 scenic kilometers (6 miles) past La Capelière. A rough dirt road rising above water on both sides greets travelers; it's time to get out of your car and stroll (though you can drive on for a few miles to Phare de la Gacholle). This is a critical reproduction area for flamingos (about 5,000 offspring annually), so it's your best chance to see groups of mamas and papas up close and personal. If you rented a mountain bike, now would be the right time to use it: It's about eight bumpy but engaging miles between water and sand dunes to Stes-Maries-de-la-Mer.

For the fastest way back to Arles, backtrack to D-37 at Villeneuve, then follow D-36. If driving to Stes-Maries-de-la-Mer, there are several parking lots and plenty of on-street parking for drivers.

By Bus: Buses serve the Camargue (stopping at Camarguais Museum and Stes-Maries-de-la-Mer) from Arles' bus station (bus #20, 5/day Mon–Sat, 3/day Sun, 1 hour, tel. 04 90 96 36 25).

Sights in the Camargue

Camarguais Museum (Musée Camarguais)—Located in a traditional Camargue barn on the road to Stes-Maries-de-la-Mer, this well-designed folk museum does a good job of describing the natural features and cultural traditions of the Camargue. The costumes, tools, and helpful exhibits come with some English explanations (look for handouts and small screens), and there's a two-mile nature trail (€5; May–Sept daily 9:00–12:30 & 13:00–18:00; Oct–April Wed–Mon 10:00–12:30 & 13:00–17:00, closed Tue; 8 miles from Arles on D-570 toward Stes-Maries-de-la-Mer at Mas du Pont de Rousty farmhouse, tel. 04 90 97 10 82).

Stes-Maries-de-la-Mer—At the western end of the Camargue lies this whitewashed, Spanish-feeling seafront town with acres of flamingos, bulls, and horses at its doorstep. From the bus stop, walk to the church (10 minutes) to get oriented. The place is so popular that it's best avoided on weekends and during holidays.

It's a French Coney Island—a trinket-selling, perennially windy place.

The town is also famous as a mecca for the Roma (also known as Gypsies). Every May, Roma from all over Europe pile in their caravans and migrate to Stes-Maries-de-la-Mer to venerate the statue of Saint Sarah. Legend has it that Mary Magdalene made landfall here in a boat with no oars after an epic journey across the Mediterranean from Egypt. Fleeing persecution for practicing the new and unpopular Christian faith, she was accompanied by two other "Stes-Maries": Mary Jacobe, the mother of the apostle James, and Mary Salome, the mother of the apostles James and John. Also in the boat was "Black Sarah," an Egyptian servant. Sarah collected alms for the poor; over time, her request for hand-outs became associated with the Roma people, who embrace her as their patron saint. Today's impressive spectacle to honor Sarah is like a sprawling flea market spilling out from the town.

At other times, the town of Stes-Maries-de-la-Mer has little to offer except its beachfront promenade, bullring, and towering five-belled fortified church. The church interior is worth a look for its unusual decorations and artifacts, including the statue of St. Sarah (free, €2 to climb to roof for Camargue and sea views). Avoid the women with flowers and the assertive palm readers, who often cluster near the church—they want your money, not your friendship.

Most tourists come to take a horse, a jeep, or a bike into the Camargue—and there's no lack of outfits ready to take you for a ride. The TIs in Arles (see page 61) and Stes-Maries-de-la-Mer have long lists (Stes-Maries-de-la-Mer TI open daily April–Sept 9:00–19:00, until 20:00 in summer, Oct–March 9:00–17:00, tel. 04 90 97 82 55, www.saintesmaries.com). You can rent bikes (for the ride out to La Digue de la Mer) and get advice on the best route at Le Vélo (19 rue de la République, tel. 04 90 97 74 56). Jeep excursions run about €30 for 2.5 hours; Camargue-Decouverte is one of many outfits based in Arles (1 rue Emile Fassin, tel. 04 90 96 69 20, www.camargue-decouverte.com—French-only website). Les Cabanes de Cacharel gives top-notch horseback tours (€13/1 hour—too short to see much, €25/2 hours, €37/3 hours, route de Cacharel in Stes-Maries-de-la-Mer, tel. 04 90 97 84 10, www .camargueacheval.com—French-only website, info@camarguea cheval.com).

Aigues-Mortes—This strange walled city, on the western edge of the Camargue (20 miles from Nîmes), was built by Louis IX as a jumping-off point for his Crusades to the Holy Land. Although Aigues-Mortes was a strategically situated royal port city, it was actually never near the sea—ships reached it via canals that were dug through an immense lagoon. Today its tall towers and thick fortifications seem oddly out of place, surrounded by nothing but salt marshes and flamingos. The name "Aigues-Mortes" means "Dead Waters," which says it all. Skip it unless you need more souvenirs and crowded streets, although drivers going between Nîmes and Arles can detour to Aigues-Mortes for a quick-and-easy taste of the Camargue. Aigues-Mortes and Nîmes are linked by buses (6/day, 50 minutes) and trains (6/day, 45 minutes).

AVIGNON

Famous for its nursery rhyme, medieval bridge, and brooding Palace of the Popes, contemporary Avignon (ah-veen-yohn) bustles and prospers behind its mighty walls. During the 68 years (1309–1377) that Avignon starred as the *Franco Vaticano*, it grew from a quiet village into a thriving city. With its large student population and fashionable shops, today's Avignon is an intriguing blend of medieval history, youthful energy, and urban sophistication. Street performers entertain the international throngs who fill Avignon's ubiquitous cafés and trendy boutiques. If you're here in July, be prepared for big crowds and higher prices, thanks to the rollicking theater festival. (Reserve your hotel far in advance.) Clean, sharp, and popular with tourists, Avignon is more impressive for its outdoor ambience than for its museums and monuments.

Orientation to Avignon

The cours Jean Jaurès, which turns into rue de la République, runs straight from the Centre-Ville train station to place de l'Horloge and the Palace of the Popes, splitting Avignon in two. The larger eastern half is where the action is. Climb to Le Jardin du Rochers des Doms for the town's best view, consider touring the pope's immense palace, lose yourself in Avignon's back streets (you can follow my "Discovering Avignon's Back Streets" self-guided walk), and find a shady square to call home. Avignon's shopping district fills the traffic-free streets near where rue de la République meets place de l'Horloge.

Tourist Information
The main TI is between the Centre-Ville train station and the old town, at 41 cours Jean Jaurès (April–Oct Mon–Sat 9:00–18:00—

until 19:00 in July, Sun 9:45–17:00; Nov–March Mon–Fri 9:00–18:00, Sat 9:00–17:00, Sun 10:00–12:00; tel. 04 32 74 32 74, www.avignon-tourisme.com). From April through mid-October, branch TI offices are open inside the St. Bénezet Bridge entrance (daily 10:00–13:00 & 14:00–18:00) and inside Les Halles market (Fri–Sun 10:00–13:00, closed Mon–Thu). At any TI, get the helpful map. If you're staying awhile, pick up the free *Guide Pratique* (info on bike rentals, hotels, apartment rentals, events, and museums).

Everyone should pick up the free **Avignon Passion Pass** (valid 15 days, for up to five family members). Get the pass stamped when you pay full price at your first sight, and then receive reductions at the others (for example, €2 less at the Palace of the Popes and €3 less at the Petit Palais). The discounts add up—always show your Passion Pass when buying a ticket. The pass comes with the Avignon "Passion" map and guide, which includes several good (but tricky-to-follow) walking tours.

Arrival in Avignon

By Train

Avignon has two train stations: TGV (linked to downtown by frequent shuttle buses) and Centre-Ville. While most TGV trains serve only the TGV train station, some serve Centre-Ville—verify your station in advance.

TGV Station (Gare TGV): This shiny new station, on the outskirts of town, has no baggage storage (bags can be stored only at Centre-Ville Station).

To get to the city center, take the *navette*/**shuttle bus** (marked *Navette/Avignon Centre*; €1.20, buy ticket from driver, 3/hour, 15 minutes). To find the bus stop, leave the station by the north exit *(sortie nord)*, walk down the stairs, and find the long bus shelter to the left. In downtown Avignon you'll arrive at a stop just inside the city walls, in front of the post office on cours Président Kennedy (see the map on page 112). From here you're three blocks from the city's main TI, and two blocks from Centre-Ville Station. A **taxi** ride between the TGV station and downtown Avignon costs about €16–20 (to find taxis, exit the TGV station via *sortie nord*).

To pick up a **rental car** at the TGV train station, walk out the south exit *(sortie sud)* to find the *location de voitures* in the parking lot. If you're driving directly to Arles, St. Rémy-de-Provence, Les Baux, or the Luberon, leave the station, following signs to *Avignon Sud*, then *La Rocade*. You'll soon see exits to Arles (best for St. Rémy and Les Baux) and Cavaillon (for Luberon villages).

If you're heading from the Avignon TGV train station to the **Arles train station,** catch the direct SNCF bus from the TGV station's bus stop (10/day, 1 hour, schedule available at any information booth inside the TGV station).

Centre-Ville Station (Gare Avignon Centre-Ville): All non-TGV trains (and a few TGV trains) serve the central station. You can stash your bags here—exit the station to the left and look for the *consignes* sign (confirm closing time when you leave your bag). To reach the town center, cross the busy street in front of the station and walk through the city walls onto cours Jean Jaurès. The TI is three blocks down, at #41.

By Bus

The dingy bus station *(gare routière)* is 100 yards to the right as you leave the Centre-Ville train station (beyond and below Ibis Hôtel).

By Car

Drivers entering Avignon follow *Centre-Ville* and *Gare SNCF* (train station) signs. You'll find central pay lots (about €10/half-day, €14/day) in the garage next to Centre-Ville Station, at the Parking Jean Jaurès under the ramparts across from the train station; or at the Parking Palais des Papes (follow signs on the riverside road, boulevard St. Lazare, just past St. Bénezet Bridge). There are two free lots nearby with free shuttle buses to the center (follow *P Gratuit* signs): One is just across Daladier Bridge (pont Daladier); the other is along the river past the Palace of the Popes, just northeast of the walls. Leave nothing in your car. Hotels have advice for smart overnight parking and can get you big discounts at pay lots.

Helpful Hints

Book Ahead for July: During the July theater festival, rooms are sparse—reserve very early, or stay in Arles (see page 78) or St. Rémy (page 101).

Local Help: David at **Imagine Tours** (a nonprofit group whose goal is to promote this region) can help with hotel emergencies or tickets to special events (mobile 06 89 22 19 87, www.imagine-tours.net, imagine.tours@gmail.com).

Internet Access: The TI has a current list of Internet cafés, or ask your hotelier.

English Bookstore: Try **Shakespeare Bookshop** (Tue–Sat 9:30–12:00 & 14:00–18:30, closed Sun–Mon, 155 rue Carreterie, in Avignon's northeast corner, tel. 04 90 27 38 50).

Baggage Storage: You can leave your bags at Centre-Ville train station (see "Arrival in Avignon," earlier).

Laundry: The launderette at 66 place des Corps-Saints, where

Avignon

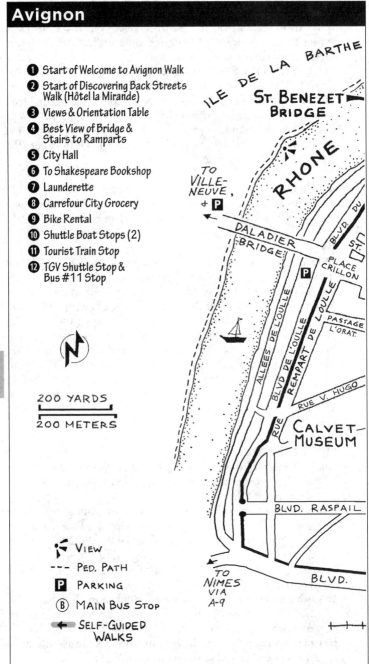

1. Start of Welcome to Avignon Walk
2. Start of Discovering Back Streets Walk (Hôtel la Mirande)
3. Views & Orientation Table
4. Best View of Bridge & Stairs to Ramparts
5. City Hall
6. To Shakespeare Bookshop
7. Launderette
8. Carrefour City Grocery
9. Bike Rental
10. Shuttle Boat Stops (2)
11. Tourist Train Stop
12. TGV Shuttle Stop & Bus #11 Stop

AVIGNON

ILE DE LA BARTHE

ST. BENEZET BRIDGE

RHONE

TO VILLE-NEUVE, & P

DALADIER BRIDGE

BLVD. DU ST.

PLACE CRILLON

P

ALLEES DE L'OULLE

BLVD. DE L'OULLE

REMPART DE L'OULLE

PASSAGE L'ORAT.

RUE V. HUGO

RUE

CALVET MUSEUM

BLVD. RASPAIL

TO NIMES VIA A-9

BLVD.

200 YARDS
200 METERS

View
Ped. Path
P Parking
B Main Bus Stop
Self-Guided Walks

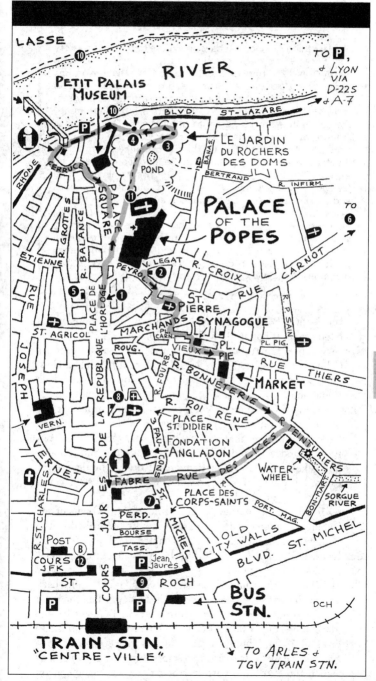

Festival d'Avignon

The last thing Avignon needs is an excuse to party. Still, every July since 1947, a theater festival crashes the city, creating a Mardi Gras–like atmosphere. Contemporary theater groups come from throughout Europe, and each year the festival showcases a different theater director or artist. The program is announced in May, and most tickets are booked immediately—hotels are 80 percent full by March. The festival is indoors, but venues overflow onto the streets. The organizers need 20 different locations for the performances, from actual theater spaces to small chapels to the inner courtyard of the Palace of the Popes, which seats 2,000. There's also a "fringe festival," called Avignon-Off, which adds another 100 venues and countless amateur performances; and a children's theater festival, with storytellers, dance, musicals, and marionettes. In July the entire city is a stage, with mimes, fire-breathers, singers, and musicians filling the streets. Most of the performances are in French, some are in English, and many dance performances don't require language at all (www.festival-avignon.com and www.avignonleoff.com).

rue Agricol Perdiguier ends, has English instructions and is handy to most hotels (daily 7:00–20:00).

Grocery Store: Carrefour City is central and has long hours (Mon–Sat 7:00–21:00, Sun 9:00–12:00, next to McDonald's, 2 blocks from the TI, toward place de l'Horloge on rue de la République).

Bike Rental: You'll see many **Vélopop** city bikes stationed at key points in Avignon, making one-way and short-term rental a breeze. But note that the machines only accept American Express and chip-and-PIN cards (see page 16). You can also rent bikes and scooters at **Provence Bike** (52 boulevard St. Roch, tel. 04 90 27 92 61, www.provence-bike.com). You'll enjoy riding on the Ile de la Barthélasse, but biking is better in Isle-sur-la-Sorgue (described in the Hill Towns of the Luberon chapter) and Vaison la Romaine (described in the Orange and the Côtes du Rhône chapter).

Car Rental: The TGV train station has the car-rental agencies (open long hours daily).

Shuttle Boat: A free shuttle boat, the *Navette Fluviale*, plies back and forth across the river (as it did in the days when the town had no functioning bridge) from near St. Bénezet Bridge (daily July–Aug 11:00–21:00, Sept–June roughly 10:00–12:30 & 14:00–18:00, 3/hour). It drops you on the peaceful Ile de la Barthélasse, with its riverside restaurant (see page 133), grassy walks, and bike rides with terrific city views. If you stay on

Avignon at a Glance

▲▲**Le Jardin du Rochers des Doms** Park and ramparts at the hilltop where Avignon was first settled, with great views of the Rhône River Valley and the famous broken bridge. **Hours:** Daily April–Sept 7:30–20:00, Oct–March 7:30–18:00. See page 118.

▲▲**St. Bénezet Bridge** The "pont d'Avignon" of nursery-rhyme fame, once connecting the Pope's territory to France. **Hours:** Daily mid-March–Oct 9:00–19:00, until 20:00 July and Sept, until 21:00 in Aug, Nov–mid-March 9:30–17:45. See page 119.

▲▲**Scenic Squares** Numerous hide-and-seek squares ideal for postcard-writing and people-watching—pick your favorite: place des Corps-Saints, place St. Pierre, place des Châtaignes (adjacent to place St. Pierre), place Crillon, place St. Didier (near recommended Caveau du Théâtre Restaurant), and the big place Pie (see map on page 112). **Hours:** Always open.

▲**Palace of the Popes** Fourteenth-century Gothic palace built by the popes who made Avignon their home. **Hours:** Daily mid-March–Oct 9:00–19:00, until 20:00 July and Sept, until 21:00 in Aug, Nov–mid-March 9:30–17:45. See page 120.

▲**Tower of Philip the Fair** Massive tower across St. Bénezet Bridge, featuring the best view over Avignon and the Rhône basin. **Hours:** April–Sept daily 10:00–12:30 & 14:00–18:30; Oct–Nov Tue–Sat 10:00–12:30 & 14:00–17:00, closed Sun–Mon; closed Dec–March. See page 125.

Petit Palace Museum "Little palace" displaying the Church's collection of medieval Italian painting and sculpture. **Hours:** June–Sept Wed–Mon 10:00–13:00 & 14:00–18:00, closed Tue; Oct–May Wed–Mon 9:30–13:00 & 14:00–17:30, closed Tue. See page 118.

Synagogue Thirteenth-century synagogue rebuilt in a Neoclassical Greek-temple style. **Hours:** Mon–Fri 10:00–12:00 & 15:00–17:00, closed Sat–Sun. See page 123.

Fondation Angladon-Dubrujeaud Museum with a small but enjoyable Postimpressionist collection, including art by Cézanne, Van Gogh, Daumier, Degas, and Picasso. **Hours:** Tue–Sun 13:00–18:00, closed Mon. See page 124.

Calvet Museum Fine-arts museum with a good collection and English audioguide. **Hours:** Wed–Mon 10:00–13:00 & 14:00–18:00, closed Tue. See page 124.

AVIGNON

the island for dinner, check the schedule for the last return boat—or be prepared for a pleasant 25-minute walk back to town.

Commanding City Views: For great views of Avignon and the river, walk or drive across Daladier Bridge, or ferry across the Rhône on the *Navette Fluviale* (described earlier). I'd take the boat across the river, walk the view path to Daladier Bridge, and then cross back over the bridge (45-minute walk over mostly level ground). You can enjoy other impressive vistas from the top of Le Jardin du Rochers des Doms, from the tower in the Palace of the Popes, and from the end of the famous, broken St. Bénezet Bridge.

Tours in Avignon

Walking Tours—The TI offers informative two-hour English walking tours of Avignon (€11, discounted with Avignon Passion Pass, April–Oct Wed and Fri–Sat at 10:00, depart from main TI; Nov–March on Sat only, depart from Palace of the Popes).

Tourist Trains—The little train leaves regularly from in front of the Palace of the Popes and offers a decent overview of the city, including Le Jardin du Rochers des Doms and St. Bénezet Bridge (€7, 2/hour, 40 minutes, mid-March–mid-Oct daily 10:00–19:00, English commentary).

Guided Excursions—Several minivan tour companies based in Avignon offer tours to destinations described in this book, including Pont du Gard, the Luberon, and the Camargue (about €65–75/person for all-day tours). See "Tours of Provence" on page 46 (note that guides Madeleine Vedel and François Marcou, as well as Imagine Tours, are all based in Avignon).

Self-Guided Walks

Combine these two walks—one ("Welcome to Avignon") covering the major sights, the other ("Discovering Avignon's Back Streets") along the lanes less taken—to get beyond the surface of this historic city.

▲▲Welcome to Avignon

Before starting this walk—which connects the city's top sights—be sure to pick up the Avignon Passion Pass at the TI, then show it when entering each attraction to receive discounted admission (explained earlier, under "Tourist Information").

• *Start your tour where the Romans did, on place de l'Horloge, in front of City Hall (Hôtel de Ville).*

Place de l'Horloge

This café square was the town forum during Roman times and the market square through the Middle Ages. (Restaurants here offer good people-watching, but they also have less ambience and low-quality meals—you'll find better squares elsewhere to hang your beret in.) Named for a medieval clock tower that the City Hall now hides (find plaque in English), this square's present popularity arrived with the trains in 1854. Walk a few steps to the center of the square, and look down the main drag, rue de la République. When the trains came to Avignon, proud city fathers wanted a direct, impressive way to link the new station to the heart of the city (just like in Paris)—so they plowed over homes to create rue de la République and widened place de l'Horloge. This main drag's Parisian feel is intentional—it was built not in the Provençal manner, but in the Haussmann style that is so dominant in Paris (characterized by broad, straight boulevards lined with stately buildings).

• *Walk uphill past the carousel (public WCs behind). You'll see a golden statue of Mary, floating high above the buildings. Veer right at the street's end, and continue into...*

Palace Square (Place du Palais)

This grand square is lined with the Palace of the Popes, the Petit Palais, and the cathedral. In the 1300s the entire headquarters of the Catholic Church was moved to Avignon. The Church bought Avignon and gave it a complete makeover. Along with clearing out vast spaces like this square and building this three-acre palace, the Church erected more than three miles of protective wall (with 39 towers), "appropriate" housing for cardinals (read: mansions), and residences for its entire bureaucracy. The city was Europe's largest construction zone. Avignon's population grew from 6,000 to 25,000 in short order. (Today, 13,000 people live within the walls.) The limits of pre-papal Avignon are outlined on city maps: Rues Joseph Vernet, Henri Fabre, des Lices, and Philonarde all follow the route of the city's earlier defensive wall.

The Petit Palais (Little Palace) seals the uphill end of the square and was built for a cardinal; today it houses medieval paintings (museum described later). The church just to the left of the Palace of the Popes is Avignon's cathedral. It predates the Church's purchase of Avignon by 200 years. Its small size reflects Avignon's modest, pre-papal population. The gilded Mary was added in 1854, when the Vatican established the doctrine of her Immaculate Conception. Mary is taller than the Palace of the Popes by design: The Vatican never accepted what it called the "Babylonian Captivity" and had a bad attitude about Avignon long after the pope was definitively back in Rome. There hasn't been a French pope since the Holy See returned to Rome—over 600 years. That's what I call a grudge.

Directly across the square from the palace's main entry stands a cardinal's residence, built in 1619 (now the Conservatoire National de Musique). Its fancy Baroque facade was a visual counterpoint to the stripped-down Huguenot aesthetic of the age. During this time, Provence was a hotbed of Protestantism—but, buried within this region, Avignon was a Catholic stronghold. Notice the stumps in front and nearby. Nicknamed *bites* (slang for the male anatomy), they effectively keep cars from double-parking in areas designed for people. Many of the metal ones slide up and down by remote control to let privileged cars come and go.

• *You can visit the massive* **Palace of the Popes** *(described on page 120) now, but it works better to visit that palace at the end of this walk, then continue directly to the "Back Streets" walk, described later.*

Now is a good time to take in the...

Petit Palace Museum (Musée du Petit Palais)

This former cardinal's palace now displays the Church's collection of mostly medieval Italian painting (including one delightful Botticelli) and sculpture. All 350 paintings deal with Christian themes. A visit here before going to the Palace of the Popes helps furnish and populate that otherwise barren building, and a quick peek into its courtyard shows the importance of cardinal housing (€6, €2 English brochure, some English explanations posted; June–Sept Wed–Mon 10:00–13:00 & 14:00–18:00, closed Tue; Oct–May Wed–Mon 9:30–13:00 & 14:00–17:30, closed Tue; at north end of Palace Square, tel. 04 90 86 44 58).

From Palace Square we'll head up to the rocky hilltop where Avignon was first settled, then drop down to the river. With this short loop, you can enjoy a park, hike to a grand river view, and visit Avignon's beloved broken bridge—an experience worth ▲▲.

• *Start by climbing to the church level, then take the switchback ramps up to...*

▲▲Le Jardin du Rochers des Doms

Though the park itself is a delight—with a sweet little café (good prices for food and drinks) and public WCs—don't miss the climax: a panoramic view of the Rhône River Valley and the broken bridge (park gates open daily April–Sept 7:30–20:00, Oct–March 7:30–18:00). For the best views (and the favorite make-out spot for local teenagers later in the evening), find the

terrace behind the odd zodiac display (across the grass from the pond-side park café, facing the statue of Jean Althen). On a clear day, the tallest peak you see, with its white limestone cap, is Mont Ventoux ("Windy Mountain"). Below and just to the right, you'll spot free passenger ferries shuttling across the river (great views from path on other side of the river), and—tucked amidst the trees on the far side of the river—a highly recommended restaurant, Le Bercail. The island in the river is the Ile de la Barthélasse, a nature preserve where Avignon can breathe.

St. André Fortress (across the river on the hill; see the info plaque to the left) was built by the French in 1360, shortly after the pope moved to Avignon, to counter the papal incursion into this part of Europe. The castle was across the border, in the kingdom of France. Avignon's famous bridge was a key border crossing, with towers on either end—one was French, and the other was the pope's. The French one, across the river, is the Tower of Philip the Fair (described on page 125).

• *From this viewpoint, take the stairs to the left (closed at night) down to the tower. As the stairs spiral down, just before St. Bénezet Bridge, catch a glimpse of the...*

Ramparts

The only bit of the rampart you can walk on is accessed from St. Bénezet Bridge (pay to enter—see next). When the pope arrived in the 1360s, small Avignon had no town wall...so he built one. What you see today was restored in the 19th century.

• *When you come out of the tower on street level, take the right-side exit and walk left along the river. Pass under the old bridge to find its entrance shortly after.*

▲▲St. Bénezet Bridge (Pont St. Bénezet)

This bridge, whose construction and location were inspired by a shepherd's religious vision, is the "pont d'Avignon" of nursery-

rhyme fame. The ditty (which you've probably been humming all day) dates back to the 15th century: *Sur le pont d'Avignon, on y danse, on y danse, sur le pont d'Avignon, on y danse tous en rond* ("On the bridge of Avignon, we will dance, we will dance, on the bridge of Avignon, we will dance all in a circle").

But the bridge was a big deal even outside of its kiddie-tune fame. Built between 1171 and 1185, it was the only bridge crossing the mighty Rhône in the Middle Ages. It was damaged several times by floods and subsequently rebuilt, until 1668, when most of it was knocked down by a disastrous icy flood. Lacking a government stimulus package, the townsfolk decided not to rebuild this time, and for more than a century, Avignon had no bridge across the Rhône. While only four arches survive today, the original bridge was huge: Imagine a 22-arch, 3,000-foot-long bridge extending from Vatican territory to the lonely Tower of Philip the Fair, which marked the beginning of France (see displays of the bridge's original length). A Romanesque chapel on the bridge is dedicated to St. Bénezet. Though there's not much to see on the bridge, the audioguide included with your ticket tells a good enough story. It's also fun to be in the breezy middle of the river with a sweeping city view.

Cost and Hours: €4.50, €13 combo-ticket includes Palace of the Popes, same hours as the Palace of the Popes (next), tel. 04 90 27 51 16. The ticket booth is housed in what was a medieval hospital for the poor (funded by bridge tolls). Admission includes a small room dedicated to the song of Avignon's bridge and your only chance to walk a bit of the ramparts (enter both from the tower).

• *To get to the Palace of the Popes from here, exit left, then turn left again back into the walls. Walk to the end of the short street, then turn right following signs to* Palais des Papes. *Look for the brown signs leading left under the passageway. After a block of uphill walking, find the stairs to the palace.*

▲Palace of the Popes (Palais des Papes)

In 1309 a French pope was elected (Pope Clément V). At the urging of the French king, His Holiness decided that dangerous Italy was no place for a pope, so he moved the whole operation to Avignon for a secure rule under a supportive king. The Catholic Church literally bought Avignon (then a two-bit town), and popes resided here until 1403. Meanwhile, Italians demanded a Roman pope, so from 1378 on, there were twin popes—one in Rome and one in Avignon—causing a schism in the Catholic Church that wasn't fully resolved until 1417.

A visit to the mighty yet barren papal palace comes with an audioguide that leads you along a one-way route and does a credible job of overcoming the complete lack of furnishings. It teaches the basic history while allowing you to tour at your own pace.

As you wander, ponder that this palace—the largest surviving Gothic palace in Europe—was built to

accommodate 500 people as the administrative center of the Holy See and home of the pope. This was the most fortified palace of the age (remember, the pope left Rome to be more secure). Nine popes ruled from here, making this the center of Christianity for 100 years. You'll walk through the pope's personal quarters (frescoed with happy hunting scenes), see many models of how the various popes added to the building, and learn about its state-of-the-art plumbing. The rooms are huge. The "pope's chapel" is twice the size of the adjacent Avignon cathedral.

The last pope checked out in 1403 (escaping a siege), but the Church owned Avignon until the French Revolution in 1789. During this interim period, the pope's "legate" (official representative, normally a nephew) ruled Avignon from this palace. Avignon residents, many of whom had come from Rome, spoke Italian for a century after the pope left, making it a linguistic ghetto within France. In the Napoleonic age, the palace was a barracks, housing 1,800 soldiers. You can see cuts in the wall where high ceilings gave way to floor beams. Climb the tower (Tour de la Gâche) for grand views and a rooftop café with surprisingly good food at very fair prices.

A room at the end of the tour (called *la boutellerie*) is dedicated to the region's wines, of which they claim the pope was a fan. Sniff "Le Nez du Vin"—a black box with 54 tiny bottles designed to develop your "nose." (Blind-test your travel partner.) The nearby village of Châteauneuf-du-Pape is where the pope summered in the 1320s. Its famous wine is a direct descendant of his wine. You're welcome to taste here (€6 for three to five fine wines and souvenir tasting cup).

Cost and Hours: €10.50 (more for special exhibits), €13 combo-ticket includes St. Bénezet Bridge, daily mid-March–Oct 9:00–19:00, until 20:00 July and Sept, until 21:00 in Aug, Nov–mid-March 9:30–17:45, last entry one hour before closing, tel. 04 90 27 50 74, www.palais-des-papes.com.

• *You'll exit at the rear of the palace, where my "Back Streets" walking tour begins (described next). Or, to return to Palace Square, make two rights after exiting the palace.*

▲▲Discovering Avignon's Back Streets

Use the map in this chapter or the TI map to navigate this easy, level, 30-minute walk. This self-guided tour begins in the small square (place de la Mirande) behind the Palace of the Popes. If you've toured the palace, this is where you exit. Otherwise, from the front of the palace, follow the narrow, cobbled rue Peyrollerie—carved out of the rock—around the palace on the right side as you face it.

• *Our walk begins at the...*

Hôtel la Mirande: Located on the square, Avignon's finest hotel welcomes visitors. Find the atrium lounge and consider a coffee break amid the understated luxury (€12 afternoon tea served daily 15:00–18:00, includes a generous selection of pastries). Inspect the royal lounge and dining room (recommended on page 132); cooking demos are offered in the basement below. Rooms start at about €400 in high season.

• *Turn left out of the hotel and left again on rue Peyrollerie ("Coppersmiths Street"), then take your first right on rue des Ciseaux d'Or. On the small square ahead you'll find the...*

Church of St. Pierre: The original chestnut doors were carved in 1551, when tales of New World discoveries raced across Europe. (Notice the Indian headdress, top center of left-side door.) The fine Annunciation (eye level on right-side door) shows Gabriel giving Mary the exciting news in impressive Renaissance 3-D. Now take 10 steps back from the door and look way up. The tiny statue breaking the skyline of the church is the pagan god Bacchus, with oodles of grapes. What's he doing sitting atop a Christian church? No one knows. The church's interior holds a beautiful Baroque altar. For recommended restaurants near the Church of St. Pierre, see "Eating in Avignon," later.

• *With your back to the church, follow the alley to the right, which was covered and turned into a tunnel during the town's population boom. It leads into...*

Place des Châtaignes: The cloister of St. Pierre is named for the chestnut *(châtaigne)* trees that once stood here (now replaced by plane trees). The practical atheists of the French Revolution destroyed the cloister, leaving only faint traces of the arches along the church side of the square.

• *Continue around the church and cross busy place Carnot to the Banque Chaix. Across the small lane to the right of the bank, find the classy...*

15th-Century Building: With its original beamed eaves showing, this is a rare vestige from the Middle Ages. Notice how this building widens the higher it gets. A medieval loophole based taxes on ground-floor square footage—everything above was tax-free. Walking down the pedestrian street, rue des Fourbisseurs ("Street of the Animal Furriers"), notice how the top floors almost meet. Fire was a constant danger in the Middle Ages, as flames leapt easily from one home to the next. In fact, the lookout guard's primary responsibility was watching for fires, not the enemy. Virtually all of Avignon's medieval homes have been replaced by safer structures.

• *Turn left from rue des Fourbisseurs onto the traffic-free rue du Vieux Sextier ("Street of the Balance," for weighing items); another left under the first arch leads 10 yards to Avignon's...*

Synagogue: Jews first arrived in Avignon with the Diaspora (exile) of the first century. Avignon's Jews were nicknamed "the Pope's Jews" because of the protection that the Vatican offered to Jews expelled from France. Although this synagogue dates from the 1220s, in the mid-19th century it was completely rebuilt in a Neoclassical Greek-temple style by a non-Jewish architect. This is the only synagogue under a rotunda that you'll see anywhere. It's an intimate, classy place dressed with white colonnades and walnut furnishings. To visit the synagogue, press the buzzer (free, Mon–Fri 10:00–12:00 & 15:00–17:00, closed Sat–Sun, 2 place Jerusalem, tel. 04 90 55 21 24).

• *Retrace your steps to rue du Vieux Sextier and turn left, then continue to the big square and find the big, boxy...*

Market (Les Halles): In 1970, the town's open-air market was replaced by this modern one. The market's jungle-like green wall reflects the changes of seasons and helps mitigate its otherwise stark exterior (open Tue–Sun until 13:00, closed Mon, small TI inside open Fri–Sun). Step inside for a sensual experience of organic breads, olives, and festival-of-mold cheeses. The rue des Temptations cuts down the center. Cafés and cheese shops are on the right—as far as possible from the stinky fish stalls on the left.

Follow your nose away from the fish and have a coffee with the locals.

• *Exit out the back door of Les Halles, turn left on rue de la Bonneterie ("Street of Hosiery"), and track the street for five minutes to the plane trees, where it becomes...*

Rue des Teinturiers: This "Street of the Dyers" is a tie-dyed, tree- and stream-lined lane, home to earthy cafés and galleries. This was the cloth industry's dyeing and textile center in the 1800s (a *teinturier* is a dyer). The stream is a branch of the Sorgue River. Those stylish Provençal fabrics and patterns you see for sale everywhere were first made here, after a pattern imported from India.

About three small bridges down, you'll pass the Grey Penitents chapel on the right. The upper facade shows the GPs, who dressed up in robes and pointy hoods to do their anonymous good deeds back in the 13th century (long before the KKK dressed this way). As you stroll on, you'll see the work of amateur sculptors, who have carved whimsical car barriers out of limestone.

Trendy restaurants on this atmospheric street are recommended later, under "Eating in Avignon."

• *Farther down rue des Teinturiers, you'll come to the...*

Waterwheel: Standing here, imagine the Sorgue River—which hits the mighty Rhône in Avignon—being broken into

several canals in order to turn 23 such wheels. In about 1800, waterwheels powered the town's industries. The little cogwheel above the big one could be shoved into place, kicking another machine into gear behind the wall. (For more on the Sorgue River and its waterwheels, see my self-guided walk of Isle-sur-la-Sorgue on page 197.)

• *To return to the real world, double back on rue des Teinturiers and turn left on rue des Lices, which traces the first medieval wall. (Lice is the no-man's-land along a wall.) After a long block you'll pass a striking four-story building that was a home for the poor in the 1600s, an army barracks in the 1800s, a fine-arts school in the 1900s, and is a deluxe condominium today (much of this neighborhood is going high-class residential). Eventually you'll return to rue de la République, Avignon's main drag.*

More Sights in Avignon

AVIGNON

Most of Avignon's top sights are covered by the walking tours, described earlier. With more time, consider these options.

Fondation Angladon-Dubrujeaud—Visiting this museum is like being invited into the elegant home of a rich and passionate art collector. It mixes a small but enjoyable collection of art from Postimpressionists (including Paul Cézanne, Vincent van Gogh, Honoré Daumier, Edgar Degas, and Pablo Picasso) with re-created art studios and furnishings from many periods. It's a quiet place with a few superb paintings (€6, Tue–Sun 13:00–18:00, closed Mon, 5 rue Laboureur, tel. 04 90 82 29 03, www.angladon.com).

Calvet Museum (Musée Calvet)—This fine-arts museum impressively displays its collection, highlighting French Baroque works. This museum goes ignored by most, but you'll find a few diamonds in the rough upstairs: Géricault, Soutine, and one painting each from Manet, Sisley, Bonnard, Dufy, and Vlamnick (€6, includes audioguide, Wed–Mon 10:00–13:00 & 14:00–18:00, closed Tue, in the quieter western half of town at 65 rue Joseph Vernet, antiquities collection a few blocks away at 27 rue de la République—same hours and ticket, tel. 04 90 86 33 84, www.musee-calvet.org).

Near Avignon, in Villeneuve-lès-Avignon

▲**Tower of Philip the Fair (Tour Philippe-le-Bel)**—Built to protect access to St. Bénezet Bridge in 1307, this massive tower offers a terrific view over Avignon and the Rhône basin. It's best late in the day (€2.10; April–Sept daily 10:00–12:30 & 14:00–18:30; Oct–Nov Tue–Sat 10:00–12:30 & 14:00–17:00, closed Sun–Mon; closed Dec–March). To reach the tower from Avignon, drive (5 minutes, cross Daladier Bridge, follow signs to *Villeneuve-lès-Avignon*), or take bus #11 (2/hour, catch bus in front of post office on cours Président Kennedy, second shelter down—see map on page 112).

Sleeping in Avignon

Hotel values are better in Arles, though I've found some good values in Avignon and have listed them below. Avignon is particularly popular during its July festival (see sidebar on page 114), when you must book ahead (expect inflated prices). Drivers should ask about parking deals.

Near Avignon's Centre-Ville Station

The first five listings are a five-to-ten-minute walk from the Centre-Ville train station. (For hotels Colbert, Parc, and Splendid, turn right off cours Jean Jaurès on rue Agricol Perdiguier.)

$$$ **Hôtel Bristol***** is a big, professionally run place on the main drag, offering predictable "American" comforts, including spacious public spaces, large rooms decorated in neutral tones,

---

Sleep Code

(€1 = about $1.25, country code: 33)
S = Single, **D** = Double/Twin, **T** = Triple, **Q** = Quad, **b** = bathroom, **s** = shower only, * = French hotel rating system (0-4 stars). Unless otherwise noted, credit cards are accepted and English is spoken.

To help you easily sort through these listings, I've divided the rooms into three categories, based on the price for a standard double room with bath:

$$$ **Higher Priced**—Most rooms €85 or more.
$$ **Moderately Priced**—Most rooms between €65-85.
$ **Lower Priced**—Most rooms €65 or less.

Prices can change without notice; verify the hotel's current rates online or by email. For other updates, see www.ricksteves.com/update.

Avignon Hotels & Restaurants

1. Hôtel Bristol
2. Hôtel Colbert
3. Hôtel du Parc
4. Hôtel le Splendid
5. Hôtel Boquier
6. Hôtel d'Europe
7. Hôtel Mercure Cité des Papes
8. Hôtel Pont d'Avignon
9. Hôtel Médiéval
10. To Le Clos du Rempart & Lumani B&Bs
11. To Auberge Bagatelle (Hostel) & Jardin de Bacchus Rooms
12. Church of St. Pierre Eateries
13. Place Crillon Eateries
14. Place des Corps-Saints Eateries
15. Restaurant Françoise
16. La Cave des Passages Wine Bar
17. L'Empreinte Restaurant
18. To Restaurant Numéro 75
19. L'Isle Sonnante Restaurant
20. La Cantina Restaurant
21. Le Caveau du Théâtre Rest.
22. Hôtel la Mirande Restaurant
23. La Vache à Carreaux Rest.
24. L'Epice and Love Rest.
25. Le Bercail Rest.
26. Carrefour City Grocery

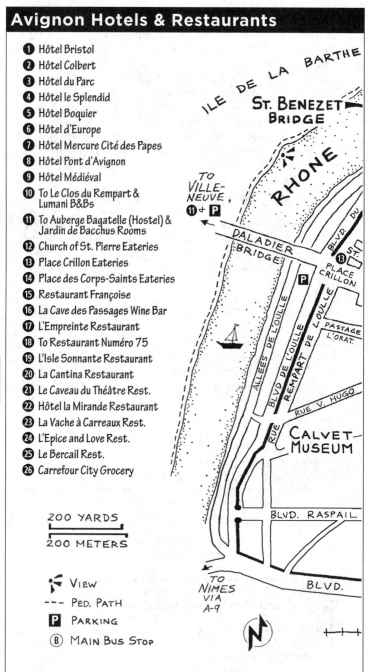

200 YARDS
200 METERS

VIEW
PED. PATH
P PARKING
B MAIN BUS STOP

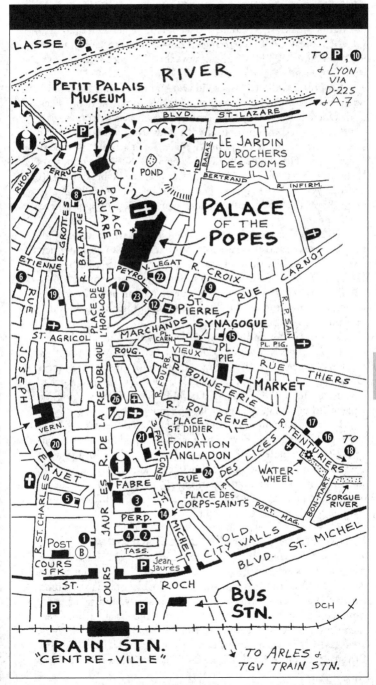

LASSE 25

RIVER

Petit Palais
Museum

TO P, 10
& LYON
VIA
D-225
& A-7

BLVD. ST-LAZARE

P

FERRUCE

RHONE

PALACE SQUARE

R. GROTTES

R. BALANCE

POND

LE JARDIN
DU ROCHERS
DES DOMS

BAÑAS

BERTRAND

R. INFIRM.

8

PALACE
OF THE
POPES

ETIENNE

6

RUE

19

PLACE DE L'HORLOGE

PEYROL

7

V. LEGAT

22

R. CROIX

23

RUE

CARNOT

R. P. SAIN

9

12

ST. PIERRE

SYNAGOGUE

15

ST. AGRICOL

MARCHANDS

PL.
CARN.

PL.
PIE

PL. PIG.

JOSEPH

ROUG.

VIEUX

R. FOURB.

R. BONNETERIE

RUE
THIERS

VERN.

26

R. ROI
RENE

MARKET

20

VERNET

R. ST. CHARLES

21

3 FAC. CONS.

PLACE
ST. DIDIER

Fondation
Angladon

17

R. TEINTURIERS

16

TO
18

DES LICES

WATER-
WHEEL

BON-MART.

SORGUE
RIVER

FABRE

24

RUE

PLACE DES
CORPS-SAINTS

PORT. MAG.

5

3

PERD.

14

MICHEL

OLD
CITY WALLS

ST. MICHEL

JAURES R. DE LA REPUBLIQUE

ST.

1

POST

B

4

2

TASS.

COURS JFK

P

Jean
Jaures

ROCH

BLVD. ST. MICHEL

BUS
STN.

DCH

P

P

TRAIN STN.
"CENTRE-VILLE"

TO ARLES &
TGV TRAIN STN.

AVIGNON

duvets on the beds, a big elevator, air-conditioning, and a generous buffet breakfast (standard Db-€88–103, bigger Db-€126, Tb/Qb-€153, breakfast-€12, parking-€12, 44 cours Jean Jaurès, tel. 04 90 16 48 48, fax 04 90 66 22 72, www.bristol-hotel-avignon.com, contact@bristol-avignon.com).

$$ Hôtel Colbert** is a solid two-star hotel and a good mid-range bet, with richly colored, comfortable rooms in many sizes. Your efficient hosts—Patrice, Annie, and *le chien* Brittany—care for this restored manor house, with its warm public spaces and sweet little patio. It's a popular place, so it's best to book in advance (Sb-€65, small Db-€78, bigger Db-€84–100, some tight bathrooms, no triples available, creative homemade breakfast-€10, air-con, Wi-Fi, 7 rue Agricol Perdiguier, tel. 04 90 86 20 20, fax 04 90 85 97 00, www.lecolbert-hotel.com, contact@avignon-hotel-colbert.com).

$$ Hôtel du Parc* is a spotless value with white walls, some tiny bathrooms, and stone accents. Since it's likely to be under new ownership for 2011, these prices are *très* tentative (S-€32, Sb-€45, Ds-€65, Db-€70, Ts-€75; no TVs, phones, or air-con; tel. 04 90 82 71 55, fax 04 90 85 64 86, http://perso.modulonet.fr/hoduparc, hotel.parc@modulonet.fr). This place is homier than Hôtel le Splendid, across the street.

$ Hôtel le Splendid* rents 17 acceptable rooms with faux-wood floors, most of which could use a little attention (Sb-€48, Db-€62, bigger Db with air-con-€72, Tb with air-con-€82, three Db apartments-€92, Internet access and Wi-Fi, 17 rue Agricol Perdiguier, tel. 04 90 86 14 46, fax 04 90 85 38 55, www.avignon-splendid-hotel.com, splendidavignon@gmail.com).

$ At Hôtel Boquier**, engaging Madame Sendra offers 12 quiet, good-value, and homey rooms under wood beams in a central location (small Db-€58, bigger Db-€72, Tb-€80, Qb-€94, air-con, Internet access and Wi-Fi, steep and narrow stairways to some rooms and no elevator, parking-€7, near the TI at 6 rue du portail Boquier, tel. 04 90 82 34 43, fax 04 90 86 14 07, www.hotel-boquier.com, contact@hotel-boquier.com).

In the Center, near Place de l'Horloge

$$$ Hôtel d'Europe****, with Avignon's most prestigious address, lets peasants sleep royally without losing their shirts—but only if you land one of the 10 surprisingly reasonable "standard" rooms. Enter a shady courtyard, linger in the lounges, and savor every comfort. The hotel is located on the handsome place Crillon, near the river (standard Db-€200, superior Db-€360, prestige Db-€495, breakfast-€17, elevator, Internet access, garage-€17, near Daladier Bridge at 12 place Crillon, tel. 04 90 14 76 76, fax 04 90 14 76

71, www.heurope.com, reservations@heurope.com). The hotel's restaurant is Michelin-rated (one star) and serves an upscale €48 *menu* in its formal dining room or front courtyard.

$$$ Hôtel Mercure Cité des Papes*** is a modern chain hotel within spitting distance of the Palace of the Popes. It has 89 smartly designed, small rooms (Sb-€135, Db-€145–180, promotional deals best if booked 15 days ahead, many rooms have views over place de l'Horloge, air-con, elevator, 1 rue Jean Vilar, tel. 04 90 80 93 00, fax 04 90 80 93 01, www.mercure.com, h1952@accor.com).

$$$ Hôtel Pont d'Avignon***, just inside the walls near St. Bénezet Bridge, is part of the same chain as the Hôtel Mercure Cité des Papes, with the same prices for its 87 rooms (direct access to a garage makes parking easier than at the other Mercure hotel, elevator, on rue Ferruce, tel. 04 90 80 93 93, fax 04 90 80 93 94, www.mercure.com, h0549@accor.com).

$$ Hôtel Médiéval** is burrowed deep a few blocks from the Church of St. Pierre. Built as a cardinal's home, this massive stone mansion has a small garden and friendly-as-they-get Mike at the helm. It has 35 wood-paneled, air-conditioned, unimaginative rooms (Sb-€49, Db-€62–77, bigger Db or Tb-€85–92, kitchenettes available but require 3-night minimum stay, Wi-Fi, 5 blocks east of place de l'Horloge, behind Church of St. Pierre at 15 rue Petite Saunerie, tel. 04 90 86 11 06, fax 04 90 82 08 64, www.hotel medieval.com, hotel.medieval@wanadoo.fr).

Chambres d'Hôte

$$$ At **Le Clos du Rempart,** a 10-minute walk from the center, Madame Assad rents two comfortable rooms and one apartment on a peaceful courtyard with Middle Eastern decor (Db-€120–150 depending on season and room size, 2-bedroom apartment for 4 with kitchen-€800–1,100/week, includes breakfast, cash only, air-con, Wi-Fi, 1 parking spot in garage, inside the walls east of the Palace of the Popes at 35–37 rue Crémade—call or check website for directions, tel. & fax 04 90 86 39 14, www.closdurempart.com, aida@closdurempart.com).

$$$ Lumani provides the ultimate urban refuge just inside the city walls, a 15-minute walk from the Palace of the Popes. In this graceful old manor house, gentle Elisabeth and Jean welcome guests to their art-gallery-cum-bed-and-breakfast that surrounds a fountain-filled courtyard with elbow room. She paints, he designs buildings, and both care about your experience in Avignon. The five rooms are decorated with flair; no two are alike, and all overlook the shady garden (small Db-€100, big Db-€140, Db suites-€170, extra person-€30, includes breakfast, credit cards OK except American Express, Internet access and Wi-Fi, music studio,

AVIGNON

parking–€10 or easy on street, 37 rue de Rempart St Lazare, tel. 04 90 82 94 11, www.avignon-lumani.com, lux@avignon-lumani.com).

On the Outskirts of Town

$ Auberge Bagatelle's hostel offers dirt-cheap beds, lively atmosphere, café, grocery store, launderette, great views of Avignon, and campers for neighbors (D-€44, Ds-€48, T-€60, Ts-€67, Tb-€82, Q-€73, Qb-€100, dorm bed-€18, includes breakfast, across Daladier Bridge on Ile de la Barthélasse, bus #10 from main post office, tel. 04 90 86 71 31, fax 04 90 27 16 23, www.auberge bagatelle.fr, auberge.bagatelle@wanadoo.fr).

Near Avignon

$$$ At Jardin de Bacchus, just 15 minutes northwest of Avignon and convenient to Pont du Gard, enthusiastic and English-speaking Christine and Erik offer three rooms in their rural farmhouse overlooking little Tavel's famous vineyards (Db-€85–105, €30 extra for one-night stays, breakfast-€10, fine dinner possible, Wi-Fi, tel. 04 66 90 28 62, www.jardindebacchus.fr, jardinde bacchus@free.fr). For details on their cooking classes, see page 473 in the appendix; to learn about their small-group food and wine tours, check their website.

Eating in Avignon

Skip the overpriced places on place de l'Horloge and find a more intimate location for your dinner. Avignon has many delightful squares filled with tables ready to seat you.

Near the Church of St. Pierre

The church divides two enchanting squares. One is quiet and intimate, the other is lively.

L'Epicerie, sitting alone on an intimate square, serves the highest-quality and highest-priced cuisine around the Church of St. Pierre, with a focus on products from the south of France. Expect lots of color and a dash of spice (€18–24 *plats,* closed Sun off-season, cozy interior good in bad weather, 10 place St. Pierre, tel. 04 90 82 74 22).

On Place des Châtaignes: Pass under the arch by L'Epicerie restaurant and enter enchanting place des Châtaignes, with a fun commotion of tables. Peruse your options. The **Crêperie du Cloître** makes mediocre dinner crêpes and salads (daily, cash only).

Vietnamese **Restaurant Nem,** tucked in the corner, is family-run (*menus* from €12, cash only). **Pause Gourmande** is a small, lunch-only eatery with €9 *plats du jour,* and always has a veggie option (closed Sun).

Place Crillon

This more refined square just off the river attracts a stylish crowd and houses a variety of dining choices. Traditional French **Restaurant les Artistes** and *italiano* **La Piazza** are both popular and owned by the same folks (good €11 lunch deals, €17 dinner *menus* with fine choices, daily, tel. 04 90 82 23 54). **La Comédie** serves €9 crêpes and salads with mod seating (closed Sun).

Place des Corps-Saints

You'll find several youthful and reasonable eateries with tables sprawling under big plane trees on this locally popular square. **Bistrot à Tartines** specializes in—you guessed it—*tartines* (big slices of toast smothered with toppings), and has the coziest interior and best desserts on the square (€8 *tartines* and salads, daily, tel. 04 90 85 58 70). I also enjoy the €10 pizzas and friendly service at **Le Pili** (daily, tel. 04 90 27 39 53). **Zeste** is a friendly, modern deli offering fresh soups, pasta salads, wraps, smoothies, and more. Get it to go, or eat inside or on the scenic square—all at unbeatable prices (closed Sun, tel. 09 51 49 05 62).

By the Market (Les Halles)

Here you'll find a good selection of eateries with good prices. **Restaurant Françoise** is a pleasant café and tea salon, where fresh-baked tarts—savory and sweet—and a variety of salads and soups make a healthful meal, and vegetarian options are plentiful (€7–12 dishes, Mon–Sat 8:00–19:00, closed Sun, free Wi-Fi, 6 rue Général Leclerc, tel. 04 32 76 24 77).

Rue des Teinturiers

This "tie-dye" street has a wonderful concentration of eateries popular with the natives, and justifies the long walk. It's a trendy, youthful area, recently spiffed up with a canalside ambience and little hint of tourism. Survey the eateries listed here before choosing (all line up near the waterwheel).

    La Cave des Passages makes a colorful pause before dinner. The owners enjoy serving you a fragrant €2.50 glass of regional wine. Choose from the blackboard by the bar that lists all the bottles open today, then join the gang outside by the canal. In the evening, this place is a hit with the young local crowd for its wine and weekend concerts (Mon–Sat 10:00–15:00 & 18:00–1:00 in the morning, closed Sun, no food in evening, across from waterwheel

AVIGNON

at 41 rue des Teinturiers).

L'Empreinte is good for North African cuisine. Choose a table in its tent-like interior, or sit canalside on the cobbles (copious couscous or *tajine* for €13–16, take-out and veggie options available, daily, 33 rue des Teinturiers, tel. 04 32 76 31 84).

Restaurant Numéro 75 is worth the walk (just past where the cobbles end on rue des Teinturiers). It fills the Pernod mansion (of *pastis* liquor fame) and a large, romantic courtyard with outdoor tables. The menu is limited to Mediterranean cuisine, but everything's *très* tasty. It's best to go with the options offered by your young black-shirted server (€20 two-course lunch *menu* with wine and coffee, dinner *menus:* €27/appetizer and main course or main course and dessert, €33/3 courses; Mon–Sat 12:00–14:00 & 20:00–22:00, closed Sun, 75 rue Guillaume Puy, tel. 04 90 27 16 00).

Elsewhere in Avignon

At **L'Isle Sonnante,** join chef Boris and wife Anne to dine intimately in their formal and charming one-room *bistrot.* You'll choose from a small menu offering only fresh products and will be served by owners who care (*menus* from €30, closed Sun–Mon, 100 yards from the carousel on place de l'Horloge at 7 rue Racine, tel. 04 90 82 56 01, best to book ahead).

La Cantina delivers fine Italian cuisine in a beautiful courtyard (€15 pizzas, €20–30 *plats*, closed Sun evening, 83 rue Joseph Vernet, tel. 04 90 85 99 04).

Le Caveau du Théâtre is a welcoming place where Richard invites diners to have a glass of wine or dinner at a sidewalk table, or inside in one of two carefree rooms (€13 *plats*, €18 *menus*, fun ambience for free, closed for lunch Sat and all day Sun, 16 rue des Trois Faucons, tel. 04 90 82 60 91).

Hôtel la Mirande is the ultimate Avignon splurge. Reserve ahead here for understated elegance and Avignon's top cuisine (€35 lunch *menu*, €105 dinner tasting *menu*; closed Tue–Wed—but for a price break, dine in the kitchen with the chef on these "closed" days for €85–140 including wine; behind Palace of the Popes, 4 place de la Mirande, tel. 04 90 86 93 93, www.la-mirande.fr).

La Vache à Carreaux is a unique place with a passion for cheese in all its forms (non-cheese dishes are also available). The decor is as warm as the welcome, the wine list is extensive and reasonable, and it's a hit with the locals—so reserve ahead (€12–20 *plats*, daily, just behind Palace of the Popes at 14 rue Peyrolerie, tel. 04 90 80 09 05).

At **L'Epice and Love** (the name is a fun French-English play on words, pronounced "lay peace and love"), English-speaking owner Marie creates a playful atmosphere in her cozy, friendly restaurant. A few colorfully decorated tables and tasty meat, fish, and vegetarian dishes at good prices greet the hungry traveler (*menus* from €16, daily, 30 rue des Lices, tel. 04 90 82 45 96).

Across the River

Le Bercail offers a fun opportunity to get out of town (barely) and take in *le fresh air* with a terrific riverfront view of Avignon, all while enjoying inexpensive Provençal cooking served in big portions. Book ahead, as this restaurant is popular (*menus* from €17, serves late, daily April–Oct, tel. 04 90 82 20 22). To get there, take the free shuttle boat (located near St. Bénezet Bridge) to the Ile de la Barthélasse, turn right, and walk five minutes. As the boat usually stops running at about 18:00 (except in July–Aug, when it runs until 21:00), you can either taxi home or walk 25 minutes along the pleasant riverside path and over Daladier Bridge.

Avignon Connections

Trains

Remember, there are two train stations in Avignon: the suburban TGV Station, and the Centre-Ville Station in the city center (€1.20 shuttle buses connect to both stations, buy ticket from driver, 3/hour, 15 minutes). TGV trains usually serve the TGV train station only, though a few depart from Centre-Ville train station (check your station). Only Centre-Ville Station has baggage storage (see "Arrival in Avignon" on page 110). Car rental is available only at the TGV Station. Some cities are served by slower local trains from Centre-Ville Station as well as by faster TGV trains from the TGV Station; I've listed the most convenient stations for each trip.

   From Avignon's Centre-Ville Station by Train to: Arles (11/day, 20 minutes, less frequent in the afternoon), **Orange** (15/day, 15 minutes), **Nîmes** (14/day, 30 minutes), **Isle-sur-la-Sorgue** (10/day on weekdays, 5/day on weekends, 30 minutes), **Lyon** (10/day, 2 hours, also from TGV Station—see below), **Carcassonne** (8/day, 7 with transfer in Narbonne, 3 hours), **Barcelona** (2/day, 6–9 hours, transfer in Montpellier).

   From Avignon's TGV Station to: Arles (by SNCF bus, 10/day, 1 hour), **Nice** (20/day, most by TGV, 4 hours, most require transfer in Marseille), **Marseille** (10/day, 1 hour), **Cassis** (7/day, 2 hours), **Aix-en-Provence TGV** (10/day, 25 minutes), **Lyon** (12/day, 1.5 hours, also from Centre-Ville Station—see above), **Paris'** Gare de Lyon (9/day direct, 2.5 hours; more connections with transfer, 3–4 hours), **Paris'** Charles de Gaulle airport (7/day, 3 hours).

Buses

The bus station *(gare routière)* is just past and below Ibis Hôtel, to the right as you exit the train station (info desk open Mon–Sat 8:00–19:30, closed Sun, tel. 04 90 82 07 35, staff speaks English). Nearly all buses leave from this station (buy tickets on bus, small bills only). The biggest exception is the SNCF bus service from the Avignon TGV train station to Arles (explained on page 86). The Avignon TI has schedules. Service is reduced or nonexistent on Sundays and holidays. Check your departure time beforehand and make sure to verify your destination with the driver.

From Avignon to Pont du Gard: Buses go to this famous old aqueduct (3–5/day, 40–50 minutes, departs from bus station, usually from stall #11), but the schedule doesn't work well for day-trippers from Avignon; instead, consider a taxi one-way and bus back; or for a more worthwhile day trip, see my suggested train/bus excursion that combines Nîmes and Pont du Gard (see page 135).

By Bus to Other Regional Destinations: Uzès (3–5/day Mon–Sat, none Sun, 1 hour, stops at Pont du Gard); **St. Rémy-de-Provence** (6/day, 45 minutes, handy way to visit its Wed market); **Orange** (Mon–Sat hourly, none Sun, 45 minutes—take the train instead); **Isle-sur-la-Sorgue** (6–8/day Mon–Sat, 3–4/day Sun, 45 minutes). To reach the **Côtes du Rhône** area, the bus runs to **Vaison la Romaine, Nyons, Sablet,** and **Séguret** (5/day during the school year—called *période scolaire*, 3/day otherwise, and 1/day from TGV station; 1.5 hours, all buses pass through Orange—faster to take train to Orange, and transfer to bus there). For the **Luberon** area—including **Lourmarin** and **Gordes**—first take the bus to Cavaillon (from there, take bus #8 toward Pertuis for Lourmarin, or bus #15 for Gordes).

AVIGNON

NEAR AVIGNON

Nîmes, Pont du Gard, and Uzès

Although Avignon lacks Roman monuments of its own, some of Europe's greatest Roman sights are an easy, breezy day trip away. (To get the most out of these sights, read "How About Them Romans?" on page 48 before you visit.) The Pont du Gard aqueduct is a magnificent structure to experience, as is the city it served 2,000 years ago, Nîmes, which wraps a variety of intriguing Roman monuments together in a bustling, bigger-city package. The pedestrian-friendly town of Uzès, between Nîmes and Pont du Gard, offers a refreshing break from power monuments and busy cities. Combining these three sights makes a memorable day trip into the Languedoc region. Traveling by car, you'll drive scenic roads (particularly D-979 between Uzès and Nîmes) that show off the rugged *garrigue* landscape that this area is famous for.

Planning Your Time

Consider getting away from the tourists and spending a night in classy Nîmes or cozy Uzès. If you're on a tighter schedule, don't worry—this region's sights are easy to cover in a day trip from Avignon, even without a car.

By Taxi, Train, or Bus: With only a few buses a day connecting Avignon with Pont du Gard and Uzès (3–5/day Mon–Sat, none on Sun), you need to plan carefully. If you only care about Pont du Gard and are pressed for time, consider taking a €42 taxi from Avignon there, then take the early-afternoon bus back (13:20 in 2010). But if you have the time and patience, public transit is a good option. Double-check all schedules at Avignon's bus station (tel. 08 10 33 42 73, push 3 to get an English-speaking information agent), arrive at bus stops at least five minutes early, pay the driver (no big bills), and always verify your stop and direction with the bus driver. Here are three plans to consider (unless noted, connections

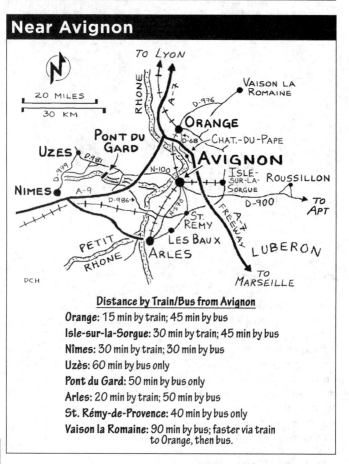

Near Avignon

20 MILES
30 KM

TO LYON

RHONE

VAISON LA ROMAINE

D-976

ORANGE

CHAT.-DU-PAPE

D-68

PONT DU GARD

UZES

D-981

AVIGNON

N-100

D-979

ISLE-SUR-LA-SORGUE

ROUSSILLON

NIMES

A-9

D-986

D-900

TO APT

N-570

ST. REMY

LES BAUX

A-7 FREEWAY

LUBERON

ARLES

PETIT RHONE

TO MARSEILLE

DCH

Distance by Train/Bus from Avignon

Orange: 15 min by train; 45 min by bus

Isle-sur-la-Sorgue: 30 min by train; 45 min by bus

Nîmes: 30 min by train; 30 min by bus

Uzès: 60 min by bus only

Pont du Gard: 50 min by bus only

Arles: 20 min by train; 50 min by bus

St. Rémy-de-Provence: 40 min by bus only

Vaison la Romaine: 90 min by bus; faster via train to Orange, then bus.

for these trips work every day but Sunday—when buses are too infrequent; I've listed bus times for 2010, so confirm these locally when planning your day). Buses take about 40–50 minutes to get to Pont du Gard from Avignon and from Nîmes; trains take 30 minutes to connect Avignon and Nîmes.

Early Riser: Take a morning bus from Avignon to Pont du Gard (8:45), then take an early-afternoon bus on to Nîmes (13:25) for some sightseeing before returning from Nîmes to Avignon (trains almost hourly).

Late Riser: Sleep in, and take the midday bus from Avignon to Pont du Gard (11:40), then take the afternoon bus (16:15) on to Nîmes. After sightseeing in Nîmes, return by train to Avignon (trains almost hourly).

Eager Beaver All-Day Trip: For a rewarding all-day excursion, begin by taking a morning train from Avignon's Centre-Ville

Station to Nîmes (about 9:00). After sightseeing there, take a mid-day bus from Nîmes to Pont du Gard (11:30 or 13:30, 40 minutes), then catch an afternoon bus to Uzès (16:20, 20 minutes). Wind down with an afternoon stroll through Uzès, and take the last bus from Uzès back to Avignon (18:30). This lands you back in Avignon at 19:30—just in time for dinner. *Bonne route!*

Nîmes

Most travelers make time in their schedules for Arles and Avignon, but ignore Nîmes. Arles and Avignon may have more touristic appeal, but Nîmes—which feels richer and surer of itself—is refreshingly lacking in overnight tourists. This thriving town of classy shops and serious businesses is studded with world-class Roman monuments and laced with traffic-free lanes. (And if you've visited the magnificent Pont du Gard, you gotta be curious where all that water went.)

Since the Middle Ages, Nîmes has exported a famous fabric: The word "denim" actually comes from here (*de Nîmes* = "from Nîmes"). Denim caught on in the United States in the 1800s, when a Bavarian immigrant, Levi Strauss, popularized its use in the American West.

Today, Nîmes is officially in the Languedoc region (for administrative purposes only), yet historically the town has been a key player in the evolution of Provence. Only 30 minutes by train from Arles or Avignon (about €8 one-way to either), and three hours from Paris on the TGV, Nîmes is worth a visit if you want a taste of today's urban Provence. The city keeps its clean and tranquil old center a secret for its well-heeled residents. (Locals admit they don't need the tourist money as much as other Provençal towns.) While most visitors understandably prefer sleeping in Arles or Avignon, a night here provides a good escape from tourist crowds and a truer taste of a Provençal city.

Orientation to Nîmes

Nîmes ("neem") has no river or natural landmark to navigate by, so it's easy to become disoriented. For a quick visit, limit yourself to the manageable triangle within the ring of roads formed by boulevard Victor Hugo, boulevard Amiral Courbet, and boulevard Gambetta.

The town's landmarks are connected by 10-minute walks: It's 10 minutes from the train station to the Arena, 10 minutes from the Arena to the Roman temple of Maison Carrée, and 10 minutes from Maison Carrée to either the Castellum or the Fountain Garden. Apart from seeing this handful of ancient monuments, appreciate the city's traffic-free old center—a delight for browsing, strolling, sipping coffee, and people-watching.

Tourist Information

The helpful TI is a few steps out the front door and across the street from Maison Carrée (Mon–Sat 8:30–19:00, Sun 10:00–18:00, 6 rue Auguste, tel. 04 66 58 38 00, www.ot-nimes.fr). Pick up the excellent *Discovering Nîmes* pamphlet, which includes a map with a description of the city's sights and museums, and a worthwhile old-town walk. You can also rent an MP3-player audioguide for a walking tour of Old Nîmes (€8, €10/2 people, leave ID as deposit).

Arrival in Nîmes

By Train and Bus: Trains and buses use the same station (handy if you're combining Pont du Gard with Nîmes). There is no baggage storage. Confirm return schedules before leaving the station, as service can be sparse. The bus station and information office are at the rear of the train station (Mon–Fri 7:30–12:30 & 14:00–18:30, closed Sat–Sun). Buses to Pont du Gard generally leave from stalls 2 or 3 (look for the shelters to the right as you walk out the back door of the train station).

The Arena is a 10-minute walk out the front of the train station. Head up the left side of avenue Feuchères, veer left at the end of the street, then curve right and you'll see the Arena (to find its entrance, walk counterclockwise around it). The Maison Carrée and TI are an enjoyable stroll from the Arena through Nîmes' traffic-free old town.

By Car: Follow signs for *Centre-Ville* and *TI*, then *Arènes Parking*, and pay to park underneath the Arena. In this huge garage, make a note of where you parked. If it's full, Parking des Feuchères is nearby (behind the train station), and Parking Maison Carrée is close to the TI.

Helpful Hints

Summer Thursdays: The "Jeudi de Nîmes" (Thursdays of Nîmes) tradition turns the entire old center of town into a festival of shops, street music, and liveliness on Thursday nights in July and August from 18:00 until late.

Internet Access: Netgames is behind Maison Carrée at 25 place du Maison Carrée (daily 9:00–24:00, lots of young gamers).

Laundry: There's a clean launderette near the recommended Hôtel la Baume at 14 rue Nationale (daily 7:00–21:00).

Taxi and Tours: Call 04 66 29 40 11 for a cab. It's about €42 to Pont du Gard.

Car Rental: At the station, you'll find **Avis** (tel. 04 66 29 66 36), **Europcar** (tel. 04 66 29 07 94), and **Hertz** (tel. 04 66 76 25 91).

Train Tickets: The small **SNCF Boutique** office, centrally located in the old town, is an easy place to check schedules or buy train tickets without having to go to the station (Tue–Sat 8:30–18:50, closed Sun–Mon, 11 rue de l'Aspic).

Local Guide: Sylvie Pagnard is a delightful guide whose walking tours are top-quality and top-price. She does regional tours and has a car (€140/3 hours, €360/8 hours, tel. 04 66 20 33 14, mobile 06 03 21 37 33, sylviepagnard@aol.com).

Tourist Train: It departs from the esplanade with the fountain, in front of the Arena (€5, daily April–Oct, nearly hourly at the bottom of the hour, does not run Nov–March, 35 minutes).

View and WCs: Ride the glass elevator to the top-floor café of the Museum of Contemporary Art for a great view over the ancient Maison Carrée and a quiet break above the world. The museum is in the glass building that faces the monument, and the elevator is inside near the front door (Tue–Sun 10:00–18:00, closed Mon). The basement has good WCs (same hours as café).

Self-Guided Walk

Welcome to Nîmes

I described Nîmes' best sights below in a logical walking order for a good daylong visit, starting from the Arena (near the train station, with easy parking underground). Many of the sights I mention are free; the major exception is the Arena.

▲▲Arena (Amphithéâtre)

Nîmes' Arena dates from about A.D. 100 and is more than 425 feet in diameter and 65 feet tall. Considered the best-preserved arena of the Roman world, it's a fine example of Roman engineering...and propaganda. In the spirit of "give them bread and circuses," it was free. No gates, just 60 welcoming arches, numbered to allow entertainment-seekers to come

and go freely. The agenda was to create a populace that was thoroughly Roman—enjoying the same activities and entertainment, all thinking as one (not unlike Americans' nationwide obsession with the same reality-TV shows). The 24,000 seats could be filled

Nîmes

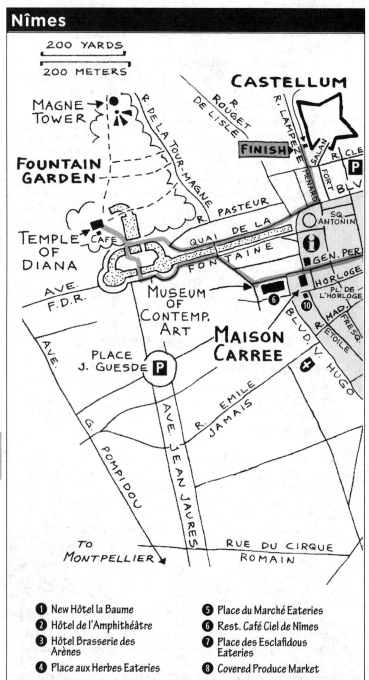

NEAR AVIGNON

200 YARDS

200 METERS

CASTELLUM

MAGNE TOWER

R. DE LA TOUR-MAGNE

R. ROUGET DE L'ISLE

R. LAMPEZE

FINISH

SALAN FORT

R. CLE

MENARD

P

FOUNTAIN GARDEN

BLV

R. PASTEUR

SQ. ANTONIN

QUAI DE LA

TEMPLE OF DIANA

CAFE

FONTAINE

GEN. PER

HORLOGE

PL. DE L'HORLOGE

AVE. F.D.R.

MUSEUM OF CONTEMP. ART

6

10

R. MAD.

FRES.

R. ETOILE

MAISON CARREE

BLVD. V. HUGO

AVE. G.

PLACE J. GUESDE

P

R. EMILE JAMAIS

POMPIDOU

AVE. JEAN JAURES

TO MONTPELLIER

RUE DU CIRQUE ROMAIN

1 New Hôtel la Baume

2 Hôtel de l'Amphithéâtre

3 Hôtel Brasserie des Arènes

4 Place aux Herbes Eateries

5 Place du Marché Eateries

6 Rest. Café Ciel de Nîmes

7 Place des Esclafidous Eateries

8 Covered Produce Market

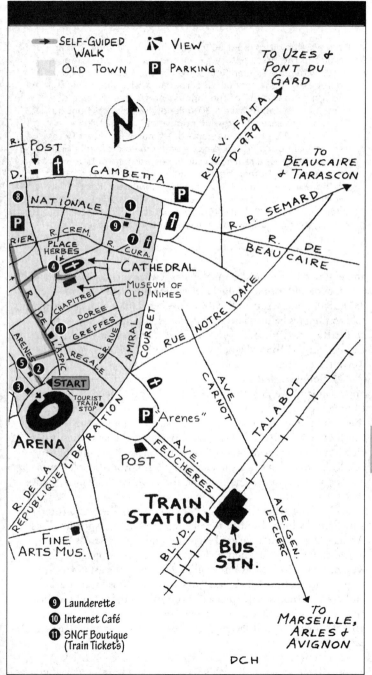

SELF-GUIDED WALK

VIEW

OLD TOWN

PARKING

TO UZES &
PONT DU
GARD

TO
BEAUCAIRE
& TARASCON

RUE V. FAITA
D-979

R. P. SEMARD

R. POST

GAMBETTA

NATIONALE

R. CREM.

PLACE
HERBES

R. CURA.

R. DE BEAUCAIRE

CATHEDRAL

MUSEUM OF
OLD NIMES

CHAPITRE

DOREE

GREFFES

AMIRAL COURBET

RUE NOTRE DAME

ARENES

REGALE

GR. RUE

DE L'ASPIC

START

TOURIST TRAIN
STOP

ARENA

R. DE LA
REPUBLIQUE LIBERATION

"Arenes"

POST

AVE. CARNOT

AVE. FEUCHERES

TALABOT

TRAIN
STATION

BUS
STN.

AVE. GEN.
LE CLERC

FINE
ARTS MUS.

BLVD.

TO
MARSEILLE,
ARLES &
AVIGNON

NEAR AVIGNON

9 Launderette
10 Internet Café
11 SNCF Boutique
(Train Tickets)

DCH

Roman Nîmes

Born a Celtic city (about 500 B.C.), Nîmes joined the Roman Empire in the first century B.C. Because it had a privileged status within the Roman Empire, Nîmes was never really considered part of the conquered barbarian world. It rated highly enough to merit one of the longest protective walls in the Roman world and to have a 30-mile-long aqueduct (Pont du Gard) built to serve its growing population.

Today, the physical remains of Roman Nîmes testify to its former importance. The city's emblem—a crocodile tied to a palm tree—is a reminder that Nîmes was a favorite retirement home for Roman officers who conquered Egypt. (The crocodile is Egypt, and the palm tree symbolizes victory.) All over town, little bronze croc-palm medallions shine on the sidewalks. In the City Hall, 400-year-old statues of crocodiles actually swing from the top of a monumental staircase.

and emptied in minutes (through passageways called *vomitoires*).

Cost and Hours: €8, includes audioguide, daily March–Oct 9:00–18:00, June–Aug until 19:00, Nov–Feb 9:00–17:00, last ticket sold 45 minutes before closing, may close for special events—check at TI. Buy the €10 combo-ticket if you plan to visit the Maison Carrée and the Tour Magne (tower in the Fountain Garden—not worth the climb).

◑ Self-Guided Tour: Climb to the very top—it's a rare opportunity to enjoy the view from the nosebleed seats of a Roman arena. An amphitheater is literally a double theater: two theaters facing each other, designed so that double the people could view a *Dirty Harry* spectacle (without the acoustics provided by the back wall of a theater stage). You may think of this as a "colosseum," but that's not a generic term. Rome's Colosseum was a one-of-a-kind arena—named for a colossal statue of Nero that stood nearby.

The floor where the action took place was the *arena* (literally, "sand," which absorbed the blood, as in bullfights today). The Arena's floor, which covered passages and storage areas underneath, came with the famous elevator for surprise appearances of wild animals. (While Rome could afford exotic beasts from the tropics, places like Nîmes made do with snarling local beasts... bulls, wild boars, lots of bears, and so on.) The standard fight was as real as professional wrestling is today—mostly just crowd-pleasing. Thumbs down and kill the guy? Maybe in Rome, but only rarely (if ever) here.

After Rome fell, and stability was replaced by Dark Age chaos, a huge structure like this was put to good use—bricked up and made a fortress (just like the Roman Arena in Arles). In the 13th century, after this region was incorporated into France, the Arena became a gated community housing about 700 people—with streets, plumbing, even gardens on the top level. Only in 1809 did Napoleon decide to scrape away the people and make this a historic monument, thus letting the ancient grandeur of Roman France shine.

Two fun multimedia exhibits bring bullfighting and gladiating to life on the Arena's ground floor (was that Kirk Douglas in those tight shorts?). Since 1850, Nîmes' Arena has been a venue for spectacles, including Spanish-style bullfights and rock concerts. ZZ Top and Stevie Wonder were among the musical gladiators on the docket in 2010.

• *From the Arena, stroll to Maison Carrée through Nîmes' "conservation zone"—the Old City. With your back to the Arena's ticket office, follow rue des Arènes into place du Marché and the heart of the...*

▲▲Old City

Those coming to Nîmes only for its famous Roman sights are enchanted by its carefully preserved old center. Here, you can study how elements in the buildings from the medieval and Renaissance times artfully survive: Shop interiors incorporate medieval brick with stone arches; windows expose Gothic finery; and Renaissance staircases grace peaceful courtyards.

Place du Marché has an inviting café ambience, including a wispy palm-tree-and-crocodile fountain (Nîmes' emblem in Roman times—see "Roman Nîmes" sidebar). **Le Courtois Café/Pâtisserie** is the class act of the square—check out its old-time interior (good lunch stop). It's been family-run since 1892. If you have a sweet tooth, let the sweet women serve you the house specialty, a chocolate-dipped *nélusko* (somewhere between a cake and a cookie—the oldest recipe of the house); or a Nîmes specialty, *caladon* (literally "cobble," like on the street—a hard honey-and-almond cookie; open daily 8:00–19:30, tel. 04 66 67 20 09).

• *Leave the square, heading past the crocodile on rue des Broquiers, then turn left on rue de l'Aspic, the town's primary shopping spine. Rue de l'Aspic leads to place de l'Horloge, the center of the old town. From here pedestrian-friendly streets fan out in all directions, including directly to Maison Carrée (described later). Take rue de la Madeleine, the first street to the right as you enter place de l'Horloge, to the...*

▲Place aux Herbes

This inviting square is the site of Nîmes' oldest market. At the center of the old town, it's a good hub for a bit of sightseeing. There are several good places to eat or to have a drink on or near the square (see "Eating in Nîmes," later). The next three sights are on or within a block of this square:

Nîmes Cathedral: While its Romanesque facade survives from the 12th century, the cathedral's interior—gutted over centuries of dynastic squabbles, Reformation, and Revolution—is unremarkable Neo-Romanesque, mostly from the 19th century.

Museum of Old Nîmes: Taking a left out of the cathedral leads to this humble single-floor museum, inhabiting a 17th-century bishop's palace. The museum highlights life in the city, starting with the Middle Ages, and provides the best chance to bring the intriguing architectural remnants of historic Nîmes to life. You'll also learn the story of indigo, 19th-century denim wear, and early Levi's (free, no English but basics are easy to understand, Tue–Sun 10:00–18:00, closed Mon, tel. 04 66 76 73 70).

Old-Time Spice Shop: L'Huilerie Epicerie is a charming time warp displaying spices and herbs, oils, and candy (Mon–Sat 9:00–12:00 & 15:00–19:00, closed Sun; a block off place aux Herbes, down the small lane past Le Petit Moka café at 10 rue des Marchands). To revel in more of Nîmes' medieval atmosphere, find the nearby Passage du Vieux Nîmes.

• *When you're ready to move on, return to place de l'Horloge, turn right, and follow rue de Gazan past the clock tower to the...*

Covered Produce Market

Les Halles Centre Commerciale looks like a big, black, modern parking garage, but the ground floor is a thriving, colorful market hall, well worth exploring (daily until 13:00).

• *A right out of the covered market on rue Général Perrier leads to the...*

▲▲Maison Carrée

This temple rivals Rome's Pantheon as the most complete and splendid building that survives from the Roman Empire. The temple radiates beauty today thanks to a recently completed two-year cleaning process. (There's nothing inside but a tacky 3-D history movie, so we'll focus on its exterior.)

The temple survived, in part, because it's been in constant use for the last thousand years—as a church, a City Hall, a private stable, archives during the Revolution, a people's art gallery after the Revolution (like Paris' Louvre), and finally as the monument you visit today. It's a textbook example of a "pseudo-peripteral temple" (surrounded by columns, half of which support the roof over a porch, and half of which merely decorate the rest of the building) and a "six-column temple" (a standard proportion—if it's six columns wide, it must be eleven columns deep).

The lettering across the front is long gone (though there is talk of replacing it), but the tiny surviving "nail holes" presented archaeologists with a fun challenge: Assuming each letter would leave a particular series of nail holes as evidence, derive the words. Archaeologists agree that this temple was built to honor Caius and Lucius, the grandsons (and adopted sons) of Emperor Augustus. And from this information, they date the temple from the year A.D. 4.

Maison Carrée ("Square House"—named before they had a word for "rectangle") was the centerpiece of a fancy plaza surrounded by a U-shaped commercial, political, and religious forum. This marked the core of Roman Nîmes. As was the case in all Roman temples, only the priest went inside. Worshippers gathered for religious rituals at the foot of the steps. Climb the steps as a priest would—starting and ending with your right foot... *dexter* (from the Latin for "right") rather than *sinister* ("left"). Put your right foot forward for good karma.

Inside, the *Heroes of Nîmes* **movie** tells the story of six heroic locals, each vying to be "the most heroic citizen of noble Nîmes." Though entertaining, this 3-D film—covering 2,000 years in 20 minutes—insults the building it fills (€4.50, every 30 minutes, daily 10:00–19:00, soundtrack in Latin and French with English subtitles).

The modern building facing the temple is Nîmes' **Carrée d'Art** ("Square of Art"), designed by British architect Lord Norman Foster. It's home to the city's Museum of Contemporary Art (Tue–Sun 10:00–18:00, closed Mon, WCs, good view café—see page 139).

• *If you haven't visited the TI yet, do it now (across the street and a few steps up from Maison Carrée; see "Tourist Information" on page 138). Then walk down rue Molière with the Museum of Contemporary Art on your left. Dogleg right until you hit the canal, then follow the canal left until you reach the...*

▲Spring of Nemo in the Fountain Garden

Centuries before the Romans arrived in Nîmes, the Spring of Nemo was here (named, like the town itself, for a Celtic god). When the Romans built a shrine to Emperor Augustus around the spring, rather than bulldoze the Nemo temple, they built alongside it and welcomed Nemo into their own pantheon (as was their more-gods-the-merrier tradition). Today, the spring remains, though the temple is gone.

Walk into the center of the Fountain Garden (Jardin de la Fontaine) and look into the canal. In the early 1700s, Nîmes needed a reliable source of water for its textile industry—to power its mills and provide water for the indigo dyes for the fabric *serge de Nîmes* (denim). About 1735, the city began a project to route a canal through the city and discovered this Roman temple. The city eventually agreed to fund a grander project that resulted in what you see today: a lavish Versailles-type park, complete with an ornate network of canals and boulevards. This was just 50 years after the construction of Versailles, and to the French, this place has a special significance. These were the first grand public gardens not meant for a king, but for the public. The industrial canals built then still wind throughout the city.

• *Hiding behind trees in the back-left corner of Fountain Garden, find the...*

▲▲Temple of Diana

This first-century "temple," which modern archaeologists now believe was more likely a Roman library, has long been considered one of the best examples of ancient stonework. Its roof—a round Roman barrel vault laced together with still-visible metal pegs—survived until a blast during the Catholic–Protestant Wars of Religion in the 1500s.

At first glance, all the graffiti is obnoxious. But it's actually part of the temple's story. For centuries, France had a highly esteemed guild of stone-, metal-, and woodworkers called the Compagnons, founded by Gothic-church builders in the Middle Ages. As part of their almost mystic training, these craftsmen would visit many buildings—including the great structures of antiquity (such as this one)—for inspiration. Walk through the side aisle for a close look at the razor-accurate stonework and the 17th-, 18th-, and 19th-century signatures of the Compagnon craftsmen inspired by this building. Notice how their signatures match their era—no-nonsense "Enlightened" chiseling of the 18th century gives way to ornate script in the Romantic 19th century.

Cost and Hours: The park and temple are free and open daily (April–mid-Sept 7:30–22:00, mid-Sept–March 7:30–18:30). Skip the hike up to Tour Magne (at top of gardens), which has two remaining levels of a Roman tower; the view is worth neither the sweat nor the €3 fee. Instead, have a coffee break or snack at the park's café, located next to the Temple of Diana.

• *To reach the next sight (about a 15-minute walk away), backtrack out of the park, turning left at the canal (quai de la Fontaine). At the busy corner, keep left and merge onto busy boulevard Gambetta. In a few blocks, turn left on rue Ménard, which leads to the...*

▲Castellum

This small excavation site, sitting next to the street, shows a modest-looking water distribution tank that was the grand finale of the 30-mile-long Pont du Gard aqueduct.

Discovered in the 1850s, this is one of only two known Roman distribution tanks (the other is in Pompeii). The water needs of Roman Nîmes grew beyond the capacity of its local springs. Imagine the jubilation on the day (in A.D. 50) that this system was finally operational. Suddenly, the town had an abundance of water—for basic needs as well as for cool extras like public fountains. Notice the plugged hole marking the end of the aqueduct, a pool, a lower water channel, and the water-distribution holes. The lower channel served top-priority needs, providing water via stone and lead pipes to the public wells that graced neighborhood squares. The higher holes—which got wet only when the supply was plentiful—routed water to the homes of the wealthy, to public baths, and to nonessential fountains.

The excavation site is free to visit and always open. (For more on this impressive example of Roman engineering, see the "Pont du Gard" section, later.)

Sleeping in Nîmes

$$$ **New Hôtel la Baume***, a few blocks from the cathedral, is a business-class hotel with 34 sizeable and well-designed rooms featuring every comfort. This beautiful Renaissance building dates from the 1600s (Sb-€115, Db-€145–150, Tb-€175, look for deals on their website, air-con, elevator, 21 rue Nationale, tel. 04 66 76 28 42, fax 04 66 76 28 45, www.new-hotel.com/labaume, nimes labaume@new-hotel.com).

$$ **Hôtel de l'Amphithéâtre**** is ideally located on a pedestrian street a spear's toss from the Arena. It's quiet—unless there's a concert at the Arena—with well-kept rooms run by helpful Hervé and Nathalie (small Db-€55–66, larger Db-€68–83, no elevator, 3 of the 15 rooms have air-con, 4 rue des Arènes, tel. 04 66 67 28 51, fax 04 66 67 07 79, hotel-amphitheatre@wanadoo.fr).

$ **Hôtel Brasserie des Arènes*** occupies a privileged location facing the Arena. Its 11 basic rooms above a modern café—some rooms with kitchenettes—provide one-star comfort at fair rates (Db-€46–54, Tb-€50–57, no air-con or elevator, 4 boulevard des

Sleep Code

(€1 = about $1.25, country code: 33)
S = Single, **D** = Double/Twin, **T** = Triple, **Q** = Quad, **b** = bathroom, **s** = shower only, * = French hotel rating system (0–4 stars). Unless otherwise noted, credit cards are accepted and English is spoken.

To help you easily sort through these listings, I've divided the rooms into three categories, based on the price for a standard double room with bath:

$$$ Higher Priced—Most rooms €85 or more.
  $$ Moderately Priced—Most rooms between €60-85.
    $ Lower Priced—Most rooms €60 or less.

Prices can change without notice; verify the hotel's current rates online or by email. For other updates, see www .ricksteves.com/update.

Arènes, tel. 04 66 67 23 05, fax 04 66 67 76 93, www.brasserie -arenes.com, hotel@brasserie-arenes.com).

Eating in Nîmes

Enjoy the elegance of Nîmes by eating lunch on one of its charming squares. Sadly, most of these cafés close for dinner.

Place aux Herbes: This square, beautifully situated in the shadow of the cathedral, boasts several popular bistros. **Restaurant ô Délices** and **Le Petit Moka** both serve fresh salads, crêpes, and *tartines.*

Place du Marché: A block from the Arena, this square is home to **Mogador Café,** serving tasty, light lunches (salads, crêpes, and lots of veggies), and **Le Courtois Café/Pâtisserie,** with its trademark desserts (described on page 143).

Overlooking the Maison Carrée: **Restaurant Café Ciel de Nîmes** fills a terrace atop the city's Norman Foster–designed contemporary art gallery, offering diners great views of the Roman temple (€10 *plats du jour*, €12 salads, €16 three-course workday lunch special, Tue–Sun 10:00–18:00, closed Mon, place de la Maison Carrée, tel. 04 66 36 71 70). Facing the temple, you'll see the terrace atop the modern building on your right.

Place des Esclafidous: Several tempting places line this cute little square two blocks behind the cathedral (find the post office on rue Crémieux and walk behind it). At **Restaurant les Magnolias** you'll dine in a cozy interior or on a peaceful terrace; meals are reasonable, and the service is friendly (*menus* from €18, big salads for €10, daily for dinner, tel. 04 66 21 64 01). **La Table de Clair** is across the square, with eclectic ambience and *très* tasty cuisine (€20–33 *menus,* dinner only, closed Sun, tel. 04 66 67 55 61).

Nîmes Connections

Trains and buses depart from the same station in Nîmes (see "Arrival in Nîmes" on page 138). If traveling by bus, plan to arrive early at the station to double-check your schedule. Ask at the bus-information office in the rear of the train station for the next bus to your destination and which stall it leaves from (most likely stall 2 or 3; look for shelters to your right as you walk outside). Buy your ticket from the driver (about €7 one-way to Pont du Gard, avoid big bills). Route numbers posted on the buses themselves usually do not correspond with those on paper timetables, so verify your destination with the driver.

From **Nîmes by Train to: Arles** (9/day, 30 minutes), **Avignon** (14/day, 30 minutes), **Aigues-Mortes** in the Camargue (6/day, 45 minutes), **Carcassonne** (8/day, 2.5 hours, transfer in Narbonne), **Paris** (10/day, 3 hours).

By Bus to: Uzès (8/day Mon–Fri, 6/day Sat, 2/day Sun, 1 hour, €8), **Pont du Gard** (5/day Mon–Sat, 2/day Sun and off-season, 40 minutes; check return times before you leave, tel. 04 66 29 27 29, www.stdgard.fr), **Aigues-Mortes** in the Camargue (6/day, 50 minutes), **Arles** (6/day, 1 hour).

Pont du Gard

Throughout the ancient world, aqueducts were like flags of stone that heralded the greatness of Rome. A visit to this sight still works to proclaim the wonders of that age. This perfectly preserved Roman aqueduct was built in about 19 B.C. as the critical link of a 30-mile canal that, by dropping one inch for every 350 feet, supplied nine million gallons of water per day (about 100 gallons per second) to Nîmes—one of ancient Europe's largest cities. Though most of the aqueduct is on or below the ground, at Pont du Gard it spans a canyon on a massive bridge—one of the most remarkable surviving Roman ruins anywhere. Wear sturdy shoes if you plan to climb around the aqueduct (footing is tricky), and bring swimwear and flip-flops if you plan to backstroke beneath the monument.

Getting to Pont du Gard

The famous aqueduct is between Remoulins and Vers-Pont du Gard on D-981, 17 miles from Nîmes and 13 miles from Avignon.

NEAR AVIGNON

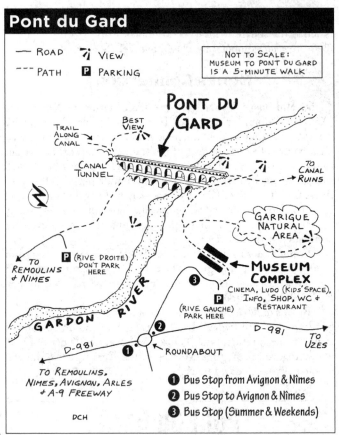

Pont du Gard

— ROAD   🏞 VIEW
--- PATH   🅿 PARKING

NOT TO SCALE:
MUSEUM TO PONT DU GARD
IS A 5-MINUTE WALK

PONT DU GARD

TRAIL ALONG CANAL

BEST VIEW

CANAL TUNNEL

TO CANAL RUINS

TO REMOULINS & NIMES

🅿 (RIVE DROITE) DON'T PARK HERE

GARRIGUE NATURAL AREA

MUSEUM COMPLEX
CINEMA, LUDO (KIDS' SPACE), INFO, SHOP, WC & RESTAURANT

③

🅿 (RIVE GAUCHE) PARK HERE

GARDON RIVER

D-981

D-981

TO UZES

②

①

ROUNDABOUT

TO REMOULINS, NIMES, AVIGNON, ARLES & A-9 FREEWAY

DCH

① Bus Stop from Avignon & Nîmes
② Bus Stop to Avignon & Nîmes
③ Bus Stop (Summer & Weekends)

By Car: Pont du Gard is a 25-minute drive due west of Avignon (follow N-100 from Avignon, tracking signs to *Nîmes* and *Remoulins,* then *Pont du Gard* and *Rive Gauche*), and 45 minutes northwest of Arles (via Tarascon on D-15). While parking is available on the Rive Droite (Right Bank), it's farther away from the museum than parking on the Rive Gauche (Left Bank). If going to Arles from Pont du Gard, follow signs to *Nîmes* (not Avignon), then follow D-986 and then D-15 to Arles.

By Bus: Buses run to Pont du Gard (on the Rive Gauche side) from Nîmes, Uzès, and Avignon. Combining Pont du Gard with Nîmes and/or Uzès makes a good day-trip excursion from Avignon (see "Planning Your Time" at the beginning of this chapter).

Buses stop at the traffic roundabout 300 yards from the aqueduct (see map above). In summer and on weekends, however, buses usually drive into the Pont du Gard site and stop at the parking lot's ticket booth. Confirm where the bus stops at the parking booth inside the Pont du Gard site.

At the roundabout, the stop for buses coming from Avignon and Nîmes (and going to Uzès) is on the side opposite Pont du Gard; the stop for buses to Nîmes and to Avignon is on the same side as Pont du Gard (a block to your left as you exit Pont du Gard onto the main road). Make sure you're waiting for the bus on the correct side of the traffic circle (stops have schedules posted), and wave your hand to signal the bus to stop for you (otherwise, it'll chug on by). Buy your ticket when you get on and verify your destination with the driver.

By Taxi: From Nîmes or Avignon it's about €42 for a taxi ride to Pont du Gard. If you're staying in Avignon and only want to see Pont du Gard (and not Nîmes or Uzès), consider splurging on a taxi to the aqueduct in the morning, then take the early-afternoon bus back.

Orientation to Pont du Gard

There are two riversides to Pont du Gard: the Left Bank (Rive Gauche) and Right Bank (Rive Droite). Park on the Rive Gauche, where you'll find the museums, ticket booth, ATM, cafeteria, WCs, and shops—all built into a modern plaza. You'll see the aqueduct in two parts: first the fine museum complex, then the actual river gorge spanned by the ancient bridge.

Cost and Hours: The aqueduct, museum, film, and outdoor *garrigue* nature area are all free, but parking is €15 per car (those arriving by bus or bike pay nothing). The museum is open daily May–Sept 9:00–19:00, Oct–April 9:00–17:00, closed two weeks in Jan. The aqueduct itself is open until 1:00 in the morning, as is the parking lot. Toll tel. 08 20 90 33 30, www.pontdugard.fr. The *garrigue* is always open.

Tours and Information: For an extra €6, you can rent an **audioguide** with detailed English explanations of the aqueduct. Call ahead or visit the website for information on **guided walks** on top of the aqueduct. Consider the helpful €4 English **booklet** about the *garrigue*—the extensive nature area featuring historic crops and landscapes of the Mediterranean.

Canoe Rental: Floating under Pont du Gard by canoe is an experience you won't soon forget. Collias Canoes will pick you up at Pont du Gard (or elsewhere, if pre-arranged) and shuttle you to the town of Collias. You'll float down the river to the nearby town of Remoulins, where they'll pick you up and take you back to Pont du Gard (€18/person, €9/child under 12, usually 2 hours, though you can take as long as you like, good idea to reserve the day before in July–Aug, tel. 04 66 22 85 54).

Plan Ahead for Swimming: Pont du Gard is perhaps best

enjoyed on your back and in the water—bring along a swimsuit and flip-flops for the rocks.

Sights at Pont du Gard

▲**Museum**—In this state-of-the-art museum (well-presented in English), you'll enter to the sound of water and understand the critical role fresh water played in the Roman "art of living." You'll see examples of lead pipes, faucets, and siphons; walk through a mock rock quarry; and learn how they moved those huge rocks into place and how those massive arches were made. While actual artifacts from the aqueduct are few, the exhibit shows the immensity of the undertaking as well as the payoff. Imagine the excitement as this extravagant supply of water finally tumbled into Nîmes. A relaxing highlight is the scenic video of a helicopter ride along the entire 30-mile course of the structure, from its start at Uzès all the way to the Castellum in Nîmes.

Other Activities—Several additional attractions are designed to give the sight more meaning—and they do (but for most visitors, the museum is sufficient). A corny, romancing-the-aqueduct 25-minute film plays in the same building as the museum and offers good information in a flirtatious French-Mediterranean style...and a cool, entertaining, and cushy break. The nearby kids' museum, called *Ludo*, offers a scratch-and-sniff teaching experience (in English) of various aspects of Roman life and the importance of water. The extensive outdoor *garrigue* natural area, closer to the aqueduct, features historic crops and landscapes of the Mediterranean.

▲▲▲**Viewing the Aqueduct**—A park-like path leads to the aqueduct. Until a few years ago, this was an actual road—adjacent to the aqueduct—that had spanned the river since 1743. Before you

cross the bridge, pass under it and hike about 300 feet along the riverbank for a grand viewpoint from which to study the world's second-highest standing Roman structure. (Rome's Colosseum is only 6 feet taller.)

This was the biggest bridge in the whole 30-mile-long aqueduct. It seems exceptional because it is: The arches are twice the width of standard aqueducts, and the main arch is the largest the Romans ever built—80 feet (so it wouldn't get its feet wet). The bridge is about 160 feet high and was originally about 1,100 feet long. Today, 12 arches are missing, reducing the length to 790 feet.

Though the distance from the source (in Uzès) to Nîmes was only 12 miles as the eagle flew, engineers chose the most economical route, winding and zigzagging 30 miles. The water made the trip in 24 hours with a drop of only 40 feet. Ninety percent of the aqueduct is on or under the ground, but a few river canyons like this required bridges. A stone lid hides a four-foot-wide, six-foot-tall chamber lined with waterproof mortar that carried the stream for more than 400 years. For 150 years, this system provided Nîmes with good drinking water. Expert as the Romans were, they miscalculated the backup caused by a downstream corner, and had to add the thin extra layer you can see just under the lid to make the channel deeper.

The bridge and the river below provide great fun for holiday-goers. While parents suntan on rocks, kids splash into the gorge from under the aqueduct. Some daredevils actually jump from the aqueduct's lower bridge—not knowing that crazy winds scrambled by the structure cause painful belly flops (and sometimes even accidental deaths). For the most refreshing view, float flat on your back underneath the structure.

The appearance of the entire gorge changed in 2002, when a huge flood flushed lots of greenery downstream. Those floodwaters put Roman provisions to the test. Notice the triangular-shaped buttresses at the lower level—designed to split and divert the force of any flood *around* the feet of the arches rather than *into* them. The 2002 floodwaters reached the top of those buttresses. Anxious park rangers winced at the sounds of trees crashing onto the ancient stones...but the arches stood strong.

The stones that jut out—giving the aqueduct a rough, unfinished appearance—supported the original scaffolding. The protuberances were left, rather than cut off, in anticipation of future repair needs. The lips under the arches supported wooden templates that allowed the stones in the round arches to rest on something until the all-important keystone was dropped into place. Each stone weighs four to six tons. The structure stands with no mortar—taking full advantage of the innovative Roman arch, made strong by gravity.

Hike over the bridge for a closer look and the best views. Steps lead up a high trail (marked *panorama*) to a superb viewpoint (go right at the top; best views are soon after the trail starts descending). You'll also see where the aqueduct meets a rock tunnel. Walk through the tunnel and continue for a bit, following a trail that meanders along the canal's path.

Back on the museum side, steps lead up to the Rive Gauche (parking lot) end of the aqueduct, where you can follow the canal path along a trail (marked with red-and-white horizontal lines) to find some remains of the Roman canal. You'll soon reach another *panorama* with great views of the aqueduct. Hikers can continue along the path, following the red-and-white markings that lead through a forest, after which you'll come across more remains of the canal (much of which are covered by vegetation). There's not much left to see because of medieval cannibalization—frugal builders couldn't resist the precut stones as they constructed local churches (stones along the canal were easier to retrieve than those high up on the aqueduct). The path continues for about 15 miles, but there's little reason to go farther. However, there is talk of opening the ancient quarry...someday.

Uzès

Like Nîmes and Pont du Gard, this intriguing, less-trampled town is officially in Languedoc, not Provence. Uzès (oo-zehs) feels like it

must have been important—and it was, as a bishopric from the fifth century until 1789. It's best seen slowly on foot, with a long coffee break in its arcaded and mellow main square, place aux Herbes (not so mellow during the colorful Wednesday morning market and even bigger all-day Saturday market).

By car, Uzès is 10 minutes from Pont du Gard and 30 minutes from Nîmes and Avignon. It offers a welcome small-town break from serious sightseeing. Go local and stay overnight here. Arrive on Tuesday or Friday nights to enjoy the next morning's market.

The town itself—traffic-free and tastefully restored—is the sight. In spite of all those bishops, there are no important museums. You can follow the TI's self-guided walking tour, but skip the dull, overpriced Palace of the Duché de Uzès (€12, French-only tour). The town's tasteful boutiques are numerous, as are English-speakers. (The toy shop Au Bois de mon Coeur, under the arcade at 8 Place aux Herbes, has special treats for kids.) The unusual circular tower called Tour Fenestrelle is all that remains of a 12th-century cathedral. Even if you're not a plant enthusiast, pop into the **Medieval Garden,** a "living herbarium" with plants thought to have curative qualities. The garden is at the foot of the King's and Bishop's towers. The €4 entrance fee includes a little shot of lemongrass tea lovingly delivered by the volunteers who care for this sight (April–Sept daily 14:00–18:00 plus 10:30–12:30 on Sat–Sun and daily in July–Aug, until 17:00 in Oct, closed Nov–March, English handout and some information posted, tel. 04 66 22 38 21).

The **Musée du Bonbon** of Haribo (think Gummi Bears) lies just outside Uzès and makes a worthwhile detour for the kids (July–Aug daily 10:00–20:00; Sept–June Tue–Sun 10:00–13:00 & 14:00–18:00, closed Mon; last entry one hour before closing, 1.5 miles from Uzès on the road to Avignon and Pont du Gard, tel. 04 66 22 74 39).

Getting to Uzès

Uzès is a short hop west of Pont du Gard. It's well-served by **bus** from Nîmes (8/day Mon–Fri, 6/day Sat, 2/day Sun, 1 hour, €8), but less so from Avignon (3–5/day Mon–Sat, none Sun, 1 hour, stops at Pont du Gard). **Drivers** will circle the old town on the busy ring road. The TI and both hotels that I list are on this ring road.

Tourist Information

The TI sits at the top of the ring road (on place Albert 1er). Pick up the brief self-guided tour brochure in English (June–Sept Mon–Fri 9:00–18:00, Sat–Sun 10:00–13:00 & 14:00–17:00; Oct–May Mon–Fri 10:00–12:30 & 14:00–18:00, Sat 10:00–13:00, closed Sun; tel. 04 66 22 68 88, www.uzes-tourisme.com).

Sleeping in Uzès

(€1 = about $1.25, country code: 33)
Pale-green signs direct drivers to hotels from the ring road.

$$$ Hôtel du Général d'Entraigues*** is a cool 15th-century stone-cozy hotel with 36 rooms and hard-to-find staff. It combines traditional and modern touches with a flowery terrace and pool (Db-€70–185, most about €90, skip the €13 continental breakfast, air-con in most rooms; coming from Pont du Gard or Nîmes, it's virtually the first building you see on the ring road; place de l'Evêché, tel. 04 66 22 32 68, fax 04 66 22 57 01, www.leshotels particuliers.com, entraigues@leshotelsparticuliers.com).

$$$ L'Hostellerie Provençale** is an intimate place with nine *très* cushy rooms just off the ring road a few blocks after the TI. It's well-known for its adorable and delectable restaurant. The splendid rooftop terrace is ideal for breakfast and sunsets—bring your own wine (Db-€105–145, air-con, Wi-Fi, parking garage-€10, 4-course dinner *menus* from €36, 1 rue de la Grande Bourgade,

tel. 04 66 22 11 06, fax 04 66 75 01 03, www.hostellerieprovencale
.com, contact@hostellerieprovencale.com).

Eating in Uzès

When the weather cooperates, it's hard to resist meals on place aux Herbes, which is lined with appealing café options. **Terroires** serves modern, light cuisine such as *tartines,* tapas, and great salads, all made with regional products (€13 *plats,* closed Mon).

The creative **Bistro Burger** serves gourmet Charolais burgers and great salads, each for about €10. It has good wines by the glass. Beware: Only Americans eat their burgers with their hands—the French use a knife and fork (many options including kids' and vegetarian *menus,* July–Aug daily 12:00–22:00, Sept–June closed Mon–Tue, 19 place aux Herbes, tel. 04 66 20 21 03).

Le Bec à Vin is one of the most atmospheric places in town. Owner Frédéric will spoil you with delicious beef dishes served inside a 14th-century vaulted room or in one of the three shady interior courtyards surrounded by medieval walls (*plats* from €14, *menus* from €27, closed Mon, 6 rue Entre-les-Tours, tel. 04 66 22 41 20).

Le Zanelli Italian, dishing up pizzas and more, is located on the most prized terrace in the center of Uzès, place Nicolas Froment (allow €8–18, daily July–Aug, otherwise closed Tue–Wed, tel. 04 66 03 01 93).

To dine well indoors, find the restaurant **La Parenthèse** in the recommended **l'Hostellerie Provençale** (described earlier).

L'Authentic Fromagerie is the place to go to cheese up for your picnic. Charming Roland is happy to offer samples of his French cheese specialties (daily, 9 rue Nicolas Froment, tel. 04 66 04 01 37).

ORANGE
AND THE COTES
DU RHONE

Orange • Châteauneuf-du-Pape • Vaison la Romaine • Best of the Côtes du Rhône Villages • More Côtes du Rhône Drives

The sunny Côtes du Rhône wine road—one of France's best—starts at Avignon's doorstep. It winds north through a mountainous landscape carpeted with vines, peppered with warm stone villages, and presided over by the Vesuvius-like Mont Ventoux. The wines of the Côtes du Rhône (grown on the *côtes*, or hillsides, of the Rhône River Valley) are easy on the palate and on your budget. But this hospitable place offers more than famous wine—its hill-capping villages inspire travel posters, its Roman ruins inspire awe, and the people you'll meet are welcoming...and, often, as excited about their region as you are. Yes, you'll have good opportunities for enjoyable wine-tasting, but there is also a soul to this area...if you take the time to look.

Located 30 minutes north of Avignon, the ancient town of Orange has vineyards on its outskirts. But it's because of its well-preserved Roman Theater that Orange gets (and deserves) attention.

Planning Your Time

Vaison la Romaine is the small hub of this region, offering limited bus connections with Avignon and Orange, bike rental, and a mini-Pompeii in the town center. Nearby, you can visit the impressive Roman Theater in Orange, drive to the top of Mont Ventoux, follow my self-guided driving tour of Côtes du Rhône villages and wineries, and pedal to nearby towns for a breath of fresh air. The vineyards' centerpiece, the Dentelles de Montmirail mountains, are laced with a variety of exciting trails ideal for hikers.

To explore this area, allow two nights for a good start. Drivers should head for the hills (read this chapter's self-guided driving tour before deciding where to stay). Those without wheels find that Vaison la Romaine is the only practical home base (or, maybe better, consider a minivan tour).

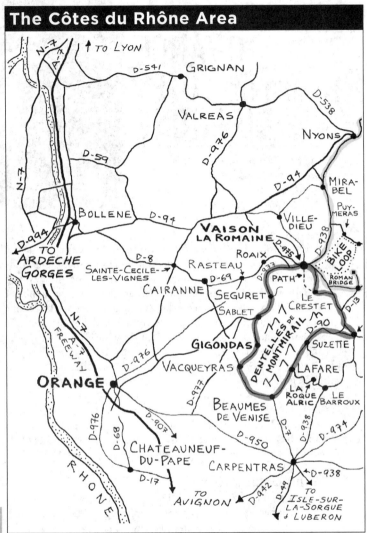

The Côtes du Rhône Area

Getting Around the Côtes du Rhône

By Car: Pick up Michelin Local maps #332 or #527 to navigate your way around the Côtes du Rhône. (Landmarks like the Dentelles de Montmirail and Mont Ventoux make it easy to get your bearings.) I've described my favorite driving route in a self-guided driving tour on page 176.

If your plan is to connect the Côtes du Rhône with the scenic **Luberon** (see next chapter), you can do it via Mont Ventoux (follow signs to *Malaucène*, then to *Mont Ventoux*, allowing 2 hours to

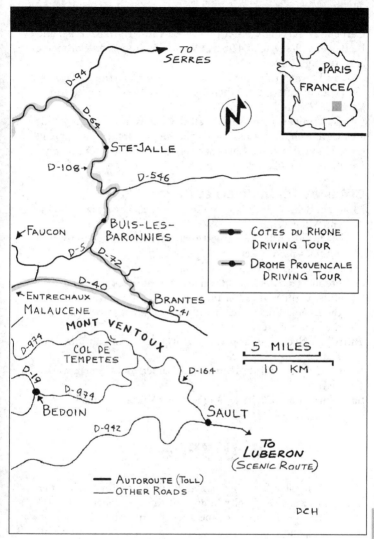

TO
SERRES

D-94

D-64

PARIS
FRANCE

N

STE-JALLE

D-108

D-546

FAUCON

BUIS-LES-
BARONNIES

D-5

D-72

D-40

ENTRECHAUX
MALAUCENE

BRANTES
D-41

MONT VENTOUX

D-974

COL DE
TEMPETES

D-164

D-19

D-974

BEDOIN

SAULT

D-942

TO
LUBERON
(SCENIC ROUTE)

- COTES DU RHONE
  DRIVING TOUR
- DROME PROVENCALE
  DRIVING TOUR

5 MILES
10 KM

— AUTOROUTE (TOLL)
— OTHER ROADS

DCH

Roussillon). This route is one of the most spectacular in Provence. Or, faster, you can zip to the Luberon by taking the autoroute via Orange and Cavaillon. A third, more direct route takes you through the traffic-snarled, difficult-to-navigate city of Carpentras, which should be avoided. Get advice from your hotelier.

By Bus: Buses run to Vaison la Romaine from Orange and Avignon (3–5/day, 45 minutes from Orange, 1.5 hours from Avignon) and connect several wine villages (including Gigondas, Sablet, and Beaumes de Venise) with Vaison la Romaine and

Nyons to the north. Another line runs from Vaison la Romaine to Carpentras, serving Crestet (below Le Crestet), Malaucène, and Le Barroux (2/day, tel. 04 90 36 09 90). Both routes provide scenic rides through this area.

By Train: Trains get you as far as Orange (from Avignon: 15/day, 15 minutes); from there buses make the 45-minute trip to Vaison la Romaine.

By Minivan Tour: Various all-day minivan excursions to this area leave from Avignon. For a wine-focused tour, I recommend several individuals who can expertly guide you through the region. For all tours to this area, see "Tours of Provence" on page 46.

Côtes du Rhône Market Days

Monday: Bedoin (intimate market, between Vaison la Romaine and Mont Ventoux)

Tuesday: Vaison la Romaine (great market with produce and antiques/flea market)

Wednesday: Malaucène (good and less-touristy market with produce and antiques/flea market, near Vaison la Romaine), Buis-les-Barronies (on recommended loop drive north into the Drôme Provençale), and Sault (handy if you're driving to the Luberon area)

Thursday: Nyons (great market with produce and antiques/flea market) and Vacqueyras

Friday: Châteauneuf-du-Pape (small market) and Carpentras (big market)

Saturday: Sainte-Cécile-les-Vignes, near Vaison la Romaine

Orange

Orange is notable for its Roman arch and grand Roman Theater. Orange was a thriving city in ancient times—strategically situated on the Via Agrippa, connecting the important Roman cities of Lyon and Arles. It was actually founded as a comfortable place for Roman army officers to enjoy their retirement. Even in Roman times, professional military men retired with time for a second career. Does the emperor want thousands of well-trained, relatively young guys hanging around Rome? No way. What to do? "How about a nice place in the south of France...?"

Orientation to Orange

Tourist Information

The unnecessary TI is located next to the fountain and parking area at 5 cours Aristide Briand (April–Sept Mon–Sat 9:30–18:30, Sun 10:00–13:00 & 14:00–18:30; Oct–March Mon–Sat 10:00–13:00 & 14:00–17:30, closed Sun; tel. 04 90 34 70 88).

Arrival in Orange

By Train: Orange's **train station** is a level 20-minute walk from the Roman Theater (or an €8 taxi ride, mobile 06 09 51 32 25). The recommended Hôtel de Provence across from the station will keep your bags (see "Sleeping in Orange," later). To walk into town from the train station, head straight out of the station (down avenue Frédéric Mistral), merge left onto Orange's main shopping street (rue de la République), then turn left on rue Caristie; you'll run into the Roman Theater's massive stage wall.

By Bus: Buses stop at the gare SNCF and at place Pourtoules, two blocks from the Roman Theater (walk to the hill and turn right to reach the theater, bus station tel. 04 90 34 15 59, www.vaucluse.fr/86-reseau-departemental.htm).

By Car: Follow *Centre-Ville* signs, then *Théâtre Antique* signs, and park as close to the Roman Theater's huge wall as possible—the easiest option is Parking Théâtre Antique (by the fountain and the TI). Those coming from the autoroute will land here by following *Centre-Ville* signs; others should follow *Centre-Ville* signs, then *Office du Tourisme* signs, to find this parking. To reach the theater, walk to the hill and turn left.

Sights in Orange

▲▲**Roman Theater (Théâtre Antique)**—Orange's ancient theater is the best-preserved in existence, and the only one in Europe with its acoustic wall still standing. (Two others in Asia Minor also survive.)

Cost and Hours: €8, drops to €7 one hour before closing but doesn't include audioguide; daily April–Sept 9:00–18:00, until 19:00 in summer, Oct–March 9:30–17:30 except Nov–Feb until 16:30, tel. 04 90 51 17 60, www.theatre-antique.com. Your ticket includes an informative audioguide, a fun film covering 2,000 years of history (called *Phantom of the Theater*), and entrance to the small museum across the street (Musée d'Art et d'Histoire). Pop into the museum to see a few theater details and a rare grid used as the official property-ownership registry—each square represented a 120-acre plot of land.

THE CÔTES DU RHÔNE

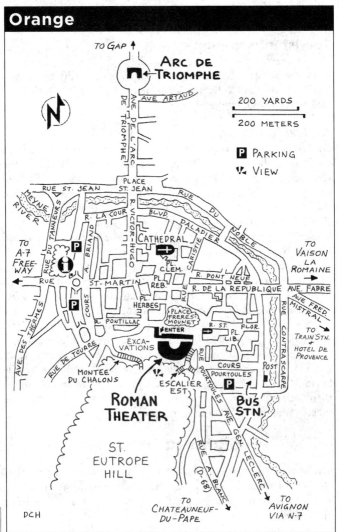

Orange

TO GAP ↑

ARC DE TRIOMPHE

AVE ARTAUD

AVE. DE L'ARC DE TRIOMPHE

200 YARDS
200 METERS

P PARKING
↙ VIEW

MEYNE RIVER

RUE ST. JEAN

PLACE ST. JEAN

RUE ST. JEAN

R. LA COUR

BLVD. PALADIER

RUE DU NOBLE

TO A-7 FREEWAY

RUE DU TANNEURS

A. BRIAND

R. VICTOR-HUGO

J. BRIAND

CATHEDRAL

PL. CLEM.

CARISTIE

R. PONT NEUF

TO VAISON LA ROMAINE

RUE

ST.-MARTIN

PL. REB.

R. DE LA RÉPUBLIQUE

AVE. FABRE

AVE FRED MISTRAL

COURS A. BRIAND

PL. HERBES

PLACE FRÈRES MOUNET

ENTER

R. ST. FLOR.

PL. LIB.

RUE CONTRASCARPE

TO TRAIN STN. & HOTEL DE PROVENCE

R. PONTILLAC

EXCAVATIONS

RUE DE TOURRE

AVE. DES THERMES

MONTÉE DU CHALONS

↙

ESCALIER EST

RUE POURTOULES

COURS POURTOULES

P

Post

ROMAN THEATER

BUS STN.

ST. EUTROPE HILL

AVE. GEN. LECLERC

RUE A. BLANC (D-68)

TO CHATEAUNEUF-DU-PAPE →

TO AVIGNON VIA N-7

DCH

Cheap Trick: Vagabonds wanting to see the theater for free can hike up nearby stairs (called *escalier est;* off rue Pourtoules) to view it from the bluff high above.

Cafés: The café in the theater has reasonably priced snacks and lunches and great views. A shaded café-filled square (place de la République) is two blocks from the theater up rue Ségond Weber.

❷ Self-Guided Tour: After you enter (to the right of the actual theater), you'll see a huge dig—the site of the Temple to the Cult of the Emperor. Look for signs to the worthwhile movie (English subtitles) that gives you a good visual sense of how the theater looked to the Romans.

Enter the theater, then climb the steep stairs to find a seat high up to appreciate the acoustics (eavesdrop on people by the stage). Contemplate the idea that 2,000 years ago, Orange residents enjoyed grand spectacles with high-tech sound and lighting effects—such as simulated thunder, lightning, and rain.

A grandiose Caesar overlooks everything, reminding attendees of who's in charge. If it seems like you've seen this statue before,

you probably have. Countless sculptures identical to this one were mass-produced in Rome and shipped throughout the empire to grace buildings like this theater for propaganda purposes. To save money on shipping and handling, only the heads of these statues were changed with each new ruler. The permanent body wears a breastplate emblazoned with the imperial griffon (body of a lion, head and wings of an eagle) that only the emperor could wear. When a new emperor came to power, new heads were made in Rome and shipped off throughout the empire to replace the pop-off heads on all these statues. (Imagine Barack Obama's head on George W. Bush's body.)

Archaeologists believe that a puny, vanquished Celt was included at the knee of the emperor, touching his ruler's robe respectfully—a show of humble subservience to the emperor. It's interesting to consider how an effective propaganda machine can con the masses into being impressed by their leader.

The horn has blown. It's time to find your seat: row 2, number 30. Sitting down, you're comforted by the "EQ GIII" carved into the seat (*Equitas Gradus* #3...three rows for the Equestrian order). You're not comforted by the hard limestone bench (thinking it'll probably last 2,000 years). The theater is filled with 10,000 people. Thankfully, you mix only with your class, the nouveau riche—merchants, tradesmen, and city big shots. The people seated above you are the working class, and way up in the "chicken roost" section is the scum of the earth—slaves, beggars, prostitutes, and youth hostellers. Scanning the orchestra section (where the super-rich sit on real chairs), you notice the town dignitaries hosting some visiting VIPs.

OK, time to worship. They're parading a bust of the emperor from its sacred home in the adjacent temple around the stage. Next is the ritual animal sacrifice called *la pompa* (so fancy, future generations will use that word for anything full of such...pomp). Finally, you settle in for an all-day series of spectacles and dramatic entertainment. All eyes are on the big stage door in the middle—where the Julia Robertses and Brad Pitts of the day will appear. (Lesser actors come out of the side doors.)

The play is good, but many come for the halftime shows—jugglers, acrobats, and striptease dancers. In Roman times, the theater was a festival of immorality. An ancient writer commented, "The vanquished take their revenge on us by giving us their vices through the theater."

With an audience of 10,000 and no amplification, acoustics were critical. A roof originally covered the stage, somewhat like the glass-and-iron stage roof you see today (recently installed to protect the stage wall). The original was designed not to protect the stage from the weather, but to project the voices of the actors into the crowd. For further help, actors wore masks with leather caricature mouths that functioned as megaphones. The side walls originally rose as high as the stage wall and supported a retractable roof that gave the audience some protection from the sun. After leaving the theater, look up to the stage wall from the outside and notice the supports for poles that held the roof in place.

The Roman Theater was all part of the "give them bread and circuses" approach to winning the support of the masses (not unlike today's philosophy of "give them tax cuts and *American Idol*"). The spectacle grew from 65 days of games per year when the theater was first built (and when Rome was at its height) to about 180 days each year by the time Rome finally fell.

In the fourth century (under Christian emperor Constantine), the church forced many theaters to close their doors. Later, during the barbarian invasions, the stage wall became a protective wall and the theater became a secure residence for many. Amazingly, people squatted here until the 19th century. You can still see traces of some buildings within the theater.

▲**Roman "Arc de Triomphe"**—Technically the only real Roman arches of triumph are in Rome's Forum, built to commemorate various emperors' victories. The great Roman arch of Orange is actually a municipal arch erected (in about A.D. 19) to commemorate a general named Germanicus, who protected the town. The 60-foot-tall arch is on a noisy traffic circle (north of city center, on avenue Arc de Triomphe).

Sleeping in Orange

(€1 = about $1.25, country code: 33)

$$ **Hôtel de Provence****, at the train station, is air-conditioned, quiet, comfortable, and affordable. Friendly Madame Verbe

runs this traditional place with grace (Db-€60–75, Tb-€75–95, small rooftop pool, café, 60 avenue Frédéric Mistral, tel. 04 90 34 00 23, fax 04 90 34 91 72, www.hoteldeprovence84.com, hoteldeprovence84@orange.fr).

Orange Connections

From Orange by Train to: Avignon (15/day, 15 minutes), **Arles** (4/day direct, 35 minutes, more frequently with transfer in Avignon), **Lyon** (16/day, 2 hours).

By Bus to: Châteauneuf-du-Pape (1/day, none Sun, 30 minutes), **Vaison la Romaine** (3–5/day, 45 minutes), **Avignon** (Mon–Sat hourly, none Sun, 45 minutes—take the train instead). Buses to Vaison la Romaine and other wine villages depart from the gare SNCF and from place Pourtoules (turn right out of the Roman Theater, and right again onto rue Pourtoules).

Near Orange: Châteauneuf-du-Pape

This most famous of the Côtes du Rhône wine villages is busy with tourists eager to sample its famous product and stroll its climb-

ing lanes. While I prefer the less-famous wine villages farther north (described under "The Best of the Côtes du Rhône Villages," later in this chapter), this welcoming wine-drenched town makes an easy day trip from Avignon, and works well with a visit to nearby Orange.

Châteauneuf-du-Pape means "New Castle of the Pope," named for the pope's summer retreat—now a ruin capping the beautiful-to-see but little-to-do hill town (more interesting during the Friday market). Wine-loving popes planted the first

vines here in the 1300s. The pope's crest is embossed on all bottles of this deservedly famous wine.

Approaching from Avignon, signs announce, "Here start the vineyards of Châteauneuf-du-Pape." Pull over and stroll into a vineyard with a view of the hill town. Notice the rocky soil—perfect for making a good wine grape. Those stones retain the sun's heat (plentiful here) and force the vines to struggle, resulting in a lean grape—lousy for eating, but ideal for producing big wines (see "Côtes du Rhône Wines" on page 56). Eight different grapes are blended to make the local specialty, which has been strictly controlled for 80 years. Grenache is the most prominent grape in the blend. The most interesting white wines in Provence are also made

THE COTES DU RHONE

here (a blend of up to five grapes), but the reds are what attract most visitors.

The **Wine Museum** (Musée du Vin) provides useful background for your Côtes du Rhône exploration (free, daily 9:00–12:00 & 14:00–18:00, on route d'Avignon, at start of the village if coming from Avignon, tel. 04 90 83 70 07). After a brief self-guided tour of the winemaking process (English explanations in the notebooks reward good students), enjoy a tasting. You'll need to tell them what you want; see "French Wine Lingo" on page 54. For a clear contrast, taste a "ready-to-drink" wine (*prêt à boire;* preh tah bwar), then a wine from "old vines" (*vieille vignes;* vee-yay-ee veen-yuh).

To visit the town itself, park below and follow signs up the hill toward *Château.* The **TI,** next to the Casino market on place du Portail, has a long list of wineries that welcome visitors (Mon–Sat 9:00–12:30 & 14:00–18:00, closed Sun, tel. 04 90 83 71 08). Appealing streets fan out from here, most with cellars selling the famous wine.

A good place to sample Châteauneuf-du-Pape wines is at Daniele Brunel's **The Best Vintage Cave.** Speaking fluent English and offering wines from 20 different producers (including her own), Daniele provides a good introduction to area wines. The youngest member of the famous Brunel wine family, Daniele represents a new generation of winemakers who combine traditional values and modern techniques (daily May–Sept 9:30–18:00, near place du Portail at 7 rue de la République, tel. 04 90 83 31 75, www .the-best-vintage.com).

Eating in Châteauneuf-du-Pape: You'll find several appealing eateries around the main square (place du Portail), and up the pedestrian street Rue Joseph Ducos. **Le Pistou** serves salads and *menus* from €13. If you have the energy and the funds, follow signs up the hill to **Le Verger des Papes,** a restaurant where you can splurge both on the terrace views and on their traditional and sophisticated cuisine (daily for lunch and dinner except closed Sun evening, €19 lunch *menu,* €29 dinner *menu,* 4 rue Montée du Château, tel. 04 90 83 50 40).

Côtes du Rhône

The Côtes du Rhône region features classic Provençal scenery, characteristic villages, cozy wineries, fields of fragrant lavender, and excellent restaurants. If you're sleeping in this area, Vaison la Romaine is a handy home base. Then delve into the region's highlights by following my self-guided driving tour. With more time, dig deeper into the Côtes du Rhône with a drive up Mont Ventoux, a spin around the Drôme Provençale, or a visit to the Ardèche Gorges.

Vaison la Romaine

With quick access to vineyards, villages, and Mont Ventoux, this lively little town of 6,000 makes a great base for exploring

the Côtes du Rhône region by car or by bike. You get two villages for the price of one: Vaison la Romaine's "modern" lower city has worthwhile Roman ruins and a lone pedestrian street. (The big square, place Montfort, has great potential and is scheduled to be redone by 2011.) The car-free medieval hill town looms above, with meandering cobbled lanes, a dash of art galleries and cafés, and a ruined castle with a good view from its base. (Vaison la Romaine is also a good place to have your hair done, since there are more than 20 hairdressers in this small town.)

Orientation to Vaison la Romaine

The city is split in two by the Ouvèze River. The Roman Bridge connects the more modern lower town (Ville-Basse) with the hill-capping medieval upper town (Ville-Haute).

Tourist Information

The superb TI is in the lower city, between the two Roman ruin sites, at place du Chanoine Sautel (July–Aug Mon–Sat 9:00–19:00, Sun 9:00–12:00; Sept–June Mon–Sat 9:00–12:00 & 14:00–17:45, Sun 9:00–12:00 & 14:00–19:00

Vaison la Romaine

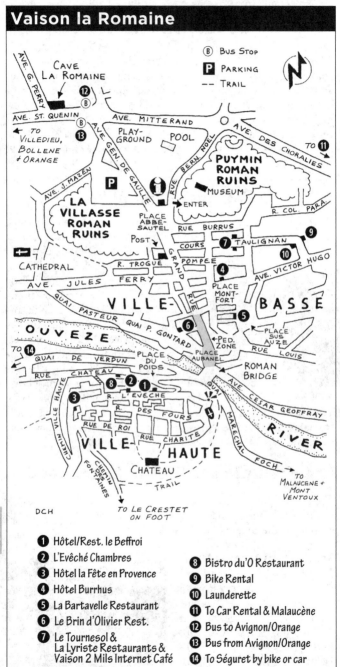

B Bus Stop
P Parking
-- Trail

Cave La Romaine
AVE. G. PERRY
AVE. ST. QUENIN
TO VILLEDIEU, BOLLENE & ORANGE
AVE. MITTERAND
PLAY-GROUND
POOL
PUYMIN ROMAN RUINS
MUSEUM
AVE. DES CHORALIES
TO
RUE BERN. NOEL
AVE. GEN. DE GAULLE
AVE. J. MAZEN
P
LA VILLASSE ROMAN RUINS
PLACE ABBE-SAUTEL
ENTER
R. COL. PARA
RUE BURRUS
COURS
POMPEE
TAULIGNAN
AVE. VICTOR HUGO
Post
R. TROGUE
CATHEDRAL
AVE. JULES
FERRY
GRAND
RUE
PLACE MONT-FORT
VILLE-
BASSE
OUVEZE
QUAI PASTEUR
QUAI P. GONTARD
Ped. Zone
PLACE SUS AUZE
RUE LOUIS
PLACE AUBANEL
QUAI DE VERDUN
RUE
CHATEAU
TO
PLACE DU POIDS
ROMAN BRIDGE
QUAI MARECHAL FOCH
AVE. CESAR GEOFFRAY
RIVER
CHEMIN VILLE HAUTE
RUE L'EVECHE
RUE DES FOURS
RUE DE ROI
RUE CHARITE
VILLE-HAUTE
CHEMIN DES FONTAINES
CHATEAU
TRAIL
TO MALAUCENE & MONT VENTOUX
TO LE CRESTET ON FOOT
DCH

1 Hôtel/Rest. le Beffroi
2 L'Evêché Chambres
3 Hôtel la Fête en Provence
4 Hôtel Burrhus
5 La Bartavelle Restaurant
6 Le Brin d'Olivier Rest.
7 Le Tournesol & La Lyriste Restaurants & Vaison 2 Mils Internet Café

8 Bistro du'O Restaurant
9 Bike Rental
10 Launderette
11 To Car Rental & Malaucène
12 Bus to Avignon/Orange
13 Bus from Avignon/Orange
14 To Séguret by bike or car

except closed Sun Oct–April; tel. 04 90 36 02 11). Say *bonjour* to *charmante* and ever-so-patient Valerie—get bus schedules, ask about festivals and evening programs, and pick up information on walks from Vaison la Romaine. Ask for the English pamphlets on biking and hiking—they have maps and instructions for several bike and walking loops, ranging from easy half-day trips to all-day affairs.

Arrival in Vaison la Romaine

By Bus: The unmarked bus stop to Orange and Avignon is in front of the Cave la Romaine winery. Buses from Orange or Avignon drop you across the street (3–5/day, 45 minutes from Orange, 1.5 hours from Avignon). Tell the driver you want the stop for the *Office de Tourisme*. When you get off the bus, walk five minutes down avenue Général de Gaulle to reach the TI and recommended hotels.

    By Car: Follow signs to *Centre-Ville*, then *Office de Tourisme;* parking is free across from the TI—most parking is free in Vaison la Romaine as well.

Helpful Hints

Market Day: Sleep in Vaison la Romaine on Monday night, and you'll wake to an amazing Tuesday market. But be warned: Mondays are quiet during the day, as many shops close (but sights are open). If you spend a Monday night, avoid parking at market sites, or you won't find your car where you left it (if signs indicate *Stationnement Interdit le Mardi,* don't park there—ask your hotel where you can park).

Internet Access: Try **Vaison 2 Mils** at 51 cours Taulignan (tel. 04 90 36 23 24).

Laundry: The self-service **Laverie la Lavandière** is on cours Taulignan, near avenue Victor Hugo (daily 8:00–22:00). The friendly owners, who work next door at the dry cleaners, will do your laundry while you sightsee—when you pick up your laundry, thank them with a small tip (dry cleaners open Mon–Sat 9:00–12:00 & 15:00–19:00, closed Sun).

Bike Rental: Try **Mag 2 Roues,** in the lower town on cours Taulignan (tel. 04 90 28 80 46).

Taxi: To get a taxi, call 04 90 36 00 04 or 06 22 28 24 49.

Car Rental: Wallgreen has a few cars for rent at **Vaison Pneus** (closed Sun, avenue Marcel Pagnol, tel. 04 90 28 73 54). The TI has a list of other car rental agencies.

Local Guide: Let sincere and knowledgeable **Anna-Marie Melard** bring those Roman ruins to life for you (€55/1.3-hour tour, tel. 04 90 36 50 48).

Cooking Classes: Charming, easygoing **Barbara Schuerenberg** offers reasonably priced cooking classes from her home in

Vaison la Romaine (€70, includes lunch, tel. 04 90 35 68 43, www.cuisinedeprovence.com, barbara@cuisinedeprovence .com).

Sights in Vaison la Romaine

Roman Ruins—Ancient Vaison la Romaine had a treaty that gave it the preferred "federated" relationship with Rome (rather than simply being a colony). This, along with a healthy farming economy (olives and vineyards), made it a most prosperous place...as a close look at its sprawling ruins demonstrates. About 6,000 people called Vaison la Romaine home 2,000 years ago. When the barbarians arrived, the Romans were forced

out, and the townspeople fled into the hills (see the sidebar on page 178). Here's something to ponder: The town has only recently reached the same population it had during its Roman era.

Vaison la Romaine's Roman ruins are split by a modern road into two sites: Puymin and La Villasse. Each is well-presented with some English information panels (less necessary if you use the audioguide), offering a good look at life during the Roman Empire. The Roman town extended all the way to the river, and its forum lies under place Montfort. What you can see is only a small fraction of the Roman town's extent—most is still buried under today's city.

Visit **Puymin** first. Nearest the entry are the scant but impressive ruins of a sprawling mansion. Find the faint remains

of a colorful frescoed wall. Climb the hill to the good little museum (pick up your audioguide here; exhibits also explained in English loaner booklet). Behind the museum is a 6,000-seat theater that is well used today, with just enough seats for the whole town (of yesterday and today). Back across the modern road in **La Villasse,** you'll explore a "street of shops" and the foundations of more houses. You'll also see a few wells, used before Vaison's two aqueducts were built.

Cost and Hours: €8 Roman ruins combo-ticket includes both ruins, helpful audioguide, and cloister at the Notre-Dame

THE COTES DU RHONE

de Nazareth Cathedral (see below); daily April–Sept 9:30–18:00, Oct–March 10:00–12:00 & 14:00–17:00.

Lower Town (Ville-Basse)—Vaison la Romaine's nondescript modern town stretches from its car-littered main square, place Montfort. Cafés grab the north side of the square, conveniently sheltered from the prevailing mistral wind, enjoying the generous shade of the ubiquitous plane *(platane)* trees (cut back each year to form a leafy canopy; see sidebar on page 267). A 10-minute walk below place Montfort, the stout **Notre-Dame de Nazareth Cathedral**—with an evocative cloister—is a good example of Provençal Romanesque (cloister entry-€1.50, or covered by €8 Roman ruins combo-ticket, daily 15:00–19:00). The pedestrian-only Grand Rue is a lively shopping street leading to the small river gorge and the Roman Bridge.

Roman Bridge—The Romans cut this sturdy, no-nonsense vault into the canyon rock 2,000 years ago, and it has survived ever since. Find the information panel at the new town end of the bridge. Until the 20th century, this was the only way to cross the Ouvèze River. The stone plaque on the wall *(Septembre 22-92...)* shows the high-water mark of the record flood that killed 30 people and washed away the valley's other bridges. The flood swept away the modern top of this bridge...but couldn't budge the 55-foot Roman arch.

Upper Town (Ville-Haute)—Although there's nothing of particular importance to see in the fortified medieval old town atop the hill, the cobbled lanes and enchanting fountains make you want to break out a sketchpad. Vaison la Romaine had a prince-bishop since the fourth century. He came under attack by the Count of Toulouse in the 12th century. Anticipating a struggle, the prince-bishop abandoned the lower town and built a château on this rocky outcrop (about 1195). Over time, the rest of the townspeople followed, vacating the lower town and building their homes at the base of the château behind the upper town's fortified wall.

To reach the upper town, hike up from the Roman Bridge (passing memorials for both world wars) through the medieval gate, under the lone tower crowned by an 18th-century wrought-iron bell cage. The château is closed, but a steep, uneven trail to it rewards hikers with a sweeping view.

▲▲**Market Day**—In the 16th century, the pope gave Vaison la Romaine market-town status. Each Tuesday morning since then, the town has hosted a farmers market. Today merchants gather with gusto, turning the entire place into a festival of produce and Provençal products. This market is one of France's best, but it can challenge claustrophobes. Be warned that parking is a real headache unless you arrive early (see "Helpful Hints" on page 169; for tips on enjoying market day, see the Shopping chapter).

Wine-Tasting—Cave la Romaine, a five-minute walk up avenue Général de Gaulle from the TI, offers a variety of good-value wines from nearby villages in a pleasant, well-organized tasting room (daily 8:30–12:00 & 14:00–18:30, avenue St. Quenin, tel. 04 90 36 55 90, www.cave-la-romaine.com).

Hiking—The TI has good information on relatively easy hikes into the hills above Vaison la Romaine. It's about 1.25 hours to the tiny hill town of Le Crestet, though views begin immediately. To find this trail, drive or walk past the upper town (with the castle just on your left), find the *chemin des Fontaines*, and stay the course as far as you like (follow yellow *Crestet* signs). Cars are not allowed on the road after about a mile. I prefer taking a taxi to Le Crestet and walking back (Le Crestet is described on page 180). The TI also has information on a loop hike from Vaison la Romaine to Crestet (a newer village below the older hillside town of Le Crestet)—it follows the same path to Le Crestet, with a different return route.

Biking—This area is not particularly flat, and if it's hot and windy, bike-riding is a dicey option. But if the air's calm, the five-mile ride to cute little Villedieu (recommended restaurant listed on page 189) is a delight. The bike route is signed along small roads; you'll find signs from Vaison la Romaine to Villedieu at the roundabout past Cave La Romaine toward Orange (see map on page 168). With a bit more energy, you can pedal beyond Villedieu on the lovely road to Mirabel (from Villedieu, follow signs to *Nyons*). Or get a good map and connect the following villages for an enjoyable 11-mile loop ride: Vaison la Romaine, St. Romain-en-Viennois, Puyméras (with a recommended restaurant—see page 187), Faucon, and St. Marcellin-lès-Vaison. The TI and bike shop have good information on mountain-biking trails.

Swimming—For a fun river swim beneath a fine Roman bridge, drive or bike to the Ouvèze River near Entrechaux, and find the St. Michel Bridge (described on page 191).

Sleeping in Vaison la Romaine

Hotels in Vaison la Romaine are a good value. Those in the medieval upper town (Ville-Haute) are quieter, cozier, and cooler, but require a 15-minute walk to the TI and Roman ruins. If staying at one of the first three places, follow signs to *Cité Médiévale* and park just outside the upper village entry (driving into the Cité Médiévale itself is a challenge, with tiny lanes and nearly impossible parking).

Sleep Code

(€1 = about $1.25, country code: 33)
S = Single, **D** = Double/Twin, **T** = Triple, **Q** = Quad, **b** = bathroom, **s** = shower only, * = French hotel rating system (0-4 stars). Unless otherwise noted, credit cards are accepted and English is spoken.

To help you sort easily through these listings, I've divided the rooms into three categories based on the price for a standard double room with bath:

$$$ Higher Priced—Most rooms €85 or more.
  $$ Moderately Priced—Most rooms between €55-85.
    $ Lower Priced—Most rooms €55 or less.

Prices can change without notice; verify the hotel's current rates online or by email. For other updates, see www.ricksteves.com/update.

If you have a car, consider staying in one of the charming Côtes du Rhône villages near Vaison la Romaine (see "Sleeping Along the Côtes du Rhône" on page 185).

$$$ Hôtel le Beffroi*** hides deep in the upper town, just above a demonstrative bell tower (you'll hear what I mean). It offers 16th-century red-tile-and-wood-beamed-cozy lodgings with nary a level surface. The rooms—split between two buildings a few doors apart—are Old World comfy, and some have views. You'll also find tasteful public spaces, a garden with view tables (light meals available in the summer), a small pool with more views, and animated Nathalie at the reception (standard Db-€95–120, superior Db-€150, Tb-€175, rue de l'Evêché, tel. 04 90 36 04 71, fax 04 90 36 24 78, www.le-beffroi.com, info@le-beffroi.com). The hotel's restaurant offers *menus* from €28.

$$$ L'Evêché Chambres, almost next door to le Beffroi in the upper town (look for the ivy), is a five-room melt-in-your-chair B&B. The owners (the Verdiers) own the art boutique across the street, have an exquisite sense of interior design, and are passionate about books, making this place feel like a cross between a library and an art gallery (Sb-€75–85, standard Db-€85–90, Db suite-€115–140, the *solanum* suite is worth every euro, Tb-€120–160, Internet access and Wi-Fi, rue de l'Evêché, tel. 04 90 36 13 46, fax 04 90 36 32 43, http://eveche.free.fr, eveche@aol.com).

$$ Hôtel la Fête en Provence, conveniently located for drivers at the entry to the medieval upper town, has a variety of room shapes and sizes. All the rooms are chiffon-comfortable, and several have small kitchenettes. Rooms are located around a calming courtyard, and there's a pool and Jacuzzi next door (standard Db-€80, bigger Db with king-size bed and bath-€110, extra person-€15, Cité Médiévale, tel. & fax 04 90 36 36 43, www .hotellafete-provence.com, fete-en-provence@wanadoo.fr). Their apartments (€155) sleep up to six people, and come with a kitchenette and sitting area.

$ Hôtel Burrhus** is part art gallery, part funky hotel—and the best value in the lower town. It's a central, laid-back, go-with-the-flow place, with a broad terrace over the raucous place Montfort (the double-paned windows are effective, but for maximum quiet, request a back room). Its floor plan will confound even the ablest navigator. The bigger, newer rooms—with contemporary decor, bigger bathrooms, and air-conditioning—are worth the extra euros for most travelers (Db-€55–61, newer Db-€71–88, Qb apartment-€140, extra bed-€15, air-con, free Internet access and Wi-Fi, 1 place Montfort, tel. 04 90 36 00 11, fax 04 90 36 39 05, www.burrhus.com, info@burrhus.com).

Eating in Vaison la Romaine

Vaison la Romaine offers a handful of excellent places—arrive by 19:30 or reserve ahead, particularly on weekends. And while you can eat very well on a moderate budget in Vaison, it's well worth venturing to nearby Côtes du Rhône villages to eat (see "Eating Along the Côtes du Rhône" on page 187). Wherever you dine, begin with a fresh glass of Muscat from the nearby village of Beaumes de Venise.

La Bartavelle is a fine place to savor traditional French cuisine in the lower town. Owner Berangère (bear-ahn-zher) has put together a tourist-friendly mix-and-match menu of local options. You get access to the top-end selections even on the €22 bottom-end *menu*—just fewer courses. Be sure to reserve ahead (closed Mon, small terrace outside, air-con and pleasant interior, 12 place de Sus Auze, tel. 04 90 36 02 16).

Le Brin d'Olivier is the most romantic place I list, with soft lighting, hushed conversations, earth tones, and a menu that celebrates Provence (€29 *menu*, closed Wed, 4 rue du Ventoux, tel. 04 90 28 74 79).

Le Tournesol offers a good €18 dinner, mostly Provençal dishes, rose walls, and friendly service. I love the *aubergine feuilleté* (eggplant puff pastry) and lamb with cheese. Show this book to get a free *kir* (daily, 30 cours Taulignan, tel. 04 90 36 09 18, owner Patrick speaks a little English).

La Lyriste, named for the loudest "singing" *cigale* (cicada), puts cuisine above decor. Marie serves what hubby Benoit cooks. Both are shy, yet proud of their restaurant. There's a fine *menu* for

€19, but go for the slightly pricier *menus,* which are inventive and *très delectable* (closed Mon, indoor and outdoor seating, 45 cours Taulignan, tel. 04 90 36 04 67).

Bistro du'O, in the upper village, is the buzz of Vaison's yuppie crowd. Reserve ahead and you'll dine on soft leather chairs under soaring stone arches and enjoy mouthwatering cuisine that is creatively presented yet affordable (*menus* from €29, closed Sun, rue du Château, tel. 04 90 41 72 90).

Hôtel le Beffroi's garden is just right for a light dinner in the summer (*menus* from €28, hotel recommended earlier).

Vaison la Romaine Connections

The most central bus stop is at Cave Vinicole.

From Vaison la Romaine by Bus to: Avignon (5/day during school year—called *période scolaire,* otherwise 3/day, 1.5 hours; much faster to bus to Orange and train from there), **Orange** (3–5/day, 45 minutes), **Nyons** (3–5/day, 45 minutes), **Crestet** (lower village below Le Crestet, 2/day, 5 minutes), **Carpentras** (2/day, 45 minutes). Bus info: tel. 04 90 36 05 22.

The Best of the Côtes du Rhône Villages

Officially, the Côtes du Rhône vineyards follow the Rhône River from just south of Lyon to Avignon. Our focus is the southern section of the Côtes du Rhône, centering on the small area between Châteauneuf-du-Pape and Vaison la Romaine. This area is best toured by car or bike. My self-guided driving tour starts in the village of Séguret, then returns to Vaison la Romaine and winds clockwise around the Dentelles de Montmirail, visiting the mountaintop village of Le Crestet, adorable little Suzette, and the renowned wine villages of Beaumes de Venise and Gigondas. I've listed several wineries *(domaines)* along the way. Before you go, study up with "Provençal Wine-Tasting 101" on page 55. Even if wine isn't your thing, don't miss this scenic drive.

Planning Your Time

Although seeing the Côtes du Rhône is possible as a day trip by car from Arles or Avignon, you'll have a more enjoyable and intimate experience if you sleep in one of the villages (my favorite accommodations are listed under "Sleeping Along the Côtes du Rhône" on page 185).

With a car, the best one-day plan is to take the driving tour described below (allow an entire day for the 80-mile round-trip from Avignon). Try to get the first two stops done before lunch (most wineries are closed 12:00–14:00; call ahead if possible), then complete the loop in the afternoon. Some wineries are closed on Sundays, holidays, and during the harvest (mid-Sept). This route is picnic-friendly, but there are few shops along the way—stock up before you leave.

Getting Around the Côtes du Rhône Villages

This area is clearly easiest if you have four wheels. Without a car, it's tougher, but a representative sampling is doable by **bike** (for ideas, see "Biking" on page 172) or by **bus** (3–5 buses/day from Avignon and Orange stop at several Côtes du Rhône villages; consider taking the bus one-way, then returning by taxi). For less effort and more expense, **Wine Safari Tours** is happy to follow this route (see "Tours of Provence" on page 46).

Self-Guided Driving Tour

The Côtes du Rhône Wine Road

This tour introduces you to the characteristic best of the Côtes du Rhône wine road. While circling the rugged Dentelles de Montmirail mountain peaks, you'll experience all that's unique about this region: its natural beauty, glowing limestone villages, inviting wineries, and rolling hills of vineyards. As you drive, notice how some vineyards grow at angles—they're planted this way to compensate for the strong effect of the mistral wind.

This trip provides a crash course in Rhône Valley wine, an excuse to meet the locals who make the stuff, and breathtaking scenery—especially late in the day, when the famous Provençal sunlight causes colors to absolutely pop.

Remember that the wineries you'll visit are serious about their wines—and hope that you'll take them seriously, too. At private wineries, tastings are not happy-go-lucky chances to knock down a few glasses and buy a cap with the property's label on it. Show genuine interest in the wines, and buy some if you enjoyed your tastes.

The many fine restaurants along the way are another highlight of the route. I've mentioned some of my favorites; you'll find much more detail about these under "Eating Along the Côtes du Rhône" on page 187.

Our tour starts just south of Vaison la Romaine in little Séguret. This town is best for a visit early or late, when it's quieter. (If you get a late start or prefer ending your tour here, begin the tour in Le Crestet—stop #3—and save the first two stops for last.)
• *From Vaison la Romaine, the easiest way to reach Séguret is to follow signs for Orange, then look for the turnoff to Séguret in a few minutes.*

THE COTES DU RHONE

Côtes du Rhône Driving Tour

SCENIC VINEYARD DRIVE

BIKE LOOP

5 MILES

10 KM

WINERY

TO NYONS & GRIGNAN

D-94

MIRABEL

TO ARDECHE GORGES

D-94

D-7

VILLE-DIEU

PUYMERAS

FAUCON

TO BUIS-LE-BARONNIES

VAISON LA ROMAINE

D-938

D-8

ROAIX

RASTEAU

CAIRANNE

D-69

D-975

ENTRE-CHAUX

D-5

D-40

TO ORANGE & AVIGNON

SÉGURET

D-88

SABLET

❷

❶

PATH

❸

D-13

LE CRESTET

TO BRANTES

GIGONDAS

❽

DENTELLES DE MONTMIRAIL

D-90

❹

❺ SUZETTE

MALAUCENE

D-974

VACQUEYRAS

❻

LAFARE

D-19

TO MONT VENTOUX

BEDOIN

D-977

❼

LA ROQUE ALRIC

LE BARROUX

D-974

TO MONT VENTOUX

BEAUMES DE VENISE

D-7

D-938

D-974

TO ORANGE & A-7

D-950

CARPENTRAS

D-942

D-49

D-938

D-942

TO AVIGNON

TO ISLE-SUR-LA-SORGUE & LUBERON

DCH

❶ Séguret

❷ Domaine de Mourchon Winery

❸ Le Crestet

❹ Le Col de la Chaîne Mountain Pass

❺ Suzette

❻ Domaine de Coyeux Winery

❼ Domaine de Durban Winery

❽ Gigondas

The Life of a Hill Town in Provence

Heat-seeking northerners have made Provence's hill towns prosperous and worldly. But before the 1960s, nobody wanted to live in these sun-drenched, rock-top settings. Like lost ships in search of safe harbor, the people of long ago took refuge here only out of necessity.

When the Romans settled Provence (125 B.C.), they brought stability to the warring locals, and hill-towners descended en masse to the Roman cities (such as Arles, Orange, Nîmes, and Vaison la Romaine). There they enjoyed theaters, fresh water from aqueducts, and commercial goods brought via the Roman road that stretched from Spain to Italy (passing along the northern edge of the Luberon).

When Rome fell (A.D. 476), barbarians swept in to rape and pillage, forcing locals back up into the hills, where they'd stay for almost 1,000 years. These "Dark Ages" were when many of the villages we see today were established. Most grew up around castles, since peasants depended on their lord for security. The hill-towners gathered stones from nearby fields and built their homes side by side to form a defensive wall, terracing the hillsides to maximize the scarce arable land. They would gather inside heavy-stone Romanesque churches to pray for salvation. Medieval life was not easy behind those walls—there were barbarians, plagues, crop failures, droughts, thieves, wars, and the everyday battle with gravity.

As the Renaissance approached, and Provence came under the protection of an increasingly centralized French nation, barbarian invasions dwindled. Just when the hill-towners thought the coast was clear to relocate down below, France's religious wars (1500s) chased them back up. As Protestants and Catholics duked it out, hilltop villages prospered, welcoming refugees. Little Séguret (pop. 100 today) had almost 1,000 residents; the village of Mérindol (near Avignon) sprouted from nowhere; and Fort de Buoux (near Apt, nothing but ruins today) was an impregnable fortress (see page 227). The turmoil of the Revolution (1789) continued to make the above-the-fray hill towns desirable.

Over the next century, hill towns slept peacefully as the rest of France modernized. Most of the hill towns you'll visit housed

THE COTES DU RHONE

By bike, or for a more scenic drive, cross to the Cité Médiévale side of the river in Vaison la Romaine, then follow D-977 signs downriver to Séguret.

❶ Séguret

Blending onto the hillside with a smattering of shops, two cafés, made-to-stroll lanes, and a natural spring, this hamlet is understandably popular. Séguret makes for a good coffee or dinner stop between 200 and 600 people and were self-sufficient, producing just what was needed (farmers, lawyers, and telemarketers were at equilibrium). Many town fountains and communal washrooms date from this time. Animals were everywhere, outnumbering humans four to one.

But 20th-century life down below required fewer stairs—and was closer to the convenience of trains, planes, and automobiles. So after World War I, down the hill-towners moved. To build in the flatlands, they pillaged the hill towns' stones, roof tiles, you name it, leaving those villages in ruin. By mid-century, most of these lovely villages became virtual ghost towns (in 1965, Le Crestet had but 15 residents—less than a third of its current, still-tiny population).

In recent years, hill towns have bounced back. Lavender production took off, and the government launched irrigation projects. But most of all, real estate boomed as Parisians, northern Europeans, and (to a lesser extent) North Americans discovered the rustic charm of hill-town life. They invested huge sums—far more than most locals could afford—to turn ancient stone structures into modern vacation homes (in many cases, buying several houses and combining them into one). Today's hill towns survive in part thanks to these outsiders' deep pockets.

Today, many villages have organizations to preserve their traditions and buildings (such as Les Amis de Séguret, or "Friends of Séguret"). Made up of older residents, groups like these raise money, sponsor festivals and dances, and even write collective histories of their villages. Many fear that younger folks won't have the motivation to carry on this tradition.

But hope springs eternal, as there may be a movement of locals back to these villages. Some northerners are finding hill-town life less romantic as their knee replacements fail. Meanwhile, the popularity of organic produce is making it financially viable for hill-town farmers with smaller plots to pursue their healthy dreams of living off the land. Finally, the Internet has allowed some hill-towners to live in remote villages and tele-commute, rather than move into bigger cities. Could the cycle be restarting? Armed with their laptops, will hill-towners once again prosper when the next wave of barbarians comes?

(restaurants recommended on page 188).

Séguret's name comes from the Latin word *securitas* (meaning "secure"). The bulky entry arch came with a massive gate, which drilled in the message of the village's name. In the Middle Ages, Séguret was patrolled 24/7—they never took their *securitas* for granted. Walk through the arch. To appreciate how the homes' outer walls provided security in those days, drop down the first passage on your right (near the fountain). These exit passages, or *poternes*, were needed in periods of peace to allow the town to expand below.

Find Séguret's open washbasin *(lavoir)*, a hotbed of social activity and gossip over the ages. The basins behind the fountain (now planted) were reserved for washing animals (which outnumbered residents in the Middle Ages); the larger ones (on the left) were for laundry only. Public washbasins like this were used right up until World War II. Farther on, the community bread oven *(four banal)* was used for festivals and celebrations. Rue Calade leads to the unusual 12th-century church for views (the circular village you see below is Sablet). This rock-sculpted church is usually closed, but it's worth a look from the outside. High above, a castle once protected Séguret, but all that's left today is a tower that you can barely make out (trails provide access). At Christmas, this entire village transforms itself into one big crèche scene—a Provençal tradition that has long since died out in other villages. To sleep well or have a fine meal with lavish views, land a room or a table at the recommended **La Table du Comtat,** just beyond the rock-sculpted church.

• *Signs near Séguret's parking will lead you up, up and away to our next stop, Domaine de Mourchon.*

❷ Domaine de Mourchon

This high-flying new winery has become the buzz of the Côtes du Rhône by blending state-of-the-art technology with traditional

winemaking methods (a dazzling ring of stainless-steel vats holds wines grown on land plowed by horses). The wines are winning the respect of international critics, yet the (Scottish) owners seem eager to help anyone understand Rhône Valley wines. Language is not an issue here, nor is a lack of stunning views. Free and informative English tours of the

vineyards are offered once a week (Easter–Sept Wed at 17:00, check website or call to verify; open Mon–Fri 10:00–12:00 & 14:00–18:00, plus April–Sept Sat 14:00–18:00, tel. 04 90 46 70 30, www.domainedemourchon.com).

• *Next, return to Vaison la Romaine and follow signs toward* Carpentras/Malaucène. *After passing through Crestet, you'll come to Le Crestet (on D-938). Look for signs leading up to* Le Village *and park at its entry.*

❸ Le Crestet

This village—founded after the fall of the Roman Empire, when people banded together in high places like this for protection from marauding barbarians—followed the usual hill-town evolution (see sidebar). The outer walls of the village did double duty as ramparts and house walls. The castle above (from about A.D. 850) provided a final safe haven when the village was attacked.

The Bishop of Vaison la Romaine was the first occupant, lending little Le Crestet a certain prestige. With about 500 residents in 1200, Le Crestet was a very important town in this region, reaching its zenith in the mid-1500s, when 660 people called it home. Le Crestet's gradual decline started when the bishop moved to Vaison la Romaine in the 1600s, though the population remained fairly stable until World War II. Today, about 35 people live within the walls year-round (about 55 during the summer).

Wander the peaceful lanes and appreciate the amount of work it took to put these stones in place. Notice the elaborate water channels. Le Crestet was served by 18 cisterns in the Middle Ages, and disputes over water were a common problem. The peaceful church (might be closed, €0.50 turns the lights on) has a beautiful stained-glass window behind the altar. Imagine hundreds of people living here, and animals roaming everywhere. Get to the top of town. The village's only business, the recommended café-restaurant **Le Panoramic,** has an upstairs terrace with a view that justifies the name...even if the food is overpriced and mediocre.

Walkers can return to Vaison la Romaine along a scenic footpath. The trail leaves from the very top of the village, at the upper, non-château end. Look for the brown sign, which indicates that it's eight kilometers (5 miles) to Vaison la Romaine, and—in a few steps—turn right, following the yellow sign that shows it's 5.1 kilometers (3 miles) to Vaison la Romaine.

• *Drivers should carry on and reconnect with the road below, following signs to* Malaucène. *As you near Malaucène, look for the huge boules courts separated by logs (on your left). Entering Malaucène, turn right on D-90 (direction: Suzette) just before the gas station. As you climb to the mountain pass, look for signs on the left to* Le Col de la Chaîne *(Chain Pass). From this point on, the scenery gets better fast.*

❹ Le Col de la Chaîne Mountain Pass

Get out of your car at the pass (about 1,500 feet) and enjoy the breezy views. Wander about. The peaks in the distance—thrusting up like the back of a stegosaurus or a bad haircut (you decide)—are the Dentelles de Montmirail, a small range running just nine miles basically north to south and reaching 2,400 feet in elevation. This region's land is constantly shifting. Those rocky tops were the result of a gradual uplifting of the land, then were blown bald by the angry mistral wind. Below, pine and oak trees mix with scotch broom, which blooms brilliant yellow in May and June. The village

THE CÔTES DU RHONE

below the peaks is Suzette (you'll be there soon). The yellow-signed hiking trail leads to the castle-topped village of Le Barroux (3.5 miles, mostly downhill).

The scene is lovely and surprisingly undeveloped. You can thank the lack of water for the absence of more homes or farms in this area. Water is everything in this parched region, and if you don't have ready access to it, you can't build or cultivate the land. (Some farmers have drilled down as far as 1,300 feet to try to find water.) With no water at hand, farmers here lie awake at night worrying about fire. Hot summers, dry pines, and windy days make a scary recipe for fast-traveling fires.

Now turn around and face Mont Ventoux. Are there clouds in the horizon? You're looking into the eyes of the Alps (behind Ventoux), and those "foothills" help keep Provence sunny.

• *Time to push on. You'll pass countless yellow trail signs along this drive. (The Dentelles provide fertile ground for walking trails.) To sleep nearby, try* **La Ferme Dégoutaud,** *just ahead (described on page 187). With the medieval castle of Le Barroux topping the horizon in the distance (off to the left), drive on to little...*

❺ Suzette

Tiny Suzette floats on its hilltop, with a small 12th-century chapel, one café, a handful of residents, and the gaggle of houses where they live. Park in Suzette's lot, below, then find the big orientation board above the lot (Rome is 620 kilometers—385 miles—away). Look out to the broad shoulders of Mont Ventoux. At 6,000 feet, it always seems to have some clouds hanging around. If it's clear, the top looks like it's snow-covered; if you drive up there, you'll see it's actually white stone (see the Mont Ventoux drive on page 189). If it's very cloudy, the mountain takes on a dark, foreboding appearance.

Look to the village. A sign asks you to *Respectez son Calme* (respect its peace). Suzette's homes once lived in the shadow of an imposing castle, destroyed during the religious wars of the mid-1500s. The recommended **Les Coquelicots** café makes a good lunch or drink stop. Good picnic tables lie just past Suzette on our route. Back across the road from the orientation table is a tasting room for **Château Redortier** wines (English brochure and well-explained list of wines provided; skip their whites, but try the good rosés and reds).

• *If you're enjoying the views and can't get enough of this landscape, consider adding this 20-minute detour from Suzette: Drive down to Le Barroux, then loop back to D-90 via the rock-swirled village of La Roque Alric, and rejoin our route in La Fare.*

Otherwise, continue from Suzette in the direction of Beaumes de Venise. You'll drop down into the lush little village of La Fare.

Cicadas *(Cigales)*

In the countryside, listen for *les cigales*. They sing in the heat and are famous for announcing the arrival of summer. (Locals say their song also marks the coming of the tourists...and more money.) People here love these ugly, long-winged bugs, an integral part of Provençal life. You'll see souvenir cicadas made out of every material possible. If you look closely—they are well-camouflaged—you can find live specimens on tree trunks and branches. Cicadas live for about two years, all but the last two weeks of which are spent quietly underground as larvae. But when they go public, their chirping begins with each sunrise and goes nonstop until sunset.

Here, joyriders can take another 20-minute detour into the mountains by taking a sharp right on entering the village, following *Dentelles de Montmirail* signs. The Domaine de Cassan winery lies near the end of the road that also leads to the Col du Cayron hiking trail (to the village of Gigondas). Your partner could drop you off and meet you in Gigondas (it's a 1.5-hour walk over the pass).

But La Fare's best wine-tasting opportunity is back on our route just after leaving the village, at...

❻ Domaine de Coyeux

The private road winds up and up to this impossibly beautiful setting, with the best views of the Dentelles I've found. Olive trees

line the final approach, and *Le Caveau* signs lead to a modern tasting room (you may need to ring the buzzer). The owners and staff are formal and take your interest in their wines seriously—skip this stop if you only want a quick taste or are not interested in buying. These wines have earned their excellent reputation (and are now available in the US). Start

with their delectable Côtes du Rhône Villages red, and finish with their trademark dry and sweet Muscats (wines range from €7 to €13 per bottle, Mon–Sat 10:00–12:00 & 14:00–18:00, closed Sun except May–Aug, tel. 04 90 12 42 42, some English spoken). After tasting, take time to wander about the vineyards.

• *Drive on toward Beaumes de Venise. You'll soon pass the recommended* **Côté Vignes**, *a fine place for lunch or dinner. Next you'll drop out of the hills as you approach Beaumes de Venise. To find the next winery, keep*

THE CÔTES DU RHÔNE

right at the first Centre-Ville *sign as the road bends left, then carefully track* Domaine de Durban *signs for three scenic miles to...*

❼ Domaine de Durban

Find the small tasting room and let your young hostess take your taste buds on a tour. This *domaine* produces appealing whites, reds, and Muscats. Start with the 100 percent Viognier (€4.50 a bottle), then try their Viognier–Chardonnay blend. Their rosé is light and refreshing (and cheap). Their three reds are very different from one another: One is fruity, one is tannic (aged in oak), and one has some fruit and tannin. Finish with their popular

Muscat de Venise (wines are €4–10/bottle, Mon–Sat 9:00–12:00 & 14:00–18:30, closed Sun, tel. 04 90 62 94 26). Picnics are not allowed, and the grass is off-limits, though strolling amid the gorgeous vineyards is OK.

• *Retrace your route to Beaumes de Venise, turn left at the bottom, then make a quick right and navigate through Beaumes de Venise, following signs for* Vacqueyras. *At a big roundabout, you'll pass Beaumes de Venise's massive* cave coopérative, *which represents many growers in this area (big selection, but too slick for my taste; daily 8:30–12:30 & 14:00–19:00). Continue following signs for* Vacqueyras *(a famous wine village with a Thursday market and another* cave coopérative*), and then signs for* Gigondas *and* Vaison par la route touristique. *As you enter Gigondas, follow signs to the TI and park on or near the tree-shaded square.*

❽ Gigondas

This town produces some of the region's best reds and is ideally situated for hiking, mountain-biking, and driving into the mountains. The **TI** has a list of wineries, *chambres d'hôte*, and good hikes or drives (Mon–Sat 10:00–12:30 & 14:00–18:00, likely closed Sun, place du Portail, tel. 04 90 65 85 46, www.gigondas-dm.fr). The €2.50 *Chemins et Sentiers du Massif des Dentelles* hiking map is helpful, though not critical, because routes are well-signed. The blue route makes a good one-hour round-trip high above Gigondas to superb views (walk up the steep road from the Mairie next to the TI and follow blue markers toward the Dentelles). You can extend this hike into a three-hour loop. At the least, take a short walk through the village lanes above the TI—the church is an easy destination with good views over the heart of the Côtes du Rhône vineyards.

You'll find several good tasting opportunities on the main square. **Le Caveau de Gigondas** is best, where Sandra and Barbara await your visit with a large and free selection of tiny bottles for sampling, filled directly from the barrel (daily 10:00–12:00 & 14:00–18:30, 2 doors down from TI, tel. 04 90 65 82 29). Here you can compare wines from a variety of private producers in an intimate, low-key surrounding. The provided list of wines is helpful. A self-imposed gag rule (intended to keep staff from favoring the production of a single winery in this co-op showcase) makes it hard to get a strong recommendation here, so it's best to know what you want (see "French Wine Lingo" on page 54).

You'll find a small grocery store and several eating options in the village. Diagonally across from the TI, the shaded red tables of **Du Verre à l'Assiette** ("From Glass to Plate") entice lunchtime eaters (also good interior ambience, €10 salads, €14 *plats*, daily, place du Village, tel. 04 90 12 36 64). To dine very well or sleep nearby, find the recommended **Hôtel les Florets,** a half-mile above town (closed Wed).

• *From Gigondas, follow signs to the circular wine village of Sablet— with generally inexpensive yet tasty wines (the TI and wine cooperative share a space in the town center)— then past Séguret and back to Vaison la Romaine, where our tour ends.*

If you haven't had your fill, consider adding on some...

Villages North of the Côtes du Rhône Drive

Cairanne, toward Orange from Vaison la Romaine, is a pleasant village producing fine wines with one of the best wine *coopératives* in this region. **Grignan,** 30 minutes north of Vaison la Romaine at the northern limit of Provence, is impressively set on a rocky spur and features one of Provence's grandest châteaux (French-only tours).

Sleeping Along the Côtes du Rhône

(€1 = about $1.25, country code: 33)
These accommodations are along the self-guided driving tour route described above. They offer a great opportunity for drivers who want to experience rural France and get better values.

Near Vaison la Romaine

These accommodations are within a 10-minute drive of Vaison la Romaine.

$$$ Domaine de Cabasse*** is a lovely spread flanked by vineyards at the foot of Séguret (with a walking path to the village). Winemaking is their primary business (tastings possible), though the hotel is well-run by its relaxed staff. The 13 rooms have retained a simple Old World feel. All the rooms have decks, and a big pool is at your disposal. From the entry gate—which opens automatically...and slowly—the place appears more formal than it is (Db-€125–140, Wi-Fi in lobby, on D-23 between Sablet and Séguret, tel. 04 90 46 91 12, fax 04 90 46 94 01, www.cabasse.fr, info@cabasse.fr). The restaurant offers a satisfying, though limited, €28 dinner *menu* served inside or out.

$$$ Hôtel les Florets**, a half-mile above Gigondas, is surrounded by pine trees at the foothills of the Dentelles de Montmirail. It comes with a huge terrace that Van Gogh would have loved, thoughtfully designed rooms, and a fine restaurant (standard Db-€100–110, superior Db-€125–160, annex rooms are best, tel. 04 90 65 85 01, fax 04 90 65 83 80, www.hotel-lesflorets.com, accueil@hotel-lesflorets.com). For more details about the hotel's restaurant, see page 189.

$$$ Domaine des Tilleuls***, 10 minutes from Vaison la Romaine in workaday Malaucène, is a winning, well-priced refuge, and the most family-friendly place I list. (Welcoming owners Arnould and Dominique have three kids.) Its 20 country-modern rooms fill an old farmhouse overlooking lovely grounds with name-sake linden trees *(tilleuls)*, a sandbox, toys, and a large pool. If you missed market day in Vaison la Romaine, sleep here Tuesday night and wake to a bustling market (Db-€84–100, Tb/Qb-€108–120, breakfast-€13, Wi-Fi, well-signed in Malaucène on the route to Mont Ventoux, tel. 04 90 65 22 31, fax 04 90 65 16 77, www.hotel-domainedestilleuls.com, info@hotel-domainedestilleuls.com).

$$ La Table du Comtat is ideal if you want to sleep in adorable little Séguret. Rooms are simple and traditional, and a fair value. Some have views; the terrace and restaurant are a serious draw. The hotel is closed Wednesday, except in July and August—start your stay on a different day of the week (Db-€90–110, no air-con, tel. 04 90 46 91 49, www.table-comtat.fr, direction@table-comtat.fr).

$$ L'Ecole Buissonnière Chambres is run by an engaging Anglo-French team, Monique and John, who share their peace and quiet 10 minutes from Vaison la Romaine. This creatively restored farmhouse has three character-filled half-timbered rooms, and convivial public spaces. Getting to know John, who has lived all over the south of France and even worked as a *gardian* (cowboy) in the Camargue, is worth the price of the room; he's also generous with his knowledge of the area. The outdoor kitchen allows guests to picnic in high fashion in the tranquil garden (Db-€56–65, Tb-€75–79, Qb-€90–97, includes breakfast, cash only, Wi-Fi;

between Villedieu and Buisson on D-75—leave Vaison following signs to *Villedieu,* then follow D-51 toward Buisson and turn left onto D-75; tel. 04 90 28 95 19, ecole.buissonniere@wanadoo.fr). Ask about their all-inclusive stay for groups of four to seven people (includes pickup at airport or train station, winery and region tour).

Near Suzette
$$ La Ferme Dégoutaud, a 20-minute drive from Vaison la Romaine, is a splendidly situated, roomy, and utterly isolated *chambre d'hôte* about halfway between Malaucène and Suzette (well-signed, a mile down a dirt road). Animated Véronique (minimal English) rents three country-cozy rooms with many thoughtful touches, a view pool, table tennis, picnic-perfect tables, and a barbecue at your disposal (Db-€72, Tb-€82, Qb-€92, includes breakfast, tel. & fax 04 90 62 99 29, www.degoutaud.fr, le.degoutaud @wanadoo.fr).

Eating Along the Côtes du Rhône

Drivers enjoy a wealth of country-Provençal dining opportunities in rustic settings, handy to many of the rural accommodations. Many of these eateries are described in my self-guided driving tour route (earlier); I've listed them by distance from Vaison la Romaine (nearest to farthest). Most are within a 10-minute drive of Vaison la Romaine. All have some outdoor seating and should be considered for lunch or dinner.

La Girocedre is an enchanting place to eat lunch or dinner if you have a car and it's nice outside. Just three picturesque miles from Vaison la Romaine in adorable Puyméras, this place offers a complete country-Provençal package: outdoor tables placed just-so in a lush garden, warm interior decor, and real Provençal cuisine (€18 three-course lunch *menus,* €26 dinner *menus,* closed Mon, tel. 04 90 46 50 67).

Auberge d'Anaïs, at the end of a dirt road 10 minutes from Vaison la Romaine, is another find—and a true Provençal experience. Outdoor tables gather under cheery lights with grand views and reliable cuisine. Ask for a table *sur la terrasse* (€10 lunch *menu,* good three-course dinner *menus* from €16, closed Mon, tel. 04 90 36 20 06). From Vaison la Romaine, follow signs to *Carpentras,* then *St. Marcellin;* signs will guide you from there.

Le Panoramic, in hill-capping Le Crestet, serves average salads, pizzas, and *plats* for more than you should spend at what must be Provence's greatest view tables. Come for a drink and view, but if you're really hungry, eat elsewhere (open daily for lunch and dinner, €28 *menus,* tel. 04 90 28 76 42). Drivers should pass on the

THE COTES DU RHONE

Lavender

Whether or not you travel to Provence during the late-June and July lavender blossom, you'll see and smell examples of this particularly local product everywhere—in shops, on tables in restaurants, and in your hotel room. And if you come during lavender season, you'll experience one of Europe's great color events, where rich fields of purple lavender meet equally rich yellow fields of sunflowers. While lavender season is hot, you'll find the best fields in the cooler hills, because the flowers thrive at higher altitudes. The flowers are harvested in full bloom (beginning in mid-July), then distilled to extract the oils for making soaps and perfume. For a good explanation of this process, visit the Museum of Lavender in Coustellet (see page 218).

And though lavender seems like an indigenous part of the Provence scene, it wasn't cultivated here until about 1920, when it was imported by the local perfume-makers. Because lavender is not native to Provence, growing it successfully requires great care. Three kinds of lavender are grown in Provence: true lavender (traditionally used by perfume-makers), spike lavender, and lavandin (a cloned hybrid of the first two). Today, a majority of Provence lavender fields are lavandin—which is also mass-produced at factories, a trend that is threatening to put the true lavender grower out of business.

Some of the best lavender fields bloom near Vaison la Romaine. Lavender blooms later the higher you go; the ones described here are listed from lowest to highest elevations. For an impressive display, drive north of Vaison la Romaine and ramble the tiny road between Valréas and Vinsobres (D-190 and D-46). You'll see more beautiful fields along D-538 between Nyons and Dieulefit, and still more if you climb Mont Ventoux to Sault (described on page 190).

first parking lot in Le Crestet and keep climbing to park at place du Château. The restaurant is to your right as you face the view.

Domaine de Cabasse lets you dine surrounded by vineyards at a relaxed wine estate/hotel, though you must book ahead. Even with its limited-selection €28 *menu*, it more than merits the short drive from Vaison la Romaine (see hotel listing earlier).

La Table du Comtat, in charming little Séguret, allows you to combine a village visit with a fine meal and finer views over vineyards and villages. Book a window table in advance, and come while there's still light (€20 lunch *menu*, €38 dinner *menu*, classic

French cuisine, closed Wed–Thu, tel. 04 90 46 91 49). See hotel listing, earlier.

Hôtel les Florets, in Gigondas, is a traditional, family-run place that's worth the drive. Dinners are a sumptuous blend of classic French cuisine and Provençal accents, served with class by English-speaking Thierry. The marvelous terrace makes your meal even more memorable (*menus* from €30, restaurant closed Wed, service can be slow). See hotel listing, earlier.

La Maison Bleue, on Villedieu's adorable little square, is a pizza-and-salad place with great outdoor ambience. Skip it if the weather forces you inside (open for lunch and dinner, closed Mon, tel. 04 90 28 97 02).

Les Coquelicots, a tiny eatery surrounded by vines and views in minuscule Suzette, is a sweet spot. The food is scrumptious (owner/chef Frankie insists on fresh products), and the setting is memorable. Try the *Assiette Provençale,* his omelets with herbs, or any of his grilled meats and fish (May–Sept usually closed Tue evening and all day Wed, Oct–April open weekends only, tel. 04 90 65 06 94).

Côté Vignes, off a short dirt road between Suzette and Beaumes de Venise, is a lighthearted wood-fired-everything place with outdoor tables flanked by fun interior dining. Young Corrine runs the restaurant with enthusiasm; try the Camembert cheese flambé with lettuce, potatoes, and ham (€9 salads and good pizza, *menus* from €18, closed Tue evening and Wed, tel. 04 90 65 07 16).

More Côtes du Rhône Drives

For further explorations of the Côtes du Rhône region, consider these suggestions: a scenic mountaintop, an off-the-beaten-path countryside ramble, and an impressive gorge.

▲Mont Ventoux and Lavender

The drive to Mont Ventoux is worth ▲▲▲ if skies are crystal-clear, or in any weather between late June and the end of July, when the lavender blooms. It also provides you a scenic connection between the Côtes du Rhône villages and the Luberon. Allow an hour to drive to the top of this 6,000-foot mountain, where you'll be greeted by cool temperatures, crowds of visitors, and acres of white stones.

Mont Ventoux is Provence's rooftop, with astonishing Pyrenees-to-Alps views—but only if it's really clear (which it usually isn't). But even under hazy skies, it's an interesting place. The top combines a barren and surreal lunar landscape with souvenirs, bikers, and hikers. All that chalky mess you see was once the bottom of a sea. Miles of poles stuck in the rock identify the route (the top is usually snowbound Dec–April). **Le Vendran** restaurant (near the old observatory and Air Force control tower) offers snacks and meals with commanding views. An orientation board is available on the opposite side of the mountaintop.

Between Mont Ventoux and the Luberon, you'll duck into and out of several climate zones and remarkably diverse landscapes. The scene alternates between limestone canyons, lush meadows, and wildflowers. Thirty minutes east of Mont Ventoux, lavender fields forever surround the rock-top village of **Sault** (pronounced "soh"), which produces 40 percent of France's lavender essence. Sault, a welcoming town in any season, goes unnoticed by most hurried travelers. It's a slow-down-and-smell-the-lavender kind of place, with a sociable "mountain market" on Wednesdays.

Getting to Mont Ventoux: To reach Mont Ventoux from Vaison la Romaine, go to Malaucène, then wind up D-974 for 40 minutes to the top (or start at cute little Bedoin, which has a local Monday market; from there D-974 offers a longer, prettier route to the top). If continuing to Sault (a worthwhile detour when the lavender blooms) or on to the Luberon (worthwhile anytime—see next chapter), follow signs to *Sault*, then *Gordes*. The *Les Routes de la Lavande* brochure suggests driving and walking routes in the area (available online at www.routes-lavande.com or at Sault TI, tel. 04 90 64 01 21).

Drôme Provençale Loop Drive

This meander north into the Drôme Provençale gets you away from popular tourist areas and combines more appealing scenery with overlooked towns and villages (see map on pages 158–159). This drive delivers relatively subtle rewards and works best for travelers with sufficient time to joyride. I'd only do it on Thursdays, when it's market day in Nyons, or on Wednesdays, when it's market day in Buis-les-Barronies. If the wind is howling, the drive provides some relief, as you'll be in and out of gorges and protected by mountain slopes. Allow most of a day for this up-and-down, curve-filled drive, particularly if it's market day in Nyons.

From Vaison la Romaine, drive to **Nyons,** an attractive mid-size town set along a river and against the hills. Here you'll find a Roman bridge with views, an olive mill, a lavender distillery, a handful of walking streets, and an arcaded square—all with few tourists. Nyons is famous for its rollicking Thursday market (until 12:30) and for producing France's best olives, which you can taste at its well-organized *coopérative* (daily 9:00–12:00 & 14:00–19:00, interesting museum about olives, on place Olivier de Serres, tel. 04 75 26 95 00).

From Nyons, head for the hills following signs to *Gap* on D-94, then follow signs to *St. Jalles* on D-64. Little **St. Jalles** hovers above the road, with a pretty Romanesque church (usually closed), two cafés (Café de Lavande overhangs the river, providing a fine backdrop for a drink, lunch, or a snack), and a small winery making crisp whites and easy reds (Domaine de Rieu Frais, Mon–Sat 10:00–12:00 & 14:00–18:00, closed Sun, tel. 04 75 27 31 54, best to call ahead and let them know you're coming).

From St. Jalles, cross the bridge following D-108 and *Buis-les-Barronnies* signs, and start your ascent over the rocky mountains. Prepare for miles of curves, territorial views, and no guardrails. Drop down (er, drive down) and meet the Ouvèze River, then follow it into bustling **Buis-les-Barronnies** (with all the services, including many cafés and an attractive old town to stroll). Buis-les-Barronnies is the linden tree capital of France and hosts an earthy outdoor market on Wednesdays with produce and crafts.

From Buis-les-Barronnies, continue south on D-5, then turn left toward Eygaliers on D-72. Follow this slow, serpentine road along the back side of Mont Ventoux and go all the way to the jewel of this trip: **Brantes,** one of Provence's most spectacularly located villages. Stop here for some fresh air and a look at the local pottery.

Finally, follow signs back to *Vaison la Romaine* along the faster, less curvy D-40. A few minutes before Vaison la Romaine, you'll pass through pleasing little Entrechaux. If you have energy for one more stop, take the short detour toward St. Marcellin at the roundabout just before entering Entrechaux, and follow *Vallée de l'Ouvèze* signs. You'll come to the Roman-era **St. Michel Bridge,** with good swimming and intriguing rock-cut channels the Romans used for mixing mortar (from lime and sand). Cross the narrow bridge and park on the other side.

▲Ardèche Gorges (Gorges de l'Ardèche)

These gorges, which wow visitors with abrupt chalky-white cliffs, follow the Ardèche River through immense canyons and thick forests. To reach the gorges from Vaison la Romaine, drive west 45 minutes, passing through Bollène and Pont Saint-Esprit to Vallon Pont d'Arc (the tourist hub of the Ardèche Gorges). From Vallon Pont d'Arc, you can canoe along the peaceful river through some of the canyon's most spectacular scenery and under the rock arch of Pont d'Arc (half-day, all-day, and 2-day trips possible; less appealing in summer, when the river is crowded and water levels are low), and learn about hiking trails that get you above it all (**TI** tel. 04 75 88 04 01, www.vallon-pont-darc.com, French only). If continuing north toward Lyon, connect Privas and Aubenas, then head back on the autoroute. Endearing little **Balazuc**—a village north of the gorges, with narrow lanes, flowers, views, and a smattering of cafés and shops—makes a great stop.

HILL TOWNS
OF THE LUBERON
France's Answer to Italy's Tuscany

Just 30 miles east of Avignon, the Luberon region hides some of France's most captivating hill towns and sensuous landscapes. Those intrigued by Peter Mayle's books love joyriding through the region, connecting I-could-live-here villages, crumbled castles, and meditative abbeys. Mayle's bestselling *A Year in Provence* marked its 20th anniversary in 2010. The book describes the ruddy local culture from an Englishman's perspective as he buys a stone farmhouse, fixes it up, and adopts the region as his new home. *A Year in Provence* is a great read while you're here— or, better yet, get it as an audio book and listen while you drive.

The Luberon terrain in general (much of which is a French regional natural park) is as enticing as its villages. Gnarled vineyards and wind-sculpted trees separate tidy stone structures from abandoned buildings—little more than rock piles—that seem to challenge city slickers to fix them up. Mountains of limestone bend along vast ridges, while colorful hot-air balloons survey the sun-drenched scene from above. The wind is an integral part of life here. The infamous mistral wind, finishing its long ride in from Siberia, hits like a hammer (see the *"Le Mistral"* sidebar on page 59).

Planning Your Time

There are no obligatory museums, monuments, or vineyards in the Luberon. Treat this area like a vacation from your vacation. Downshift your engine. Brake for the views, and get out of your car to take a walk. Get on a first-name basis with a village.

To enjoy the ambience of the Luberon, you'll want at least one night and a car (only Isle-sur-la-Sorgue—and, to a lesser extent, Lourmarin—are accessible by train or bus). Allow a half-day for Isle-sur-la-Sorgue if it's market day (less time if not). Add more time if you want to paddle the Sorgue River or pedal between villages (canoe trips and bike rental described on page 201). You'll also want a full day for the Luberon villages.

For the ultimate Luberon experience, drivers should base themselves in or near Roussillon. To lose the tourists, set up in St-Saturnin-lès-Apt or Saignon. If you lack wheels or prefer streams to hills and like a little more action, stay in Isle-sur-la-Sorgue, located within striking distance of Avignon and just outside the Luberon. Adequate train service from Avignon and Marseille, and some bus service, connect Isle-sur-la-Sorgue with the real world. Level terrain, tree-lined roads, and nearby villages make Isle-sur-la-Sorgue good for biking.

The village of Lourmarin works as a southern base for visiting Luberon sights, as well as Aix-en-Provence, Cassis, and Marseille. Determined travelers can take a bus from Avignon or Aix-en-Provence to reach Lourmarin.

Getting Around the Luberon

By Car: Luberon roads are scenic and narrow. With no major landmarks, it's easy to get lost in this area—and you will get lost, trust me—but getting lost is the point. Pick up Michelin map #332 or #527 to navigate.

If connecting this region with the **Côtes du Rhône,** avoid driving through Carpentras (terrible traffic, confusing signage). If you're in a hurry, use the autoroute from Cavaillon and get off in Orange (if you plan to visit that town), or use the exit before Orange Centre (exit #22) to get to the villages. If time is not an issue, drive via Mont Ventoux—one of Provence's most spectacular routes (see page 189).

By Bus: Isle-sur-la-Sorgue is accessible by bus from Avignon, with several daily trips and a central stop at the post office (6–8/day Mon–Sat, 3–4/day Sun, 45 minutes). Buses link Lourmarin with Avignon (3/day, 1.5 hours, transfer in Cavaillon) and Aix-en-Provence (3/day, 1.25 hours, transfer in Pertuis), making it a workable village stop between these cities. Without a car or minivan tour, skip the more famous hill towns of the Luberon.

By Train: Trains get you to Isle-sur-la-Sorgue (station called "L'Isle–Fontaine de Vaucluse") from Avignon (10/day on weekdays, 5/day on weekends, 30 minutes) or from Marseille (8/day, 1–2 hours). If you're day-tripping by train, check return times before leaving the station.

By Minivan Tour: Dutchman Mike Rijken, who runs **Wine Safari,** offers tours of this area, as do several other Avignon-based companies (see "Tours of Provence" on page 46).

By Taxi: Contact **Luberon Taxi** (based in Maubec off D-3, mobile 06 08 49 40 57, www.luberontaxi.com, contact@lub? ron taxi.com).

THE LUBERON

By Bike: Hardy bikers can ride from Isle-sur-la-Sorgue to Gordes, then to Roussillon, connecting other villages in a full-day loop ride (30 miles round-trip to Roussillon and back, with lots of hills). Many appealing villages are closer to Isle-sur-la-Sorgue and offer easier biking options (see "Biking" on page 201).

Luberon Area Market Days

Monday: Cavaillon (produce and antiques/flea market)

Tuesday: Gordes and Lacoste (both small)

Wednesday: Sault (produce and antiques/flea market)

Thursday: Roussillon (cute) and Isle-sur-la-Sorgue (good, but smaller than its Sunday market)

Friday: Lourmarin (very good) and Bonnieux (pretty good)

Saturday: Apt (huge produce and antiques/flea market)

Sunday: Isle-sur-la-Sorgue (granddaddy of them all, produce and antiques/flea market), Coustellet (very good and less touristy), and St-Saturnin-lès-Apt

Isle-sur-la-Sorgue

This sturdy market town—literally, "Island on the Sorgue River"—sits within a split in its crisp, happy little river. It's a workaday town, with a gritty charm that feels refreshingly real after so many adorable villages. It also makes a good base for exploring the Luberon (15 minutes by car, doable by hardy bikers) and Avignon (30 minutes by car or train) and can work for exploring the Côtes du Rhône by car (allow an hour to Vaison la Romaine).

After the arid cities and villages elsewhere in Provence, the presence of water at every turn is a welcome change. In Isle-sur-la-Sorgue—called the "Venice of Provence"—the Sorgue River's extraordinarily clear and shallow flow divides like cells, producing water, water everywhere. The river has long nourished the region's economy. The fresh spring water of the Sorgue's many branches has provided ample fish, irrigation for crops, and power for local industries for centuries. Today, antiques shops power the town's economy—every other shop seems to sell some kind of antique.

Orientation to Isle-sur-la-Sorgue

Although Isle-sur-la-Sorgue is renowned for its market days (Sun and Thu), it's otherwise a pleasantly average town with no important sights and a steady trickle of tourism. It's calm at night and dead on Mondays. The town revolves around its river, the church square, and two pedestrian-only streets, rue de la République and rue Carnot.

Tourist Information

The TI has information on hiking, biking itineraries, and a line on rooms in private homes, all of which are outside of town (Mon–Sat 9:00–12:30 & 14:30–18:00, Sun 9:00–12:30, in town center next to church, tel. 04 90 38 04 78, www.oti-delasorgue.fr).

Arrival in Isle-sur-la-Sorgue

By Car: Traffic is a mess and parking is a headache on market days (all day Sunday and Thursday mornings). Circle the ring road and look for parking signs, or give up and find the pay lot behind the post office (PTT). There are several lots just west of the roundabout at Le Bassin (marked on the map on page 198). You'll also pass freestyle parking on roads leaving the city. Don't leave anything visible in your car.

By Train: Remember that the train station is called "L'Isle–Fontaine de Vaucluse." To reach my recommended hotels, walk straight out of the station and turn right on the ring road.

By Bus: The bus from Avignon drops you near the post office (PTT, ask driver for "*luh pay-tay-tay*"), a block from the recommended Hôtel les Névons.

Helpful Hints

Shop Hours: The antiques shops this town is famous for are open Saturday to Monday only.

Internet Access: Your best option is the centrally located **Gécosystem** (rue Carnot 40, tel. 04 90 15 40 16).

Bookstore: You'll find a handful of English novels at **La Marque-Page de l'Isle,** where the pedestrian street rue de la République meets Notre-Dame des Anges church (Tue–Sat 7:00–12:30 & 15:00–19:00, Sun–Mon 7:00–12:30).

Laundry: It's at the **Centre Commercial Super U** supermarket, on the ring road at the roundabout, on Cours Fernande Peyre (daily 9:00–19:00).

The Luberon

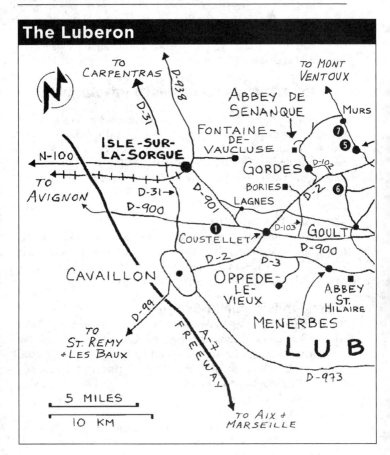

Supermarket: A well-stocked **Spar** market is on the main ring road, near the Peugeot Car shop and the train station (Mon–Sat 8:30–12:30 & 15:00–19:00, Sun 15:00–19:00). A smaller, more central **Casino** market is on pedestrian rue de la République (Tue–Sun 7:30–12:30 & 15:30–19:30, closed Mon).

Bike Rental: Christophe at **Isles 2 Roues,** by the train station, rents good bikes (€15/day, closed Sun–Mon, must show your passport, 10 avenue de la Gare, tel. 04 90 38 19 12). **Vélo Services** is also fine (on the northern side of ring road at 1 quai Clovis Hugues, mobile 06 82 58 35 02, www.europbike -provence.fr).

Taxi: Call 06 13 38 32 11.

Public WC: A WC is in the parking lot between the post office (PTT) and the Hôtel les Névons.

Hiking: The TI has good information on area hikes; most trails

TO MONT VENTOUX

— AUTOROUTE (TOLL)
— OTHER ROADS
++ RAIL

• PARIS
FRANCE

D-943
ST-SATURNIN-LES-APT
JOUCAS
D-2
ROUSSILLON
RUSTREL
D-22
LE COLORADO PROVENCAL
LE CHENE
APT
D-943
D-209
VIENS
ST. MARTIN
D-90
D-900
ST. JULIEN BRIDGE
SAIGNON
TO GRAND CANYON DU VERDON
BUOUX
FORT DE BUOUX
LACOSTE
BONNIEUX
E R O N
LOURMARIN
D-943
TO AIX & MARSEILLE
DCH

❶ Chambres Sous l'Olivier
❷ Le Clos des Cigales Chambres
❸ Hôtel les Sables d'Ocre
❹ La Petite Ecole Rest.
❺ Hostellerie des Commandeurs
❻ La Ferme de la Huppe Hôtel
❼ Le Mas du Loriot Hôtel
❽ Mas del Sol Chambres
❾ Mas Perréal Chambres
❿ Château de la Canorgue Winery

are accessible by short drives, and you can use a taxi to get there.

Self-Guided Walk

Wandering Isle-sur-la-Sorgue

The town has crystal-clear water babbling under pedestrian bridges stuffed with flower boxes, and its old-time carousel is always spinning. For this walk (shown on the map on the next page), navigate by the town's splintered streams and nine mossy waterwheels, which, while still turning, power only memories of the town's wool and silk industries.

• *Start your tour at the church next to the TI—where all streets seem to converge—and make forays into the town from there. Go first to the church.*

Notre-Dame des Anges: This 12th-century church has a

THE LUBERON

Isle-sur-la-Sorgue

1. La Prévôté Hôtel/Rest.
2. Hôtel les Névons
3. To Le Pont des Aubes Chambres, Chambres Sous l'Olivier & L'Ousteau de l'Isle Rest.
4. Hôtel/Rest. les Terrasses du Bassin
5. Le Caveau de la Tour de l'Isle Wine Bar & Casino Market
6. Fromenterie Bakery & Bus from Avignon
7. Bus to Avignon
8. Café de France & La Marque-Page de l'Isle (Bookstore)
9. To Launderette
10. Gécosystem Internet
11. Spar Market
12. Bike Rental (2)
13. Delices de Luberon Shop
14. Riverfront Stroll to Partage des Eaux (Swimming)
15. Antique Toy & Doll Museum

festive Baroque interior and feels too big for today's town. Walk in. The curls and swirls and gilded statues date from an era that was all about Louis XIV, the Sun King. This is propagandist architecture, designed to wow the faithful into compliance. (It was made possible thanks to profits generated from the town's river-powered industries.) When you enter a church like this, the heavens should open up and assure you that whoever built it had celestial connections (daily 10:00–12:00 & 15:15–17:00, Mass on Sun at 10:30).

Outside the church, notice the buildings' faded facades around you, recalling their previous lives (Fabrique de Chausseures was a shoemaker; *meubles* means furniture). Admire Fauque Beyret's antique facade. Isle-sur-la-Sorgue retains a connection to its past uncommon in this renovation-happy region.

• *With your back to the church entry, angle to the left and wander down rue Danton to lose the crowds and find...*

Three Waterwheels: These big, forgotten waterwheels have been in business here since the 1200s, when they were first used

THE LUBERON

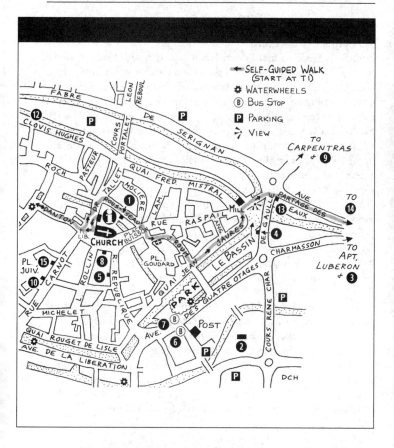

for grinding flour. Paper, textile, silk, and woolen mills would later find their power from this river. At its peak, Isle-sur-la-Sorgue had 70 waterwheels like this, and in the 1800s the town competed with Avignon as Provence's cloth-dyeing and textile center. Those stylish Provençal fabrics and patterns you see for sale everywhere were made possible by this river.

• *Double back to the church, turn left under the arcade, then find the small stream just past the TI. Breakaway streams like this run under the town like subways run under Paris. Take a right on the first street after the stream; it leads under a long arch (along rue J. J. Rousseau). Follow this straight, and veer slightly right at place F. Buisson and walk to the main river, then follow it left. You'll come to...*

THE LUBERON

Le Bassin: Literally translated as a "pond," this is where the Sorgue River crashes into the town and separates into many branches. Track as many branches as you can see (Frank Provost hides a big one), and then find the round lookout point for the best perspective (carefully placed lights make this a beautiful sight after dark). Fishing was the town's main industry until the waterwheels took over. In the 1300s, local fishermen provided the pope with his fresh-fish quota. They trapped them in nets and speared them while standing on skinny, flat-bottomed boats. Several streets are named after the fish they caught—including rue de l'Aiguille ("Eel Street") and rue des Ecrevisses ("Crayfish Street").

The sound of the rushing water reminds us of the power that rivers can generate. With its source (a spring) a mere five miles away, the Sorgue River never floods and has a constant flow and temperature in all seasons. Despite its exposed (flat) location, Isle-sur-la-Sorgue prospered in the Middle Ages, thanks to the natural protection this river provided. Walls with big moats once ran along the river, but they were destroyed during the French Revolution.

• *Cross the busy roundabout, and walk to the neon orange* **Delices de Luberon** *store. Find the small tasting table with 12 scrumptious tapenades. Walk behind the store to find the river and take a refreshing...*

Riverfront Stroll: Follow the main river upstream, along the bike/pedestrian lane, as far as you like. The little road meanders about a mile, following the serene course of the river, past waterfront homes and beneath swaying trees. It ends at the Hôtel le Pescador and a riverfront café. The wide and shallow Partage des Eaux, where the water divides before entering Isle-sur-la-Sorgue, is perfect for a cool swim on a hot day.

Sights in Isle-sur-la-Sorgue

▲▲**Market Days**—The town erupts into a carnival-like market frenzy each Sunday and Thursday, with hardy crafts and local produce. The Sunday market is astounding and famous for its antiques; the Thursday market is more intimate (see market tips in the Shopping chapter). Find a table across from the church at the Café de France and enjoy the scene.

Antique Toy and Doll Museum (Musée du Jouet et de la Poupée Ancienne)—The town's lone sight is a fun and funky toy museum with more than 300 dolls displayed in three small rooms (€3.50, kids-€1.50; July–Sept Mon–Sat 10:30–18:30, Sun 11:00–18:00; Oct–June Tue–Fri 13:00–18:00, Sat–Sun 11:00–17:00, closed Mon; call ahead to reconfirm opening times, 26 rue Carnot, mobile 06 09 10 32 66).

Near Isle-sur-la-Sorgue

Fontaine-de-Vaucluse—You'll read and hear a lot about this overrun village, impressively located at the source of the Sorgue River, where the medieval Italian poet Petrarch mourned for his love, Laura. The river seems to magically appear from nowhere (the actual source is a murky, green waterhole) and flows through the town past a lineup of cafés, souvenir shops, and wall-to-river tourists. The setting is beautiful—with cliffs jutting to the sky and a ruined castle above—but the trip is worth it only if the spring is flowing. *Sans* flowing spring, this is the most overrated sight in France. Ask your hotelier if the spring is active, and arrive early or late to avoid crowds. It's a good bike ride here from Isle-sur-la-Sorgue (about four miles).

Arriving by car, you'll pay to park (about €3), and then walk about 20 minutes along the sparkling river to *la source* (the spring), located in a cave at the base of the cliff. (It's an uphill hike for the last part.) The spring itself is the very definition of anticlimactic, unless it's surging. At those times, it's among the most prolific water producers in the world, with a depth no one has yet been able to determine.

The path to the spring is lined with distractions. The only stops worth your time are the riverfront cafés—**Philip's** offers the best seats—and the **Moulin à Papier,** a reproduction of a 17th-century paper mill. Here you'll see the value of harnessing the river's power. In the mill, a 22-foot-diameter paddle wheel turns five times a minute, driving hammers that pound paper for up to 36 hours (free, daily 9:00–19:00). As you watch the hammers pound away, imagine Isle-sur-la-Sorgue's waterwheels and the industries they once powered. The shop inside sells paper in every size.

Canoe Trips on the Sorgue—A better reason to travel to Fontaine-de-Vaucluse is to canoe down the river. A guide escorts small groups in canoes, starting in Fontaine-de-Vaucluse and ending in Isle-sur-la-Sorgue; you'll return to Fontaine-de-Vaucluse by shuttle bus (call for departure times; a shuttle bus will pick you up in Isle-sur-la-Sorgue). If you're *really* on vacation, take this five-mile, two-hour trip. **Kayaks Verts** is a family operation run by happy-go-lucky Michel, who speaks "small English" (€19/person, tel. 04 90 20 35 44).

Biking—Isle-sur-la-Sorgue is ideally situated for short biking forays into the mostly level terrain. Pick up a biking itinerary at the TI. These towns make easy biking destinations from Isle-sur-la-Sorgue: Velleron (5 miles north, flat, a tiny version of Isle-sur-la-Sorgue with waterwheels, fountains, and an evening farmer's market Mon–Sat 18:00–20:00); Lagnes (3 miles east, a pretty and well-restored hill town with views from its ruined château); and

THE LUBERON

Fontaine-de-Vaucluse (5 miles northeast, gently uphill, described on previous page). Allow 30 miles and many hills for the round-trip ride to Roussillon. (A bike-rental company in Isle-sur-la-Sorgue is listed on page 196.)

Sleeping in Isle-sur-la-Sorgue

Pickings are slim for good sleeps in Isle-sur-la-Sorgue, though the few I've listed provide solid values.

$$$ La Prévôté* has the town's highest-priced digs. Its five meticulously decorated rooms—located above a classy restaurant—are decorated in earth tones, with high ceilings, a few exposed beams, and beautiful furnishings. Helpful Séverine manages the hotel while chef-hubby Jean-Marie controls the kitchen (standard Db-€135, larger Db-€160, suite Db-€180, no air-con or elevator, Internet access and Wi-Fi, rooftop deck with Jacuzzi, no parking, one block from the church at 4 rue J. J. Rousseau, tel. & fax 04 90 38 57 29, www.la-prevote.fr, contact@la-prevote.fr).

$$ Hôtel les Névons, two blocks from the center (behind the post office), is concrete motel–modern outside, but a fair value within. The staff is eager to please, and you have two wings to choose from: the new wing, with cavernous (by local standards) and well-appointed rooms; or the old wing, with humble, but cheaper rooms. There are several family suites and a roof deck with 360-degree views around a small pool (old wing—Db-€61; new wing—huge Db-€70, Tb-€90, Qb-€95; good but pricey breakfast, air-con, Internet access, Wi-Fi in lobby, easy parking, 205 chemin des Névons, push and hold the gate button a bit on entry, tel. 04 90 20 72 00, fax 04 90 20 56 20, www.hotel-les-nevons.com, info @hotel-les-nevons.com).

$$ Le Pont des Aubes Chambres has two huggable rooms in an old green-shuttered farmhouse right on the river a mile from town. Borrow a bike or a canoe. From here you can cross a tiny bridge and walk 15 minutes along the river into Isle-sur-la-Sorgue, or cross the street to the recommended L'Ousteau de l'Isle restaurant. Charming Martine speaks English, while husband Patrice speaks smiles (Db-€75, Tb-€90, 1-room apartments-€380–450/week, cash only, a mile from town toward Apt, next to Pain d'Antan Boulangerie at 189 route d'Apt, tel. & fax 04 90 38 13 75, http: //perso.wanadoo.fr/lepontdesaubes, patriceaubert@wanadoo.fr).

$ Hôtel les Terrasses du Bassin rents eight spotless rooms with designer touches over a good restaurant on Le Bassin, where the river waters separate before running through town. Several rooms look out over Le Bassin, a few have queen-size beds, and there's some traffic noise (Db-€64, extra bed-€10, air-con, Wi-Fi, 2 avenue Charles de Gaulle, tel. 04 90 38 03 16, fax 04 90 38 65

Sleep Code

(€1 = about $1.25, country code: 33)
S = Single, **D** = Double/Twin, **T** = Triple, **Q** = Quad, **b** = bathroom, **s** = shower only, * = French hotel rating system (0-4 stars). Unless otherwise noted, credit cards are accepted and English is spoken.

To help you sort easily through these listings, I've divided the rooms into three categories based on the price for a standard double room with bath:

$$$ Higher Priced—Most rooms €90 or more.
$$ Moderately Priced—Most rooms between €60-90.
$ Lower Priced—Most rooms €60 or less.

Prices can change without notice; verify the hotel's current rates online or by email. For other updates, see www .ricksteves.com/update.

61, www.lesterrassesdubassin.com, corinne@lesterrassesdubassin .com).

Near Isle-sur-la-Sorgue

$$$ Chambres Sous l'Olivier, located five minutes east of Isle-sur-la-Sorgue, is well-situated for exploring the hill towns of the Luberon and Isle-sur-la-Sorgue. Its six lovely rooms are housed in a massive 150-year-old farmhouse with lounges that you and your entire soccer team could spread out in. Julien and Carole will take care of your every need, and will cook you a full-blown dinner with wine for €30 per person (Db-€90–135, Tb-€120, two-room Tb-€180, three-room suite for up to six people-€220, prices include breakfast; credit cards not accepted—pay with cash, euro travelers checks, or bank transfer; pool; route d'Apt, tel. 04 90 20 33 90, www.chambresdhotesprovence.com, souslolivier@orange .fr). It's below Isle-sur-la-Sorgue, about 25 minutes from Avignon toward Apt on D-900 (near Petit Palais—don't go to Lagnes by mistake). Look for signs 200 yards after the big sign to *le Mas du Grand Jonquier,* on the right.

Eating in Isle-sur-la-Sorgue

Inexpensive restaurants are easy to find in Isle-sur-la-Sorgue, but consistent quality is another story. The restaurants I list offer good value, but none of them is really "cheap." For inexpensive meals, troll the riverside cafés for today's catch. Dining on the river is a unique experience in this arid land famous for its hill towns, and shopping for the perfect table is half the fun. Riverside picnics work well here (the Fromenterie bakery, listed below, stocks mouthwatering quiche and more).

Begin your dinner with a glass of wine at the cozy **Le Caveau de la Tour de l'Isle** (the wine bar hides in the rear, Tue–Sun 9:30–12:30 & 15:30–20:00, closed Mon, 12 rue de la République, tel. 04 90 20 70 25).

Les Terrasses du Bassin has moderate prices, good choices, and a cool riverfront location (terrace dining available). The hardworking owners are dedicated to providing a good value and welcoming service. Come for a full meal or just a *plat* (€10 lunch salads and starters, €16 dinner *plats*, €24–34 dinner *menu*, closed Tue–Wed Oct–May, 2 avenue Charles de Gaulle, tel. 04 90 38 03 16).

La Prévôté is a place to really do it up. Its dining room is covered in wood beams, the outdoor patio is peaceful, and the ambience is country-classy but not stuffy. A branch of the Sorgue runs under the restaurant, visible through glass windows (*menus* from €50, save room for amazing cheese platter, closed Tue–Wed, 4 rue J. J. Rousseau, on narrow street that runs along left side of church as you face it, tel. 04 90 38 57 29).

L'Ousteau de l'Isle, a mile from the town center, dishes up regional cuisine with a modern twist and a friendly welcome. Skip the modern interior and ask for a table *sur la terrasse* (dinner *menus* from €27, lunch *menu* for €17, closed Tue–Wed, 147 chemin de Bosquet, tel. 04 90 20 81 36). From Isle-sur-la-Sorgue's center, follow signs toward *Apt*, and turn right at Pain d'Antan Boulangerie; or walk 20 minutes along the river and cross the small bridge to chemin de Bosquet.

The **Fromenterie** bakery next to the post office (PTT) sells decadent quiche, monster sandwiches, desserts, wine, and other drinks—in other words, everything you need to picnic (open daily until 20:00).

The Heart of the Luberon

A 15-minute drive east of Isle-sur-la-Sorgue brings you to this protected area, where canyons and ridgelines rule, and land developers take a back seat. Still-proud hill towns guard access to winsome valleys, while carefully managed vineyards (producing inexpensive wines) play hopscotch with cherry groves, lavender fields, and cypress trees.

Peter Mayle's *A Year in Provence* nudged tourism in this area into overdrive. A visit to Mayle's quintessential Provence includes many of the popular villages and sights described in this chapter. While the hill towns can be seen as subtly different variations on the same theme, each has a distinct character. Look for differences: the color of shutters, the pattern of stones, the way flowers are planted, or the number of tourist boutiques. Every village has something to offer—it's up to you to discover and celebrate it.

Stay in or near Roussillon. By village standards, Roussillon is always lively, and it struggles to manage its popularity. When restaurant-hunting, read descriptions of the villages in this chapter—many good finds are embedded in the countryside. For aerial views high above this charmed land, consider a hot-air balloon trip (see page 210).

Planning Your Time

With a car and one full day, I'd linger in Roussillon in the morning, visit the St. Julien Bridge, then have lunch nearby in Lacoste or Bonnieux. After lunch, continue the joyride past Ménerbes to Oppède-le-Vieux, then return through Coustellet and Gordes. With a second full day, I'd start by climbing the Fort de Buoux, then lunch nearby. After lunch, continue to Saignon and Viens, then loop back via Le Colorado Provençal and St-Saturnin-lès-Apt.

I've described sights at each stop listed above, but you'll need to be selective—you can't see them all. Read through your options and choose the ones that appeal most. Slow down and get to know a few places well, rather than dashing between every stop you can cram in. The best sight is the dreamy landscape between the villages.

Roussillon

With all the trendy charm of Santa Fe on a hilltop, photogenic Roussillon requires serious camera and café time (and €3 for parking). Roussillon has been a protected village since 1943 and has benefited from a complete absence of modern development. An enormous deposit of ochre gives the earth and its buildings that distinctive red color and provided this village with its economic base until shortly after World War II. This place is popular; it's best to visit early or late in the day.

Roussillon

1. Le Clos de la Glycine Hôtel
2. Hôtel Rêves d'Ocres
3. To Madame Cherel,
   Le Clos des Cigales Chambres &
   Hôtel Les Sables d'Ocre
4. Le Bistrot de Roussillon,
   Café Couleur & Le Castrum Rest.
5. Librairie du Luberon
   (Bookshop, Rest. & Internet)
6. Orientation Plaque,
   View & Start of Walk

OCHRE CLIFFS

P (Ocres)

POSTE AVE. BURLIERE

To 3,
OCHRE CONSERVATORY,
D-900 TO
BONNIEUX &
D-104 TO
GOULT & APT

Post P (Pasquier)
WC

TO
ST-SATURNIN-LES-APT
& RUSTREL
VIA D-227

RUE DE L'ARCADE

(Fontaine) P

PLACE MATHIEU

BELL TOWER
ST. MICHEL

PLACE MAIRIE

RUE RONDE

RUE DES BOURGADES

TO MURS,
JOUCAS &
GORDES
VIA D-2

D-2

MONT ROUGE

(St. Michel) P

WC

RUE DE LA PORTE HEUREUSE

WC

P (Sablons)

P PARKING
↙ VIEW
▥▥ STEPPED STREETS

N

2

D-169

DCH

TO
GORDES & JOUCAS

Orientation to Roussillon

Roussillon sits atop Mont Rouge (Red Mountain) at about 1,000 feet above sea level, and requires some uphill walking to reach. Exposed ochre cliffs form the village's southern limit.

Tourist Information

THE LUBERON

The little TI is in the center, across from the David restaurant. If in need of accommodations, leaf through their good binders describing area hotels and *chambres d'hôte*. Walkers should get info on trails from Roussillon to nearby villages (TI open April–Oct Mon–Sat

9:30–12:00 & 13:30–18:00, closed Sun except in summer; Nov–March Mon–Sat 14:00–17:30, closed Sun; tel. 04 90 05 60 25).

Arrival in Roussillon

Parking lots are available at every entry to the village. The closest two lots are on the northern edge (Parking Sablons, by the recommended Hôtel Rêves d'Ocres) and on the southern flank, closer to the ochre cliffs (Parking Pasquier). If you approach from Gordes or Joucas, you'll park at Sablons. If you're coming from D-900 and the south, you'll land at Pasquier (but don't park there on Wednesday night, because Thursday is Roussillon's market day). Leave nothing valuable showing in your car.

Helpful Hints

An ATM is next to the TI. Internet access and a modest selection of English books is available at the delightful **Librairie du Luberon** on the main square (daily 10:00–18:00, tel. 04 90 71 55 72; its restaurant is described later, under "Eating in Roussillon").

Self-Guided Walk

Welcome to Roussillon

This quick walk will take you through Roussillon's village to its ochre cliffs.

• *To begin the walk, climb a few minutes from either parking lot (passing the Hollywood set–like square under the bell tower and the church) to the summit of...*

▲The Village

Find the orientation plaque and the dramatic viewpoint, often complete with a howling mistral. During the Middle Ages, a castle stood where you are, on the top of Red Mountain (Mont Rouge), and watched over the village below. Though nothing remains of the castle today, the strategic advantage of this site is clear. Count how many villages you can identify, and then notice how little sprawl there is in the valley below. Because the Luberon

is a natural reserve (Parc Naturel Régional du Luberon), development is strictly controlled.

A short stroll down leads to the church. Duck into the pretty 11th-century Church of St. Michel, and appreciate the natural air-conditioning and the well-worn center aisle. The white interior tells you that the stone

THE LUBERON

Boules (Pétanque)

The game of *boules*—also called *pétanque*—is the horseshoes of Provence and the Riviera. It's played in every village, almost exclusively by men, on level dirt areas kept specifically for this

purpose. It was invented here in the early 1900s, and today every French boy grows up playing *boules* with Papa and *Ton-Ton* (Uncle) Jean. It's a social-yet-serious sport, and endlessly entertaining to watch—even more so if you understand the rules.

Boules is played with heavy metal balls (*boules,* about the size of baseballs) and a small wooden target ball (*le cochonnet,* about the size of a table tennis ball). Whoever gets his *boule* closest to the *cochonnet* wins. It's most commonly played in teams of two, though individual competition and teams of three are not uncommon. (There are *boules* leagues and professional players who make little money but are national celebrities.) Most teams have two specialists, a *pointeur* and a *tireur.* The *pointeur* goes first and tries to lob his balls as close to the target as he can. The *tireur's* job is to blast away opponents' *boules.*

Here's the play-by-play: Each player gets three *boules.* A coin toss determines which team goes first. The starting team scratches a small circle in the dirt, in which players must stand (with both feet on the ground) when launching their *boules.* Next, the starting team tosses the *cochonnet* (about 6–10 yards)—that's the target. The *boule* must be tossed underhand, and can be rolled, thrown sky-high, or rocketed at its target. Most lob it like a slow pitch in softball, with lots of backspin. The starting team's *pointeur* shoots, then the other team's *pointeur* shoots until he gets closer. Once the second team lands a *boule* closer, the first team is back up. If the opposing team's *boule* is very near the *cochonnet,* the *tireur* will likely attempt to knock it away. If the team decides that they can lob one in closer, the *pointeur* shoots.

Once all *boules* have been launched, the tally is taken. This is where it gets tense, as the difference in distance often comes down to millimeters. Faces are drawn, lips are pursed, and eyes are squinted as teams try to sort through the who's-closer process. I've seen all kinds of measuring devices, from shoes to belts to tape measures. The team with the ball closest to the target receives one point, and the teams keep going until someone gets 13 points.

came from elsewhere, and the WWI memorial plaque over the side door suggests a village devastated by the war (over 40 died from little Roussillon).

On leaving the church, look across the way to the derelict building, a reminder of Roussillon's humble roots. After World War II, when the demand for ochre faded, this became a dusty, poor village. Adding to the town's economic woes, many residents fled for an easier life below, with level streets and modern conveniences. Abandoned buildings like this presented a serious problem (common throughout France)...until the tourists discovered Roussillon, and people began reinvesting in the village. This building is still looking for a buyer.

• *Continue down to the village.*

Notice the clamped-iron beams that shore up old walls. Examine the different hues of yellow and orange. These lime-finished exteriors, called *chaux* (literally, "limes"), need to be redone about every 10 years. Locals choose their exact color...but in this town of ochre, it's never white. The church tower that you walk under once marked the entrance to the fortified town. Just before dropping down to the square, turn right and find the gigantic 150-year-old grapevine that decorates Restaurant la Treille. This is what you get when you don't prune.

Linger over *un café,* or—if it's later in the day—*un pastis,* in what must be the most picturesque village square in Provence (place de la Mairie). Watch the stream of shoppers. Is anyone playing *boules* at the opposite end? You could paint the entire town without ever leaving the red-and-orange corner of your palette. Many do. While Roussillon receives its share of day-trippers, mornings and evenings are romantically peaceful on this square. The Librairie du Luberon bookshop on the square's corner deserves a visit (nice top-floor restaurant).

• *With the cafés on your right, drop downhill past the lineup of shops and turn right past the TI to find the parking lot just beyond. Animals grazed here for centuries. It was later turned into a school playground. When tourists outnumbered students, it became a parking lot. Walk past the parking lot with the cliffs on your left and find the...*

▲▲Ochre Cliffs

Roussillon was Europe's capital for ochre production until World War II. A stroll to the south end of town, beyond the upper parking lot, shows you why: Roussillon sits on the world's largest known

THE LUBERON

ochre deposit. A radiant orange path leads through the richly colored ochre canyon, explaining the hue of this village (€2.50, ask about combo-tickets with the Ochre Conservatory—described below; daily 9:00–17:00, until 19:00 in summer; beware—light-colored clothing and orange powder don't mix).

Ochre is made of iron oxide and clay. When combined with sand, it creates the yellowish-red pigments you see in the buildings around you. Although ochre is also produced in the US and Italy, the quality of France's ochre is considered *le best*.

The value of Roussillon's ochre cliffs was known even in Roman times. Once excavated, the clay ochre was rinsed with water to separate it from sand, then bricks of the stuff were dried and baked for deeper hues. The procedure for extracting the ochre did not change much over 2,000 years, until ochre mining became industrialized in the late 1700s. Used primarily for wallpaper and linoleum, ochre use reached its zenith just before World War II. (After that, cheaper substitutes took over.)

Sights near Roussillon

Ochre Conservatory (Conservatoire des Ocres et Pigments Appliqués)—If the ochre cliffs inspire you, visit this colorful, interesting exposition, about a half-mile below Roussillon toward Apt on D-104. Fifty-minute tours of a reconstructed ochre factory explain how ochre is converted from an ore to a pigment, from extraction to shipping (€6, €8.50 combo-ticket with ochre cliffs—call ahead for tour times, conservatory open daily 9:00–13:00 & 14:00–18:00, July–Aug 9:00–19:00; tours are in French, but most guides will explain the basics in English; short English handout available, great gift shop, tel. 04 90 05 66 69, www.okhra.com).

Hot-Air Balloon Flight—Ply the calm morning air above the Luberon in a hot-air balloon. The Montgolfières–Luberon outfit has two flight options: the Four-Star Flight (€255, 1.5 hours in balloon, allow 3 hours total, includes picnic and champagne) and the economy-class Tourist Flight (€160, 45 minutes, includes glass of bubbly). For either flight, meet on the main road below Joucas at 7:00 (reserve a few days ahead, maximum 12 passengers, tel. 04 90 05 76 77, fax 04 90 05 74 39, www.montgolfiere-luberon.com).

Goult—Bigger than its sister hill towns, this surprisingly quiet village seems content to be away from the tourist path. Wander up the hill to the panoramic view and windmill, and consider its many good restaurants—where you won't have to compete with tourists for a table. **La Bartavelle** is the best in town and has reasonable prices. When it's warm, tables spill along a quiet alley. Reservations several days in advance are essential (*menus* from €40, closed Tue–Wed, rue du Cheval Blanc, tel. 04 90 72 33 72).

Sleeping in Roussillon

(€1 = about $1.25, country code: 33)

The TI posts a list of hotels and *chambres d'hôte*. Parking is free if you sleep in Roussillon—ask your hotelier where to park. The village offers three good-value accommodations—conveniently, one for each price range.

$$$ Le Clos de la Glycine* provides Roussillon's plushest accommodations, with nine gorgeous rooms located dead-center in the village (Db-€140–160, big Db-€180, loft suite with deck and view-€275, Wi-Fi, located at the refined restaurant David—so they prefer you pay for half-pension, across from the TI on place de la Poste, tel. 04 90 05 60 13, fax 04 90 05 75 80, www.luberon-hotel.com, le.clos.de.la.glycine@wanadoo.fr).

$$ Hôtel Rêves d'Ocres is a solid two-star value, run by eager-to-help Sandrine and Yvan. It's ochre-colored, warm, and comfortable, with 16 mostly spacious and tastefully designed rooms—some with musty bathrooms. Eight smaller rooms have view terraces, but are *très* cozy. There's also a lovely lounge where you can stretch out (Sb-€60, Db without balcony-€76, Db with balcony-€80, Tb-€95, Qb-€115, meek air-con, Internet access, Wi-Fi, route de Gordes, tel. 04 90 05 60 50, fax 04 90 05 79 74, www.hotel-revesdocres.com, hotelrevesdocres@wanadoo.fr). Coming from Gordes and Joucas, it's the first building you pass in Roussillon.

$ Madame Cherel rents ramshackle rooms that are barely this side of a youth hostel. A shared view terrace and good reading materials are available, and the beds have firm mattresses (D-€45–49, family suite available, includes breakfast, cash only, 3 blocks from upper parking lot, between the gas station and school, La Burlière, tel. 04 90 05 71 71, mulhanc@hotmail.com). Chatty and sincere Cherel speaks English and is a wealth of regional travel tips.

Near Roussillon

The next two listings are for drivers only, and are most easily found by turning north off D-900 at the *Roussillon/Les Huguets* sign. It's the second turn-off to Roussillon coming from Avignon. Joucas, St-Saturnin-lès-Apt, and Lacoste (all described later in this chapter) also have good beds near Roussillon.

$$$ Le Clos des Cigales, run by friendly Philippe, has five blue-shuttered, stylish bungalows. Two are doubles, three are two-room suites with tiny kitchenettes, and all have private patios facing a big pool. When you arrive, you'll understand the name—the cacophony from the *cigales* (cicadas) is deafening (Db-€85–115, Tb-€115, Qb-€135, includes breakfast, Wi-Fi, table tennis,

THE LUBERON

hammock, 5 minutes from Roussillon toward Goult on D-104, tel. & fax 04 90 05 73 72, www.leclosdescigales.com, philippe.lherbeil @wanadoo.fr).

$$ Hôtel les Sables d'Ocre** is a modern resort kind of place, with 22 motelesque rooms, a big pool, the greenest grass around, air-conditioning, and fair rates (Db-€70, spring for the Db with garden balcony-€84, Tb loft-€100–120, a half-mile after leaving Roussillon toward Apt at intersection of D-108 and D-104, tel. 04 90 05 55 55, fax 04 90 05 55 50, www.roussillon-hotel.com, sables docre@free.fr).

Eating in Roussillon

Choose ambience over cuisine if dining in Roussillon, and enjoy any of the eateries on the main square. It's a festive place, where children twirl while parents dine, and dogs and cats look longingly for leftovers. Restaurants change with the mistral here—what's good one year disappoints the next. Consider my suggestions and go with what looks best (or look over my recommendations in other Luberon villages). Look also at the hotels listed in Joucas (see page 214)—all offer quality cuisine at fair prices, just a few minutes' drive from Roussillon. The first three places listed next share the same square and offer similar values. One should always be open.

At **Le Bistrot de Roussillon,** Johan offers the most consistent value on the square, with excellent salads (try the *salad du bistrot*) and *plats* for the right price. There's a breezy terrace in back and a comfy interior (€15 for a filling salad and dessert, €13 *plats*, daily, tel. 04 90 05 74 45).

Café Couleur and **Le Castrum** flank Le Bistrot de Roussillon, offering similar atmosphere and prices, but less-steady quality.

Librairie du Luberon, opposite the above-listed restaurants on the square, hides a slick top-floor restaurant/*salon de thé* above its bookstore. Have lunch or a drink outside on the splendid terrace, or inside surrounded by books—for a price (€19 *plats*, restaurant closed Mon).

Near Roussillon, in Le Chêne

The following is just one of many excellent eateries that lie a short drive from Roussillon; for others, don't miss the "Luberon Restaurants that Justify the Trip" sidebar.

La Petite Ecole is where locals go for fine cuisine at affordable prices. The perfect team—host Denis and chef Sophie—enthusiastically welcome travelers and locals into their nine-table restaurant (more tables outside). It's in an old schoolhouse with an unimpressive roadside location (but you won't care). This is a real experience—the food is fresh and very Provençal. Arrive when

Luberon Restaurants that Justify the Trip

Many of the restaurants in the countryside around Roussillon are worth a detour. Use the list below as a quick reference, then flip to the full descriptions (page numbers noted) of those that sound most appealing. All of these are within a 20-minute drive from Roussillon. Remember that Isle-sur-la-Sorgue is a manageable 30-minute drive from Roussillon.

Ideal for Dinner

La Petite Ecole, in a converted schoolhouse in Le Chêne, is popular with locals for its reasonably priced Provençal cuisine (closed Tue–Wed; see page 212).

Hôtel des Voyageurs, located in St-Saturnin-lès-Apt, is another local favorite (closed all day Wed and Thu for lunch, 15-minute drive from Roussillon; see page 225).

L'Auberge de la Loube is the ultimate country/Provençal experience. But, because it makes for a long after-dinner drive, many find it's best for lunch (closed Sun eve and all day Mon and Thu; see page 228).

Hostellerie des Commandeurs is inexpensive, traditional, friendly, and a solid value that's good for families (closed Wed, in Joucas—a 5-minute drive from Roussillon; see page 214).

Le Fournil, in Bonnieux, has good food and a photogenic terrace (closed for dinner Mon, closed for lunch Mon–Tue and Sat; see page 220).

Le Bistrot de Roussillon, on the village square with a terrace out back, has excellent salads and *plats* priced just right (open daily; see page 212).

Best Places to Lunch

Le Fournil in Bonnieux (with a fair-value lunch *menu*), **Le Bistrot de Roussillon,** and **L'Auberge de la Loube** are all listed for dinner, above—but are also top lunch stops. Here are some others to consider:

Bar/Restaurant de France, in Lacoste, is an easygoing eatery with sensational view tables and good *plats,* omelets, and salads (daily, lunch only off-season; see page 222).

L'Auberge des Seguins is a corner of paradise awaiting those who survive the climb to Fort de Buoux (daily; see page 228).

Auberge du Presbytère, in the village of Saignon, offers a slow, tasty lunch by the fountain on one of Provence's most handsome squares (closed Wed; see page 226).

Le Petit Jardin Café, in remote Viens, offers an unpretentious lunch or dinner stop, with cozy interior tables, a garden terrace, and reasonable prices (closed Wed; see page 226).

they open at 19:30 to score a table, or reserve ahead. There's an outdoor terrace, but I like the inside scene (€21 two-course *menus*, €29 three-course *menus*, cheaper at lunch, closed Sun–Mon, below Roussillon on D-900 in Le Chêne, tel. 04 32 52 16 41).

Joucas

This understated, quiet, and largely overlooked village slumbers below the Gordes buzz. Vertical stone lanes with carefully arranged flowers and well-restored homes play host to aspiring Claude Monets and a smattering of locals. There's not much to do or see here, except eat, sleep, and just be. Joucas has one tiny grocery, a view café, one pharmacy, a good kids' play area, and one good-value accommodation option. Sleep here for a central location and utter  silence. For views, walk past the little fountain in the center and up the steep lanes as high as you want.

Several **hiking** trails leave from Joucas. Gordes and Roussillon are each three miles away, uphill. Even better, hikers can take the three-mile hike to the attractive village of Murs, with several cafés/restaurants, though it's easier in the other direction (yellow signs point the way from the top of the village). You don't have to go far to enjoy the natural beauty on this trail.

Sleeping and Eating in Joucas

$$ Hostellerie des Commandeurs**, run by soft Sophie, has modern, comfortable, and clean rooms in the village of Joucas. It's kid-friendly, with a big pool and a sports field/play area next door. Ask for a south-facing room *(coté sud)* for the best views, or a north-facing room *(coté nord)* if it's hot. All rooms have showers (Db-€64–68, extra bed-€16, small fridges, above park at village entrance, tel. 04 90 05 78 01, fax 04 90 05 74 47, www.les commandeurs.com, hostellerie@lescommandeurs.com). The simple restaurant offers tasty cuisine at fair prices (three-course *menus* from €20, succulent lamb, memorable crème brûlée with lavender, restaurant closed Wed).

Near Joucas
$$$ La Ferme de la Huppe*** has a Gordes address, but it's closer, physically and spiritually, to Joucas. This small farmhouse-elegant hacienda makes an excellent mini-splurge. Ten low-slung rooms

gather on two levels behind the stylish pool. The decor is tasteful, understated, and rustic (small Db-€140, bigger Db-€170, much bigger Db-€200, includes good breakfast, small fridges, air-con, Wi-Fi; between Joucas and Gordes on D-156 road to Goult, just off D-2; tel. 04 90 72 12 25, fax 04 90 72 25 39, www.laferme delahuppe.com, info@lafermedelahuppe.com). Dine poolside or in the smart dining room (€46 three-course *menu* or €62 six-course tasting *menu*).

$$$ **Le Mas du Loriot** is another worthwhile almost-in-Joucas value. Gentle owners Alain and Christine have carved the ideal escape out of an olive grove, with eight soothing rooms, private terraces, a generous pool, and home-cooked dinners—all at fair prices and with a view to remember (Db-€105–135, extra bed-€20, €32 four-course dinners available four nights a week—when half-pension is a smart idea, Internet access, on D-102 between Joucas and Murs, tel. 04 90 72 62 62, Wi-Fi, fax 04 90 72 62 54, www.masduloriot.com, hotel@masduloriot.com).

More Luberon Towns

Le Luberon is packed with appealing villages and beautiful scenery, but it has only a handful of must-see sights. I've grouped them by area to make your sightseeing planning easier (see the Luberon map at the beginning of this chapter). Busy D-900 slices like an arrow through the heart of the Luberon, dividing the region in half. The more popular and visited section lies above D-900 (with Roussillon and Gordes), while the villages to the south seem a bit less trampled.

The busiest sights are in and near Gordes; I've listed those first, to encourage you to avoid afternoon crowds. Beyond that, you're free to connect the stops however you please. Rambling the Luberon's spaghetti network of small roads is a joy, and getting lost comes with the territory—go with it. None of the sights listed below is a must-see, but all are close to each other. Pick up a good map (Michelin maps #332 and #527 work for me).

THE LUBERON

Gordes and Nearby Sights

Gordes

In the 1960s, Gordes was a virtual ghost town of derelict buildings. But now it's thoroughly renovated and filled with people who live in a world without calluses. Many Parisian big shots and wealthy

foreigners have purchased and restored older homes here, putting property values out of sight for locals—and creating gridlock and parking headaches (come early).

Ponder a region that in the last 35 years has experienced such a dramatic change. Post-World War II, the Luberon was mired in poverty. By 1970, the Luberon had recovered but was still unknown to most travelers. Locals led simple lives and had few ambitions. Then came the theater festival in Avignon, bringing directors who wanted to re-create perfect Provençal villages on film. Parisians, Swiss, Brits, and a few Americans followed, willing to pay any price for their place in the Provençal sun. Property taxes increased—as did the cost of *une bière* at the corner café—and all too soon, villagers found themselves with few affordable options.

The village's setting is striking. As you approach Gordes, make a hard right at the impressive view of the place (you'll find some parking along the small road). Beyond here, the village has little of interest, except its many boutiques and its Tuesday market (which ends at 13:00). The town's 11th-century castle houses a mildly interesting collection of contemporary art.

There are two sights near Gordes—the Abbey Notre-Dame de Sénanque and the Village des Bories—both well-marked from Gordes and described below.

Near Gordes

Abbey Notre-Dame de Sénanque—

This still-functioning and beautifully situated Cistercian abbey was built in 1148 as a back-to-basics reaction to the excesses of Benedictine abbeys. The Cistercians strove to be separate from the world and to recapture the simplicity, solitude, and poverty of the early Church. To succeed required industrious self-sufficiency—a skill these monks excelled at.

THE LUBERON

Their movement spread and colonized Europe with a new form of Christianity. By 1200 there were more than 500 such monasteries and abbeys in Europe.

The abbey is best appreciated from the outside, and is worth the trip for its splendid and remote setting alone. Come early or late, stop at a pullout for a bird's-eye view as you descend, then wander the abbey's perimeter with fewer tourists. The abbey church (Eglise Abbatiale) is open and highlights the utter simplicity sought by these monks. The beautiful bookshop is worth a look as well (Cistercians know how to turn a profit). In late June through much of July, the lavender fields that surround the abbey make for breathtaking pictures and draw loads of visitors, making it more important to arrive early or late.

The abbey itself can only be visited on a 50-minute, French-only tour with an English handout. The interior, which doesn't

measure up to the abbey's spectacular setting, is not worth it for most people. The tour covers Sénanque's church, the small cloisters, the refectory, and a *chauffoir*, a small heated room where monks could copy books year-round (€7, includes tour—about 6/day Mon–Sat; Mon–Sat 10:00–12:00 & 13:30–18:00, Sun 14:00–18:00, tel. 04 90 72 05 72, www.senanque.fr). You can also attend Mass (usually Sun at 10:00, Mon at 8:30, Tue–Sat at 12:00, check website or call to confirm). A small monastic community still resides here. For more on monasteries, see the "Medieval Monasteries" sidebar, later.

If your next destination is near Roussillon, Bonnieux, or Apt, leave the abbey opposite the way you arrived, following signs to *Gordes*, then *Roussillon*, then follow *Murs* and *Joucas*...and enjoy the ride.

Village des Bories—A lengthy stone-bordered dirt road sets the mood for this mildly entertaining open-air museum of stone huts *(bories)*. The vertical stones you see on the walls as you approach the site were used as counterweights to keep these walls, built without mortar, intact. The "village" you tour is made up of dry-laid stone structures, proving that there has always been more stone than wood in this rugged region. Stone villages like this predated the Romans—some say by 2,000 years. This one was inhabited for 200 years (from about 1600 to 1800). *Bories* can still be seen in fields throughout the Luberon; most are now used to store tools or hay. A look around these hills confirms the supply of building materials: The trees are small and gnarled (not good for construction), but white stone grows everywhere.

The Village des Bories is composed of five "hamlets." You'll duck into several homes and see animal pens, a community oven, and more (identified in English). Study the "beehive" stone-laying method and imagine the time it took to construct. The villagers had no scaffolds or support arches—just hammers and patience (€6, buy €4 booklet of English translations to learn more, daily June–Sept 9:00–20:00, Oct–May 9:00–17:30).

Bouillon Olive Mill and Museum of Glass (Moulin des Bouillons and Musée de l'Histoire du Verre)—This fun museum park is a true Back Door experience. Find an hour and fork it over to two charming women who will explain to you (in English) the mill and the museum. Start with Carole at the olive mill, which has been in use for more than 2,000 years. You'll learn about this ancient practice, including how olive oil and its products are made. The Roman remains are nice, but they take a back seat to the massive 400-year-old oak olive press.

Then wander with the chickens through a small park and modern sculpture garden to the solar-paneled, bunker-like Museum of Glass. Here Béatrice will teach you about the historic importance of glass from Roman times to contemporary glassblowing. You'll learn about the medieval art of stained glass and see modern glass made by the museum's benefactor, Madame Frédérique Duran. The newest exhibit describes the use of glass to dispose of nuclear waste (€5 apiece for mill or museum, €7.50 for both, April–Oct Wed–Mon 10:00–12:00 & 14:00–18:00, closed Tue, by appointment in winter, tel. 04 90 72 22 11). It's well-signed between Gordes, Coustellet, and St. Pantaleon on D-148.

Museum of Lavender (Musée de la Lavande)—Located halfway between Gordes and Isle-sur-la-Sorgue in Coustellet, this surprisingly interesting museum does a good job explaining the process of lavender production with interesting exhibits and good English information (with an audioguide, a film, and posted explanations at the exhibits). It's popular with tour groups, smells great inside, and offers the ultimate "if they made it with lavender, we sell it" gift shop (€6, daily May–Sept 9:00–19:00, Oct–April 9:00–13:00 & 14:00–18:00, in Coustellet just off D-900 toward Gordes, tel. 04 90 76 91 23). For more on this fragrant flower, see page 188.

THE LUBERON

Villages and Sights South of Roussillon

These villages and sights below Roussillon and D-900 feel less visited than places north of this busy road. You'll need a good half-day to visit them all (see the map on page 196 to get oriented). They work well in the order described below, with lunch in Bonnieux or Lacoste (see "Luberon Restaurants that Justify the Trip" sidebar, earlier). The first sight is situated south of Roussillon, where D-108 crosses D-900.

St. Julien Bridge (Pont St. Julien)

This delicate three-arched bridge survives as a testimony to Roman engineers—and to the importance of this rural area 2,000 years

ago. It's the only surviving bridge on what was the main road from northern Italy to Provence—the primary route used by Roman armies. The 215-foot-long Roman bridge was built from 27 B.C. to A.D. 14. Mortar had not yet been invented, so (as with Pont du Gard) stones were carefully set in place. Amazingly, the bridge survives today, having outlived Roman marches, hundreds of floods, and decades of automobile traffic. A new bridge finally rerouted traffic from this beautiful structure in 2005.

Walk below the bridge. Notice how thin the layer of stone seems between the arch tops and the road. Those open niches weren't for statues, but instead allowed water to pass through when the river ran high. (At its current trickle, that's hard to fathom.) Walk under an arch and examine the pockmarks in the side—medieval thieves in search of free bronze stole the clamps.

Château de la Canorgue Winery

Well-signed halfway between the St. Julien Bridge and Bonnieux, this pretty winery makes even prettier wines at reasonable prices (average bottle is €10). They also make it easy for travelers, with a welcoming tasting room offering the full range of wines—from Viognier and Chardonnay whites to rosés and rich reds. Owner-in-waiting and winemaker Nathalie greets guests on weekdays. Compare the *Vendanges de Nathalie* with the *vin du pays* for a good contrast in reds (Mon-Sat 10:00–12:00 & 14:00–18:00, closed Sun, tel. 04 90 75 81 01).

Bonnieux

Spectacular from a distance, this town disappoints me up close. It lacks a pedestrian center, though the Friday-morning market

Medieval Monasteries

France is littered with medieval monasteries, and Provence is no exception. Most have virtually no furnishings (they never had many), which leaves the visitor with little to reconstruct what life must have been like in these cold stone buildings a thousand years ago. A little history can help breathe life into these important yet underappreciated monuments.

After the fall of the Roman Empire, monasteries arose as refuges of peace and order in a chaotic world. While the pope got rich and famous playing power politics, monasteries worked to keep the focus on simplicity and poverty. Throughout the Middle Ages, monasteries were mediators between Man and God. In these peacefully remote abbeys, Europe's best minds struggled with the interpretation of God's words. Every sentence needed to be understood and applied. Answers were debated in universities and contemplated in monasteries.

St. Benedict established the Middle Ages' most influential monastic order (Benedictine) in Monte Cassino, Italy, in A.D. 529. He scheduled a rigorous program of monastic duties that combined manual labor with intellectual tasks. His movement spread north and took firm root in France, where the abbey of Cluny (Burgundy) eventually controlled more than 2,000 dependent abbeys and vied with the pope for control of the Church. Benedictine abbeys grew dot-com rich, and with wealth came excess (king-size beds and Wi-Fi). Monks lost sight of their purpose and became soft and corrupt. In the late 1100s, the determined and charismatic St. Bernard rallied the Cistercian order by going back to the original rule of St. Benedict. Cistercian abbeys thrived as centers of religious thought and exploration from the

briefly creates one. The main reason to visit here is to enjoy its excellent restaurants and views.

Eating in Bonnieux: **Le Fournil** has marvelous food, a postcard-perfect terrace, and outdoor tables around a tranquil fountain. The interior is uninviting (unless you dig caves and modern decor), so book an outdoor table or skip it (€15 lunch *plats*, €42 dinner *menus*, closed for dinner Mon, closed for lunch Mon–Tue and Sat, next to TI, tel. 04 90 75 83 62).

Sleeping near Bonnieux: The country-elegant *chambre d'hôte* **$$$ Mas del Sol,** ideally situated between Bonnieux and Lacoste, is perfect for connoisseurs of the Luberon. Young Lucine and Richard Massol rent five bright, spacious rooms that come with

13th through the 15th centuries.

Cistercian abbots ran their abbeys like little kingdoms, doling out punishment and food to the monks, and tools to peasant farmers. Abbeys were occupied by two groups: the favored monks from aristocratic families (such as St. Bernard) and a larger group of lay brothers from peasant stock, who were given the heaviest labor and could join only the Sunday services.

Monks' days were broken into three activities: prayer, reading holy texts, and labor. Monks lived in silence and poverty with few amenities—meat was forbidden, as was cable TV. In summer, they ate two daily meals; in winter, just one. Monks slept together in a single room on threadbare mats covering solid-rock floors.

With their focus on work and discipline, Cistercian abbeys became leaders of the medieval industrial revolution. Among the few literate people in Europe, monks were keepers of technological knowledge—about clocks, waterwheels, accounting, foundries, gristmills, textiles, and agricultural techniques. Abbeys became economic engines that helped drive France out of its Middle Aged funk.

As France (and Europe) slowly got its act together in the late Middle Ages, cities re-emerged as places to trade and thrive. Abbeys gradually lost their relevance in a brave new humanist world. Kings took over abbot selection, further degrading the abbeys' power, and Gutenberg's movable type made monks obsolete. The French Revolution closed the book on abbatial life, with troops occupying and destroying many abbeys. The still-functioning Abbey Notre-Dame de Sénanque, near Gordes, is a rare survivor.

views and a big breakfast. The setting is unbeatable, and the stylish pool and gardens will calm your nerves (Db-€100–140, tel. 04 90 75 94 80, www.mas-del-sol.com, lemasdelsol@wanadoo.fr). From D-900, take the D-36 turnoff to Bonnieux and look for *Mas del Sol* signs after about four kilometers.

Lacoste

Little Lacoste slumbers across the valley from Bonnieux in the shadow of its looming castle. Climb through this photogenic village of arches and stone paths, passing American art students (from the Savannah College of Art and Design) showing their work. Support an American artist, learn about the art, and then keep climbing and climbing to the ruined castle base. The view of Bonnieux from the base of Lacoste's castle is as good as it gets.

The Marquis de Sade (1740–1814) lived in this castle for more than 30 years. Author of dirty novels, he was notorious for hosting orgies behind these walls, and for kidnapping peasants

THE LUBERON

for scandalous purposes. He was eventually arrested and imprisoned for 30 years and, thanks to him, we have a word to describe his favorite hobby—sadism. Today, clothing designer Pierre Cardin is spending a fortune renovating the castle in lavish fashion, complete with a concert hall that now hosts a summer theater and opera festival. Some locals are critical of Cardin, who they say is buying up the town to create his own "faux-Provence." Could "Cardism" be next?

Eating in Lacoste: If it's time for lunch, find the **Bar/ Restaurant de France**'s outdoor tables overlooking Bonnieux and savor the view (inexpensive, good omelets, daily, lunch only off-season, tel. 04 90 75 82 25).

Abbey St. Hilaire

A dirt road off D-103 between Lacoste and Ménerbes leads down to this long-forgotten and pint-size abbey. There's not much to see here—it's more about the experience. The tranquility and isolation sought by monks 800 years ago are still palpable in the simple church and modest cloisters. Once a Cistercian outpost for the bigger abbey at Sénanque, Abbey St. Hilaire is now owned by Carmelite Friars. The lone stone bench in front is picnic-ready, and a rugged WC is cut into the rock (across the courtyard). Leave nothing valuable in your car at this remote site.

Ménerbes

Ménerbes is (in)famous as the village that drew author Peter Mayle's attention to this region, but offers little of interest (unless you're into corkscrews). If you must explore Ménerbes, stash your car, then follow *Eglise* signs to the end of the village and find the heavy Romanesque church (closed and under renovation) and graveyard (good views in all directions). You're face-to-face with the Grand Luberon ridge. Notice the quarry carved into its side, where the stone for this village came from. Foodies can duck into the snazzy **Maison de la Truffe et du Vin,** which offers "truffle discovery workshops" (call for schedule, tel. 04 90 72 52 10). The **Corkscrew Museum** (Musée du Tire-Bouchon) lies a kilometer below Ménerbes and is worth a stop if you're a corkscrew enthusiast or want to taste their wines (Domaine de la Citadelle). They have 1,200 corkscrews on display in glass cases and a well-stocked gift shop (€4 for the "museum," includes tasting, daily 10:00–12:00 & 14:00–19:00, tel. 04 90 72 41 58).

Oppède-le-Vieux

This windy barnacle of a town clings with all its might to its hillside. There's one boutique, two cafés, and a dusty little square at the base of a short, ankle-twisting climb to a pretty little church and ruined castle. This off-the-beaten-path fixer-upper of a village was completely abandoned in 1910, and today has a ghost town–like feel (it once housed 200 people). The inhabited village below has a rugged character and shows little inclination for boutiques and smart hotels. It's ideal for those looking to perish in Provence.

Plan your ascent to the castle. It's 20 minutes straight up, but the Luberon views justify the effort. (After making this walk, you'll understand why locals abandoned it for more level terrain.) Small information panels provide a worthwhile background in English as you climb. Walk under the central arch of the building across from Le Petit Café and climb. After walking under the arch, look back to notice the handsome building it supports. At the fork, either way works—though the path to the right is easier. Find the little church terrace. From here, tiled rooftops paint a delightful picture with the grand panorama; the flat plain of the Rhône delta is visible off to the left. The colorful **Notre-Dame d'Alidon church** (1588) is generally open (9:30–18:30; depends on village volunteers who are eager to answer questions). There's been a church on this site for 1,000 years. Pick up the English text and imagine having to climb this distance at least every Sunday—for your entire life. Notice the pride locals have for their church: You'll see new gold-leaf accents and other efforts to spruce up the long-abandoned building. The steps to chapels on the right were necessary, thanks to the church's hillside setting. Wander above the church. Mountain goats can climb on what remains of the castle (pay attention—there are no rails).

Once you're back down, consider a light lunch or an overnight at **Le Petit Café** (cheap lunches with views of the castle ruins, simple but comfy Db-€60–70, big Db-€90, includes breakfast, Jacuzzi, sauna, rooftop terrace, tel. 04 90 76 74 01, www.petitcafe .fr, café open for dinner May–Oct but closed Thu).

Getting There: To find Oppède-le-Vieux from D-900, follow signs to *Oppède* and *Oppède le Village*, then *Oppède-le-Vieux*, and drive toward le Grand Luberon massif. You'll follow a long, one-way loop and be forced to park a few hundred yards from the village (unless you're sleeping there), for which you'll get to pay €3.

THE LUBERON

Villages and Sights East of Roussillon: La Provence Profonde

Provence is busy with tourists, but there are still plenty of characteristic and less-discovered places to explore. The area east of Roussillon feels quieter and less touristed—come here to get a sense of how most villages were before they became "destinations." Here are the key sights in the order that you'll pass them coming from Roussillon or Joucas. Allow a full day to complete this loop. If all you have is a half-day, head straight for the Fort de Buoux (see map on page 196).

St-Saturnin-lès-Apt

Most tourists pass by this pleasant town (with a lively Sunday market) on their way to more famous destinations. I couldn't find a souvenir shop. Ditch your car below the main entry to the town (just below the old city) and walk up the main drag past the Hôtel Hubert (rue de la République). You'll come to a striking church that's a fine example of Provençal Romanesque, with a tall, rounded spire (the interior is often closed). From here, find the ramp with *Le Château* signs and climb. The ruined "château" grows right out of the rock, making it difficult to tell the man-made from the natural. Go left as you enter and hike as high as the sun allows with no shade—faded green dots guide you up.

It's a scamperer's paradise, with views that rank among the best village-top vistas I found in Provence. The small chapel at the very top is closed, so there's no reason to climb all the way up. To get back down, find your way through the small opening to the little dam.

Sleeping and Eating in or near St-Saturnin-lès-Apt: For a warm welcome, stay at **$$$ Mas Perréal** just outside St-Saturnin-lès-Apt. American Kevin and his Parisian wife, Elisabeth, left no stone unturned as they restored their lovely farmhouse. Elisabeth teaches French—that's how Kevin met her—and still gives lessons (book in advance). This place features sumptuous rooms (each with its own terrace), a pool, 360-degree views (they own the vineyards and orchards around you), elaborate American-size breakfasts that change weekly, and no language barrier (Db-€125–140, includes big breakfast, tel. 04 90 75 46 31, fax 04 90 04 88 08, www.mas perreal.com, elisabeth-kevin@masperreal.com). Mas Perréal is off D-943, between St-Saturnin-lès-Apt and D-900. Coming from

D-900, turn left at Moulin d'Huile d'Olive, continue 1.2 kilometers (three-quarters of a mile), cross one "major" road, then look for signs on your right.

$ Hôtel des Voyageurs*, with amiable owners Nadine and Alain (who speak no English), is a time-warp that has survived

many Provençal trends without changing its look or product. The basic budget accommodations gather around uneven floors and a frumpy upstairs terrace that only an artist could love (modest but nice Db-€57–66, big Db-€70). The Old World restaurant, with pink-and-rose tablecloths above vintage floor tiles, serves traditional cuisine that locals adore (*menus* from €20, closed all day Wed and Thu for lunch, tel. 04 90 75 42 08, fax 04 90 75 50 58, hotel.rest.voyageur@orange.fr). It's at the base of the old village—look for signs.

Le Colorado Provençal

This park has ochre cliffs similar to Roussillon's, but they're spread over a larger area, with well-signed trails. If hiking through soft,

orange sand through Bryce Canyon–like rocks strikes your fancy, follow signs toward the village of *Rustrel*, the gateway to Le Colorado Provençal.

The park is located a kilometer below Rustrel off D-22, between Apt and Gignac. There are two parking lots. Skip the sprawling lot on D-22 with the big signs and snack stands—it's more expensive and leaves you 15 minutes from the trails. The less-expensive and more-convenient *Parking Municipal* at the trailhead is 200 yards toward Apt from the big parking lot (look for small signs to *Colorado Provençal* off D-22, allow €3.50 for parking). There's no entry fee to the park, which is always open, with parking attendants available from about 9:00 until 17:00 or 18:00.

For the best walk, cross the little footbridge and follow either the Cheminée de Fée or the Sahara trail. (Trails are color-coded and easy to follow, allow about 30–40 minutes for each with modest elevation gain; Cheminée de Fée is more impressive, but steeper.) Light-colored clothing is a bad choice. Signs remind you to please remain on the trails and not to climb the cliffs.

Viens

Located about 15 minutes uphill and east of Le Colorado Provençal (turn right when leaving Colorado), this village is where Luberon locals go to get away. With a set-

ting like this, it's surprising that modest Viens is not more developed. The panoramas are higher and more vast than around Roussillon (with some lavender fields), and the vegetation is more raw. Walk the streets of the old town (bigger than it first appears) and visit the few shops scattered about. Find the courtyard of the old château, then find the lone stone arch overlooking the view. This is how Gordes must have looked before it became chic.

Eating in Viens: **Le Petit Jardin Café,** just below the town's only phone booth, fits perfectly in this unpretentious town. Come for a drink and rub shoulders with locals (notice the photos on the walls); or, better, have a meal and meet Madame and Monsieur Aubert. Dine in the small traditional interior, or outside on a garden terrace (*menu du jour*-€13 on weekdays, more elaborate €22 *menu* on weekends, lunch served 12:00–14:00, closed Wed, tel. 04 90 75 20 05). A small **grocery store** and a **bakery** are a few blocks past the café, toward St. Martin de Castillon.

To reach the next village (Saignon), follow signs to *St. Martin de Castillon,* then turn right on D-900 toward Apt.

Saignon

Sitting high atop a rock spur, this village looks down onto Apt, a city of only 11,500—which from here looks like a megalopolis after all these tiny villages. You can peek into the too-big-for-this-village Romanesque church (Notre-Dame de la Pitié) and admire its wood doors and tympanum, then follow *Le Rocher* signs through the village up to the "ship's prow." If you need to see it all, climb to the Le Rocher Bellevue for grand views over lavender fields (about three stories of stairs to the top). There's a handful of cafés, a cushy hotel (described below), and a grocery store in the linear village's center. Parking is best just above the town (hike or drive farther above town for sensational views over Saignon).

Sleeping and Eating in Saignon: **$$$ Auberge du Presbytère*** houses some of the most appealing rooms I list in Provence, on one of the region's most handsome little squares. This vine-strewn place is family-run, so expect kids underfoot. Three rooms come with private terraces, but all combine a homey feel with exquisite furnishings and bathrooms you can stretch out in (Db-€70–120, bigger Db-€155, Tb/Qb loft-€155, massive studio with terrace-€200). The restaurant is what draws most to Saignon. Enjoy lunch fountain-side on the square, or eat inside at dinner (*plats* from €20, *menus* €33–38, restaurant closed Wed; place de la Fontaine, tel. 04 90 74 11 50, fax 04 90 04 68 51, www.auberge -presbytere.com, reception@auberge-presbytere.com).

Buoux

Buoux (pronounced "by-oox"), a way-off-the-beaten-path village, is home to two memorable restaurants and Provence's without-a-doubt best ruined castle. A trip to this far-flung corner rewards with rocky canyons, acres of lavender, and few tourists. Start early and climb to the castle before the heat rises, then have a long, well-earned lunch nearby (see recommendations under "Eating in Buoux," later). If you liked Les Baux but weren't so fond of the crowds and don't need an audioguide, you'll love it here.

Buoux is south of Apt on D-113 between Saignon and Lourmarin. Ambitious travelers can combine a visit to Buoux with Lourmarin and Bonnieux.

Sights in Buoux

▲▲Fort de Buoux

The remains of this remote ridge-top castle are a playground for energetic lovers of crumbled ruins and grand views. You need good

legs and stable shoes to navigate the steep, uneven footing.

Floating like a cloud above the valleys below, the fort is easy to miss—it blends with the limestone rock cliffs that dominate the landscape. The long, rocky outcrop has been inhabited since prehistoric times. In the Middle Ages, it was home to hundreds of residents and a powerful castle that controlled a vast area. Like Les Baux, the fort was destroyed in the 1500s during the wars of religion (it was a Protestant base) and again in the 1600s by a paranoid King Louis XIII (see "The Life of a Hill Town in Provence" on page 178).

Madame la Caretaker lives in the flowery house where you buy your ticket (€3). Get the English map and start climbing. The map suggests a one-way route through the rocky ruins. You'll start with what's left of the village, then scramble around rock piles along the long outcrop to the castle remains, once home to hundreds of residents. You'll also climb around the remains of homes, a church, cisterns, and medieval storage silos.

THE LUBERON

The unforgettable highlight of this castle is a three-story stone spiral staircase. Cut into the cliffs, it leads back down to the base (follow the faded white arrows as you leave the ruins). The staircase is steep and has no handrails and big steps, so be very careful—or return the way you came.

Getting There: To reach the fort from Apt and the north, drive through Buoux, pass L'Auberge de la Loube, drop down, and follow signs to *Fort de Buoux* (and *L'Aubergere des Seguins*). If coming from the south, follow signs to *Apt*, then *L'Aubgere des Seguins* and *Fort de Buoux*. Park in the dirt lot and walk about 15 minutes up a dirt road to the foot of the fort.

Sleeping in Buoux

$ L'Auberge des Seguins is a stone's throw from the parking area for the fort. It's a lush and simple Shangri-la kind of place at the end of the valley, with confident young Amélie (and hound Miette) in charge. The rambling old farm is purposefully un-manicured—guests are encouraged to enjoy the natural beauty. The 28 rooms are simple, clean, and squirreled about the place: Some require a dirt path to reach, and some are built into the rocky cliff. Kids love it (there's also a big pool, but it's not heated). This place is a very good value unless you need things just so (half-pension with good dinner-€60/person, €40/person if you sleep in the cool dorm rooms, tel. 04 90 74 16 37, www.aubergedesseguins.com, aubergedesseguins@gmail.com). See also "Eating in Buoux," next.

Eating in Buoux

L'Auberge de la Loube ("Inn of the Wolf") is up the road from the fort in Buoux village and delivers the ultimate in Provençal country-coziness. Plan to stay awhile and enjoy the superb cuisine and setting (indoors or out) and eccentric owner, Monsieur Leporati. You'll understand why it was one of Peter Mayle's favorites. Call a day ahead to secure a table (allow €24 for lunch—more on Sun, €33 for dinner, cash only, reasonable wine list, closed Sun eve and all day Mon and Thu, tel. 04 90 74 19 58).

L'Auberge des Seguins (also listed under "Sleeping in Buoux," above) has a good restaurant and a small café with bar food and snacks. The choices are limited, but the produce is very fresh—manager Amélie brags that they only use the small refrigerator for ice cream (€10–15 lunch options, €25 dinner *menu*, indoor and outdoor seating, closed Mon for lunch).

Lourmarin

The southernmost Luberon village of Lourmarin has a good Friday market, a beautiful Renaissance château on its fringe, and an enchanting town center.

Lourmarin sits on a level plain and feels strangely peaceful and happy, away from the more-visited villages in the heart of the Luberon. This self-assured and lovely town accommodates a healthy (mostly French) tourist demand without feeling overrun. It's the best Luberon village to enjoy in the winter when other, better-known towns rattle about with few residents and little commercial activity.

Existentialist writer Albert Camus *(The Stranger)* lived in Lourmarin in the 1950s and is buried here, lending it a certain fame that persists today. Author Peter Mayle moved here not so long ago, adding to the village's cachet...and now you're here, too. Lourmarin makes a good base for touring the southern Luberon, Aix-en-Provence, and even Marseille and maybe Cassis. From here you can tour big cities, beaches, and castles, returning every night to the comfort of your village.

Getting There: Three buses per day link Lourmarin to Avignon (1.5 hours), and to Aix-en-Provence (1.25 hours, bus to Pertuis leaves 3/day, transfer there to bus bound for Aix-en-Provence, 2/hour).

Orientation to Lourmarin

Tourist Information

The TI is located on place Henri Barthélémy (Mon–Sat 10:00–12:30 & 15:00–18:00, closed Sun, tel. 04 90 68 10 77).

Theft Alert: There have been a rash of break-ins at parking lots in Lourmarin. Park centrally, and leave nothing visible in your car.

Sights In Lourmarin

Château de Lourmarin—The impressive château looks across a grassy meadow at the village and offers a rare-in-this-region look inside a Renaissance château. Tour the château on your own, with the help of its decent English handout and posted

THE LUBERON

explanations. You'll see several well-furnished rooms, a nice kitchen, gorgeous exterior galleries, and a slick double spiral staircase in stone (€5.50, daily May–Sept 10:00–11:30 & 14:30–17:30, Oct–April until 16:00, tel. 04 90 68 15 23).

Friday Market—This little town erupts into a market frenzy every Friday until 13:00. Sleep here Thursday night and awake to the commotion, arrive early, or prepare for a good walk from your car.

Sleeping in Lourmarin

Try to sleep here on a Thursday, so you can awake to Friday's market. The good-value Villa St. Louis and Les Chambres de la Cordière sit across from each other at the very eastern end of the town center.

$$$ At **Les Olivettes,** Joseph and Elizabeth DeLiso rent five apartments just a five-minute walk from the village center. The apartments are well-furnished and very comfortable, with kitchens, living rooms, CD players, and Internet access. They are rentable by the week or half-week (one-bedroom unit-€430/3 nights, two-bedroom unit-€842/3 nights, these prices promised in 2011 for Rick Steves readers, credit cards OK, avenue Henri Bosco, tel. 04 90 68 03 52, www.olivettes.com, lourmarin@olivettes.com).

$$ **Villa St. Louis** is a splendid place. It's a cross between a museum, a grand old manor home, and a garage sale. The fun and slightly eccentric owner, Madame Bernadette, adds charm to a house packed with character. The dreamy backyard is ideal for a siesta (hammock provided) and picnics. The rooms are like Grandma's, and there's a common room with a fridge (Db-€65–75, includes breakfast, cash only, secure parking, loaner bikes, 35 rue de Henri Savournin, tel. 04 90 68 39 18, fax 04 90 68 10 07, www.villasaintlouis.com, villasaintlouis@wanadoo.fr).

$$ **Les Chambres de la Cordière** is a cool getaway. Owner Françoise's goal is to make you feel at home. Six cozy rooms are tucked into one of the village's oldest buildings (c. 1582), with a tiny courtyard and welcoming cats (Db-€65–70, Tb-€85, Qb-€100, includes breakfast; four rooms come with mini-kitchens—the two with full kitchens are usually rented only by the week for about €450, cash only, rue Albert Camus, tel. & fax 04 90 68 03 32, www.cordiere.com, cordiereluberon@aol.com).

Eating in Lourmarin

All roads seem to converge on the postcard-perfect intersection near **Café de la Fontaine,** where you can enjoy a light meal or  snack inside or out—or choose from several cafés. The following listings are within a block of this intersection.

Restaurant l'Antiquaire, with stylish decor, is *the* place to eat well in Lourmarin (indoor seating only, €32 *menu,* €40 bouillabaisse possible if ordered ahead, closed Sun–Mon, indoors only but air-con, a block up from Café de la Fontaine on 9 rue du Grand Pré, tel. 04 90 68 17 29).

Le Bistrot de Lourmarin cooks up modern Provençal fare at fair prices in a welcoming, relaxed atmosphere (€15 *plats,* €26 *menu,* closed Sun and Thu, 2 avenue Philippe de Girard, tel. 04 90 68 29 74).

La Recreation, across the street, features a welcoming terrace and regional cuisine with vegetarian options (€16–20 *plats,* €26 *menus,* closed Wed except in summer, next to the TI on avenue Philippe de Girard, tel. 04 90 68 23 73).

MARSEILLE, CASSIS & AIX-EN-PROVENCE

In the rush to get between Avignon and the Riviera, most travelers zip through the eastern fringe of Provence. That's a shame, as this area nurtures compelling cities and a strikingly beautiful coastline, all in a tight package. I cover three different-as-night-and-day places, each worthy of a slice of your time. Marseille is an untouristy, semi-seedy-but-vibrant port city with 2,600 years of history. The nearby coastal village of Cassis offers the perfect antidote to the big city. And just inland, popular and polished Aix-en-Provence is the yin to Marseille's yang, with beautiful people to match its lovely architecture.

Marseille

Those who think of Marseille as the "Naples of France"—a big, gritty, dangerous port—are missing the boat. Today's Marseille (mar-say), though hardly pristine, is closer to the "Barcelona of France." It's a big, gritty port, *sans* question, but it has a distinct culture, a proud spirit, and a populace determined to clean up its act. That's a tall order, but they're off to a fair start. Thousands of Marseille's historic buildings are undergoing a massive renovation  program, and a new tramway system is up and running. In 2013 Marseille takes over as European Capital of Culture, allowing it to show off its cultural highlights.

Marseille, Cassis & Aix-en-Provence

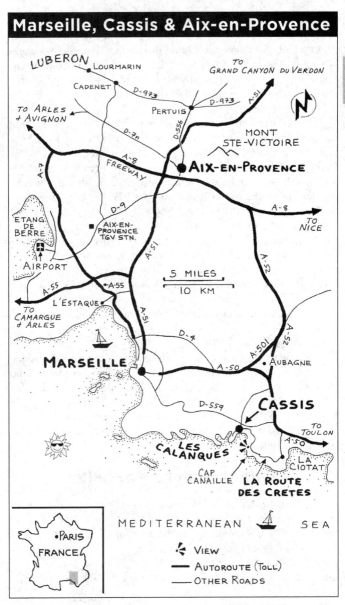

France's oldest (600 B.C.) and second-biggest city (and Europe's third-largest port) owns a history that goes back to ancient Greek times—and challenges you to find its charm. Marseille is a world apart from France's other leading cities, and has only one essential sight to visit—Notre-Dame de la Garde. Here the city is the museum, the streets are its paintings, and the happy-go-lucky residents provide its ambience.

The influence of immigrants matters: More than 25 percent of the city's population came from countries in North Africa. You're likely to hear as much Arabic as French. These migrants have created residential ghettos where nary a word of French is uttered—infuriating anti-immigrant French people certain that this will be the destiny for the rest of "their" country (see "Vive la Différence" sidebar).

Most tourists leave Marseille off their itinerary—it doesn't fit their idea of the French Riviera or of Provence (and they're right). But it would be a shame to come to the south of France and not experience the region's leading city and namesake of the French national anthem. By train, it's made-to-order for a half-day visit—the TGV line makes it just a three-hour trip from Paris. This much-maligned city seems eager to put on a welcoming face.

Planning Your Time

For a stimulating four-hour tour of Marseille that covers the basics, walk from the train station down La Canebière, wander around the Old Port, climb to the La Charité Museum (ideal lunch café), find the cathedral, then return to the port and take the shuttle ferry across to the new town (with the best eating options). Finally, take a bus, tourist train, or taxi up to Notre-Dame de la Garde before returning to the station.

Orientation to Marseille

Marseille is big, with 820,000 people, so keep it simple and focus on the area immediately around the Old Port (Vieux Port). A main boulevard (La Canebière) meets the colorful Old Port at a cluster of small (and skippable) museums and the TI. The Panier district is the old town, blanketing a hill that tumbles down to the port. The harborside is a lively, broad promenade lined with inviting eateries, amusements, and a morning fish market. Everything described here (except Notre-Dame de la Garde) is within a 30-minute walk of the train station.

Vive la Différence

Marseille is one of Europe's greatest cultural melting pots. An important trading center since ancient times, Marseille has long been defined by the waves of immigrant peoples who have called this beautiful setting home. Accessible by land and sea to North Africa, Spain, Italy, and Greece, Marseille once attracted Phoenicians, Greeks, and Romans. Today, Marseille houses France's largest concentration of immigrants: 200,000 of its more than 800,000 residents are Muslim; 80,000 are Jewish (Marseille has had a large Jewish population since the Jews were expelled from Spain in 1492); 80,000 are Armenian Orthodox (escaping Ottoman injustices); and there are 70,000 Comorans (from a group of islands in the Indian Ocean).

There's a spirit of cooperation among Marseille's immigrants, who understand that what benefits one group helps them all. While anti-Semitic and anti-government riots have disrupted other parts of France in recent years (Paris in particular), gritty Marseille has remained quiet. Unlike in Paris, immigrants in Marseille live in the city center, not the suburbs, so they are more visible (and hard to ignore). And though unemployment is high among immigrants, it is not as high as in Parisian suburbs. The commercial port, a thriving high-tech industry, and tourism (mostly from cruise ships) fuel Marseille's economy. The city also has invested mightily in jobs programs and city-center renovation projects that have benefited its lower-income residents.

Marseille engenders a strong sense of identity apart from France (and the French language) that unites this city's diverse population. Locals see themselves as *Marseillais* (marsay-ay) first, and as French second (or third, after their native country). Locals' fierce pride is manifested in their passion for Olympique de Marseille, the city's soccer team. Since 1899 *Marseillais* have lived and died with the fate of their team. (A few years ago, I was here the day that 30,000 Marseille fans were boarding trains to Paris for the France finals.) The Olympique de Marseille has made a point of creating a team that looks like the city by recruiting players from North African countries (Zinédine Zidane is the most famous example). The strategy seems to have worked—Marseille has won the French Cup more than any other team in France.

Immigrant populations are booming in cities throughout Europe, challenging local governments to accommodate them. Many would do well to study Marseille.

In 2009 the city unveiled both a smart new tramway line and a cheap public bike system called le Vélo (similar to Vélib' bikes in Paris)—though visitors won't find much use for either.

Tourist Information

The main TI is right at the **Old Port** (Mon–Sat 9:00–19:00, Sun 10:00–17:00, 4 La Canebière, tel. 08 26 50 05 00, www.marseille -tourisme.com). Pick up the good city map, the flier with a self-guided walk through the old town, and information on museums and the weekly walking tours.

Arrival in Marseille

By Train: St. Charles Station (Gare St. Charles) is busy, modern, and user-friendly. Many services are along or outside of track A, including WCs (€0.50), baggage storage (daily 8:15–21:00), and a quiet waiting area *(Salle d'Attente)*. If you exit the station at track A to Square Narvik, you'll see car rental and Hôtel Ibis on your left; access to the old city by foot is to

the right. With your back to the tracks, turn right to find shops, many food options (including McDonald's), and the bus station (with airport buses and more). To get from the train station to the Old Port, you can walk, take the Métro, or catch a taxi.

On **foot** it's an exhilarating 15-minute downhill gauntlet along grimy streets from the station to the Old Port. Leave the station through the exit at track A (by the big departure board), veer right, and admire the view from atop the stairs (Toto, we're not in Cassis anymore). That's Notre-Dame de la Garde overlooking the city—pretty cool. Walk down the stairs and straight on boulevard d'Athènes, which becomes boulevard Dugommier. Turn right at McDonald's onto the grand boulevard, La Canebière, which leads directly to the port and the main TI.

By **Métro** it's an easy subterranean trip from the train station to the Old Port: Go down the escalator opposite track E and buy a ticket (from the machines or inside the *Accueil* office, €2 ticket is good for one hour of travel on Métro and buses, all-day pass costs about €5). Descend the long escalator, and take the blue line #1 (direction: La Timone) two stops to Vieux Port. Following *Sortie la Canebière* exit signs, you'll pop out at the TI (and smell the fish market). To return to the station from here, take the blue line #1 (direction: La Rose) two stops and get off at the stop called Gare SNCF.

If you take a **taxi,** allow €10 to the port and €15 to Notre-Dame de la Garde—though train station cabbies may refuse these short trips if business is hopping (tel. 04 91 02 20 20). Taxis along

Marseille at a Glance

▲▲**Notre-Dame de la Garde** Marseille's landmark sight: a huge Romanesque-Byzantine basilica, towering above everything, with panoramic views. **Hours:** Daily in summer 7:00-20:00, until 19:00 in winter. See page 246.

▲**Marine Museum** Grandiose building with small exhibit on the city's maritime history. **Hours:** Tue-Sun June-Sept 10:00-18:00, Oct-May 10:00-17:00, closed Mon year-round. See page 242.

▲**Old Port** Economic heart of town, featuring lots of boats and a fish market, all protected by two impressive fortresses. **Hours:** Port—always open; fish market—daily until 13:00. See page 243.

▲**La Charité Museum** Housed in a beautiful building with Celtic, Greek, Roman, and Egyptian artifacts, plus temporary exhibits. **Hours:** Tue-Sun June-Sept 11:00-18:00, Oct-May 10:00-17:00, closed Mon year-round. See page 244.

Marseille History Museum Shows off the city's remarkable history with artifacts from Caesar to Louis XIV. **Hours:** Mon-Sat 12:00-19:00, closed Sun. See page 242.

Cathédrale de la Nouvelle Major Impressive striped cathedral with floor and wall mosaics. **Hours:** Daily 10:00-12:00 & 14:00-18:00. See page 244.

Arab Markets Taste of North Africa in downtown Marseille. **Hours:** Open long hours daily. See page 239.

Fashion Museum Sparse collection of dresses from the last half-century. **Hours:** Tue-Sun June-Sept 11:00-18:00, Oct-May 10:00-17:00, closed Mon year-round. See page 242.

Château d'If Island with fortress-turned-prison, featured in Alexandre Dumas' *The Count of Monte Cristo*. **Hours:** Boats depart daily from quai des Belges, usually on the hour 9:00-17:00. See page 246.

the port will take you on shorter rides.

By Car: Drivers who are good in big, crazy cities can navigate Marseille. Leaving the autoroute, signs to *Vieux Port, Centre-Ville,* and *Office du Tourisme* take you right to the Old Port. At the port, turn left and let the blue *P* signs direct you into an underground lot with 625 spaces. Locals claim pay lots are patrolled and safe.

By Plane: Marseille's airport (Aéroport Marseille–Provence), about 16 miles north of the city center, is small and easy to navigate (tel. 04 42 14 14 14, www.marseille.aeroport.fr). Frequent buses run to Marseille's St. Charles train station (€9, 3/hour, 25 minutes) and to Aix-en-Provence (stops at Aix-en-Provence's TGV station or bus station, 2/hour, 30 minutes, www.rdt13.fr). A five-minute shuttle bus trip connects the airport to a nearby train station, called Vitrolles Aéroport. This station is handy for its direct service to cities west of Marseille, including Arles, Avignon, and Nîmes. (You can also take a train from this station into Marseille, but the bus described above is easier and more frequent.) For destinations east of Marseille (such as Cassis, Nice, or Italy), take the bus to Marseille's Gare St. Charles and connect by train from there. If you need to sleep near the airport, consider Hôtel Louisiana (see page 248).

Helpful Hints

Pickpockets: As in any big city, thieves thrive in crowds and target tourists. Wear your money belt, and assume any commotion is a smokescreen for theft.

Car Rental: All the major companies are represented at St. Charles Station (see "Arrival in Marseille," earlier).

Bus #60 to the Basilica: This handy bus scoots you from the Old Port up to Notre-Dame de la Garde in 10 minutes for about a €2 round-trip (ticket is good for one hour, pay driver, 3/hour). Ask the driver for the Notre-Dame de la Garde stop (where most are going). To return to the port, you can board the bus at this same stop.

Soccer Matches: *Le football* is to Marseille what American football is to Green Bay: Frenzied fans go crazy, and star-worship is always temporary. One of the best-ever soccer players was raised here: Zinédine Zidane (known to Americans mostly for his notorious head-butt of an opponent during the 2006 World Cup finals). If you're here during soccer season (end of July to mid-May), consider getting tickets to a match (every other Sat, tickets start at about €15, ask at the TI or at the **FNAC** store in La Centre Bourse behind the Marine Museum—see page 242). To get to the soccer stadium (Stade Vélodrome), take Métro line 2 (direction: Ste. Marguerite) to the stop called Point du Prado.

Tours in Marseille

Ask at the TI about occasional **walking tours** in English (usually Sat afternoons, about €7) and two-hour **taxi tours** with recorded information in English (arranged through the TI, €90/up to 4 people).

Le Petit Train's helpful little tourist trains with skimpy recorded information make two routes through town. Both leave at least hourly from the port (across from TI). The more interesting Notre-Dame de la Garde route (#1) saves you the 30-minute climb to the basilica's fantastic view, and runs along a nice section of Marseille's waterfront (€7, allow one hour round-trip, including 20 minutes to visit the church, runs daily, April–Oct usually every 20 minutes 10:00–13:00 & 14:00–18:30, March and Nov hourly, Dec–Feb 5/day, tel. 04 91 25 24 69). I'd skip the Vieux Marseille route (#2), which toots you through the Panier district—better done on foot (€6, 40 minutes, April–Oct only).

Le Grand Tour's double-decker buses with open seating up top offer a 16-stop, hop-on, hop-off route that is very similar to Le Petit Train's routes. The pricey buses depart from next to the Petit Train stop and run only once an hour, leaving you too long at most stops. Skip these buses (€18 for one-day pass).

Sights in Marseille

I've listed these sights in roughly the order that you come to them as you approach the Old Port on La Canebière. I've also included some commentary to help you connect the dots (see the map on pages 240–241).

• *Start by the McDonald's at the corner of La Canebière and boulevard Dugommier.*

Along La Canebière

The boulevard La Canebière (pronounced "can o' bee-air") with its new facelift—and classy tramway—is the celebrated main drag of Marseille. Strolling this stubby thoroughfare, you feel surrounded by a teeming, diverse city. Two blocks before the harbor, you'll find three museums and a stylish shopping district. The boulevard dead-ends at the Old Port's fish market and TI.

Arab Markets—Marseille's huge Moroccan, Algerian, and Tunisian populations give the city a special spice. For a taste of

MARSEILLE

Marseille

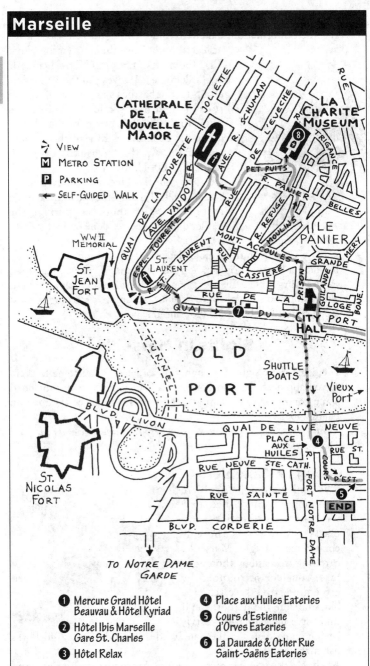

1. Mercure Grand Hôtel Beauvau & Hôtel Kyriad
2. Hôtel Ibis Marseille Gare St. Charles
3. Hôtel Relax
4. Place aux Huiles Eateries
5. Cours d'Estienne d'Orves Eateries
6. La Daurade & Other Rue Saint-Saëns Eateries

MARSEILLE

7 Le Souk & Les Galinettes
  Chez Madie Restaurants

8 La Charité Museum Café

9 Arab Markets

10 Le Petit Trains Departure
  Point & Taxi Stand

11 Bus #60 Stop & Boat
  Dock for Island &
  Calanques Cruises

12 McDonald's & Start of
  Self-Guided Walk

Africa, leave La Canebière by turning left at the second street onto rue Longue des Capucins and walk down a few blocks (to rue d'Aubagne). Suddenly you're immersed in an exotic and fragrant little medina filled with commotion—and no one's speaking French. Stop by **Soleil d'Egypte** and try a *bourek* wrap (apple and ground round) or, better, try the *pastilla* wrap (chicken, almonds, onions, and egg). Double back to La Canebière on rue d'Aubagne, stopping to pick up dessert (Tunisian pastries) at **La Carthage** bakery.

• *Continue down La Canebière. The grand triumphal arch you see far to the right at cours Belsunce marks the historic gateway to the city of Aix-en-Provence. Next, the big building that seals the street to the left at rue Ferréol is Marseille's préfecture, or regional administration. Now, cross back to the north side of La Canebière and you'll come to the...*

Fashion Museum (Musée de la Mode)—The exhibits here are as skimpy as most of its dresses, with two rooms full of creative and colorful outfits from the 1950s to today (€3, Tue–Sun June–Sept 11:00–18:00, Oct–May 10:00–17:00, closed Mon year-round, 11 La Canebière, in Espace Mode Mediterranée).

For more fashion, cross back over La Canebière, continue across place du Général de Gaulle (passing the merry-go-round), and find the tiny rue de la Tour, Marseille's self-proclaimed "rue de la Mode." It's lined with shops proudly displaying the latest fashions, mostly from local designers. Just beyond that is the 1920s Art Deco facade of Marseille's opera house.

• *Near the end of La Canebière, on the right side, find the tall, grandiose chamber of commerce building that houses the...*

▲Marine Museum—Step inside (free entry) and take in the grand 1860s interior. A relief on the ceiling shows great moments in Marseille's history and a large court with a United Nations of plaques, reminding locals how their commerce comes from trade around the world.

The small ground-floor exhibit on the city's maritime history starts (to the right as you enter) with an impressive portrait of Emperor Napoleon III (who called for the building's construction) and his wife. Sketches show the pomp surrounding its grand opening. The next room traces the growth of the city through charts of its harbor, and the following rooms display models of big ships over the centuries (€2, Tue–Sun June–Sept 10:00–18:00, Oct–May 10:00–17:00, closed Mon year-round, tel. 04 91 39 33 33).

• *In La Centre Bourse, the modern shopping center behind the chamber of commerce, you'll find the...*

Marseille History Museum (Musée d'Histoire de Marseille)—Come here for a French-only introduction to Marseille's remarkable history, including the remains of an old Roman ship and bits of a Greek vessel—both found here (€2, no English, Mon–Sat 12:00–19:00, closed Sun, tel. 04 91 90 42 22).

• *The TI is back across La Canebière, a short block down from the Marine Museum. After checking in at the TI, cross the big street and get close to the...*

Old Port (Vieux Port)

Protected by two impressive fortresses at its mouth, Marseille's Vieux Port has long been the economic heart of town. These citadels were built in the 17th century under Louis XIV, supposedly to protect the city. But locals figured the forts were actually designed to keep an eye on Marseille—a city that was essentially autonomous until

1660, and a challenge to thoroughly incorporate into the growing kingdom of France.

Today, the serious shipping is away from the center, and the Old Port is the happy domain of pleasure craft. The fish market

along quai des Belges (where you're standing) thrives each morning (unless the wind kept the boats home the day before). The stalls are gone by 13:00, but the smells linger. Looking out to sea from here, Le Panier (the old town) rises to your right. The harborfront below Le Panier was destroyed in 1943 by the Nazis, who didn't want a tangled refuge for resistance fighters so close to the harbor. Today, it's been rebuilt with modern condos and trendy restaurants.

• *Walk around the right side of the port and find the small ferry dock (La Ligne du Ferry Boat) that crosses the port. You'll be back here soon. But for now, turn around and find the City Hall.*

Le Panier District (Old Town)

Until the mid-19th century, Marseille was just the hill-capping old town and its fortified port. Today, it's the best place to find the town's soul. The ornate **City Hall** (Hôtel de Ville) stands across from the three-masted sailboat and the little shuttle ferry. Its bust of Louis XIV overlooks the harbor. Rue de la Prison leads behind the City Hall and up the hill (where we're headed shortly). At the crest of the hill—the highest point in the old town—is the peaceful place des Moulins, named for the 15 windmills that used to spin and grind from this windy summit. (Today, only the towers of three windmills remain.)

• *Walk up the broad stairway, passing the City Hall, turn left at the top, then track the brown signs up—and up some more—to la Vieille Charité. As you walk, read the thoughtful English-information plaques (posted on iron stands at points of historic interest) and listen for the sounds of local life being played out, on the streets and in the rooms just above.*

▲**La Charité Museum (Centre de la Vieille Charité)**—Now a museum, this was once a poorhouse. In 1674 the French king

decided that all the poor people on the streets were bad news. He built a huge triple-arcaded home to house a thousand needy subjects. In 1940 the famous architect Le Corbusier declared it a shame that such a fine building was so underappreciated. Today, the striking building—wonderfully renovated and beautiful in its arcaded simplicity—is used as a collection of art galleries surrounding a Pantheonesque church. You can stroll around the courtyard for free. (Good WCs are in the far-left corner.)

The pediment of the church features the figure of Charity taking care of orphans (as the state did with this building). She's flanked by pelicans (symbolic of charity, for the way they were said to pick flesh from their own bosom to feed their hungry chicks, according to medieval legend). The ground floor outside the church houses temporary exhibits. Upstairs you'll find rooms with interesting collections of Celtic (c. 300 B.C.), Greek, and Roman artifacts from this region. There's also a surprisingly good Egyptian collection, and masks from Africa and the South Pacific (€3–6 depending on exhibits, no English information, Tue–Sun June–Sept 11:00–18:00, Oct–May 10:00–17:00, closed Mon year-round, idyllic restaurant/bar, tel. 04 91 14 58 80).

• *From La Charité, cross the small cobbled triangular square, turn right on rue du Petit Puits, and follow the street down, curving left, then right, to find...*

Cathédrale de la Nouvelle Major—Bam. This huge, striped cathedral seems lost out here, away from the action and above the nondescript cruise-ship port. The cathedral was built in the late 1800s to replace the old cathedral that the city had outgrown. It's more impressive from the outside, but worth a quick peek inside for its floor and wall mosaics over the nave (daily 10:00–12:00 & 14:00–18:00).

• *Return to the Old Port by walking up the tree-lined esplanade de la Tourette. Marseille's sprawling modern port is behind you and becomes visible as you climb.*

The Great Maritime Port of Marseille (GPMM)—The economy of Marseille is driven by its modern commercial ports, which extend 30 miles west from here (a nearby canal links Marseille inland via the Rhône River, adding to the port's importance). Over 100 million tons of freight pass through this port each year (60 percent of which is petroleum), making this one of Europe's top three ports. Container traffic is significant but is hampered by crippling strikes for which the left-leaning city is famous. By contrast, cruise-ship tourism has taken off in a big way, bringing more than 550,000 passengers to Marseille each year.

• *Keep walking. A fabulous view awaits you at the bend.*

View Terrace—Voilà! This is one of the best views of Marseille, with Notre-Dame de la Garde presiding above, and twin forts below protecting the entrance to the Old Port. The ugly, boxy building marked "Memorial" at the base of the fort (below and to your right) is a memorial to those lost during the Nazi occupation of the city in World War II. The small church to your left is the Church of St. Laurent, which once served as a parish church for sailors and fishermen—notice the lighthouse-like tower.

• *Continue down the steps back to the Old Port.*

From the Old Port to the New Town

Halfway along the promenade (quai du Port), at the City Hall, you'll see the fun little **shuttle boat** that ferries locals across the harbor to the new town (free, every 10 minutes 7:00–19:20, lunch break from about 12:00–13:15). Note the unusual two-way steering wheel as you sail. You'll dock in the new town—which, because of the 1943 bombings, is actually older than the "old" town along the harborfront.

Directly in front of the ferry landing, you'll find popular bars and brasseries, good for a quick meal or memorable drink. Wander in along place aux Huiles, make your way left, and find a smart pedestrian zone crammed with cafés and restaurants (see "Eating in Marseille," later).

• *Our walk is over. Don't miss a trip up to Notre-Dame de la Garde, described next.*

Overlooking the Old Port

▲▲**Notre-Dame de la Garde**—Crowning Marseille's highest point, 500 feet above the harbor, is the city's landmark sight. This

massive Neo-Romanesque–Byzantine basilica, built in the 1850s during the reign of Napoleon III, is a radiant collection of domes, gold, and mosaics. The monumental statue of Mary and the Baby Jesus towers above everything (Jesus' wrist alone is 42 inches around, and the statue weighs nine tons). And though people come here mostly for the commanding city view, the interior will bowl you over (open daily in summer 7:00–20:00, until 19:00 in winter, cafeteria and WCs just below the view terrace). This hilltop has served as a lookout, as well as a place of worship, since ancient times. Climb to the highest lookout for an orientation table and the best views. Those islands straight ahead are the Iles du Frioul, including the island of If—where the Count of Monte Cristo spent time (described below).

Getting There: To reach the church, you can hike 30 minutes straight up from the harbor. To save some sweat, catch a taxi (about €10), hop on bus #60, or ride the tourist train—all stop on the harborfront near the fish market (see map on page 240 and "Helpful Hints" on page 238).

Offshore Islands and Calanques

Château d'If—When King François I visited Marseille in the 16th century, he realized the potential strategic importance of a fort on the uninhabited island of If (one of the Islands of Frioul), just outside the harbor. His château was finished in 1531. The impregnable fortress, which never saw battle, became a prison—handy for locking up Protestants during the Counter-Reformation. Among its illustrious inmates was José Faria, a spiritualist priest who was the idol of Paris and whom Alexandre Dumas immortalized in *The Count of Monte Cristo*. Since 1890 the château has been open to the public. Tour boats take tourists to this French Alcatraz, where the required two-hour stay will leave you sensitive to the count's predicament. I'd bypass this prison (€10 round-trip, €5 château entry, 30-minute trip, usually depart daily on the hour 9:00–17:00, get the latest at the TI).

Islands of Frioul (Îles du Frioul)—These islands, which offer a nature break from the big city with a few hiking paths and cafés, are another 15 minutes away (round-trip with Château d'If-€10, boats run daily on the half-hour 9:30–17:30, get the latest at the TI).

Calanques **Cruises**—For those who won't get to Cassis, **Croisières Marseille Calanques** offers day trips to the dramatic fjord-like inlets known as *calanques,* east of Marseille (€15/2 hours, €25/3 hours, tel. 08 25 13 68 00, www.croisieres-marseille -calanques.com). Boats depart from the Old Port across from the TI. To read up on *calanques,* see page 254.

Sleeping in Marseille

Stay in Marseille only if you want a true urban experience. Hotel values and ambience are better 20 minutes away in Cassis (see page 256).

$$$ Mercure Grand Hôtel Beauvau** lets you buy away the gritty reality outside your door with business-class comfort (Db-€190, Db with port view-€270, rates are frequently reduced, Wi-Fi in little lobby, 4 rue Beauvau, tel. 04 91 54 91 00, fax 04 91 54 15 76, www.accorhotels.com, h1293@accor.com).

$$ Hôtel Ibis Marseille Gare St. Charles, with 180 rooms (which often are fully booked), is a worthwhile value because it's right at the train station—on the left as you exit (Db-€85–105, €10 less on weekends, extra bed-€10, check for deals on their website, air-con, elevator, Square Narvick, tel. 04 91 95 62 09, fax 04 91 50 68 42, www.ibishotel.com, h1390@accor.com).

$$ Hôtel Kyriad, a block off the port behind the TI, is a shade musty but offers relative quiet and livable comfort at good rates (Db-€95, Db with king-size bed-€103, Tb-€115, air-con, elevator, Wi-Fi, 6 rue Beauvau, tel. 04 91 33 02 33, fax 04 91 33 21 34, www.kyriad.com, kyriad.vieux-port@wanadoo.fr).

$ Hôtel Relax, humble and homey, is run by sweet Houria (pronounced "oo-ree-ah," which means "Liberty" in Arabic—she's Algerian), her husband, Ali, and their son. Despite its downtown location, it has little traffic noise and a lobby any poodle would love. Book this place ahead. Half of the simple rooms overlook a classy square—worth requesting, as the back-side rooms can be gloomy (back-side Db-€62, Db on square-€67, no triples or quads, rooms have tight bathrooms with step-up showers, air-con, Wi-Fi,

---

Sleep Code

(€1 = about $1.25, country code: 33)
S = Single, **D** = Double/Twin, **T** = Triple, **Q** = Quad, **b** = bathroom,
s = shower only, * = French hotel rating system (0-4 stars).
Unless otherwise noted, credit cards are accepted and English
is spoken.

To help you sort easily through these listings, I've divided
the rooms into three categories based on the price for a
standard double room with bath:

  $$$ Higher Priced—Most rooms €100 or more.
    $$ Moderately Priced—Most rooms between €70-100.
     $ Lower Priced—Most rooms €70 or less.

Prices can change without notice; verify the hotel's
current rates online or by email. For other updates, see www
.ricksteves.com/update.

---

just 2 blocks off harbor on place de l'Opéra at 4 rue Corneille, tel.
04 91 33 15 87, fax 04 91 55 63 57, www.hotelrelax.fr, hotelrelax
@free.fr).

Near the Airport: **$ Hôtel Louisiana*** is cheap and has easy
train connections to Marseille. If you have an early flight, consider
bedding down here. Rooms are small but clean, and the restaurant
serves affordable meals (Db-€50–60; Impasse Pythagore, Z.I.
de Couperigne, 13127 Vitrolles; tel. 04 42 15 09 30, www.hotel
-louisiana.com, hotel.louisiana@yahoo.fr).

Eating in Marseille

In the New Town: For the best combination of trendiness, variety,
and a fun people scene, eat in the new town, on or near quai de
Rive-Neuve (on the left side of the Old Port as you look out to
sea). Look for place aux Huiles, cours d'Estienne d'Orves, and
rue Saint-Saëns for a melting pot of international eateries ranging
from giant salads and fresh seafood to crêpes, Vietnamese dishes,
Belgian waffles, and Buffalo wings. Come here for ambience, not
for top cuisine. **La Daurade** is worth considering, with fresh seafood at fair prices served in a classy setting (€18 *menus*, €20 bouillabaisse, closed Wed, 36 rue Saint-Saëns, tel. 04 91 33 82 42).

Near the Old Port: For good views *en terrasse,* go to the other
side of the port. Have a real Moroccan dinner at **Le Souk** (€16
couscous and *tajine* dishes, €20 three-course *menu,* intimate and
authentic interior, closed Mon, 100 quai du Port, tel. 04 91 91
29 29). If you must have bouillabaisse, try **Les Galinettes Chez**

Madie (€26 *menu*, €35/person for bouillabaisse, closed Sun, 138 quai du Port, tel. 04 91 90 40 87).

Near La Charité: **La Charité Museum** has a lovely, quiet courtyard café (lunch only).

Marseille Connections

Marseille is well-served by TGV and local trains, and is the hub for many smaller stations in eastern Provence.

From Marseille by Train to: Cassis (20/day, 25 minutes), **Aix-en-Provence** Centre-Ville station (2/hour, 45 minutes), **Antibes** (16/day, 2.5 hours), **Nice** (18/day, 2.5 hours), **Arles** (20/day, 1.5 hours), **Avignon TGV** (10/day, 1 hour), **Paris** (hourly, 3.25 hours), **Isle-sur-la-Sorgue** (8/day, 1–2 hours).

From Marseille's Train Station by Bus to: Marseille Airport (3/hour, 25 minutes), **Cassis** (8/day, 50 minutes), **Aix-en-Provence** (4/hour, 50 minutes).

From Marseille's Métro Castellane by Bus to: Cassis (10/day, 40 minutes).

Cassis

Hunkered below impossibly high cliffs, Cassis (kah-see) is an unpretentious port town that gives travelers a sunny time-out from their busy vacation. Two hours away from the fray of the Côte d'Azur, Cassis is a poor man's St-Tropez. Outdoor cafés line the small port on three sides, where boaters clean their crafts as they chat up café clients. Cassis is popular with the French and close enough to Marseille to be busy on weekends and all summer. Come to Cassis to dine portside, swim in the glimmering-clear water, and explore its rocky *calanques* (inlets).

Orientation to Cassis

The Massif du Puget mountain hovers over little Cassis, with hills spilling down to the port. Cap Canaille cliff rises from the southeast, and the famous *calanques* inlets hide along the coast northwest of town. Hotels, restaurants, and boats line the attractive little port.

Tourist Information

The TI is in the modern building in the middle of the port among the boats (Mon–Sat 9:00–12:30 & 14:00–18:00, Sun 10:00–12:30 except July–Aug 9:00–19:00, quai des Moulins, toll tel. 08 92 25

98 92—€0.34/minutes, www.ot-cassis.fr, info@ot-cassis.com). If you're going to Marseille, pick up a map here.

Arrival in Cassis

By Train: Cassis' hills forced the train station to be built two miles away, and those last two miles can be a challenge. It's a small station with limited hours (no baggage storage, ticket windows open Mon–Fri 6:15–13:15 & 13:45–20:45, Sat–Sun 9:30–13:15 & 13:45–18:10). If you need to buy tickets when the station is closed, use the machines (coins only).

A **taxi** into town costs €10 with baggage and is well worth the expense unless a bus is soon to arrive (see below). If there's no taxi waiting, call 04 42 01 78 96 (a pay phone is outside the train station). Otherwise, it's a 50-minute walk into town (turn left out of the station and follow signs).

Marcouline **buses** link the station with the town center, but service is spotty (about hourly with longer intervals in the afternoon, schedule posted at all stops). Call the TI in advance to get the schedule and plan your arrival accordingly—but be ready to take a taxi. The bus drops you at the Casino stop in Cassis: From here, turn right on rue de l'Arène and walk downhill five minutes to reach the port.

By Bus: Regional buses (including those from Marseille) stop a five-minute walk from the port on avenue du 11 Novembre (stop is labeled Gendarmerie).

By Car: There are two exits from the autoroute for Cassis; the second (coming from Aix-en-Provence) costs €1 more in tolls but saves you 10 minutes, provides easy access to La Route des Crêtes (described later under "Sights in Cassis"), and offers memorable views.

The hills above Cassis can make it difficult to navigate. Hotels are signed, though the blue signs can be tricky to follow, so pay attention. Hotel parking is minimal (read each hotel's listing carefully as some have more parking than others), and the traffic is worse the closer you get to the port. Outside of summer, drivers arriving by 10:00 usually can find curbside parking (about €1/hour, free 18:00–9:00); latecomers likely will need to park in one of the well-marked pay lots above the port (Parking de la Viguerie is closest but often full, and their *Abonnés* entrance is for locals only). Parking Daudet, up the road from Parking de la Viguerie, usually has better availability. If you are driving on weekends in May, June, and September, or any day in July and August, take advantage of the free parking with shuttle service from Parking les Gorguettes high above the town (well-signed).

Helpful Hints

Market Days: The market hops on Wednesdays and Fridays until 12:30 (on the streets around the Hôtel de Ville).

Beaches: Cassis' beaches are pebbly. The big beach behind the TI is sandier than others, though water shoes still help. You can rent a mattress with a towel (about €15/day) and pedal boats (about €10/hour). Underwater springs just off the Cassis shore make the water clean, clear, and a bit cooler than at other beaches.

Internet Access: Avelit Télécom is a few blocks from the port, across from Parking la Viguerie, on avenue de la Viguerie (at #23, tel. 04 42 98 81 94).

Grocery Store: The **Casino** market is next door to Hôtel le Liautaud (daily 8:30–12:30 & 15:30–20:00, Sun until 18:00).

Laundry: There is no self-service launderette in Cassis.

Wine Tasting: Le Chai Cassidain is a wine bar that welcomes visitors, with red-leather stools and a good selection of regional wines offered by the bottle or by the glass (daily 10:00–13:00 & 15:00–22:00 and often later, 4 blocks from port at 6 rue Séverin Icard, tel. 04 42 01 99 80).

Taxi: Call 04 42 01 78 96 or find the main taxi stand across from Hôtel Cassitel by the *boules* court.

Tourist Train: The little white *train touristique*, with commentary in French and English, will take you on a worthwhile 45-minute circuit out to the peninsula on the Port-Miou *calanque* and back (€6, March–Oct, afternoons only, catch it next to the TI, tel. 04 42 01 09 98).

Self-Guided Tour

Cassis Visual Tour from the Port

Find a friendly bench in front of Hôtel le Golfe—or, better, enjoy a drink at their café—and read this quick town intro.

Cassis was born more than 2,500 years ago (on the hill with the castle ruins, across the harbor). Ligurians, Phoenicians, maybe

Greeks, certainly Romans, and plenty of barbarians all found this spot to their liking. Parts of the castle date from the eighth century, and the **fortress walls** were constructed in the 13th century to defend against seaborne barbarian raids. The Michelin family

Cassis

1 Best Western Hôtel la Rade
2 Hôtel le Golfe
3 Hôtel/Rest. le Clos des Arômes
4 Hôtel Cassitel
5 Hôtel de France
6 Hôtel Laurence
7 To Mahogany Hôtel de la Plage & Le Jardin d'Emile Hôtel
8 El Sol, L'Oustau de la Mar, Bar Canaille & Chez César Rests.
9 Le 8 et Demi Café & Grand Marnier Crêpes
10 Le Grand Large Restaurant
11 La Girondole Restaurant
12 Le Napoléon Restaurant
13 Le Chai Cassidain Wine Bar
14 Avelit Télécom Internet Café
15 Casino Grocery
16 Tourist Train (Afternoon Only)
17 Motorboat Rental & WC
18 Pedal Boat Rental
19 Kayak Rental
20 To Bus Stop for Marseille

B BUS STOP TO/FROM TRAIN STATION
T TAXI STAND
P PARKING

To P Daudet

BLVD. JAURÈS
AVE. VIGUERIE
RUE ST-CLAIR
R. DU JEUNE ANA-
QUAI BARTH.
AVE. DARDANELLES
AVE. L-AMIRAL GANT.

TO CALANQUES PLAGE DU BESTOUAN (BEACH), & 7

TO CALANQUES

PORT

PROMENADE ARISTIDE

MEDITERRANEAN

100 YARDS
100 METERS

recently sold the fortress to investors who wanted to turn it into a luxury hotel. Cassis' planning commission had other ideas.

In the 18th century, when things got safer, people moved their homes back to the waterfront. Since then, Cassis has made its living through fishing, quarrying its famous white stone, and producing well-respected white wines—which, conveniently, pair well with the local seafood dishes, and *bien sûr*, with tourists like us.

With improvements in transportation following the end of World War II, tourism rose gradually in Cassis, though crowds are still sparse by Riviera standards. While foreigners overwhelm nearby resorts, Cassis is popular mostly with the French and still feels unspoiled. The town's protected status limits the height of the buildings along the waterfront. Cassis' port is home to some nice

boats...but they're chump change compared to the glitzier harbors farther east.

The big cliff towering above the castle hill is **Cap Canaille.** Europe's highest maritime cliff, it was sculpted by receding glaciers (wrap your brain around that concept), and today drops 1,200 feet straight down. You can—and should—drive or taxi along the top for staggering views (see "Above Cassis: La Route des Crêtes" on page 256). Return to this bench at sunset, when the Cap glows a deep red.

If you can overcome your inertia, walk to your right, then veer left on top of the short wall in front of the public WCs. The rocky shore over your right shoulder looks cut away just for sunbathers. But Cassis was once an important **quarry,** and stones were sliced right out of this beach for easy transport to ships. The Statue of Liberty's base sits on this rock, and even today, Cassis stone remains highly valued throughout the world...but yesterday's quarrymen have been replaced by today's sunbathers.

Sights in Cassis

▲▲▲The *Calanques*

Until you see these exotic Mediterranean fjords—with their trans-lucent blue water, tiny intimate beaches, and stark cliffs plunging

into the sea or forming rocky promon-tories—it's hard to understand what all the excitement is about.

Calanques (kah-lahnk) are narrow, steep-sided valleys partially flooded by the sea, surrounded by rugged white cliffs usually made of limestone (quar-ries along the *calanques* have provided building stone for centuries). The word comes from the Corsican word *calanca*, meaning "inlet"—the island of Corsica also has *calanques*. These inlets began as underwater valleys carved by the seaward flow of water at rivermouths, and were later gouged out deeper by glaciers. About 12,000 years ago, when the climate warmed and glaciers retreated at the end of the last Ice Age, the sea level rose partway up the steep rocky sides of the *calanques*. Today the cliffs harbor a unique habitat that includes rare plants and nesting sites for unusual raptors.

The most famous inlets are in the Massif des Calanques, which runs along a 13-mile stretch of the coast from Marseilles to Cassis. This area and part of the surrounding region will become a national park in 2011.

You can hike, or cruise by boat or kayak, to many *calanques*. Bring plenty of water, sunscreen, and anything else you need for the day, as there's nary a baguette for sale. Don't dawdle—to limit crowds and because of fire hazards, the most popular *calanques* can be closed to visitors between 11:00 and 16:00 in high season (late June–mid-Sept) and on weekends. When they are "closed," the only way to see the *calanques* is by boat or kayak. The TI can give you plenty of advice.

Cruising the *Calanques*: Several boats offer trips of various lengths (3 *calanques*-€13, 2/hour, 45 minutes; 5 *calanques*-€15, 3/day, one hour; 8–10 *calanques*-€19, 1–3/day, 2 hours; tel. 04 42 01 90 83, www.calanques-cassis.com). The three-*calanque* tour is most popular. Tickets are sold (and boats depart) from a small booth on the port opposite the Hôtel Lieutaud. *Prochain départ* means "next departure." Boats vary in size (some seat up to 100). Closer to the TI, Didier Crespi offers more personal cruises on his smaller boat *Le Calendal* (seats 12 max). His commentary is in French only, but he can give you the basics in English (3 *calanques*-€13, one hour, drop by or call for the day's schedule, mobile 06 63 35 66 51).

Hiking to the *Calanques*: The trail lacing together *calanques* Port-Miou, Port-Pin, and d'En-Vau will warm a hiker's heart. Views are glorious and the trail is manageable if you have decent shoes (though shade is minimal).

For most, the best *calanque* by foot is Calanque Port-Pin, about an hour from Cassis (30 minutes after the linear, boat-lined Calanque Port-Miou, which also works as a destination if time is short). Calanque Port-Pin is intimate and well-forested, with a small beach. The most spectacular *calanque* to hang out at is **Calanque d'En-Vau,** but it's a two-hour hike one-way from Cassis with a steep descent to the beach at the end. In summer (mid-June–mid-Sept), access is strictly controlled, and this *calanque* is closed by 11:00.

The TI's map of Cassis gives a general idea of the *calanques* trail, though you don't really need a map. Start along the road behind Hôtel le Golfe and walk past Plage du Bestouan, then look for green hiker signs to *Calanque Miou* (pay attention to your route for an easier return). You'll climb up, then drop down residential streets, eventually landing at the foot of Calanque Port-Miou, where the dirt trail begins. Follow signs to *Calanques Port-Pin* and *d'En Vau,* walking 500 yards along a wide trail and passing through an old quarry.

You're now on the *GR (Grande Randonnée)* trail, indicated by red, white, and green markers painted on rocks, trees, and other landmarks. Follow those markers as they lead uphill (great views at top), then connect to a rough stone trail leading down to Calanque Port-Pin (nice beach, good scampering). The trail continues from here back up and on to Calanque d'En Vau. *Bonne route!*

Other Ways to Reach the *Calanques*: From about mid-April to mid-October, you can rent a **kayak** in Cassis—or in nearby Port Miou, which is closer to the *calanques* (one-seater-€25/4 hours, two-seater-€40/4 hours, tel. 04 42 01 80 01 in Cassis, mobile 06 75 70 00 73 in Port Miou). The TI has brochures for more kayak companies. You can also take a **kayak tour** (€35/half-day, €55/day, €30/sunset tour, depart from nearby town of La Ciotat, advance reservations smart, mobile 06 12 95 20 12, www.provencekayak mer.fr). If the hiking trails are closed, this is the only way you'll be able to get to those *calanques* beaches.

You can rent a small motorboat without a special boating license (€100/half-day, €140/day, €700 cash or credit-card imprint as deposit; at Loca'Bato office, a few steps away from Hôtel le

Golfe; mobile 06 73 11 63 65). Another option is a **skippered boat rental** (up to 8 people, about €250/half-day, €440/day, ask at TI).

▲▲Above Cassis: La Route des Crêtes

If you have a car, or are willing to spring for a taxi (€30 for a 30-minute trip, 4 people per taxi), you must take this remarkable drive. Ride straight up to the top of Cap Canaille and toward the next town, La Ciotat. It's a twisty road, providing access to numbingly high views over Cassis and the Mediterranean. From Cassis, follow signs to *La Ciotat/Toulon*, then *La Route des Crêtes*. The towns just east of Cassis (La Ciotat, Bandol, etc.) do not merit a detour. This road is occasionally closed (because of strong winds or road repair), though you can usually get partway up—before investing time and money in this trip, check at the TI.

Sleeping in Cassis

(€1 = about $1.25, country code: 33)

Cassis hotels are laid-back places with less polish but lower rates than those on the Riviera (rooms average about €80). Some close from November to March, but those that stay open offer good discounts. All are busy on weekend and summer nights, when many can come with late-night noise (though most hotels have effective double-paned windows). Book early for sea views. Most hotels have free Wi-Fi and a few invaluable parking spots that you can reserve when booking your room. None of the places I list have elevators.

Near the Port or in Town

$$$ Best Western Hôtel la Rade*** sits on a ring road above the northwest corner of the port, with good views from its lovely poolside deck and welcoming lounge. It's the most professional place I recommend. You'll pay for the view, the pool, and the relatively—for Cassis—plush and tasteful rooms (standard Db-€120, bigger Db-€170, suites-€225–250, extra bed-€15, free Internet access and Wi-Fi, parking-€15, route des Calanques, 1 avenue de Dardanelles, tel. 04 42 01 02 97, fax 04 42 01 01 32, www.hotel-cassis.com, larade@hotel-cassis.com).

$$ Hôtel le Golfe**, over an easygoing (but not late-night) café, has good rates, air-conditioning, English-speaking Christine at the desk, and the best views of the port. Half of its basic-but-cute little blue-and-yellow rooms come with port views and small balconies and are worth booking ahead (Db with view and some noise-€85–95, Db without view-€75–85, extra bed-€18, 2 extra beds-€25, no Wi-Fi, dim lighting, 3 parking spaces-€8/day, nearby garage-€10/day, 3 place Grand Carnot, tel. 04 42 01 00 21, fax 04 42 01 92 08, www.legolfe-cassis.fr, contact@legolfe-cassis.fr).

$$ Hôtel le Clos des Arômes** is a simple, quieter retreat. This place has appealing ambience with public spaces you can stretch out in. *Très provençal*, it has a big courtyard terrace and a good restaurant. The rooms have old furnishings, so-so beds, poor lighting, and no air-conditioning (some have ceiling fans), but the place works in spite of these things (standard Sb-€50, Db-€75, bigger Db-€85, Tb/Qb-€95, Wi-Fi in reception area only, near Parking la Viguerie at 10 rue Abbé Paul Mouton, tel. 04 42 01 71 84, fax 04 42 01 31 76, www.le-clos-des-aromes.com, closdes aromes@orange.fr). It's best to book by phone or fax.

$$ Hôtel Cassitel**, located on the harbor over a lively café (noisy on weekends) has comfortable rooms with air-conditioning and Wi-Fi. In some rooms the shower and sink are open to the room (offering little privacy within the room), and in all rooms the double-paned windows filter most portside noise (standard Db-€75–80, large Db-€90–100, extra bed-€13, parking garage-€12/day, place Clemenceau, tel. 04 42 01 83 44, fax 04 42 01 96 31, www.hotel-cassis.com, cassitel@hotel-cassis.com).

$$ Hôtel de France** is a good place for drivers on a budget. It's a few blocks up from the port, so it's fairly quiet and has parking near the front door. Rooms are pastel soft, air-conditioned, and well-maintained (Db-€85, with breakfast and parking-€100, free Wi-Fi, above the Casino on avenue du Revestel, tel. 04 42 01 72 21, www.hoteldefrancemaguy.com, hoteldefrancemaguy @gmail.com).

$ Hôtel Laurence** offers Cassis' best budget beds, in small but relatively clean, tasteful, and air-conditioned rooms. Some come with decks and views. You must call a few days ahead to confirm your reservation (Db-€50–70, Db with balcony-€70–80, Db with view terrace-€77–90, extra bed-€13, cash only, closed in winter, 2 blocks off the port beyond Hôtel Cassitel at 8 rue de l'Arène, tel. 04 42 01 88 78, fax 04 42 01 81 04, www.cassis-hotel-laurence .com, contact@cassis-hotel-laurence.com). Animated Nadia runs the reception.

On Plage du Bestouan

The next two hotels are a 10-minute walk from the port on the next beach west, Plage du Bestouan. Easy parking makes them good for drivers.

$$$ Mahogany Hôtel de la Plage*** faces the beach with a concrete exterior and mod interior, generous public spaces, and 30 well-conceived, quite comfortable, and mostly spacious rooms at acceptable rates (same price for Db with modern decor, deck, and sea view, as for bigger suite-like Db with Provencal decor but no view-€155–175, suite with view Db-€200–230, includes breakfast, air-con in all but six rooms, Internet access, Wi-Fi in reception

area only, parking-€15, Plage du Bestouan, tel. 04 42 01 05 70, fax
04 42 01 34 82, www.hotelmahogany.com, info@hotelmahogany
.com).

$$$ Le Jardin d'Emile** is a villa-hotel located below the
Mahogany Hôtel de la Plage. It's a charming little refuge with rich
colors inside and out, plush rooms, and a green garden. Six of the
seven rooms have decks, and three have sea views (Db-€140, extra
bed-€30, air-con, free and secure parking, Plage du Bestouan,
tel. 04 42 01 80 55, fax 04 42 01 80 70, www.lejardindemile.fr,
provence@lejardindemile.fr).

Eating in Cassis

Peruse the lineup of tempting restaurants along the port, window-
shop the recommended places below, and then decide for your-
self (all have good interior and exterior seating). You can have
a ham-and-cheese crêpe or go all-out for bouillabaisse with the
same great view. Arrive by 19:30 for the view tables. Picnickers can
enjoy a beggars' banquet at the benches at Hôtel le Golfe or on the
beach, or discover your own quiet places along the lanes away from
the port (small grocery stores open until 19:30). Local wines are
terrific: red from Bandol and whites/rosés from Cassis.

Dining Portside

The first four places offer €23–28 *menus* and are ideally situated
side by side, allowing diners to comparison shop. I've enjoyed good
meals at each of them.

El Sol is sharp and popular with discerning diners (closed
Sun eve and all day Mon, 20 quai des Baux, tel. 04 42 01 76 10).

L'Oustau de la Mar is a good choice, with a loyal following,
fair prices, and welcoming owner Dominique. Try the *dos de loup
de mer à la crème d'olives*—a whitefish smothered in a delectable
sauce (closed Thu, 20 quai des Baux, tel. 04 42 01 78 22).

Bar Canaille specializes in fresh seafood platters, oysters, and
other shellfish (closed Tue, 22 quai des Baux, tel. 04 42 01 72 36).

Chez César was most popular with locals on my last visit,
with good prices and selection (€25 *marmite de pêcheur*—a poor
man's bouillabaisse, €12.50 *plats, menus* from €22, closed Sun–
Mon, 21 quay des Baux, tel. 04 42 01 75,).

Le 8 et Demi serves crêpes, pizza, salads, and good Italian
gelato on plastic tables with front-and-center portside views (closed
Thu, 8 quai des Baux, tel. 04 42 01 94 63).

The **Grand Marnier crêpe stand** cooks delicious dessert
crêpes to go for €3—the Grand Marnier crêpe rules. This is ideal
for strollers (next to Le 8 et Demi).

Dining Away from the Port

Le Clos des Arômes, listed earlier under "Sleeping in Cassis," is the place to come for a refined, candlelit dinner. Dine on a lovely enclosed terrace (€26 *menu*, closed all day Mon and Tue–Wed for lunch, tel. 04 42 01 71 84).

Le Grand Large is indeed large and owns the scenic beach-front next to the TI. Come here for a quiet drink before dinner, or to dine seaside rather than portside (€27 *menu* with good choices, open daily, Plage de Cassis, tel. 04 42 01 81 00).

La Girondole is an easy place for families, with cheap pizza, pasta, and salads. It's a block off the port (open daily in summer, take-away also possible, closed Tue off-season, 1 rue Thérèse Rastit, tel. 04 42 01 13 39).

Le Napoléon attracts budget travelers with good prices, sufficient quality, and a big selection (€12 two-course *menu*, €16 three-course *menu*, closed Sun–Mon, 14 rue Général Bonaparte, tel. 04 42 01 80 84).

Cassis Connections

Cassis' train station is two miles from the port. Shuttle buses meet some trains on weekdays, and taxis are reasonable (for details, see "Arrival in Cassis" on page 250). All destinations below require a transfer in Marseille.

From Cassis by Train to: Marseille (20/day, 25 minutes), **Aix-en-Provence** (12/day, 1.5 hours), **Arles** (7/day, 2 hours), **Avignon TGV** (7/day, 2 hours), **Nice** (14/day, 3 hours, transfer in Marseille or Toulon), **Paris** (7/day, 4 hours).

Aix-en-Provence

Aix-en-Provence is famous for its outdoor markets, beautiful people, and ability to embrace the good life. It was that way when the French king made the town his administrative capital of Provence, and it's that way today. For a tourist, Aix-en-Provence (the "Aix" is pronounced "X") is happily free of any obligatory turnstiles. And there's not a single ancient sight to see. It's just a wealthy town filled with 140,000 people—most of whom, it seems, know how to live well and look good.

Aix-en-Provence's 40,000 students (many from other countries) give the city a youthful energy and its well-deserved nickname, "Sex-en-Provence."

Orientation to Aix-en-Provence

With no "must-see" sights (unless you're a student), Aix works well as a day trip, and is best on days when the most markets thrive (Tue, Thu, and Sat). The city can be seen in a 1.5-hour stroll from the TI or train station, though connoisseurs of southern French culture will want more time to savor this lovely place.

Cours Mirabeau (the grand central boulevard) divides the stately, quiet Mazarin Quarter from the lively old town. In the old sections, picturesque squares are connected by fine pedestrian shopping lanes, many of which lead to the cathedral.

Tourist Information

The TI anchors the west end of cours Mirabeau at La Rotonde traffic circle (although be aware that it will probably move to an adjacent location sometime in 2011). Get the walking-tour brochure *In the Footsteps of Cézanne*, with the best city-center map and a good overview of excursions in the area. The TI has other maps that cover areas beyond old Aix (Mon–Sat 8:30–19:00, Sun 10:00–13:00 & 14:00–18:00, longer hours in the summer, shorter hours in the winter, 2 place du Général de Gaulle, tel. 04 42 16 11 61, www.aixenprovencetourism.com). English-language **walking tours** of the old town are offered at 10:00 on Tuesdays, Thursdays, and Saturdays (€8, depart from the TI).

Arrival in Aix-en-Provence

By Train: Aix-en-Provence has two train stations: Centre-Ville, near the city center; and the faraway TGV station. Neither has baggage storage.

Arrival at the Centre-Ville Station: It's a breezy 10-minute stroll to the TI and pedestrian area (cross the boulevard and walk straight up avenue Victor Hugo, turn left at first intersection, still on Victor Hugo; TI is on the left when you reach La Rotonde, the big traffic circle).

Arrival at Aix-en-Provence TGV Station: Shuttle buses *(navettes)* connect the distant, futuristic TGV station with Aix-en-Provence's city-center bus station, described below (€4, 3/hour, 20 minutes). From the tracks, follow signs for *Navette–Direction Aix Centre* to the

end of the hall and downstairs (buses leave from an underpass below the tracks).

If you're headed from Aix's city center to the TGV station, the *navette* buses usually depart from stall #4 at the bus station (schedule posted). To find the TGV by car from Aix-en-Provence, get on the A-51 autoroute toward *Marseille,* get off at the first exit (Les Milles), and track signs for another 10 minutes.

By Bus: From the sidewalk bus station *(gare routière)*, it's a 10-minute walk to the TI: Head uphill to the flowery roundabout and turn left toward the splashing fountain (La Rotonde, the big traffic circle by the TI). There is talk of relocating the *gare routière* that most residents don't take seriously—still, beware of possible changes.

By Plane: Buses link Marseille's airport with the bus station in Aix-en-Provence (2/hour, 35 minutes, www.navetteaixtgvair port.com).

By Car: The city is very well-signed (yellow for hotels, green for parking). First, follow signs to *Centre-Ville,* then the yellow signs to your hotel. If your hotel has parking, use it. Otherwise, once you've spotted your hotel sign, follow green signs to park in the first pay lot you see (I've noted the closest parking to each hotel under "Sleeping in Aix-en-Provence," later). Day-trippers should look for the La Rotonde parking area (near the TI) or park in any pay lot near the old city. Allow €14 for 24 hours of parking.

Helpful Hints

Markets: Aix-en-Provence bubbles over with photogenic open-air morning markets in several of its squares: **Richelme** (produce daily, my favorite), **Palace of Justice** (flea market Tue, Thu, and Sat), and **L'Hôtel de Ville** (flower market Tue, Thu, and Sat; book market first Sun of each month). Most pack up at 13:00, except the book market, which runs all day. It's well worth planning your visit for a market day, as these markets are the sightseeing highlights of the town. WineInProvence leads market tours (see "Wine Tasting and Cooking Classes" on page 264).

Internet Access: There are many options; ask your hotelier or the TI for suggestions.

English Bookstore: Located on the quiet side of Aix-en-Provence, the low-key **Paradox Bookshop** has a modest collection of adult and children's books, a good selection of tourist guides (Cassis, Arles, Avignon, and so on), and a small supply of American grocery staples such as peanut butter. The owner, Ms. Graillon, carries my guidebooks, speaks fluent English, and is a good source for information (Mon–Sat 10:00–12:30 & 14:00–18:30, closed Sun, 15 rue du 4 Septembre, tel. 04 42 26 47 99).

AIX-EN-PROVENCE

Aix-en-Provence

TO CEZANNE'S STUDIO

NOTRE-DAME

BLVD.

BLVD. JEAN JAURES

ST. SAUVEUR

FINISH

OLD

R. BON. PAST.

⑭

⑮

MUSEE ETIENNE DE ST. JEAN

TO

TO AVIGNON

FORUM DES CARDEURS

⑤ ⑬

RUE CORD.

Post

COURS SEXTIUS

R. LISSE DES CORD.

City Hall

⑤ ⑬

⑳

D'ENT. ⑥

RICHELME SQUARE

⑰

PLACE RAMUS

FOCH

⑪

TO LUBERON

BLVD. DE LA REPUBLIQUE

㉔

BERNAD. ⑪

⑫

R. ESP.

ESPARIAT

⑥

NAZ.

㉒

BONAPARTE

R. VICTOR LEYDET

㉓

Post

COURS →

⑳

LA ROTONDE (PLACE DE GAULLE)

START

③

MAZARIN

GOYRAND VILLARS

VICTOR HUGO AVE.

CARDI-

R. LAPIERRE

ⓘ

RUE GONTARD

HUGO BLVD.

AVE. DES BELGES

R. DESPLACES

①

P

BUS STN. & TGV SHUTTLE BUS

AVE. EUR.

P

㉔

TRAIN STATION

TO MARSEILLE, CASSIS & TGV STATION

1. Hôtel/Rest. Cézanne
2. Grand Hôtel Negre Coste
3. Hôtel Saint Christophe
4. To Chambre d'Hôte Pavillon de la Torse
5. L'Epicerie Chambres
6. Hôtel le Manoir & Pasta Cosy Rest.
7. Hôtel Cardinal
8. Hôtel des Quatre Dauphins & Paradox Bookshop
9. Thé à Thème Rest.
10. Chez Feraud Rest.
11. Les Agapes Rest. & Launderette
12. Charlotte Restaurant
13. Le Papagayo Café, Paniers des Salades & Juste en Face Rest.
14. Café l'Archevêché
15. La Médina de Fez Rest.
16. Boulangere de la rue Tournefort (24-hr bakery)
17. O'Shannon's Pub
18. Restaurants Aux Deux Garçons & Le Grillon
19. La Brochurie Restaurant & Launderette
20. Maison Béchard Patisserie
21. Café de l'Unic & Brûlerie Richelme
22. Monoprix (Groceries)
23. Electric Minibus Stop
24. Car Rental (2)

200 YARDS
200 METERS

➡ SELF-GUIDED WALK
🅿 PARKING

DCH

Laundry: There's a launderette at 11 rue des Bernadines, and another at 3 rue Fernand Dol (both daily 8:00–19:00).

Supermarket: Monoprix, on cours Mirabeau two long blocks up from La Rotonde, has a grocery store in the basement (Mon–Sat 8:30–21:00, closed Sun).

Taxi: Call 04 42 27 71 11 or 06 16 23 82 39.

Car Rental: Hertz is across from the Centre-Ville train station (43 avenue Victor Hugo, tel. 04 42 27 91 32), and **Europcar** is near La Rotonde (55 boulevard de la République, tel. 08 25 89 69 76). All major companies have offices at the TGV station.

Wine Tasting and Cooking Classes: At **WineInProvence,** smart, young, and enthusiastic Americans Hilary and Brian are eager to help you discover French wine and food in a fun loft apartment just off a market square. Their dream is to show you a side of Provence that you wouldn't otherwise see—through the lens of French food and wines (2-hour tasting of 5 French wines-€50, 5-hour cooking and wine-tasting class-€150, mobile 06 47 30 77 31, www.wineinprovence.com, contact@wineinprovence.com). Hilary and Brian also lead tours of Aix's open markets and specialty food shops, allowing you to experience shopping for food in Provence like a local. You'll meet their favorite cheese-makers, bakers, and produce vendors (€75, 2 hours).

Famous Local Product: Signs at fancy bakeries advertise *calissons d'Aix,* the city's homemade pastries (which don't do much for me). They're made with almond paste—kind of like a marzipan cake—and make good souvenirs. I prefer the *macarons.*

Dark Sunglasses: You may want to pick up a pair of especially dark glasses (to be more discreet when appreciating the beautiful people of Aix-en-Provence).

Tours in Aix-en-Provence

Local Guides—Caroline Bernard speaks great English and enjoys teaching visitors the wonders of her city (bernardcaro@aol.com, or contact her through the TI). **Catherine d'Antuono** is a smart, capable guide for Aix-en-Provence and the region (mobile 06 17 94 69 61, tour.designer@provence-travel.com). Americans Brian and Hilary, of **WineInProvence,** lead tours of Aix-en-Provence's markets (see "Wine Tasting and Cooking Classes," above).

Electric Minibus Joyride—For a mere €0.50, take an orientation ride on a *Diabline*—a six-seater electric-powered minibus. It leaves every 10 minutes from the La Rotonde fountain, opposite the TI (Mon–Sat 8:30–13:00 & 15:00–19:30, none on Sun, 40 minutes round-trip). You can also wave down the young drivers anywhere

Aix-en-Provence History

Aix-en-Provence was founded in about 120 B.C. as a Roman military camp on the site of a thermal hot spring (in France, "Aix" refers to a city built over a hot spring). The Romans' mission: to defend the Greek merchants of Marseille against the local Celts. Strategically situated Aix-en-Provence was the first Roman base outside Italy—the first foreign holding of what would become a vast empire. (The region's name—Provence—comes from its status as the first Roman province.) But Rome eventually fell, and the barbarians destroyed Aix-en-Provence in the fourth century. Through the Dark Ages, Aix-en-Provence's Roman buildings were nibbled to nothing by people needing the pre-cut stone. No buildings from Roman Aix-en-Provence survive.

Aix-en-Provence was of no importance through the Middle Ages. Because the area was once owned by Barcelona, Provence has the same colors as Catalunya: gold and red. In 1481 the Count of Provence died. He was hairless (according to my guide). Without a hair, Provence was gobbled up by France. When Aix-en-Provence was made the district's administrative center, noble French families moved in, kicking off the city's beautiful age (belle époque). They built about 200 *hôtels particuliers* (private mansions)—many of which survive today—giving Aix-en-Provence its classy appearance. As you wander around the town, look up, peek in, and notice the stately architecture with its grandiose extra touches.

Aix-en-Provence thrived thanks to its aristocratic population. But when the Revolution made being rich dicey, Aix-en-Provence's aristocracy and clergy fled. Aix-en-Provence entered the next stage of its history as the "Sleeping Beauty city." Later in the 19th century, the town woke up and resumed its familiar, pretentious ways. In Aix-en-Provence, the custom of rich people being bobbed along in sedan chairs survived longer than anywhere else in France. After the Revolution, you couldn't have servants do it—but you could hire pallbearers in their off-hours to give you a lift. If being ostentatious ever became the norm...it happened in Aix-en-Provence.

and hop on. There are two routes (A and B); ask the driver for a map when you board. Line A gives you a better overview of the city and runs a route similar to the self-guided walk described below. It also gets you near Cézanne's Studio. Designed with local seniors in mind, the minibus provides a fun (and less glamorous) slice-of-life experience in Aix-en-Provence.

Petit Train—Rest your feet and discover Aix-en-Provence's historic center on a 50-minute tour on the little train, while listening to English commentary (€6, departs from La Rotonde fountain). Ask about the longer tours that cover Cézanne's steps.

Self-Guided Walk

Welcome to Aix-en-Provence

I've listed these streets, squares, and sights in the order of a handy, lazy orientation stroll. This walk is highlighted on the map on page 262.

• Start across from the TI, on cours Mirabeau near the small fountain.

La Rotonde: In the 1600s, the roads from Paris and Marseille met just outside the Aix-en-Provence town wall at a huge roundabout called La Rotonde. From here locals enjoyed a sweeping view of open countryside before entering the town. As time passed, Aix-en-Provence needed space more than fortifications. The wall was destroyed and replaced by a grand boulevard (cours Mirabeau). A modern grid-plan town, the Mazarin Quarter, arose across the boulevard from the medieval town (to the right as you look up cours Mirabeau). In 1860, to give residents water and shade, the town graced La Rotonde with a fountain and the boulevard with trees. Voilà: The modern core of Aix-en-Provence was created.

• Saunter up cours Mirabeau.

Cours Mirabeau: This "Champs-Elysées of Provence" divides the higgledy-piggledy old town and the stately Mazarin Quarter. Designed for the rich and famous to strut their fancy stuff, cours Mirabeau survives much as it was: a single lane for traffic and an extravagant pedestrian promenade, shaded by plane trees (see sidebar) and lined by 17th- and 18th-century mansions for the nobility. Rich folks lived on the right side (in the Mazarin  Quarter); common folk lived on the left side (in the old town). Cross-streets were gated to keep everyone in their place.

The street follows a plan based on fours: 440 meters long, 44 meters wide, plane trees (originally elms) 4 meters apart, and deco-

Plane Trees

Stately old plane trees line roads and provide canopies of shade for town squares all over southern France. These trees are a part of the local scene.

The plane tree is a hybrid of the Asian and American sycamores—created accidentally in a 16th-century Oxford botanical garden. The result was the perfect city tree: fast-growing, resistant to urban pollution, and hearty (it can survive with little water and lousy soil). The plane tree was imported to southern France in the 19th century to replace the traditional elm trees. Napoleon planted them along roads to give his soldiers shade for their long marches. Plane trees were used to leaf up grand boulevards as towns through-out France—including Aix-en-Provence—built their Champs-Elysées wannabes.

rated by 4 fountains. The "mossy fountains," covered by 200 years of neglect, trickle with water from the thermal spa that gave Aix its first name (and make steamy sights on cold winter days). At the end of the boulevard, a statue celebrates the last count of Provence, under whose rule this region joined France.

Cours Mirabeau was designed for showing off. Today, it remains a place for *tendance* (trendiness)—or even *hyper-tendance*. Show your stuff and strut the broad sidewalk. As you stroll up the boulevard, stop in front of Aix's oldest and most venerated *patisserie*, **Maison Béchard** (12 cours Mirabeau), and get a whiff coming from the vent under the entry. Grab a seat in an upscale café and observe.

• *From the mossy fountain at rue du 4 Septembre, turn right onto Aix-en-Provence's quiet side, the pleasing little place des Quatre Dauphins. This marks the center of the...*

Mazarin Quarter (Quartier Mazarin): Built in a grid plan during the reign of King Louis XIV, the Mazarin Quarter remains a peaceful, elegant residential neighborhood—although each of its mansions now houses several families rather than just one. Study the quarter's Baroque and Neoclassical architecture (from the 17th and 18th centuries). The square's Fountain of the Four Dolphins, inspired by Bernini's fountains in Rome, dates from an age when Italian culture set the Baroque standard across Europe.

Wander up rue Cardinale to the **Musée Granet,** which faces a handsome square and features Aix's home-grown artists (including a few paintings by Cézanne—see sidebar on page 270). The vertical St. Jean de Malte church sits across from the museum.

• *Return to the cours Mirabeau and pop into #53, the venerable...*

Aux Deux Garçons: This café, once frequented by Paul Cézanne, is now popular with—and controlled by—the local mafia. Don't take photos here (and don't open a competing café—the mafia is a serious problem for many independent restaurateurs in Aix). Still, it's worth a peek for its beautiful circa-1790 interior and, for many, worth the higher (mafia-inflated) prices for the sidewalk setting. The Cézanne family hat shop was next door (#55). Cézanne's dad must have been some hatter. He parlayed that successful business into a bank, then into greater wealth, setting up his son to be free to enjoy his artistic pursuits.

• *From here we'll enter the lively Old Town, where pedestrian streets are filled with strolling beauties and romantic street musicians. This is the place in Aix-en-Provence for shopping. Leave cours Mirabeau down the tiny passage Agard, 10 steps past Aux Deux Garçons. It leads to the* **Palace of Justice Square,** *which hosts a bustling flea market (Tue, Thu, and Sat mornings). If the market is on, dally awhile. Leave this square heading left along the first street you crossed to enter it. The street you're on, rue Marius Reinaud, hosts the top designer shops in town. Pause several blocks down at the peaceful courtyard square called...*

Place d'Albertas: This sweet little square was created by the guy who lived across the street. He hated the medieval mess of buildings facing his mansion, so he drew up a harmonious facade with a fountain, and hired an architect to build his ideal vision and mask the ugly neighborhood. The neighbors got a nice new facade, and the rich guy got the view of his dreams. The long-overdue restoration of this once run-down square is making a remarkable difference. But since only two-thirds of the property owners agreed to help fund the work, one third remains undone.

• *From here turn right on rue Aude, the main street of medieval Aix-en-Provence (which turns into rue du Maréchal Foch and eventually leads to the cathedral). Notice how effectively the green bollards keep cars from parking in this virtual car-free zone. Notice also the side streets, with their traffic-barrier stumps that lower during delivery hours. Stop where rue du Maréchal Foch crosses rue de la Fauchier for a decadent* macaron *sensation at* **Brunet Chocolatier** *(ooh la la). Make your way to...*

Richelme Square (Place Richelme): This wonderful square

hosts a lively market, as it has since the 1300s (daily 7:00–13:00). It's the perfect Provençal scene—lovely buildings, plane trees, farmers selling local produce, and a guy in the goat-cheese stall near the Bar de l'Horloge who looks just like Paul Cézanne—or Jerry Garcia, if that's more your style. (He works Tue, Thu, and Sat and is fully aware of his special good looks; drop by for a sample and a photo if you like.) The cafés at the end of the square are ideal for market observation. To savor the market scene, pause for a drink at **Café de l'Unic** (also draws a lively and young pre-dinner crowd). To experience the best coffee and hot chocolate in Aix, grab an outdoor stool and go local at **Brûlerie Richelme** (Tue–Sat 8:30–18:15, closed Sun–Mon).

• *One block uphill is the stately...*

L'Hôtel de Ville Square (Place de l'Hôtel de Ville): This square, also known as place de la Mairie, is anchored by a Roman

column. Stand with your back to the column and face the Hôtel de Ville. The center niche of this 17th-century City Hall once featured a bust of Louis XIV. But since the Revolution, Marianne (the Lady of the Republic) has taken his place. As throughout Europe, the three flags represent the region (Provence), country (France), and the European Union. Provence's flag carries the red and yellow of Catalunya (the region in Spain centered on Barcelona) because the counts of Provence originated there. The coat of arms over the doorway combines the Catalan flag and the French fleur-de-lis.

The 18th-century building on your left was once the town's corn exchange (today it's a letter exchange). Its exuberant pediment features figures representing the two rivers of Provence: old man Rhône and madame Durance. While the Durance River floods frequently (here depicted overflowing its frame), it also brings fertility to the fields (hence the cornucopia).

Back toward the Hôtel de Ville (where you're heading), the 16th-century bell tower was built in part with stones scavenged from ancient Roman buildings—notice the white stones at the tower's base. The niche above the arch once displayed the bust of the king. Since the Revolution, it has housed a funerary urn that symbolically honors all who gave their lives for French liberty. Under the arch, a small plaque honors the American 3rd Division that liberated the town in 1944 (with the participation of French troops; Aix-en-Provence got through World War II relatively unscathed).

History aside, the square is a delight for its colorful morning

Paul Cézanne in Aix-en-Provence

Post-Impressionist artist Paul Cézanne (1839–1906) loved Aix-en-Provence. He studied law at the university (opposite the cathedral), and produced most of his paintings in and around Aix-en-Provence—even though this conservative town didn't understand him or his art. Today the city fathers milk anything remotely related to his years here. But because the conservative curator of the town's leading art gallery, the Granet Museum, decreed "no Cézannes," you can see only a few of Cézanne's lesser original paintings in Aix-en-Provence. Bad curator.

Instead, fans of the artist will want to pick up the *In the Footsteps of Cézanne* self-guided-tour flier at the TI, and follow the bronze pavement markers around town.

Cézanne's **last studio** (Atelier Cézanne)—preserved as it was when he died—is open to the public. It's a 30-minute walk from the TI, or you can get there on electric minibus A (see "Tours in Provence," earlier). Although there is no art here, his tools and personal belongings make it almost interesting for enthusiasts—I'd skip it. If you must go, it's best (and essential in high season) to reserve a visit time in advance at the TI or at www.aixenprovencetourism.com (€6, daily July–Aug 10:00–18:00, April–June and Sept 10:00–12:00 & 14:00–18:00, Oct–March until 17:00, English-language tours usually at 16:00 or 17:00, 2 miles from TI at 9 avenue Cézanne, tel. 04 42 16 10 91, www.atelier-cezanne.com).

markets: flowers (Tue, Thu, and Sat) and old books (Sun). On non-market days and each afternoon, café tables replace the market stalls.

• *Stroll under the bell tower and up rue Gaston de Saporta, to the yellow-bannered...*

Musée Etienne de St. Jean: This museum fills a 17th-century mansion with a scant collection of artifacts. The building interior itself is of most interest. Pop in for a look at the grand staircase and fancy ceilings. The exhibits include lots of *santons*—painted clay figurines popular in old-time manger scenes (€4, pick up the English handout, April–Sept Tue–Sun 10:00–13:00 & 14:00–18:00, Oct–March until 17:00, closed Mon, 17 rue Gaston de Saporta).

• *A block farther uphill, facing the historic university building (where Cézanne studied), is the...*

Cathedral of the Holy Savior (Saint-Sauveur): This church was built atop the Roman forum—likely on the site of a pagan temple. As the cathedral grew with the city, its interior became a parade of architectural styles. The many-faceted interior is at once confusing and fascinating, with three distinct sections: Standing at the entrance, you face the Romanesque section; to the left are the Gothic and then the Baroque sections. We'll visit each in turn.

In the **Romanesque section,** branching off to the right is the baptistery, with its early Christian (fourth-century) Roman font. It's big enough for immersion, which was the baptismal style in Roman times. Also notice that it's eight-sided, symbolizing eternity: one side more than the seven days it took God to create everything. The font is surrounded by ancient columns with original fourth-century capitals below a Renaissance cupola. Farther down is the door to the 12th-century cloister (visits on the half-hour except 12:00–14:00, or just open the outer door and peer through the iron gate). Beyond that, find the closet-sized architectural footprint of the original Christian chapel from the Roman era.

In the **Gothic section,** two organs flank the nave: One works, but the other is a prop, added for looks...an appropriately symmetrical Neoclassical touch, as was the style in the 18th century. The precious door (facing the street from this section) is carved of chestnut with a Gothic top (showing sibyls, or ancient female prophets) and Renaissance lower half (depicting prophets). Because it faces the street, it's covered by a second, protective door (viewable on request).

In the **Baroque section,** don't miss the finely detailed three-paneled altar painting of the burning bush (15th century, by Nicolas Froment).

• *Your tour is over. Walking back through town, drop by a designer bakery to try a calisson, Aix-en-Provence's local pastry (see "Helpful Hints," earlier). Or, for fewer calories and just as much fun, marvel at a town filled with people who seem to be living life very, very well.*

Sleeping in Aix-en-Provence

(€1 = about $1.25, country code: 33)

Hotel rooms, starting at about €60, are surprisingly reasonable in this highbrow city. Reserve ahead, particularly on weekends. Hotel stars have less meaning here. The best values are on the quiet side of cours Mirabeau in the Mazarin Quarter.

$$$ Hôtel Cézanne**, a block up from the Centre-Ville train station, delivers professional service with a smile. The lobby and 55 plush, spacious rooms are *très* modern, with every creature comfort (and cool faucets). This stylish place pampers guests with an efficient, English-speaking staff (including your chef, adorable Christianne) and amenities like a daily champagne "brunch" that comes with French toast, omelets, and smoked salmon (€20, served until noon, try the French toast with honey and the truffle omelet) and free nonalcoholic drinks from your minibar (standard Db-€190, deluxe Db-€260, some king-size beds, air-con, elevator, free parking if you book ahead, free and easy Internet access and Wi-Fi, 40 avenue Victor Hugo, tel. 04 42 91 11 11, fax 04 42 91 11 10, www.hotelaix.com, hotelcezanne@hotelaix.com).

$$$ Chambre d'Hôte Pavillon de la Torse is an upscale B&B in a park-like setting. A lane of plane trees escorts you

down a private lane into this urban retreat. Pass the 25-meter lap pool surrounded by gardens that Louis would appreciate, then get to know eager-to-help American Mary and Frenchman François, who offer every amenity (Db-€150–210, €20 less Nov and March; extra bed-€20 for kids who must be 5 or older, €40 for adults; 2-night minimum, includes breakfast, Internet access and Wi-Fi, easy parking, 15-minute walk south of the old city at 69 cours Gambetta, tel. 09 50 58 49 96, www.latorse.com, contact@latorse.com).

$$$ L'Epicerie Chambres is a fun place with an avid collector as owner. The reception is a nostalgic general store, and the five rooms are well-conceived and very comfortable (Sb-€80, Db-€100, Tb suite-€130, includes breakfast, air-con, €25 three-course dinner must be booked ahead, a block off forum des Cardeurs at 12 rue du Cancel, mobile 06 08 85 38 68, www.unechambre enville.eu).

$$ Grand Hôtel Negre Coste** occupies a privileged position at the center of cours Mirabeau. This once grand, now not-so-grand hotel houses a formal staff and traditional rooms in need of a facelift, but may have rooms when others don't (Db-€95–115, big Db-€150, air-con, Internet access and Wi-Fi, private garage-€10, 33 cours Mirabeau, tel. 04 42 27 74 22, fax 04 42 26 80 93, www .hotelnegrecoste.com, contact@hotelnegrecoste.com).

$$ Hôtel Saint Christophe**, a basic business hotel with fair-enough rates, is located behind the TI and above a swanky brasserie. It has 58 tight but well-equipped rooms, some with small terraces (Db-€95–105, mezzanine suite sleeps up to 4-€115–155, air-con, elevator, parking garage-€12, 2 avenue Victor Hugo, tel. 04 42 26 01 24, fax 04 42 38 53 17, www.hotel-saintchristophe.com, saintchristophe@francemarket.com).

$$ Hôtel le Manoir*, built on the heavy arches of a medieval monastery, is modest, peaceful, and central. The decor is strictly traditional and furnishings are worn, though the setting is ideal (small Db-€66, standard Db-€80–99, Tb-€92–100, Qb-€115, elevator, limited free parking, 8 rue d'Entrecasteaux, tel. 04 42 26 27 20, fax 04 42 27 17 97, www.hotelmanoir.com, infos@hotel manoir.com).

$$ Hôtel Cardinal** is a solid value on Aix-en-Provence's classy side, across cours Mirabeau from the pedestrian zone. It's a shy, rose-colored hotel with 29 traditionally furnished rooms and a hopelessly confusing floor plan (Sb-€64, Db-€74, cavernous Db suite in nearby annex-€114, elevator, Wi-Fi, closest parking is Mignet, 24 rue Cardinale, tel. 04 42 38 32 30, fax 04 42 26 39 05, www.hotel-cardinal-aix.com, hotel.cardinal@wanadoo.fr).

$$ Hôtel des Quatre Dauphins** is a sweet little place in the quiet quarter with soft rooms, Old World decor, and excellent rates (Db-€70–85, bigger Db-€90–105, Tb-€120, air-con, Wi-Fi, closest parking is Mignet, 54 rue Roux Alphéran, tel. 04 42 38 16 19, fax 04 42 38 60 19, www.lesquatredauphins.fr, lesquatredauphins @wanadoo.fr).

Eating in Aix-en-Provence

In Aix-en-Provence, you can dine on bustling squares, along a grand boulevard, or in little restaurants on side streets (where you'll find the best values). Cours Mirabeau is good for desserts and drinks, as are many of the outdoor places lining leafy squares. Aix is filled with tempting but mediocre restaurants. To eat higher on the food chain, try one of the following places.

In the Old Town

Thé à Thème delivers wonderful lunches and early dinners at colorful tables, with cheery ambience inside and on the charming back terrace. The portions are big and the prices are small, making this a popular place with locals. Call ahead for an outside table (€10 *plats,* wonderful desserts, Tue–Sat 9:30–18:00, closed Sun–Mon, 7 rue Mignet, tel. 04 42 63 04 05).

Chez Feraud, in a lovely vine-covered building, is a good choice for a refined dinner of authentic Provençal dishes. Here, clients speak in hushed voices, the table settings are carefully arranged, and Mama serves with formal grace while son handles the grill (€30 *menu,* 8 rue du Puits Juif, tel. 04 42 63 07 27).

Pasta Cosy is unique, serving a Franco-Italian fusion of original dishes in a small, cozy setting (inside and out). Welcoming owner Fabien greets every client with the same enthusiasm and ensures good service and top quality (his wife is le chef). Be tempted by their rich Pastacosy dish (pasta cooked inside a wheel of parmesan cheese). Try the *fiocchetti* (pasta cooked with pears and gorgonzola) or the gourmet white truffle pasta. Desserts are homemade and delicious. The reasonably priced wine list features wines from Burgundy and Provence (closed Sun, across from Hôtel le Manoir at 5 rue d'Entecasteaux, tel. 04 42 38 02 28).

Les Agapes is a top choice for Provençal cuisine, offering generous portions, good prices, and attentive service (€20–25 *menus*, 11 rue des Bernardines, tel. 04 92 70 45 45).

Charlotte is Aix's low-key, down-and-dirty diner, where locals come for a good meal at a good price in simple surroundings. The entrance is the epitome of low-profile (€19 three-course *menu* only, no à la carte, 32 rue des Bernadines, tel. 04 42 26 77 56).

Hôtel Cézanne, recommended earlier in "Sleeping in Aix-en-Provence," serves up a gourmet champagne brunch à la francaise. For €20 you can feast on a great selection of omelets (made with caramelized goat cheese or truffles) and sample real French toast (brunch served daily 7:00–12:00, 40 avenue Victor Hugo, www .hotelaix.com).

On Forum des Cardeurs: Just off L'Hôtel de Ville Square, the forum des Cardeurs is café-crammed. Browse the selection from top to bottom, then decide. **Le Papagayo** has a good selection of salads and a quiche of the day (big €14 salads, open daily for lunch and dinner, 22 forum des Cardeurs, tel. 04 42 23 98 35). **Paniers des Salades** is *the* place for salads (€10 buys a salad big enough for two; the goat-cheese salad is particularly good, 34 forum des Cardeurs, tel. 04 42 21 35 80). **Juste en Face,** facing Papagayo, features excellent grilled meats (the duck and rabbit are tasty) and Mediterranean cuisine, specializing in North African *tajine*—a vegetable-based stew usually served with meat (€16 *plats*, open daily, 6 rue Verrerie, tel. 04 42 96 47 70).

On and near Place des Martyrs de la Resistance: A short block below the cathedral, this quiet square is good for a light meal. **Café l'Archevêché** is a fine bet for café fare and is understandably proud of its pizzas (lunch only except June–mid-Sept, tel. 04 42 21 43 57). For a change of pace, find **La Médina de Fez** a few blocks away, offering authentic Moroccan cuisine at fair prices (*menus* from €19, closed Mon, 35 rue Campra, tel. 04 42 21 68 58).

Le Late-Night Hunger: Aix is the only French city I know of with a 24/7 bakery. Find **Boulangere de la rue Tournefort** at the non-Rotonde end of cours Mirabeau (on the left side of the building that seals the street's upper end, tel. 04 42 38 21 32). Their chocolate-chip cookies are a rare treat.

Bar Hopping: For the young—and young at heart—the best action centers on rue de la Verrerie. **O'Shannon's Pub** (#30) makes a great starting point for your evening out.

Along Cours Mirabeau

If you're interested in a delicious view more than delicious food, eat with style on cours Mirabeau.

Aux Deux Garçons has always been the place to see and be seen: a vintage brasserie with door-to-door waiters in aprons, a lovely interior, and well-positioned outdoor tables with properly placed silverware on white tablecloths. It's busy at lunch but quiet for dinner (€20 *plats*, two-course *menus* from €28, great steak *tartare*, open daily, 53 cours Mirabeau, tel. 04 42 26 00 51). Even if you're not eating here, pop in to see the decor (see page 268).

Le Grillon is a younger, more boisterous, and less pricey choice for dinner on cours Mirabeau (white tablecloths, €15 *plats*, €24 *menu*). Its bar is a hit with locals for the prime seating: front and center on the boulevard's strolling fashion show (open daily for lunch and dinner, corner of rue Clémenceau and cours Mirabeau, tel. 42 27 58 81).

In the Mazarin Quarter

La Brocherie dishes up French rather than Provençal cuisine. Its stone-rustic, indoors-only ambience is best for cooler days. This family-owned bistro—run by Messieurs Soudain and Tourville—is deep in the Mazarin Quarter and highlights food from the farm (it's about beef). Dig into the hearty self-service salad buffet (all you can eat, €12) and meats grilled over a wood fire (skip the fish options). The €20 *menu* includes the salad bar (closed Sun, indoor seating only, 5 rue Fernand Dol, tel. 04 42 38 33 21).

Aix-en-Provence Connections

Remember, Aix-en-Provence has both a TGV station and a Centre-Ville train station (see "Arrival in Aix-en-Provence" on page 260). In some cases, destinations are served from both stations; I've listed the station with the best connection.

From Aix-en-Provence's Centre-Ville Station by Train to: Marseille (2/hour, 45 minutes), **Cassis** (12/day, 1.5 hours, transfer in Marseille), **Arles** (10/day, 2.25 hours, transfer in Marseille; train may separate midway—be sure you're in section going to Arles).

From Aix-en-Provence's TGV Station by Train to: Avignon TGV (10/day, 25 minutes), **Nice** (10/day, 3.5 hours, usually change in Marseille), **Paris** (14/day, 3 hours, may require transfer in Lyon).

From Aix-en-Provence by Bus to: Marseille (4/hour, 50 minutes), **Marseille airport** (2/hour, 35 minutes), **Lourmarin** (1.25 hours total—bus to Pertuis leaves 2/hour, transfer there to Avignon-bound bus, 3/day).

THE FRENCH RIVIERA

THE FRENCH RIVIERA

La Côte d'Azur

A hundred years ago, celebrities from London to Moscow flocked to the French Riviera to socialize, gamble, and escape the dreary weather at home. Today, budget vacationers and heat-seeking Europeans fill belle époque resorts at France's most sought-after fun-in-the-sun destination.

The region got its nickname from turn-of-the-20th-century vacationing Brits, who simply extended the Italian Riviera west to France. Their original definition of the French Riviera only went as far as Nice, though the Riviera label has been stretched even farther westward since these Victorian Brits strolled their promenade. Today, this summer fun zone—which, for our purposes, runs from St-Tropez to the Italian border—is *La Côte d'Azur* to the French. All of my French Riviera destinations are on the sea, except for a few hill towns and the Gorges du Verdon.

This sunny sliver of land has been inhabited for more than 3,000 years. Ligurians were first, then Greeks, then Romans—who, as usual, had the greatest impact. After the fall of Rome, Nice became an important city in the Kingdom of Provence (along with Marseille and Arles). In the 14th century Nice's leaders voted to throw their beach towel in with the Duke of Savoy's mountainous kingdom (also including several regions of northern Italy), which would later evolve into the Kingdom of Sardinia. It was not until 1860 that Nice (and Savoy) became a part of France—the result of a citywide vote made possible by Napoleon III and the King of Sardinia.

Nice has world-class museums, a splendid beachfront promenade, a seductive old town, and all the drawbacks of a major city (traffic, crime, pollution, and so on). The day-trip possibilities are easy and exciting: Monte Carlo welcomes everyone and will happily take your cash; Antibes has a thriving port and silky sand beaches;

The French Riviera

and image-conscious Cannes is the Riviera's self-appointed queen, with an elegant veneer hiding...very little. Yacht-happy St-Tropez swims alone an hour west (halfway to Cassis and Marseille). The Riviera's overlooked interior transports travelers to a world apart, with cliff-hanging villages, impossibly steep canyons, and alpine scenery—a refreshing alternative to the beach scene.

Choose a Home Base

My favorite home bases are Nice, Antibes, and Villefranche-sur-Mer.

Nice is the region's capital and France's fifth-largest city. With convenient train and bus connections to most regional sights, this is the most practical base for train travelers. Urban Nice also has a full palette of museums (most of which are free), a beach scene that rocks, the best selection of hotels in all price ranges, and good

THE FRENCH RIVIERA

nightlife options. A car is a headache in Nice, though it's easily stored at one of the many pricey parking garages or for free at an outer tram station.

Nearby **Antibes** is smaller, with a bustling center, a lively night scene, great sandy beaches, grand vistas, good walking trails, and a much-admired Picasso Museum. Antibes has frequent train service to Nice and Monaco, and quick connections by train or car to Grasse. It's also an easy place for drivers, with light traffic and easy hotel parking.

Villefranche-sur-Mer is the romantic's choice, with a serene setting and small-town warmth. It has finely ground pebble beaches; quick public transportation to Nice, Monaco, and Cap Ferrat; easy parking; and a small selection of hotels in most price ranges.

Planning Your Time

Ideally, allow a day and a half for Nice itself, an afternoon to explore inland hill towns, a day for Italianesque Villefranche-sur-Mer and lovely Cap Ferrat, a day for Monaco and the Corniches, and—if time allows—a day for Antibes and Cannes. Consider using two different Riviera bases, and enjoy each for a couple of nights—Villefranche-sur-Mer pairs well with Antibes or Nice. And if you must do St-Tropez, visit it while traveling to or from destinations farther west (such as Cassis, Aix-en-Provence, and Arles) and avoid it on weekend afternoons, as well as all summer.

Monaco has a unique energy at night, and Antibes works well by day (good beaches and hiking) and night (fine choice of restaurants and a lively after-hours scene). Hill town–loving naturalists should add a night or two inland to explore the charming hill-capping hamlets near Vence.

Depending on the amount of time you have in the Riviera, here are my recommended priorities:

3 days: Nice, Villefranche-sur-Mer with Cap Ferrat, and Monaco

5 days, add: Antibes and maybe Cannes, and hill towns near Vence

7 days, add: Grand Canyon du Verdon and St-Tropez

Helpful Hints

Medical Help: Riviera Medical Services has a list of English-speaking physicians all along the Riviera. They can help you make an appointment or call an ambulance (tel. 04 93 26 12 70, www.rivieramedical.com).

Closed Days: The following sights are closed on Mondays: the Modern and Contemporary Art Museum, the Fine Arts Museum, and cours Saleya market in Nice, along with

Antibes' Marché Provençal market from September through May. On Tuesdays the Chagall, Matisse, and Archaeological museums in Nice are closed.

Events: The Riviera is famous for staging major events. Unless you're actually taking part in the festivities, these events give you only room shortages and traffic jams. Here are the three biggies in 2011: **Nice Carnival** (Feb 18–March 8, www .nicecarnaval.com), **Grand Prix of Monaco** (May 26–29, www.grand-prix-monaco.com), and Festival de Cannes, better known as the **Cannes Film Festival** (May 11–22, www .festival-cannes.com).

Local Guides: Sylvie Di Cristo offers terrific full-day tours throughout the French Riviera in a car or minivan. She adores educating people about this area's culture and history, and loves adapting her tour to your interests, from overlooked hill towns to wine, cuisine, art, or perfume (€170/person for 2–3 people, €120/person for 4–6 people, €100/person for 7–8 people, 2-person minimum, mobile 06 09 88 83 83, www .frenchrivieraguides.net, sylvie.di.cristo@wanadoo.fr).

Sofia Villavicencio can expertly guide you in Nice and around the Riviera. Her English is flawless, and art is her passion (€135/half-day, €200/full-day, tel. 04 93 32 45 92, mobile 06 68 51 55 52, sofia.villavicencio@laposte.net).

Minivan Tours: The TI and most hotels have information on minivan excursions from Nice (roughly €50–60/half-day, €80–110/day). **Med-Tour** is one of many (tel. 04 93 82 92 58, mobile 06 73 82 04 10, www.med-tour.com); **Tour Azur** is another (tel. 04 93 44 88 77, www.tourazur.com). **Revelation Tours** specializes in English-language excursions (tel. 04 93 53 69 85, www.revelation-tours.com). All also offer private tours by the day or half-day (check with them for their outrageous prices, about €90/hour).

Getting Around the Riviera

By Train and Bus: Trains and buses do a good job of connecting places along the coast (with views along many sections), and buses provide reasonable service to some inland hill towns (for details on all the connections, see "**Getting Around the Riviera**" in the Nice chapter, on page 292).

Nice makes the most convenient base for day trips, though public transport also works well from smaller Riviera towns like Antibes and Villefranche-sur-Mer. And though trains are faster, buses are cheaper (€1 for most trips) and more frequent to destinations near Nice. St-Tropez is remote, requiring a bus or boat connection. Details are provided under each destination's "Connections" section. For a scenic inland train ride, take the narrow-gauge train into the Alps (see page 305). Never board a train without a ticket or valid pass—fare inspectors don't accept any excuses, and the minimum fine is €70.

By Car: After Paris, this is France's second most challenging region to drive in. Beautifully distracting vistas (natural and human), loads of Sunday-driver tourists, and an overabundance of cars make for a dangerous combination; pay extra attention while driving down here. Parking can be tricky for the same reasons, so have patience and consider using buses or trains. Have lots of coins ready for parking and for autoroute tolls.

The Riviera is awash with scenic roads. To sample some of the Riviera's best scenery, drivers should find the splendid coastal road between Cannes and Fréjus (D-6098 from Cannes/D-550 from Fréjus, old route N-98), which works well when connecting the Riviera with Provence. If it weren't for the Mediterranean sea below, you'd swear you were in Arizona (in Fréjus, follow signs to *Centre-Ville,* then *Cannes par la Bord de la Mer;* from Cannes, drive to the western end of town and follow *La Napoule* signs to reach the road).

Drivers should also scour the three Corniches between Nice and Monaco (see page 358) and take my recommended inland hill-towns drive (on page 422). Farther inland, the Grand Canyon du Verdon patiently awaits, with breathtaking gorges and alpine scenery. But even if you have a car, consider the convenience that trains and buses offer for basic sightseeing between Monaco and Cannes.

By Boat: Trans Côte d'Azur offers boat service from Nice to Monaco or to St-Tropez from June into September, as well as between Cannes and St-Tropez (tel. 04 92 98 71 30, www.trans-cote-azur.com). For details, see "Getting Around the Riviera from Nice" (page 292).

The Riviera's Art Scene

The list of artists who have painted the Riviera reads like a Who's Who of 20th-century art. Pierre-Auguste Renoir, Henri Matisse, Marc Chagall, Georges Braque, Raoul Dufy, Fernand Léger, and Pablo Picasso all lived and worked here—and raved about the region's wonderful light. Their simple, semi-abstract, and—most importantly—colorful works reflect the Riviera. You'll experience the same landscapes they painted in this bright, sun-drenched region, punctuated with views of the "azure sea." Try to imagine the Riviera with a fraction of the people and development you see today.

Top Art Sights of the Riviera

These are listed in order of importance.

Fondation Maeght (St-Paul-de-Vence)
Chagall Museum (Nice)
Picasso Museum (Antibes)
Matisse Museum (Nice)
Museum of the Annonciade (St-Tropez)
Chapel of the Rosary (Vence)
Modern and Contemporary Art Museum (Nice)
Renoir Museum (Cagnes-sur-Mer)
Fine Arts Museum (Nice)

But the artists were mostly drawn to the uncomplicated life-style of fishermen and farmers that has reigned here since time began. As the artists grew older, they retired in the sun, turned their backs on modern art's "isms," and painted with the wide-eyed wonder of children, using bright primary colors, basic outlines, and simple subjects.

A dynamic concentration of well-organized modern- and contemporary-art museums (many described in this book) litter the Riviera, allowing art-lovers to appreciate these masters' works while immersed in the same sun and culture that inspired them. Many of the museums were designed to blend pieces with the surrounding views, gardens, and fountains, thus highlighting that modern art is not only stimulating, but sometimes simply beautiful.

Entire books have been written about the modern-art galleries of the Riviera. If you're a fan, do some studying before your visit to be sure you know about that far-out museum of your dreams. Even if you aren't usually turned on by modern art, take the opportunity to experience the region's brilliant display of it by visiting the Fondation Maeght in St-Paul-de-Vence, and the Chagall and Matisse museums in Nice.

The Riviera's Cuisine Scene

The Riviera adds a Mediterranean flair to the food of Provence. While many of the same dishes served in Provence are available throughout the Riviera (see "Provence's Cuisine Scene" on page 51), there are differences, especially if you look for anything Italian or from the sea. The proximity to the water and historic ties to Italy are clear in this region's dishes.

La salade niçoise (nee-swahz) is where most Riviera meals start.

A true specialty from Nice, this salad has many versions, though most include a base of green salad topped with green beans, boiled potatoes (sometimes rice), tomatoes (sometimes corn), anchovies, olives, hard-boiled eggs, and lots of tuna. Every café and restaurant adds its own twist to this filling dish that goes down well on sultry days.

For lunch on the go, look for a *pan bagnat* (like a *salade niçoise* stuffed into a hollowed-out soft roll). Other tasty bread treats include *pissaladière* (bread dough topped with onions, olives, and anchovies), *fougasse* (a spindly, lace-like bread sometimes flavored with nuts, herbs, olives, or ham), and *socca* (a thin chickpea crêpe, seasoned with pepper and olive oil and often served in a paper cone by street vendors).

Invented in Nice, ravioli and potato gnocchi can be found on menus everywhere (ravioli can be stuffed with a variety of fillings, but it's best with seafood). Thin-crust pizza and *pâtes fraîches* (fresh pasta) are generally a good value throughout the Riviera.

Bouillabaisse is the Riviera's most famous dish; look for it in any seafront village or city. It's a spicy fish stew based on recipes handed down from sailors in Marseille. It must contain at least four types of fresh fish, though most have five to twelve kinds. A true bouillabaisse never has shellfish. The fish—cooked in a tomato-based stock and flavored with saffron (and sometimes anise and orange)—is separated from the stock before serving. The cook then heightens the flavor of the stock by adding toasted croutons and a dollop of *rouille* sauce (a thickened reddish mayonnaise heady with garlic and spicy peppers). This dish often requires a minimum order of two even though it can cost up to €40–60 per person.

Those on a budget can enjoy other seafood soups and stews. Less pricey than bouillabaisse but equally good is the local *soupe de poisson* (fish soup). It's flavored like bouillabaisse, with anise and orange, and served with croutons and *rouille* sauce. For a less colorful but still tasty soup, look for *bourride,* a creamy fish concoction thickened with an aioli garlic sauce instead of the red *rouille;* or *baudroie,* a fishy soup cooked with vegetables and garlic.

The Riviera specializes in all sorts of fish and shellfish. Other options include *"fruits de mer,"* or platters of seafood (including tiny shellfish, from which you get the edible part only by sucking really hard); herb-infused mussels; stuffed sardines; squid (slowly simmered with tomatoes and herbs); and tuna *(thon)*. The popular *loup flambé au fenouil* is grilled sea bass, flavored with fennel and torched with *pastis* prior to serving.

Cheese and dessert dishes of the Riviera are indistinguishable from those in Provence. Refer to "Provence's Cuisine Scene" (page 51) for suggestions.

You're better off avoiding fixed-price *menus* at most places and just ordering a first course and a main course, or a main course and dessert. I prefer licking my dessert on an after-dinner waterfront stroll (works great in all three home bases I recommend).

Unfortunately, memorable restaurants that showcase the Riviera's cuisine are more difficult to find than in neighboring Provence. Because most visitors come more for the sun than the food, and because the clientele is predominantly international, many restaurants aim for the middle and are hard to tell apart. When dining on the Riviera, I look for views and ambience more than top-quality cuisine.

Wines of the Riviera

Do as everyone else does: Drink wines from Provence. Bandol (red) and cassis (white) are popular and from a region nearly on the Riviera. The only wines made in the Riviera are Bellet rosé and white, the latter often found in fish-shaped bottles. For more on Provençal wine, see page 55.

NICE

Nice (sounds like "niece"), with its spectacular Alps-to-Mediterranean surroundings, is an enjoyable big-city highlight of the Riviera. Its traffic-free old city mixes Italian and French flavors to create a spicy Mediterranean dressing, while its broad seaside walkways invite lounging and people-watching. Nice may be nice, but it's hot and jammed in July and August—reserve ahead and get a room with air-conditioning *(une chambre avec climatisation)*. Everything you'll want to see in Nice is either within walking distance, or a short bus or tram ride away.

Orientation to Nice

Everything of interest lies between the beach and the train tracks (about 15 blocks apart—see map on page 288). The city revolves around its grand place Masséna, where pedestrian-friendly avenue Jean Médecin meets Old Nice and the Albert 1er parkway (with quick access to the beaches). It's a 20-minute walk (or a €10 taxi ride) from the train station to the beach, and a 20-minute walk along the promenade from the fancy Hôtel Negresco to the heart of Old Nice.

A 10-minute ride on the smooth-as-silk tramway takes you through the center of the city, connecting the train station, place Masséna, Old Nice, the bus station, and the port (from nearby place Garibaldi). The tram and all city and regional buses cost only €1 per trip, making this one of the cheapest and easiest cities in France to get around in (see "Getting Around Nice," later).

Tourist Information

Nice's helpful TI has three locations: at the **airport** (in Terminal 1, daily 8:00–21:00, closed Sun off-season), next to the **train station** (usually busy; summer Mon–Sat 8:00–20:00, Sun 9:00–18:00; rest of year Mon–Sat 9:00–19:00, Sun 10:00–17:00), and facing the **beach** at 5 promenade des Anglais (usually quiet, daily 9:00–18:00, until 20:00 July–Aug, closed Sun off-season, toll tel. 08 92 70 74 07—€0.34/minute, www.nicetourisme.com). Pick up the thorough *Practical Guide to Nice* and a free Nice map (or find a better one at your hotel). You can also get information here on day trips (including maps of Monaco or Antibes; details on boat excursions; and bus schedules to Eze-le-Village, La Turbie, or Vence).

Arrival in Nice

By Train: All trains stop at Nice's main station, Nice-Ville (baggage storage at the far right with your back to the tracks, lockers open daily 8:00–21:00). The station area is gritty and busy: Never leave your bags unattended and don't linger here longer than necessary.

Turn left out of the station to find a **TI** next door. Continue a few more blocks down for the Gare Thiers **tram stop** (this will take you to place Masséna, the old city, bus station, and port). Board the tram heading toward the right, direction Pont Michel (see "Getting Around Nice," later). You'll find many recommended hotels a 10- to 20-minute walk down the same street (those listed under "Between Nice Etoile and the Sea," on page 311), though it's easier taking the tram to place Masséna and walking from there.

To walk to other recommended hotels (those listed under "Between the Train Station and Nice Etoile" on page 310 and "Between Boulevard Victor Hugo and the Sea" on page 312), cross avenue Thiers in front of the station, go down the steps by Hôtel Interlaken, and continue walking down avenue Durante. Follow this same route for the fastest path from the station to the beach—avenue Durante turns into rue des Congrés. You'll soon reach the heart of Nice's beachfront promenade.

Taxis and **buses to the airport** (#23 and #99) wait in front of the train station. **Car rental** offices are to the right as you exit the station.

By Bus: Nice's bus station *(gare routière)* is sandwiched between boulevard Jean Jaurès and avenue Félix Faure, next to the old city. Cross boulevard Jean Jaurès to enter Old Nice, or cross avenue Félix Faure to get to my recommended hotels near Nice Etoile. Trams run along boulevard Jean Jaurès; take the tram in the direction of Las Planas to reach place Masséna and the train station.

By Car: To reach the city center on the autoroute from the

Nice

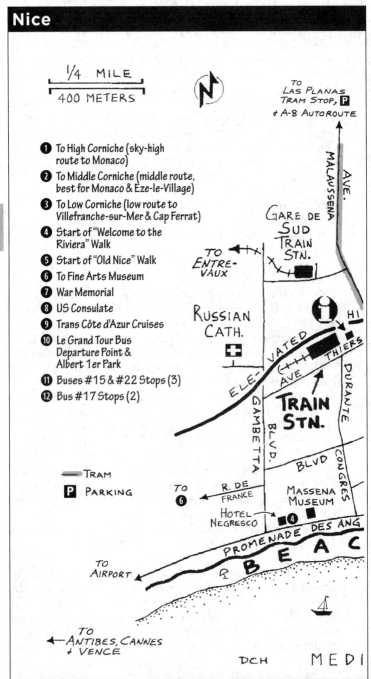

1/4 MILE
400 METERS

TO
LAS PLANAS
TRAM STOP, P
& A-8 AUTOROUTE

1 To High Corniche (sky-high route to Monaco)
2 To Middle Corniche (middle route, best for Monaco & Eze-le-Village)
3 To Low Corniche (low route to Villefranche-sur-Mer & Cap Ferrat)
4 Start of "Welcome to the Riviera" Walk
5 Start of "Old Nice" Walk
6 To Fine Arts Museum
7 War Memorial
8 US Consulate
9 Trans Côte d'Azur Cruises
10 Le Grand Tour Bus Departure Point & Albert 1er Park
11 Buses #15 & #22 Stops (3)
12 Bus #17 Stops (2)

TRAM
P PARKING

NICE

TO
ENTRE-
VAUX

GARE DE
SUD
TRAIN
STN.

AVE. MALAUSSENA

RUSSIAN
CATH.

HI

THIERS

ELEVATED AVE

GAMBETTA BLVD.

TRAIN
STN.

DURANTE

BLVD

CONGRES

TO
6

R. DE
FRANCE

MASSENA
MUSEUM

HOTEL
NEGRESCO

4

PROMENADE DES ANG

TO
AIRPORT

BEAC

TO
ANTIBES, CANNES
& VENCE

DCH

MEDI

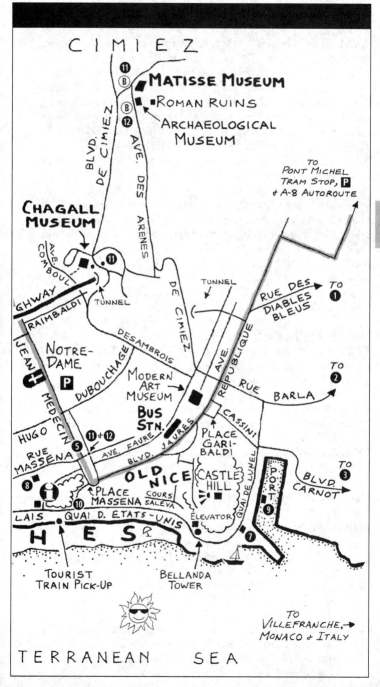

west, take the first Nice exit (for the airport—called Côte d'Azur, Central) and follow signs for *Nice Centre* and *Promenade des Anglais*. (Be ready to cross three left lanes of traffic as soon as you get off the autoroute.) Try to avoid arriving at rush hour (usually Mon–Fri 8:00–9:30 & 17:00–19:30), when promenade des Anglais grinds to a halt. Hoteliers know where to park (allow €15–26/day). The parking garage at the Nice Etoile shopping center on avenue Jean Médecin is pricey but near many of my recommended hotels (ticket booth on third floor, about €20/day, €11 from 20:00–8:00). The garage next to the recommended Hôtel Ibis at the train station has better rates. All on-street parking is metered (9:00–18:00 or 19:00), but usually free all day Sunday.

You can avoid driving in the center—and park for free—by ditching your car at a parking lot at a remote tram stop (Las Planas is best) and taking the tram into town (€1, 15 minutes, 10/hour, don't leave anything in your car, tramway described later under "Getting Around Nice"). From the A-8 autoroute, take the *Nice Nord* exit and find the Las Planas tram station (see map on page 288).

By Plane: For information on Nice's handy airport, see "Nice Connections" at the end of this chapter.

Helpful Hints

Theft Alert: Nice has its share of pickpockets. Thieves target fanny packs: Have nothing important on or around your waist, unless it's in a money belt tucked out of sight. Don't leave anything visible in your car, be wary of scooters when standing at intersections, don't leave things unattended on the beach while swimming, and stick to main streets in Old Nice after dark.

US Consulate: You'll find it at 7 avenue Gustave V (tel. 04 93 88 89 55, fax 04 93 87 07 38, http://france.usembassy.gov/nice .html, usca.nice@orange.fr).

Canadian Consulate: It's at 2 place Franklin (tel. 04 93 92 93 22, fax 04 93 92 55 51).

Medical Help: Riviera Medical Services has a list of English-speaking physicians. They can help you make an appointment or call an ambulance (tel. 04 93 26 12 70, www.rivieramedical .com).

Museums: Some Nice museums (Chagall, Matisse, Archae-ological) are closed on Tuesdays, while others (Modern and Contemporary Art, Fine Arts) close on Mondays. City museums are free of charge—so all of the sights in this chapter (except the Chagall Museum and the Russian Cathedral) cost zilch to enter, making rainy-day options a swinging deal here.

Internet Access: There's no shortage of places to get online in Nice—they're everywhere. Ask at your hotel, or just look up as you walk (keep your eye out for the @ symbol).

English Bookstore: The Cat's Whiskers has an eclectic selection of novels and regional travel books, including mine (Tue–Sat 10:00–12:00 & 14:00–19:00, closed Sun–Mon, 26–30 rue Lamartine—see map on page 308, tel. 04 93 80 02 66).

Laundry: You'll find launderettes everywhere in Nice—ask your hotelier for the nearest one. The self-service **Point Laverie** is centrally located (daily 8:00–20:00, at the corner of rue Alberti and rue Pastorelli, next to Hôtel Vendôme—see map on page 308).

Grocery Store: The big **Monoprix** on avenue Jean Médecin and rue Biscarra has it all, including deli counter, bakery, and cold drinks (Mon–Sat 8:30–21:00, closed Sun, see map on page 318). You'll also find many small grocery stores (some open Sun and/or until late hours) near my recommended hotels.

Renting a Bike (and Other Wheels): Roller Station rents bikes (*vélos*, €5/hour, €10/half-day, €15/day), rollerblades (*rollers*, €6/day), Razor-type scooters (*trotinettes*, €6/half-day, €9/day), and skateboards (€6/half-day, €9/day). You'll need to leave your ID as a deposit (daily 9:30–19:00, July–Aug until 20:00, next to yellow awnings of Pailin's Asian restaurant at 49 quai des Etats-Unis—see map on page 308, another location at 10 rue Cassini near place Garibaldi, tel. 04 93 62 99 05, owner Eric). If you need more power, try the electric-assisted bikes or scooters at **Energy Scoot** (2 rue St. Philippe, near the promenade des Anglais and avenue Gambetta, tel. 04 97 07 12 64).

Car Rental: Renting a car is easiest at Nice's airport, which has offices for all the major companies. You'll also find most companies represented at Nice's train station and near Albert 1er Park.

English Radio: Tune in to Riviera-Radio at FM 106.5.

Views: For panoramic views, climb Castle Hill (see page 305), or take a one-hour boat trip (described later, under "Tours in Nice").

Beach Gear: To make life tolerable on the rocks, swimmers should buy a pair of the cheap plastic beach shoes sold at many shops (flip-flops fall off in the water). **Go Sport** at #13 on place Masséna sells beach shoes, flip-flops, and cheap sunglasses (daily 10:00–19:00—see map on page 314).

Getting Around Nice

Although you can walk to most attractions in Nice, smart travelers make good use of the buses and tram. Both are covered by the same single-ride €1 ticket (good for 74 minutes in one direction, including transfers between bus and tram; can't be used for a round-trip). An all-day pass is €4 (valid on local buses and trams, as well as buses to nearby destinations—see "Getting Around the Riviera From Nice," below).

The **bus** is handy for reaching the Chagall and Matisse museums and the Russian Cathedral. Make sure to validate your ticket in the machine just behind the driver—watch locals do it and imitate.

Nice's new **tramway** makes an "L" along avenue Jean Médecin and boulevard Jean Jaurès, and connects the main train station (Gare Thiers stop), place Masséna (Masséna stop, a few blocks' walk from the sea), Old Nice (Opéra-Vieille Ville), the bus station (Cathédrale-Vieille Ville), and the Modern and Contemporary Art Museum and port (Place Garibaldi). It also comes within a few blocks of the Gare du Sud train station  (Libération stop)—the departure point for the scenic Chemins de Fer de Provence trains (see page 305).

Taking the tram in the direction of Pont Michel takes you from the train station toward the beach and bus station (direction Las Planas goes the other way). Buy tickets at the machines on the platforms (coins only, no credit cards). Choose the English flag to change the display language, turn the round knob and push the green button to select your ticket, press it twice at the end to get your ticket, or press the red button to cancel. Once you're on the tram, validate your ticket by inserting it into the top of the white box, then reclaiming it.

Taxis are useful for getting to Nice's outlying sights, and worth it if you're nowhere near a bus or tram stop (figure €15 from promenade des Anglais). They normally only pick up at taxi stands *(tête de station)*, or you can call 04 93 13 78 78.

The hokey **tourist train** gets you up Castle Hill (see "Tours in Nice," later in this chapter).

Getting Around the Riviera from Nice

Nice is perfectly situated for exploring the Riviera by public transport. Monaco, Eze-le-Village, Villefranche-sur-Mer, Antibes, St-Paul-de-Vence, Grasse, and Cannes are all within about a one-hour bus or train ride. Fares are cheap, but you need plenty of change to buy train tickets from machines at smaller, unstaffed stations and to buy bus tickets from drivers (who can't make change for large bills).

By Train: There is no faster way to move about the Riviera

Public Transportation in the Nice Region

Many key Riviera destinations are connected by direct bus or train service from Nice, and some are served by both. Because bus fare is only €1, the pricier train is only a better choice when it saves you time (which it generally does). You make the call—both modes of transportation work well.

All prices are one-way. Unless otherwise noted, the following bus frequencies are for Monday–Saturday (Sunday often has limited or no service).

Destination	Bus from Nice	Train from Nice
Villefranche-sur-Mer	4/hr daily, 15 min	2/hr, 10 min, €1.90
Cap Ferrat	about 2/hr daily, 30 min*	none
Monaco	4/hr Mon–Sat, 3/hr Sun, 45 min	2/hr, 20 min, €3.60
Menton	4/hr Mon–Sat, 3/hr Sun, 1 hr	2/hr, 25 min, €3.70
Antibes	2-4/hr, 1-1.5 hrs	2/hr, 15–30 min, €4
Cannes	2-4/hr, 1.5-1.75 hrs	2/hr, 30–40 min, €6.20
St-Paul-de-Vence	every 40 min, 45 min	none
Vence	every 40 min, 50 min	none
Grasse	every 40 min, 1.25 hr	1/hr, 1.25 hr, €7.20
Eze-le-Village	16/day, 25 min	none
La Turbie	4/day, 45 min	none

*A more frequent bus to Cap Ferrat entails a longer walk. Buses also run from Monaco to Eze-le-Village and to La Turbie, allowing travelers to triangulate Nice, Monaco, and Eze-le-Village or La Turbie for a good all-day excursion—ending up back in Nice (see page 389 for details).

than by train. Speedy trains link the Riviera's beachfront destinations—Cannes, Antibes, Nice, Villefranche-sur-Mer, Monaco, Menton, and the inland perfume town of Grasse (see sidebar for approximate travel times and one-way prices). All trains serving Nice arrive at and depart from the Nice-Ville station. Never board a train without a ticket or a valid pass. Fare inspectors don't accept excuses, and you'll pay a fine of at least €70.

By Bus: At Nice's ramshackle bus station on boulevard Jean

Jaurès, you'll find several bus companies and WCs (but no baggage storage). You can get timetables and prices from the English-speaking clerk at the information desk (Mon–Sat 8:00–12:00 & 13:00–17:00, closed Sun, tel. 04 93 85 61 81), or at Nice's TIs. Buy tickets from the driver. Television monitors by the central bus bays list platforms, destinations, and departure times.

Buses are an amazing deal. Any one-way ride costs €1 (except on express airport buses)—whether you're riding 15 minutes to Villefranche-sur-Mer, 45 minutes to Monaco, or an hour to Antibes. Two private bus companies provide service to Riviera destinations: the more important Ligne d'Azur (www.lignedazur.com, in English) and the smaller TAM. The same tickets work on buses for both companies (and for local buses and trams within Nice)—you can even transfer between the buses of the two different companies. The €1 single ticket (called **"Ticket Azur"**), available on all Ligne d'Azur buses, lets you take a one-way ride anywhere within the bus system (if you board a TAM bus and want to transfer, ask for a transfer: *un ticket correspondance*). The €4 all-day ticket **(Carte Journée)** is good on Nice's city buses and tramway, as well as on buses throughout the region. This all-day ticket makes sense if you plan to take the bus to museums, use the tramway several times, or are going to the airport (you must validate your ticket on every trip).

Express buses to and from the airport (#98 and #99) require the €4 all-day ticket, so savvy riders pack in other bus and/or tram rides on the day of their flight.

By Boat: From June to mid-September, Trans Côte d'Azur offers scenic trips from Nice to Monaco and Nice to St-Tropez. Boats leave in the morning and return in the evening, giving you all day to explore your destination. Drinks and WCs are available on board.

Boats to **Monaco** depart at 9:30 and 16:00, and return at 11:00 and 18:00 (€32 round-trip, €27 if you don't get off in Monaco, 45 minutes each way, June–Sept Tue, Thu, and Sat only).

Boats to **St-Tropez** depart at 9:00 and return at 19:00 (€55 round-trip, 2.5 hours each way; July–Aug Tue–Sun, no boats Mon; late June and early Sept Tue, Thu, and Sun only). Reservations are required for both boats, and tickets for St-Tropez often sell out, so book a few days ahead (tel. 04 92 98 71 30 or 04 92 00 42 30, www.trans-cote-azur.com, croisieres@trans-cote-azur.com). The boats leave from Nice's port, bassin des Amiraux, just below Castle Hill—look for the blue ticket booth *(billeterie)* on quai de Lunel (see map on page 288). The same company also runs one-hour round-trip cruises along the coast to Cap Ferrat (see "Tours in Nice," next).

Tours in Nice

Bus Tour—Le Grand Tour Bus provides a 12-stop, hop-on, hop-off service on an open-deck bus with headphone commentary (2/hour, 1.5-hour loop) that includes the promenade des Anglais, the old port, Cap de Nice, and the Chagall and Matisse museums on Cimiez Hill (€20/1-day pass, €23/2-day pass, cheaper for seniors and students, €10 for last tour of the day at about 18:00, some hotels offer €3 discounts, buy tickets on bus, main stop is near where promenade des Anglais and quai des Etats-Unis meet, across from plage Beau Rivage, tel. 04 92 29 17 00). This tour is a pricey way to get to the Chagall and Matisse museums, but it's an acceptable option if you also want a city overview. Check the schedule if you plan to use this bus to visit the Russian Cathedral, as it may be faster to walk there.

Tourist Train—For €7 (or €3 for children under 9) you can spend 40 embarrassing minutes on the tourist train tooting along the promenade, through the old city, and up to Castle Hill. This is a sweat-free way to get to Castle Hill...but so is the elevator, which is much cheaper (every 30 minutes, daily 10:00–18:00, June–Aug until 19:00, recorded English commentary, meet train near Le Grand Tour Bus stop on quai des Etats-Unis, tel. 04 93 62 85 48).

▲**Boat Cruise**—Here's your chance to join the boat parade and see Nice from the water. On this one-hour star-studded tour, you'll cruise in a comfortable yacht-size vessel to Cap Ferrat and past Villefranche-sur-Mer, then return to Nice with a final lap along promenade des Anglais. It's a scenic trip (the best views are from the seats on top), and worthwhile if you won't be hiking along the Cap Ferrat trails that provide similar views.

French (and sometimes English-speaking) guides play Robin Leach, pointing out mansions owned by some pretty famous people, including Elton John (just as you leave Nice, it's the soft-yellow square-shaped place right on the water), Sean Connery (on the hill above Elton, with rounded arches and tower), and Microsoft co-founder Paul Allen (in saddle of Cap Ferrat hill, above yellow-umbrella beach with sloping red-tile roof). Guides also like to point out the mansion where the Rolling Stones recorded *Exile on Main Street* (between Villefranche-sur-Mer and Cap Ferrat). I wonder if this gang ever hangs out together (€15; May–Oct Tue–Sun 2/day, usually at 11:00 and 15:00, no boats Mon; March–April Tue–Wed, Fri, and Sun at 15:00; no boats Nov–Feb; call ahead to verify schedule, arrive 30 minute early to get best seats, drinks and WCs available). For directions to the dock and contact information, see "Getting Around the Riviera From Nice—By Boat," earlier.

Walking Tours—The TI on promenade des Anglais organizes weekly walking tours of Old Nice in French and English (€12,

NICE

Nice at a Glance

▲▲▲**Chagall Museum** The world's largest collection of Chagall's work, popular even with people who don't like modern art. **Hours:** Wed–Mon 10:00–17:00, May–Oct until 18:00, closed Tue. See page 298.

▲▲▲**Promenade des Anglais** Nice's four-mile sun-struck seafront promenade. **Hours:** Always open. See page 297.

▲▲**Old Nice** Charming old city offering enjoyable atmosphere and a look at Nice's French-Italian cultural blend. **Hours:** Always open. See page 330.

▲**Matisse Museum** A worthwhile collection of Henri Matisse's paintings. **Hours:** Wed–Mon 10:00–18:00, closed Tue. See page 299.

▲**Modern and Contemporary Art Museum** Ultramodern museum with enjoyable collection from the 1960s–1970s, including Warhol and Lichtenstein. **Hours:** Tue–Sun 10:00–18:00, closed Mon. See page 302.

▲**Russian Cathedral** Finest Orthodox church outside of Russia. **Hours:** Mon–Sat 9:00–12:00 & 14:30–18:00, Sun 14:30–18:00, until 17:00 off-season. See page 304.

▲**Castle Hill** Site of an ancient fort boasting great views—especially in early mornings and evenings. **Hours:** Park closes at 20:00 in summer, earlier off-season. Elevator runs daily 10:00–19:00, until 20:00 in summer. See page 305.

Fine Arts Museum Lush villa shows off impressive paintings by Monet, Sisley, Bonnard, and Raoul Dufy. **Hours:** Tue–Sun 10:00–18:00, closed Mon. See page 303.

Molinard Perfume Museum Small museum tracing the history of perfume. **Hours:** Daily July–Aug 10:00–19:00, Sept–June 10:00–13:00 & 14:00–18:30, sometimes closed Mon off-season. See page 303.

May–Oct only, usually Sat morning at 9:30, 2.5 hours, reservations necessary, depart from TI, tel. 08 92 70 74 07). They also have evening art walks on Fridays at 19:00.

Nice's cultural association (Centre du Patrimoine) offers incredibly cheap €5 walks on varying themes (in English, minimum 5 people). Call 04 92 00 41 90 a few days ahead to make a reservation. Most tours start at their office at 75 quai des Etats-

Unis; look for the red plaque next to Musée des Ponchettes (see map on page 314).

Local Guides—Sofia Villavicencio and Sylvie Di Cristo each give expert tours of Nice (for contact info, see page 281). Lovely Pascale Rucker tailors her tours in Nice to your interests. Book in advance, though it's also worth a try on short notice (€140/half-day, €230/day, tel. & fax 04 93 87 77 89, mobile 06 16 24 29 52).

Les Petits Farcis Cooking Tour and Classes—Charming Canadian Francophile Rosa Jackson, a food journalist and Cordon Bleu–trained cook, offers popular cooking classes in Old Nice. Her single-day classes include a morning trip to the open-air market on cours Saleya to pick up ingredients, and an afternoon session spent creating an authentic Niçois meal from your purchases (€195/person, mobile 06 81 67 41 22, www.petitsfarcis.com).

NICE

Sights in Nice

Walks and Beach Time

▲▲▲**Promenade des Anglais and Beach**—Meandering along Nice's four-mile seafront promenade on foot or by bike is a must.

This stretch is *the* place to be in Nice, from the days when wealthy English tourists filled the grand seaside hotels to today's Europeans seeking fun in the sun.

For a self-guided walk of this strip, see the Welcome to the Riviera Walk chapter. To rev up the pace of your promenade saunter, rent a bike and glide along the coast in both directions (about 30 minutes each way; for rental info see "Helpful Hints," earlier). Both of the following paths start along promenade des Anglais.

The path to the **west** stops just before the airport, at perhaps the most scenic *boules* courts in France. Pause here to watch the old-timers while away their afternoon tossing shiny metal balls (for more on this game, see page 208). If you take the path heading **east,** you'll round the hill—passing a scenic cape and the town's memorial to both world wars—to the harbor of Nice, with a chance to survey some fancy yachts. Pedal around the harbor and follow the coast past the Corsica ferry terminal (you'll need to carry your bike up a flight of steps). From there the path leads to an appealing tree-lined residential district.

And of course, there's the **beach.** Settle in to the smooth pebbles and consider your options: you can play beach volleyball, table tennis, or *boules;* rent paddleboats, personal watercraft, or windsurfing equipment; explore ways to use your zoom lens and pretend you're a paparazzo; or snooze on a comfy beach bed.

To rent a spot on the beach, compare rates, as prices vary—beaches on the east end of the bay are usually cheaper (chair and mattress—*chaise longue* and *transat*-€12–18, umbrella-€3–5, towel-€4). Some hotels have special deals with certain beaches for discounted rentals (check with your hotel for details). Consider having lunch in your bathing suit (€12 salads and pizzas in bars and restaurants all along the beach). Or, for a peaceful café au lait on the Mediterranean, stop here first thing in the morning before the crowds hit. *Plage Publique* signs explain the 15 beach no-nos (translated into English).

▲▲**Wandering Old Nice (Vieux Nice)**—Offering an intriguing look at Nice's melding of French and Italian cultures, the old city is a fine place to linger. Enjoy its narrow lanes, bustling market squares, and colorful people.

For details on this neighborhood, see the Old Nice Walk chapter.

Museums and Monuments

To bring culture to the masses, the city of Nice has nixed the entry fee to all municipal museums—so it's free to enter all of the following sights except the Chagall Museum and the Russian Cathedral. Cool.

The first two museums (Chagall and Matisse) are a long walk northeast of Nice's city center. Because they're in the same direction and served by the same bus line (buses #15 and #22 stop at both museums), it makes sense to visit them on the same trip. From place Masséna, the Chagall Museum is a 10-minute bus ride or a 30-minute walk, and the Matisse Museum is a 20-minute bus ride or a one-hour walk.

▲▲▲**Chagall Museum (Musée National Marc Chagall)**—

Inspired by the Old Testament, modern artist Marc Chagall custom-painted works for this building, which he considered a "House of Brotherhood." In typical Chagall style, these paintings are lively, colorful, and simple (some might say simplistic). The museum is a can't-miss treat for Chagall fans, and a hit even for people who usually don't like modern art.

For a complete self-guided tour of the museum, and directions on how to get here, see the Chagall Museum Tour chapter.

Cost and Hours: €7.50, free first Sun of the month (but crowded), open Wed–Mon 10:00–17:00, May–Oct until 18:00, closed Tue year-round, avenue Docteur Ménard, tel. 04 93 53 87 20, www.musee-chagall.fr.

▲**Matisse Museum (Musée Matisse)**—This small museum contains the world's largest collection of Henri Matisse paintings. It offers a painless introduction to the artist, whose style was shaped by Mediterranean light and by fellow Côte d'Azur artists Pablo Picasso and Pierre-Auguste Renoir. The collection is scattered throughout several rooms with a few worthwhile works, though it lacks a certain *je ne sais quoi* when compared to the Chagall Museum.

Cost and Hours: Free, Wed–Mon 10:00–18:00, closed Tue, 164 avenue des Arènes de Cimiez, tel. 04 93 81 08 08, www.musee-matisse-nice.org. The museum is housed in a beautiful Mediterranean mansion set in an olive grove amid the ruins of the Roman city of Cemenelum. Part of the ancient Roman city of Nice, Cemenelum was a military camp that housed as many as 20,000 people.

Getting to the Matisse Museum: It's a long uphill walk from the city center. Take the bus (details follow) or a cab (about €15 from promenade des Anglais). Once here, walk into the park to find the pink villa. **Buses #15, #17,** and **#22** offer regular service to the Matisse Museum from just off place Masséna on rue Sacha Guitry (Masséna Guitry stop, a block east of the Galeries Lafayette department store—see map on page 288; 20 minutes; note that bus #17 does not stop at the Chagall Museum). **Bus #20** connects the port to the museum. On any bus, get off at the Arènes–Matisse bus stop. (For bus tips on leaving the museum, see the end of this listing.)

Background: Henri Matisse, the master of leaving things out, could suggest a woman's body with a single curvy line—letting the viewer's mind fill in the rest. Ignoring traditional 3-D perspective, he used simple dark outlines saturated with bright blocks of color to create recognizable but simplified scenes composed into a decorative pattern to express nature's serene beauty. You don't look "through" a Matisse canvas, like a window; you look "at" it, like wallpaper.

Matisse understood how colors and shapes affect us emotionally. He could create either shocking, clashing works (Fauvism) or geometrical, balanced, harmonious ones (later pieces). Whereas other modern artists reveled in purely abstract design,

Henri Matisse
(1869–1954)

Here's an outline of Henri Matisse's busy life:

1880s and 1890s—At age 20, Matisse, a budding lawyer, is struck down with appendicitis. Bedridden for a year, he turns to painting as a healing escape from pain and boredom. After recovering, he studies art in Paris and produces dark-colored, realistic still lifes and landscapes. His work is exhibited at the Salons of 1896 and 1897.

1897–1905—Influenced by the Impressionists, he experiments with sunnier scenes and brighter colors. He travels to southern France, including Collioure (on the coast near Spain), and seeks still more light-filled scenes to paint. His experiments are influenced by Vincent van Gogh's bright, surrealistic colors and thick outlines, and by Paul Gauguin's primitive visions of a Tahitian paradise. From Paul Cézanne, he learns how to simplify objects into their basic geometric shapes. He also experiments (like Cézanne) with creating the illusion of 3-D not by traditional means, but by using contrasting colors for the foreground and background.

1905—Back in Paris, Matisse and his colleagues (André Derain and Maurice de Vlaminck) shock the art world with an exhibition of their experimental paintings. The thick outlines, simple forms, non-3-D scenes, and—most of all—bright, clashing, unrealistic colors seemed to be the work of "wild animals" *(fauves)*. Fauvism is hot, and Matisse is instantly famous. (Though notorious as a "wild animal," Matisse himself was a gentle, introspective man.)

1906–1910—After just a year, Fauvism is out, and African masks are in. This "primitive" art form inspires Matisse to simplify and distort his figures further, making them less realistic but more expressive.

1910–1917—Matisse creates his masterpiece paintings. Cubism is the rage, pioneered by Matisse's friend and rival for the World's

Matisse (almost) always kept the subject matter at least vaguely recognizable. He used unreal colors and distorted lines not just to portray what an object looks like, but to express its inner nature (even inanimate objects). Meditating on his paintings helps you connect with nature—or so Matisse hoped.

As you tour the museum, look for Matisse's favorite motifs—including fruit, flowers, wallpaper, and sunny rooms—often with a

Best Painter award, Pablo Picasso. Matisse dabbles in Cubism, simplifying forms, emphasizing outline, and muting his colors. But ultimately it proves to be too austere and analytical for his deeply sensory nature. The Cubist style is most evident in his sculpture.

1920s—Burned out from years of intense experimentation, Matisse moves to Nice (spending winters there from 1917, settling permanently in 1921). Luxuriating under the bright sun, he's reborn, and he paints colorful, sensual, highly decorative works. Harem concubines lounging in their sunny, flowery apartments epitomize the lush life.

1930s—A visit to Tahiti inspires more scenes of life as a sunny paradise. Matisse increases playing around with the lines of the figures he draws to create swirling arabesques and decorative patterns.

1940s—Duodenal cancer (in 1941) requires Matisse to undergo two operations and confines him to a wheelchair for the rest of his life. Working at an easel becomes a struggle for him, and he largely stops painting in 1941. But as World War II ends, Matisse emerges with renewed energy. Now in his 70s, he explores a new medium: Paper cutouts pasted onto a watercolored surface (découpages on gouache-prepared surface). The medium plays to his strengths: The cutouts are essentially blocks of bright color (mostly blue) with a strong outline. Scissors in hand, Matisse says, "I draw straight into the color." (His doctor advises him to wear dark glasses to protect his weak eyes against the bright colors he chooses.) In 1947, Matisse's book *Jazz* is published, featuring the artist's joyful cutouts of simple figures. Like jazz music, the book is a celebration of artistic spontaneity. And like music in general, Matisse's works balance different tones and colors to create a mood.

1947-1951—Matisse's nurse becomes a Dominican nun in Vence. To thank her for her care, he spends his later years designing a chapel there. He oversees every aspect of the Chapel of the Rosary (Chapelle du Rosaire) at Vence, from the stained glass to the altar to the colors of the priest's robe (see page 427). Though Matisse is not a strong Christian, the church exudes his spirit of celebrating life and sums up his work.

1954—Matisse dies.

window opening onto a sunny landscape. Another favorite subject is the *odalisque* (harem concubine), usually shown sprawled in a seductive pose and with a simplified, masklike face. You'll also see a few souvenirs from his travels, which influenced much of his work.

Viewing the Collection: Enter the museum at park level from the door opposite the olive grove (not the basement entry). Take one of the free museum handouts, which provide minimal English information on the collection. The museum features temporary exhibits about Matisse that change frequently.

Rooms on the entry level usually house paintings from Matisse's formative years as a student (1890s). Notice how quickly his work evolves: from dark still lifes to colorful Impressionist works to more abstract pieces, all in a matter of a few years. A beige banner describes his "discovery of light," which the Riviera (and his various travels to sun-soaked places like Morocco and Tahiti) brought to his art. You may see photographs of his apartment on cours Saleya, which is described in my Old Nice Walk chapter.

Other rooms on this floor may highlight Matisse's fascination with dance and the female body (these subjects sometimes move upstairs). You'll see pencil and charcoal drawings, and a handful of bronze busts; he was fascinated by sculpture. *The Acrobat*—painted only two years before Matisse's death—shows the artist at his minimalist best. Look also for the orange-bearded 1905 portrait of Matisse by André Derain.

The floor above features sketches and models of Matisse's famous Chapel of the Rosary in nearby Vence (see page 427) and related religious works. On the same floor, you may find paper cutouts from his *Jazz* series, more bronze sculptures, various personal objects, and linen embroideries inspired by his travels to Polynesia.

The bookshop, WCs, and additional temporary exhibits are in the basement levels. The fantastic wall-hanging near the bookshop—Matisse's colorful paper cutout *Flowers and Fruits*—shouts, "Riviera!"

Leaving the Museum: When leaving the museum, find the stop for buses #15 and #22 (frequent service downtown and stops en route at the Chagall Museum): Turn left out of the Matisse Museum into the park and keep straight, exiting the park at the Archeological Museum, then turn right. Pass the bus stop across the street (#17 goes to the city center but not the Chagall Museum, and #20 goes to the port), and walk to the small roundabout. Cross the roundabout to find the shelter (facing downhill) for buses #15 and #22 by the apartment building with the oval portico (see map on page 288).

▲Modern and Contemporary Art Museum (Musée d'Art Moderne et d'Art Contemporain)—This ultramodern museum features an explosively colorful, far-out, yet manageable collection focused on American and European-American artists from the 1960s and 1970s (Pop Art and New Realism styles are highlighted). The exhibits cover three floors and include a few works by Andy Warhol, Roy Lichtenstein, and Jean Tinguely, and small models of

Christo's famous wrappings. You'll find rooms dedicated to Robert Indiana, Yves Klein, and Niki de Saint Phalle (my favorite). The temporary exhibits can be as appealing to modern-art–lovers as the permanent collection: Check the museum website for what's playing. Don't leave without exploring the rooftop terrace.

For a succinct introduction to modern art on the Riviera, see the French Riviera chapter.

Cost and Hours: Free, Tue–Sun 10:00–18:00, closed Mon, about a 15-minute walk from place Masséna, near bus station on promenade des Arts, tel. 04 93 62 61 62, www.mamac-nice.org.

Fine Arts Museum (Musée des Beaux-Arts)—Housed in a sumptuous Riviera villa with lovely gardens, this museum holds 6,000 works from the 17th to 20th centuries. Start on the first floor and work your way up to experience an appealing array of paintings by Monet, Sisley, Bonnard, and Raoul Dufy, as well as a few sculptures by Rodin and Carpeaux (free, Tue–Sun 10:00–18:00, closed Mon, 3 avenue des Baumettes, inconveniently located at the western end of Nice, take buses #12 or #23 from the train station or bus #38 from the bus station to the Rosa Bonheur stop, tel. 04 92 15 28 28, www.musee-beaux-arts-nice.org).

Molinard Perfume Museum—The Molinard family has been making perfume in Grasse (about an hour's drive from Nice—see page 431) since 1849. Their Nice store has a small museum in the rear that illustrates the story of their industry. Back when people believed water spread the plague (Louis XIV supposedly bathed less than once a year), doctors advised people to rub fragrances into their skin and then powder their body. At that time, perfume was a necessity of everyday life.

Tiny Room 1 shows photos of the local flowers, roots, and other parts of plants used in perfume production. Room 2 explains the earliest (18th-century) production method. Petals would be laid out in the sun on a bed of animal fat, which would absorb the essence of the flowers as they baked. Petals were replaced daily for two months until the fat was saturated. Models and old photos show the later distillation process (660 pounds of lavender produced only a quarter-gallon of essence). Perfume is "distilled like cognac and then aged like wine." The small bottles on the table in the corner demonstrate the role of the "blender" and the perfume mastermind called the "nose" (who knows best). Notice the photos of these lab-coat-wearing perfectionists. Of the 150 real "noses" in the world, more than 100 are French. You are welcome to enjoy the testing bottles.

Cost and Hours: Free, daily July–Aug 10:00–19:00, Sept–June 10:00–13:00 & 14:00–18:30, sometimes closed Mon off-season, just between beach and place Masséna at 20 rue St. François de Paule, see map on page 314, tel. 04 93 62 90 50, www.molinard.com.

Other Nice Museums—Both of these museums are acceptable rainy-day options, and free of charge.

The **Archaeological Museum** (Musée Archéologique) displays various objects from the Romans' occupation of this region. It's convenient—just below the Matisse Museum—but has little of interest to anyone but ancient Rome aficionados. You also get access to the Roman bath ruins...which are, sadly, overgrown with weeds (free, very limited information in English, Wed–Mon 10:00–18:00, closed Tue, near Matisse Museum at 160 avenue des Arènes de Cimiez, tel. 04 93 81 59 57, www.musee-archeologique -nice.org).

The **Masséna Museum** (Musée Masséna), like Nice's main square, is named in honor of Jean-André Masséna, a commander during France's Revolutionary and Napoleonic Wars (for more on him, see page 331). This beachfront mansion is worth a gander for its lavish decor and lovely gardens alone (pick up your free ticket at the boutique just outside).

The ground floor shows rotating exhibits, and the upstairs floors offer a folk-museum-like look at Nice through the years, with antique posters, models of the old casino destroyed in World War II (La Jetée Promenade, described on page 327), many 18th- and 19th-century paintings (mostly by artists from Nice), and other collections relevant to the city's tumultuous history. Find the images of Nice before they covered the river that runs under place Masséna. You'll also come across some Napoleon paraphernalia; Josephine's cape and tiara are impressive, and I'd look good in Napoleon's vest. Check out the paintings of the Italian patriot and Nice favorite Giuseppe Garibaldi, as well as his burial sheet (free, daily 10:00–18:00, 35 promenade des Anglais, tel. 04 93 91 19 10).

▲**Russian Cathedral (Cathédrale Russe)**—Nice's Russian Orthodox church—claimed by some to be the finest outside Russia—is worth a visit. Five hundred rich Russian families wintered in Nice in the late 19th century. Since they couldn't pray in a Catholic church, the community needed a worthy Orthodox house of worship. Czar Nicholas I's widow provided the land (which required tearing down her house), and Czar Nicholas II gave this church to the Russian community in 1912. (A few years later, Russian comrades who *didn't* winter on the Riviera assassinated him.) Here in the land of olives and anchovies, these proud onion domes seem odd. But, I imagine, so did those old Russians.

Step inside (pick up English info sheet). The one-room interior is filled with icons and candles, and the old Russian music adds to the ambience. The wall of icons (iconostasis) divides things between the spiritual world and the temporal world of the worshippers. Only the priest can walk between the two worlds, by using the "Royal Door." Take a close look at items lining the front (starting in the left corner). The angel with red boots and wings—the protector of the Romanov family—stands over a symbolic tomb of Christ. The tall black hammered-copper cross commemorates the massacre of Nicholas II and his family in 1918. Notice the Jesus icon to the right of the Royal Door. According to a priest here, as worshippers meditate, staring deep into the eyes of Jesus, they enter a lake where they find their soul. Surrounded by incense, chanting, and your entire community...it could happen. Farther to the right, the icon of the unhappy-looking Virgin and Child is decorated with semiprecious stones from the Ural Mountains. Artists worked a triangle into each iconic face—symbolic of the Trinity.

Cost and Hours: €3, Mon–Sat 9:00–12:00 & 14:30–18:00, Sun 14:30–18:00, until 17:00 off-season, chanted services Sat at 17:30 or 18:00, Sun at 10:00, no tourist visits during services, no short shorts, 17 boulevard du Tzarewitch, tel. 04 93 96 88 02, www .acor-nice.com. The park around the church stays open at lunch and makes a fine setting for picnics.

Getting to the Russian Cathedral: It's a 10-minute walk from the train station. Exit the station to the right onto avenue Thiers, turn right on avenue Gambetta, go under the freeway, and turn left following *Eglise Russe* signs. Or, from the station, take any bus heading west on avenue Thiers and get off at avenue Gambetta (then follow the previous directions).

▲**Castle Hill (Colline du Château)**—Nice was first settled on this hill, which offers sweeping views over the city—best by far in the early morning or late in the day (park closes at 20:00 in summer, earlier off-season). You can get to the top by foot, by elevator (€0.70 one-way, €1.10 round-trip, runs daily 10:00–19:00, until 20:00 in summer, next to beachfront Hôtel Suisse), or by pricey tourist train (described under "Tours in Nice" on page 295). Up top you'll find cafés and an extensive play area for kids.

For more on Castle Hill, see the Welcome to the Riviera Walk chapter.

Near Nice: Scenic Railway

Narrow-Gauge Train into the Alps (Chemins de Fer de Provence)—Leave the tourists behind and take the scenic train-bus-train combination that runs between Nice and Digne through canyons, along whitewater rivers, and through many tempting villages (Nice to Digne: €19, 25 percent discount with railpass, 4/day,

3.5 hours, departs Nice from the South Station—Gare du Sud—about 10 blocks behind the main train station, two blocks from the Libération tram stop, 4 rue Alfred Binet, tel. 04 97 03 80 80, www .trainprovence.com).

Start with an 8:50 departure and go as far as you want. Little **Entrevaux** is a good destination that feels forgotten and still stuck in its medieval shell (€10, 1.5 scenic hours from Nice). Climb high to the citadel for great views. The train ends in **Digne-les-Bains,** where you can catch a main-line train (covered by railpasses) to other destinations—or, better, take the bus (free with railpass, quick transfer if you get the 8:50 train from Nice) to **Veynes** (4/day, 1.5 hours). From there you can catch the most scenic two-car train to **Grenoble** (5/day, 2 hours), then take a train to Annecy (arriving about 18:50).

To do the entire trip from Nice to Annecy in one day, you must start with the 8:50 departure, but I'd rather spend a night in one of the tiny villages en route. **$ Hôtel Beauséjour** in little Annot, about two hours from Nice, makes a fun and reasonable getaway (Db-€55–65, tel. 04 92 83 21 08, www.francebeausejour.com). Farther along, in remote Clelles, you'll find the **$ Hôtel Ferrat****, a basic family-run mountain hacienda at the base of Mont Aiguille, with a swimming pool and a good restaurant (Db-€56–65, tel. 04 76 34 42 70, fax 04 76 34 47 47, hotel.ferrat@wanadoo.fr).

Nightlife in Nice

Promenade des Anglais, cours Saleya, and rue Masséna are all worth an evening walk. Nice's bars play host to a happening late-night scene, filled with jazz, rock, and trolling singles. Most activity focuses on Old Nice. Rue de la Préfecture is ground zero for bar life, though place Rossetti and rue Droite are also good targets. **Distilleries Ideales** is a good place to start or end your evening, with a lively international crowd and a fun interior (where rues de la Poissonnerie and Barillerie meet, happy hour 18:00–20:00). **Wayne's Bar** is a happening spot for the younger, English-speaking backpacker crowd (15 rue Préfecture). Along the promenade des Anglais, the plush bar at **Hôtel Negresco** is fancy-cigar old English.

Plan on a cover charge or expensive drinks where music is involved. If you're out very late, avoid walking alone. Nice is well-known for its lively after-dark action; if Nice's nightlife doesn't meet your needs, head for the town of Juan-les-Pins (page

403). For more relaxed and accessible nightlife, consider nearby Antibes (page 391).

Sleeping in Nice

Don't look for charm in Nice. Go for modern and clean, with a central location and, in summer, air-conditioning. The rates listed here are for April through October. Prices generally drop €15–30 November through March, but go sky-high in 2011 during the Nice Carnival (Feb 18–March 8), the Cannes Film Festival (May 11–22), and Monaco's Grand Prix (May 26–29). Between the film festival and the Grand Prix, the second half of May is very tight every year. Nice is also one of Europe's top convention cities, and June is convention month here. Reserve early if visiting May through August, especially during these times. For parking, ask your hotelier (several hotels have limited private parking), or see "Arrival in Nice—By Car" on page 287.

I've divided my sleeping recommendations into three areas: between the train station and Nice Etoile shopping center (easy access to the train station and Old Nice via the sleek new tramway, 20-minute walk to promenade des Anglais); between Nice Etoile and the sea (east of avenue Jean Médecin, good access to Old Nice and the sea at quai des Etats-Unis); and between boulevard Victor Hugo and the sea (a somewhat classier area, offering better access to the promenade des Anglais but longer walks to the train station and Old Nice). I've also listed a hotel near the airport and a hostel on the outskirts.

Sleep Code

(€1 = about $1.25, country code: 33)
S = Single, **D** = Double/Twin, **T** = Triple, **Q** = Quad, **b** = bathroom, **s** = shower only, ***** = French hotel rating (0-4 stars). Hoteliers speak English; the hotels have elevators and accept credit cards unless otherwise noted.

To help you sort easily through these listings, I've divided the rooms into three categories based on the price for a standard double room with bath:

$$$ Higher Priced—Most rooms €110 or more.
  $$ Moderately Priced—Most rooms between €75-110.
    $ Lower Priced—Most rooms €75 or less.

Prices can change without notice; verify the hotel's current rates online or by email. For other updates, see www.ricksteves.com/update.

Nice Hotels

NICE

TO 19,
LAS PLANAS
TRAM STOP &
A-8 AUTOROUTE

TO
CHAGALL
MUSEUM
ON FOOT

TRAIN
STATION

TO
RUSSIAN
CHURCH

HIGHWAY

BLVD RAIM.
ASSALIT
PERTINAX
P. PARIS

TZAR.

ELEVATED

THIERS

BELGIQUE
ALSACE

RUE

NOTRE
DAME
R. FOCH

SUISSE
ITALIE

PAGANINI

BISCARRA

AVE

GAMBETTA

AVE

RUE HEROLD

AVE GEORGES

NOD

AUBER

DURANTE

GOU-

BARQUIS-

CLEMENCEAU

P. DEROUL.

NICE
ETOILE
SHOPPING
MALL

BLVD.

BLVD. DE LOYE

R. GIUGLIA

RUE BERLIOZ

RUE VERDI

ROSSINI

RUE

HUGO

ALPH. KARR

LONGCHAMP

MEDECIN

RUE

VICTOR

JOFFRE

R. LIBERTE

BLVD.

RUE DE RIVOLI

MAR. MEYERBEER

DALPOZZO

CONGRES

BUFFA

RUE MASSENA

R. CRONSTADT

DE

FRANCE

PLACE
MASSENA

RUE

MUSEE
MASSENA

VERDUN

ALBERT
1er
PARK

R. DE

QUAI

PROMENADE DES ANGLAIS

B   E   A   C   H

TOURIST TRAIN
PICK-UP

TO 20

M E D I T E R R A N E A N

❶ Hôtel Ibis Nice Centre Gare

❷ Hôtel Belle Meunière

❸ Hôtel Durante

❹ Hôtel St. Georges

❺ Auberge de Jeunesse
les Camélias

❻ B&B Nice Home Sweet Home

❼ Hôtel Masséna

❽ Hôtel Suisse

❾ Hôtel Mercure Marché aux Fleurs

❿ Hôtel Vendôme & Launderette

⓫ Hôtel Lafayette

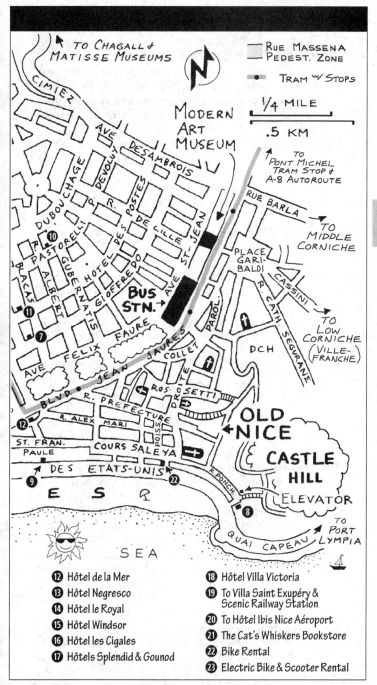

NICE

TO CHAGALL & MATISSE MUSEUMS

CIMIEZ

MODERN ART MUSEUM

RUE MASSENA PEDEST. ZONE

TRAM w/ STOPS

¼ MILE

.5 KM

AVE. DESAMBROIS

DEVOLUY

R. DES POSTES

R. DE LILLE

ST-JEAN

RUE BARLA

TO PONT MICHEL TRAM STOP & A-8 AUTOROUTE

TO MIDDLE CORNICHE

PLACE GARIBALDI

CASSINI

R. CATH. SEGURANE

TO LOW CORNICHE (VILLE-FRANCHE)

DUBOUCHAGE

PASTORELLI

R. ALBERTI

BLACAS

GUBERNATIS

HOTEL DES

GIOFFREDO

AVE. PAROL.

BUS STN.

FELIX FAURE

JEAN JAURES

BLVD. J. COLLET

DCH

AVE.

ROSSETTI

R. DROITE

OLD NICE

CASTLE HILL

R. ALEX MARI

R. PREFECTURE

R. POISS.

ELEVATOR

ST. FRAN. PAULE

COURS SALEYA

DES ETATS-UNIS

R. PONCH.

E S R

TO PORT LYMPIA

SEA

QUAI CAPEAU

⑫ Hôtel de la Mer
⑬ Hôtel Negresco
⑭ Hôtel le Royal
⑮ Hôtel Windsor
⑯ Hôtel les Cigales
⑰ Hôtels Splendid & Gounod
⑱ Hôtel Villa Victoria
⑲ To Villa Saint Exupéry & Scenic Railway Station
⑳ To Hôtel Ibis Nice Aéroport
㉑ The Cat's Whiskers Bookstore
㉒ Bike Rental
㉓ Electric Bike & Scooter Rental

Check hotel websites for deals (which are more common at larger hotels).

Between the Train Station and Nice Etoile

This area offers Nice's cheapest sleeps, though most hotels near the station ghetto are overrun, overpriced, and loud. The following hotels are the pleasant exceptions (most are near avenue Jean Médecin), and are listed in order of proximity to the train station, going toward the beach.

$$ Hôtel Ibis Nice Centre Gare**, 100 yards to the right as you leave the station, gives those in need of train station access a secure refuge in this seedy area. It's modern, with two-star business comfort (Db-€90–105, air-con, Wi-Fi, bar, café, 14 avenue Thiers, tel. 04 93 88 85 85, fax 04 93 88 58 00, www.ibishotel.com, h1396@accor.com).

$$ At Hôtel Durante**, you know you're on the Mediterranean as soon as you enter this cheery, way-orange building with its rooms wrapped around a flowery courtyard. Every one of its quiet rooms overlooks a spacious, well-maintained patio/garden with an American-style Jacuzzi. The rooms are good enough (mostly big beds) and the price is right enough (Ds-€72–80, bigger Db-€100–150, Tb-€130–170, air-con, Wi-Fi, 16 avenue Durante, tel. 04 93 88 84 40, fax 04 93 87 77 76, www.hotel-durante.com, info@hotel-durante.com).

$$ Hôtel St. Georges**, five blocks from the station toward the sea, has a backyard garden, reasonably clean and comfortable high-ceilinged rooms, orange tones, blue halls, fair rates, and friendly Houssein at the reception (Sb-€85, Db-€85–100, Tb with 3 beds-€120, extra bed-€20, air-con, Wi-Fi, 7 avenue Georges Clemenceau, tel. 04 93 88 79 21, fax 04 93 16 22 85, www.hotel saintgeorges.fr, contact@hotelsaintgeorges.fr).

$ Hôtel Belle Meunière*, in a fine old mansion built for Napoleon III's mistress, offers cheap beds and private rooms a block below the train station. Lively and youth hostel–esque, this simple but well-kept place attracts budget-minded travelers of all ages with basic-but-adequate rooms and charismatic Mademoiselle Marie-Pierre presiding (with perfect English). Tables in the front yard greet guests and provide opportunities to meet other travelers (bunk in 4-bed dorm-€23 with private bath, €18 with shared bath, Db-€60, includes breakfast, Wi-Fi, laundry service, 21 avenue Durante, tel. 04 93 88 66 15, fax 04 93 82 51 76, www.belle meuniere.com, hotel.belle.meuniere@cegetel.net).

$ Auberge de Jeunesse les Camélias is a laid-back youth hostel with a great location and modern facilities. Rooms accommodate between four and eight people in bunk beds (136 beds in all) and come with showers and sinks—WCs are down the hall. Reservations must be made on the website in advance or on the same day by phone. If you don't have a reservation, call by 10:00—or, better, try to snag a bunk in person. The place is popular but worth a try for last-minute availability (€23/bed, one-time €15 extra charge without hostel membership, includes breakfast, rooms closed 11:00–15:00 but can leave bags, Internet access, laundry, kitchen, safes, bar, 3 rue Spitalieri, tel. 04 93 62 15 54, www.hihostels.com, nice-camelias@fuaj.org).

$ B&B Nice Home Sweet Home is a great value. Gentle Genevieve (a.k.a. Jennifer) Levert rents out three large rooms and one small single in her home. Her rooms are simply decorated, with high ceilings, big windows, lots of light, and space to spread out. One room comes with private bath; otherwise, it's just like at home...down the hall (S-€31–38, D-€61–70, Db-€65–75, Tb-€74–84, Q-€80–90, includes breakfast, air-con units available in summer, no elevator, two floors up, washer/dryer-€5, kitchen access, 35 rue Rossini at intersection with rue Auber, mobile 06 19 66 03 63, www.nicehomesweethome.com, glevert@free.fr).

Between Nice Etoile and the Sea

These hotels are either on the sea or within an easy walk of it, and are the closest to Old Nice.

$$$ Hôtel Masséna**, in a classy building a few blocks from place Masséna, is a "professional" hotel (popular with tour groups) with 100 rooms at almost-reasonable rates and mod public spaces (5 small Db-€160, larger Db-€200, still larger Db-€295, extra bed-€30, skip the €20 breakfast, call same day for special rates—prices drop big time when hotel is not full, sixth-floor rooms have balconies, reserve parking ahead-€25/day, 58 rue Giofreddo, tel. 04 92 47 88 88, fax 04 92 47 88 89, www.hotel-massena-nice.com, info@hotel-massena-nice.com).

$$$ Hôtel Suisse*, below Castle Hill, has Nice's best ocean and city views for the money, and is surprisingly quiet given the busy street below. Rooms are quite comfortable, the decor is classy, and the staff is professional. There's no reason to sleep here if you don't land a view, so I've listed prices only for view rooms—many of which have balconies (Db-€170–205, extra bed-€36, breakfast-€15, 15 quai Rauba Capeu, tel. 04 92 17 39 00, fax 04 93 85 30 70, www.hotels-ocre-azur.com, hotel.suisse@hotels-ocre-azur.com).

$$$ Hôtel Mercure Marché aux Fleurs* is ideally situated across from the sea and behind cours Saleya. Rooms are tastefully designed and well-maintained (some with beds in a loft). Prices are reasonable, though rates vary dramatically depending on demand: Be sure to check their website for deals (standard Db-€135, superior Db-€165 and worth the extra euros, sea view-€50 extra, air-con, 91 quai des Etats-Unis, tel. 04 93 85 74 19, fax 04 93 13 90 94, www.hotelmercure.com, h0962@accor.com). Don't confuse this Mercure with the four others in Nice.

$$$ Hôtel Vendôme*** gives you a whiff of the belle époque, with pink pastels, high ceilings, and grand staircases in a mansion set off the street. Its public spaces are delightful. The rooms are modern and come in all sizes; the best have balconies (on floors 4 and 5)—request *une chambre avec balcon* (Sb-€115, Db-€150, Tb-€165, air-con, Internet access and Wi-Fi, book ahead for limited parking-€12/day, 26 rue Pastorelli, tel. 04 93 62 00 77, fax 04 93 13 40 78, www.vendome-hotel-nice.com, contact@vendome -hotel-nice.com).

$$$ Hôtel Lafayette***, in a handy location a block behind the Galeries Lafayette department store, is a great value. The hotel may look average from the outside, but inside it's comfortable and homey, with 18 well-designed, mostly spacious rooms, all one floor up from the street. It's family-run by Kirill, Tina, and young Victor. Rooms not overlooking rue de l'Hôtel des Postes are quieter and worth requesting (standard Db-€105–120, spacious Db-€115–130, extra bed-€24, coffee service in rooms, air-con, no elevator, 32 rue de l'Hôtel des Postes, tel. 04 93 85 17 84, fax 04 93 80 47 56, www.hotellafayettenice.com, info@hotellafayette nice.com).

$$ Hôtel de la Mer** is a humble place with an enviable position overlooking place Masséna, just steps from Old Nice (it's among the closest of my listings to the old town). Although this small hotel has a few rough edges, new (and very helpful) owner Pierre seems to be on top of things, the beds are firm, and it's quiet (small Db-€100, bigger Db facing place Masséna-€130, Tb-€145, air-con, Wi-Fi, 4 place Masséna, tel. 04 93 92 09 10, fax 04 93 85 00 64, www.hoteldelamernice.com, hotel.mer@wanadoo.fr).

Between Boulevard Victor Hugo and the Sea

These hotels are either on the beach or within walking distance, and closest to promenade des Anglais.

$$$ Hôtel Negresco**** owns Nice's most prestigious address on promenade des Anglais and knows it. Still, it's the kind of place that, if you were to splurge just once in your life.... Rooms are opulent (see page 326 for more description), and tips are expected (viewless Db-€360, Db with sea view-€460–580, view suite-€770– 1,900, breakfast-€30, Old World bar, 37 promenade des Anglais, tel. 04 93 16 64 00, fax 04 93 88 35 68, www.hotel-negresco-nice .com, reservations@hotel-negresco.com).

$$$ Hôtel le Royal*** stands shoulder-to-shoulder on promenade des Anglais with the big boys (the Negresco, Palais, and Westminster hotels). With 140 rooms, big lounges, and hallways that stretch forever, it feels a bit institutional. But the prices are reasonable considering the solid air-conditioned comfort and terrific location—and sometimes they have rooms when others don't (viewless Db-€125, Db with sea view-€155–175, bigger view room-€175–195 and worth it, extra person-€25, 23 promenade des Anglais, tel. 04 93 16 43 00, fax 04 93 16 43 02, www.hotel-royal -nice.cote.azur.fr, royal@vacancesbleues.com).

$$$ Hôtel Windsor*** is a snazzy garden retreat that feels like a cross between a modern-art museum and a health spa. Some of the contemporary rooms, designed by modern artists, defy explanation. It has a full-service bar, a small outdoor swimming pool and gym (both free for guests), an €11 sauna, €55 massages, and full meal service in the cool, shaded garden area (standard Db-€125, bigger Db-€155, big Db with balcony-€180, extra bed-€20, rooms over garden worth the higher price, air-con, Internet access and Wi-Fi, 11 rue Dalpozzo, tel. 04 93 88 59 35, fax 04 93 88 94 57, www.hotelwindsornice.com, reservation@hotelwindsor nice.com).

$$$ Hôtel les Cigales*** is one of my favorites. It's a smart little pastel place with tasteful decor, 19 plush rooms (most with tub-showers), air-conditioning, and a nifty upstairs terrace, all well-managed by friendly Mr. Valentino, with Veronique and Elaine. Book directly through the hotel and show this book for a surprise treat on arrival (standard Db-€135–160, Tb-€160–180, free Wi-Fi, 16 rue Dalpozzo, tel. 04 97 03 10 70, fax 04 97 03 10 71, www.hotel-lescigales.com, info@hotel-lescigales.com).

$$$ Hôtel Splendid**** is a worthwhile splurge if you miss your Marriott. The panoramic rooftop pool, Jacuzzi, bar, restaurant, and breakfast room almost justify the cost...but throw in solid rooms (four of the six floors are non-smoking), a free gym, spa services, and air-conditioning, and you're as good as home (Db-€235, deluxe Db with terrace-€280, suites-€360–410, breakfast-€16, check website for special deals, parking-€24/day, 50 boulevard Victor Hugo, tel. 04 93 16 41 00, fax 04 93 16 42 70, www .splendid-nice.com, info@splendid-nice.com).

$$$ Hôtel Gounod*** is behind Hôtel Splendid, and because the two share the same owners, Gounod's guests are allowed free access to Splendid's pool, Jacuzzi, and other amenities. Don't let the lackluster lobby fool you—most rooms are richly decorated, with high ceilings and air-conditioning (Db-€170, palatial 4-person suites-€270, parking-€15/day, 3 rue Gounod, tel. 04 93 16 42 00, fax 04 93 88 23 84, www.gounod-nice.com, info@gounod -nice.com).

$$$ Hôtel Villa Victoria*** is managed by cheery Marlena, who welcomes travelers into this spotless, classy old building with a green awning and an open, attractive lobby overlooking a generous garden. Rooms are traditional and well-kept, with space to

Old Nice Hotels & Restaurants

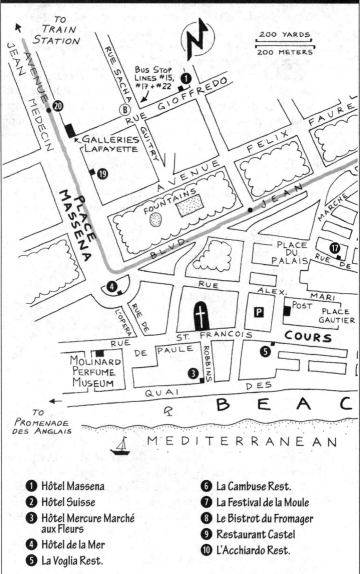

1. Hôtel Massena
2. Hôtel Suisse
3. Hôtel Mercure Marché aux Fleurs
4. Hôtel de la Mer
5. La Voglia Rest.
6. La Cambuse Rest.
7. La Festival de la Moule
8. Le Bistrot du Fromager
9. Restaurant Castel
10. L'Acchiardo Rest.

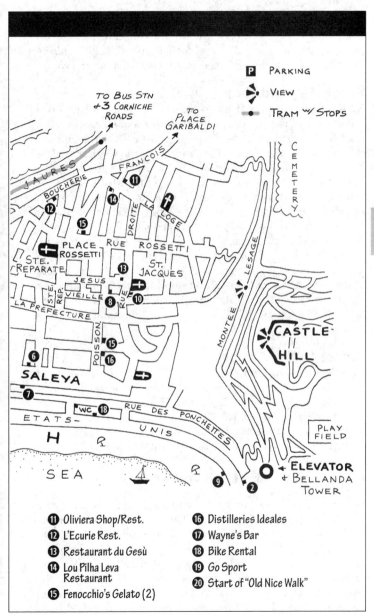

NICE

Legend:
- **P** PARKING
- **⚐** VIEW
- **━●━** TRAM w/ STOPS

TO BUS STN & 3 CORNICHE ROADS

TO PLACE GARIBALDI

JAURES

BOUCHERIE

FRANCOIS

DROITE

LA LOGE

CEMETERY

LESAGE

PLACE ROSSETTI

STE. REPARATE

RUE ROSSETTI

ST. JACQUES

JESUS

STE. REP.

VIEILLE

LA PREFECTURE

POISSON

SALEYA

MONTEE

CASTLE HILL

WC

RUE DES PONCHETTES

ETATS-UNIS

PLAY FIELD

H   R

SEA

R

ELEVATOR & BELLANDA TOWER

- ⓫ Oliviera Shop/Rest.
- ⓬ L'Ecurie Rest.
- ⓭ Restaurant du Gesù
- ⓮ Lou Pilha Leva Restaurant
- ⓯ Fenocchio's Gelato (2)
- ⓰ Distilleries Ideales
- ⓱ Wayne's Bar
- ⓲ Bike Rental
- ⓳ Go Sport
- ⓴ Start of "Old Nice Walk"

stretch out (streetside Db-€150, garden-side Db-€180, Tb-€160–185, suites-€210–235, breakfast-€15, air-con, minibar, Wi-Fi, parking-€18, 33 boulevard Victor Hugo, tel. 04 93 88 39 60, fax 04 93 88 07 98, www.villa-victoria.com, contact@villa-victoria.com).

Barely Beyond Nice

$ Villa Saint Exupéry, a service-oriented hostel, is a haven two miles north of the city center. Its amenities and 60 comfortable, spick-and-span rooms create a friendly climate for budget-minded travelers of any age. Often filled with energetic youth, the place can be noisy. There are units for one, two, and up to six people. Many have private bathrooms and views of the Mediterranean—some come with balconies. You'll also find a laundry room, complete kitchen facilities, and a lively bar. There's easy Internet access with a wall of computers in the lobby and Wi-Fi in all the rooms (bed in dorm-€30/person, S-€50–70, Db-€60–90, Tb-€115, includes big breakfast, no curfew; take bus #23 from the airport or train station, or take the tram—direction: Las Planas—to the Compte de Falicon stop and walk 10 minutes; ask about free pickup at train station, 22 avenue Gravier, toll-free tel. 08 00 30 74 09, fax 04 92 09 82 94, www.vsaint.com, reservations @vsaint.com).

Closer to the Airport

$$ Hôtel Ibis Nice Aéroport** offers a handy port-in-the-storm for those with early flights or just stopping in for a single night (Db-€78–98 when no special events in town, parking-€7, 359 promenade des Anglais, tel. 04 93 83 30 30, fax 04 93 21 19 43, www.ibisnice.com, reception@ibisnice.com). Hotel chains Etap, Campanile, and Novotel also have hotels at the airport.

Eating in Nice

Remember, you're in a resort. Seek ambience and fun, and lower your palate's standards. Italian is a low-risk and regional cuisine. The listed restaurants are concentrated in neighborhoods close to my recommended hotels. Promenade des Anglais is ideal for picnic dinners on warm, languid evenings. Old Nice has the best and busiest dining atmosphere (and best range of choices), while the Nice Etoile area is more local, convenient, and also offers a good range of choices. To feast cheaply, eat on rue Droite in Old Nice, or explore the area around the train station. For a more peaceful meal, head for nearby Villefranche-sur-Mer (see page 356). Allow yourself one dinner at a beachfront restaurant in Nice, and for terribly touristy trolling, wander the wall-to-wall eateries lining rue Masséna. Yuck.

In Old Nice

Nice's dinner scene converges on cours Saleya (koor sah-lay-yuh), which is entertaining enough in itself to make the generally mediocre food a good deal. It's a fun, festive spot to compare tans and mussels. Even if you're eating elsewhere, wander through here in the evening. For locations, see the map on page 314.

La Voglia is all about good Italian food at fair prices. It's popular with locals, lively, and offers fun inside and outside seating (€14 pizza and pasta, open daily, at the western edge of cours Saleya at 2 rue St Francois de Paule, tel. 04 93 80 99 16).

La Cambuse is a classy place by cours Saleya standards, and may be the only restaurant along here that doesn't try to reel in passersby. The cuisine is Franco-Italian with an emphasis on Italy. There's attentive service and good seating indoors and out (€14 starters, €18–24 *plats*, 5 cours Saleya, tel. 04 93 80 82 40).

La Festival de la Moule is a simple, touristy place for lovers of mussels (or for just plain hungry folks). For €14 you get all-you-can-eat mussels (11 sauces possible) and fries in a youthful outdoor setting. Let twins Alex and Marc tempt you with their spicy and cream sauces—be daring and try several (other bistro fare available, across the square from la Cambuse, 20 cours Saleya, tel. 04 93 62 02 12).

Le Bistrot du Fromager's owner is crazy about cheese and wine. Come here to escape the heat and dine in cool vaulted cellars surrounded by shelves of wine. All dishes use cheese as their base ingredient, although you'll also find pasta, ham, and salmon (with cheese, of course). This is a good choice for vegetarians (€10 entrees, €12–14 *plats*, €6 desserts, closed Sun, just off place de Gésu at 29 rue Benoit Bunico, tel. 04 93 13 07 83).

Restaurant Castel is a fine eat-on-the-beach option, thanks to its location at the very east end of Nice looking over the bay. You almost expect Don Ho to step up and grab a mic. Lose the city hustle and bustle by dropping down the steps below Castle Hill. The views are unforgettable even if the cuisine is not; you can even have lunch at your beach chair if you've rented one here (€10/half-day, €14/day). Dinner here is best: Arrive before sunset and find a waterfront table perfectly positioned to watch evening swimmers get in their last laps as the sky turns pink and city lights flicker on. Linger long enough to merit the few extra euros the place charges (€16 salads and pastas, €20–26 main courses, 8 quai des Etats-Unis, tel. 04 93 85 22 66).

Dining Cheap *à la Niçoise*

Try at least one of these five places—not just because they're terrific budget options, but primarily because they offer authentic *niçoise* cuisine.

Nice Restaurants

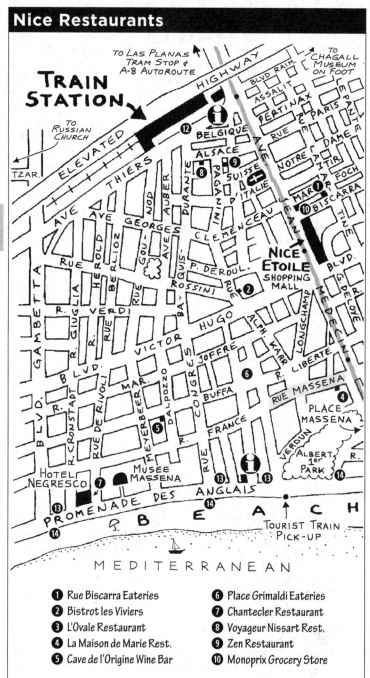

NICE

1 Rue Biscarra Eateries
2 Bistrot les Viviers
3 L'Ovale Restaurant
4 La Maison de Marie Rest.
5 Cave de l'Origine Wine Bar
6 Place Grimaldi Eateries
7 Chantecler Restaurant
8 Voyageur Nissart Rest.
9 Zen Restaurant
10 Monoprix Grocery Store

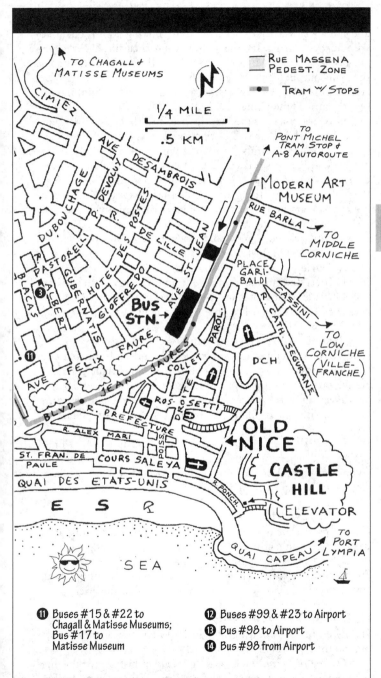

NICE

- ⑪ Buses #15 & #22 to Chagall & Matisse Museums; Bus #17 to Matisse Museum
- ⑫ Buses #99 & #23 to Airport
- ⑬ Bus #98 to Airport
- ⑭ Bus #98 from Airport

L'Acchiardo, hidden away in the heart of Old Nice, is a dark and homey eatery that does a good job mixing a loyal clientele with hungry tourists. Its simple, hearty *niçoise* cuisine is served for fair prices by gentle Monsieur Acchiardo. The small plaque under the menu outside says it's been run by father and son since 1927 (€7 starters, €14 *plats,* €5 desserts, cash only, closed Sat–Sun, indoor seating only, 38 rue Droite, tel. 04 93 85 51 16).

Oliviera venerates the French olive. This shop/restaurant sells a variety of oils, offers free tastings, and serves a menu of dishes paired with specific oils (think of a wine pairing). Welcoming owner Nadim, who speaks excellent English, knows all of his producers and provides "Olive Oil 101" explanations with his tastings (best if you buy something afterward or have a meal). You'll learn how passionate he is about his products, and once you come to taste, you'll want to stay and eat (€14–22 main dishes, Tue–Sat 10:00–22:00, closed Sun–Mon, indoor seating only, 8 bis rue du Collet, tel. 04 93 13 06 45).

L'Ecurie, a favorite for Nice residents, is off the beaten path in Old Nice. The cuisine is a mix of traditional *niçoise* and Italian specialties, and the ambience is warm inside and out (€23 three-course *menu,* €11 wood-fired pizza, open daily, 4 rue du Marché, tel. 04 93 62 32 62).

Restaurant du Gesù, a happy-go-lucky greasy spoon, squeezes plastic tables into a slanting square deep in the old city (sailors accustomed to dining off-balance will feel right at home). Arrive early or join the mobs waiting for an outside table; better yet, have fun in the soccer-banner–draped interior. The *raviolis sauce daube* is popular (€10 pizzas and pastas, closed Sun, 1 place du Jésus, tel. 04 93 62 26 46).

Lou Pilha Leva delivers fun and cheap lunch or dinner options with *niçoise* specialties and outdoor-only benches that are swimming in pedestrians (open daily, located where rues de la Loge and Centrale meet in Old Nice).

And for Dessert…

Gelato-lovers should save room for the tempting ice-cream stands in Old Nice. **Fenocchio** is the city's favorite, with mouth-watering displays of 86 flavors ranging from tomato to lavender to avocado—all of which are surprisingly good (daily March–Nov until 24:00, two locations: 2 place Rossetti and 6 rue de la Poissonnerie).

Eating near Nice Etoile

If you're not up for eating in Old Nice, try one of these spots around the Nice Etoile shopping mall.

On rue Biscarra: An appealing lineup of bistros overflowing with outdoor tables stretches along the broad sidewalk on traffic-

free rue Biscarra (just east of avenue Jean Médecin behind Nice
Etoile, all closed Sun). Come here to dine with area residents away
from the tourists. These three places are all good choices, with
good interior and exterior seating: **Le Cenac** seems most popular
and features cuisine from southwest France (like duck, foie gras,
and omelets with cep mushrooms, €14–23 *plats*). **L'Authentic** has
the most creative cuisine and comes with two memorable owners: burly Philippe and sleek Laurent (€22 two-course *menus,* €25
three-course *menus,* reasonable pasta dishes, tel. 04 93 62 48 88).
Le 20 sur Vin is a neighborhood favorite with a cozy, wine-bar-
meets-café ambience. It offers *(bien sûr)* good wines at fair prices,
and basic bistro fare (tel. 04 93 92 93 20).

Bistrot les Viviers attracts those who require attentive service and authentic *niçoise* cuisine with a big emphasis on fish. This
classy splurge offers two intimate settings as different as night
and day: a soft, formal restaurant (€50 *menu,* €28–35 *plats*), and a
relaxed *bistrot* next door (€35 weekday *menu,* €25–32 *plats,* bouilla-
baisse-€41, bourride-€25). I'd reserve a table in the atmospheric
bistrot, where some outdoor seating is available (restaurant closed
Sun, *bistrot* open daily, 5-minute walk west of avenue Jean Médecin
at 22 rue Alphonse Karr, tel. 04 93 16 00 48).

L'Ovale is a find. Named for the shape of a rugby ball, how
this ever-so-local and rugby-loving café survives in a tourist mecca,
I'll never know. It's a welcoming, well-run bistro with quality food
at respectable prices. Dine inside on big *plats* for €13; consider
their specialty, *cassoulet* (€35 for two people, though it's enough
for three); or enjoy *la planche de charcuterie* as a meaty, filling first
course. The *salade de manchons* with duck and walnuts is incredible (excellent €17 three-course *menu,* €12 monster salads, closed
Sun, air-con, 29 rue Pastorelli, tel. 04 93 80 31 65). Effervescent
Johanna ensures good service.

La Maison de Marie is a surprisingly good-quality refuge
off touristy rue Masséna, where most other restaurants serve
mediocre food to tired travelers. Enter through a deep-red arch
to a bougainvillea-draped courtyard, and enjoy the fair prices and
good food that draw neighborhood regulars and out-of-towners
alike. The interior tables are as appealing as those in the courtyard
(*menus* from €22, open daily, look for the square red sign at 5 rue
Masséna, tel. 04 93 82 15 93).

Near Promenade des Anglais

Cave de l'Origine is a warm, local spot run by kind Isabelle and
Carlo, where you'll find a quality food shop *(épicerie)* and wine bar/
bistrot serving a small selection. Carlo loves talking about his all-
natural wines and other products. Stop by for a glass of wine, to
peruse the shop, or better, to reserve a table for a meal (€10 starters,

NICE

€19 *plats,* open Tue–Sat for lunch, Thu–Sat for dinner, reservations smart, indoor seating only; shop open Tue–Sat 10:00–20:00, closed Sun–Mon; 3 rue Dalpozzo, tel. 04 83 50 09 60).

Place Grimaldi nurtures several appealing restaurants with good indoor and outdoor seating along a broad sidewalk and under tall sycamore trees. **Crêperie Bretonne** is the only crêperie I list in Nice (€8 dinner crêpes, closed Sun, 3 place Grimaldi, tel. 04 93 82 28 47). **Le Grimaldi** is popular for its café fare (€12 pasta and pizza, €15–19 *plats,* closed Sun, 1 place Grimaldi, tel. 04 93 87 98 13).

Chantecler has Nice's most prestigious address—inside the Hôtel Negresco. This is everything a luxury restaurant should be: elegant, soft, and top-quality. If your trip is ending in Nice, call or email for reservations—you've earned this splurge (*menus* from €90, closed Mon–Tue, 37 promenade des Anglais, tel. 04 93 16 64 00, chantecler@hotel-negresco.com).

Near the Train Station

Both of the following restaurants provide good indoor and outdoor seating.

Voyageur Nissart has blended good-value cuisine with cool Mediterranean ambience and friendly service since 1908. Alexis and Max could not be kinder hosts, making this a top option for those on a budget (€16 three-course *menus,* €7 fine *salade niçoise,* €10 *plats,* closed Mon, 19 rue d'Alsace-Lorraine, tel. 04 93 82 19 60).

Zen provides a Japanese break from French cuisine. Its friendly staff, pleasing contemplative decor, and tasty specialties draw a strong following (€16 three-course *menu,* €8–13 sushi, open daily, 27 rue d'Angleterre, tel. 04 93 82 41 20).

Nice Connections

For rough train, bus, and boat schedules from Nice to nearby towns, see "Getting Around the Riviera from Nice" on page 292. Note that most long-distance train connections to other French cities require a change in Marseille. The Grande Ligne train to Bordeaux (serving Antibes, Cannes, Toulon, Arles, Carcassonne, and other stops en route) requires a reservation.

From Nice by Train to: Marseille (18/day, 2.5 hours), **Cassis** (14/day, 3 hours, transfer in Toulon or Marseille), **Arles** (11/day, 3.75–4.5 hours, most require transfer in Marseille or Avignon), **Avignon** (20/day, most of which are by TGV, 4 hours, most require transfer in Marseille), **Paris'** Gare de Lyon (10/day, 6 hours, may require change; 11-hour night train goes to Paris' Gare d'Austerlitz), **Aix-en-Provence** TGV station (10/day, 3.5 hours, may require transfer in Marseille or Toulon), **Chamonix** (4/day, 10 hours, 3 transfers), **Beaune** (7/day, 7 hours, 1–2 changes), **Munich**

(4/day, 12–13 hours with 2–4 transfers, night trains possible via Italy), **Interlaken** (6/day, 9–11 hours, 2–5 transfers), **Florence** (6/day, 7–9 hours, 1–3 transfers), **Milan** (7/day, 5–5.5 hours, all require transfers), **Venice** (5/day, 8–9 hours, all require transfers), **Barcelona** (1/day via Montpelier, 10.5 hours, more with multiple changes).

Nice's Airport

Nice's easy-to-navigate airport (Aéroport de Nice Côte d'Azur) is on the Mediterranean, a 20- to 30-minute drive west of the city center. Planes leave about hourly to Paris (one-hour flight, about the same price as a train ticket, check www.easyjet.com for the cheapest flights to Paris' Orly airport). The two terminals (Terminal 1 and Terminal 2) are connected by frequent shuttle buses *(navettes)*. Both terminals have banks, ATMs, taxis, baggage storage (open daily 6:00–23:00), and buses to Nice. The TIs for Nice and Monaco are in Terminal 1 (tel. 08 20 42 33 33 or 04 89 88 98 28, www.nice.aeroport.fr).

Taxis into the center are expensive considering the short distance (figure €35 to Nice hotels and €55 to Villefranche-sur-Mer, 10 percent more 19:00–7:00 and all day Sun). Taxis stop outside door *(Porte)* A-1 at Terminal 1 and outside *Porte* A-3 at Terminal 2. Notorious for overcharging, Nice taxis are not always so nice. If your fare for a ride into town is much higher than €35 (or €40 at night or on Sun), refuse to pay the overage. If this doesn't work, tell the cabbie to call a *gendarme* (police officer). It's always a good idea to ask for a receipt *(reçu)*.

Airport shuttle vans work with some of my recommended hotels, but they only make sense when going *to* the airport, not when arriving on an international flight. Unlike taxis, shuttle vans offer a fixed price that doesn't rise on Sundays, early mornings, or evenings. Prices are best for groups (figure €25 for one person, and only a little more for additional people). **Nice Airport Shuttle** is one option (€25/one person, €32/two people, mobile 06 60 33 20 54, www.nice-airport-shuttle.com), or ask your hotelier for recommendations.

Three bus lines connect the airport with the city center, offering good alternatives to high-priced taxis. **Bus #99** (airport express) runs from both terminals to Nice's main train station (€4, 2/hour, 8:00–21:00, 30 minutes, drops you within a 10-minute walk of many recommended hotels). To take this bus *to* the airport, catch it right in front of the train station (departs on the half-hour). If your hotel is within walking distance of the station, #99 is a breeze.

Bus #98 serves both terminals, and runs along promenade des Anglais to Nice's main bus station *(gare routière)*, which is near Old Nice (€4, 3/hour, from the airport 6:00–23:00, to the airport until 21:00, 30 minutes, see map on page 318 for stops). The slower, cheaper local **bus #23** serves only Terminal 1, and makes every stop between the airport and train station (€1, 5/hour, 6:00–20:00, 40 minutes, direction: St. Maurice).

For all buses, buy tickets in the information office just outside either terminal, or from the driver. To reach the bus information office and stops at Terminal 1, turn left after passing customs and exit the doors at the far end. Buses serving Terminal 2 stop across the street from the airport exit (information kiosk and ticket sales to the right as you exit).

If you take bus #98 or #99, hang on to your €4 ticket—it's good all day on any public bus and the tramway in Nice, and for buses between Nice and nearby towns (see page 293 for details). Note that if you take your big bag onto any non-airport bus, you may be charged an extra €5.

To get to **Villefranche-sur-Mer** from the airport, take bus #98 to Nice's bus station *(gare routière)*, then transfer to the Villefranche-sur-Mer bus (bus #100, use same ticket).

To reach **Antibes,** take bus #250 from Terminal 1 (€8, about 2/hour, 40 minutes). For **Cannes,** take bus #210 from either terminal (2/hour, 30 minutes on freeway). Pricey express buses (line #110) run directly to **Monaco** from the airport (€18, hourly, 50 minutes), but you'll save money by transferring in Nice to a Monaco-bound bus.

WELCOME TO THE RIVIERA WALK

From the Promenade des Anglais to Castle Hill

This leisurely, level walk begins on the promenade des Anglais (near the landmark Hôtel Negresco) and ends on Castle Hill above Old Nice. While the entire walk is enjoyable at any time, the first half makes a great pre- or post-dinner stroll. Timing your stroll to end up on Castle Hill (this walk's grand finale) at sunset is a smart move. Allow one hour at a promenade pace to reach the elevator up to Castle Hill. A quick visit to the Masséna Museum (free, daily 10:00–18:00, see page 304), next to the starting point of this walk, sets the Riviera stage for this stroll.

The Walk Begins

Promenade des Anglais

Welcome to the Riviera. There's something for everyone along this four-mile-long seafront circus. Watch the Europeans at play, admire the azure Mediterranean, anchor yourself on a blue seat, and prop your feet up on the made-to-order guardrail. Later in the day, come back to join the evening parade of tans along the promenade.

For now, stroll like the belle époque English aristocrats for whom the promenade was paved (see map on page 318). The broad sidewalks of the promenade des Anglais ("walkway of the English") were financed by upper-crust English tourists who wanted a safe place to stroll and admire the view. The walk was done in marble in 1822 for aristocrats who didn't want to dirty their shoes or smell the fishy gravel. This grand promenade leads to the old city and Castle Hill.

• *Start at the pink-domed...*

Hôtel Negresco

Nice's finest hotel is also a historic monument, offering up the city's most expensive beds (see page 312) and a free "museum" interior (always open—provided you're dressed decently, absolutely no beach attire). The hotel underwent a massive renovation in 2010, so expect some changes to the following description.

March straight through the lobby (as if you're staying here) into the exquisite **Salon Royal,** a cozy place for a drink and a frequent host to art exhibits (opens at 11:00). The chandelier hanging from the Eiffel-built dome is made of 16,000 pieces of crystal. It was built in France for the Russian czar's Moscow palace...but because of the Bolshevik Revolution in 1917, he couldn't take delivery. Read the explanation of the bucolic dome scene, painted in 1913 for the hotel, then saunter around the perimeter counterclockwise. If the bar door is open (after about 15:00), wander up the marble steps for a look. Farther along, nip into the toilets for either an early 20th-century powder room or a Battle of Waterloo experience. The chairs nearby were typical of the age (cones of silence for an afternoon nap sitting up).

The hotel's Chantecler **restaurant** is one of the Riviera's best (allow €90 per person before drinks; described on page 322). A few years ago, it lost one of its Michelin stars, so you'll understand if the staff doesn't smile. In France, big-time chefs are like famous athletes: People know about them and talk about who's hot and who's not. Cooking is serious business—a few years ago, a famous Burgundian chef lost a star and committed suicide. On your way out, pop into the **Salon Louis XIV** (right of entry lobby as you leave), where the embarrassingly short Sun King models his red platform boots (English descriptions explain the room).

Once outside, turn left and walk past the bar to the back to see the hotel's original **entrance** (grander than today's)—in the 19th century, classy people stayed out of the sun, and any posh hotel that cared about its clientele would design its entry on the shady north side.

• *Cross the promenade des Anglais, and—before you begin your seaside promenade—grab a blue seat and gaze out to the...*

Bay of Angels (Baie des Anges)

Face the water. The body of Nice's patron saint, Réparate, was supposedly escorted into this bay by angels in the fourth century. To your right is where you might have been escorted into France—

RIVIERA WALK

Nice's airport, built on a massive landfill. On that tip of land way beyond the runway is Cap d'Antibes. Until 1860, Antibes and Nice were in different countries—Antibes was French, but Nice was a protectorate of the Italian kingdom of Savoy-Piedmont, a.k.a. the Kingdom of Sardinia. (During that period, the Var River—just west of Nice—was the geographic border between these two peoples.) In 1850 the people here spoke Italian and ate pasta. As Italy was uniting, the region was given a choice: Join the new country of Italy or join good old France (which was enjoying good times under the rule of Napoleon III). The vast majority voted in 1860 to go French...and voilà!

The first green hill to your left (Castle Hill) marks the end of this walk. Farther left lies Villefranche-sur-Mer (marked by the tower at land's end, and home to lots of millionaires), then Monaco (which you can't see, with more millionaires), then Italy (with lots of, uh, Italians). Behind you are the foothills of the Alps (Alpes Maritimes), which trap threatening clouds, ensuring that the Côte d'Azur enjoys sunshine more than 300 days each year. While half a million people live here, pollution is carefully treated—the water is routinely tested and very clean.

• *With the sea on your right, begin...*

Strolling the Promenade

The block next to Hôtel Negresco houses a lush park and the Masséna Museum of city history (described on page 304 and worth a short detour). Nearby sit two other belle époque establishments: the West End and Westminster **hotels,** both boasting English names to help those original guests feel at home (the West End is now part of the Best Western group...to help American guests feel at home). These hotels symbolize Nice's arrival as a tourist mecca a century ago, when the combination of leisure time and a stable economy allowed visitors to find the sun even in winter.

As you walk, be careful to avoid the green bike lane. You'll pass a number of separate **beaches**—some private, others public. In spite of the rocks, they're still a popular draw. You can rent

gear—about €12–18 for a *chaise longue* (long chair) and a *transat* (mattress), €3–5 for an umbrella, and €4 for a towel—and kick back. You'll also pass several beach restaurants (a highly recommended experience). Some of these eateries serve breakfast, all serve lunch, some do dinner, and a few have beachy bars... tailor-made for a break from this

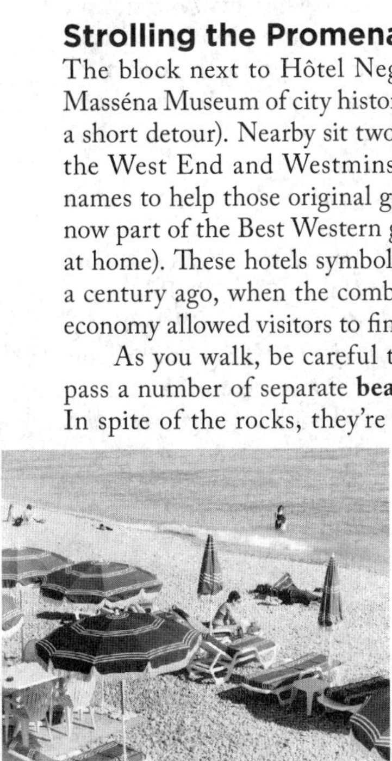

(vertical text in right margin) RIVIERA WALK

walk. A few promote package deals, including a lounge chair, an umbrella, a locker, and a meal, all for about €26. Why all this gear rental? In Europe, most beach-going families take planes or trains, since parking and gas are pricey (even worse than in the US) and traffic is ugly. So, unlike my family's beach trips, they can't stuff chairs, coolers, and the like in the trunk of their car and park right near the beach.

Even a hundred years ago, there was sufficient tourism in Nice to justify building its first **casino** (a leisure activity imported from Venice). Part of an elegant casino, La Jetée Promenade stood on those white-covered pilings just offshore, until the Germans destroyed it during World War II. (The Masséna Museum has images and models of the elaborate building.)

Although La Jetée Promenade is gone, you can still see the striking 1927 Art Nouveau facade of the Palais de la Méditerranée, a grand casino, hotel, and theater. This intimidating edifice was built during the great Depression by American financier Frank Jay Gould, who was looking for a better return on his investments when America's economy was tanking. It soon became the grandest casino in Europe, and today is one of France's most exclusive hotels.

The unappealing Casino Ruhl stands nearby. Anyone can drop in for some one-armed-bandit fun, but to play the tables at night you'll need to dress up and bring your passport. **Albert 1er Park** is named for the Belgian king who enjoyed wintering here. While the English came first, the Belgians and Russians were also big fans of 19th-century Nice. That tall statue at the edge of the park commemorates the 100-year anniversary of Nice's union with France.

Continue along the promenade, past the park. You're now on **quai des Etats-Unis** ("quay of the United States"). This name was given as a tip-of-the-cap to the Americans for finally entering World War I in 1917. Five minutes past the Hôtel Suisse (brilliant views as you walk), there's a monumental **war memorial** sculpted out of the rock in honor of the thousands of local boys who died serving their country in World Wars I and II.

• *Take the elevator next to the Hôtel Suisse up to Castle Hill (elevator runs daily 10:00–19:00, until 20:00 in summer, €0.70 one-way, €1.10 round-trip).*

Castle Hill (Colline du Château)

This hill—in an otherwise flat city center—offers sensational views over Nice, the port (to the east), the foothills of the Alps, and the Mediterranean. The views are best early or at sunset, or whenever the weather's clear (park closes at 20:00 in summer, earlier off-season). Nice was founded on this hill. Its residents were crammed onto the hilltop until the 12th century, as it was too risky to live in the flatlands below. Today you'll find a waterfall, a playground, two cafés (with fair prices), and a cemetery—but no castle—on Castle Hill.

• *Your tour is finished. Enjoy the vistas. To walk down to Old Nice, follow signs from just below the upper café to* Vieille Ville *(not Le Port), turn right at the cemetery, and then look for the walkway down on your left. If you're planning a boat tour (one hour, see page 295 for details), follow the* Le Port *signs to the bassin des Amiraux.*

OLD NICE WALK

*From Place Masséna
to Place Rossetti*

This self-guided walking tour gives you a helpful introduction to Nice's bicultural heritage and its most interesting neighborhoods. Allow about an hour at a leisurely pace for this level walk, including a stop for coffee and *socca* (chickpea crêpe). It's best done in the morning (while the outdoor market thrives and the *socca*'s hot), and preferably not on a Sunday, when many shops are closed. Because this walk ends near the bus station, it works well on the way to an afternoon bus excursion (e.g., to Monaco, Villefranche-sur-Mer, Cap Ferrat, or the inland hill towns). This walk is also a joy at night, when fountains glow and pedestrians control the streets.

The Walk Begins

• *Start on avenue Jean Médecin, near the Café Ritz, a block north of the Galleries Lafayette department store (see map on page 288).*

Avenue Jean Médecin

Nice's newly renovated "main street," once a nightmare of cars and delivery vehicles tangling with pedestrians, has been turned into a pedestrian and cyclist nirvana. As you walk along this major street, notice how quiet it is. Now think of a major street like this in your city, teeming with vehicles; then imagine it without the cars and trucks. Bravo, Nice. I used to avoid this street at all costs. Now I can't get enough of it. Places like the Café Ritz flourish in an environment of generous sidewalks and no traffic.

• *Stroll toward place Masséna and drink in the Italianesque colors and street theater that surround you. Find a bench on place Masséna.*

Place Masséna

This vast square pays tribute to Jean-André Masséna, a French military leader during the Revolutionary and Napoleonic Wars.

He's not just another pretty face in a long lineup of French military heroes, but is considered among the greatest commanders in history—anywhere, anytime. Napoleon thought of him as "the greatest name of my military Empire." No wonder this city is proud of him.

This grand *place* is Nice's drawing room, where old meets new, and where the tramway bends between the bus and train stations. The square's black-and-white pavement feels like an elegant outdoor ballroom, with the sleek tram waltzing across its dance floor. The men you see on pedestals high above are modern-art additions that arrived with the new tram. For a mood-altering experience, return after dark and watch the illuminated figures float above. Place Masséna is at its sophisticated best after the sun goes down.

There's also no better place than place Masséna to appreciate the city's Italian heritage (standing here makes me feel as if I'm in Venice's St. Mark's Square). The rich colors of the buildings reflect the taste of previous Italian rulers, back when Nice's residents rooted for Italian soccer teams. The fountains are the product of more recent tastes—to save money, they only have high pressure after 17:00. The distant hills behind the fountains separate Nice from Villefranche-sur-Mer, and that Italianesque clock tower is barely beyond Nice's bus station.

Look west across place Masséna and down a grassy parkway. You're standing on Nice's historic river, the Paillon. It's been covered since the late 1800s and runs under place Masséna, then under the parkway to the sea. For centuries this river was Nice's natural defense to the north and west (the sea protected the south, and Castle Hill defended the east). Imagine the fortified wall that once ran along its length from the hills behind you to the sea.

With the arrival of tourism in the 1800s, Nice spread north, beyond the river to your right (where your hotel is probably located). The modern can't-miss-it sculpture in the parkway is meant to represent the "curve of the French Riviera"—whatever that means—but looks more like an answer to local skateboarders' prayers. The tram is the first of three planned routes, and is Nice's first serious stab at managing its debilitating traffic problems.

• *Cross the square toward the Caisse d'Epargne Côte d'Azur bank, and*

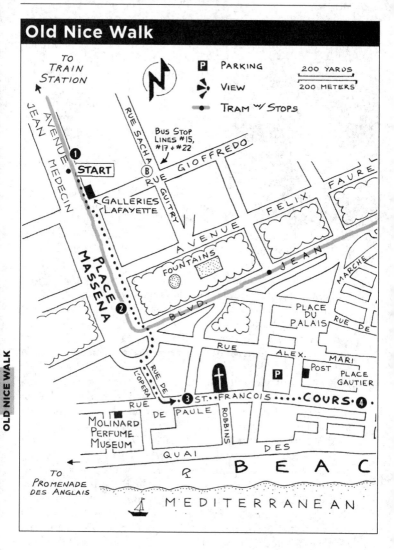

walk between the curved buildings along rue de l'Opéra, turning left on...

Rue St. François de Paule

You've entered Old Nice. Peer into the **Alziari** olive-oil shop at #14 (on the right, Mon–Sat 8:30–12:00 & 14:00–1900, closed Sun). Dating from 1868, the shop produces top-quality stone-ground olive oil. The proud and charming owner, Gilles Piot, claims that stone wheels create less acidity (since metal grinding builds up heat). Locals fill their own containers from the huge vats (the

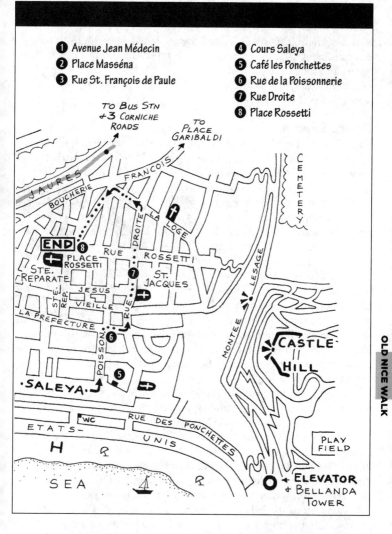

1. Avenue Jean Médecin
2. Place Masséna
3. Rue St. François de Paule
4. Cours Saleya
5. Café les Ponchettes
6. Rue de la Poissonnerie
7. Rue Droite
8. Place Rossetti

TO BUS STN
& 3 CORNICHE
ROADS

TO
PLACE
GARIBALDI

CEMETERY

JAURES

BOUCHERIE

FRANCOIS

LA LOGE

DROITE

END 8
PLACE
ROSSETTI

RUE

ROSSETTI

STE.
REPARATE

ST.
JACQUES

STE.
REP.

JESUS

VIEILLE

LA PREFECTURE

RUE

POISSON

6

5

SALEYA

WC

RUE DES PONCHETTES

ETATS-

UNIS

LESAGE

MONTEE

CASTLE
HILL

PLAY
FIELD

SEA

ELEVATOR
& BELLANDA
TOWER

OLD NICE WALK

cheapest one is peanut oil, not olive oil). Consider a gift for the olive oil–lover on your list. (Some may want to backpedal one block to the **Molinard** perfume shop and museum before continuing—see page 303.)

A block down on the left (at #7), **Pâtisserie Auer's** grand old storefront has changed little since the pastry shop opened in 1820 (closed Sun). The writing on the window says, "Since 1820 from father to son." The gold royal shields on the back wall remind shoppers that Queen Victoria indulged her sweet tooth here.

Across the street is Nice's grand **opera house,** dating from the same era. Imagine this opulent jewel back in the 19th century, buried deep in the old town of Nice. With all the fancy big-city folks wintering here, this rough-edged town needed some high-class entertainment. The four statues on top represent theater, dance, music, and song.

• *Continue on, sifting your way through souvenirs to the cours Saleya (koor sah-lay-yuh).*

Cours Saleya

Named for its broad exposure to the sun *(soleil)*, this commotion of color, sights, smells, and people has been **Nice's main market square** since the Middle Ages (produce market held Tue–Sun until 13:00—on Mon, an antiques market takes center stage). Amazingly, part of this square was a parking lot until 1980, when the mayor of Nice had an underground garage built.

The first section is devoted to the Riviera's largest flower market (all day Tue–Sun and in operation since the 19th century). Here you'll find plants and flowers that grow effortlessly and ubiquitously in this climate, including the local favorites: carnations, roses, and jasmine. Fresh flowers are perhaps the best value in this otherwise pricey city.

The boisterous produce section trumpets the season with mushrooms, strawberries, white asparagus, zucchini flowers, and more—whatever's fresh gets top billing.

Place Pierre Gautier (also called Plassa dou Gouvernou—bilingual street signs include the old Niçoise language, an Italian dialect) is where farmers set up stalls to sell their produce and herbs directly. For a great market overview, climb the steps by Le Grand Bleu restaurant; you may have to step over the trash sacks.

Look up to the **hill** that dominates to the east. The city of Nice was first settled up there by Greeks (circa 400 B.C.). In the Middle Ages, a massive castle stood there with soldiers at the ready. Over time, the city grew down to where you are now. With the river guarding one side and the sea the other, this mountain fortress seemed strong—until Louis XIV leveled it in 1706. Nice's medieval seawall ran along the line of two-story buildings where you're standing.

Now, look across place Pierre Gautier to the large "palace." The **Ducal Palace** was where the kings of Sardinia (the city's Italian rulers until 1860) would reside when in Nice. Today, it's police headquarters.

Resume your stroll down the center of cours Saleya, stopping when you see La Cambuse restaurant on your left. In front, hovering over the black-barrel fire with the paella-like pan on top, is the self-proclaimed **Queen of the Market,** Thérèse (tehr-ehz). When she's not looking for a husband, Thérèse is cooking *socca,* Nice's chickpea crêpe specialty (until about 13:00). Spend €3 for a wad of *socca* (careful—it's hot, but good). If she doesn't have a pan out, that means it's on its way (watch for the frequent scooter deliveries). Wait in line...or else it'll be all gone when you return.

• *Continue down cours Saleya. The fine golden building that seals the end of the square is where Henri Matisse spent 17 years with a brilliant view onto Nice's world. If you're in the mood, the **Café les Ponchettes** is perfectly positioned for a people-watching break. If not, turn left a block before the end of the square and head down...*

Rue de la Poissonnerie

Look up at the first floor of the first building on your right. **Adam and Eve** are squaring off, each holding a zucchini-like gourd. This scene (post-apple) represents the annual rapprochement in Nice to make up for the sins of a too-much-fun Carnival (Mardi Gras). Residents of Nice have partied hard during Carnival for more than 700 years (Feb 18–March 8 in 2011).

Now, walk a few doors down to #6 (right side). That filthy **iron grille** above the door allows air to enter the building, but keeps out uninvited guests. You'll see lots of these open grilles in Old Nice. They were part of a clever system that sucked in cool air from the sea, circulating it through homes and blowing it out through vents in the roof.

A few steps away, check out the small **Baroque church** (Notre-Dame-de-l'Annonciation) dedicated to St. Rita, the patron saint of desperate causes. She holds a special place in locals' hearts, making this the most popular church in Nice.

• *Turn right on the next street, where you'll pass Old Nice's most happening café/bar **(Distilleries Ideales)**, with a lively happy hour (18:00–20:00) and a Pirates of the Caribbean–style interior. Now turn left on "Right" Street (rue Droite), and enter an area that feels like a Little Naples.*

Rue Droite

In the Middle Ages, this straight, skinny street provided the most direct route from wall to wall, or river to sea. Stop at **Esipuno's bakery** (at place du Jésus, closed Mon–Tue) and say *bonjour* to the friendly folks. Thirty years ago, this baker was voted the best in France—the trophies you see were earned for bread-making, not bowling. His son now runs the place. Notice the firewood stacked by the oven. Try the house specialty, *tourte aux blettes* (pastry stuffed with pine nuts, raisins, and white beets).

Farther along, at #28, Thérèse (whom you met earlier) cooks her *socca* in the wood-fired oven here before she carts it to her barrel on cours Saleya. The balconies of the mansion in the next block mark the **Palais Lascaris** (1647, gorgeous at night), a rare souvenir from one of Nice's most prestigious families. It's worth popping inside for its Baroque Italian architecture, antique musical instruments, tapestries, and furniture (free, Wed–Mon 10:00–18:00, closed Tue). Look up and make faces back at the guys under the balconies.

• *Turn left on the rue de la Loge, then left again on rue Centrale, to reach...*

Place Rossetti

The most Italian of Nice's piazzas, place Rossetti feels more like Roma than Nice. This square comes alive after dark. Fenocchio is popular for its many gelato flavors, ranging from classic to innovative (daily March–Nov 9:00–24:00; mouth-watering preview at www.fenocchio.fr).

Walk to the fountain and stare back at the church. This is the **Cathedral of St. Réparate**—an unassuming building for a major city's cathedral. It was relocated here in the 1500s, when Castle Hill was temporarily converted to military-only. The name comes from Nice's patron saint, a teenage virgin named Réparate whose martyred body floated to Nice in the fourth century accompanied by angels (remember the Bay of Angels?). The interior of the cathedral gushes Baroque, a response to the Protestant Reformation. With the Catholic Church's Counter-Reformation, the theatrical energy of churches was cranked up—with re-energized, high-powered saints and eye-popping decor.

• *Our tour is over. If you're re-energized, take a walk up* **Castle Hill***. To get there, cross place Rossetti and follow the lane leading uphill (see Castle Hill description at the end of the previous Welcome to the Riviera Walk chapter). If it's early enough and you're up for a day trip, take a left outside the church and you'll eventually arrive at the bus station.*

CHAGALL MUSEUM TOUR

Musée Chagall

Even if you're suspicious of modern art, this museum—with the world's largest collection of Marc Chagall's work in captivity—is a delight. After World War II, Chagall returned from the United States to settle in Vence, not far from Nice. Between 1954 and 1967 he painted a cycle of 17 large murals designed for, and donated to, this museum. These paintings, inspired by the biblical books of Genesis, Exodus, and the Song of Songs, make up the "nave," or core, of what Chagall called the "House of Brotherhood."

Orientation

Cost: €7.50, free first Sun of the month (but crowded).

Hours: Wed–Mon 10:00–17:00, May–Oct until 18:00, closed Tue year-round.

Getting There: You can reach the museum, located on avenue Docteur Ménard, by bus or on foot.

　　Buses #15 and #22 serve the Chagall Museum from the Masséna Guitry stop, near place Masséna (5/hour Mon–Sat, 3/hour Sun, €1; stop faces eastbound on rue Sacha Guitry, a block east of Galeries Lafayette department store—see map on page 288). The museum's bus stop (called Musée Chagall, shown on the bus shelter) is on boulevard de Cimiez (walk uphill from the stop to find the museum).

　　To **walk** from central Nice to the Chagall Museum (30 minutes), go to the train-station end of avenue Jean Médecin and turn right onto boulevard Raimbaldi. Walk four long blocks along the elevated road, then turn left onto avenue Raymond Comboul, and follow *Musée Chagall* signs.

Information: Although Chagall would suggest that you explore his works without help, the free audioguide gives you detailed explanations of his works and covers temporary exhibits. The free *Plan du Musée* helps you locate the rooms, though you can do without, as the museum is pretty simple. Tel. 04 93 53 87 20, www.musee-chagall.fr.

Leaving the Museum: To take **buses** #15 or #22 back to downtown Nice, turn right out of the museum, then make another right down boulevard de Cimiez, and catch the bus heading downhill. To continue on to the Matisse Museum, catch buses #15 or #22 using the uphill stop located across the street. **Taxis** usually wait in front of the museum. It's about €12 for a ride to the city center.

To **walk** to the train station area from the museum (20 minutes), turn left out of the museum grounds, then left again on the street behind it (avenue Docteur Ménard). As the street bends right, take the ramps and staircases down on your left, turn left at the bottom, cross under the freeway and the train tracks, then turn right on boulevard Raimbaldi to reach the station.

Length of This Tour: Allow one hour.

Cuisine Art and WCs: An idyllic café (€10 salads and *plats*) awaits in the corner of the garden. A spick-and-span WC is next to the ticket desk (there's one inside, too).

The Tour Begins

This small museum consists of six rooms: two rooms with the 17 large murals, two rooms for special exhibits, an auditorium with stained-glass windows, and a mosaic-lined pond (viewed from inside). In the main hall you'll find the core of the collection (Genesis and Exodus scenes). The adjacent octagonal room houses five paintings—the Song of Songs room.

• *Buy your ticket, pass through the garden, and enter the museum at the baggage-check counter (daypacks must be checked). Find the main hall filled with Chagall's colorful paintings of...*

Old Testament Scenes

Each painting is a lighter-than-air collage of images that draw from Chagall's Russian folk-village youth, his Jewish heritage, biblical themes, and his feeling that he existed somewhere between heaven and earth. He believed that the Bible was a synonym for nature, and that color and biblical themes were key ingredients for understanding God's love for his creation. Chagall's brilliant blues and reds celebrate nature, as do his spiritual and folk themes. Notice the focus on couples. To Chagall, humans loving each other mirrored God's love of creation.

The paintings are described below in the order you should see

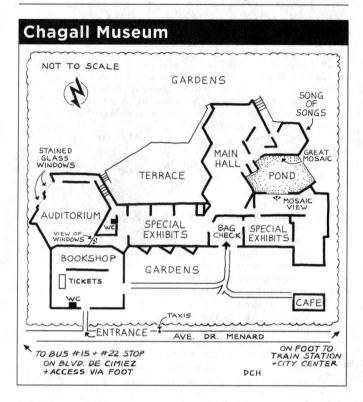

them, going counterclockwise around the room (some paintings might be on loan to other museums). Look for posted explanations of each work in English.

Abraham and the Three Angels

In the heat of the day, Abraham looked up and saw three men. He said, "Let a little food and water be brought, so you can be refreshed..." (Genesis 18:1–5)

Abraham refreshes God's angels on this red-hot day and, in return, they promise Abraham a son (in the bubble, at right), thus making him the father of the future Israelite nation.

The Sacrifice of Isaac

Abraham bound his son Isaac and laid him on the altar. Then he took the knife to slay his son. But the angel of the Lord called out to him from heaven, "Abraham!" (Genesis 22:9–11)

Tested by God, Abraham prepares to kill his only son, but the angel stops him in time. Notice that Isaac is posed exactly as Adam is in *The Creation* (described below). Abraham's sacrifice echoes three others: the sacrifice all men must make (i.e., Adam,

Chagall's Style

Chagall uses a deceptively simple, almost childlike style to paint a world that's hidden to the eye—the magical, mystical world below the surface. Here are some of his techniques:

- **Deep, radiant colors,** inspired by Expressionism and Fauvism (an art movement pioneered by Matisse and other French painters).

- **Personal imagery,** particularly from his childhood in Russia— smiling barnyard animals, fiddlers on the roof, flower bouquets, huts, and blissful sweethearts.

- **A Hasidic Jewish perspective,** the idea that God is everywhere, appearing in everyday things like nature, animals, and humdrum activities.

- **A fragmented Cubist style,** multifaceted and multidimensional, a perfect style to mirror the complexity of God's creation.

- **Overlapping images,** like double-exposure photography, with faint imagery that bleeds through, suggesting there's more to life under the surface.

- **Stained-glass-esque technique** of dark, deep, earthy, "potent" colors, and simplified, iconic, symbolic figures.

- **Gravity-defying compositions,** with lovers, animals, and angels twirling blissfully in midair.

- **Happy (not tragic) mood** depicting a world of personal joy, despite the violence and turmoil of world wars and revolution.

- **Childlike simplicity,** drawn with simple, heavy outlines, filled in with Crayola colors that often spill over the lines. Major characters in a scene are bigger than the lesser characters. The grinning barnyard animals, the bright colors, the magical events presented as literal truth...Was Chagall a lightweight? Or a lighter-than-air-weight?

the everyman), the sacrifice of atonement (the goat tied to a tree at left), and even God's sacrifice of his own son (Christ carrying the cross, upper right).

The Creation

God said, "Let us make man in our image, in our likeness..." (Genesis 1:26)

A pure-white angel descends through the blue sky and carries a still-sleeping Adam from radiant red-yellow heaven to earth. Heaven is a whirling dervish of activity, spinning out all the events of future history, from the tablets of the Ten Commandments to the Crucifixion—an overture of many images that we'll see in later paintings. (Though not a Christian, Chagall saw the Crucifixion as a universal symbol of man's suffering.)

Moses Receives the Ten Commandments

The Lord gave him the two tablets of the Law, the tablets of stone inscribed by the finger of God... (Exodus 31:18)

An astonished Moses is tractor-beamed toward heaven, where God reaches out from a cloud to hand him the Ten Commandments. While Moses tilts one way, Mount Sinai slants the other, leading our eye up to the left, where a golden calf is being worshipped by the wayward Children of Israel. But down to the right, Aaron and the menorah assure us that Moses will set things right. In this radiant final panel, the Jewish tradition—after a long struggle—is finally established.

Driven from Paradise

So God banished him from the Garden of Eden...and placed cherubim and a flaming sword to guard the way... (Genesis 3:23–24)

An angel drives them out with a fire hose of blue (there's Adam still cradling his flaming-red coq), while a sparkling yellow sword prevents them from ever returning. Deep in the green colors, the painting offers us glimpses of the future—Eve giving birth (lower-right corner) and the yellow sacrificial goat of atonement (top right).

Paradise

God put him in the Garden of Eden...and said, "You must not eat from the tree of the knowledge of good and evil..." (Genesis 2:15–17)

Paradise is a rich, earth-as-seen-from-space pool of blue, green, and white. Amoebic, still-evolving animals float around Adam (celibately practicing yoga) and Eve (with lusty-red hair). On the right, an angel guards the tempting tree, but Eve offers an apple, and Adam reaches around to sample the forbidden fruit.

The Rainbow

God said, "I have set my rainbow in the clouds as a sign of the covenant between me and the earth." (Genesis 9:13)

A flaming angel sets the rainbow in the sky, while Noah rests beneath it and his family offers a sacrifice of thanks. The pure-white rainbow's missing colors are found radiating from the features of the survivors.

Jacob's Ladder

He had a dream in which he saw a ladder resting on the earth with

Marc Chagall
(1887-1985)

1887-1910: Russia
Chagall is born in the small town of Vitebsk, Belarus. He's the oldest of nine children in a traditional Russian Hasidic Jewish family. He studies realistic art in his hometown. In St. Petersburg, he is first exposed to the Modernist work of Paul Cézanne and the Fauves.

1910-1914: Paris
A patron finances a four-year stay in Paris. Chagall hobnobs with the avant-garde and learns technique from the Cubists, but he never abandons painting recognizable figures or his own personal fantasies. (Some say his relative poverty forced him to paint over used canvases, which gave him the idea of overlapping images that bleed through. Hmm.)

1914-1922: Russia
Returning to his hometown, Chagall marries Bella Rosenfeld (1915), whose love will inspire him for decades. He paints happy scenes despite the turmoil of wars and the Communist Revolution. Moving to Moscow (1920), he paints his first large-scale works, sets for the New Jewish Theatre. These would inspire many of his later large-scale works.

1923-1941: France and Palestine
Chagall returns to France. In 1931 he travels to Palestine, where the bright sun and his Jewish roots inspire a series of gouaches (opaque watercolor paintings). These gouaches would later inspire 105 etchings to illustrate the Bible (1931-1952), which would eventually influence the 17 large canvases of biblical scenes in the Chagall Museum (1954-1967).

1941-1947: United States/World War II
Fearing persecution for his Jewish faith, Chagall emigrates to New York, where he spends the war years. The Crucifixion starts to appear in his paintings—not as a Christian symbol, but as a representation of the violence mankind perpetrates on itself. In 1947 his beloved Bella dies, and he stops painting for months.

1947-1985: South of France
After the war, Chagall returns to France, eventually settling in St-Paul-de-Vence. In 1952 he remarries. His new love, Valentina Brodsky, plus the southern sunshine, bring Chagall a revived creativity—he is extremely prolific for the rest of his life. He experiments with new techniques and media—ceramics, sculpture, book illustrations, tapestry, and mosaic. In 1956 he's commissioned for his first stained-glass project. Eventually he does windows for cathedrals in Metz and Reims, and a synagogue in Jerusalem (1960). The Chagall Museum opens in 1973.

CHAGALL MUSEUM TOUR

its top reaching to heaven, and the angels of God were ascending and descending on it... (Genesis 28:12)

In the left half, Jacob (Abraham's grandson) slumps asleep and dreams of a ladder between heaven and earth. On the right, a spinning angel with a menorah represents how heaven and earth are bridged by the rituals of the Jewish tradition.

Jacob Wrestles with an Angel

So Jacob wrestled with him till daybreak. Jacob said, "I will not let you go unless you bless me..." (Genesis 32: 24, 26)

Jacob holds on while the angel blesses him with descendants (the Children of Israel) and sends out rays from his hands, creating, among others, Joseph (stripped of his bright-red coat and sold into slavery by his brothers).

Noah's Ark

Then he sent out a dove to see if the water had receded... (Genesis 8:8)

Adam and Eve's descendants have become so wicked that God destroys the earth with a flood, engulfing the sad crowd on the right. Only righteous Noah (center), his family (lower right), and the animals (including our yellow goat) are spared inside an ark. Here Noah opens the ark's window and sends out a dove to test the waters.

Moses Brings Water from the Rock

The Lord said, "Strike the rock, and water will come out of it for the people to drink..." (Exodus 17:5–6)

In the brown desert, Moses nourishes his thirsty people with water miraculously spouting from a rock. From the (red-yellow) divine source, it rains down actual (blue) water, but also a gush of spiritual yellow light.

Moses and the Burning Bush

The angel of the Lord appeared to him in flames of fire from within a bush... (Exodus 3:2)

Horned Moses—Chagall depicts him according to a medieval tradition—kneels awestruck before the burning bush, the event that calls him to God's service. On the left, we see Moses after the call, his face radiant, leading the Israelites out of captivity across the Red Sea, while Pharaoh's men drown (lower half of Moses' robe). The Ten Commandments loom ahead.

• *Return to* Moses Receives the Ten Commandments, *then walk past a stained-glass window on your way to the octagonal room.*

CHAGALL MUSEUM TOUR

Song of Songs

Song of Solomon 7:11
*Come, my lover, let us go to the countryside,
let us spend the night in the villages.*
Song of Solomon 5:2
I slept but my heart was awake.
Song of Solomon 2:17
*Until the day breaks and the shadows flee,
turn, my lover, and be like a gazelle or
like a young stag on the rugged hills.*
Song of Solomon 3:4
I held him and would not let him go.
Song of Solomon 7:7
*Your stature is like that of the palm, and your
breasts like clusters of fruit.*

Song of Songs

Chagall wrote, "I've been fascinated by the Bible ever since my earliest childhood. I have always thought of it as the most extraordinary source of poetic inspiration imaginable. As far as I am concerned, perfection in art and in life has its source in the Bible, and exercises in the mechanics of the merely rational are fruitless. In art as well as in life, anything is possible, provided there is love."

Chagall enjoyed the love of two women in his long life—his first wife, Bella, then Valentina, who gave him a second wind as he was painting these late works. Chagall was one of the few "serious" 20th-century artists to portray unabashed love. Where the Bible uses the metaphor of earthly, physical, sexual love to describe God's love for humans, Chagall uses unearthly colors and a mystical ambience to celebrate human love. These red-toned canvases are hard to interpret on a literal level, but they capture the rosy spirit of a man in love with life. The sidebar above reflects the order of the verses displayed in the painting.

• *Head back toward the entry and turn left at* The Sacrifice of Isaac *to find...*

The Pond

The great mosaic reflected in the pond evokes the prophet Elijah in his chariot of fire (from the Second Book of Kings)—with Chagall's addition of the 12 signs of the zodiac, which he used to symbolize Time.

• *Return to the main hall, veer left, and exit the hall to the right. Pass through the exhibition room with temporary displays. At the end, you'll find...*

The Auditorium

This room is worth a peaceful moment to enjoy three Chagall stained-glass windows: the creation of light, elements, and planets (a visual big bang that's four "days" wide); the creation of animals, plants, man and woman, and the ordering of the solar system (two "days" wide, complete with fish and birds still figuring out where they belong); and the day of rest, with angels singing to the glory of God (the narrowest—only one "day" wide). If you like these windows, make sure to visit the cathedral in Reims on a future trip.

VILLEFRANCHE-SUR-MER, CAP FERRAT, AND EZE-LE-VILLAGE

Between Nice and Monaco lies the Riviera's richest stretch of real estate, paved with famously scenic roads (called the Three Corniches) and peppered with cliff-hanging villages, million-dollar vistas, and sea-splashed walking trails connecting beach towns. Fifteen minutes from Nice, little Villefranche-sur-Mer stares across the bay to woodsy and exclusive Cap Ferrat. The eagle's-nest Eze-le-Village and the Corniche-topping La Trophée des Alpes (in La Turbie) survey the scene from high above.

Villefranche-sur-Mer

In the glitzy world of the Riviera, Villefranche-sur-Mer offers travelers an easygoing slice of small-town Mediterranean life.

From here convenient day trips allow you to gamble in style in Monaco, saunter the promenade des Anglais in Nice, or drink in immense views from Eze-le-Village. Villefranche-sur-Mer feels Italian, with soft-orange buildings; steep, narrow streets spilling into the sea; and pasta on most menus. Luxury sail-ing yachts glisten in the bay—an inspiration to those lazing along the harborfront to start saving when their trips are over. Cruise ships make occasional calls to Villefranche-sur-Mer's famously deep harbor, creating periodic rush hours of frenetic shoppers and happy boutique owners. Sand-pebble beaches, a handful of inter-

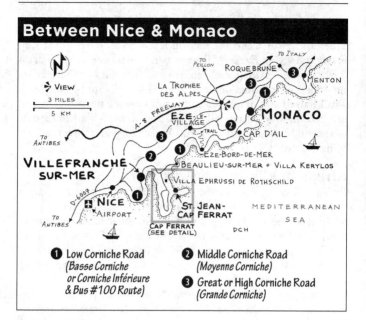

Between Nice & Monaco

N

VIEW

3 MILES
5 KM

TO ITALY

TO PEILLON

ROQUEBRUNE

MENTON

LA TROPHEE DES ALPES

A-8 FREEWAY

EZE-LE-VILLAGE

TRAIL

MONACO

CAP D'AIL

TO ANTIBES

VILLEFRANCHE-SUR-MER

EZE-BORD-DE-MER

BEAULIEU-SUR-MER + VILLA KERYLOS

VILLA EPHRUSSI DE ROTHSCHILD

D-6007

NICE

AIRPORT

ST. JEAN-CAP FERRAT

MEDITERRANEAN SEA

TO ANTIBES

CAP FERRAT (SEE DETAIL)

DCH

❶ Low Corniche Road (Basse Corniche or Corniche Inférieure & Bus #100 Route)

❷ Middle Corniche Road (Moyenne Corniche)

❸ Great or High Corniche Road (Grande Corniche)

esting sights, and quick access to Cap Ferrat keep other visitors just busy enough.

Originally a Roman port, Villefranche-sur-Mer was overtaken by fifth-century barbarians. Villagers fled into the hills, where they stayed and farmed their olives. In 1295 the Duke of Provence—like many in coastal Europe—was threatened by the Saracen Turks. He asked the hillside olive farmers to move down to the water and establish a front line against the invaders, thus denying the enemy a base from which to attack Nice. In return for tax-free status, they stopped farming, took up fishing, and established *Ville-* (town) *franche* (without taxes). Since there were many such towns, this one was specifically "Tax-free town on the sea" *(sur Mer)*. In about 1560, the Duke of Savoy built an immense, sprawling citadel in the town (which you can still tour). And today, while the town has an international following (including Tina Turner), two-thirds of its 8,000 people call it their primary residence. That makes Villefranche-sur-Mer feel more like a real community than many neighboring Riviera towns.

Orientation to Villefranche-sur-Mer

Tourist Information

The TI is in the park named jardin François Binon, below the main bus stop, labeled Octroi (July–Aug daily 9:00–19:00; Sept–June Mon–Sat 9:00–12:00 & 14:00–18:00, closed Sun; 20-minute

walk or €10 taxi ride from train station, tel. 04 93 01 73 68, www
.villefranche-sur-mer.com). Pick up schedules for buses #81 to Cap
Ferrat and #83 to Eze-le-Village (via an easy transfer). Also ask for
the brochure detailing a self-guided walking tour of Villefranche-
sur-Mer and information on boat rides (usually mid-June–Sept).
The TI also has a simple brochure-map showing the walks around
neighboring Cap Ferrat and information on the Villa Ephrussi de
Rothschild's gardens, though this book's map and directions are
sufficient (see "Cap Ferrat," later).

Arrival in Villefranche-sur-Mer

By Bus: Take bus #100 or #81 from Nice (the bus bays are adjacent
at Nice's *gare routière*) or bus #100 from Monaco, to the Octroi stop
in Villefranche-sur-Mer (see "Villefranche-sur-Mer Connections,"
later). The Octroi stop is at the jardin François Binon, just above
the TI. To reach the old town, walk past the TI down avenue
Général de Gaulle, take the first stairway on the left, then make a
right at the street's end.

By Plane: Allow an hour from Nice's airport to Villefranche-
sur-Mer. Take express bus #98 from Nice's airport to its bus station (€4, 3/hour, 30 minutes), then transfer to bus #100 or #81 to
Villefranche-sur-Mer (4/hour on #100, 3/hour Sun; about 2/hour
on #81; 15 minutes). One €4 ticket covers the whole trip.

By Train: Not all trains stop in Villefranche-sur-Mer (you may
need to transfer to a local train in Nice or Monaco). Villefranche-
sur-Mer's train station is a 15-minute walk along the water from
the old town and many of the hotels listed in this chapter. Find
your way down toward the water, and turn right to walk into town.
Taxis to my recommended hotels cost €15, but they don't wait here
and prefer longer rides; call instead, and pray the phone is working
(for taxi telephone numbers, see the next page).

By Car: From Nice's port, follow signs for *Menton, Monaco,*
and *Basse Corniche*. In Villefranche-sur-Mer, turn right at the
TI (first signal after Hôtel la Flore) for parking and hotels. For a
quick visit to the TI, park at the pay lot just below the TI. A bit
farther down, you'll find free parking in the small lot off avenue
Verdun, and—beyond that—more parking down in the moat
areas within the boundaries of the citadel (well-signed from main
road—look for *Parking Fossés*). There's a more secure pay lot on
the water across from Hôtel Welcome, and some hotels also have
their own parking.

Helpful Hints

Market Day: A fun bric-a-brac market enlivens Villefranche-
sur-Mer on Sundays (on place Amélie Pollonnais by Hôtel
Welcome, and in jardin François Binon by the TI). On

Saturday mornings, a small food market sets up near the TI (only in jardin François Binon). A small trinkets market springs to action on place Amélie Pollonnais whenever cruise ships grace the harbor.

Last Call: Villefranche-sur-Mer makes a great base for day trips, but the last bus back from Nice or Monaco is at about 20:00. After that, take the train or a cab.

Internet Access: Two options sit side by side on place du Marché. **Chez Net,** an "Australian International Sports Bar Internet Café," has American keyboards, whereas **L'Ex Café** has French keyboards. Both are open daily, have Wi-Fi, and let you enjoy a late-night drink while surfing the Internet.

Laundry: The town has two launderettes, both owned by Laura and located just below the main road on avenue Sadi Carnot. At the upper *pressing moderne,* Laura does your wash for you—for a price (Tue–Sun 9:00–12:30 & 15:00–18:30, closes Sat at 17:00, closed Mon, next to Hôtel Royal Riviera, tel. 04 93 01 73 71). The lower *laverie* is self-service only (daily 7:00–20:00, opposite 6 avenue Sadi Carnot).

Electric Bike Rental: If you plan to explore Cap Ferrat but don't feel like walking, consider renting an electric bike from Henri at **Eco-Loc.** The adventurous can also try this as an alternative to taking the bus to Cap Ferrat, Eze-le-Village, or even Nice (although the road to Nice is awfully busy). You get about 25 miles on a fully charged battery (less on hilly terrain—after that you're pedaling; €5/hour, €20/day, April–Sept daily 9:00–17:30, deposit and ID required, best to call for reservations 24 hours in advance; helmets, locks, baskets, and child seats available; find the small tent on the port next to Café Calypso, mobile 06 66 92 72 41).

Taxi: For a reliable taxi in Villefranche-sur-Mer, call or email **Didier** (mobile 06 15 15 39 15, taxididier.villefranchesurmer @orange.fr). If he's busy, beware of taxi drivers who over-charge—the normal weekday, daytime rate to central Nice is about €35; to the airport, figure €50–60; one-way to Cap Ferrat is about €20, and to Eze-le-Village is about €35. The five-minute trip from the waterfront up to the main street level (to bus stops on the Low Corniche) should be less than €10. Ask your driver to write down the price before you get in, and get a receipt when you pay (mobile 06 09 33 36 12 or 06 39 32 54 09).

Minibus: Little **minibus #80** will save you the sweat of going from the harbor up the hill, but it only runs once per hour (daily 7:00–19:00, €1). It travels from the port to the top of the hill, stopping near Hôtel la Fiancée du Pirate and the stop for buses #82 and #112 to Eze-le-Village, before going

Villefranche-sur-Mer

1 Hôtel Welcome & Souris Gourmande Rest.
2 Hôtel Villa Vauban
3 Hôtel la Flore
4 To Hôtel la Fiancée du Pirate & Minibus Route
5 Hôtel de la Darse
6 Le Cosmo Bistrot/Brasserie
7 La Grignotière Restaurant
8 La Serre Restaurant
9 La Mère Germaine Rest.
10 Casino Grocery
11 Internet: Chez Net Bar & L'Ex Café
12 Boat Rides & Electric Bike Rental
13 Launderette
14 Octroi Bus Stop (from Nice; to Monaco & Cap Ferrat)
15 Octroi Bus Stop (to Nice; from Monaco & Cap Ferrat)

TO 4, EZE-LE VILLAGE & MONACO VIA MIDDLE CORNICHE ROAD

AVE. ALBERT 1er
POST
AVE. CH. JEUN.
AVE. JOF.
AVE. FOCH
JARDIN BINON
PLAY AREA
AVENUE DE GAULLE
PLAY AREA
QUAI CORDERIE

200 YARDS
200 METERS

AVE. PRINCESSE GRACE

TO MONT-ALBAN FORT & NICE

P   PARKING
T   TAXI STAND
⌇   STEPPED STREETS

DCH

VILLEFRANCHE-SUR-MER

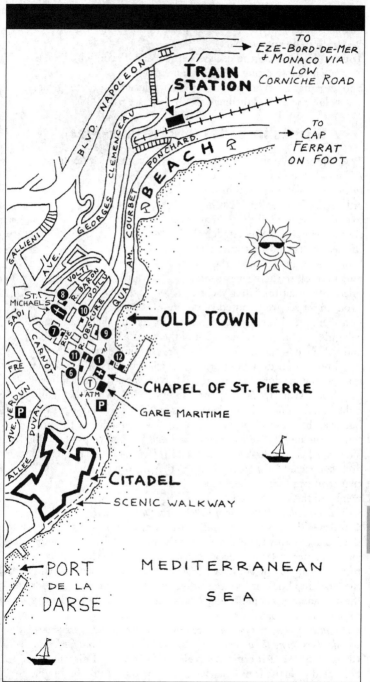

TO EZE-BORD-DE-MER & MONACO VIA LOW CORNICHE ROAD

TRAIN STATION

TO CAP FERRAT ON FOOT

BLVD. NAPOLEON

GEORGES CLEMENCEAU

AM. COURBET

PONCHARD

BEACH

QUAI

GALLIENI

AVE. VOLTI

R. BARON

POL.

R. OBSCURE

RUE

SADI CARNOT

FRE

AVE. VERDUN

DUVAL

ALLEE

ST. MICHAEL'S

OLD TOWN

CHAPEL OF ST. PIERRE

GARE MARITIME

CITADEL

SCENIC WALKWAY

PORT DE LA DARSE

MEDITERRANEAN SEA

8

10

7

9

11

1

12

6

T

ATM

P

P

to the outlying suburban Nice Riquier train station (only convenient if you're already on minibus, must transfer to train to downtown Nice).

Tourist Train: Skip the useless white **Petit Train,** which goes nowhere interesting (€6, 20-minute ride).

Sports Fans: Lively *boules* action takes place each evening just below the TI and the huge soccer field (see page 208).

Sights in Villefranche-sur-Mer

The Harbor—Browse Villefranche-sur-Mer's minuscule harbor.

Although the town was once an important fishing community, only eight families still fish here to make money. Find the footpath that leads beneath the citadel to the sea (by the port parking lot). Stop where the path hits the sea and marvel at the scene: a bay filled with beautiful sailing yachts. (You might see well-coiffed captains being ferried in by dutiful mates to pick up their statuesque call girls.) Local guides keep a list of the world's 100 biggest yachts and talk about some of them as if they're part of the neighborhood.

Looking far to the right, that last apartment building on the sea was the headquarters for the US Navy's Sixth Fleet following World War II, and remained so until 1966, when de Gaulle pulled France out of the military wing of NATO. (The Sixth Fleet has been based in Naples ever since.) A wall plaque at the bottom of rue de l'Eglise commemorates the US Navy's presence in Villefranche. Now look left into the hills and notice the impressive arch-supported Low Corniche road that leads to Monaco. Until that road was built in 1860, those hills were free of any development...all the way to Monaco.

• *You are standing at the base of Villefranche's massive...*

Citadel—The town's mammoth castle was built in the 1500s by the Duke of Savoy to defend against the French. When the region joined France in 1860, it became just a barracks. In the 20th century, the city had no military use for the space, and started using the citadel to house its police station, city hall, a summer outdoor theater, and two art galleries. There's still only one fortified entry to this huge complex.

• *To continue along this footpath, see "Seafront Walks," later; otherwise, wander back along the harbor toward the Hôtel Welcome and find the...*

Chapel of St. Pierre (Chapelle Cocteau)—This chapel, decorated by artist Jean Cocteau, is the town's cultural highlight.

Cocteau was a Parisian transplant who adored little Villefranche-sur-Mer and whose career was distinguished by his work as an artist, poet, novelist, playwright, and filmmaker. Influenced by his pals Marcel Proust, André Gide, Edith Piaf, and Pablo Picasso, Cocteau was a leader among 20th-century avant-garde intellectuals. At the door, Marie-France—who is passionate about Cocteau's art—collects a €2.50 donation for a fishermen's charity. She then sets you free to enjoy the chapel's small but intriguing interior. She's happy to give some explanations if you ask.

In 1955 Jean Cocteau covered the barrel-vaulted chapel with heavy black lines and pastels. Each of Cocteau's surrealist works—the Roma (Gypsies) of Stes-Maries-de-la-Mer who dance and sing to honor the Virgin, girls wearing traditional outfits, and three scenes from the life of St. Peter—is explained in English. Is that Villefranche-sur-Mer's citadel in the scene above the altar? (Tue–Sun 10:00–12:00 & 15:00–19:00, closed Mon and when Marie-France is tired, below Hôtel Welcome).

A few blocks north along the harbor (past Hôtel Welcome), rue de May leads to the mysterious **rue Obscura**—a covered lane running 400 feet along the medieval rampart. This street served as an air-raid shelter during World War II. Much of the lane is closed indefinitely for repair.

Boat Rides (Promenades en Mer)—These little cruises provide a seaborne perspective of this beautiful area (€11 for 1-hour cruise around Cap Ferrat, departs Wed at 17:00 July–Aug only; €17 for 2-hour cruise as far as Monaco—but doesn't actually stop there—departs Wed and Sat at 15:00 June–Sept; no trips Oct–May, boats depart from the harbor across from Hôtel Welcome, call to confirm the ever-changing schedule, reservations a must, tel. 04 93 76 65 65, www.amv-sirenes.com).

You can be your own skipper and rent a motor boat at **Dark Pelican** (€75–90/half-day, €130/day, deposit required, on the harbor at the Gare Maritime, tel. 04 93 01 76 54, www.darkpelican.com).

St. Michael's Church—The town church, a few blocks up rue de l'Eglise from the harbor, features an 18th-century organ and a fine statue of a recumbent Christ—carved, they say, from a fig tree by a galley slave in the 1600s.

Seafront Walks—A seaside walkway originally used by customs agents to patrol the harbor leads under the citadel and connects the old town with the interesting workaday harbor (port de la Darse). At the port you'll find a few cafés, France's Institute of Oceanography (an outpost for the University of Paris oceanographic studies), and an 18th-century dry dock. This scenic walk turns downright romantic after dark—if you're sleeping elsewhere, take an ice-cream-licking stroll here. You can also wander along

Villefranche-sur-Mer's waterfront and continue beyond the train station for postcard-perfect views back to Villefranche-sur-Mer (ideal in the morning—go before breakfast). You can even extend your walk to Cap Ferrat (see "Getting to Cap Ferrat" on page 360).

Hike up to Mont-Alban Fort—This fort, with a remarkable setting on the high ridge that separates Nice and Villefranche-sur-Mer, makes a good destination for hikers needing to stretch their legs (also accessible by car). Get information at the Villefranche TI, then walk on the main road toward Nice about 200 yards past Hôtel Versailles. Look for wood trail signs labeled *Escalier de Verre* and climb about 45 minutes as the trail makes long switchbacks through the woods up to the ridge. Find your way to Mont-Alban Fort and its view terrace (though it's not possible to enter the fort). Bus #30 from Nice gets close, as does bus #80 from Villefranche's port. The views west over Nice, east over Villefranche, and north to the mountains are mesmerizing. There's talk of turning the fort into an exhibition hall for modern art.

Sleeping in Villefranche-sur-Mer

You have a handful of good hotels to choose from in Villefranche-sur-Mer. The ones I list have sea views from at least half of their rooms—well worth paying extra for.

$$$ Hôtel Welcome*** easily has the best location in Villefranche-sur-Mer, anchored right on the water in the old town, with all 32 balconied rooms overlooking the harbor. The lobby opens to the water, and the mellow wine bar lowers my pulse. You'll pay top price for all the comforts in this smart hotel (Sb-€99, "comfort" Db-€196, bigger "superior" Db-€230, suites-€340–380, extra bed-€35, air-con, elevator, parking garage-€17–25/day, 3 quai Amiral Courbet, tel. 04 93 76 27 62, fax 04 93 76 27 66, www.welcomehotel.com, resa@welcomehotel.com).

$$$ Hôtel Villa Vauban*** is a small villa two blocks below the TI, with nine simple and huggable rooms. Many have balconies and sea views, and most come with Old World bathrooms. The cheaper rooms on the lower level are a tad musty. Amiable British expat Alan Powers adds a personal touch that's rare in this area, making the place feel more like an intimate B&B (Db with small view-€95–130, Db with big sea view-€125–170, Db suite with sea view-€140–190, air-con, Wi-Fi, 11 avenue Général de Gaulle, tel. & fax 04 93 55 94 51, www.hotelvillavauban.com, info@hotel villavauban.com).

$$$ Hôtel la Flore*** is a good Villefranche value if your idea of sightseeing is to enjoy the view from your spacious bedroom deck (most rooms have one) or the pool. It's a 15-minute uphill walk from the old town, but the parking is free, and the bus stops

Sleep Code

(€1 = about $1.25, country code: 33)
S = Single, **D** = Double/Twin, **T** = Triple, **Q** = Quad, **b** = bathroom, **s** = shower only, * = French hotel rating (0–4 stars). Unless otherwise noted, credit cards are accepted and English is spoken.

To help you sort easily through these listings, I've divided the rooms into three categories based on the price for a standard double room with bath:

$$$ Higher Priced—Most rooms €130 or more.
$$ Moderately Priced—Most rooms between €80–130.
$ Lower Priced—Most rooms €80 or less.

Prices can change without notice; verify the hotel's current rates online or by email. For other updates, see www.ricksteves.com/update.

for Nice and Monaco are close (Db with no view-€100–135, Db with view and deck-€140–160, larger Db with even better view and bigger deck-€170–210, Db mini-suite-€220, Qb loft with huge terrace-€220, extra bed-€34, 15 percent cheaper Oct–March, online deals, air-con, elevator; just off main road high above harbor—go 2 blocks from TI toward Nice, at 5 boulevard Princesse Grace de Monaco; tel. 04 93 76 30 30, fax 04 93 76 99 99, www.hotel-la -flore.fr, hotel-la-flore@wanadoo.fr).

$$ Hôtel la Fiancée du Pirate is a family-friendly refuge that's best suited for drivers, as it's high above Villefranche-sur-Mer on the Middle Corniche (although it is on bus lines #82 and #112 to Eze-le-Village and Monaco). Don't let the streetside appearance deter you: Eager-to-please Eric and Laurence offer 15 bright and comfortable rooms, along with a large pool, a pleasant garden, a roomy lounge area (with board games), and a breakfast terrace with partial views of Cap Ferrat and the sea. Choose between rooms in the main building or below on the garden patio. Parking and Wi-Fi are free, the beds are firm, all rooms are air-conditioned, and the big breakfast features homemade crêpes. Light lunches, salads, and snacks are available during the day (Db-€120–140, Tb-€155, Qb-€185, 8 boulevard de la Corne d'Or, Moyenne Corniche N7, tel. 04 93 76 67 40, fax 04 93 76 91 04, www.fianceedupirate.com, info@fianceedupirate.com).

$ Hôtel de la Darse** is a shy, unassuming little hotel burrowed in the shadow of its highbrow neighbors. This low-profile alternative on the water at Villefranche-sur-Mer's old port is a great budget option. It's less central—figure 10 minutes of level walking to the harbor, but a steep 15-minute walk up to the main road and buses. The rooms facing the sea are worth the extra few euros for their million-dollar-view balconies (view Db-€87, view Tb-€100, Qb-€113, most with air-con and some noise on weekend nights, book well ahead for these). Rooms on the quieter garden side are sharp and have air-con but no view (Sb-€63, Db-€72; extra bed-€10, up to 4 floors, no elevator, good-value breakfast; from TI walk or drive down avenue Général de Gaulle; walkers should turn left shortly after Hôtel Villa Vauban into the jardins de Narvik and follow steps to bottom, then turn right at the old Port de la Darse; parking usually available nearby, tel. 04 93 01 72 54, fax 04 93 01 84 37, www.hotel-dela-darse-villefranche-sur-mer .cote.azur.fr, hoteldeladarse@wanadoo.fr).

Eating in Villefranche-sur-Mer

Comparison-shopping is half the fun of dining in Villefranche-sur-Mer. Make an event out of a pre-dinner stroll through the old city. Check what looks good on the lively place Amélie Pollonnais (next to Hôtel Welcome), where the whole village seems to converge at night; saunter the string of pricey candlelit places lining the waterfront; and consider the smaller, wallet-friendlier eateries embedded in the old city's walking streets. Arm yourself with a gelato from any ice-cream shop and enjoy a floodlit, post-dinner stroll along the sea.

Le Cosmo Bistrot/Brasserie takes center stage on place Amélie Pollonnais with a great setting—a few tables have views to the harbor and to Cocteau chapel's facade (after some wine, Cocteau pops). Manager Arnaud runs a tight-but-friendly ship and offers well-presented, tasty meals with good wines (I love their red Bandol). Ask for the daily suggestions and consider the €12 *omelette niçoise* (€13–16 fine salads and pastas, €15–27 *plats*, open daily, place Amélie Pollonnais, tel. 04 93 01 84 05).

Disappear into Villefranche-sur-Mer's walking streets and find cute little **La Grignotière,** serving generous and delicious €18 *plats*, and plenty of other options. The mixed seafood grill is a smart order, as is the spaghetti and *gambas* (shrimp). They also offer a hearty €30 *menu*, but good luck finding room for it. Gregarious Michel speaks English fluently and runs the place with his sidekick Bridget. Dining is primarily inside, making this a good choice for cooler days (daily May–Oct, closed Wed Nov–April, 3 rue Poilu, tel. 04 93 76 79 83).

La Serre, nestled below the church in the old town, is a simple place with a hardworking owner. Sylvie serves well-priced meals to a loyal local clientele, always with a smile. Choose from the many pizzas (all named after US states and €10 or less), salads, and meats; or try the good-value, €17 three-course *menu* (open daily, cheap house wine, 16 rue du May, tel. 04 93 76 79 91).

La Mère Germaine, right on the harbor, is the only place in town classy enough to lure a yachter ashore. It's dressy, with formal service and a price list to match. The name commemorates the current owner's grandmother, who fed hungry GIs during World War II. Try the bouillabaisse, served with panache (€72/person with 2-person minimum, €45 mini-version for one, €41 *menu,* open daily, reserve harborfront table, tel. 04 93 01 71 39).

Souris Gourmande ("Gourmet Mouse") is handy for a made-to-order sandwich, either to take away or to eat there (€5 sandwiches, daily 11:00–22:00, closed Fri in winter, at base of steps behind Hôtel Welcome). Sandwich in hand, you'll find plenty of great places to enjoy a harborside sit.

There's a handy **Casino market/grocery store** a few blocks above Hôtel Welcome at 12 rue Poilu (Thu–Tue 7:30–12:30 & 15:00–19:30, Wed 7:30–13:00 only).

For Drivers: If you have a car and are staying a few nights, take the short drive up to Eze-le-Village or, better still, La Turbie. If it's summer (June–Sept), the best option of all is to go across to Cap Ferrat's plage de Passable for a before-dinner drink or a dinner you won't soon forget (recommendations listed under each destination later in this chapter).

Villefranche-sur-Mer Connections

The last bus leaves Nice for Villefranche-sur-Mer at about 19:45; the last bus from Villefranche-sur-Mer to Nice departs at about 20:50; and trains runs later (until 24:00). Never board a train without a ticket or valid pass—inspectors don't accept excuses. The minimum fine is €70.

From Villefranche-sur-Mer by Bus to: Beaulieu-sur-Mer (#81, about 2/hour daily, 10 minutes; or #100, 4/hour Mon–Sat, 3/ hour Sun, 10 minutes), **Monaco** (#100, 4/hour Mon–Sat, 3/hour Sun, 25 minutes), **Nice** (#100, 4/hour Mon–Sat, 3/hour Sun, 15 minutes; or #81, 2/hour daily, 15 minutes). Remember, all buses in this area cost €1 per ride, regardless of your destination (buy from driver). A ticket is good for 74 minutes in one direction and for transfers but not round-trips. In Villefranche-sur-Mer, all bus stops are along the main drag; the most convenient is the Octroi stop, just above the TI.

By Train to: Monaco (2/hour, 10 minutes), **Nice** (2/hour, 10 minutes), **Antibes** (2/hour, 40 minutes).

To Cap Ferrat: The best public-transit option is **bus #81,** which follows a circular route from Nice through Villefranche-sur-Mer, Beaulieu-sur-Mer, then to all Cap Ferrat stops, ending at the port in St. Jean-Cap-Ferrat (2/hour daily until 19:30, 15 minutes from Villefranche to St. Jean). The twice-as-frequent Nice-to-Monaco **bus #100** stops at Villefranche-sur-Mer, then leaves you at the edge of Cap Ferrat (a 20-minute walk to Villa Ephrussi de Rothschild or plage de Passable). A **taxi** to Cap Ferrat costs about €20. It's a 50-minute **walk** to the key sights on the Cap (see "Getting to Cap Ferrat" on page 360).

The Three Corniches

Nice, Villefranche-sur-Mer, and Monaco are linked by three coastal routes: the Low, Middle, and High Corniches. The roads are nicknamed after the decorative frieze that runs along the top of a building (cornice). Each Corniche (kor-neesh) offers sensational views and a different perspective. You can find the three routes from Nice by driving up boulevard Jean Jaurès past the bus station *(gare routière)*. For the Low Corniche, follow signs to N-98 *(Monaco par la Basse Corniche)*, which leads past Nice's port. Shortly after the turnoff to the Low Corniche, you'll see signs for N-7 *(Moyenne Corniche)* leading to the Middle Corniche. Signs for the High *(Grande)* Corniche appear a bit after that; follow D-2564 to *Col des 4 Chemins* and the *Grande Corniche*.

Low Corniche: The Basse Corniche (also called "Corniche Inférieure") strings ports, beaches, and seaside villages together for a traffic-filled ground-floor view. It was built in the 1860s (along with the train line) to bring people to the casino in Monte Carlo. When this Low Corniche was finished, many hill-town villagers descended to the shore and started the communities that now line the sea. Before 1860, the population of the coast between Villefranche-sur-Mer and Monte Carlo was zero. Think about that as you make the trip today.

Middle Corniche: The Moyenne Corniche is higher, quieter, and far more impressive. It runs through Eze-le-Village (described in this chapter) and provides breathtaking views over the Mediterranean, with several scenic pullouts. (The ones above Villefranche-sur-Mer are the best.)

High Corniche: Napoleon's crowning road-construction achievement, the Grande Corniche caps the cliffs with staggering views from almost 1,600 feet above the sea. It is actually the Via Aurelia, used by the Romans to conquer the West.

Villas: Driving from Villefranche-sur-Mer to Monaco, you'll come upon impressive villas. A particularly grand entry leads to the sprawling estate built by King Leopold II of Belgium in the 1920s.

Those driving up to the Middle Corniche from Villefranche-sur-Mer can look down on this yellow mansion and its lush garden, which fill an entire hilltop. This estate was later owned by the Agnelli family (of Fiat fame and fortune), and then by the Safra family (American bankers).

The Best Route: For a ▲▲▲ route, **drivers** should take the Middle Corniche from Nice or Villefranche-sur-Mer to Eze-le-Village; from there, follow signs to the *Grande Corniche* and *La Turbie (La Trophée des Alpes)*, then finish by dropping down into Monaco. **Buses** travel each route; the higher the Corniche, the less frequent the buses (4/hour on Low, 12/day on Middle, and 5/day on High; get details at Nice's bus station). There are no buses between Eze-le-Village and La Turbie (45-minute walk), though buses do connect Nice and Monaco with La Turbie.

If traveling by bus, follow my self-guided bus tour to Monaco (at the end of this chapter), then consider returning to Nice or Villefranche-sur-Mer by bus via Eze-le-Village, or to Nice via La Turbie (see "Monaco Connections" on page 389).

The following villages and sights are listed from west to east, in order of how you'll reach them when going from Villefranche-sur-Mer to Monaco.

Cap Ferrat

This exclusive peninsula, rated ▲▲, decorates Villefranche-sur-Mer's bay views. Cap Ferrat is a peaceful eddy off the busy Nice–Monaco route (Low Corniche). You could spend a leisurely day on this peninsula, wandering the sleepy port village of St. Jean-Cap-Ferrat (a.k.a. St. Jean), touring the Villa Ephrussi de Rothschild mansion and gardens and the nearby Villa Kérylos, and walking on sections of the beautiful trails that follow the coast. If you have a house here, former Microsoft mogul Paul Allen is your neighbor.

Tourist Information: The main TI is between the port and Villa Ephrussi (Mon–Fri 9:00–16:00, closed Sat–Sun, 59 avenue Denis Séméria, bus #81 stops here at *Office du Tourisme*). A smaller TI is in the village of St. Jean-Cap-Ferrat (unpredictable hours, likely Sat–Sun 10:00–17:00, closed Mon–Fri, 5 avenue Denis Séméria). The two TIs share a phone number and email address (tel. 04 93 76 08 90, office-tourisme@saintjeancapferrat.fr).

Planning Your Time

Here's how I'd spend a day on the Cap: From Nice or Villefranche-sur-Mer, take the bus (#81) to the Villa Ephrussi de Rothschild stop (called Passable), then visit the villa. Walk 30 minutes,

CAP FERRAT

mostly downhill, to St. Jean-Cap-Ferrat for lunch (many options, including grocery shops for picnic supplies) and poke around the village. Consider the 45-minute walk on the plage de Paloma trail (ideal for picnics). After lunch, follow a beautiful 30-minute trail to Villa Kérylos in Beaulieu-sur-Mer and tour that villa. Return to Villefranche-sur-Mer, Nice, or points beyond by train or bus. (Drivers should skip the drive on the loop road around Cap Ferrat's peninsula.)

You can add Eze-le-Village to this day if you skip the small town of St. Jean-Cap-Ferrat and walk directly from Villa Ephrussi de Rothschild to Villa Kérylos. Take bus #100 (direction: Monaco) from the stop near Villa Kérylos and get off at the Gare d'Eze stop, where you meet bus #83 that shuttles up and up to the village (one €1 ticket covers both buses, get #83 schedule at a TI or check online at www.lignedazur.com).

Warning: Late-afternoon buses back to Villefranche-sur-Mer or Nice along the Low Corniche can be slammed (worse on weekends), potentially leaving passengers stranded at stops for long periods. To avoid this, either take the train or board bus #81 on the Cap itself (before it gets crowded).

Getting to Cap Ferrat

From Nice or Villefranche-sur-Mer: Bus #81 runs to all Cap Ferrat stops (daily, 2/hour until 19:30). For Villa Ephrussi de Rothschild, get off at the Passable stop (allow 30 minutes from Nice's *gare routière* and 10 minutes from Villefranche-sur-Mer's Octroi stop). Schedules are posted at stops or get one from a TI. The times listed for *Direction Le Port/Cap Ferrat* are when buses depart from Nice's *gare routière*—allow about 10 minutes after that for Villefranche-sur-Mer. The return bus (direction: Nice) begins in St. Jean-Cap-Ferrat village.

The more frequent (4/hour Mon–Sat, 3/hour Sun) **bus #100** to Monaco drops you at Cap Ferrat's edge (Ange Gardien or Pont St. Jean stops); from there, you can walk 20 minutes to Villa Ephrussi de Rothschild (after crossing over main road from bus stop, look for the center alleyway—chemin des Moulins—running straight up the Cap, turn left at the end, go down a stone stairway, then turn right on the small road).

It's also quick by **car** (take the Low Corniche) or **taxi** (allow €20 one-way from Villefranche-sur-Mer, €50 from Nice).

You can also **walk** 50 minutes from Villefranche-sur-Mer to Cap Ferrat: Go past the train station along the small beach lane, then climb the steps at the far end of the beach and walk parallel to the tracks. Continue straight past the mansions (with ornate gates) and take the first right on avenue de Grasseuil. You'll see signs to *Villa Ephrussi de Rothschild,* then to Cap Ferrat's port.

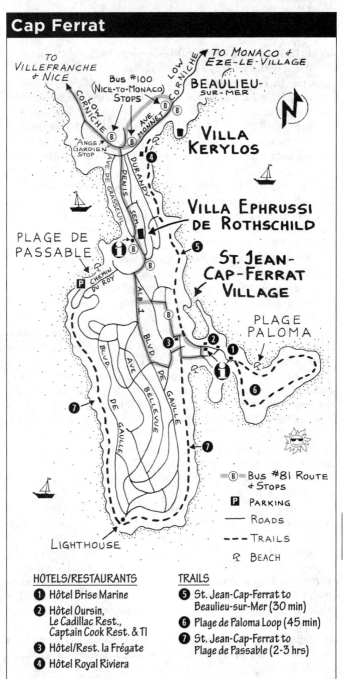

Cap Ferrat

TO VILLEFRANCHE & NICE

TO MONACO & EZE-LE-VILLAGE

LOW CORNICHE

LOW CORNICHE

BEAULIEU-SUR-MER

Bus #100 (Nice-to-Monaco) Stops

AVE MONNET

"ANGE GARDIEN" STOP

VILLA KERYLOS

AVE DE GRASSEUIL

DENIS SEM.

DURANDY

VILLA EPHRUSSI DE ROTHSCHILD

PLAGE DE PASSABLE

CHEMIN DU ROY

St. JEAN-CAP-FERRAT VILLAGE

PLAGE PALOMA

ALB. 1

BLVD

BLVD DE GAULLE

AVE DE GAULLE

AVE BELLEVUE

LIGHTHOUSE

B Bus #81 Route & Stops
P Parking
— Roads
- - - Trails
♝ Beach

CAP FERRAT

HOTELS/RESTAURANTS

❶ Hôtel Brise Marine
❷ Hôtel Oursin,
Le Cadillac Rest.,
Captain Cook Rest. & TI
❸ Hôtel/Rest. la Frégate
❹ Hôtel Royal Riviera

TRAILS

❺ St. Jean-Cap-Ferrat to
Beaulieu-sur-Mer (30 min)
❻ Plage de Paloma Loop (45 min)
❼ St. Jean-Cap-Ferrat to
Plage de Passable (2-3 hrs)

Sights on Cap Ferrat

▲Villa Ephrussi de Rothschild—In what seems like the ultimate in Riviera extravagance, Venice, Versailles, and the Côte d'Azur come together in the pastel-pink Villa Ephrussi. Rising above Cap Ferrat, this 1905 mansion has views west to Villefranche-sur-Mer and east to Beaulieu-sur-Mer.

Start with the well-furnished belle époque **interior** (helpful English handout provided). Upstairs, an 18-minute film (with English subtitles) gives you good background on the life of rich and eccentric Beatrice, Baroness de Rothschild, the French woman from an important banking family who built and furnished the place. As you stroll through the halls, you'll pass rooms with royal furnishings and personal possessions, including her bathroom case for cruises. A fancy tearoom serves drinks and lunch with a view (11:00–17:30).

But the gorgeous **gardens** are why most come here. Designed in the shape of a ship, the gardens were motivated by Beatrice's many ocean-liner trips. Her small army of gardeners even dressed like sailors. Behind the mansion, stroll through the seven lush gardens re-created from locations all over the world. The sea views from here are amazing. Don't miss the Alhambra-like Spanish gardens, the rose garden at the far end, and the view back to the house from the "Temple of Love" gazebo.

Cost and Hours: Palace and gardens-€10, skippable tour of upstairs-€3 extra, combo-ticket with Villa Kérylos-€15—valid for one week; mid-Feb–Oct daily 10:00–18:00, July–Aug until 19:00; Nov–mid-Feb Mon–Fri 14:00–18:00, Sat–Sun 10:00–18:00; tel. 04 93 01 33 09, www.villa-ephrussi.com. Kids will enjoy the free treasure-hunt booklet. Parking is tricky; there's a small turnaround at the top. The nearest bus stop is Passable, just a few minutes after turning onto Cap Ferrat—be ready (only via bus #81, 10-minute walk uphill to the villa).

Walks from Villa Ephrussi: It's a lovely 30-minute stroll, mostly downhill and east, from Villa Ephrussi to Villa Kérylos in Beaulieu-sur-Mer (described on page 366) or to the port of St. Jean-Cap-Ferrat. To get to either, make a hard left at the stop sign below Villa Ephrussi and follow signs along a small road toward the Hôtel Royal Riviera on avenue Henri Honoré (see map on page 361). When the road comes to a T, keep going straight, passing a green gate down a pedestrian path, which ends at a trail—go left to reach Villa Kérylos, or head right to get to St. Jean-Cap-Ferrat (be careful to follow the path left at the Villa Sonja Rello). It's about 15 minutes to either destination once you join this path.

CAP FERRAT

To get to plage de Passable, on the west side of the Cap, turn left along the main road just below Villa Ephrussi and find signs in 50 yards (5 minutes down, at least 10 minutes back up).

Plage de Passable—This pleasant beach, located below Villa Ephrussi, comes with great views of Villefranche-sur-Mer and a rough, pebbly surface. It's a peaceful beach, popular with families. Half is public (free, with shower), and the other half is run by a small restaurant (€20 includes changing locker, lounge chair, and shower; reserve ahead in summer or on weekends as this is a prime spot, kayak rental available, tel. 04 93 76 06 17). If ever you were to do the French Riviera rent-a-beach ritual, this is the place.

To park near the beach (figure about €6/day), follow signs past it, and go around the bend to a surprise lot. If it's full, follow signs over the hill and around to Lido Parking, a few steps from plage de Passable.

For me, the best reason to come here is for dinner. Beg, borrow, or steal a way to arrive here before sunset, then watch as darkness descends and lights flicker over Villefranche-sur-Mer's heavenly setting. At **Restaurant de la Plage Passable,** enjoy a surprisingly elegant dining experience to the sounds of children still at play on the beach. Notice the streetlights that illuminate the path of the Low and Middle Corniches (€12–16 starters, €18–27 *plats,* open daily late May–mid-Sept, until 20:00 in good weather April–late May and mid-Sept–Oct, tel. 04 93 76 06 17).

St. Jean-Cap-Ferrat—This quiet village port (also called St.

Jean) lies in Cap Ferrat's center, yet off most tourist itineraries. St. Jean houses yachts, boardwalks, views, and boutiques packaged in a "take your time, darling" atmosphere. It's a few miles off the busy Nice-to-Monaco road—convenient for drivers, yet it feels overlooked. A string of restaurants line the port, with just enough visitors to keep them in business. St. Jean is especially peaceful at night.

There's a small TI in the village center with limited hours (see page 359). The bus stop back to Villefranche-sur-Mer is a block above the port near Hôtel la Frégate (if you need a taxi, call 04 93 76 86 00). The hiking trail to Beaulieu-sur-Mer (with access to Villa Ephrussi) begins past the beach, to the left of the port as you look out to the water (details below).

▲▲Walks Around Cap Ferrat—The Cap is perfect for a walk, as you'll find well-maintained foot trails covering most of its length.

CAP FERRAT

Depending on how much time you have, there are three easy, mostly level options (30 minutes, 45 minutes, or 2–3 hours). The TIs in Villefranche-sur-Mer and St. Jean-Cap-Ferrat have maps of Cap Ferrat with walking paths marked, or you can use this book's directions (below) and map (page 361). During segments of all of

the hikes, you can make out the three Corniche roads cut into the side of the massive cliffs.

Between St. Jean-Cap-Ferrat and Beaulieu-sur-Mer (30 minutes): A level walk takes you past sumptuous villas, great views, and fun swimming opportunities. From St. Jean-Cap-Ferrat's port, walk along the harbor with the water on your right, and work your way past the beach. Head up the steps to promenade Maurice Rouvier and continue; before long you'll see smashing views of the whitewashed Villa Kérylos (and you might be able to make out the hill town of Eze-le-Village crowning the last peak on the right across the bay). To get from Beaulieu-sur-Mer to St. Jean-Cap-Ferrat, start walking at Villa Kérylos (with the sea on your left) toward the Hôtel Royal Riviera, and find the trail (be careful to stay left at the Villa Sonja Rello about halfway down). You can also reach this trail by walking 10 minutes downhill from Villa Ephrussi (described above).

Plage de Paloma Loop Trail (45 minutes): Just east of St. Jean's port, a sea-soaked, view-loaded trail offers you a terrific sampling of Cap Ferrat's beauty for a modest effort. From the port, walk or drive about a quarter-mile east (with the port on your left, passing Hôtel La Voile d'Or); you'll find the trailhead where the road comes to a T—look for a *Plage Paloma* sign. (Parking is available at the port or on streets near plage de Paloma.) Cross the small dirt park to start the trail, and do this walk counterclockwise. The trail is level and paved, yet uneven enough that good shoes are helpful. Plunk your picnic on one of the benches along the trail, or eat at the café on plage de Paloma at the end of the walk (sandwiches and salads). If time is tight, walk up the road toward *Plage Paloma* signs and find the trail for great views.

Plage de Passable to St. Jean-Cap-Ferrat (2–3 hours): For a longer hike that circles the Cap, follow the signs below Villa Ephrussi marked *Plage Passable* (10 minutes downhill on foot from the villa, parking available near the trailhead). Walk down to the beach (you'll find a good café that's ideal for lunch), turn left, and cross the beach. Go along a paved road behind a big apartment building, and after about 300 feet, take the steps down to the trail

(Sentier Littoral). Near the end of the trail, you'll pass by the port of St. Jean-Cap-Ferrat, where you have three options: take bus #81 back to Villefranche-sur-Mer, walk back to Villa Ephrussi and plage de Passable via the shorter inland route (by reversing the directions under "Walks from Villa Ephrussi," earlier), or continue on to Beaulieu-sur-Mer and take a bus to Monaco or Nice.

Sleeping on Cap Ferrat

(€1 = about $1.25, country code: 33)
The sleepy village of St. Jean-Cap-Ferrat offers surprisingly good values, probably because it's off the main route (and less convenient if you don't have a car).

$$$ Hôtel Brise Marine*,** flanked by tall palm trees and graced with gardens and a view terrace, is a peaceful retreat. Run by a gentle mother-son team, this aged mansion—with faded, Old World character—feels lost in a time warp. Many of its spacious rooms come with sensational views, and some have small balconies (view Db with balcony-€185, view Db without balcony-€160, breakfast-€14, air-con, Wi-Fi, minibar, secure parking-€14, ideally located between the port and plage de Paloma at 58 avenue Jean Mermoz, tel. 04 93 76 04 36, fax 04 93 76 11 49, www.hotel-brise marine.com, info@hotel-brisemarine.com).

$$ Hôtel Oursin** is central to the port, with 14 respectably priced and surprisingly well-appointed rooms all on one floor. Run by mother-and-son team Chantal and Aubrey, it's a welcoming, humble place with white walls, and feels more like a B&B than a hotel (smaller Db without air-con-€80, bigger Db with air-con and upgraded bathroom-€110, larger Db with port views-€125, €20 less Oct–April, 1 avenue Denis Séméria, tel. & fax 04 93 76 12 55, www.hoteloursin.com, reception@hoteloursin.com).

$ Hôtel/Restaurant la Frégate, a simple, family-run place, overlooks the port with 10 spotless, no-frill rooms. Some have good views, while others overlook the garden courtyard (Db-€54–69 with no air-con and no view, Db-€86 with air-con and view, reserved owners, 11 avenue Denis Séméria, tel. 04 93 76 04 51, fax 04 93 76 14 93).

Eating on Cap Ferrat

For **picnics,** the short pedestrian street in St. Jean-Cap-Ferrat has all you need (grocery store, bakery, charcuterie, and pizza to go), and you'll have no trouble finding portside or seaside seating. Plage de Paloma is a 10- minute walk away.

Le Cadillac is *the* place for outdoor seating and café fare in St. Jean-Cap-Ferrat. It's at the top of the small pedestrian street

CAP FERRAT

(good €13 pizza, €16 *plats,* daily, 1 rue Mermoz, tel. 04 93 76 16 44).

Captain Cook is sweet little eatery that takes its fish seriously. There's a small patio in front, a bigger one out back (no view), and a cozy interior between (good €26 *menu,* ask about bouillabaisse, closed Wed, a few steps past the port toward plage de Paloma at 11 avenue Jean Mermoz, tel. 04 93 76 02 66).

Near Cap Ferrat: Villa Kérylos

This town, right on the Low Corniche road (just after Cap Ferrat), is busy with traffic. It's a good place to pick up the hiking trail to St. Jean-Cap-Ferrat, and to visit the unusual **Villa Kérylos.** In 1902, an eccentric million-aire modeled his new mansion after a Greek villa from the island of Delos from about 200 B.C. No expense was spared in re-creating this Greek fan-tasy, from the floor mosaics to

Carrara marble columns to exquisite wood furnishings. The rain-powered shower is fun, and the included audioguide will increase your Greek IQ. The ceramics workshop—open only high season and weekend afternoons—offers a chance to test your talents (€9, combo-ticket with Villa Ephrussi de Rothschild-€15—valid for one week; mid-Feb–Oct daily 10:00–18:00, July–Aug until 19:00; Nov–mid-Feb Mon–Fri 14:00–18:00, Sat–Sun 10:00–18:00; tel. 04 93 01 47 29, www.villa-kerylos.com).

Getting to and from Villa Kérylos

Drivers should park near the casino in Beaulieu-sur-Mer, not on the villa's access road. The Monaco–Nice bus #100 (4/hour Mon–Sat, 3/hour Sun, 20 minutes from Nice or Monaco) drops you at the Eglise stop at the Hôtel Metropole in Beaulieu (turn right off the bus and find signs to Villa Kérylos). Trains (2/hour, 10 min-utes from Nice or Monaco) leave you a 10-minute walk away: Turn left out of the train station and left again down the main drag. Walk to the end, turn right, then find signs to Villa Kérylos. The walking trail from Villa Kérylos to Cap Ferrat and Villa Ephrussi de Rothschild begins on the other side of the bay, beneath Hôtel Royal Riviera.

Eze-le-Village

Floating high above the sea, flowery and flawless Eze-le-Village (don't confuse it with the seafront town of Eze-Bord-de-Mer) is

entirely consumed by tourism. This *village d'art et de gastronomie* (as it calls itself) nurtures perfume outlets, upscale boutiques, steep cobbled lanes, and magnificent views. Touristy as this place certainly Eze, its stony state of preservation and magnificent hilltop setting over the Mediterranean may draw you away from the beaches. Day-tripping by bus to Eze-le-Village from Nice, Monaco, or Villefranche-sur-Mer works well, provided you know the bus schedules (ask at TIs or check www.lignedazur.com; Villefranche-sur-Mer requires a transfer).

Getting to Eze-le-Village

There are two Ezes: Eze-le-Village (the spectacular hill town) and Eze-Bord-de-Mer (a modern beach resort far below Eze-le-Village). Eze-le-Village is about 20 minutes east of Villefranche-sur-Mer on the Middle Corniche.

From Nice and upper Villefranche-sur-Mer, buses #82 and #112 provide 16 buses per day to Eze-le-Village (eight on Sun, 25 minutes). Take bus #80 from the center of Villefranche-sur-Mer uphill to the stop in front of Hôtel la Fiancée du Pirate to make this connection.

From Nice, Villefranche, or Monaco, you can also take the train or the Nice–Monaco bus to Eze-Bord-de-Mer, getting off at the Gare d'Eze stop. From here, take the #83 shuttle bus straight up to Eze-le-Village (8/day, daily 9:45–18:00, schedule is posted at the stop but it's best to know schedule before you go).

To connect Eze-le-Village directly with Monte Carlo in Monaco, take bus #112 (7/day Mon–Sat, none on Sun, 25 minutes).

There are no direct buses from Villefranche-sur-Mer to Eze-le-Village, and there are no buses between La Turbie (La Trophée des Alpes) and Eze-le-Village (40-minute walk).

You could take a pricey taxi between the two Ezes or from Eze-le-Village to La Turbie (allow €25 one-way, mobile 06 09 84 17 84).

Orientation to Eze-le-Village

Bus stops and parking lots weld the town to the highway (Middle Corniche) that passes under its lowest wall. Eze-le-Village's main parking lot is a block below the town's entry. The stop for buses to Nice is across the road by the Avia gas station, and the stops for buses to Eze-Bord-de-Mer and Monaco are on the village side of the main road, near the Casino Market. The helpful **TI,** in the lot's far corner, has bus schedules (April–Oct daily 9:00–18:00, July–Aug until 19:00; Nov–March Mon–Sat 9:00–18:30, closed Sun; place de Gaulle, tel. 04 93 41 26 00, www.eze-riviera.com). English-language tours of the village and gardens are available for €8 (call to arrange in advance). Public WCs are located just behind the TI and in the village behind the church, though the cleanest and best-smelling are at either perfume showroom.

Self-Guided Walk

Welcome to Eze-le-Village
• *From the TI and parking lot, wander uphill into the town. You'll come to an exclusive hotel gate and the start of a steep trail down to the beach, marked* Eze/Mer. *For a panoramic view and an ideal picnic perch, walk 80 steps down this path (for more details, see "Trail to Eze-Bord-de-Mer," later). Continuing up into the village, find the steps just after the ritzy hotel gate and climb to...*

Place du Centenaire: In this square, a stone plaque in the flower bed celebrates the 100th anniversary of the 1860 plebiscite, the time when all 133 Eze residents voted to leave the Italian Duchy of Savoy and join France. Vive la France! A town map here helps you get oriented.

• *Now pass through the once-formidable town gate (designed to keep the Ottomans out) and climb into the 14th-century village. You'll find occasional English information plaques on walls in the old city that together give a good history of the village. Wandering the narrow lanes, follow signs to the...*

Château Eza: This was the winter getaway of the Swedish royal family from 1923 until 1953; today it's a hotel. The château's tearoom (Salon de Thé), on a cliff overlooking the jagged Riviera and sea, offers you the most scenic coffee or beer break you'll ever enjoy—for a price. The sensational view terrace is also home to an expensive-but-sensational restaurant. Reserve well ahead for dinner (€7 beer, €50 lunch *menus,* allow €110 for dinner, open daily, tel. 04 93 41 12 24, www.chateaueza.com, info@chateaueza.com).

• *The uphill lanes end at the hilltop castle ruins—now blanketed by the...*

Jardins d'Eze: Here you'll find a prickly festival of cactus. Since 1949, these ruins have been home to 400 different plants 1,300 feet above the sea (€5, open daily, hours change frequently but usually May–Sept 9:00–19:00, Oct–April until dusk, well-described in English, tel. 04 93 41 10 30). At the top, you'll be treated to a commanding 360-degree view, with a helpful *table d'orientation.* On a crystal-clear day (they say...), you can see Corsica. The castle was demolished by Louis XIV in 1706. Louis destroyed castles like this all over Europe (most notably along the Rhine), because he didn't want to risk having to do battle with rebellious nobles inside them at some future date.

• *As you descend, drop by the...*

Eze Church: Though built during Napoleonic times, it has an uncharacteristic Baroque fanciness—a reminder that 300 years of Savoy rule left the townsfolk with an Italian savoir faire and a sensibility for decor.

Sights in Eze-le-Village

Perfume Factory Fragonard—This factory, with its huge tour-bus parking lot, lies on the Middle Corniche, 350 feet below Eze-le-Village. Designed for tour groups, it cranks them through all day long. If you've never seen mass tourism in action, this place will open your eyes. (The gravel is littered with the color-coded stickers each tourist wears so that the salespeople know which guide gets the kickback.) Drop in for an informative and free tour, which can last anywhere from 20 to 40 minutes depending on the walking ability of the group (daily 9:00–18:00, but best Mon–Fri 9:00–11:00 & 14:00–15:30, when the "factory" actually has people working, tel. 04 93 41 05 05). You'll see how the perfume and scented soaps are made and bottled before you're herded into the gift shop.

For a more personal and intimate (but unguided) look at perfume, cross the main road in Eze-le-Village to visit the **Gallimard** shop. Explore the small museum and let the lovely ladies show you their scents (daily 9:00–18:30, handy and free WCs).

Trail to Eze-Bord-de-Mer—This steep trail leaves Eze-le-Village from the foot of the hill-town entry, near the fancy hotel gate, and descends 1,300 feet to the sea along a no-shade, all-view trail. Allow 45 minutes at a steady but manageable pace (good walking shoes are essential). Once in Eze-Bord-de-Mer, you can catch a bus or train to all destinations between Nice and Monaco. While walking this trail in the late 1800s, Friedrich Nietzsche was moved to write his unconventionally spiritual novel, *Thus Spoke Zarathustra.*

Eating in Eze-le-Village

To enjoy Eze-le-Village in relative peace, visit at sunset and stay for dinner. There's a handy **Casino** market at the foot of the village by the bus stop (daily 8:00–20:00) and a sensational picnic spot at the beginning of the trail to Eze-Bord-de-Mer. **Le Cactus** serves cheap crêpes, salads, and sandwiches at outdoor tables near the entry to the old town (daily, tel. 04 93 41 19 02). For a real splurge, dine at **Château Eza** (described earlier).

La Trophée des Alpes

High above Monaco, on the Grande (High) Corniche in the over-looked village of La Turbie, lies one of this region's most evocative historic sights (with dramatic views over the entire country of Monaco as a bonus). Rising well above all other buildings, this massive Roman monument, rated ▲▲, commemorates Augustus Caesar's conquest of the Alps and its 44 hostile tribes. It's exciting to think that, in a way, La Trophée des Alpes celebrates a victory that kicked off the Pax Romana—joining Gaul and Germania, freeing up the main artery of the Roman Empire, and linking Spain and Italy. (It's depressing to think that it's closed on Mondays, if that's your only chance to visit.)

Walk around the monument and notice how the Romans built a fine, quarried-stone exterior, filled in with rubble and coarse concrete. Flanked by the vanquished in chains, the towering inscription tells the story: It was erected "by the senate and the people to honor the emperor." The structure served no military purpose when built, though it was fortified in the Middle Ages (like the Roman Arena in Arles) as a safe haven for villagers. When Louis XIV ordered the destruction of the area's fortresses in the early 18th century, he sadly included this one. The monument later became a quarry before being restored in the 1930s and 1940s with money from the Tuck family of New Hampshire.

The one-room **museum** shows a reconstruction and translation of the dramatic inscription, which lists all the feisty alpine tribes that put up such a fight. Escorts from the museum take people up to the monument, but it's not worth waiting for.

Cost and Hours: €5, Tue–Sun mid-May–mid-Sept 9:30–13:00 & 14:30–17:30, off-season 10:00–13:00 & 14:30–17:00, closed

Mon year-round, tel. 04 93 41 20 84.

La Turbie: The sweet old village of La Turbie sees almost no tourists, but it has plenty of cafés and restaurants (see "Eating in La Turbie," below). To stroll the old village, park in the main lot on place Neuve (follow *Monaco* signs one block from the main road to find it), then walk behind the post office and find brick footpaths—they lead through a village with nary a shop.

Getting to and from La Trophée des Alpes (in La Turbie)

By **car,** take the High Corniche to La Turbie, ideally from Eze-le-Village (La Turbie is 10 minutes east of, and above, Eze-le-Village), then look for signs to *La Trophée des Alpes.* Once in La Turbie, you can park in the lot in the center of town (place Neuve, follow *Monaco* signs for a short block) and walk from there (walk 5 minutes around the old village, with the village on your right); or drive to the site by turning right in front of La Régence Café. Those coming from farther afield can take the efficient A-8 to the La Turbie exit. To reach Eze-le-Village from La Turbie, follow signs to *Nice,* and then look for signs to *Eze-le-Village.*

You can also get here on **bus** #116 from Nice (5/day, 45 minutes, €1, last bus returns to Nice at about 18:00) or on bus #114 from Monaco (6/day, 3/day Sat morning only, none on Sun, 20 minutes, €1). La Turbie's bus stop is across from the PTT/post office on place Neuve (to reach La Trophée des Alps, walk around the old village, with the village on your right—5 minutes).

On **foot,** Eze is a 45-minute roadside walk downhill from La Turbie (no buses). There's a bike lane for half of the trip, but the rest is along a fairly quiet road with no shoulder. Follow D-2564 from La Turbie to Eze-le-Village, and don't miss the turnoff for D-45. The views of Eze are magnificent as you get close.

Eating in La Turbie

To eat very well, find **La Terrasse,** the Riviera's most welcoming restaurant (I'm not kidding—free calls are encouraged from their phone anywhere, anytime; there's a computer at your disposal; and the Wi-Fi is free). Tables gather under sun shades and everyone seems to be on a first-name basis. The sea lies miles below (that point of land is Cap Ferrat), but most diners are more interested in the meal than the view. Let Helen, Jacques, and Annette tempt you to return for dinner at sunset, and book ahead for a table with a view (€8–11 salads, great €12.50 *plats du jour,* €19.50 three-course *menu* includes glass of wine, steak tartare is a specialty, daily, near the PTT/post office at the main parking lot, 17 place Neuve, tel. 04 93 41 21 84).

LA TROPHEE DES ALPES

Quickie Riviera Bus Tour from Nice to Monaco

Don't have a car? You can still enjoy the trip from Nice to Monaco (and on to Menton, described on page 390). Although most travelers see the Riviera from their train window as they zoom along the coast, the public bus affords a far better view of the dramatic crags, dreamy villas, and much-loved beaches that make it Europe's coast with the most.

This tour works best if you take the bus from Nice, ride the entire Nice–Monaco–Menton route (one scenic hour), enjoy Menton, then see Monaco (or you may find time for another stop) on the way back to Nice. To minimize bus and sightseeing crowds, time it so that you're on the bus by 9:00, but beware: Monte Carlo's casino does not open until 14:00 most days. Alternatively, come for late-afternoon sightseeing and stay into the evening. (Keep in mind that afternoon buses back to Nice are often crammed and agonizingly slow after Villefranche-sur-Mer—at these times, the train is a better solution.)

Riding the bus couldn't be easier. Bus #100 runs four times an hour along the Low Corniche (daily 6:00–20:00, 3/hour on Sun, departs from Nice bus station). One simple €1 ticket (buy from the driver) is good for 74 minutes, no matter how far you go. Since bus fares are cheap, consider hopping on and off at great viewpoints (the next bus will be by soon). Riding from Nice toward Monaco, grab a seat on the right-hand side. All stops have names (usually posted on the shelter or bus stop sign)—I'll identify the ones that matter along this route. Keep your eyes peeled for town names and bus stops as we go.

It's easiest to get a good seat if you board the bus in Nice's bus station (or if you go before 9:00). If there's a long line, you could wait for the next bus to be assured of a view seat (buses start from here and run every 15 minutes). At the Nice bus station, TV monitors list the platform, destination, and time for the next departure. You're looking for bus #100 to *destination: Monaco/Menton* (most likely from stall 17). Pay the driver as you get on, and be assertive with the crowds trying to board.

Many bus drivers on this line seem to be in training for the 2011 Monaco Grand Prix—so hold on tight.

Self-Guided Bus Tour

This Nice-to-Monaco route along the Low Corniche was inaugurated with the opening of the Monte Carlo Casino in 1863. It was designed to provide easy and safe access from Nice (and the rest of France) to the gambling fun in Monaco. Here's what you'll see along the way:

In Nice: Shortly after the bus pulls out, you'll get a quick glimpse of Nice's snazzy Museum of Modern Art on the left before passing through place Garibaldi (easy transfer to the tram on your way back), with its linden trees and statue of Giuseppe Garibaldi (one of the men credited with uniting Italy in the 1860s) at the center.

Nice Harbor: This harbor was built in the 1700s. Before then, boats littered Nice's beaches. You'll see some yachts, an occasional cruise ship, and the daily ferry to Corsica. The one-hour boat tour along Cap Ferrat and Villefranche-sur-Mer leaves from the right side, about halfway down (see page 295). If you get on or off here on your return, it's a pleasant 30-minute walk around the point to or from the promenade des Anglais.

From Nice to Villefranche-sur-Mer: As you glide away from Nice, look back for views of the harbor, Castle Hill, and the sweeping Bay of Angels. Imagine the views from the homes below, and imagine 007 on his deck admiring a sunset (the soft, yellow, rounded tower ahead near the top of the hill is part of Sean Connery's property). Elton John's home is higher up the hill (and out of view).

You'll soon pass the now-closed Hôtel Maeterlinck, one of several luxury hotels to go belly-up in recent years (now slated for condo-conversion). Next, you'll come to the yacht-studded bay of Villefranche-sur-Mer and the peninsula called Cap Ferrat— playground of the rich and famous, marked by its lighthouse on the point just across the bay. This bay is a rare natural harbor along the Riviera. Since it's deeper than Nice's, it hosts the huge cruise ships.

Villefranche-sur-Mer: To see Villefranche-sur-Mer, get off at the stop labeled *Octroi* (for more on charming Villefranche, see page 346). After passing through Villefranche-sur-Mer, look for sensational views back over the town. Looking ahead, the Baroness Rothschild's pink Villa Ephrussi, with its red-tiled roof, breaks the horizon on Cap Ferrat's peninsula. A little farther to the right is "Baron" Paul Allen's home (with a sloping red-tiled roof). Keep an eye out as the road arcs to the right—the Rolling Stones recorded 1972's *Exile on Main Street* (one of your co-author's favorites) in the basement of a mansion below where you see the *l'Ange Gardien* signs.

Cap Ferrat: To visit Villa Ephrussi de Rothschild or to walk the seaside paths of Cap Ferrat, get off at the stop marked *Pont St. Jean* (after the Total station). Cross back over the main road; then, to walk to Villa Ephrussi (20 minutes) or to the village of St. Jean-Cap-Ferrat (45 minutes), find the walkway that runs up the center of the Cap (see "Getting to Cap Ferrat" on page 360 for details).

As you leave Cap Ferrat on our bus tour, remember that this road was built in 1860 to bring customers to Monaco. Before then, there was no development along this route, all the way to Monaco.

Beaulieu-sur-Mer: To visit Villa Kérylos, get off at the Eglise stop, in front of the Hôtel Metropole. Just after the town of Beaulieu-sur-Mer, the cliffs create a microclimate and a zone nicknamed "Little Africa." (The bus stop is labeled *Petite Afrique*.) Exotic vegetation (including the only bananas on the Riviera) grows among private, elegant

villas that made Beaulieu-sur-Mer *the* place to be in the 19th century.

Eze-Bord-de-Mer: A few minutes after leaving Beaulieu-sur-Mer, be ready for scant, short-lived views way up to the fortified town of Eze-le-Village. After passing under through a rock arch, you'll swing around a big bend going left: Eze-le-Village crowns the ridge in front of you. To reach Eze-le-Village, the #83 shuttle bus makes the climb from the Gare d'Eze stop in Eze-Bord-de-Mer (daily, 8/day, shares the same eastbound stop used by bus #100).

Cap d'Ail: After passing through several tunnels, you emerge at Cap d'Ail. The huge, yellowish hospital-like building below (what color is that, anyway?) once thrived as a luxury hotel popular with the Russian aristocracy. Now it's popular with condo-commandos. At the first stop in the village of Cap d'Ail (labeled *Cap d'Ail-Edmonds*), look above at the switchbacks half-way up the barren hillside. It was at the bend connecting these two switchbacks that Princess Grace Kelly (the former American movie star) was killed in a car crash in 1982. You can get off here and walk a lovely beach trail that will take you to Monaco in 30 minutes.

Monaco (three bus stops): Cap d'Ail borders Monaco—you're about to leave France. You'll pass by some pretty junky development along this no-man's-land stretch. Eventually, to the right, just before the castle-topped hill (Monaco-Ville), is Monaco's Fontvieille district, featuring tall, modern apartments all built on land reclaimed from the Mediterranean. The first Monaco stop (Place d'Armes) is best for visiting the palace and other old-town sights in Monaco-Ville.

If you stay on the bus, you'll pass through the tunnel, then emerge to follow the road that Grand Prix racers (like your driver) speed along. In late May you'll see blue bleachers and barriers set up for the big race.

You'll pass the second Monaco stop (Stade Nautique), then enjoy the harbor and city views as you climb to the last Monaco stop (Casino). Get off here for a glimpse at the gambling action (a plush, terraced garden leads down to the casino) and an easy walk back into Monte Carlo. For information on Monaco, see the next chapter. If you stay on the bus for a few more minutes, you'll be back in France, and in 15 more minutes you'll reach the end of the line, **Menton** (described on page 390).

Bonne route!

MONACO

Despite high prices, wall-to-wall daytime tourists, and a Disney-esque atmosphere, Monaco is a Riviera must. Monaco is on the go. Since 1929, cars have raced around the port and in front of the casino in one of the world's most famous auto races, the Grand Prix de Monaco (May 26–29 in 2011; see sidebar later in this chapter). The modern breakwater—constructed elsewhere and towed in by sea—enables big cruise ships to dock here. The district of Fontvieille, reclaimed from the sea, bristles with luxury high-rise condos. But don't look for anything too deep in this glittering tax haven. Two-thirds of its 30,000 residents live here because there's no income tax—leaving fewer than 10,000 true Monegasques.

This minuscule principality (0.75 square mile) borders only France and the Mediterranean. The country has always been tiny, but it used to be...less tiny. In an 1860 plebiscite, Monaco lost two-thirds of its territory when the region of Menton voted to join France. To compensate, France suggested that Monaco build a fancy casino and promised to connect it to the world with a road (the Low Corniche) and a train line. This started a high-class tourist boom that has yet to let up.

Although "independent," Monaco is run as a piece of France. A French civil servant appointed by the French president—with the blessing of Monaco's prince—serves as state minister and manages the place. Monaco's phone system, electricity, water, and so on, are all French.

The death of Prince Rainier in 2005 ended his 56-year career of enlightened rule. Today Monaco is ruled by Prince

Rainier's unassuming son, Prince Albert Alexandre Louis Pierre, Marquis of Baux. At 50-some years old, Prince Albert has long been considered Europe's most eligible bachelor—though he has admitted to fathering two children out of wedlock—but finally got engaged in 2010. A graduate of Amherst College, Albert is a bobsled enthusiast who raced in several Olympics, and an avid environmentalist who seems determined to clean up Monaco's tarnished tax-haven, money-laundering image. (Monaco is infamously known as a "sunny place for shady people.")

Monaco is big business, and Prince Albert is its CEO. Its famous casino contributes only 5 percent of the state's revenue, whereas its 43 banks—which offer an attractive way to hide your money—are hugely profitable. The prince also makes money with a value-added tax (19.6 percent, the same as in France), plus real estate and corporate taxes.

The glamorous romance and marriage of the American actress Grace Kelly to Prince Rainier added to Monaco's fairy-tale mystique. Grace Kelly (Prince Albert's mother) first came to Monaco to star in the 1955 Hitchcock movie *To Catch a Thief,* in which she was filmed racing along the Corniches. Later, she married the prince and adopted the country. Tragically, in 1982 Monaco's much-loved Princess Grace died in a car wreck on that same Corniche. She was just 52 years old.

Monaco is a special place: There are more people in Monaco's philharmonic orchestra (about 100) than in its army (about 80 guards). The princedom is well-guarded, with police and cameras on every corner. (They say you could win a million dollars at the casino and walk to the train station in the wee hours without a worry...and I believe it.) Stamps are so few that they increase in value almost as soon as they're printed. And collectors snapped up the rare Monaco versions of euro coins (with Prince Rainier's portrait) so quickly that many Monegasques have never even seen one.

Orientation to Monaco

The principality of Monaco consists of three distinct tourist areas: Monaco-Ville, Monte Carlo, and La Condamine. Monaco-Ville

fills the rock high above everything else and is referred to by locals as Le Rocher ("The Rock"). This is the oldest section, home to the Prince's Palace and all the sights except the casino. Monte Carlo is the area around the casino. La Condamine is the port (which divides Monaco-Ville and Monte Carlo). From here

Monaco

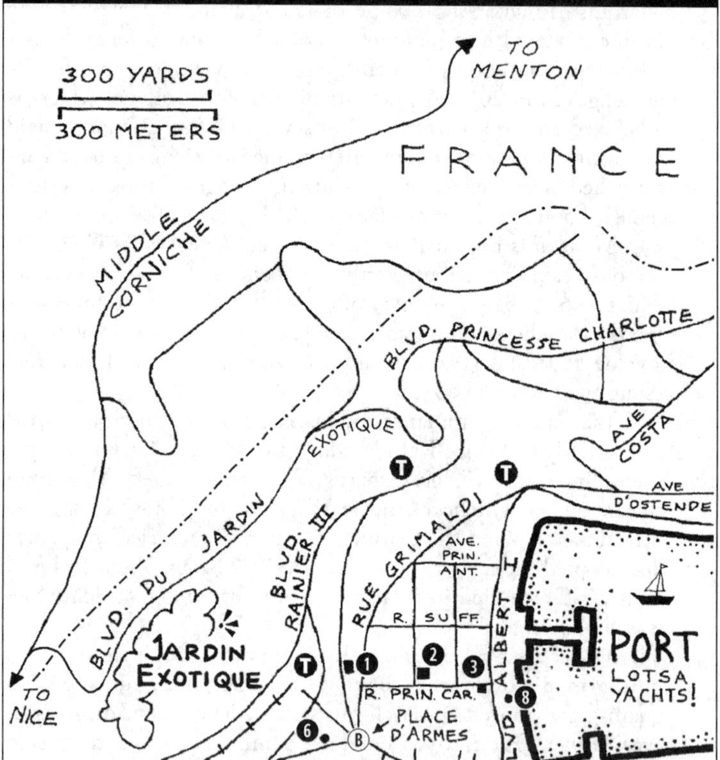

300 YARDS
300 METERS

TO MENTON

F R A N C E

MIDDLE CORNICHE

BLVD. PRINCESSE CHARLOTTE

AVE. COSTA

EXOTIQUE

AVE. D'OSTENDE

JARDIN DU

BLVD. DU

RUE GRIMALDI

AVE. PRIN. ANT.

R. SUFF.

BLVD. RAINIER III

JARDIN EXOTIQUE

TO NICE

PORT
LOTSA YACHTS!

BLVD. ALBERT I

R. PRIN. CAR.

PLACE D'ARMES

AVE. DE LA PORTE NEUVE

RAMPE MAJOR

POST

P

PLACE DE LA VISIT.

PRINCE'S PALACE
& NAPOLEON COLLECTION

CATHEDRAL

OLD TOWN

JARDIN BOTANIQUE

FONTVIEILLE

MONACO

ACCESS TO TRAIN STATION

Parking

Local Bus Stop

View

Border

MEDITERRANEAN SEA

TO MENTON

BLVD. REP.

BLVD. DES MOULINS

AVE. F. LARVOTTO

AVE. SPE

AVE.

PARK

LOEWS CASINO

CASINO

PLACE DU CASINO

PALAIS DES CONGRES & P "Le Casino"

MONTE CARLO

MONACO-VILLE

MONTE CARLO STORY & P "Le Palais"

COUSTEAU AQUARIUM

1 Hôtel de France
2 Huit et Demi Restaurant
3 Crock'in Café
4 Boulangerie
5 Palace Square: Start of Self-Guided Walk
6 Bus #100 to Nice: Place d'Armes Stop
7 Bus #100 from Nice: Place d'Armes Stop
8 Bus #100 to/from Nice: Stade Nautique Stop
9 Bus #100 to Nice: Casino Stop
10 Bus #100 from Nice: Casino Stop
11 Bus #112 to Eze-le-Village & #114 to La Turbie

MONACO

it's a 25-minute walk up to the Prince's Palace or to the casino, or three minutes by local bus (see "Getting Around Monaco," later). A fourth, less-interesting area, Fontvieille, forms the west end of Monaco and was reclaimed from the sea by Prince Rainier in the 1970s.

The surgical-strike plan for most travelers is to start at Monaco-Ville (where you'll spend the most time), wander down along the port area, and finish by gambling away whatever you have left in Monte Carlo (the casino doesn't open until 14:00). You can walk the entire route in about 1.5 hours, or take three bus trips and do it in 15 minutes.

Tourist Information
The main TI is at the top of the park, above the casino (Mon–Sat 9:00–19:00, Sun 10:00–12:00, 2 boulevard des Moulins, tel. 00-377/92 16 61 16 or 00-377/92 16 61 66, www.visitmonaco.com). A branch TI is in the train station (Tue–Sat 9:00–17:00, closed Sun–Mon except July–Aug). From June to September you might find information kiosks in the Monaco-Ville parking garage and on the port. There is also a TI desk for Monaco in Terminal 1 of Nice's airport.

Arrival in Monaco
By Bus from Nice and Villefranche-sur-Mer: See my "Quickie Riviera Bus Tour from Nice to Monaco" on page 372 to plan your route and for tips. Bus riders need to pay attention, since stops are not announced. Cap d'Ail is the town before Monaco, so be on the lookout after that (the last stop before Monaco is called Cimitière). You'll enter Monaco through the modern cityscape of high-rises of the Fontvieille district. When you see the rocky outcrop of old Monaco, be ready to get off.

There are three stops in Monaco. Listed in order from Nice, they are Place d'Armes (in front of a tunnel at the base of Monaco-Ville's rock), Stade Nautique (center on the port), and Casino (near the casino on avenue d'Ostende). The Place d'Armes stop is the best starting point. From there you can walk up to Monaco-Ville and the palace (10 minutes straight up), or catch a quick local bus (line #1 or #2, details below). To reach the bus stop and steps up to Monaco-Ville, cross the street right in front of the tunnel and walk with the rock on your right for about 200 feet (good WCs at the local-bus stop). To begin at the Casino stop, walk uphill to the Häagen-Dazs and turn right to find the casino.

For directions on returning to Nice by bus, see "Monaco Connections," near the end of this chapter.

By Train from Nice: This loooooong underground train station is in central Monaco, about a 15-minute walk to the casino or to the port, and about 25 minutes to the palace. The station has no baggage storage.

The TI and ticket windows are up the escalator at the Italy end of the station. There are three exits from the train platform level (one at each end and one in the middle).

To reach Monaco-Ville and the palace from the station, take the platform-level exit at the Nice end of the tracks (signed *Sortie Fontvieille/Monaco Ville*), which leads through a long tunnel (TI annex at end) to the foot of Monaco-Ville; turn left at the end of the walkway and hike 15 minutes up to the palace, or take the bus (#1 or #2).

To reach Monaco's port and the casino, take the mid-platform exit, closer to the Italy end of the tracks. Follow *Sortie la Condamine* signs down the steps and escalators, then follow *Accès Port* signs until you pop out at the port, where you'll see the stop for buses #1 and #2. It's a 25-minute walk from the port to the palace (to your right) or 20 minutes to the casino (up avenue d'Ostende to your left), or a short trip via buses #1 or #2 to either.

If you plan to return to Nice by train after 20:30, when ticket windows close, buy your return tickets now or be sure to have about €4 in coins (the ticket machines only take coins).

To take the short-but-sweet coastal **walking path** into Monaco's Fontvieille district, get off the train at Cap d'Ail, which is one stop before Monaco. Turn left out of the little station and walk 50 yards up the road, then turn left again, going downstairs and under the tracks. Turn left onto the coastal trail, and hike the 20 minutes to Fontvieille. You'll end up at Pointe des Douaniers. Once there, it's a 20-minute uphill hike to Monaco's sights (or hop on bus #100).

By Car: Follow *Centre-Ville* signs into Monaco (warning: traffic can be a problem), then watch for the red-letter signs to parking garages at *Le Casino* (for Monte Carlo) or *Le Palais* (for Monaco-Ville). You'll pay about €10 for four hours.

Helpful Hints

Telephone Tip: To call Monaco from France, dial 00, then 377 (Monaco's country code) and the eight-digit number. Within Monaco, simply dial the eight-digit number.

Minivan Tours from Nice: Several companies offer daytime and nighttime tours of Monaco, allowing you freedom to gamble without worrying about catching the last train or bus home (see "Getting Around the Riviera" on page 281).

Loop Trip by Bus: You can visit Monaco by bus, then take a bus from Monaco directly to Eze-le-Village (#112, no Sun bus) or La Turbie (#114, no Sun bus), then return to Nice by bus from there. For details, see "Monaco Connections," later.

MONACO

Monaco at a Glance

▲**Casino of Monte Carlo** Classy casino that saved Monaco's economy. **Hours:** Slots and some gaming rooms—open at 14:00, elegant game rooms—some open Mon–Fri at 16:00 and Sat–Sun at 15:00, others at 21:00 or 22:00. Must have passport and adhere to dress code.

Prince's Palace Prince Albert's extravagant residence. **Hours:** April–Oct daily 10:00–18:00, closed Nov–March.

Napoleon Collection The prince's private collection of Napoleonic stuff, from medals, swords, and guns, to his cool *chapeau*. **Hours:** Same as Prince's Palace.

Changing of the Guard Big ceremony for a tiny nation. **Hours:** Daily at 11:55 on the palace square.

Cathedral of Monaco Final resting place for Princess Grace and Prince Rainier. **Hours:** Daily 8:30–18:45, until 18:00 in winter.

Cousteau Aquarium Jacques Cousteau's cliff-hugging aquarium. **Hours:** Daily July–Aug 9:30–19:30, April–June and Sept 9:30–19:00, Oct–March 10:00–18:00.

Monte Carlo Story Film Informative 35-minute film describing Monaco's sexy history. **Hours:** Showings usually at 14:00, 15:00, 16:00, and 17:00, morning showings possible—ask.

Stamp Shopping Collector stamps sold at Monaco's post offices. **Hours:** Mon–Sat 9:00–12:00 & 13:00–17:00, closed Sun.

Jardin Exotique Cliffside botanical garden mixing thousands of cacti and fantastic views. **Hours:** Daily mid-May–mid-Sept 9:00–19:00, mid-Sept–mid-May 9:00–18:00 or dusk.

Getting Around Monaco

By Local Bus: Buses #1 and #2 link all areas with fast and frequent service (single ticket-€1, 10 tickets-€6, day pass-€3, pay driver, 10/hour, fewer on Sun, buses run until 21:00). You can split a 10-ride ticket with your travel partners, since you're unlikely to take more than two or three rides in Monaco.

By Open Bus Tour: You could pay €17 for a hop-on, hop-off open-deck bus tour that makes 12 stops in Monaco, but I wouldn't. This tour doesn't go to the best view spot in the Jardin Exotique (described on page 387) and, besides, most of Monaco is walkable. If you want a scenic tour of the principality that includes its best views, pay €1 to take local bus #2, and stay on board for a full loop (or hop on and off as you please).

By Tourist Train: "Monaco Tour" tourist trains begin at the aquarium and pass by the port, casino, and palace (€7, 2/hour, 10:30–18:00 in summer, 11:00–17:00 in winter depending on weather, 30 minutes, recorded English commentary).

By Taxi: If you've lost track of time at the casino, you can call the 24-hour taxi service (tel. 08 20 20 98 98)...provided you still have enough money to pay for the cab home.

Self-Guided Walk

Welcome to Monaco-Ville

All of Monaco's sights (except the casino) are in Monaco-Ville, packed within a few cheerfully tidy blocks. This walk makes a tidy loop around Monaco-Ville.

• *To get from anywhere in Monaco to the palace square (Monaco-Ville's sightseeing center, home of the palace and the Napoleon Collection), take bus #1 or #2 to place de la Visitation (end of the line). Turn right as you step off the bus and walk five minutes straight down the street leading from the left corner of the little square. You'll pass the post office, a worthwhile stop for its collection of valuable Monegasque stamps (we'll go there later—to visit it now, see page 384).*

If you're walking up from the port, the well-marked lane leads you directly to the palace.

Palace Square (Place du Palais): This square is the best place to get oriented to Monaco. Facing the palace, go to the right and look out over the city (er...principality). This rock gave birth to the

little pastel Hong Kong look-alike in 1215, and it's managed to remain an independent country for most of its nearly 800 years. Looking beyond the glitzy port, notice the faded green roof above and to the right: It belongs to the casino that put Monaco on the map. The famous Grand Prix runs along the port, and then up the ramp to the casino. And Italy is so close, you can almost smell the pesto. Just beyond the casino is France again (which flanks Monaco on both sides)—you could walk one-way from France to France, passing through Monaco in about 60 minutes.

The odd statue of a woman with a fishing net is dedicated to **Prince Albert I's** glorious reign (1889–1922). Albert was a

Renaissance man with varied skills and interests. He had a Jacques Cousteau–like fascination with the sea (and built Monaco's famous aquarium), and was a determined pacifist who made many attempts to dissuade Germany's Kaiser Wilhelm II from becoming involved in World War I. It was Albert I's dad, Charles III, who built the casino.

• *Now walk toward the palace and find the statue of the monk grasping a sword.*

Meet **François Grimaldi,** a renegade Italian dressed as a monk, who captured Monaco in 1297 and began the dynasty that still rules the principality. Prince Albert is his great-great-great... grandson, which gives Monaco's royal family the distinction of being the longest-lasting dynasty in Europe.

• *Walk to the opposite side of the square.*

At the Louis XIV cannonballs, look down at Monaco's newest area, the reclaimed-from-the-sea **Fontvieille** district, which has seen much of Monaco's post–World War II growth (residential and commercial—notice the lushly planted building tops). Prince Rainier continued—some say, was obsessed with—Monaco's economic growth, creating landfills (topped with apartments, such as Fontvieille), flashy ports, more beaches, and a new rail station. Today, thanks to Prince Rainier's efforts, tiny Monaco is a member of the United Nations. (If you have kids with you, check out the nifty play area just below.)

• *If you're into stamps, detour down rue Comte Félix Gastaldi, then follow the jog to the right onto rue Emile de Loth to find the...*

Post Office: Philatelists and postcard-writers with panache can buy—or just gaze in awe at—this post office's impressive collection of Monegasque stamps (Mon–Sat 9:00–12:00 & 13:00–17:00, closed Sun, tel. 00-377/93 15 28 63).

• *Backpedal a few steps to the...*

Prince's Palace (Palais Princier): A medieval castle sat where Monaco's palace is today. Its strategic setting has had a lot to do with Monaco's ability to resist attackers. Today, Prince Albert lives in the palace, whereas Princesses Stephanie and Caroline live down the street a few blocks. The palace guards protect the prince 24/7 and still stage a **Changing of the Guard** ceremony with all the pageantry of an important nation (daily at 11:55, fun to watch but jam-packed). Audioguide tours take you through part of the prince's lavish palace in 30 minutes. The rooms are well-furnished and impressive, but interesting only if you haven't seen a château lately (€8 combo-ticket includes audioguide and the Napoleon Collection, April–Oct daily 10:00–18:00, last entry 30 minutes before closing, closed Nov–March, tel. 00-377/93 25 18 31).

• *Next to the palace entry is the...*

Napoleon Collection: Napoleon occupied Monaco after

MONACO

the French Revolution. This is the prince's private collection of items Napoleon left behind: military medals, swords, guns, letters, and—best—his hat. I found this collection more interesting than the palace (€4 includes audioguide, €8 combo-ticket includes Prince's Palace, same hours as palace).

• *With your back to the palace, leave the square through the arch to the right (under the most beautiful police station I've ever seen) and find the...*

Cathedral of Monaco (Cathédrale de Monaco): The somber but beautifully lit cathedral, rebuilt in 1878, shows that Monaco cared for more than just its new casino. It's where centuries of Grimaldis are buried, and where Princess Grace and Prince Rainier were married. Circle slowly behind the altar (counterclockwise). The second tomb is that of Albert I, who did much to put Monaco on the world stage. The second-to-last tomb—inscribed *"Gratia Patricia, MCMLXXXII"*—is where Princess Grace was buried in 1982. Prince Rainier's tomb lies next to Princess Grace's (daily 8:30–18:45, until 18:00 in winter).

• *As you leave the cathedral, find the 1956 wedding photo of Princess Grace and Prince Rainier (keep an eye out for other photos of the couple as you walk), then walk left through the immaculately maintained Jardin Botanique, with more fine views. Find the...*

Cousteau Aquarium (Musée Océanographique): Prince Albert I built this impressive, cliff-hanging aquarium in 1910 as a monument to his enthusiasm for things from the sea. The aquarium, which Captain Jacques Cousteau directed for 32 years, has 2,000 different specimens, representing 250 species. The bottom floor features Mediterranean fish and colorful tropical species (all nicely described in English). My favorite is the zebra lionfish, though I'm keen on eels too. Rotating exhibits occupy the entry floor. Upstairs, the fancy Albert I Hall houses a museum (included in entry fee, very little English information) and features ship models, whale skeletons, oceanographic instruments and tools, and scenes of Albert and his beachcombers hard at work. Find the display on Christopher Columbus with English explanations. Don't miss the elevator to the rooftop terrace view, where you'll also find convenient WCs and a reasonable café (€13, kids-€7, daily July–Aug 9:30–19:30, April–June and Sept 9:30–19:00, Oct–March 10:00–18:00; down the steps from Monaco-Ville bus stop, at the opposite end of Monaco-Ville from

Le Grand Prix Automobile de Monaco

Each May, the Grand Prix de Monaco (May 26–29 in 2011) focuses the world's attention on this little country. The race started as an enthusiasts' car rally by the Automobile Club of Monaco (and is still run by the same group, more than 80 years later). The first race, held in 1929, was won by a Bugatti at a screaming average speed of...48 mph (today's cars double that speed). To this day, drivers consider this one of the most important races on their circuits.

By Grand Prix standards, it's an unusual course, running through the streets of this tiny principality, sardined between mountains and sea. The hilly landscape means that the streets are narrow, with tight curves, steep climbs, and extremely short straightaways. Each lap is about two miles, beginning and ending at the port. Cars climb along the sea from the port, pass in front of the casino, race through the commercial district, and do a few dandy turns back to the port. The race lasts 78 laps, and whoever is still rolling at the end wins (most don't finish).

The Formula 1 cars look like overgrown toys that kids might pedal up and down their neighborhood street (if you're here a week or so before the race, feel free to browse the parking structure below Monaco-Ville, where many race cars are kept). Time trials to establish pole position begin three days before the race, which is always on a Sunday. In 2011, the time trials take place on May 26, 27, and 28, and the race itself is on May 29 (www.yourmonaco.com/grand_prix). More than 150,000 people attend the gala event; like the nearby film festival in Cannes, it's an excuse for yacht parties, restaurant splurges, and four-digit bar tabs at luxury hotels. During this event, hotel rates in Nice and beyond rocket up (even for budget places).

the palace; tel. 00-377/93 15 36 00, www.oceano.mc).

• *The red-brick steps, across from the aquarium to the right, lead up to buses #1 and #2, both of which run to the port, the casino, and the train station. To walk back to the palace and through the old city, turn left at the top of the brick steps. For a brief movie break, take the escalator to the right of the aquarium as you leave it and drop into the parking garage, then take the elevator down and find the...*

Monte Carlo Story: This informative 35-minute film gives an entertaining and informative account of Monaco's fairytale history, from fishing village to jet-set principality, and offers a comfortable, soft-chair break from all that walking. The last part of the film was added to the original version after the death of Prince Rainier, which is why your sound stops early (€7, headphone commentary in English; daily showings usually on the hour at 14:00, 15:00, 16:00, and 17:00; there may be a morning showing for groups that you can join—ask, tel. 00-377/93 25 32 33).

Sights in Monaco

Above Monaco-Ville

Jardin Exotique—This cliffside municipal garden, located above Monaco-Ville, has eye-popping views from France to Italy. It's a fascinating home to more than a thousand species of cacti (some giant) and other succulent plants, but probably worth the entry only for view-loving botanists (some posted English explanations provided). Your ticket includes entry to a skippable natural cave and an anthropological museum, as well as a not-to-be-missed view snack bar/café (€7, daily mid-May–mid-Sept 9:00–19:00, mid-Sept–mid-May 9:00–18:00 or until dusk, tel. 00-377/93 15 29 80). Bus #2 runs here from any stop in Monaco, and makes for a worthwhile mini tour of the country, even if you don't visit the gardens. You can get similar views over Monaco for free from behind the souvenir stand at the Jardin's bus stop; or, for even grander vistas, cross the street and hike toward La Turbie.

In Monte Carlo

▲**Casino**—Monte Carlo, which means "Charles' Hill" in Spanish, is named for the prince who presided over Monaco's 19th-century makeover. Begin your visit opposite Europe's most famous casino, in the park above the pedestrian-unfriendly traffic circle. In the mid-1800s, olive groves stood here. Then, with the construction

of casino and spas, and easy road and train access, one of Europe's poorest countries was on the Grand Tour map—*the* place for the vacationing aristocracy to play. Today, Monaco has the world's highest per-capita income.

The casino is intended to make us feel comfortable while losing money. Charles Garnier designed the place (with an opera house inside) in 1878, in part to thank the prince for his financial help in completing Paris' Opéra Garnier (which the architect also designed). The central doors provide access to slot machines, private gaming rooms, and the opera house. The private gaming rooms occupy the left wing of the building.

Count the counts and Rolls-Royces in front of Hôtel de Paris (built at the same time, visitors allowed in the hotel, no shorts, www.montecarloresort.com), then strut inside past the slots to the sumptuous atrium. This is the lobby for the opera house (open only for performances). There's a model of the opera at the end of the room, and marble WCs on the right. If you're over 21, you can try your luck at the one-armed bandits (push button on slot machines to claim your winnings). If it's before 20:00, shorts are allowed at the slots, though you'll need decent attire to go any farther. After 20:00, shorts are off-limits everywhere.

The scene, flooded with camera-toting tourists during the day, is great at night—and downright James Bond–like in the private rooms. The park behind the casino offers a peaceful café and a good view of the building's rear façade and of Monaco-Ville.

If paying an entrance fee to lose money is not your idea of fun, you can access all games for free in the plebeian, American-style Loews Casino, adjacent to the old casino.

Cost and Hours: The slot machines and the first gaming rooms *(salons européens)* open daily at 14:00. Slots are free, but you'll pay €10 to enter *les salons européens*. Most of the glamorous private game rooms open Mon–Fri at 16:00 and Sat–Sun at 15:00, though some don't open until 21:00 or 22:00. Here you can rub elbows with high rollers—provided you're 18 or older (bring your passport for proof) and properly attired (tie and jacket for men, dress standards for women are far more relaxed—only tennis shoes are a definite no-no). Men might be able to rent a tie and jacket at a nearby store (ask at the TI or casino before you go, casino tel. 00-377/92 16 20 00, www.montecarlocasinos.com).

Take the Money and Run: The stop for buses returning to Nice and Villefranche-sur-Mer, and for local buses #1 and #2, is at the top of the park, above the casino on avenue de la Costa (under the arcade to the left). To get back to the train station from the casino, take bus #1 or #2 from this stop, or walk about 15 minutes down avenue d'Ostende (just outside the casino) toward the port, and follow signs to *Gare SNCF* (see map).

Sleeping and Eating in Monaco

(€1 = about $1.25, country code: 377)

$$ Hôtel de France, run by friendly Sylvie, is centrally located, spotlessly maintained, reasonably priced, and perfectly pleasant. Its extensive renovation should be complete in time for your visit; expect air-conditioning and higher prices than those printed here—check their site for updated rates (Db-€90–125, Tb-€110–

155, includes breakfast, Wi-Fi, 6 rue de la Turbie, near west exit from train station, tel. 00-377/93 30 24 64, fax 00-377/92 16 13 34, www.monte-carlo.mc/france, hotel-france@monte-carlo.mc).

Several cafés serve basic, inexpensive fare (day and night) on the port. I prefer the eateries that line the flowery and traffic-free rue de la Princesse Caroline, which runs between rue Grimaldi and the port. The best this street has to offer is **Huit et Demi.** It has a white-tablecloth-meets-director's-chair ambience, mostly outdoor tables, and cuisine worth returning for (€13 salads, €14 pizzas, €18–24 *plats*, closed Sat for lunch and all day Sun, 7 rue de la Princesse Caroline, tel. 00-377/93 50 97 02). For a simple and cheap salad or sandwich, find the **Crock'in** café farther down at 2 rue de la Princesse (closed Sun, tel. 04 93 15 02 78).

In Monaco-Ville you'll find incredible *pan bagnat* (*salade niçoise* sandwich), quiche, and sandwiches at the yellow-bannered **Boulangerie,** a block off Palace Square (open daily until 19:00, 8 rue Basse). Try a *barbajuan* (a spring roll–size beignet with wheat, rice, and parmesan), the *tourta de bléa* (pastry stuffed with pine nuts, raisins, and white beets), or the focaccia sandwich (salted bread with herbs, mozzarella, basil, and tomatoes, all drenched in olive oil). For dessert, order the *fougasse monégasque* (a soft-bread pastry topped with sliced almonds and anise candies). Monaco-Ville has many pizzerias, *crêperies,* and sandwich stands, but the neighborhood is dead at night. If you're here in the evening, eat near the port.

Monaco Connections

From Monaco by Train to: Nice (2/hour, 20 minutes, €3.60), **Villefranche-sur-Mer** (2/hour, 10 minutes), **Antibes** (2/hour, 45–60 minutes).

By Bus to: Nice (#100, 4/hour Mon–Sat, 3/hour Sun, 45 minutes, €1), **Nice Airport** (#110 express on the freeway, hourly, 50 minutes, €18), **Villefranche-sur-Mer** (#100, 4/hour Mon–Sat, 3/hour Sun, 25 minutes, €1), **Eze-le-Village** (#112, 7/day Mon–Sat, none on Sun, 25 minutes), **La Turbie** (#114, 6/day Mon–Fri, 3/day Sat morning only, none on Sun, 20 minutes), **Menton** (#100, 4/hour Mon–Sat, 3/hour Sun, 15 minutes).

The Monaco-to-Nice bus (#100) is not identified at every stop—verify with a local by asking, *"Direction Nice?"* There's a handy stop below Monaco-Ville at place d'Armes (on the main road to Nice in front of the Brasserie Monte Carlo). Another is a few blocks above the casino on avenue de la Costa (under the arcade to the left of Barclays Bank).

Buses #112 (to Eze-le-Village) and #114 (to La Turbie) depart Monaco from place de la Crémaillère, one block above the main

TI and casino park. Walk up rue Iris with Barclays Bank to your left, curve right, and find the bus shelter across the street by the green Costa à la Crémaillère café. Bus numbers for these routes are not posted, but this is the stop.

Last Call: The last bus leaves Monaco for Villefranche-sur-Mer and Nice at about 20:00; the last train leaves Monaco for Villefranche-sur-Mer and Nice at about 23:30. If you plan to leave Monaco by train after 20:30, buy your tickets in advance (since the window will be closed), or bring enough coins for the machines.

Near Monaco: Menton

If you wish the Riviera were less glitzy and more like a place where humble locals take their families to lick ice cream and make sand castles, visit Menton (15 minutes by bus beyond Monaco). Menton feels like a poor man's Nice. It's unrefined and unpretentious, with lower prices, fewer rentable umbrellas, and lots of Italians day-tripping in from just over the border (five miles away). There's not an American in sight.

Though a bit rough, the Menton beach is a joy. An inviting promenade lines the beach, and seaside cafés serve light meals and salads (much cheaper than in Nice). A snooze or stroll here is a lovely Riviera experience. From the promenade, a pedestrian street leads through town. Small squares are alive with jazz bands playing crowd-pleasers under palm trees.

Stepping into the old town—which blankets a hill capped by a fascinating cemetery—you're immersed in a pastel-painted, yet dark and tangled Old World scene with (strangely) almost no commerce. A few elegant restaurants dig in at the base of the towering centuries-old apartment flats. The richly decorated Baroque St. Michael's Church (midway up the hill) is a reminder that, until 1860, Menton was a thriving part of the larger state of Monaco. Climbing past sun-grabbing flower boxes and people who don't get out much anymore, the steep stepped lanes finally deposit you at the ornate gate of a grand cemetery that fills the old castle walls. Explore the cemetery, which is the final resting place of many aristocratic Russians (buried here in the early 1900s) and offers breathtaking Mediterranean views.

Getting to Menton: While trains serve Menton regularly, the station is a 15-minute walk from the action. Buses are more convenient, as they drop visitors right on the beach promenade (#100, 4/hour Mon–Sat, 3/hour Sun, 1 hour from Nice, 15 minutes past Monaco, €1; see my self-guided bus tour on page 372).

ANTIBES, CANNES, AND ST-TROPEZ

The Riviera opens up west of Nice with bigger, sandier beaches and an overabundance of tasteless beachfront development. Ancient Antibes and superficial Cannes buck the slap-it-up high-rise trend, each with thriving centers busy with pedestrians and yachts. Trendy St-Tropez, a scenic 1.5-hour drive from Antibes, marks the western edge of the French Riviera.

Antibes

Antibes has a down-to-earth, easygoing ambience that's rare in this area. Its old town is a maze of narrow streets and red-tile roofs rising above the blue Med, protected by twin medieval towers and wrapped in extensive ramparts. Visitors making the short trip from Nice can browse Europe's biggest yacht harbor, snooze on a sandy beach, loiter through an enjoyable old town, and hike along a sea-swept trail. The town's cultural claim to fame, the Picasso Museum, shows off its great collection in a fine old building.

Though much smaller than Nice, Antibes has a history that dates back just as far. Both towns were founded by Greek traders in the fifth century B.C. To the Greeks, Antibes was "Antipolis"—the town *(polis)* opposite *(anti)* Nice. For the next several centuries, Antibes remained in the shadow of its neighbor. By the turn of the 20th century, the town was a military base—so the rich and famous partied elsewhere. But when the army checked out after World War I, Antibes was "discovered" and enjoyed a particularly roaring '20s—with the help of party animals like Rudolph Valentino and the rowdy (yet silent) Charlie Chaplin. Fun-seekers even invented water-skiing right here in the 1920s.

ANTIBES

Orientation to Antibes

Antibes' old town lies between the port and boulevard Albert 1er and avenue Robert Soleau. Place Nationale is the old town's hub of activity. The restaurant-lined rue Aubernon connects the port and the old town. Stroll along the sea between the old port and place Albert 1er (where boulevard Albert 1er meets the water). The best beaches lie just beyond place Albert 1er, and the walk is beautiful. Good play areas for children  are along this path and on place des Martyrs de la Résistance (close to recommended Hôtel Relais du Postillon).

Tourist Information

Antibes has three TIs: one in a kiosk at the **train station** (April–Sept only, Mon–Sat 9:00–18:00, closed Sun), one near the **port** at 32 boulevard d'Aguillon (Mon–Sat 10:00–12:00 & 13:30–18:00, closed Sun), and the main TI on **place Général de Gaulle** where the fountains squirt (July–Aug daily 9:00–19:00; Sept–June Mon–Sat 9:00–12:30 & 13:30–18:00, Sun 9:00–12:00; tel. 04 97 23 11 11, www.antibesjuanlespins.com). At any TI, pick up the excellent city map and the self-guided walking tour of old Antibes. The Nice TI has Antibes maps and the Antibes TI has Nice maps—plan ahead.

Arrival in Antibes

By Train: Bus #14 runs every 20 minutes from the train station (bus stop 50 yards to right as you exit station) to the *gare routière* (bus station; near the main TI and old town), and continues to the fine plage de la Salis with quick access to the Phare de la Garoupe trail. **Taxis** usually are usually waiting in front of the train station.

To **walk** to the port, the old town, and the Picasso Museum (15–20-minute walk), cross the street in front of the station, skirting left of the Piranha Café, and follow avenue de la Libération downhill as it bends left. At the end of the street, the port will be in front of you and the old town to the right.

To walk directly to my hotels and to the main TI (15-minute walk to TI), cross the street to the Piranha Café, turn right, and stay the course for about eight blocks on avenue Robert Soleau until you reach the fountain-soaked place Général de Gaulle.

The last train back to Nice leaves at about midnight.

By Bus: Slow bus #200 stops a few blocks from the TI

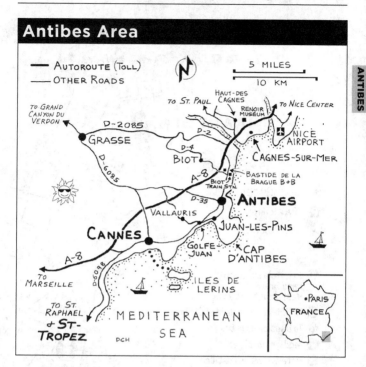

(turn right as you leave the TI to find the stops just off boulevard Dugommier: buses from Nice and to Cannes stop on avenue Aristide Briand—second shelter down; buses to Nice and from Cannes stop on boulevard Gustave Chancel). The airport bus (#250) drops you behind the train station (see "Helpful Hints," later). Buses from other destinations use the **bus station** at the edge of the old town on place Guynemer, a block below the main TI on place Général de Gaulle (info desk open Mon–Sat 7:30–19:00, closed Sun, www.envibus.fr).

By Car: Day-trippers follow signs to *Centre-Ville*, then *Port Vauban*, and park near the old town walls (first 30 minutes free, then about €2.50/hour). Walk into the old town through the last arch on the right.

If you're sleeping here, follow *Centre-Ville* signs, then signs to your hotel, and get advice from your hotelier on where to park. (Most hotels have free parking.) The most appealing hotels in Antibes are easiest by car. Antibes works well for drivers; compared to Nice, parking is easy, it's a breeze to navigate, and it's a convenient springboard for the Inland Riviera. Pay parking is usually available at Antibes' train station, so drivers can ditch their cars here and day-trip from Antibes by train.

Antibes

TO ❸, FORT CARRE & NICE

FOOT-BRIDGE

AVE. DU 11 NOV.

AVE. DE LA LIB.

TRAIN STN.

TO ⑳

➜ SELF-GUIDED WALK

P PARKING

ONE-WAY STREET

AVE. GRAND CAV.

AVE. ROBERT

AVE. THIERS

BLVD. GAMBETTA

SOLEAU

VAUBAN

RUE

❶ To Hôtels La Jabotte,
Beau Site &
Restaurant de Bacon

❷ To Hôtel Pension le Mas Djoliba

❸ To Bastide de la Brague

❹ Modern Hôtel

❺ Hôtel Relais du Postillon

❻ Epicerie de la Place Market

❼ La Marmite Restaurant

❽ La Taverne du Safranier

❾ L'Aubergine Restaurant

❿ Le Broc en Bouche Restaurant

⓫ Le Vauban Restaurant

⓬ Le Brulot & Le Brulot Pasta

⓭ Les Vieux Murs Restaurant

⓮ l'Outil du Web Internet

⓯ Heidi's English Bookshop

⓰ Launderette

⓱ CityZen Bikes

⓲ Avis Car Rental

⓳ Hertz Car Rental

⓴ Europcar Car Rental

㉑ Boat Rental

㉒ Bus #200 from Nice &
to Cannes

㉓ Bus #200 from Cannes

㉔ Bus #14 Stop

AVE. BRIAND

BLVD. DUG

BLVD. CHANCEL

PLACE DE GAULLE

BLVD. WILSON

BLVD. T

BLVD. M.

200 YARDS

200 METERS

TO ❷ ← RUE

ANTIBES

Helpful Hints

Monday, Monday: Avoid Antibes on Mondays, when all sights are closed.

Internet Access: Centrally located **l'Outil du Web** is two blocks from place Général de Gaulle TI—walk toward the train station (Mon–Fri 9:30–18:00, Sat 9:30–13:00, closed Sun, 11 avenue Robert Soleau, tel. 04 93 74 11 86).

English Bookstore: Heidi's English Bookshop has a welcoming vibe and a great selection of new and used books, with many guidebooks—including mine (Mon–Fri 10:00–19:00, Sat–Sun 11:00–18:00, 24 rue Aubernon).

Laundry: Smiling **Madame Hallepau** will do your laundry while you swim. Her launderette is above the market hall on rue de la Pompe (Mon–Fri 8:30–12:00 & 15:00–18:30, closed Sat–Sun).

Grocery Store: Picnickers will appreciate Casino's **Epicerie de la Place market** (daily until 22:00 in summer, until 21:00 off-season, where rue Sade meets place Nationale).

Bike and Scooter Rental: Centrally located **CityZen Bikes** rents scooters and bikes—electric or pedal (clever name, near the main TI at 22 boulevard Dugommier, tel. 04 93 74 56 46, www.cityzenbikes.fr). The TI can give you more bike-rental options. See "Walks and Hikes" on page 402 for possible biking destinations.

Taxi: For a taxi, call 08 25 56 07 07 or 04 93 67 67 67.

Car Rental: The big-name agencies have offices in Antibes. The most central are **Avis** (32 boulevard Albert 1er, tel. 04 93 34 65 15) and **Hertz** (across from the train station at 52 avenue Robert Soleau, tel. 04 93 61 18 15). **Europcar** is less central, at 106 route de Grasse (tel. 04 93 34 79 79). These offices are closed Mon–Sat 12:00–14:00 and Sundays.

Boat Rental: You can motor your own seven-person yacht thanks to **Antibes Bateaux Services** (€300/half-day, at the small fish market on the port, mobile 06 15 75 44 36, www.antibes-bateaux.com).

Airport Bus: Bus #250 runs from near the train station to Nice's airport (€8, 2/hour, 40 minutes; cross over the tracks on the pedestrian bridge—it's the last shelter to the right, stop from the airport is labeled *Vautrin,* stop going to the airport is labeled *Passerelle*).

Getting Around Antibes

Though most sights and activities are walkable, buses are a great value in Antibes, allowing three hours of travel for €1 (one-way or round-trip). **Bus #2** provides access to the best beaches, the path to La Phare de la Garoupe, and the Cap d'Antibes trail (all described later in this chapter). It runs from the bus station down boulevard Albert 1er, with stops every few blocks (daily 7:00–19:00, every 40 minutes). **Bus #14** is also useful, linking the train station, bus station, old town, and plage de la Salis. Pick up a schedule for return times for these and other regional buses at the bus station (for more on buses, see "Arrival in Antibes," earlier).

A **tourist train** offers circuits around old Antibes, the port, the ramparts, and to Juan-les-Pins (€7, departs from place de la Poste, mobile 06 03 35 61 35).

Self-Guided Walk

Welcome to Antibes

This 40-minute walk will help you get your bearings, and works well day or night.

• *Begin at the old port (Vieux Port) at the southern end of avenue de Verdun. Stand across from the archway with the clock (parking right there).*

Old Port: Locals claim that this is Europe's first and biggest pleasure-boat harbor, with 1,600 stalls. The port was enlarged in the 1970s to accommodate ever-expanding yacht dimensions. The work was financed by wealthy yacht owners (mostly Saudi Arabian) eager for a place to park their aircraft carriers. That old four-pointed structure crowning the opposite end of the port is **Fort Carré** (described later in this chapter), which protected Antibes from foreigners for more than 500 years.

The pathetic remains of a once-hearty **fishing fleet** are moored in front of you. The Mediterranean is pretty much fished out. Most of the seafood you'll eat here comes from fish farms or the Atlantic.

• *With the port on your left, pass the sorry fleet and find the entry to the shell-shaped **plage de la Gravette**, a normally quiet public beach tucked right in the middle of old Antibes.*

Wander up the ramp to the round lookout to better appreciate the scale of the ramparts that protected this town. Because Antibes was the last fort before the Italian border, the French king made sure the ramparts were top-notch. Those twin towers crowning the old town are the church's bell tower and the tower topping Château Grimaldi (today's Picasso Museum). Forested Cap d'Antibes is the point of land in the distance to the left, with a terrific sea-soaked walking trail (see "Cap d'Antibes Hike" on page 402). Looking east toward Nice, I'm not sure what the white mesh-man sculpture is all about, but I know it was created by the same artist who did the pedestal-top statues on place Masséna in Nice (see page 331).

• *Admirers of mega-sized toys will want to wander farther out along the port (others can skip to the next paragraph).*

Continuing along the port leads you past historic maps and images of Antibes' port to a controlled entry point that pedestrians are welcome to enter (along the ochre path). Welcome to the **"quai des Milliadaires"** (billionaires' dock), where yacht-length envy inspires unfathomable conspicuous consumption. The Union Jacks fluttering above most boats are the flag of the Cayman Islands—can you say tax dodge? The people you see on the boats are busy keeping them meticulously clean...for the 5–10 days a year these boats actually sail somewhere.

Restoration work on that big tower, the Bastion Saint Jaume (intended for special exhibits and events), may be completed by your visit.

• *Now let's backtrack to where we started and enter Antibes' old town through the arch under the clock.*

Old Town: Today, the town is the haunt of a large community of English, Irish, and Aussie boaters who help crew those giant yachts in Antibes' port. (That helps explain the Irish pubs and English bookstores.) Continue straight and uphill (halfway up on the right, you'll pass rue Clemenceau, which leads to the heart of the old town), and you'll arrive at Antibes' **market hall** (daily until 13:00, except closed Mon Sept–May). This hall does double duty—market by day, restaurants by night (a fun place for dinner).

Go left where the market starts (rue Chessel) and find Antibes' pretty pastel **Church of the Immaculate Conception,** built on the site of a Greek temple (worth a peek inside). A church has stood on this site since the 12th century. This one served as the area's cathedral until the mid-1200s. The stone bell tower stands apart from the church and predates it by 600 years, when it was part of the city's defenses. Those heavy stones were pillaged from Antibes' Roman monuments.

Looming above the church on prime real estate is the white-stone **Château Grimaldi,** where you'll find Antibes' prized

Picasso Museum (for a self-guided tour, see the next page). This site has been home to the acropolis of the Greek city of Antipolis, a Roman fort, and a medieval bishop's palace (once connected to the cathedral below). Later still, the château was the residence of the Grimaldi family (who still rule Monaco). Its proximity to the cathedral symbolized the sometimes too-cozy relationship between society's two dominant landowning classes: the Church and the nobility. (In 1789, the French Revolution changed all that.)

• *After visiting the Picasso Museum, exit it to the left. Work your way through a warren of pretty lanes, then head out to the water, and turn right along the ramparts (that's some view!). As you walk, notice the ground-floor level of the homes to your right (watch out for cars).*

The homes in this area make up a special Antibes community called **La Commune Libre du Safranier.** A group of public-spirited residents banded together in the 1960s to preserve this most traditional of Antibes neighborhoods, where small homes line narrow lanes and sidewalk plantings are meticulously maintained. To best explore this picturesque community, turn right on place du Safranier along the stone wall with the wire-top fence, pass the recommended Taverne du Safranier in the square below, and then turn right up the bricked lane.

• *To continue your walk, return to the path along the sea and find the* **History and Archaeology Museum** *(described later, under "Sights in Antibes").*

Before going in, stop on the terrace above the museum, where you'll get a clear view of **Cap d'Antibes,** crowned by its lighthouse and studded with mansions (see "Cap d'Antibes Hike" on page 402). The Cap was long the refuge of Antibes' rich and famous, and a favorite haunt of F. Scott Fitzgerald and Ernest Hemingway.

After taking a quick spin through the museum, continue hugging the shore past place Albert 1er until you see the views back to old Antibes. Benches and soft sand await (a few copies of famous artists' paintings of Antibes are placed on bronze displays along the beach walkway). You're on your own from here—energetic walkers can continue to the view from the Phare de la Garoupe (see page 402); others can return to old Antibes and poke around in its peaceful back lanes.

Sights in Antibes

▲▲**Picasso Museum (Musée Picasso)**—Sitting serenely where the old town meets the sea, this compact three-floor museum offers a manageable collection of Picasso's paintings, sketches, and ceramics. Picasso lived in this castle for four months in 1946, when he cranked out an amazing amount of art. He was elated by the end of World War II, and his works show a celebration of color and a rediscovery of light after France's long nightmare of war. Picasso was also reenergized by his young and lovely companion, Françoise Gilot (with whom he would father two children). The resulting collection (donated by Picasso) put Antibes on the tourist map.

Cost and Hours: €6; mid-June–mid-Sept Tue–Sun 10:00–18:00, July–Aug Wed and Fri until 20:00; mid-Sept–mid-June Tue–Sun 10:00–12:00 & 14:00–18:00; closed Mon year-round, last entry 30 minutes before closing, tel. 04 92 90 54 20, www.antibes-juanlespins.com/eng/culture/musees.

⊘ Self-Guided Tour: Start outside in the sculpture garden for the view. Pause to appreciate Picasso's working environment (and wonder why he only spent four months here).

The museum's interior is a calm place of white walls, soft arches, and ample natural light—a great space for exhibiting art. The ground floor houses a permanent collection of 20th-century works by Hans Hartung and his partner, Anna-Eva Bergman, who, like Picasso, both donated their paintings to the museum. Their work blends well with what you'll see by Picasso. The first floor up usually holds a small collection of works by Nicolas de Staël and temporary exhibits of other artists' work.

The museum's highlight is on the top floor, where you'll find the permanent collection of Picasso's works. Visitors are greeted by a large image of Picasso and a display of photographs of the artist at work and play during his time in Antibes. Tour the floor clockwise, noticing the focus on sea creatures, tridents, and other marine themes (*oursin* is a sea urchin, *poulpe* is an octopus, and *poisson* is, well, fishy). *Nature Morts* means still life, and you'll see many of these in this collection.

The first gallery room houses several famous works, including the lively, frolicking, and big-breasted *La Joie de Vivre* painting (from 1946). This Greek bacchanal sums up the newfound freedom in a newly liberated France and sets the tone for the rest of the collection. You'll also see the colorless three-paneled *Satyr, Faun and Centaur with Trident* and several ceramic creations (the bull rocks).

Next, look for a room filled with ink sketches labeled *Figures Feminines* that challenge the imagination—these show off Picasso's skill as a cartoonist and caricaturist. Then look for the Basque fishermen and several Cubist-style nudes *(nus couchés)*, one painted on plywood—Picasso loved experimenting with materials and different surfaces (I particularly like the crayon sketches).

Farther along, don't miss the wall devoted to his ceramic plates. Inspired by a visit to a ceramics factory in nearby Vallauris, Picasso was smitten by the texture of soft clay and devoted a great deal of time to exploring this medium—producing over 2,000 pieces in one year. In the same room, the wall-sized painting *Ulysses and the Sirens* screams action and anxiety.

History and Archaeology Museum (Musée d'Histoire et d'Archéologie)—More than 2,000 years ago, Antibes was the center of a thriving maritime culture. It was an important Roman city with aqueducts, theaters, baths, and so on. This museum—the only place to get a sense of the city's ancient roots—displays Greek, Roman, and Etruscan odds and ends in two simple halls (no English descriptions, though the small museum brochure offers some background in English). Your visit starts at an 1894 model of Antibes and continues past displays of Roman coins, cups, plates, and scads of amphorae. The lanky lead pipe connected to a center box was used as a bilge pump; nearby is a good display of Roman anchors (€3, Tue–Sun 10:00–13:00 & 14:00–17:00, closed Mon, on the water between Picasso Museum and place Albert 1er, tel. 04 93 34 00 39.

▲Market Hall (Marché Provençal)—The daily market bustles under a 19th-century can-opy, with flowers, produce, Provençal products, and beach accessories (in the old town, behind Picasso Museum on cours Masséna). The market wears many hats: produce daily until 13:00, handicrafts Thursday through Sunday in the afternoon, and fun out-door dining in the evenings (market closed Mon Sept–May).

Other Markets and Squares—Antibes' lively antiques/flea market fills place Nationale and place Audiberti (next to the port) on Thursdays and Saturdays (7:00–18:00). Its clothing market winds through the streets around the post office (rue Lacan) on Thursdays (9:00–18:00). Place Général de Gaulle, a pleasing, palm-studded, and fountain-flowing square in Antibes' modern city, is the trendy place to be seen.

Fort Carré—This impressively situated citadel, dating from 1487, was the last fort inside France. It protected Antibes from Nice, which until 1860 was part of Italy. You can tour this unusual four-pointed fort for the fantastic views over Antibes, but there's little to see inside (€3, includes tour in French, Tue–Sun June–Sept

10:00–18:00, Oct–May 10:00–16:30, closed Mon, 30-minute walk from Antibes along avenue 11 Novembre, easy parking nearby).

▲**Beaches *(Plages)*—**The best beaches stretch between Antibes' port and Cap d'Antibes. The first you'll cross is the plage Publique (no rentals required). Next are the groomed plages de la Salis and du Ponteil, with mattress, umbrella, and towel rental. All are busy but manageable in summer and on weekends, with cheap snack stands and exceptional views of the old town. The closest beach to the old town is at the port (plage de la Gravette), which seems calm in any season.

Walks and Hikes

From place Albert 1er (where boulevard Albert 1er meets the beach), you get a good view of plage de la Salis and Cap d'Antibes. That tower on the hill is your destination for the first walk described below. The longer "Cap d'Antibes Hike" begins on the next beach, just over that hill. The two hikes are easy to combine by bus, bike, or car.

▲▲**Chapelle et Phare de la Garoupe**—The territorial views—best in the morning, skippable if hazy—from this viewpoint more than merit the 20-minute uphill climb from the plage de la Salis (a few blocks after Maupassant Apartments, where the road curves left, follow signs and the rough, cobbled chemin du Calvaire up to lighthouse tower). An orientation table explains that you can see from Nice to Cannes and up to the Alps. Take buses #2 or #14 to the plage de la Salis stop and find the trail a block ahead. By car or bike, follow signs for *Cap d'Antibes*, then look for *Chapelle et Phare de la Garoupe* signs.

▲**Cap d'Antibes Hike (Sentier Touristique Piétonnier de Tirepoil)**—At the end of the mattress-ridden plage de la Garoupe (over the hill from Phare de la Garoupe lighthouse) lies a terrific

trail around the tip of Cap d'Antibes. The beautiful path undulates above a splintered coastline splashed by turquoise water and peppered with exclusive mansions. You'll walk for two miles, then head inland along small streets, ending at the recommended Hôtel Beau-Site (and bus stop). You can walk as far as you'd like and then double back, or do the whole loop (allow 2.5 hours at most, use the TI's Antibes map). Bring good shoes, as the walkway is uneven and slippery in places. Sundays are busiest.

To get to the trail from Antibes, take bus #2 (catch it at the bus station, along boulevard Albert 1er, or at plage de la Salis) for about 15 minutes to the La Fontaine stop at Hôtel Beau-Site (return stop is 50 yards away on opposite side, get return times at station). Walk 10 minutes down to plage de la Garoupe and start from there.

By car or bike, follow signs to *Cap d'Antibes,* then to *plage de la Garoupe,* and park there.

The trail begins at the far-right end of plage de la Garoupe.

Near Antibes

Juan-les-Pins—The low-rise town of **Juan-les-Pins,** sprawling across the Cap d'Antibes isthmus from Antibes, is where the action is...after hours. It's a modern beach resort with good beaches, plenty of lively bars and restaurants, and a popular jazz festival in July. The town is also famous for its clothing boutiques that stay open until midnight in high season (people are too busy getting tan to shop at normal hours). As locals say, "Party, sleep in, shop late, party more." Buses, trains, and even a tourist train (see "Getting Around Antibes" on page 396) make the 10-minute trip to and from Antibes constantly.

Marineland and Parc de la Mer—A few backstrokes from Antibes, Parc de la Mer is a world of waterslides, miniature golf, exhibits, and more. Marineland anchors this sea-park extravaganza with French-language shows featuring dolphins, sea lions, and killer whales (Marineland only—€37, kids-€28, €2 more in July–Aug and €6 less in winter; Aquasplash waterslide park—€25, kids-€20, closed in winter; various combo-tickets available for Aquasplash waterslides, miniature golf, and other attractions; daily 10:00–19:00, until 23:00 July–Aug, tel. 04 93 33 49 49, www .marineland.fr).

Getting There: The park is a short walk from the train station in nearby Biot (5 minutes from Antibes) and about 15 minutes from Antibes' bus station on buses #200 or #7. By car, the park is signed from RN-7, several miles from Antibes toward Nice.

Renoir Museum (Musée Renoir)—Halfway between Antibes and Nice, above Cagnes-sur-Mer, Pierre Auguste Renoir found his Giverny. This is where the artist spent the last 12 years of his life (1907–1919) tending his gardens, painting, and even dabbling in sculpture (despite suffering from rheumatoid arthritis). His home has been converted into a small museum, where visitors get a very personal look into Renoir's later years. You'll see his studio, wheelchair, and bedroom, stroll in his gardens, and enjoy several of his and other artists' paintings of people and places around Cagnes-sur-Mer. It's a pleasant place and a must-see for his fans (€3, Wed–Mon May–Sept 10:00–12:00 & 14:00–18:00, Oct–April until 17:00, closed Tue year-round, chemin des Collettes, tel. 04 93 20 61 07, www.cagnes-tourisme.com/renoir-museum.php).

Getting There: Take bus #200 to Cagnes-sur-Mer (ask the driver for stop closest to the museum: *Musée Renoir? Quel arrêt?*, mew-zay reh-nwah kehl ah-reh), then walk uphill 15 minutes to the museum. The train stops downhill from the museum as well (40-minute uphill walk to the museum—take a cab). Drivers go to Cagnes-sur-Mer, then follow brown *Musée Renoir* signs.

More Day Trips from Antibes—Antibes is halfway between Nice and Cannes (easy train and bus service to both), and close to the artsy pottery and glassblowing village of **Biot,** home of the Fernand Léger Museum as well as the Parc de la Mer (mentioned above). Biot village is easy to reach on bus #10 from Antibes' train station (daily, every 40 minutes). The Biot train station is a 45-minute walk below the village—take bus #10 from here. The best parking is just above the town, allowing direct access to its pretty pedestrian street.

Another pottery center, **Vallauris,** is a striking hill town and a must for lovers of blown glass. Picasso fans will enjoy his murals in the Chapel of War and Peace (bus #8 from place de la Libération in Antibes, or take bus #200 or the train to Golfe-Juan-Vallauris—3/hour, 6 minutes, get details at local TIs).

Sleeping in Antibes

My favorite Antibes hotels are best by car or taxi, though walkers and bus users can manage as well. Pickings are slim when it comes to centrally located hotels in this city, where restaurants are a dime a dozen but hotels play hard to get. Air-conditioning is rare.

Outside the Town Center

$$$ Hôtel la Jabotte**, hidden along an ignored alley a block from the famous beaches and a 15-minute walk from the old town, is a cozy place that defies the rules. Yves, Claude, and dog Tommy have turned a small beach villa into a boutique hotel with personality: The colors are rich, the decor shows a personal touch, and most rooms have individual terraces facing a small, central

Sleep Code

(€1 = about $1.25, country code: 33)
S = Single, **D** = Double/Twin, **T** = Triple, **Q** = Quad, **b** = bathroom,
s = shower only, ***** = French hotel rating (0–4 stars). Unless
otherwise noted, credit cards are accepted and English is
spoken.

To help you sort easily through these listings, I've divided
the rooms into three categories based on the price for a
standard double room with bath:

$$$ Higher Priced—Most rooms €100 or more.
$$ Moderately Priced—Most rooms between €70-100.
$ Lower Priced—Most rooms €70 or less.

Prices can change without notice; verify the hotel's
current rates online or by email. For other updates, see www
.ricksteves.com/update.

garden where you'll get to know your neighbor. Rooms are not
air-conditioned, but fans are provided (Db-€115–130, includes
good breakfast and a few parking spots, Wi-Fi, 13 avenue Max
Maurey, take the third right after passing the big Hôtel Josse,
tel. 04 93 61 45 89, fax 04 93 61 07 04, www.jabotte.com, info
@jabotte.com).

$$$ Hôtel Beau Site*** is my only listing on Cap d'Antibes, a
10-minute drive from the old town. It's a terrific value if you want
to get away...but not *too* far away. (But if you don't have a car, you
may feel isolated.) This place is a sanctuary, with sweet Nathalie in
charge as well as a pool, a comfy patio garden, and free parking.
Rooms are spacious and comfortable, and several have balconies
(standard Db-€90, bigger Db-€125, even bigger Db-€160, family
rooms-€175–230, extra bed-€25; huge breakfast-€13, continen-
tal breakfast-€7.50, air-con, Wi-Fi, bikes available, 141 boule-
vard Kennedy, tel. 04 93 61 53 43, fax 04 93 61 78 16, www.hotel
beausite.net, hbeausit@club-internet.fr). From the hotel, it's a
10-minute walk down to the plage de la Garoupe and a nearby
hiking trail (described earlier, under "Walks and Hikes").

$$$ Hôtel Pension le Mas Djoliba*** is a fair splurge that's
better for drivers but also workable for walkers (10-minute walk
from plage de la Salis, 15 minutes to old Antibes, and 30 minutes
to the train station). Reserve early for this traditional, bird-chirp-
ing, flower-filled manor house where no two rooms are the same.
From May to September, they definitely prefer (but won't insist)
that you dine here. It's hard to pass up once you see the setting:

After a busy day of sightseeing, dinner by the pool is a treat. The cuisine is average but copious. Some rooms are small, but the bigger rooms are well worth the additional cost, and several come with small decks (Sb-€130, Db-€120–200, several good family rooms-€200–280, figure €100–115 per person with breakfast and dinner; air-con, Wi-Fi, cool *boules* court and loaner balls, avenue de Provence; from boulevard Albert 1er, look for grey signs as you approach the beach and turn right up avenue Gaston Bourgeois; tel. 04 93 34 02 48, fax 04 93 34 05 81, www.hotel-djoliba.com, contact@hotel-djoliba.com).

$$ Bastide de la Brague is an easygoing seven-room bed-and-breakfast hacienda up a dirt road above Marineland (10-minute drive east of Antibes). It's run by a fun-loving family (wife Isabelle, who speaks English, hubby Franck, and Mama). Rooms are quite comfortable, air-conditioned, and affordable; several are made for families. Request the tasty €22 home-cooked dinner (includes apéritif, wine, and coffee) and enjoy a family dining experience. There's enough space to stretch out, and they adore kids (Db-€80–100, Tb/Qb-€100–120, includes breakfast, free Wi-Fi and computer with printer for guests, 55 avenue No. 6, Antibes 06600, tel. 04 93 65 73 78, www.bbchambreantibes.com, bastidebb06 @gmail.com). Franck is happy to take guests on a private boat tour of the coast (allow €40/person for all afternoon, 4-person minimum). From Antibes, follow signs that read *Nice par Bord de la Mer,* turn left toward Brague and Marineland, then right at the roundabout (toward Groules), then take the first left and follow signs. Antibes bus #10 drops you five minutes away, and the Biot train station and bus #200 are a 15-minute walk (ask for details when you book). If you arrange it in advance, they'll pick you up at the train station in Antibes or Biot.

In the Town Center

$$ Modern Hôtel**, in the pedestrian zone near the bus station, is a solid value for budget-conscious travelers. The 17 standard-size rooms—each with air-conditioning, bright decor, and Wi-Fi—are simple, spick-and-span, and well-run by Laurence (Sb-€60–70, Db-€68–88, 1 rue Fourmillière, tel. 04 92 90 59 05, fax 04 92 90 59 06, www.modernhotel06.com, modern-hotel@wanadoo.fr).

$$ Hôtel Relais du Postillon** is a mellow place on a central square above a peaceful café. There are a few cheap true singles and 12 well-designed doubles with small balconies but no air-conditioning (Sb-€50, Db-€69–98, price varies by room size, most have tight bathrooms, Wi-Fi, 8 rue Championnet, tel. 04 93 34 20 77, fax 04 93 34 61 24, www.relaisdupostillon.com, relais@relais dupostillon.com).

Eating in Antibes

Antibes is a fun place to dine out. You can eat on a budget, enjoy a good meal at an acceptable price, or join the party just inside the

walls on boulevard d'Aguillon, on place Nationale, or—my favorite—under the festive Marché Provençal (all are filled with tables and tourists). The options are endless. Take a walk and judge for yourself, and be tempted by these suggestions. Romantics should picnic at the beach (the **Epicerie de la Place market** is open late; see "Helpful Hints" on page 396). Everyone should stroll along the ramparts after dinner.

La Marmite owner Patrick offers diners an honest, unpretentious budget value in old Antibes, with eight tables, helpful service, and delicious seafood choices but no air-conditioning (*menus* from €16, closed Mon, 20 rue James Close, tel. 04 93 34 56 79).

La Taverne du Safranier, hiding in a small square a block from the sea, feels right out of a movie. It's a cheery place away from the rest, where you'll order from colorful chalkboard menus and dine under grapevines and happy lights (seafood is their forte, €11 pasta, €14–24 *plats*, €28 three-course *menu*, closed Mon, place du Safranier, tel. 04 93 34 80 50).

L'Aubergine delivers fine cuisine at fair prices—including good vegetarian options—served with no hurry in an intimate room rich with color. Arrive early to get a table (€32 bouillabaisse, *menus* from €23, opens at 18:30, closed Wed, 7 rue Sade, tel. 04 93 34 55 93).

Le Broc en Bouche is part cozy wine bar, part bistro, and part collector's shop. Come early to get a seat at this cool little place and enjoy well-prepared dishes from a selective list (€23 *plats*, closed Tue–Wed, 8 rue des Palmiers, tel. 04 93 34 75 60).

Le Vauban is run by a young couple who draw a local following with their handsome interior, smart tableware, and reliable cuisine at fair prices (€29 three-course *menu*, closed Tue, opposite 4 rue Thuret, tel. 04 93 34 33 05).

Le Brulot is an Antibes institution with two restaurants—Le Brulot and Le Brulot Pasta—that sit almost side-by-side a short block below Marché Provençal on rue Frédéric Isnard. Join Antibes residents at the very popular **Le Brulot,** known for its Provençal cuisine and meats cooked on an open fire. It's a small place, overflowing onto the street, with a few outside tables and a dining room below. Try the aioli (€19 *menus*, closed Sun, at #2, tel. 04 93 34 17 76). **Le Brulot Pasta** is family-friendly and goes Italian with excellent pizza (the €11 *printanière* is tasty and huge) and big portions of pasta, served in air-conditioned comfort under stone arches (daily, at #3, tel. 04 93 34 19 19).

Les Vieux Murs is a romantic splurge with a candlelit, red-toned interior overlooking the sea. The outside tables are worth booking ahead—but pass on the upstairs room (€46 dinner *menu*, €30 lunch *menu*, open daily June–mid-Sept, closed Mon off-season, valet parking available, along ramparts beyond Picasso Museum at 25 promenade de l'Amiral de Grasse, tel. 04 93 34 06 73).

Restaurant de Bacon is often picked as Antibes' best restaurant, thanks to its top-notch bouillabaisse and views of Antibes. Located on Cap d'Antibes, past the plage de la Salis, it's simple from the outside (no sign), but lovely on the inside, and made for seafood-lovers (*menus* from €50, allow €70 for bouillabaisse, closed Mon–Tue and Oct–Feb, boulevard de Bacon, tel. 04 93 61 50 02).

Antibes Connections

From Antibes by Train: TGV and local trains serve Antibes' little station. Trains go to **Cannes** (2/hour, 15 minutes), **Nice** (2/hour, 15–30 minutes, €4), **Grasse** (1/hour, 40 minutes), **Villefranche-sur-Mer** (2/hour, 40 minutes), **Monaco** (2/hour, 45–60 minutes), and **Marseille** (16/day, 2.5 hours).

By Bus: Handy bus #200 ties everything together, but runs at a snail's pace when traffic is bad (Mon–Sat 4/hour, Sun 2–3/hour, any ride costs €1). This bus goes west to **Cannes** (35 minutes); and east to near **Biot** village (15 minutes—bus #10 is better, described on page 404), **Cagnes-sur-Mer** (and its Renoir Museum, 25 minutes), and **Nice** (1–1.5 hours). Bus #250 links to **Nice Airport** (2/hour, 40 minutes).

Cannes

Cannes (pronounced "can"), famous for its film festival (May 11–22 in 2011), is the sister city of Beverly Hills. That says it all. When I asked the TI for a list of museums and sights, they just smiled. Cannes—with big, exclusive hotels lining mostly private stretches of perfect, sandy beach—is for strolling, shopping, dreaming of meeting a movie star, and lounging on the seafront. Cannes has little that's unique to offer the traveler...except a mostly off-limits film festival and quick access to two undeveloped islands. You can buy an ice-cream cone at the train station and see everything before you've had your last lick. Money is what Cannes has always been about—wealthy people come here to make the scene, so there's always enough *scandale* to go around. The king of Saudi Arabia purchased a serious slice of waterfront just east of town and built his compound with no regard to local zoning regulations. Money talks on the Riviera...and always has.

Orientation to Cannes

Don't sleep or drive in Cannes. Day-trip in by train or bus. It's a breeze, as trains and buses run frequently along the Riviera, and they all stop in Cannes (train is faster, bus is cheaper; for details, see "Cannes Connections" on page 413). Buses arrive next to the train station. If you must drive, store your car at the parking garage next to the train station.

Turn left out of the train station (baggage storage available 8:30–20:30), find the busy **TI,** and pick up the nifty little city map (Mon–Sat 9:00–13:00 & 14:00–18:00, closed Sun, tel. 04 93 99 19 77, www.cannes.fr). On Sundays, when the train station TI is closed, drop by the glamorously quiet main TI, in the film festival building at 1 boulevard de la Croisette (daily 9:00–19:00).

Self-Guided Walk

Do the Cannes Cancan

This self-guided walking tour will take you to Cannes' sights in a level, one-hour walk at a movie-star pace. Well-kept WCs are available in the lobbies of any large hotel you pass.

• *From the train station TI, cross the street and walk for five unimpressive minutes down rue des Serbes to the beachfront. Cross the busy boulevard de la Croisette and make your way past snack stands to the sea. Find the round lookout and get familiar with...*

The Lay of the Land: Cannes feels different from its neighbors to the east. You won't find the distinctive pastel oranges and pinks of Old Nice and Villefranche-sur-Mer. Cannes was never part of Italy—and through its architecture and cuisine, it shows.

Face the water. The land jutting into the sea on your left is actually two islands, St. Honorat and Ste. Marguerite. **St. Honorat** has been the property of monks for over 500 years; today its abbey, vineyards, trails, and gardens can be visited by peace-seeking travelers. **Ste. Marguerite,** which you also can visit, is famous for the stone prison that housed the 17th-century Man in the Iron Mask (whose true identity remains unknown).

Now look to your right. Those striking mountains sweeping down to the sea are the Massif de l'Esterel. Their red-rock outcrops oversee spectacular car and train routes (see page 281). Closer in, the hill with the medieval tower caps Cannes' old town (Le Suquet). This hilltop offers grand views and pretty lanes, but little else. Below the old town, the port welcomes yachts of all sizes... provided they're big.

Face inland. On the left, find the modern, rust-colored building that's home to the famous film festival (we'll visit there soon). Back the other way, gaze up the boulevard. That classy building with twin black-domed roofs is Hôtel Carlton, our eventual target and as far as we'll go together in that direction.

• *Continue with the sea on your right and stroll the...*

Promenade (La Croisette): You're walking along boulevard de la Croisette—Cannes' famed two-mile-long promenade. First popular with kings who wintered here after Napoleon fell, the elite parade was later joined by British aristocracy. Today, boulevard de la Croisette is fronted by some of the most expensive apartments and hotels in Europe. If it's lunchtime, you might try one of the beach cafés—Brad Pitt  did. **Plage le Goéland's** café has fair-enough prices and appealing decor (€13 mussels, €15 roasted chicken, daily, closest private beach to the Film Festival Hall, tel. 04 93 38 22 05).

• *Stop when you get to...*

Hôtel Carlton: This is the most famous address on boulevard de la Croisette (allow €1,200–5,800 per night). Face the beach. The iconic Cannes experience is to slip out of your luxury hotel (preferably this one), into a robe (ideally, monogrammed with your initials), and onto the beach—or, better yet, onto the pier (this avoids getting irritating sand on your carefully oiled skin). While you may not be doing the "fancy hotel and monogrammed robe" ritual on this Cannes excursion, you can—for about €18—rent a chair and umbrella and pretend you're tanning for a red-carpet

Handy Cannes and St-Tropez Phrases

Where is a movie star?	*Où est une vedette?*
I am a movie star.	*Je suis une vedette.*
I am rich and single.	*Je suis riche et célibataire.*
Are you rich and single?	*Etes-vous riche et célibataire?*
Are those real?	*Ils sont des vrais?*
How long is your yacht?	*Quelle est la longeur de votre yacht?*
How much did that cost?	*Combien coûtait-il?*
You can always dream...	*On peut toujours rêver...*

premiere. Cannes does have a few token public beaches, but most

beaches are private and run by hotels like the Carlton. You could save money by sunning among the common folk, but the real Cannes way to flee the rabble and paparazzi is to rent a spot on a private beach (best to reserve ahead in July–Aug).

Cross over and wander into the hotel—you're welcome to browse (except during the festival). Ask for a hotel brochure, verify room rates, check for availability. Can all these people really afford this? Imagine the scene here during the film festival (see anyone famous?). A surprisingly affordable café (considering the cost of a room) lies just beyond.

• *You can continue your stroll down La Croisette, but I'm doubling back to the dull orange building that is Cannes'...*

Film Festival Hall: Cannes' film festival (Festival de Cannes), staged since 1939, completes the "Big Three" of Riviera events

(with Monaco's Grand Prix and Nice's Carnival). The hall where the festival takes place—a busy-but-nondescript convention center—sits like a plump movie star on the beach. You'll recognize the formal grand entryway—but the red carpet won't be draped for your visit. Find the famous (Hollywood-style) handprints in the sidewalk all around. To get inside during the festival, you have to be a star (or a photographer—some 3,000 paparazzi attend the gala event, and most bring their own ladders to get above the crowds). Though off-limits to us, the festival is all that matters around here—and worth a day trip if you're here while it's on. The town buzzes with mega-star energy, press passes, and revealing dresses. Locals claim that it's the world's third-biggest media event, after the Olympics and the World Cup (soccer). The festival prize is the Palme d'Or (like the Oscar for Best Picture). The French press can't cover the event enough, and the average Jean in France follows it as Joe would the World Series in the States. In 2008, the French surprised everyone by winning the prize for the first time in 21 years, for the unhyped, realistic drama *Entre les Murs (The Class*, about a teacher's struggles in a Paris middle school). The Thai film *Uncle Boonmee Who Can Recall His Past Lives* took the prize in 2010.

• *Around the other side of the festival hall is the port (Gare Maritime).*

The Port and Old Town (Le Suquet): The big-boy yachts line up closest to the Film Festival Hall. After seeing this yacht frenzy, everything else looks like a dinghy. Boat service to St-Tropez and the nearby islands of St. Honorat and Ste. Marguerite depart from the far side of the port (at quai Laubeuf; see "Sights in Cannes," below, for boat info).

Cannes' oldest neighborhood, Le Suquet, crowns the hill past the port. Locals refer to it as their Montmartre. It's artsy and charming, but it's a steep 15-minute walk above the port, with little of interest except the panoramic views from its ancient church, Notre-Dame-de-l'Espérance (Our Lady of Hope).

• *To find the views from Le Suquet, walk past the bus station at the northwest corner of the port and find your way up cobbled rue Saint-Antoine (next to the Café St. Antoine). Turn left on place du Suquet, and then follow signs to* Traverse de la Tour *for the final leg.*

Cue music. Roll end credits. Our film is over. For further exploration, look for Cannes' "underbelly" between Le Suquet and the train station—narrow lanes with inexpensive cafés and shops that regular folks can afford.

Sights in Cannes

Shopping—Cannes is made for window-shopping (the best streets are between the station and the waterfront). For the trendiest boutiques, stroll down handsome rue d'Antibes (it parallels the sea about three blocks inland). Rue Meynadier anchors a pedestrian zone with more affordable shops closer to the port. To bring home a real surprise, consider cosmetic surgery. Cannes is well-known as *the* place on the Riviera to have your face (or other parts) realigned.

Excursions to St. Honorat and Ste. Marguerite Islands—Boats ferry tourists 15 minutes to these twin islands just off

Cannes' shore (€12 round-trip, daily 9:00–18:00, 1–2/hour, www .trans-cote-azur.com, no ferry runs between two islands). The islands offer a refreshing change from the frenetic mainland, with almost no development, good swimming, and peaceful walking paths. On Ste. Marguerite you can visit the castle and cell where the mysterious Man in the Iron Mask was imprisoned (good little museum with decent English explanations featuring cargo from a sunken Roman vessel). On St. Honorat you can hike seafront trails and visit the abbey where monks still live and pray.

Yachters' Itinerary—If you're visiting Cannes on your private yacht, here's a suggested itinerary:

1. Take in the Festival de Cannes and the accompanying social scene. Organize an evening party on your boat.
2. Motor over to Monte Carlo for the Grand Prix, scheduled—conveniently for yachters—just after the film festival.
3. Drop by Porto Chervo on Sardinia, one of the few places in the world where your yacht is "just average."
4. Head west to Ibiza and Marbella in Spain, where your friends are moored for the big party scene.

Eating in Cannes

For a tasty, easy lunch in Cannes, consider **Fournil St. Nicholas.** You'll get mouthwatering quiche and sandwiches and exquisite salads at affordable prices (leaving the train station, turn right and walk a few blocks to 5 rue Venizelos, tel. 04 93 38 81 12).

Cannes Connections

TGV and local trains serve Cannes' station. Buses stop next to the train station.

    From Cannes by Train to: Antibes (2/hour, 15 minutes), **Nice** (2/hour, 30–40 minutes, €6), **Grasse** (roughly 1/hour, 30 minutes).

    By Bus: Bus #200 heads east from Cannes along the Riviera (Mon–Sat 4/hour, Sun 2–3/hour, €1 for any destination), stopping at **Antibes** (35 minutes), and **Nice** (1.5–1.75 hours). Trip duration depends on traffic. Bus #210 is an express on the freeway to **Nice Airport** (2/hour, 30 minutes).

By Boat: Trans Côte d'Azur runs boat excursions from Cannes to **St-Tropez** (€42 round-trip, 75 minutes each way; July–mid-Sept daily 2/day; June and late Sept 1/day Tue, Thu, and Sat–Sun only; no service Oct–May; tel. 04 92 98 71 30, fax 04 92 00 42 31, www .trans-cote-azur.com). This boat trip is popular—book a few days ahead from June to September.

St-Tropez

St-Tropez is a busy, charming, and traffic-free port town smoth-ered with fashion boutiques, elegant restaurants, and luxury boats. If you came here for history or quaintness, you caught the wrong yacht. But if you have more money than you know what to do with, you're home. There are 5,700 year-round residents... and more than 100,000 visitors daily in the summer. Come in the winter if you can.

As with many seaside villages in southern France, the pas-tel beauty of St-Tropez was first discovered by artists. Paul Signac introduced several of his friends to St-Tropez in the late 1800s, giving the village its first notoriety. But it wasn't until Brigitte Bardot made the scene here in the 1956 film *...And God Created Woman* that St-Tropez became synonymous with Riviera glamour. Since then, it's the first place that comes to mind when people think of the jet  set luxuriating on Mediterranean beaches. For many, the French Riviera begins here and runs east to Menton, on the Italian border.

The village itself is the attraction, as the nearest big beach is miles away. Wander the harborfront, where fancy yachts moor stern-in, their carefully coiffed captains and first mates enjoying *pu-pus* for happy hour—they're seeing and being seen. Take time to stroll the back streets while nibbling a chocolate-and-Grand Marnier crêpe.

Orientation to St-Tropez

St-Tropez lies between its famous port and the hilltop Citadelle (with great views). The network of lanes between the port and Citadelle are strollable in a Carmel-by-the-Sea sort of way.

Tourist Information

The TI is starboard on the port (to you landlubbers, that's to the right as you face the sea), where quai Suffren and quai Jean Jaurès meet (daily April–Oct 9:30–12:30 & 14:00–19:00, July–Aug until 20:00, Nov–March until 18:00, tel. 08 92 68 48 28, www.ot-saint -tropez.com). Pick up their good, free walking-tour in English (usually inserted into a larger tourist brochure), ask about events in town, and get maps and bus information if you plan to hike along the coast.

Arrival in St-Tropez

For bus and boat details, see "St-Tropez Connections," at the end of this chapter.

By Bus: Buses leave you a few minutes' walk to the port, near the parking lot—Parking du Vieux Port—on avenue Général de Gaulle.

By Boat: Boats from St. Raphael deposit you by the Parking du Vieux Port, a five-minute walk to the port.

By Car: Prepare for traffic in any season—worse on weekends (forget driving on Sunday afternoons), always ugly during summer, and downright impossible between St-Tropez and St. Maxime on weekends. You can avoid this bottleneck by taking the autoroute to Le Luc, and following the windy D-558 to St-Tropez from here (via La Garde-Freinet and Port Grimaud).

The last few miles to St-Tropez are along a too-long, two-lane road with one way in, one way out, and too many people going exactly where you're going. There are two main parking lots (both about €2.50/hour): Parking des Lices (near all recommended hotels) and Parking du Vieux Port (best for day-trippers).

Self-Guided Walk

Welcome to St-Tropez

This quick, scenic walk is best done with the TI's walking-tour brochure.

• *Begin at the round tower (Bureau du Port) at the port's vessel entry, by the Parking du Vieux Port.*

Climb the steps for a fine **view.** Check out the massive crane—it's used to pull yachts that are bigger than my house out of the water for off-season maintenance. Moorage fees for the bigger yachts run €2,000 per day.

Walk around the port; notice the busy deckhands (hustling before their captains arrive) and the artists competing for room to showcase their work. Saunter around to the opposite corner of the port, and work your way to the TI.

The red-tabled café **(Le Sénéquier)** by the TI is one of the

ST-TROPEZ

St-Tropez

MEDITERRANEAN

JETTY

QUAI D'ORVES   MOLE REVEILLE

P PARKING
-- TRAILS
R BEACH
V. VIEW

ROUND TOWER

PORT

NOUVEAU PORT

MUSEUM OF THE ANNONCIADE

PLACE GRAMMONT

Q. PERI

AVE 11 NOV.

Post

RUE ALLARD

R. CHARBONS

BUS STN.

WC

DE GAULLE

RUE TISSERANDS

WC

AVE. GEN.   GEN. LECLERC

BLVD L. BLANC

QUARANTA

AVE. P. ROUSSEL

TO PORT GRIMAUD, STE. MAXIME + NICE

❶ Hôtel la Ponche
❷ Hôtel les Palmiers
❸ Hôtel Lou Cagnard
❹ Hôtel le Colombier
❺ Hôtel Sube (Bar)
❻ Le Café & Café des Arts
❼ La Table du Marché Rest.
❽ L'Auberge des Maures Rest.
❾ Boats to St. Raphael

town's most venerated, and has long attracted celebrities, including Jean-Paul Sartre. High-end cafés and restaurants line the port from here to the jetty—it doesn't seem to matter that you can't see the sea for the big yachts. See if you recognize anyone famous.

Find bulky **Tour de Portalet** at the port's end with views across the bay—to St. Maxime and out to sea. A plaque honors the American, British, and French troops that liberated Provence on August 15, 1944.

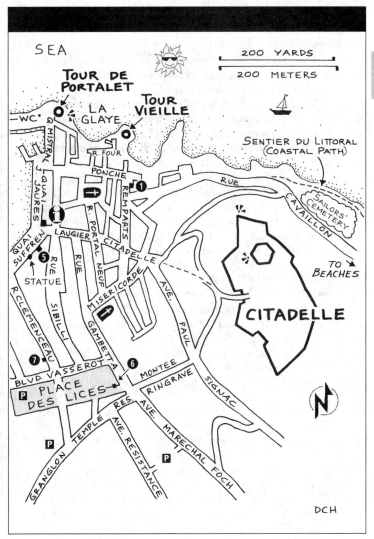

Climb the jetty for great views over St-Tropez's port, then wander past Tour Vieille to a walking path that leads around the town to small beaches and swimming opportunities. Notice how clear the water is, and how the homes seem at one with the sea. From here you can continue along the shore, or walk up to the Citadelle for more views (see below). The small lanes below the Citadelle are St-Tropez's most appealing. Work your way to the big **place des Lices** (good cafés) and see if anyone is playing *pétanque*.

Sights in St-Tropez

In the Village

Window-shopping, people-watching, tan maintenance, and savoring slow meals fill people's days, weeks, and, in some cases, lives. Here, one dresses up, sizes up one another's yachts, and trolls for a partner. While the only models you'll see are in the shop windows, Brigitte Bardot—who turns 77 in 2011—still hangs out on a bench in front of the TI signing autographs (Thu 15:00–17:30).

Museum of the Annonciade (Musée de l'Annonciade)— Though generally ignored, this museum houses an enchanting collection of works from the Post-Impressionist and Fauvist artists who decorated St-Tropez before Brigitte. Almost all canvases feature St-Tropez sights and landscapes. You'll see colorful paintings by Paul Signac, Henri Matisse, Georges Braque, Pierre Bonnard, Maurice de Vlaminck, and more. Gaze out the windows and notice how the port has changed since they were here (€5, Wed–Mon 10:00–12:00 & 14:00–18:00, closed Tue and in Nov, place Grammont, tel. 04 94 17 84 10).

La Citadelle—This old fortress offers peacocks, a tour through its history (some English information posted—pick up an English brochure), occasional special exhibits (inquire at TI), and views over St-Tropez from its high walls. Good views are free from just outside its walls (€2, €4 with special exhibits, daily June–Sept 10:00–18:00, Oct–May 10:00–12:00 & 13:00–17:30, closed in Nov, longer hours and more expensive during special exhibits, tel. 04 94 97 59 43).

Coastal Hike—The scenic Sentier du Littoral path, originally patrolled by customs agents, runs past the Citadelle for 12 miles along the coast and is marked with yellow dashes on the pavement, walls, and trees. Leave St-Tropez along the road below the Citadelle, pass the Sailors' Cemetery, and you'll join the path before long. If you're really into this, take the 20-minute bus *(la navette)* from place des Lices in St-Tropez to the Capon/Pinet stop and walk three hours back to St-Tropez (bus only runs 2/day, taxi also works, get details at TI).

Boat Excursions—Several companies offer mildly interesting tours of the bay (paralleling the Sentier du Littoral described above). Le Brigantin has reliable outings in comfortable wooden vessels with personalized English commentary. You'll learn a smidgen about St-Tropez's history and a lot about villas of the rich and famous. Conrad Hilton and John Grisham both have little bungalows, and you'll sail right past Brigitte Bardot's surprisingly modest-looking home. Redhead Victoria (from Britain) staffs the information desk on the quai Suffren and can explain the trip (€10, kids age 5–10-€5, 4/day, tel. 04 94 54 40 61).

Boules—The vast *pétanque (boules)* court on place des Lices is worth your attention. Have a drink at the recommended Le Café and take in the action. Study up on the sport (see page 208) and root for your hero.

Near St-Tropez

Port Grimaud—Although more modern than St-Tropez, Port Grimaud (located a few miles toward St. Maxime) is no less attractive or upscale. This "Venice of Provence" was reclaimed from a murky lagoon about 40 years ago, and is now lined with four miles of canals, lovely homes, and moorage for thousands of yachts. It's a fascinating look at what clever minds can produce from a swamp. Park at the lot across from the town entry (TI next to the parking lot, tel. 04 94 56 02 01), and cross the barrier and bridge into a beautiful world of privilege. Climb the church bell tower for a good panorama.

Sleeping in St-Tropez

(€1 = about $1.25, country code: 33)

Though everything seems pricey in this golden town, I've uncovered a few jewels. Sleep only in the town center, as traffic makes coming and going a royal headache. High season in St-Tropez runs from June through September, and weekends are busy year-round.

$$$ Hôtel la Ponche** offers a warm welcome and the most central, luxurious beds I could find (Db-€250–450, Db with top-floor deck and sea view-€490–680, breakfast-€20, Wi-Fi, parking-€22, near the sea, several blocks behind the TI at 3 rue des Remparts, tel. 04 94 97 02 53, fax 04 94 97 78 61, www.laponche .com, hotel@laponche.com).

$$$ Hôtel les Palmiers** is a relaxed place with a lush garden, a bar/lounge, and good rooms at normal three-star rates. It's on place des Lices, so parking is easy (standard Db-€92–125, bigger Db-€120–170, air-con, off place des Lices at 26 boulevard Vasserot, tel. 04 94 97 01 61, www.hotel-les-palmiers.com, info @hotel-les-palmiers.com).

$$$ Hôtel Lou Cagnard** looks average from the outside. But enter the courtyard garden and you'll find a pretty, well-managed, and shockingly reasonable hotel (Ds-€72, bigger Db-€95–145, higher prices are for garden-side and larger rooms, one-week minimum June–Sept, air-con, free parking, follow signs to *Parking des Lices* and you'll pass the hotel, 18 avenue Paul Roussel, tel. 04 94 97 04 24, fax 04 94 97 09 44, www.hotel-lou-cagnard.com).

$$ Hôtel le Colombier, little and adorable, is on a quiet street. Its 11 soft and comfortable rooms enclose a small, sweet garden-patio. This is a terrific value (Ds-€77, Db-€98, bigger Db with air-con-€132–160, Tb/Qb-€175–205, rates include easy parking nearby, follow *Parking des Lices* signs and look for hotel signs on left, impasse des Conquêtes, tel. 04 94 97 05 31, fax 04 94 97 32 57).

Eating in St-Tropez

There are several grocery stores in the old city. The **Casino market** is a block off the port, up rue V. Laugier.

Start or end your evening with St-Tropez's best port-view seats on the small deck at **Hôtel Sube's** bar on quai Suffren, near the TI (drinks only, fine interior).

Dining on place des Lices is a great opportunity to watch *pétanque* matches, with several appealing eateries to choose from. **Le Café** has long been the place to park your beret on this square, and serves surprisingly good cuisine. Stroll inside past the soft chairs and old wooden floor, and find one of the best zinc counters in France, complete with an atmospheric bar (daily, €20–30 *menus*, €18 *plats*, tel. 04 94 97 44 69). **Café des Arts,** at the end of the square, has good ambience inside and out, and serves pizza, salads, and *plats* for €10–15 (daily, tel. 04 94 97 02 25).

Christophe Leroy's **La Table du Marché,** just off place des Lices, is an inviting pastry shop/deli/restaurant. Delectable *menus* from €30 feature gourmet pasta, seafood, and meat dishes—and include a glass of wine (daily, 38 rue Georges Clemenceau, tel. 04 94 97 85 20).

Elsewhere in St-Tropez, **L'Auberge des Maures** has a rich, lively decor, indoor and outdoor tables, and a welcoming staff. It's a good place to go for quality Provençal cuisine (€50 *menu*, daily, 4 rue du Docteur Boutin, tel. 04 94 97 01 50).

St-Tropez Connections

From St-Tropez by Public Transportation: With no trains to St-Tropez, buses and boats are your only options. **Buses** serve St-Tropez from St-Raphaël's train station to the east (almost hourly, 1.3 hours) and from Toulon's train station to the west (7/day, 2 hours). **Boats** make the one-hour trip from St-Raphaël to St-Tropez twice daily (€15 one-way, €30 round-trip, departs St-Raphaël at 9:30 and 14:30, departs St-Tropez at 10:30 and 17:15, tel. 04 94 95 17 46, www.bateauxsaintraphael.com, or call the TI). For boats connecting St-Tropez with Nice, see page 294; with Cannes, page 414.

INLAND RIVIERA

St-Paul-de-Vence • Vence •
Grasse • Grand Canyon du Verdon

For a verdant, rocky, fresh escape from the beaches, head inland and upward. Some of France's most perfectly perched hill towns and splendid scenery hang overlooked in this region that's more famous for beaches and bikinis. A short car or bus ride away from the Mediterranean reaps big rewards: lush forests, deep canyons, and swirling hilltop villages. A longer drive (though still doable as a day trip) brings you to Europe's greatest canyon, the Grand Canyon du Verdon.

Getting Around the Inland Riviera

By Car: Driving is the most flexible way to tour this area (particularly in the off-season)—though summer and weekend traffic and parking challenges will test your patience. A one-day car rental is worth considering (see the "Helpful Hints" sections in the Nice and Antibes chapters). I describe the best route later.

By Bus: Buses get you to many of the places in this chapter. Vence, St-Paul-de-Vence, and Grasse are well-served by bus from Nice about every 40 minutes, and Grasse has train service from Nice, Antibes, and Cannes (see page 281). A few buses to Tourrettes-sur-Loup, Le Bar-sur-Loup, and Grasse leave from Vence daily except Sunday (7/day, 15 minutes to Tourrettes-sur-Loup, 35 minutes to Le Bar-sur-Loup; 4/day to Grasse, 50 minutes, tel. 04 93 42 40 79). Buses do not serve the Gorges du Loup, the village of Gourdon, or the Gorges du Verdon.

With a Local Guide: Informative and enjoyable guides **Sylvie Di Cristo** and **Sofia Villavicencio** both live in inland villages and can expertly show you around their backyards. See page 281 for contact information.

Self-Guided Driving Tour

The Inland Riviera:
From St-Paul-de-Vence to Grasse

This splendid loop drive connects St-Paul-de-Vence, Vence, Tourrettes-sur-Loup, and Grasse (all described later, in that order). It's best done by car as a day trip from the Nice/Antibes area (allow all day), though it could be done en route to the Gorges du Verdon (the most impressive part of the Grand Canyon du Verdon area, described later). Some of the villages can be linked by bus, but a car is essential to do the loop as described. Each stop is only minutes away from the next by car or bus, but allow 45 minutes to drive from Nice or Antibes to the first stop, St-Paul-de-Vence. Start early if you want to see St-Paul-de-Vence without the mobs (have breakfast at St-Paul-de-Vence's Café de la Place). If you won't be visiting the Gorges du Verdon (or if you care more about nature than art), take the exceptionally beautiful long way around from Vence to Gourdon (described below, under "Alternate Route"), and skip Tourrettes-sur-Loup and the Gorges du Loup (you won't miss them, trust *moi*). All of the bolded stops below are explained in detail later in this chapter.

The Drive Begins

Let's get started. From Nice, leave along the promenade des Anglais and head toward Cannes and Antibes. Follow *Grasse* signs, then *Vence* and *St-Paul-de-Vence* signs. On this route, you'll pass the tempting Renoir Museum in Cagnes-sur-Mer (described on page 403). Continue following *St-Paul-de-Vence* signs into the village, and park as close to the center as you can. After sampling **St-Paul-de-Vence,** visit the **Fondation Maeght** just above the town (park at the museum for free, or walk 20 minutes up from St-Paul-de-Vence, following blue signs).

After completing your course in contemporary art, find artsy **Vence,** a few miles away, with many good lunch options. From Vence visit Matisse's famous **Chapel of the Rosary** (limited opening hours—see page 427; best views of Vence are a mile beyond the chapel, where there's a turnaround).

Next, head for slippery-sloped **Tourrettes-sur-Loup** (poorly signed from Vence, follow D-2210)—or skip Tourrettes-sur-Loup and follow the "Alternate Route" described on page 424. From Tourrettes-sur-Loup, follow signs for *Pont-du-Loup* (great views of Tourrettes-sur-Loup a mile after leaving). Before long you'll see views of **Le Bar-sur-Loup,** clinging to its hillside in the distance. When you arrive at the junction of the roads to Gourdon and Le Bar-sur-Loup, look way up to your destination—the tiny soaring village of Gourdon. Sugar addicts can detour quickly down

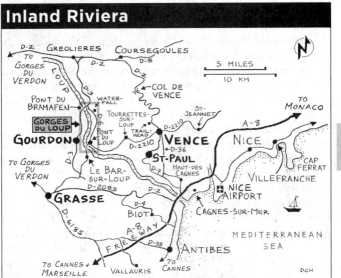

Inland Riviera

to **Pont-du-Loup** and visit the small candied-fruit factory of **Confiseries Florian.** Follow *Gourdon* and *Gorges du Loup* signs to the right and climb into the teeth of a rocky canyon, the **Gorges du Loup.** It's a mostly second-gear road that winds between severe rock faces above a surging stream. (Buses cannot enter the Gorges du Loup, so non-drivers must continue on directly to Grasse.) Several miles into the gorge, you can visit the Cascades du Saut du Loup waterfall, which may have you thinking you've made a wrong turn into Hawaii (€1, easy walk down).

The drive passes all too quickly to where the road hooks back, crossing Pont du Bramafen and up toward Gourdon. Climb above the canyon you just drove through and watch the world below miniaturize. At the top, the village of **Gourdon,** known as the "Eagle's Nest" (2,400 feet), waits for tourists with shops, good lunch options, and grand panoramas.

From Gourdon, slide downhill—passing stone quarries—

toward **Grasse.** Enjoy sensational views down to (literally) over-looked Le Bar-sur-Loup. Follow signs to *Grasse,* then *Centre-Ville,* and park at the first underground lot you come to (by the Grasse bus station). After mastering your scent in Grasse—the capital of perfume—return to your Riviera home base (allow 45 minutes to

424 Rick Steves' Provence & the French Riviera

Nice or 30 minutes to Antibes via Cannes and the autoroute), or continue to the Gorges du Verdon.

Alternate Route: If you won't be visiting the Gorges du Verdon, consider this delicious detour, which takes you a bit farther inland (ideal if staying in Vence): Follow the route described above until Vence and complete your sightseeing there, then find D-2 just before the bridge that leads to St-Jeannet, and follow signs for *Col de Vence* (the Vence pass). This road switches up and up beyond the tree line into a stones-only landscape to the pass in about 15 minutes. Great views over Vence begin a few minutes after leaving the town. (For a 45-minute uphill hike to great views over Vence and the Riviera, pass the Château St-Martin, drive another kilometer, then look for the brown trailhead sign to *Baous des Blancs*.) From the pass (3,000 feet), continue on D-2, trading rocky slabs for lush forests, pastures, and vast canyons. You'll pass the postcard-perfect village of Coursegoules (worth a photo but not a detour), then follow signs to *Gréolières*. At a roundabout just before Gréolières you'll find D-3, which leads to Nice, Gorges du Loup, and Gourdon. But first, continue a few minutes past Gréolières to the pullout barely above the village, with stirring views over the village and its ruined castle. Consider a coffee break in Gréolières before backtracking to the roundabout, following signs to *Gourdon*. After visiting Gourdon, you can continue to Grasse, or return to Nice or Antibes.

St-Paul-de-Vence

The most famous of Riviera hill towns is also the most-visited village in France. And it feels that way—like an overrun and over-restored artist-shopping-mall.  Its attraction is understandable, as every cobble and flower seems *just-so*, and the setting is memorable. Avoid visiting between 11:00 and 18:00, particularly on weekends. Arriving early makes it easier to park near the village (cars are not allowed inside St-Paul). Consider skipping breakfast at your hotel and instead eating at the local hangout, **Café de la Place,** where you can watch as waves of tourists crash into town.

The **TI,** just through the gate into the old city on rue Grande, has maps with minimal explanations of key buildings (daily 10:00–18:00, tel. 04 93 32 86 95, www.saint-pauldevence.com). If the traffic-free lane leading to the old city is jammed, take the road that veers up and left just after Café de la Place, and enter the town through its side door. Meander deep into St-Paul-de-Vence's quieter streets to find panoramic views. See if you can locate the hill town of Vence at the foot of an impressive mountain.

If you come late in the day and stay for dinner (smart plan, particularly if sleeping in Vence), splurge for a memorable dinner at **Le Tilleul.** Book ahead, as you'll be competing with locals for tables on the lovely terrace or in the cozy interior (à la carte only, allow €50/person for three courses, open daily, tel. 04 93 32 80 36).

Fondation Maeght

This inviting, pricey, and far-out private museum is situated a steep walk or short drive above St-Paul-de-Vence. Fondation Maeght (fohn-dah-shown mahg) offers an excellent introduction to modern Mediterranean art by gathering many of the Riviera's most famous artists under one roof. The founder, Aimé Maeght, long envisioned the perfect exhibition space for the artists he supported and befriended as an art dealer. He purchased this arid hilltop, planted more than 35,000 plants, and hired an architect (José Luis Sert) with the same vision.

A sweeping lawn laced with amusing sculptures and bending pine trees greets visitors. On the right, a chapel designed by Georges

Braque—in memory of the Maeghts' young son, who died of leukemia—features a moving purple stained-glass work over the altar. The unusual museum building is purposefully low-profile, to let its world-class modern-art collection take center stage. Works by Fernand Léger, Joan Miró, Alexander Calder, Georges Braque, and Marc Chagall are thoughtfully arranged in well-lit rooms. The backyard of the museum has views, a Gaudí-esque sculpture labyrinth by Miró, and a courtyard filled with the wispy works of Alberto Giacometti. The only permanent collection in the museum consists of the sculptures, though the museum tries to keep a good selection of paintings by the famous artists here year-round. For a review of modern art, see "The Riviera's Art Scene" on page 282. There's also a great gift shop and cafeteria.

Cost and Hours: €14, €5 to take photos, daily July–Sept 10:00–19:00, Oct–June 10:00–18:00, tel. 04 93 32 81 63, www.fondation-maeght.com.

Getting There: The museum is a steep uphill-but-doable 20-minute walk from St-Paul-de-Vence and the bus stop. Blue signs indicate the way (parking is usually available at the top).

Vence

Vence is a well-discovered yet appealing town set high above the Riviera. While growth has sprawled beyond Vence's old walls, and cars jam its roundabouts, the mountains are front and center and the breeze is fresh. Vence bubbles with workaday life and ample tourist activity in the day but is quiet at night, with few tourists and cooler temperatures than along the coast. Vence makes a handy base for travelers wanting the best of both worlds: a hill-town refuge near the sea. Some enjoy the Gorges du Verdon as a day trip from Vence (see the route described on page 437).

Orientation to Vence

Tourist Information

Vence's fully loaded and eager-to-help TI faces the main square at 8 place du Grand Jardin. They have bus schedules, brochures on the cathedral, and a city map with a well-devised self-guided walking tour (25 stops, incorporates informative wall plaques). They also publish a list of Vence art galleries with English descriptions of the collections. To properly engage you in French culture, the TI has information on French-language classes, and—even better— *pétanque* instructions with *boules* to rent for €3 per person (TI open July–Aug Mon–Sat 9:00–19:00, Sun 10:00–18:00; Sept–June Mon–Sat 9:00–18:00 but 10:00–17:00 in winter, Sun 10:00–17:00; tel. 04 93 58 06 38, www.ville-vence.fr).

Market day in the *cité historique* (old town) is on Tuesday and Friday mornings on place Clemenceau. There's a big all-day antiques market on place du Grand Jardin every Wednesday.

Arrival in Vence

By Bus: The bus stop (labeled l'Ara) is on a roundabout. It's a 10-minute walk to the town center along avenue Henri Isnard.

By Car: Follow signs to *cité historique,* and park where you can. A central pay lot is under place du Grand Jardin, across from the TI.

Sights in Vence

Explore the narrow lanes of the old town using the TI's worth-while self-guided tour map. Connect the picturesque streets, enjoy a drink on a quiet square, inspect an art gallery, and find the small 11th-century cathedral with its colorful Chagall mosaic of Moses (for background, see the Chagall Museum Tour chapter). If you're here later in the day, enjoy the *boules* action across from the TI (rent a set from the TI and join in).

Château de Villeneuve—This 17th-century mansion, adjoining an imposing 12th-century watchtower, bills itself as "one of the Riviera's high temples of modern art," with a rotating collection. Check with the TI to see what's playing in the temple (€5, Tue–Sun 10:00–12:30 & 14:00–18:00, closed Mon, tel. 04 93 58 15 78).

▲Chapel of the Rosary (Chapelle du Rosaire)—The chapel, a short drive or 20-minute walk from town, was designed by an

elderly and ailing Henri Matisse as thanks to the Dominican sister who had taken care of him (he was 81 when the chapel was completed—see the timeline of Matisse's life on page 300). The modest chapel is a simple collection of white walls laced with yellow, green, and blue stained-glass windows and charcoal black-on-white tile sketches. The sunlight filters through the glass and does a cheery dance across the sketches. While the chapel is the ultimate pilgrimage for serious Matisse fans, the experience may underwhelm others.

(If you've taken my self-guided tour of the Matisse Museum in Nice, you'll remember that he was the master of leaving things out.) Decide for yourself whether Matisse met the goal he set himself: "Creating a religious space in an enclosed area of reduced proportions and to give it, solely by the play of colors and lines, the dimension of infinity."

Cost and Hours: €3; Mon, Wed, and Sat 14:00–17:30; Tue and Thu 10:00–11:30 & 14:00–17:30, Sun only open for Mass at 10:00 followed by tour of chapel, closed Fri and mid-Nov–mid-Dec, 466 avenue Henri Matisse, tel. 04 93 58 03 26, http://pagesperso-orange.fr/maison .lacordaire.

Getting There: To reach the chapel from the Vence TI, turn right out of the TI and walk or drive down avenue Henri Isnard, then right on avenue Henri Matisse, following signs to *St-Jeannet* (allow 20 minutes).

Sleeping in Vence

Hôtel Miramar is a 10-minute walk above the old town. La Maison du Frêne and L'Auberge des Seigneurs are a short walk from the TI, next to the Château de Villeneuve; to reach them, turn right

Sleep Code

(€1 = about $1.25, country code: 33)
S = Single, **D** = Double/Twin, **T** = Triple, **Q** = Quad, **b** = bathroom,
s = shower only, * = French hotel rating (0–4 stars). Credit
cards are accepted and English is spoken unless otherwise
noted.

　　To help you sort easily through these listings, I've divided
the rooms into three categories based on the price for a
standard double room with bath:

　$$$　**Higher Priced**—Most rooms €100 or more.
　　$$　**Moderately Priced**—Most rooms between €70–100.
　　　$　**Lower Priced**—Most rooms €70 or less.

Prices can change without notice; verify the hotel's
current rates online or by email. For other updates, see www
.ricksteves.com/update.

out of the TI, then right again, then left. Maison Lacordaire is
next to Matisse's chapel, a 20-minute walk from the TI.

$$$ Hôtel Miramar*** is a laid-back, 18-room Mediterranean
villa perched on a ledge with grand panoramas. Friendly owner
Daniel welcomes you into this refuge, which he's filled with many
personal touches. The Old World rooms come in soothing colors,
with firm beds and worn furnishings. The pool and view ter-
race could make you late for dinner, or seduce you into skipping it
altogether—picnics are allowed (standard Db-€90–125, Db with
balcony-€120–135, Db with great view and balcony-€160, family
suite-€185, some rooms have air-con, most don't need it, bar, table
tennis, parking, turn left out of the TI and follow the brown signs to
167 avenue Bougearel, tel. 04 93 58 01 32, fax 04 93 58 20 22, www
.hotel-miramar-vence.com, contact@hotel-miramar-vence.com).

$$$ La Maison du Frêne is an art-packed B&B with four
sumptuous rooms located behind the TI. Energetic Thierry
combines his passion for contemporary art and hosting travelers
in his lovingly restored manor house (Db-€150–185, higher price
is for peak times, includes breakfast, air-con, Wi-Fi, 1 place du
Frêne, tel. 04 93 24 37 83, www.lamaisondufrene.com, contact@la
maisondufrene.com).

$$ L'Auberge des Seigneurs** is a shy little place just inside
the old town. Its six simple yet character-filled rooms—above a
cozy restaurant—have wood furnishings, red-tile floors, and ade-
quate bathrooms (spacious Sb-€65, Db-€85–100, place du Frêne,
tel. 04 93 58 04 24, fax 04 93 24 08 01, www.auberge-seigneurs
.com, sandrine.rodi@wanadoo.fr).

$$ Maison Lacordaire, adjacent to Matisse's Chapel of the Rosary, lets you sleep like a nun. This simple place has 24 rooms in two restored villas, with a sweet garden and view terrace. It's run by Dominican nuns, so be on your best behavior (Db-€43/person for required half-board, 466 avenue Henri Matisse, tel. 04 93 58 03 26, http://pagesperso-orange.fr/maison.lacordaire, dominicaines@ wanadoo.fr).

Near Vence

To melt into the Inland Riviera's quiet side, drive 15 minutes from Vence to the remarkably situated, no-tourist-in-sight hill town of St-Jeannet. Views are endless and everywhere. It's so quiet, it's hard to believe that the beach is only 10 miles away. But the best reason to visit St-Jeannet is to stay at **$$ The Frogs' House,** where Benôit and Corinne will eagerly welcome you to this region, which they are both mad about. This young couple offers a full menu of good rooms, fine meals, cooking lessons, hikes in the area, and day trips to popular destinations. If you don't have wheels, they'll happily pick you up at the train station or airport. The hotel is freshly renovated, so everything feels new. Rooms are small but sharp (Db-€74, Db with balcony-€94, includes breakfast, dinners-€25–35, tel. 04 93 58 98 05, mobile 06 28 06 80 28, www.thefrogshouse.com, info@thefrogshouse.com). There's a parking lot in the center of St-Jeannet, a few blocks from this small hotel.

Eating in Vence

Tempting outdoor eateries litter the old town; they all look good to me. Lights embedded in the old-town cobbles illuminate the way after dark.

On place Clemenceau: These two restaurants serve tasty Provençal cuisine a few doors apart on the charming place Clemenceau: **La Cassolette,** at #10, is an intimate place with reasonable prices and a romantic terrace across from the floodlit church (€28 *menus,* €14–17 *plats,* closed Thu, tel. 04 93 58 84 15). **Les Agapes,** at #4, offers limited outdoor seating, a lovely upstairs dining room, and a menu that stays fresh with each season (€24 and €30 *menus,* closed Sun–Mon, tel. 04 93 58 50 64).

At nearby **La Peyra,** enjoy a relaxed dinner salad or pasta dish outdoors to the sound of the town's main fountain (€15 "maxi salads" and *plats,* daily, 13 place du Peyra, tel. 04 93 58 67 63).

L'Auberge des Seigneurs feels more alpine than Mediterranean, and is good for a cooler day, when you can sit by the fire and watch your meat being cooked. The choices are limited and filling. Sandrine will help you decide (*menus* from €32, closed Sun–Mon; also recommended under "Sleeping in Vence," above).

Near Vence: For a very personal experience, reserve ahead for a meal with Benôit and Corinne at **The Frogs' House,** their small hotel in St-Jeannet. You'll dine in their grand kitchen and learn about local produce and recipes (€25–35 for dinner with wine and the works, see listing under "Sleeping in Vence," above). Or, drive to St-Paul-de-Vence and dine at **Le Tilleal** (described on page 425).

Hill Towns and Sights Between Vence and Grasse

The following sights are connected by the Inland Riviera self-guided driving tour on page 422.

Shortcut from Vence to the Gorges du Verdon—To save time and add scenery, skip the town of Grasse and take D-2 from Vence following Col de Vence (Vence pass), and climb above the tree line. Follow D-2 up and over, passing the photogenic villages of Coursegoules and Gréolières, and continue west following signs to *Thorenc, Valderoure,* and *Grasse,* to where the road eventually meets D-6085 (old N-85). From here, turn left, then shortly after follow signs to the right to *Draguignan* and *Gorges du Verdon,* and join the route described later, under "Le Grand Canyon du Verdon."

Tourrettes-sur-Loup—This picturesque town, hemmed in by forests, looks ready to skid down its abrupt hill. Tourrettes-sur-Loup is small, with no sprawl. Known as the *Cité des Violettes,* the village produces more violets than anywhere else in France, most of which get shipped off to end up in bottles that make you smell nice.

Park in the lot at the village center and stroll the lanes. You'll still find a smattering of arts and crafts, though much less than in the "Vence towns." Plunge deep to find good views, as well as **Tom's Ice Cream** (afternoons only, closed Mon) and a few places to eat. Wednesday is market day (on place de la Libération). Views of Tourrettes-sur-Loup await a minute away on the drive to Pont-du-Loup.

Confiseries Florian—The candied-fruit factory hides between trees down in Pont-du-Loup (though their big, bright sign is hard to miss). Ten-minute tours of their factory leave regularly, covering the candied-fruit process and explaining the use of flower petals (like violets and jasmine) in their products. Everything they make is fruit-filled—even their chocolate (with oranges). The tour ends with a tasting of the *confiture* in the dazzling gift shop (tours are free, request a tour with English commentary, daily 9:00–12:00 & 14:00–18:00, gift shop stays open during lunch, tel. 04 93 59 32 91, www.confiserieflorian.com).

Gorges du Loup—The Inland Riviera is crawling with spectacular canyons only miles from the sea. Slotted between Grasse and Vence, the Gorges du Loup is the easiest gorge to reach and works in well with a day trip from the Nice area. You can drive about five miles right up into the canyon (on D-6), passing waterfalls and sheer rock walls, then return on the gorge's rooftop (on D-3) to the "Eagle's Nest" village of Gourdon for magnificent vistas and a complete change of scenery.

Gourdon—This 2,400-foot-high, cliff-topping hamlet features grassy picnic areas, a short lineup of tourist shops, and a few good lunch options. The village's most famous building is its château, which is best enjoyed from the outside (infrequent, French-only tours of the interior). A well-marked trail (Chemin du Paradis) leads down the cliffs to Le Bar-sur-Loup (1 hour)—now *that's* steep. The far side of the village features fabulous vistas, a tiny Romanesque church, and two options for lunch with a view...

Eating in Gourdon: **La Taverne Provençale** boasts a popular spread of outdoor tables overlooking the grandeur (€10–12 omelets and pasta dishes, €18 *menu,* July–Aug daily lunch and dinner, Sept–June lunch only, place de l'Eglise, tel. 04 93 09 68

22). Just below is the most appropriately named restaurant in France, **Le Nid de l'Aigle** ("The Eagle's Nest"), which tempts travelers with fine cuisine and an equally remarkable setting with interior and exterior seating (€20 lunch *menu,* €35 dinner *menu;* July–mid-Sept daily lunch and dinner; mid-Sept–June Wed–Sun lunch only, Sat lunch and dinner, closed Mon–Tue; tel. 04 93 77 52 02).

Le Bar-sur-Loup—This town is the yin to St-Paul-de-Vence's yang: It has almost no tourist shops and little for you to do except wander the peaceful brick-lined lanes and enjoy the view. Park at the lot by the Hôtel de Ville and Syndicat d'Initiative (TI).

Grasse

Both the historic and contemporary capital of perfume, Grasse offers a contrast to the dolled-up hill towns above the Riviera. Though famous for its pricey product, Grasse's urban center is an unpolished, intriguing collection of walking lanes, peek-a-boo squares, and vertical staircases. The place feels in need of a facelift—yet also refreshingly real. Its historic alliance with Genoa explains the Italian-esque look of the old city. Still, the only good

Fragrant Grasse

Grasse has been at the center of the fragrance industry since the 1500s, when it was known for its scented leather gloves. The cultivation of aromatic plants around Grasse slowly evolved to produce ingredients for soaps and perfumes, and by the 1800s, Grasse was recognized as the center for perfume (thanks largely to its flower-friendly climate), making it a wealthy city.

It can take a ton of carefully picked petals (like jasmine)—that's about 10,000 flowers—to make about two pounds of essence. A damaged flower petal is bad news. Today, perfumes are made from as many as 500 different scents; most are imported to Grasse from countries around the world. The "blender" of these scents and the perfume mastermind is called the "nose" (who knows best). The five master "noses" who work here must study their profession longer than a doctor goes to med school (seven years). They've had to show that they had the gift before entering "nose school" (in Versailles), and they cannot drink alcohol, ever.

Skip the outlying perfumeries with French-only tours. Only three factories out of forty open their doors to visitors, and only one is worth visiting: Fragonard Perfume in Grasse.

reasons to visit Grasse are if you care about perfume, or if you're heading to or from the Gorges du Verdon.

Orientation to Grasse

Tourist Information

All sights in Grasse cluster near the main TI in the Palais du Congrès on cours Honoré Cresp, also referred to as place du Cours (July–Sept Mon–Sat 9:00–19:00, Sun 9:00–12:30 & 14:00–18:00; Oct–June Mon–Sat 9:00–12:30 & 14:00–18:00, closed Sun; tel. 04 93 36 66 66, www.grasse.fr, free cold water fountain). There's a branch TI (Grasse Espace Accueil) on place de la Foux near the bus station. At either TI, pick up an English map with a self-guided tour of the old city (handy information plaques). If heading to the Gorges du Verdon, get specifics here.

Arrival in Grasse

By Train: Fifteen trains a day connect Grasse with Nice (1.25 hours), Antibes (40 minutes), and Cannes (30 minutes). Buses #2, #3, and #4 take you from the train station to the center of town (4/hour, €1). Turn right out of the station and head to the stop on the road leading uphill (not the stop in front of the station). Ask the driver to let you off at the stop closest to *Parfumerie Fragonard;* for your return trip, go to the bus station *(gare routière)*. All buses leave from there.

By Bus: Buses run directly to Cannes in 40 minutes and to Nice in 1.25 hours. From the bus station on place de la Buanderie, it's a five-minute walk to the sights (walk one block up to boulevard du Jeu de Ballon, turn left, and take the pleasant stroll downhill to cours Honoré Cresp).

By Car: Grasse's size, hilly terrain, and inconsistent signage can confuse drivers. Those coming from Nice (via A-8), Antibes, and Cannes should follow signs to *Centre-Ville* and *Office du Tourisme* (follow *Peymeinade* signs if you lose *Centre-Ville* signs). Soon after passing the golden Fragonard perfume boutique, turn left into the Parking Honoré Cresp. This parking lot's *Sortie Parfumerie* leads you directly to the Fragonard perfume tour. Those arriving from Vence, Gourdon, and the Gorges du Verdon should follow signs to *Centre-Ville* until Hôtel le Napoleon. Make a hard left after the hotel, then a quick right, and park at the lot next to the *gare routière* (bus station). Then follow the walking directions from the bus station described above.

Sights in Grasse

▲**International Museum of Perfume (Musée International de la Parfumerie)**—This city museum is a magnificent tribute to perfume, providing a thorough examination of its history and production from ancient Greece to today. The museum is well-designed, with excellent English explanations, a good audioguide, and impressive multimedia exhibits that could keep a perfume fan busy for days. Start in the Sensorial Room, where you'll spend nine minutes getting mellow and preparing your senses for the visit. The three floors below teach you everything there is to know about perfume. Your visit ends with a cool display of perfume packages for every year since 1900 and a chance to sniff 32 key perfume ingredients (€3, includes audioguide; June–Sept daily 10:00–19:00, Sat until 21:00; Oct–May Wed–Mon 11:00–18:00, closed Tue; a block up from the main TI at 2 rue Jeu de Ballon, tel. 04 97 05 58 00, http://boutique.museesdegrasse.com).

The museum also offers a self-guided visit to their **gardens** near Grasse, featuring five acres of important plants and flowers used in perfume production (€5 combo-ticket includes museum entry, daily May–Sept 11:00–20:00, Oct–April 11:00–18:00, bus service available—schedules at museum).

Fragonard Perfume—This well-run, functioning factory, located dead-center in Grasse, provides frequent, fragrant, informative 20-minute tours and an interesting "museum" to explore while you wait. Pick up the English brochure describing what's in the museum cases, then drop down to where the tour begins. On your tour you'll learn that the difference between perfume, eau de toilette, and cologne is only a matter of perfume-percentages. You'll also learn how the product is made today, as well as how they used to do it (by pressing flowers in animal fat). The tour ends with a whiff in the elegant gift shop (daily 9:00–18:00 or 18:30, last tour at 17:00 or 18:00, just off cours Honoré Cresp at 20 boulevard Fragonard, tel. 04 93 36 44 65, www.fragonard.com).

The same company runs a two-room **museum** (Musée Provençal du Costume et du Bijou) displaying traditional dresses and jewelry (free, no English information, daily 10:00–13:00 & 14:00–18:00, a block above the *parfumerie* on the pedestrian street at 2 rue Jean Ossola). Upon leaving, you'll be given a card to be exchanged for a free gift at a shop next door.

Villa Jean-Honoré Fragonard—The home of the 18th-century Baroque painter of swirling big bodies (whose father started the smelly business) has a good collection of his paintings and repro-ductions (€3, excellent English handout; June–Sept daily 10:00–18:30; Oct–May Wed–Mon 10:00–12:30 & 14:00–18:30, closed Tue; turn left out of Fragonard Perfume and walk downhill to 23 boulevard Fragonard).

Old Grasse—Just above the Fragonard Perfume museum, rue Jean Ossola leads into the labyrinth of ancient streets that form an intriguing pedestrian area. You can follow the TI's minimalist self-guided tour with your map (takes an hour at a speedy pace) or, better, just wander and read the beige information plaques when you see them. To get a good taste of old Grasse, stroll up rue Jean Ossola (just above boulevard Fragonard), then turn right down rue Gazan to find the Romanesque cathedral opposite an unusual WWI monument (it's worth peering into the cathedral to see its tree-trunk-like columns and austere decor). Find the view terrace behind the cathedral. From here you can descend many steps to the Italian-esque place de l'Evêché (fun cafés) and work your way back up. Or skip the steps and double back to rue Jean Ossola, turn right, then make a left up bohemian rue de l'Oratoire and pop out onto my favorite square, place aux Aires (with more good eating options).

Le Grand Canyon du Verdon

Two hours north of Nice and three hours east of Avignon lies the Parc Naturel Régional du Verdon (a.k.a. Gorges du Verdon). This immense area of natural beauty is worth ▲▲▲...even to Arizonans.

For millions of years, the region currently known as Provence–Alpes–Côte d'Azur was covered by the sea. Over time, sediments and the remains of marine animals were deposited here, becoming thick layers of limestone as they were buried. Later, earth movements uplifted and erosion exposed the limestone, and the Verdon River—with help from Ice Age glaciers—carved out the gorges and its side canyons. At their deepest points, the gorges drop 2,200 feet to the river. At the bottom, the canyons can narrow to 26 feet across, while at the top, the canyon walls can spread as far as 4,700 feet apart.

The Verdon River is named for its stunning turquoise-green hue. The color comes from very fine particles of rock suspended in the water, pulverized by glaciers high at the river's source. The Verdon's unusual color is said to have inspired a religious cult among the dominant tribe of Ligurian Celts, who once ruled the region.

Planning Your Time

The Grand Canyon du Verdon, Europe's greatest canyon, offers a dilly of a detour between the Riviera and Provence (figure seven hours with modest canyon time between Nice and the Luberon or Aix-en-Provence; see my self-guided driving tour of the Inland Riviera on page 422). You can reach the canyon on a long round-trip drive from the Nice area if you leave early (easier if staying in Vence or Antibes). Some visitors prefer to stop and smell the canyon, overnighting en route (suggestions later in this chapter).

Here are some rough driving times: Riviera to Grasse—1 hour, Grasse to Balcon de la Mescla—1 hour, Balcon de la Mescla to Aiguines—1 hour, Aiguines to Moustiers-Ste-Marie—20 minutes, Moustiers-Ste-Marie to Manosque (en route to Provence)—1 hour.

Le Grand Canyon du Verdon

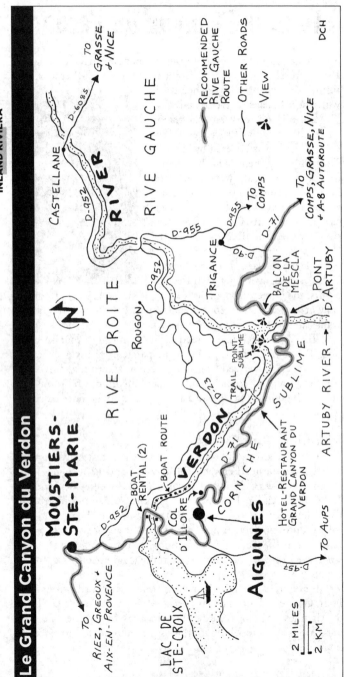

MOUSTIERS-STE-MARIE

TO RIEZ, GREOUX + AIX-EN-PROVENCE

D-952

BOAT RENTAL (2)

BOAT ROUTE

COL D'ILLOIRE

LAC DE STE-CROIX

TO AUPS

D-957

AIGUINES

HOTEL-RESTAURANT GRAND CANYON DU VERDON

CORNICHE

D-71

VERDON

ARTUBY RIVER

SUBLIME

TRAIL

POINT SUBLIME

D-23

ROUGON

RIVE DROITE

D-952

CASTELLANE

D-6085

TO GRASSE + NICE

RIVER

D-952

RIVE GAUCHE

D-955

TO COMPS

TRIGANCE

D-955

D-90

D-71

BALCON DE LA MESCLA

PONT D'ARTUBY

TO COMPS, GRASSE, NICE + A-8 AUTOROUTE

— RECOMMENDED RIVE GAUCHE ROUTE

— OTHER ROADS

🔭 VIEW

DCH

2 MILES

2 KM

Orientation to
Le Grand Canyon du Verdon

The Park Naturel Régional du Verdon, far more than just its famous canyon, is an extensive area mixing alpine scenery with misty villages, meandering streams, and seas of gentle meadows. The canyon is the heart of the park, where overpowering slabs of white and salmon-colored limestone plunge impossible distances to the snaking Verdon River far below. You need a car, ample time, and a lack of vertigo to appreciate this area. If traveling in summer or on holiday weekends, go really early or skip it. Fill your tank before leaving Grasse or Moustiers-Ste-Marie, as gas is scarce. Roads crawl along the length of the canyon on both sides *(Rive Gauche and Rive Droite)*; the *Rive Gauche* (left bank) works best for most, though both are spectacular.

The Grand Canyon du Verdon is located between the villages of Moustiers-Ste-Marie and Aiguines to the west and Castellane to the east. The most scenic driving segments are along the right (north) bank between Moustiers-Ste-Marie and the Point Sublime overlook, and along the left (south) bank between Aiguines and the Balcon de la Mescla. (Thrill-seekers head for the Castellane area, where the whitewater rafting, climbing, and serious hiking trails are best.) Picnickers will find endless choices for the perfect lunch stop.

Self-Guided Driving Tour

Grand Canyon du Verdon:
Rive Gauche (Left Bank)

For drivers connecting the Riviera with Provence via the canyon, the *Rive Gauche* (left bank) offers the most accessible and most scenic tour of the gorges. Coming from the Riviera, you'll drive the canyon from east to west. The basic route: Drive through Grasse and Digne, then turn off to hit the canyon at the Balcon de la Mescla. After seeing the canyon's most scenic stretch, you can either split off (after Aiguines) to return to the Riviera, or continue through Moustiers-Ste-Marie and on to Provence. (For drivers coming *from* Provence, this tour can be done in reverse, west to east; see "Approaching from Provence," at the end of the tour.)

The Drive Begins

The most direct route from the Riviera follows D-6185 (old N-85), which starts near Cannes (A-8 autoroute from Nice to Cannes saves time) and passes through Grasse, changing to D-6085 and continuing north toward Digne and Castellane. You'll turn left off D-6085 about 20 kilometers before Castellane, following signs to the *Gorges du Verdon* and *Draguignan* (there's an impressive medieval bridge just north of the road, about 3 kilometers before Comps-sur-Artuby, signed *La Souche*). Turn right at Comps-sur-Artuby, following signs to *Gorges du Verdon, Rive Gauche* (not *Rive Droite*).

You'll reach the canyon rim at the **Balcon de la Mescla,** the first pullout that drivers reach as they approach from Nice. The lookout on the lower side of the gift shop/café is best (you'll find a good selection of maps and books in the friendly shop).

From here you'll follow the canyon lip for about 60 serpentine minutes (including stops). You'll drive at an escargot's pace, navigating hairpin turns along the Corniche Sublime while enjoying constant views of rocky masses and vanishing-point views up the canyon. Hikes into the canyon are too long and steep for most (I've described one good hike for determined hikers). Most travelers are better off walking along the road for a bit, or, even more sublime, walking along sections of small dirt roads that lead away from the asphalt (several to choose from; two are described below). There are many small pullouts along the route, so stop frequently and get out of that car to allow the driver a look at the views.

A little beyond the Balcon de la Mescla, you can amble across Europe's highest bridge, **Pont d'Artuby,** and imagine working on its construction crew *(non, merci).* About one kilometer west of the bridge, you'll find a grassy pullout (north side) with a short two-track dirt road that allows walkers to ditch the asphalt and experience the gorges more peacefully (stash your car and follow the dirt path on foot—it's about 100 yards to the rocky edge of the canyon). You'll find an even better dirt-road option about two kilometers farther west (look for a pullout on the north side of the road) with sensational views down to the river and acres of limestone to scramble over.

About halfway through the canyon is the recommended **Hôtel-Restaurant Grand Canyon du Verdon,** clinging to its cliff like a baby to its mother. This concrete, funky place looks slapped together, but the café terrace has a table for you with stupendous views (drinks, snacks, and meals available at fair prices).

A stone's throw below the hotel is your best option for a sturdy **hike:** A posted trail leads all the way down to the river (parking available by the trailhead). It's a steep, challenging, and visually interesting 30 minutes down to the Passerelle de l'Estellie, and at least twice that long back up (good shoes and strong ankles are essential, as the rocky trail can be slippery). Once down, you can explore along the river, or cross the footbridge and prowl the right bank. Do this hike earlier in the day—in the afternoon, the high canyon walls can make darkness set in quickly. Once back up, celebrate with a drink on the hotel's terrace café.

Back along the main road, the **Col d'Illioure**—the last pass before leaving the canyon—provides sweeping views from the western portal. Park in the large pullout, where you'll find a few picnic tables scattered above and some good rock-scampering just below.

Just west of the canyon, the small village of **Aiguines** squats below waves of limestone and overlooks the long turquoise Lac de

Ste-Croix. This unspoiled village has a handful of shops, hotels, and cafés (recommended hotels listed below). It's an outdoorsy, popular-with-hikers place that most canyon visitors cruise right through. Detour onto the grounds of the 15th-century château for the view over Aiguines (with picnic benches and a fun play area for kids). The château interior is closed to the public. Aiguines' **TI** is on the main drag (Mon–Fri 9:30–12:00 & 14:00–17:30, closed Sat–Sun, allée des Tilleuls, tel. 04 94 70 21 64, www.aiguines.com).

For more views over Aiguines and the lake, stroll up to the small **Chapelle St. Pierre** at the northern edge of town and find the orientation table. From here, you can walk up the small road five minutes to the campground café, with nice tables on its broad view terrace (ideal for a pre-dinner drink or morning coffee).

From Aiguines, decide your onward route. If you're continuing to Provençal destinations, head for Moustiers-Ste-Marie and continue the tour below. If you're day-tripping from the Riviera, as you leave Aiguines follow signs for *Aups* (D-957), then *Draguignan*, then *Nice* via A-8. (If you're returning to the Riviera but want to see the Lac de Ste-Croix and Moustiers-Ste-Marie—described below—visit them before backtracking to the Aups road.)

Barely more than 30 years old, the man-made **Lac de Ste-Croix** is about six miles long and is the last stop for water flowing out of the Gorges du Verdon. For a fun lake/river experience, rent a canoe or a paddle boat at either side of the low bridge halfway between Moustiers and Aiguines. You can paddle under the bridge, then follow the aquamarine inlet upstream as far as 2.5 miles, tracing the river's route up the gorge on its final journey to the lake (€10/hour for paddle boat or canoe, figure 2 hours for a good trip).

Moustiers-Ste-Marie is another pretty Provençal face lined with boutiques—though this one comes with an impressive setting straddling a small stream at the base of the limestone cliffs of the Gorges du Verdon. The town is slammed with tourists clambering for the locally famous china and the usual Provençal kitsch. The

TI is in the center, next to the church (daily 10:00–12:30 & 14:00–18:00, place de l'Eglise, tel. 04 92 74 67 84, www.moustiers.fr). Hotel and restaurant recommendations are listed later.

You can escape some of the crowds by climbing 30 minutes on a steep, ankle-twisting path to the **Chapelle Notre-Dame de Beauvoir**—a simple chapel that has attracted pilgrims for centuries. A notebook in the chapel allows travelers to pen a request for a miracle for a loved one. For most, the chapel does not warrant the effort, though you'll get great views over the village by walking a short way up the path.

From here it's another one-and-a-half to two hours to most Provençal destinations. From Moustiers-Ste-Marie, head for Riez, then Gréoux-les-Bains. From Gréoux-les-Bains, follow signs for *Manosque,* then *Apt* for Luberon and Avignon; or use A-51 south to reach Aix-en-Provence, Cassis, Marseille, or Arles.

Approaching from Provence

Drivers coming from Provence can do the above tour from west to east (Moustiers-Ste-Marie to the Balcon de la Mescla).

All roads from Provence pass through Gréoux-les-Bains, which is about an hour northeast of Aix-en-Provence. Those coming from Cassis, Aix-en-Provence, and Arles will find A-51 north the fastest path; those coming from the Luberon and Avignon should take D-900 via Apt (turns into D-4100), then follow signs for *Manosque.* From Gréoux-les-Bains, follow signs to *Riez, Moustiers-Ste-Marie,* and *Aiguines* before entering the Grand Canyon du Verdon *(Rive Gauche).*

Leave the canyon after the Balcon de la Mescla. To get to Nice, follow signs for *Comps-sur-Artuby* (and *Draguignan* for a short distance), then *Grasse* and *Nice.* The fastest way from Grasse to Nice is via Cannes and A-8.

Sleeping and Eating near the Grand Canyon du Verdon

(€1 = about $1.25, country code: 33)
These places are listed in the order you'll reach them on the self-guided driving tour from east to west. Notice that, unlike in the rest of this book, some hotel rates in this remote area are per person and for half-pension (including breakfast and dinner).

Midway Through the Canyon

$$$ Hôtel-Restaurant Grand Canyon du Verdon** is housed in a funky structure that must have been grandfathered-in to own such an unbelievable location—2,500 feet high on the Corniche Sublime. In addition to its incredible view terrace, the hotel rents 15 basic, alpine-modern rooms, half on the canyon side (worth reserving ahead) and a few with view decks (open mid-April–mid-Oct, Db or Tb-€65–70/person with half-pension, tel. 04 94 76 91 31, fax 04 94 76 92 29, www.hotel-canyon-verdon.com, hotel .gd.canyon.verdon@wanadoo.fr).

In Aiguines

$$ Hôtel du Vieux-Château**, which has been in business for 200 years, is Aiguines' most characteristic hotel. Run by Frédéric and his energetic mama, the hotel's 10 snug rooms are red-tiled, spotless, and cool—literally, as there's little direct light (Db-€75–85, or about €60/person for half-pension, cozy restaurant open daily with simple, hearty fare and good soups, place de la Fontaine, tel. 04 94 70 22 95, fax 04 94 84 22 36, www.hotelvieuxchateau.fr, contact@ hotelvieuxchateau.fr).

$$ Hôtel Altitude 823**, just below, offers more predictable comfort with a bit less character at similar rates (€50–60/person for half-pension, tel. 04 98 10 22 17, fax 04 98 10 22 16, www.hotel -altitude823-verdon.com, altitude823@laposte.net).

In Moustiers-Ste-Marie

$$ La Bonne Auberge** offers no-frills rooms but a nice pool at the southern edge of the old town (Db-€65–85, extra bed-€16, garage-€6, route de Castellane, tel. 04 92 74 66 18, fax 04 92 74 65 11, www.bonne-auberge-moustiers.com, labonneauberge@club -internet.fr, closed Nov–March).

$ At **Restaurant/Chambres Clerissy,** Sophie offers travelers a great value and a warm welcome with four spacious and spotless rooms. It's good for families (Db-€47, Tb-€57, breakfast-€5, cash only, place du Chevalier de Blacas, in the village center across from the left transept of the church, mobile 06 33 34 06 95, tel. & fax 04 92 74 62 67, www.clerissy.fr, contact@clerissy.fr).

Eating: There is no shortage of dining options in Moustiers-Ste-Marie. The simple **Restaurant Clerissy** (whose rooms are listed above) offers inexpensive and simple meals (crêpes and pizza) and appealing indoor and outdoor tables. **Côté Jardin** is a haven of quiet a few steps south of the old town, with a pleasing garden setting and good cuisine at fair prices (*menus* from €23, closed Mon–Tue, tel. 04 92 74 68 91).

INLAND RIVIERA

TRAVELING WITH CHILDREN

With relatively few must-see museums, plenty of outdoor activities, and cooperative weather, Provence and the French Riviera are practically made for kids. This part of France has beaches, fun canoeing on safe rivers, good biking, Roman ruins to scramble over, abundant sunshine, and swimming pools everywhere. Teenagers love the seaside resorts (Cassis is best) and enjoy the hustle and bustle of cities like Avignon, Arles, Aix-en-Provence, and Nice. Younger kids tend to prefer the rural areas, which offer more swimming pools, open spaces, and parks.

To make your trip fun for everyone in the family, mix heavy-duty sights with kids' activities, such as playing miniature golf or *boules*, renting bikes or canoes, and riding the little tourist trains popular in many towns. Kids also like audioguides, available at important sights in many cities. And if you're in France near Bastille Day, remember that firecracker stands pop up everywhere on the days leading up to July 14. Putting on their own fireworks show can be a highlight for teenagers.

Minimize hotel changes by planning three-day stops. Aim for hotels with restaurants, so older kids can go back to the room while you finish a pleasant dinner.

I've listed swimming pools in many places, but be warned: Public pools in France commonly require a small, Speedo-like bathing suit for boys and men (American-style swim trunks won't do)—though they usually have these little suits to loan. At hotel pools, any type of swimsuit will do.

For breakfast, croissants are a hit, though a good *pain au chocolat* (croissant with chocolate bits) will be appreciated even more. Hot chocolate, fruit, and yogurt are usually available. For lunch and dinner, it's easy to find fast-food places and restaurants with kids' menus, or *crêperies*, which have a wide variety of fillings for both savory and dessert crêpes. For food emergencies, I travel with a plastic container of peanut butter brought from home and smuggle small amounts of jam from breakfast.

Homesick kids can keep in touch with friends with cheap international phone cards and email. Hotel Internet access and cybercafés are a godsend for parents with teenagers. Readily available Wi-Fi makes bringing a laptop worthwhile. Some parents find buying a French mobile phone—or roaming with an American mobile phone—a helpful investment; adults can stay connected to teenagers while allowing them maximum independence (see page 467). If you and your teenager both have mobile phones that work in Europe, sending each other text messages can be a relatively inexpensive way to keep in touch (much cheaper than actual phone calls).

Kids like the French adventure comics Astérix and Tintin (both available in English, sold in bigger bookstores with English sections).

It's fun to take kids to movies (even if not in English) just to see how theaters work elsewhere. Movies shown in their original language—usually with subtitles—are listed as *v.o.* at the box office. (One showing could be *v.o.* and the next could be dubbed in French, labeled *v.f.;* be aware that *v.o.* movies are hard to find outside major cities.) *Dessin animé* means "cartoon." While many live-action movies can be found in their original language with French subtitles, cartoons and kids' movies (intended for an audience that doesn't read so well yet) are almost always dubbed.

You'll find old-style merry-go-rounds in many cities, perfect for younger travelers (my daughter's goal was to ride a merry-go-round in every town...she came close). I've also identified parks with play areas when possible. Visits to local goat cheese–makers in early spring yield good kid rewards (look for *fromage fermier de chèvre* signs along the country roads). Goats are social animals and goat-cheese makers will usually let your child hold or pet one. You can also pick up some superb fresh cheese for your picnic.

The best thing I did on a recent trip was buy a set of *boules* (a.k.a. *pétanque,* a form of outdoor bowling—for the rules, see sidebar on page 208). We'd play *boules* before dinner, side by side with real players on the village court. Get your *boules de pétanque* at sporting-goods stores or larger department stores. Since they're heavy, buy a set only if you'll be driving. The *boules* also make fun, if weighty, souvenirs, and are just as enjoyable to play back at home.

Swap babysitting duties with your partner if one of you wants to take in an extra sight. And for memories that will last long after the trip, keep a family journal. Pack a small diary and a glue stick. While relaxing at a café over a *citron-pressé* (lemonade), take turns writing about the day's events and include mementos such as ticket stubs from museums, postcards, or stalks of lavender.

Before You Go

Get your kids into the spirit ahead of time using these tips:

- Pick up books at the library and rent videos. Watch or read the Madeline stories by Ludwig Bemelmans, *The Hunchback of Notre-Dame* by Victor Hugo, *The Three Musketeers* by Alexandre Dumas, or Dumas' *The Man in the Iron Mask*. *Anni's Diary of France*, by Anni Axworthy, is a fun, picture-filled book about a young girl's trip; it could inspire your children. *How Would You Survive in the Middle Ages?*, by Fiona MacDonald, is a worthwhile "guide" for kids. Serious kid-historians will devour *The Kingfisher History Encyclopedia*. For a fantastical visit to Avignon in the days of the pope, *The Lady and the Squire* by former Monty Python Terry Jones is a fun read. If your children are interested in art, get your hands on *The History of Art for Young People* by Anthony Janson and *Discovering Great Artists: Hands-On Art for Children in the Styles of the Great Masters* by MaryAnn Kohl. (Also see the recommended books and movies list, which includes some good choices for teenagers, in this book's appendix.)
- Involve your kids in trip planning. Have them read about the places that you may include in your itinerary (even the hotels you're considering), and let them help with your decisions.
- Hotel selection is critical. In my recommendations, I've identified hotels that seem particularly kid-friendly (pools, table tennis, grassy areas, easygoing owners, etc.). If you're staying for a week or more in one place, one great option is to rent a *gite* (see "*Gites* and Apartments" on page 28).

What to Bring

- Children's books in English are scarce and pricey in France. My children read much more when traveling in Europe than while at home, so don't skimp here (see list above).
- Bring peanut butter (hard to find in France)...or help your kids acquire a taste for Nutella, the tasty hazelnut-chocolate spread available everywhere. Look for organic *(bio)* stores in cities where you can find *Chocolade*, a less-sugary version of Nutella, and numerous nut butters.
- Choose items that are small and convenient for use on planes, trains, and in your hotel room: a lightweight netbook computer has a long battery life and takes little packing space, compact travel games, a deck of cards, and a handheld video game. Bring your own drawing paper, pens, and crayons, as these supplies are pricey in France.

CHILDREN

- For younger kids, Legos are easily packed and practical (it's also fun to purchase kits in Europe, where the Legos are sometimes different from those in the US).
- Budding fashionistas enjoy traveling with—and buying new outfits for—a Corelle doll or another 16-inch doll. The French have wonderful doll clothes, with a much wider selection than typically found in the US.
- For traveling with infants, car-rental agencies usually rent car seats, though you must reserve one in advance (verify the price ahead of time—you may want to bring your own). And though most hotels have some sort of crib, I brought a portable crib and did not regret it.
- Cameras are a great investment to get your kids involved.
- For longer drives, audio books can be fun for the whole family (if carefully chosen). I recommend Peter Mayle's *A Year in Provence,* available on CD (or put it on your MP3 player).

Planning Your Time

- Lower your sightseeing ambitions and prepare to savor fewer places for longer periods. Plan longer stays at fewer stops— you won't regret it.
- Don't overdo it. Tackle one key sight each day and mix in a healthy dose of fun activities.
- Follow this book's crowd-beating tips to a T. Kids despise long lines more than you do.
- Eat dinner early (19:00–19:30 at restaurants, earlier at cafés). Skip romantic eateries. Try relaxed cafés (or fast-food restaurants) where kids can move around without bothering others. Picnics work well.
- The best and cheapest toy selections are usually in department stores, like Monoprix and Galeries Lafayette.
- Let kids help choose daily activities, lead you through ancient sights, and so on.
- Keep an eye out for *mini-golfs* (miniature golf).

Top Kid-Friendly Sights and Activities

These are listed in no particular order:

- Pont du Gard. An entire wing of the museum is dedicated to kids, who can also swim or take a canoe trip on the river. See page 149.
- Cassis. Boat trip to the *calanques* or the port and beaches for teenagers. See page 254.
- Changing of the Guard in Monaco (11:55 daily). See page 384.
- Cousteau Aquarium in Monaco. See page 385.
- Pedal boats on the Mediterranean (page 297) and into the

Gorges du Verdon (page 439).
- Biking through vineyards to small villages, from Vaison la Romaine. See page 172.
- Les Baux's castle ruins, with medieval weaponry and great walls to climb. See page 91.
- Canoeing on the Ardèche River (page 191), the Sorgue River (page 201), or into the Gorges du Verdon (page 439).
- Boat trips from Nice (page 294), Villefranche-sur-Mer (page 353), or St-Tropez (page 418).
- Biking or in-line skating on the promenade des Anglais in Nice. See page 291.
- Marineland near Antibes. See page 403.
- Little tourist trains (in nearly every city).

Honorable mention goes to Arles' Ancient History Museum (page 65), horseback riding and public beaches in the Camargue (page 104), Roman arenas in Nîmes (page 139) and Arles (page 71), Cathédrale d'Images near Les Baux (page 94), the beaches of Antibes (page 402), and the narrow-gauge train ride from Nice (page 305).

SHOPPING

Provence and the Riviera offer France's best shopping outside of Paris, with a great range of reasonably priced items ideal for souvenirs and gifts. And if approached thoughtfully, shopping in the south of France can be a culturally enlightening experience. There's no better way to mix serious shopping business with travel pleasure than at the weekly markets *(marchés)* in towns and villages throughout the region. These traditional market days offer far more than fresh produce and fish; in many cases, about half the market is devoted to durable goods (baskets, tablecloths, pottery, and local fabrics)—*très* handy for gift-scavenging travelers. If you miss market day, most Provençal towns have more than enough small shops that sell local products—and more than enough kitschy souvenirs. (They're often selling the same items you can find more cheaply at weekly markets.) If you crave French fashion, the cities described in this book have unlimited boutique shopping for clothing.

In this chapter you'll find information on shopping for souvenirs, navigating market days, and browsing boutiques. For information on VAT refunds and customs regulations, see page 18. For a comparison of French to US clothing sizes, see page 498.

What to Buy

Here's a shopping list of locally made goods in Provence and the Riviera. You'll find most of these items in tourist-oriented boutiques, though many of them can be had for less on market days. If you buy more expensive, nonperishable goods, most stores will work with you to send them home.

- **Jams** *(confiture)* containing lush and often exotic fruits, such as *fruits de passion* (passion fruit), *figues* (figs), and *pastèque* or *citre* (different types of watermelon).
- **Honey** *(miel)*, particularly lavender *(lavande)* or rosemary

(romarin). Stronger palates should try the chestnut *(châtaigne)* or even oak-flavored *(chêne)* honey.

- Tins of **tapenade** (olive paste) and all kinds of **olives:** black, green, and stuffed with garlic or anchovies.

- **Olive-wood products** such as utensils and bowls. Olives are not just for nibbling; in Provence, the entire tree is used.

- Canned **pâtés,** including the buttery, rich *foie gras* (its "home" is Périgord, but you'll also find it in the markets of Provence). Canned goose, duck, and pork pâté can be imported to the US, but not beef.

- Packets of **herbs** (including the famous *herbes de Provence*), **salt** from the Camargue (look for *Fleur de Sel* for the best, and use sparingly), and bottles or tins of **olive oil** from local trees (Nyons is France's olive capital, though Les Baux is rightly proud of its olives as well). Most of these items can be found in attractive packaging that can be saved and enjoyed long after the product itself is gone.

- Sweets, including the famous *nougat de Montélimar* (a rich, chewy confection made with nuts and honey and sometimes flavored with lavender or other fragrances), *calissons* (orange-and-almond-flavored candy, shaped like the nut and originally from Aix-en-Provence), and **chocolates** from the Provençal producer Puyricard.

- **Soaps and lotions,** particularly those "perfumed" with local plants such as lavender *(lavande)*, rosemary *(romarin)*, or linden *(tilleul)*. You'll also find colorful **sachets** containing the same fragrances.

- Brightly colored **table linens.** Souleiado and Les Olivades are the most famous local manufacturers, but good-quality knockoffs can be found in most any market or store.

- **Cloth bags** with French designs for grocery shopping (these pack easily and cost pennies).

- Local **pottery** (*poterie; faïence* is hand-painted *poterie*). Terre Provence is a well-known (and pricey) brand, but many other producers offer excellent quality, usually for less. Serious potters can plan ahead to visit a pottery fair featuring the best of the regions' potters (calendar at http://artceramistes.free.fr /marches/Provence).

- *Santons,* the tiny, brightly adorned clay or wood Provençal figurines. Originally designed for traditional Christmas crèche scenes, today's *santons* ("little saints") represent all walks of life—from the local *boulanger* to the woman sewing bright Provençal cloth to the village doctor. The most famous *santon* makers are in Séguret and Aubagne. All *santon* makers belong to the *santon*-maker guild (think medieval stonecutters or woodworkers), and each *santon* is handmade and signed.

Market Day *(Jour du Marché)*

Market days are a big deal throughout France, and in no other region are they more celebrated than in Provence and the Riviera.

Markets have been a central feature of life in rural areas since the Middle Ages. No single event better symbolizes the French preoccupation with fresh products, and their strong ties to the small farmer, than the weekly market. Many locals mark their calendars with the arrival of the new season's produce.

Provence is a Mediterranean melting pot, where Italy, Spain, and North Africa intersect with France to do business. Notice the ethnic mix of the vendors (and the products they sell). Spices from Morocco and Tunisia, fresh pasta from Italy, saffron from Spain, and tapenade from Provence compete for your attention at Provence's *marchés*.

There are two kinds of weekly open-air markets: *les marchés* and *les marchés brocantes*.

Les marchés are more general in scope, more common, and more colorful, featuring products from local farmers and artisans. These markets can offer a mind-boggling array of choices, from the perishable (produce, meats, cheeses, breads, and pastries) to the nonperishable (kitchen wares, inexpensive clothing, brightly colored linens, and pottery).

Les marchés brocantes specialize in quasi-antiques and flea-market bric-a-brac. *Brocantes* markets began in the Middle Ages, when middlemen would gather to set up small stalls and sell old, flea-infested clothes and discarded possessions of the wealthy at bargain prices to eager peasants. Buyers were allowed to *rummage* through piles of aristocratic garbage.

Many *marchés* have good selections of produce and some *brocantes*. The best of all market worlds may rest in the picturesque town of Isle-sur-la-Sorgue, where, on Sunday mornings, a brilliant food *marché* tangles with an active flea market and a good selection of antiques.

I've listed days and locations for both market types throughout this book. Notice the signs as you enter towns indicating the *jours du marché* (essential information to any civilized soul, and a reminder not to park on the streets the night before—be on the lookout for *stationnement interdit* signs that mark "no parking" areas). Most *marchés* take place once a week in the town's main square, and, if large enough, they spill into nearby streets.

SHOPPING

Usually, the bigger the market, the greater the overall selection, particularly for nonperishable goods. Bigger towns (like Arles) may have two weekly markets, one a bit larger than the other, with more nonperishable goods; in other towns (including Isle-sur-la-Sorgue), the second weekly market simply may be a smaller version of the main market day. The biggest market days usually are on weekends, so that everyone can go. In the largest cities (such as Avignon and Nîmes), modern market halls have been established with produce stands and meat counters selling fresh goods daily.

Market day is as important socially as commercially—it's a weekly chance for locals to resume friendships and get the current gossip. Here neighbors can catch up on Henri's barn renovation, see photos of Jacqueline's new grandchild, and relax over *un café*. Dogs are tethered to café tables while friends exchange kisses. Tether yourself to a table and observe: three cheek-kisses for good friends (left-right-left), a fourth for friends you haven't seen in a while. (The appropriate number of kisses varies by region—Paris, Lyon, and Provence have separate standards.)

Markets begin at about 8:00, with setup commencing in the predawn hours (for some, a reason not to stay in a main-square hotel the night before market day). They usually end by 13:00. Most perishable items are sold directly from the producers—no middlemen, no Visa cards, just really fresh produce (*du pays* means "grown locally"). Sometimes you'll meet a widow selling a dozen eggs, two rabbits, and a wad of herbs tied with string. But most vendors follow a weekly circuit of markets they feel works best for them, showing up in the same spot every week, year in and year out. At a favorite market, my family has done business with the same olive vendor and "cookie man" for 19 years.

It's bad form to be in a hurry on market day. Allow the crowd to set your pace. Observe the interaction between vendor and client. Notice the joy they can find in chatting each other up. Wares are displayed with pride. Generally the rule is "don't touch"—instead, point and let them serve you. If self-serve is the norm, the seller will hand you a bag. Remember, they use metric weight. Ask for *un kilo* (about 2 pounds), *un demi-kilo* (about 1 pound—also called *une livre*), or *un quart-kilo* (pronounced "car-kilo," about half a pound). Many vendors speak enough English to assist you in your selection. Your total price will be hand-tallied on small scraps of paper and given to you. Vendors are normally honest. If you're struggling to find the correct change, just hold out your hand and they will take only what is needed. (Still, you're wise to double-check the amount you just paid for that olive tree.)

At the root of a good market experience is a sturdy shopping basket or bag. Find the vendor selling baskets and other wicker items and go local (*osier* is the French name for wicker, *cade* is the

Key Shopping Phrases

English	French	Pronounced
Just looking.	*Je regarde.*	zhuh ruh-garde
How much is it?	*Combien?*	kohm-bee-ehn
Too big/small/ expensive	*Trop grand/ petit/cher*	troh grahn/ puh-tee/sher
May I try it on?	*Je peux l'essayer?*	zhuh puh luh-say-yay
Can I see more?	*Puis-je en voir d'autres?*	pweezh ehn vwahr doh-truh
I'll think about it.	*Je vais y penser.*	zhuh vayz-ee pahn-say
I'd like this.	*Je voudrais ça.*	zhuh voo-dray sah
on sale	*solde*	sold-ay
discounted price	*prix réduit*	pree ray-dwee
big discounts	*prix choc*	pree shock

Provençal name—from the basket-making Luberon village of Cadenet); you can also find plastic and nylon versions. Most baskets are inexpensive, make for fun and colorful souvenirs, and can come in handy for odd-shaped or breakable carry-ons for the plane trip home. With basket in hand, shop for your heaviest items first. (You don't want to put a kilo of fresh apples on top of the bread you bought for your picnic.)

Markets change seasonally. In April and May, look for asparagus (green, purple, or the prized white—after being cooked, these are dipped in vinegar or homemade mayonnaise and eaten by hand). In late spring, shop for strawberries, including the best: *fraises des bois* (wild strawberries). Almost equally prized are the strawberries called *gariguettes* and *maras des bois*. Soon after, you'll see cherries and other stone fruits, plus the famously sweet Cavaillon melons (resembling tiny cantaloupes, often served cut in half with a spoonful or two of the sweet Rhône white wine Beaumes de Venise). Don't worry if these are split open—the abundance of sugar and sunshine are the cause, and the *fendus* are considered the sweetest. In late June and early September, watch for figs *(figues)*. From July through September, essential vegetables for the Provençal dish ratatouille—including eggplant, tomatoes, zucchinis, and peppers—come straight from the open fields. In the fall you'll see stands selling game birds, other beasts of the hunt, and a glorious array of wild mushrooms.

After November and throughout the winter, look for little (or big, depending on your wallet size) black truffles. Truffles preserved and sealed in jars can safely be brought back to the United States. The Luberon is one of Provence's largest truffle-producing areas. The town of Carpentras hosts a truffles-only market on Friday mornings in winter, off the main roundabout in front of a café. Listen carefully and you might hear the Provençal language being spoken between some vendors and buyers. Richerenches, Northern Provence's truffle capital, holds its own winter truffle market; during its annual truffle-themed Mass, many parishioners would give a truffle as a small offering, instead of money.

For more immediate consumption, look for local cheeses (cow, called *vache;* sheep or ewe, called *brebis;* or the Provençal favorite: goat cheese, or *chèvre,* named *picodons*). Cheeses range from very fresh (aged one day) to aged for weeks. The older the cheese, the more dried and shrunken. Some may even be speckled with edible mold. Cheeses come in many shapes (round, logs, pyramids) and various sizes (from single-bite mouthfuls to wheels that will feed you for several meals). Some are sprinkled with herbs or spices. Others are more adorned, such as those rolled in ash *(à la cendre)* or wrapped in leaves *(banon).* Watch for the locally produced *banon de banon,* a goat cheese soaked in *eau-de-vie* (the highly alcoholic "water of life"), then wrapped in chestnut leaves and tied with string—*ooh la la.*

Next, move on to the sausages (many also rolled in herbs or spices). Samples are usually free—try the *sanglier* (boar). Be on the lookout for locally produced wines or ciders (free tastings are standard) and find samples of *foie gras* (available in take-it-home tins), good with the sweet white wine of Beaumes de Venise. These items make perfect picnic fare when teamed with a crusty baguette.

Throughout Provence you'll see vendors selling paella made *sur place* (on the spot) in huge traditional round pans. Paella varies by area and chef, but most recipes include the traditional ingredients of fresh shellfish, chicken, and sausages mixed into saffron-infused rice. And throughout France you'll see vans selling sizzling, spit-roasted chicken (perfectly bagged for carrying-out) or pizza (made to your liking on the spot). *Bon appétit!*

Clothing Boutiques

Those preferring fashion over food will be happy to learn that they don't have to go to Paris to enjoy the latest trends. The stylish boutiques lining the shopping streets of Avignon, Nîmes, Aix-en-Provence, St. Rémy, Uzès, Nice, and the ultra-trendy Juan-les-Pins offer more than sufficient selection and style for the fashion-conscious. Still, they play by a different set of rules in France, and the better knowledge you have of the rules, the better player you'll be.

While many shopkeepers speak some English, an effort to speak even a minimum of French earns better service. These tips should get you off on the right track:

- In small stores, always say, *"Bonjour, Madame* or *Mademoiselle* or *Monsieur"* when entering. And remember to say *"Au revoir, Madame/Mademoiselle/Monsieur"* when leaving.
- Except in department stores, it's not normal for the customer to handle clothing. Ask first before you pick up an item: *"Je peux?"* (zhuh puh), meaning, "Can I?"
- For clothing-size comparisons between the US and France, see page 498 in the appendix.
- Forget returns (and don't count on exchanges).
- The customer is not always right; in fact, some clerks figure they're doing you a favor by waiting on you.
- Saturdays are busiest, and stores are closed on Sunday.
- Observe French shoppers, then imitate them.
- Don't feel obliged to buy. If a shopkeeper offers assistance, just say, *"Je regarde, merci,"* meaning, "Just looking, thanks."

SHOPPING

FRANCE: PAST AND PRESENT

French History in an Escargot Shell

About the time of Christ, Romans "Latinized" the land of the Gauls. With the fifth-century A.D. fall of Rome, the barbarian Franks and Burgundians invaded. Today's France evolved from this unique mix of Latin and Celtic cultures.

While France wallowed with the rest of Europe in medieval darkness, it got a head start in its development as a nation-state. In 507, Clovis, the king of the Franks, established Paris as the capital of his Christian Merovingian dynasty. Clovis and the Franks would eventually become Louis and the French. The Frankish military leader Charles Martel stopped the spread of Islam by beating the Spanish Moors at the Battle of Poitiers in 732. And Charlemagne, the most important of the "Dark Age" Frankish kings, was crowned Holy Roman Emperor by the pope in 800. Charles the Great presided over the "Carolingian Renaissance" and effectively ruled an empire that was vast for its time.

The Treaty of Verdun (843), which divided Charlemagne's empire among his grandsons, marks what could be considered the birth of Europe. For the first time, a treaty was signed in vernacular languages (French and German), rather than in Latin. This split established a Franco-Germanic divide and heralded an age of fragmentation. While petty princes took the reigns, the Frankish king ruled only Ile de France, a small region around Paris.

Vikings, or Norsemen, settled in what became Normandy. Later, in 1066, these "Normans" invaded England. The Norman king, William the Conqueror, consolidated his English domain, accelerating the formation of modern England. But his rule also muddied the political waters between England and France, kicking off a centuries-long struggle between the two nations.

Typical Church Architecture

History comes to life when you visit a centuries-old church. Even if you wouldn't know your apse from a hole in the ground, learning a few simple terms will enrich your experience. Note that not every church will have every feature, and a "cathedral" isn't a type of church architecture, but rather a designation for a church that's a governing center for a local bishop.

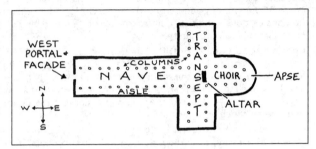

Aisles: The long, generally low-ceilinged arcades that flank the nave.

Altar: The raised area with a ceremonial table (often adorned with candles or a crucifix), where the priest prepares and serves the bread and wine for Communion.

Apse: The space beyond the altar, generally bordered with small chapels.

Choir: A cozy area, often screened off, located within the church nave and near the high altar where services are sung in a more intimate setting.

Cloister: A square-shaped series of hallways surrounding an open-air courtyard, traditionally where monks and nuns got fresh air.

Facade: The outer wall of the church's main (west) entrance, viewable from outside and generally highly decorated.

Groin Vault: An arched ceiling formed where two equal barrel vaults meet at right angles. Less common usage: term for a medieval jock strap.

Narthex: The area (portico or foyer) between the main entry and the nave.

Nave: The long, central section of the church (running west to east, from the entrance to the altar) where the congregation stood through the service.

Transept: The north–south part of the church, which crosses (perpendicularly) the east–west nave. In a traditional Latin cross-shaped floor plan, the transept forms the "arms" of the cross.

West Portal: The main entry to the church (on the west end, opposite the main altar).

Top French Notables in History

Madame and Monsieur Cro-Magnon: Prehistoric hunter-gatherers who moved to France (c. 30,000 B.C.), painted cave walls at Lascaux and Font-de-Gaume, and eventually settled down as farmers (c. 10,000 B.C.).

Vercingétorix (72–46 B.C.): This long-haired warrior rallied the Gauls against Julius Caesar's invading Roman legions (52 B.C.). Defeated by Caesar, France fell under Roman domination, resulting in 500 years of peace and prosperity. During that time, the Romans established cities, built roads, taught in Latin, and converted people to Christianity.

Charlemagne (A.D. 742–814): For Christmas in A.D. 800, the pope gave King Charlemagne the title of Emperor, thus uniting much of Europe under the leadership of the Franks ("France"). Charlemagne stabilized France amid centuries of barbarian invasions. After his death, the empire was split, carving the outlines of modern France and Germany.

Eleanor of Aquitaine (c. 1122–1204): The beautiful, sophisticated ex-wife of the King of France married the King of England, creating an uneasy union between the two countries. During her lifetime, French culture was spread across Europe by roving troubadours, theological scholars, and skilled architects pioneering "the French style"—a.k.a. Gothic.

Joan of Arc (1412–1431): When France and England fought the Hundred Years' War to settle who would rule (1337–1453), teenager Joan of Arc—guided by voices in her head—rallied the French troops. Though Joan was captured and burned as a heretic, the French eventually drove England out of their country for good, establishing the current borders. Over the centuries, the church upgraded Joan's status from heretic to saint (canonized in 1920).

François I (1494–1547): This Renaissance king ruled a united, modern nation, making it a cultural center that hosted the Italian Leonardo da Vinci. François set the tone for future absolute monarchs, punctuating his commands with the phrase, "For such is our pleasure."

Louis XIV (1638–1715): Charismatic and cunning, the "Sun King" ruled Europe's richest, most populous, most powerful nation-state. Every educated European spoke French, dressed in Louis-style leotards and powdered wigs, and built Versailles-like palaces. Though Louis ruled as an absolute monarch (distracting the nobility with courtly games), his reign also fostered the arts and philosophy, sowing the seeds of democracy and revolution.

Marie Antoinette (1755–1793): As the Austrian-born wife of Louis XVI, she came to symbolize (probably unfairly) the decadence of France's ruling class. When the Revolution broke out (1789), she was arrested, imprisoned, and executed—one of thousands who were guillotined on Paris' place de la Concorde as an enemy of the people.

Napoleon Bonaparte (1769–1821): This daring young military man became a hero during the Revolution, fighting Europe's royalty. He went on to conquer much of the Continent, become leader of France, and, eventually, rule as a dictator with the title of Emperor. In 1815 an allied Europe defeated and exiled Napoleon, reinstating the French monarchy—though future kings (including Napoleon's nephew, who ruled as Napoleon III) were subject to democratic constraints.

Claude Monet (1840–1926): Monet's Impressionist paintings captured the soft-focus beauty of the belle époque—middle-class men and women enjoying drinks in cafés, walks in gardens, and picnics along the Seine. At the turn of the 20th century, French culture reigned supreme while its economic and political clout was fading, soon to be shattered by the violence of World War I.

Charles de Gaulle (1890–1970): A career military man, de Gaulle helped France survive occupation by Nazi Germany during World War II with his rousing radio broadcasts and unbending faith in France. As president he led the country through its postwar rebuilding, divisive wars in Vietnam and Algeria (trying to preserve France's colonial empire), and turbulent student riots in the 1960s.

Contemporary French: Which recent French people will history remember? President François Mitterand (1916–1996), the driving force behind Paris' La Grande Arche and Opéra Bastille? Marcel Marceau (1923–2007), white-faced mime? Chef Paul Bocuse (b. 1926), inventor of *nouvelle cuisine?* Brigitte Bardot (b. 1934), film actress, crusader for animal rights, and popularizer of the bikini? Yves Saint Laurent (1936–2008), one of the world's greatest fashion designers? Jean-Marie Le Pen (b. 1928), founder of the far-right National Front party, with staunch anti-immigration policies? Bernard Kouchner (b. 1939), co-founder of Doctors without Borders and minister of foreign affairs under President Nicholas Sarkozy? Or Zinédine Zidane (b. 1972), France's greatest soccer player ever, whose Algerian roots helped raise the status of Arabs in France?

In the 12th century, Eleanor of Aquitaine (a separate country in southwest France) married Louis VII, king of France, bringing Aquitaine under French rule. They divorced, and she married Henry of Normandy, soon to be Henry II of England. This marital union gave England control of a huge swath of land, from the English Channel to the Pyrenees. For 300 years France and England would struggle for control of Aquitaine. Any enemy of the French king would find a natural ally in the English king.

In 1328, the French king Charles IV died without a son. The English king (Edward III), Charles IV's nephew, was interested in the throne, but the French resisted. This quandary pitted France, the biggest and richest country in Europe, against England, which had the largest army. They fought from 1337 to 1453 in what was modestly called the Hundred Years' War.

Regional powers from within France actually sided with England. Burgundy took Paris, captured the royal family, and recognized the English king as heir to the French throne. England controlled France from the Loire north, and things looked bleak for the French king.

Enter Joan of Arc, a 16-year-old peasant girl driven by religious voices. France's national heroine left home to support Charles VII, the dauphin (boy prince, heir to the throne but too young to rule). Joan rallied the French, ultimately inspiring them to throw out the English. In 1430 Joan was captured by the Burgundians, who sold her to the English, who convicted her of heresy and burned her at the stake in Rouen. But the inspiration of Joan of Arc lived on, and by 1453 English holdings on the Continent had dwindled to the port of Calais.

By 1500 a strong, centralized France had emerged, with borders similar to those today. Its kings (from the Renaissance François I through the Henrys and all those Louises) were model divine monarchs, setting the standard for absolute rule in Europe.

Outrage over the power plays and spending sprees of the kings—coupled with the modern thinking of the Enlightenment (whose leaders were the French *philosophes*)—led to the French Revolution (1789). In France it was the end of the *ancien régime*, as well as its notion that some are born to rule, while others are born to be ruled.

The excesses of the Revolution in turn led to the rise of Napoleon, who ruled the French empire as a dictator. Eventually, *his* excesses ushered him into a South Atlantic exile, and after another half-century of monarchy and empire, the French settled on a compromise role for their leader. The modern French "king" is ruled by a constitution. Rather than dress in leotards and powdered wigs, the president goes to work in a suit and carries a briefcase.

The 20th century spelled the end of France's reign as a mili-

PAST AND PRESENT

tary and political superpower. Devastating wars with Germany in 1870, 1914, and 1940—and the loss of her colonial holdings—left France with not quite enough land, people, or production to be a top player on a global scale. But the 21st century may see France rise again: Paris is a cultural capital of Europe, and France—under the EU banner—is leading the push to unify Europe as a single economic power. And if Europe becomes a superpower, Paris may yet be its capital.

Contemporary Politics in France

Today, the key political issues in France (like everywhere) are mainly about the economy. And though the French have suffered less than the US (they didn't get involved in risky home loans and are less invested in the stock market), unemployment is high (about 10 percent) and taxes are higher (about 44 percent of the gross domestic product). Other French concerns are the cultural strains caused by a steadily increasing percentage of ethnic minorities (about 10 percent of France's population is of North African descent), the extent of the European Union's power, and balancing cushy workers' benefits against the need to compete in a global marketplace. The challenge for the French leadership is to address these issues while maintaining the level of social services that the French expect from their government.

France is part of the 27-member European Union (a kind of "United States of Europe") that has successfully dissolved borders and implemented a single currency, the euro. France's governments have been decidedly pro-EU; however, its people are more skeptical. In 2005 the French voted against ratifying an EU constitution that would have increased the EU's political powers. Many French fear that a more powerful EU would ultimately result in lost job security and social benefits (a huge issue in France).

Another controversy involves the increased presence of Muslim immigrants. The French debate whether it makes sense to ban women from wearing full-body cloaks and face-veils. Does banning the veil enforce democracy...or squelch diversity?

French national politics are complex but fascinating. The two biggest parties are President Nicolas Sarkozy's center-right Popular Movement Union (UMP) and the center-left Socialists (PS).

But unlike America's two-party system, France has many small parties, and any major player must form coalitions in order to rule. There's the Democratic Movement (MoDem) party, fighting for the center of the political landscape. To the left lie the once-powerful, now-marginal Communists (PCF); the "Green" environmental party (Les Verts); and—on the extreme left—the New Anti-Capitalists (NPA). These leftists must work with the more-centrist Socialist party if they want have a national voice.

PAST AND PRESENT

Trouble in Paradise: Population Growth in Southern France

Life is not as perfect as it may appear amid the breezy, sun-kissed beaches, cities, and villages of Provence and the French Riviera. The south of France has become a melting pot of people in search of their Provençal paradise. While some say the influx into this region has invigorated the culture, many residents are feeling growing pains. Two major trends are fueling the population boom in the south: northern Europeans looking for their place in the sun, and North African immigrants looking for a better life in France.

Cheap flights and lightning-fast train service have enabled northern Europeans to experience the south of France as a weekend getaway...and a growing number are choosing to stay. Thanks to its sunny climate, relatively inexpensive homes (if you're from northern Europe), and plentiful transportation options, this region is an understandably big draw. Unfortunately, as wealthy northerners pick off local homes and inflate prices, the average Jean is losing out.

Immigration, particularly from North Africa, is another cause of the population boom. With the historic loss of able-bodied men from World Wars I and II, and native-French birth rates unable to replace those losses, France looked across the Mediterranean to its old colonies for cheap sources of manual labor. When these workers came, they brought their families, who stayed in France and had families of their own (sound familiar?). Today, France has Europe's largest Muslim population.

Five million North Africans legally reside in France—and many more live here illegally. More than 100,000 illegal immigrants arrive in France each year, about half of whom are North African. Most live in the south (more than a quarter of Marseille's population is North African). This concentration of immigrants among a very Catholic French population (Muslims outnumber Protestants 2 to 1), combined with high unemployment (20 percent compared to a national average of 10 percent), has led to the rise of racist politics. This anti-immigrant movement has been spearheaded by the National Front party, which wants to keep "France for the French." Its leader, Jean-Marie Le Pen, has referred to the growing numbers of North Africans in France as "the silent invasion." The National Front generally receives about 20 percent of this region's vote in national elections.

The French left tends to see its popularity rise when the economy is strong and fall when it's weak.

To the right of Sarkozy lies the National Front party (FN), led by 82-year-old Jean-Marie Le Pen. He campaigns for the expulsion of ethnic minorities, restoration of the French franc, and broader police powers. The situation in the country became especially tense in the fall of 2005, when disadvantaged youths (primarily of North African descent) rioted in Parisian suburbs, protesting discrimination. Although the FN only has a staunch voter base of about 13 percent nationally, rising unemployment and globalization worries have increased its following, allowing Le Pen to nudge the political agenda to the right.

The French president is elected by popular vote every five years. The prime minister is chosen by the president, then confirmed by the parliament (Assemblée Nationale), and is a very powerful position when the president's party loses its majority in parliament. With seven major parties, a single majority is rare, so it takes a coalition to confirm a prime minister. Over the past 13 years, the right has been more successful than the left in marshaling supporters. Previous President Jacques Chirac (who served two terms) and current President Sarkozy (elected in 2007) are both conservatives.

Sarkozy is pro-American (though he doesn't speak English) and pro–EU. He is tough on crime and unchecked immigration. To address a sluggish economy, he proposes a tough-love, carrot-and-stick approach—limiting the power of unions and cutting workers' benefits, while offering tax incentives to workers who work overtime (above the current 35- to 39-hour workweek). His policies are generating predictable resistance from unions: Expect at least one major strike somewhere in France during your trip.

More French eyebrows have been raised by Sarkozy's personal life. Within a year of becoming president, he divorced his wife of 11 years and married sexy Italian model-turned-singer Carla Bruni (who has been linked romantically with Mick Jagger and Eric Clapton). Google "Sarkozy" and you'll turn up almost as many hits for Carla. Their bedroom life is a constant topic of tabloid gossip, as are their eccentricities. Sarkozy likes to jog, and even wears sweats when relaxing *(quelle horreur!)*. The press has nicknamed Sarkozy "Président Bling Bling" for his love of shiny things (Ray-Ban sunglasses, expensive watches, yachts, Italian supermodels), his jet-set lifestyle, and his affinity for celebrities.

APPENDIX

Contents

Tourist Information 463
Communicating 464
Transportation 474
Resources .491
Holidays and Festivals 496
Conversions and Climate. 498
Essential Packing Checklist. 501
Hotel Reservation Form 502
French Survival Phrases. 503

Tourist Information

The French national tourist office **in the US** is a wealth of information. Before your trip, scan their website: www.franceguide.com. You can contact them to briefly describe your trip and request any information (such as city maps and schedules of upcoming festivals). To ask questions and request tourist materials (for a small shipping fee), email info.us@franceguide.com or call 514/288-1904. You can download many brochures free of charge at their website.

In France, your best first stop in a new city is generally the tourist information office (remember that these are abbreviated as **TI** in this book). Throughout Provence and the French Riviera, you'll find TIs are well organized, with English-speaking staff. A TI is a great place to get a city map, advice on public transportation (including bus and train schedules), information on special events, and recommendations for nightlife. Most TIs will help you find a room by calling hotels (for free or for a small fee) or by giving you a complete listing of available bed-and-breakfasts. Towns with a lot of tourism generally have English-speaking guides available for private hire (about $140 for a 2-hour guided town walk). Many TIs have information on the entire country or at least the region, so try to pick up maps for towns you'll be visiting later in your trip. If you're arriving in town after the office closes, call ahead or pick up a map in a neighboring town.

The French call TIs by different names: *Office de Tourisme* and *Bureau de Tourisme* are used in cities; *Syndicat d'Initiative* or *Information Touristique* are used in small towns. Also look for *Accueil* signs in airports and at popular sights. These information booths are staffed with seasonal helpers who provide tourists with limited, though generally sufficient, information. Smaller TIs are often closed from 12:00 to 14:00.

Communicating

The Language Barrier and that French Attitude

You've probably heard that the French are "mean and cold and refuse to speak English." This is an out-of-date preconception left over from the days of Charles de Gaulle—and it's especially incorrect in this region. In these southern lands kissed by the sun and sea, you'll find your hosts more jovial and easygoing (like their Italian neighbors) than in the more serious north. Still, be reasonable in your expectations: Waiters are paid to be efficient, not chatty. And Provençal postal clerks are every bit as speedy, cheery, and multilingual as ours are back home.

The biggest mistake most Americans make when traveling to France is trying to do too much with limited time. This approach is a mistake in the bustling north, and a virtual sin in the laid-back south. Hurried, impatient travelers who miss the subtle pleasures of people-watching from a sun-dappled café often misinterpret French attitudes. By slowing your pace and making an effort to understand French culture by living it, you're far more likely to have a richer experience. With the five weeks of paid vacation and 35-hour work week that many French workers consider as non-negotiable rights, your hosts can't fathom why anyone would rush through their vacation.

The French take great pride in their customs, clinging to their belief in cultural superiority despite the fact that they're no longer a world superpower. Let's face it: It's tough to keep on smiling when you've been crushed by a Big Mac, Mickey Moused by Disney, and drowned in instant coffee. Your hosts are cold only if you decide to see them that way. Polite and formal, the French respect the fine points of culture and tradition. Here, strolling down the street with a big grin on your face and saying hello to strangers is a sign

APPENDIX

of senility, not friendliness (seriously). They think that Americans, though friendly, are hesitant to pursue more serious friendships. Recognize sincerity and look for kindness. Give them the benefit of the doubt.

French communication difficulties are exaggerated. To hurdle the language barrier, bring a small English/French dictionary, a phrase book (look for mine, which contains a dictionary and menu decoder), a menu reader (if you're a gourmet eater), and a good supply of patience (for a list of survival phrases, see page 503). In transactions, a small notepad and pen minimize misunderstandings about prices; have vendors write the price down.

Though many French people—especially those in the tourist trade, and in big cities—speak English, you'll get better treatment if you learn and use the French pleasantries. If you learn only five phrases, choose these: *bonjour* (good day), *pardon* (pardon me), *s'il vous plaît* (please), *merci* (thank you), and *au revoir* (good-bye). The French value politeness. Begin every encounter with *"Bonjour* (or *S'il vous plaît), madame* or *monsieur"* and end every encounter with *"Au revoir, madame* or *monsieur."*

The French are language perfectionists—they take their language (and other languages) seriously. Often they speak more English than they let on. This isn't a tourist-baiting tactic, but timidity on their part about speaking another language less than fluently. Start any conversation with, *"Bonjour, madame* or *monsieur. Parlez-vous anglais?"* and hope they speak more English than you speak French.

Telephones

Smart travelers use the telephone to reserve or reconfirm rooms, get tourist information, reserve restaurants, confirm tour times, or phone home. When spelling out your name on the phone, you'll find that most letters are pronounced very differently in French: *a* is pronounced "ah," *e* is pronounced "eh," and *i* is pronounced "ee." To avoid confusion, say *"a,* Anne," *"e,* euro," and *"i,* Isabelle."

Generally the easiest, cheapest way to call home is to use an international phone card purchased in France. This section covers dialing instructions, phone cards, and types of phones (for more in-depth information, see www.ricksteves.com/phoning).

How to Dial

Calling from the US to France, or vice versa, is simple—once you break the code. The European calling chart later in this chapter will walk you through it.

Dialing Domestically Within France

France has a direct-dial 10-digit phone system (no area codes). To make domestic calls anywhere within France, just dial the number.

For example, the number of one of my recommended hotels in Nice is 04 97 03 10 70. That's the number you dial whether you're calling it from across the street or across the country.

Dialing Internationally to or from France

If you want to make an international call, follow these steps:

1. Dial the international access code (00 if you're calling from Europe, 011 from the US or Canada).

2. Dial the country code of the country you're calling (33 for France, or 1 for the US or Canada).

3. Dial the local number. If you're calling France, drop the initial zero of the phone number (the European calling chart lists specifics per country).

Calling from the US to France: To call the Nice hotel from the US, dial 011 (the US international access code), 33 (France's country code), then 4 97 03 10 70 (the hotel's number without its initial zero).

Calling from any European Country to the US: To call my office in Edmonds, Washington, from anywhere in Europe, I dial 00 (Europe's international access code), 1 (the US country code), 425 (Edmonds' area code), and 771-8303.

Note: You might see a + in front of a European number. When dialing the number, replace the + with the international access code of the country you're calling from (00 from Europe, 011 from the US or Canada).

Public Phones and Hotel-Room Phones

To make calls from public phones, you'll need a prepaid phone card. There are two kinds of phone cards: insertable and international. (Both types of phone card work only in France. If you have a live card at the end of your trip, give it to another traveler to use up.) Coin-op phones are virtually extinct.

Insertable Phone Cards: Called a *télécarte* (tay-lay-kart), this type of card can be used only at pay phones. These cards are handy and affordable for local and domestic calls, but more expensive for international calls. They're sold in two denominations—*une petite* costs about €7.50; *une grande* about €15—at *tabacs* (tobacco shops), newsstands, post offices, and train stations. To use the card, insert it into a slot in the pay phone. Though you can use a *télécarte* to call anywhere in the world, it's only a good deal for making quick local calls from a phone booth.

International Phone Cards: Called "code cards" (*cartes à code,* cart ah code), these are the cheapest way to make international calls from Europe—with the best cards, it costs literally pennies a minute. They can also be used to make local calls, and work from any type of phone, including your hotel-room phone (but ask at the front desk if you'll be charged for making toll-free calls).

The cards are sold at newsstand kiosks and tobacco shops *(tabacs)*. Ask the clerk which of the various brands has the best rates for calls to America. Because cards are occasionally duds, avoid the more expensive denominations. Some shops also sell cardless codes, printed right on the receipt.

To use the card, scratch to get your code, then dial the free (usually 4-digit) access number. If the access code on the card doesn't work from your hotel-room phone, try the card's 10-digit, toll-free code that starts with 08. A voice in French (followed by English) tells you to enter your code. Before or after entering your code, you may need to press (or "*touche*," pronounced toosh) the pound key (#, *dièse*, dee-ehz) or the star key (*, *étoile*, eh-twahl). At the next message, dial the number you're calling (possibly followed by pound or star key; you don't have to listen through the entire sales pitch).

Remember that you don't need the actual card to use a card account, so it's sharable. You can write down the access number and code in your notebook and share it with friends.

Hotel-Room Phones: Calling from your room can be cheap for local calls (ask for the rates at the front desk first), but is often a rip-off for long-distance calls (unless you use an international phone card, explained above). Incoming calls are free, making this a cheap way for friends and family to stay in touch (provided they have a good long-distance plan for calls to Europe and a list of your hotels' phone numbers).

US Calling Cards: These cards, such as the ones offered by AT&T, Verizon, or Sprint, are the worst option. You'll nearly always save a lot of money by using a locally purchased phone card instead.

Mobile Phones

Many travelers enjoy the convenience of traveling with a mobile phone.

Using Your Mobile Phone: Your US mobile phone works in Europe if it's GSM-enabled, tri-band or quad-band, and on a calling plan that includes international calls. Phones from T-Mobile and AT&T, which use the same GSM technology that Europe does, are more likely to work overseas than Verizon or Sprint phones (if you're not sure, ask your service provider). Most US providers charge $1.29 per minute while roaming internationally to make or receive calls, and 20–50 cents to send or receive text messages.

You'll pay cheaper rates if your phone is electronically "unlocked" (ask your provider about this); then, while in Europe,

European Calling Chart

Just smile and dial, using this key:
AC = Area Code, LN = Local Number.

European Country	Calling long distance within ...	Calling from the US or Canada to ...	Calling from a European country to ...
Austria	AC + LN	011 + 43 + AC (without the initial zero) + LN	00 + 43 + AC (without the initial zero) + LN
Belgium	LN	011 + 32 + LN (without initial zero)	00 + 32 + LN (without initial zero)
Bosnia-Herzegovina	AC + LN	011 + 387 + AC (without initial zero) + LN	00 + 387 + AC (without initial zero) + LN
Britain	AC + LN	011 + 44 + AC (without initial zero) + LN	00 + 44 + AC (without initial zero) + LN
Croatia	AC + LN	011 + 385 + AC (without initial zero) + LN	00 + 385 + AC (without initial zero) + LN
Czech Republic	LN	011 + 420 + LN	00 + 420 + LN
Denmark	LN	011 + 45 + LN	00 + 45 + LN
Estonia	LN	011 + 372 + LN	00 + 372 + LN
Finland	AC + LN	011 + 358 + AC (without initial zero) + LN	999 (or other 900 number) + 358 + AC (without initial zero) + LN
France	LN	011 + 33 + LN (without initial zero)	00 + 33 + LN (without initial zero)
Germany	AC + LN	011 + 49 + AC (without initial zero) + LN	00 + 49 + AC (without initial zero) + LN
Gibraltar	LN	011 + 350 + LN	00 + 350 + LN
Greece	LN	011 + 30 + LN	00 + 30 + LN
Hungary	06 + AC + LN	011 + 36 + AC + LN	00 + 36 + AC + LN
Ireland	AC + LN	011 + 353 + AC (without initial zero) + LN	00 + 353 + AC (without initial zero) + LN

European Country	Calling long distance within ...	Calling from the US or Canada to ...	Calling from a European country to ...
Italy	LN	011 + 39 + LN	00 + 39 + LN
Montenegro	AC + LN	011 + 382 + AC (without initial zero) + LN	00 + 382 + AC (without initial zero) + LN
Morocco	LN	011 + 212 + LN (without initial zero)	00 + 212 + LN (without initial zero)
Netherlands	AC + LN	011 + 31 + AC (without initial zero) + LN	00 + 31 + AC (without initial zero) + LN
Norway	LN	011 + 47 + LN	00 + 47 + LN
Poland	LN	011 + 48 + LN (without initial zero)	00 + 48 + LN (without initial zero)
Portugal	LN	011 + 351 + LN	00 + 351 + LN
Slovakia	AC + LN	011 + 421 + AC (without initial zero) + LN	00 + 421 + AC (without initial zero) + LN
Slovenia	AC + LN	011 + 386 + AC (without initial zero) + LN	00 + 386 + AC (without initial zero) + LN
Spain	LN	011 + 34 + LN	00 + 34 + LN
Sweden	AC + LN	011 + 46 + AC (without initial zero) + LN	00 + 46 + AC (without initial zero) + LN
Switzerland	LN	011 + 41 + LN (without initial zero)	00 + 41 + LN (without initial zero)
Turkey	AC (if there's no initial zero, add one) + LN	011 + 90 + AC (without initial zero) + LN	00 + 90 + AC (without initial zero) + LN

- The instructions above apply whether you're calling a land line or mobile phone.
- The international access codes (the first numbers you dial when making an international call) are 011 if you're calling from the US or Canada, or 00 if you're calling from virtually anywhere in Europe (except Finland, where it's 999 or another 900 number, depending on the phone service you're using).
- To call the US or Canada from Europe, dial 00, then 1 (the country code for the US and Canada), then the area code and number. In short, 00 + 1 + AC + LN = Hi, Mom!

you can simply buy a tiny **SIM card,** which gives you a European phone number. SIM cards are sold at mobile-phone stores and some newsstand kiosks for about $5–10, and generally include several minutes' worth of prepaid domestic calling time. When you buy a SIM card, you may need to show ID, such as your passport. Insert the SIM card in your phone (usually in a slot behind the battery), and it'll work like a European mobile phone. When buying a SIM card, always ask about fees for domestic and international calls, roaming charges, and how to check your credit balance and buy more time.

Many **smartphones,** such as the iPhone or BlackBerry, work in Europe—but beware of sky-high fees, especially for data downloading (checking email, browsing the Internet, watching videos, and so on). Ask your provider in advance how to avoid unwittingly "roaming" your way to a huge bill. Some applications allow for cheap or free smartphone calls over a Wi-Fi connection (see "Calling over the Internet," below).

Using a European Mobile Phone: Mobile-phone shops all over Europe sell basic phones. Phones that are "locked" to work with a single provider start at around $30; "unlocked" phones (which allow you to switch out SIM cards to use your choice of provider) start at around $60. You'll also need to buy a SIM card and prepaid credit for making calls. When you're in the phone's home country, domestic calls are reasonable, and incoming calls are free. You'll pay more if you're "roaming" in another country.

Calling over the Internet

Some things that seem too good to be true...actually are true. If you're traveling with a laptop, you can make calls using VoIP (Voice over Internet Protocol). With VoIP, two computers act as the phones, and the Internet-based calls are free (or you can pay a few cents to call from your computer to a telephone). If both computers have webcams, you can even see each other while you chat. The major providers are Skype (www.skype.com) and Google Talk (www.google.com/talk).

Useful Phone Numbers

Understand the various prefixes. France's toll-free numbers start with 0800 (like US 800 numbers, though in France you dial a 0 first rather than a 1). In France, these 0800 numbers—called *numéro vert* (green number)—can be dialed free from any phone without using a phone card. But you can't call France's toll-free numbers from America, nor can you count on reaching US toll-free numbers from France.

Any 08 number that does not have a 00 directly following is a toll call, generally costing from €0.10 to €0.50 per minute.

Emergency Needs
Police: tel. 17
Emergency Medical Assistance: tel. 15
Riviera Medical Services: tel. 04 93 26 12 70, www.rivieramedical
.com (has list of English-speaking physicians in the Riviera region
and can help make an appointment or call an ambulance)

Embassies and Consulates
US Consulate in Nice: tel. 04 93 88 89 55, fax 04 93 87 07 38 (7
avenue Gustave V, http://france.usembassy.gov/nice.html; does *not*
provide visa services—Paris is the nearest office for these services)
Canadian Consulate in Nice: tel. 04 93 92 93 22, fax 04 93 92 55
51 (2 place Franklin)
US Consulate in Marseille: tel. 04 91 54 92 00, fax 04 91 55 56 95
(place Varian Fry, http://france.usembassy.gov/marseille.html)
US Consulate and Embassy in Paris: tel. 01 43 12 22 22, emergency walk-in passport services available Mon–Fri 9:00–11:00,
non-emergency online appointments possible, closed Sat–Sun
(4 avenue Gabriel, to the left as you face Hôtel Crillon, Mo:
Concorde, http://france.usembassy.gov)
Canadian Consulate and Embassy in Paris: tel. 01 44 43 29
00, reception open daily 9:00–12:00 & 14:00–17:00 (35 avenue
Montaigne, Mo: Franklin D. Roosevelt, www.amb-canada.fr)
Australian Consulate in Paris: tel. 01 40 59 33 00, Mon–Fri
9:00–12:00 & 14:00–16:00, closed Sat–Sun (4 rue Jean Rey, Mo:
Bir-Hakeim, www.france.embassy.gov.au)

Travel Advisories
US Department of State: tel. 202/647-5225, www.travel.state.gov
Canadian Department of Foreign Affairs: Canadian tel. 800-
267-6788, www.dfait-maeci.gc.ca
US Centers for Disease Control and Prevention: tel. 800-CDC-
INFO (800-232-4636), www.cdc.gov/travel

Directory Assistance
Directory Assistance for France (some English spoken): tel. 12
Collect Calls to the US: tel. 00 00 11

Airports
Nice: Aéroport de Nice—toll tel. 08 20 42 33 33 (€0.12/minute),
www.nice.aeroport.fr
Marseille: Aéroport Marseille–Provence—tel. 04 42 14 14 14,
www.marseille.aeroport.fr
Paris: Aéroports Charles de Gaulle and Orly share the same numbers—toll tel. 3950 (€0.34/minute), www.adp.fr; Beauvais—toll
tel. 08 92 68 20 66, www.aeroportbeauvais.com

Lyon: Saint-Exupéry Airport—toll tel. 08 26 80 08 26 (€0.15/minute), www.lyon.aeroport.fr

Airlines
The following 08 numbers are toll calls; the per-minute fee generally ranges from €0.10 to €0.50.
Aer Lingus: toll tel. 08 21 23 02 67
Air Canada: toll tel. 08 25 88 08 81
Air France: tel. 3654 or toll tel. 08 20 82 36 54
Alitalia: toll tel. 08 20 31 53 15
American Airlines: tel. 01 55 17 43 41
Austrian Airlines: toll tel. 08 02 81 68 16
British Airways: toll tel. 08 25 82 54 00
Continental: tel. 01 71 23 03 35
Delta: toll tel. 08 11 64 00 05
EasyJet: toll tel. 08 26 10 33 20
Iberia: toll tel. 08 25 80 09 65
Icelandair: tel. 01 44 51 60 51
KLM: toll tel. 08 92 70 26 08
Lufthansa: toll tel. 08 92 23 16 90
Olympic: tel. 01 44 94 58 58
Royal Air Maroc: toll tel. 08 20 82 18 21
SAS: toll tel. 08 25 32 53 35
Swiss International: toll tel. 08 92 23 25 01
United: toll tel. 08 10 72 72 72
US Airways: toll tel. 08 10 63 22 22

Car Leasing in France
Europe by Car: US tel. 800-223-1516, US fax 212/246-1458, www.ebctravel.com
Auto France: US tel. 800-572-9655, US fax 201/393-7800, www.autofrance.net
Kemwel: US tel. 877-820-0668, www.kemwel.com

RV Rental
French RVs are much smaller than those you see at home.
Van It: mobile 06 70 43 11 86, www.van-it.com
Idea Merge: US tel. 888-297-0001, US fax 503/296-2625, www.ideamerge.com

Hotel Chains
Accor Hotels (huge chain, including Ibis, Mercure, and Novotel): US tel. 800-221-4542, www.accorhotels.com
Ibis Hotels: toll tel. 08 92 68 66 86, US tel. 800-221-4542, www.ibishotel.com

Mercure Hotels: toll tel. 08 25 88 33 33, US tel. 800-221-4542, www.mercure.com

Kyriad Hotels: toll tel. 08 25 02 80 38, from US dial 011 33 1 64 62 59 70, www.kyriad.com

Best Western Hotels: tel. 08 00 90 44 90, US tel. 800-780-7234, www.bestwestern.com

Country Home Rental: www.gites-de-france.fr or www.gite.com; France Homestyle, US tel. 206/325-0132, www.francehomestyle.com, info@francehomestyle.com; Ville et Village, US tel. 510/559-8080, www.villeetvillage.com, rentals@villeetvillage.com

Youth Hostels
Hostelling International, US Office: www.hiusa.org
Hostelling International, Canada Office: www.hihostels.ca

Cooking Schools
Maison d'Hôtes de Provence: In central Arles, you can take educational and convivial cooking courses with Erick Vedel (11 rue Portagnel, tel. & fax 04 90 49 69 20, www.cuisineprovencale.com).

Cuisine de Provence: Charming, easygoing Barbara Schuerenberg leads reasonably priced cooking classes from her home in Vaison la Romaine (tel. 04 90 35 68 43, www.cuisinedeprovence.com, barbara@cuisinedeprovence.com, see page 169).

Jardin de Bacchus: Northwest of Avignon, in their Tavel bed-and-breakfast, Christine and Erik offer fun cooking classes (tel. 04 66 90 28 62, www.provence-escapade.fr, jardindebacchus@free.fr, see page 130).

Les Petits Farcis: In Old Nice, Rosa Jackson teaches a variety of cooking courses, some of which include visits to the city's markets (www.petitsfarcis.com, see page 297).

Internet Access
It's useful to get online periodically as you travel—to confirm trip plans, check train or bus schedules, get weather forecasts, catch up on email, blog or post photos from your trip, or call folks back home (explained earlier, under "Calling over the Internet").

Many hotels offer a computer in the lobby with Internet access for guests. Smaller places may sometimes let you sit at their desk for a few minutes just to check your email, if you ask politely. If your hotel doesn't have access, ask your hotelier to direct you to the nearest place to get online. In the region's key cities—Nice and Avignon—you'll find plenty of coffee shops that offer Wi-Fi to travelers with laptop computers. Little hole-in-the-wall Internet-access shops, while common in the rest of Europe, are not prevalent in France. In smaller towns, post offices may offer Internet access *(cyberposte)*; buy a chip-card (about the same prices as phone cards) and you're in business.

Traveling with a Laptop: With a laptop or netbook, it's easy to get online if your hotel has Wi-Fi (wireless Internet access, pronounced "wee-fee" by the French) or a port in your room for plugging in a cable. Some hotels offer Wi-Fi for free; others charge by the minute or hour. A cellular modem—which lets your laptop access the Internet over a mobile phone network—provides more extensive coverage, but is much more expensive than Wi-Fi.

Mail

French post offices are sometimes called PTT—for "Post, Telegraph, and Telephone"—or look for signs for *La Poste*. Hours vary, though most are open weekdays 8:00–19:00 and Saturday morning 8:00–12:00. Stamps and phone cards are also sold at *tabacs*. It costs about €1 to mail a postcard to the US. Federal Express makes pricey two-day deliveries. One convenient, if pricey, way to send packages home is by using the PTT's Colissimo XL postage-paid mailing box. It costs €36–41 to ship boxes weighing 5–7 kilos (about 11–15 pounds).

You can arrange for mail delivery to your hotel (allow 10 days for a letter to arrive), but phoning and emailing are so easy that I've dispensed with mail stops altogether.

Transportation

By Car or Public Transportation?

Cars are best for groups of three or more (especially families with small kids), those packing heavy, and travelers scouring the countryside in search of the perfect hill town—a tempting plan for this region. Trains and buses are best for those going solo, blitz tourists, and city-to-city travelers.

If you plan to focus on Arles, Avignon, Aix-en-Provence, and seaside destinations along the Riviera, go by train. Stations are centrally located in each city, which makes hotel-hunting and sightseeing easy. Buses and taxis pick up where trains leave off. While bus service can be sparse, taxis are generally available and reasonable. If relying on public transportation, focus on fewer destinations, or hire one of the excellent minivan tour guides I recommend (see "Tours of Provence" on page 46).

I've included two sample itineraries—by car and by public transportation—to help you explore Provence and the French Riviera smoothly; you'll find these in the Introduction.

French Train Terms and Abbreviations

SNCF *(Société Nationale Chemins de Fer):* This is the Amtrak of France, operating all national train lines that link cities and towns.

TGV *(Train à Grande Vitesse):* SNCF's network of high-speed trains (twice as fast as regular trains), connecting major cities in France. These trains always require a reservation.

CORAIL: These trains are the next best compared with the TGV in terms of speed and comfort.

TER *(Trains Express Régionale):* These trains serve smaller stops within a region. For example, you'll find trains called TER de Bourgogne (trains operating only in Burgundy) and TER Provence (Provence-only trains).

Rapide and *Express:* Trains designated as *Rapide* stop only in major cities. *Express* trains serve long-distance destinations, stopping at both large and midsize cities.

Trains

France's rail system (SNCF) sets the pace in Europe. Its super TGV (*train à grande vitesse;* tay zhay vay) system has inspired bullet trains throughout the world. The TGV runs at 170–220 mph. Its rails are fused into one long, continuous track for a faster and smoother ride. The TGV has changed commuting patterns in much of France and put most of the country within day-trip distance of Paris. TGV trains serve these cities in Provence and the Riviera: Avignon, Arles (very few trains), Nîmes, Marseille, Orange, Aix-en-Provence, Antibes, Cannes, and Nice. Avignon and Aix-en-Provence have separate TGV stations outside of town (with bus connections into the center)—note carefully which station your train serves (either "Centre-Ville" or "TGV"; if it's not specified, then it's the central station).

At any train station, you can get schedule information, make reservations, and buy tickets for any destination.

Schedules

Schedules change by season, weekday, and weekend. Verify train times shown in this book—on the Web, visit http://bahn.hafas.de /bin/query.exe/en (Germany's excellent all-Europe schedule site), or check locally at train stations.

Bigger stations have helpful information agents (wearing red or blue vests) roaming the station and at *Accueil* offices or booths. They can answer rail questions more quickly than the information or ticket windows. Make use of their help; don't stand in a ticket line if all you need is a train schedule.

Public Transportation in Provence

APPENDIX

Railpasses

Long-distance travelers can save money with a France Railpass, sold only outside France (through travel agents or Europe Through the Back Door). For roughly the cost of a Paris–Avignon–Paris ticket, the France Railpass offers three days of travel (within a month) anywhere in France. You can add up to six more days for the cost of a two-hour ride each day. You'll save money by getting the second-class instead of the first-class version, but first class gives you more options when reserving popular TGV routes (seats are very limited for passholders, so reserving these fast trains at

least several weeks in advance is recommended). The Saverpass version gives two or more people traveling together a 15 percent discount.

Each day of use allows you to take as many trips as you want on one calendar day (you could go from Paris to Beaune in Burgundy, enjoy wine-tasting, then continue to Avignon, stay a few hours, and end in Nice—though I don't recommend it). Buy second-class tickets in France for shorter trips and spend your valuable railpass days wisely.

For a summary of railpass deals and the latest prices, check my

French Railpasses

Prices listed are for 2010 and are subject to change. For the latest prices, details, and train schedules (and easy online ordering), see my comprehensive *Guide to Eurail Passes* at www.ricksteves.com/rail.

"Saver" prices are per person for two or more people traveling together. "Youth" means under age 26. The fare for children 4–11 is half the adult individual fare or Saver fare. Kids under age 4 travel free.

FRANCE PASS

	Adult 1st Class	Adult 2nd Class	Senior 1st Class	Youth 1st Class	Youth 2nd Class
3 days in 1 month	$291	$248	$266	$215	$182
Extra rail days (max 6)	40-44	32-38	37-41	30-33	26-29

Senior = 60 and up.

FRANCE SAVERPASS

	1st Class	2nd Class
3 days in 1 month	$249	$214
Extra rail days (max 6)	36-38	30-31

FRANCE RAIL & DRIVE PASS

Any 2 rail days and 2 car days in 1 month.

Car Category	1st Class	Extra Car Day
Economy	$289	$47
Compact	297	55
Intermediate	309	67
Full-size	340	98
Premium Automatic	357	115
Minivan	336	94

Prices are per person, two traveling together, except that extra-car-day prices are paid by only one person. Solo travelers pay about $100 extra. Third and fourth persons sharing the car can buy just a regular railpass. Extra rail days (3 max) cost $39 per day. To order a Rail & Drive pass, call your travel agent or Rail Europe at 800-438-7245.
This pass is not sold by Europe Through the Back Door.

Map key:
Approximate point-to-point one-way second-class rail fares in US dollars. First class costs 50 percent more. Add up fares for your itinerary to see if a railpass will save you money.

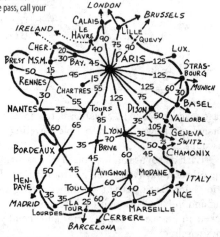

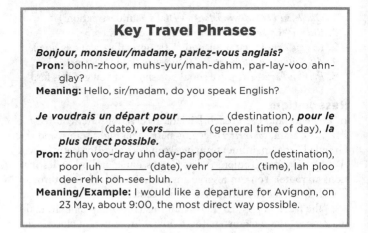

Key Travel Phrases

Bonjour, monsieur/madame, parlez-vous anglais?
Pron: bohn-zhoor, muhs-yur/mah-dahm, par-lay-voo ahn-glay?
Meaning: Hello, sir/madam, do you speak English?

Je voudrais un départ pour _____ (destination), *pour le* _____ (date), *vers*_____ (general time of day), *la plus direct possible.*
Pron: zhuh voo-dray uhn day-par poor _____ (destination), poor luh _____ (date), vehr _____ (time), lah ploo dee-rehk poh-see-bluh.
Meaning/Example: I would like a departure for Avignon, on 23 May, about 9:00, the most direct way possible.

Guide to Eurail Passes at www.ricksteves.com/rail. If you decide to get a railpass, this guide will help you know you're getting the right one for your trip.

Buying Tickets

If traveling *sans* railpass and buying as you go, remember that second-class tickets provide the same transportation for up to 33 percent less (and many regional trains to less-trafficked places often have only second-class cars).

You can buy tickets online at www.raileurope.com (a US company that delivers tickets to your home but doesn't always have the lowest rates), or better, at www.tgv-europe.com/en/home. If you choose a country other than the US and outside of western Europe, you'll be able to print tickets at home or pick them up in the station (if you choose, say, France, the site will be in French, and if you choose the US, you'll be redirected to www.raileurope.com).

On the Train: You can buy tickets on the train for a €4 surcharge, but you must find the conductor immediately upon boarding; otherwise it's a €35 minimum charge.

Automatic Train Ticket Machines

The ticket machines available at most stations are great time-savers for short trips when ticket window lines are long (but your American credit card won't work, so you'll need euro coins). Some have English instructions, but for those that don't, here is what you are prompted to do. (The default is usually what you want; turn the dial or move the cursor to your choice, and press *Validez* to agree to each step.)

1. *Quelle est votre destination?* (What's your destination?)
2. *Billet Plein Tarif* (Full-fare ticket—yes for most.)
3. *1ère ou 2ème* (First or second class; normally second is fine.)
4. *Aller simple ou aller-retour?* (One-way or round-trip?)
5. *Prix en Euro* (The price should be shown if you get this far.)

Reservations

In Provence and the French Riviera, reservations are required for any TGV train, *couchettes* (sleeping berths) on night trains, and the Grande Ligne (mainline) train between Nice and Bordeaux (serves Antibes, Cannes, Toulon, Arles, Carcassonne, and other destinations en route). You can reserve any train at any station or through SNCF Boutiques (small offices in city centers).

The fast and popular TGV trains usually fill up quickly, making reservations a challenge (particularly for railpass-holders, who are allocated a limited number of seats). It's wise to book well ahead for any TGV, especially on the busy Paris–Avignon–Nice line. Reservations cost €3 (more during peak periods) and are possible up to 90 days in advance.

Although reservations are generally unnecessary for non-TGV trains (except the Nice-Bordeaux train mentioned above), they are advisable during busy times (e.g., Fri and Sun afternoons, Sat mornings, weekday rush hours, and particularly holiday weekends; see "Major Holidays and Weekends" on page 27).

You are required to validate (*composter,* kohm-poh-stay) all train tickets and reservations. Before boarding any SNCF train, look for a yellow machine nearby to stamp your ticket or reservation. (Do not *composter* your railpass, but do validate it at a ticket window before the first time you use it.)

Baggage Check

Baggage check (*consigne,* or *Espaces Bagages*) is available only at the biggest train stations (about €4–10/bag depending on size), and is noted where available in this book (depends on security concerns, so be prepared to keep your bag). For security reasons, all luggage must carry a tag with the traveler's first and last name and current address. This applies to hand luggage, as well as bigger bags that are stowed. Free tags are available at train stations.

Train Tips

- Arrive at the station with plenty of time before your departure to find the right platform, confirm connections, and so on. *Remember that Avignon and Aix-en-Provence have separate TGV stations that are outside the town center.*
- Small stations have minimal staff; if you can't find an agent at the station, go directly to the tracks and look for the overhead

Coping with Strikes

Going on strike *(en grève)* is a popular pastime in this revolution-happy country. President Sarkozy is pushing unions to their limits, and because bargaining between management and employees is not standard procedure, workers strike to get attention. Truckers and tractors block main roads and autoroutes (they call it Opération Escargot—"Operation Snail's Pace"), baggage handlers bring airports to their knees, and museum workers make artwork off-limits to tourists. Métro and train personnel seem to strike every year—probably during your trip. What does the traveler do? You could *jetter l'éponge* (throw in the sponge) and go somewhere less strike-prone (Switzerland's lovely), or learn to accept certain events as out of your control. Strikes in France generally last no longer than a day or two, and if you're aware of them, you can usually plan around them. Your hotelier will know the latest (or can find out). Make a habit of asking your hotel receptionist about strikes, or check www.americansinfrance.net (look under "Daily Life").

sign that confirms your train stops at that track.

- Larger stations have platforms with monitors showing each car's layout (numbered forward or backward) so you can figure out where your *voiture* (car) will stop on the long platform and where to board it.

- Try to check schedules in advance. Upon arrival at a station, find out your departure possibilities. Large stations have a separate information window or office; at small stations, the regular ticket office gives information.

- If you have a rail flexipass, write the date on your pass each day you travel (before or immediately after boarding your first train).

- Validate tickets (not passes) and reservations in yellow machines before boarding. If you're traveling with a pass and have a reservation for a specific trip, you must validate the reservation.

- Before getting on a train, confirm that it's going where you think it is. For example, if you want to go to Antibes, ask the conductor or any local passenger, *"À Antibes?"* (Ah ahn-teeb; meaning, "To Antibes?")

- If a non-TGV train seat is reserved, it will usually be labeled *réservé*, with the cities to and from which it is reserved.

- Some trains split cars en route. Make sure your train car is continuing to your destination by asking, for example, *"Cette voiture va à Avignon?"* (Seht vwah-tewr vah ah ah-veen-yohn;

meaning, "This car goes to Avignon?") On my last trip, the train from Marseilles to Arles split off some cars along the way—which was not mentioned when I asked the conductor if this train went to Arles.

- If you don't understand an announcement, ask your neighbor to explain, "*Pardon madame/monsieur, qu'est-ce qui se passe?*" (kess-key-suh-pass; meaning, "Excuse me, what's going on?").
- Verify with the conductor all of the transfers you must make: "*Correspondance à?*"; meaning, "Transfer to where?"
- To guard against theft, it's best to keep your bags directly overhead. If you want to store them in the lower racks (available in most cars), make sure you can see them from your seat. If you have big bags, board early to get the best storage space. Your bags are most vulnerable to theft before the train takes off and whenever it stops.
- Note your arrival time so you'll be ready to get off.
- Use the train's free WCs before you get off (but not while the train is stopped).

Buses

You can get nearly anywhere in Provence and the Riviera by rail and bus...if you're well-organized, patient, and not in a hurry. Review my bus schedule information, and verify times at the local tourist office or bus station. Regional buses work well for some destinations not served by trains. A few bus lines are run by SNCF (France's rail system) and are included with your railpass (show railpass at station to get free bus ticket), but most bus lines are independent of the rail system and are not covered by railpasses. Train stations often have bus information where train-to-bus connections are important—and vice versa for bus companies. On Sunday, regional bus service virtually disappears.

Bus Tips
- Read the train tips described earlier, and use those that apply.
- Use TIs often to help plan your trip; they have regional bus schedules and are happy to assist you.
- Remember that service is sparse to nonexistent on Sunday. Wednesday bus schedules are often different during the school year, since school is out this day (and regional buses generally serve schools).
- Be at bus stops at least five minutes early.
- On schedules, *en semaine* means Monday through Saturday, *dimanche* is Sunday, and *jours fériés* are holidays.

Renting a Car

To rent a car in France, you must be at least 18 years old and have held your license for one year. An International Driving Permit—a translation of your driver's license—is recommended, but not required, if your driver's license has been renewed within the last year ($15 through your local AAA, plus two passport photos, www.aaa.com). However, I've frequently rented cars in France and traveled problem-free with just my US license.

Drivers under the age of 25 may incur a young-driver surcharge, and some rental companies do not rent to anyone 75 and over. If you're considered too young or old, look into leasing, which has less-stringent age restrictions (see "Leasing," later).

Research car rentals before you go. It's cheaper to arrange most car rentals from the US. Call several companies and look online to compare rates, or arrange a rental through your hometown travel agent.

Most of the major US rental agencies (such as Alamo/National, Avis, Budget, Dollar, Hertz, and Thrifty) have offices in France. It can be cheaper to use a consolidator, such as Auto Europe (www.autoeurope.com) or Europe by Car (www.ebctravel.com), but by using a middleman, you risk trading customer service for lower prices; if you have a problem with the rental company, you can't count on a consolidator to intervene on your behalf.

For the best deal, rent by the week with unlimited mileage. I normally rent the least expensive model with a stick-shift (cheaper than an automatic). Roads and parking spaces are narrow in France, so you'll do yourself a favor by renting the smallest car that meets your needs.

For a two-week rental, allow $750 per person (based on two people sharing a car), including insurance, tolls, gas, and parking. For a longer rental time, consider leasing (explained later in the chapter); you'll save money on insurance and taxes. Compare pick-up costs (downtown can be cheaper than the airport) and explore drop-off options. Returning a car at a big-city train station can be tricky; get precise details on the car drop-off location and hours. **Except in major cities, rental offices are usually closed during lunch and on Sundays.**

If you want a car for only a day or two (e.g., for the Côtes du Rhône wine route or Luberon villages), you'll likely find it cheaper to rent it in France—US-arranged rentals tend to make financial sense only for three days or more. You can rent a car on the spot just about anywhere. In many cases, this is a worthwhile splurge. All you need is your American driver's license and a major credit card (figure €65–80/day, including 100 kilometers, or 60 miles, per day).

When you pick up the car, check it thoroughly and make sure

any damage is noted on your rental agreement. Find out how your car's lights, turn signals, wipers, and gas cap function. When you return the car, make sure the agent verifies its condition with you.

A **rail-and-drive pass** (such as a EurailDrive, Selectpass Drive, or France Rail and Drive) allows you to mix car and train travel economically (sold only outside France, available from your travel agent). Generally big-city connections are best by train, and rural regions are best by car. With a rail-and-drive pass, you can take advantage of the speed and comfort of the TGV trains for longer trips, and rent a car for as little as one day at a time for day trips that can't be done without one.

The basic France Rail and Drive Pass comes with two days of car rental and two days of rail in one month. You can pick up a car in one city and drop it off in another. Though you're only required to reserve the first car day, it's safer to reserve all days, as vehicles are not always available on short notice.

Car Insurance Options

Accidents can happen anywhere, but when you're on vacation, the last thing you need is stress over car insurance. When you rent a car, you are liable for a very high deductible, sometimes equal to the entire value of the car. Limit your financial risk in case of an accident by choosing one of these three options: Buy Collision Damage Waiver (CDW) coverage from the car-rental company (figure roughly 25 percent extra), get coverage through your credit card (free, but more complicated), or buy coverage through Travel Guard.

CDW includes a very high deductible (typically $1,000–1,500). While each rental company has its own variation, basic CDW costs $15–35 a day and reduces your liability, but does not eliminate it. When you pick up the car, you'll be offered the chance to "buy down" the deductible to zero (for an additional $15–30/day; this is sometimes called "super CDW").

If you opt for **credit-card coverage,** there's a catch. You'll technically have to decline all coverage offered by the rental companies, which means they can place a hold on your card for up to the full value of the car. In case of damage, it can be time-consuming to resolve the charges with your credit-card company. Before you decide on this option, quiz your credit-card company about how it works.

Finally, you can buy car-rental insurance from **Travel Guard** ($9/day plus a one-time $3 service fee covers you for up to $35,000, $250 deductible, tel. 800-826-4919, www.travelguard.com). It's valid everywhere in Europe except the Republic of Ireland, and some Italian car-rental companies refuse to honor it. Residents of Texas and Washington state aren't eligible for this coverage.

For more on car-rental insurance, see www.ricksteves.com /cdw.

Leasing

For trips of three weeks or more, consider a tax-free lease (no VAT to pay), which also includes zero-deductible collision and theft insurance. By technically buying and then selling back the car, you save lots of money. Leasing provides you a brand-new car with unlimited mileage and a 24-hour emergency assistance program. You can lease for as little as 17 days to as long as six months, or possibly longer if you're a teacher or student on sabbatical. Car leases must be arranged in the US at least 30 to 45 days prior to departing for Europe.

Three reliable companies offer 17-day lease packages from about $1,000 for a small car and $1,400 for a midsize. They are Auto France (Peugeot cars only, US tel. 800-572-9655, www.auto france.net), Europe by Car (Peugeot, Citroën, and Renault cars, US tel. 800-223-1516, www.ebctravel.com), and Kemwel (Peugeot cars only, US tel. 877-820-0668, www.kemwel.com). Anyone age 18 or over with a driver's license is eligible. You can pick up or return cars in major cities outside of France, but you'll have to pay an additional fee.

Driving in Provence and the French Riviera

It's a pleasure to explore this region by car, but you need to know the rules.

Seat belts are mandatory for all, and children under age 10 must be in the back seat. Almost all rentals are manual by default, so if you need an automatic, you must request one in advance. Gas *(essence)* is expensive—about $7 per gallon. Diesel *(gazole)* is less—about $6 per gallon—and diesel cars get better mileage, so try to rent a diesel to save money. Be sure you know what type of fuel your car takes before you fill up. Gas is most expensive on autoroutes and cheapest at big supermarkets (closed at night and on Sun). Many gas stations close on Sunday. Your

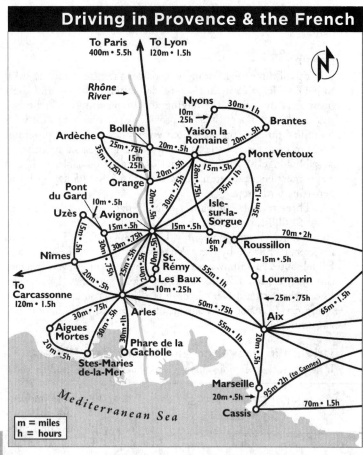

Driving in Provence & the French

To Paris
400m • 5.5h

To Lyon
120m • 1.5h

Rhône River →

Nyons
Vaison la Romaine
10m .25h
30m • 1h
Brantes
20m • .5h
Bollène
25m • .75h
20m • .5h
Ardèche
35m • 1.25h
15m .25h →
Mont Ventoux
28m • .75h
15m • .5h
35m • 1.5h
Orange
20m • .5h
20m • .5h
30m • .75h
Isle-sur-la-Sorgue
35m • 1.5h
Pont du Gard
10m • .5h
Uzès
Avignon
15m • .5h
15m • .5h
15m • .5h
16m .5h ↑
Roussillon
70m • 2h
15m • .5h →
Nîmes
30m • .75h
30m • .75h
45m 1h
St. Rémy
55m • 1h
Lourmarin
To Carcassonne
120m • 1.5h
20m • .75h
25m .5h
20m • .5h
Les Baux
10m • .25h ←
25m • .75h →
30m • .75h
Arles
50m • .75h
Aix
65m • 1.5h
Aigues Mortes
30m • .5h
30m • 1h
55m • 1h
20m • .5h
Phare de la Gacholle
20m • .5h
Stes-Maries de-la-Mer
Marseille
20m • .5h →
95m • 2h (to Cannes)
70m • 1.5h
Cassis

Mediterranean Sea

m = miles
h = hours

US credit and debit cards probably won't work at self-serve pumps; if not, either pay cash, or find gas stations with attendants. Most drivers will spend about $150 per week on gas to prowl the roads in Provence and the French Riviera.

Four hours on the autoroute costs about €25 in tolls (American credit cards not accepted), but the alternative to these super "fee-ways" usually means being marooned in countryside traffic—especially near the Riviera. Autoroutes save enough time, gas, and nausea to justify the splurge. Mix high-speed "autorouting" with scenic country-road rambling (be careful of sluggish tractors on country roads). You'll usually take a ticket when entering an autor-oute and pay when you leave. At pay points, avoid the Télepéage tollbooths and those with a credit-card icon. Look instead for green arrows above the tollbooth, which indicate they accept cash. Some exits are entirely automated, with machines taking all euro

Riviera: Distance & Time

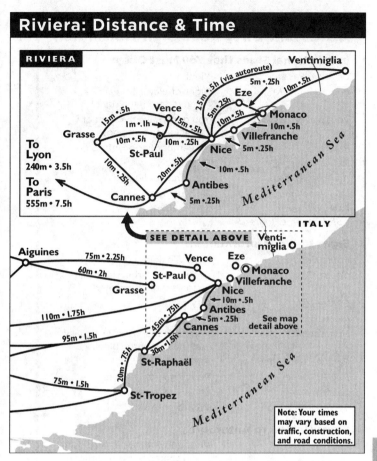

Note: Your times may vary based on traffic, construction, and road conditions.

APPENDIX

bill denominations. Shorter autoroute sections (including along the Riviera) have periodic toll booths, where you can pay by dropping coins into a basket (change given, but keep a good supply of coins handy to avoid waiting for an attendant). Autoroute gas stations usually come with well-stocked mini-marts, clean restrooms, sandwiches, maps, local products, and cheap vending-machine coffee (€1.20—I dig the *cappuccino sucré*). Many have small cafés or more elaborate cafeterias with reasonable prices.

Roads are classified into departmental (D), national (N), and autoroutes (A). D routes (usually yellow lines on maps) are often slower but the most scenic. N routes and important D routes (red lines) are the fastest after autoroutes (orange lines). Green road signs are for national routes; blue are for autoroutes. Note that some key roads in France are undergoing letter designation and number changes (mostly N roads converting to D roads). If you are

Quick-and-Dirty Road Sign Translation

Instructional Signs that You Must Obey:

Cédez le Passage	Yield
Priorité à Droite	Right-of-way is for cars coming from the right
Vous n'avez pas la priorité	You don't have the right of way (when merging)
Rappel	Remember to obey the sign
Déviation	Detour
Allumez vos feux	Turn on your lights
Doublage Interdit	No passing
Parking Interdit/ Stationnement Interdit	No parking

Signs for Your Information:

Route Barrée	Road blocked
Centre Commercial	Grouping of large, suburban stores (not city center)
Centre-Ville	City center
Feux	Traffic signals
Horadateur	Remote parking meter, usually at the end of the block
Parc de Stationnement	Parking lot
Rue Piétonne	Pedestrian-only street
Sauf Riverains	Local access only
Sortie des Camions	Work truck exit

Signs Unique to Autoroutes:

Aire	Rest stop with WCs, telephones, and sometimes gas stations
Bouchon	Traffic jam ahead
Fluide	No slowing ahead ("fluid conditions")
Péage	Toll
Télépéage	Toll booths—automatic toll payment only
Toutes Directions	All directions (passing through a city)
Autres Directions	Other directions (passing through a city)
Par temps de Pluie	When raining (modifies speed-limit signs)

using an older map, the actual route name may differ from what's on your map. Navigate by destination rather than road name...or buy a new map. There are plenty of good facilities, gas stations (most closed Sun), and rest stops along most French roads.

Because speed limits are by road type, they typically aren't posted, so it's best to memorize them:

• Two-lane D and N routes outside cities and towns: 90 km/hour
• Divided highways outside cities and towns: 110 km/hour
• Autoroutes: 130 km/hour

If it's raining, subtract 10 km/hour on D and N routes and 20 km/hour on divided highways and autoroutes. Speed-limit signs are a red circle around a number; when you see that same number again in gray with a broken line diagonally across it, this means that limit no longer applies. Speed limits drop to 30–50 km/hour in villages (always posted) and must be respected.

Beware of traffic cameras: Portable cameras are sometimes positioned to trap unsuspecting drivers, particularly in 30–50 km/hour zones. You can get busted for going even a few kilometers over the limit (believe me).

Parking is a headache in the larger cities. Ask your hotelier for ideas, and pay to park at well-patrolled lots (blue *P* signs direct you to parking lots in French cities). Parking structures usually require that you take a ticket with you and pay at a machine (called a *caisse*) on your way back to the car. Be aware that US credit cards probably won't work in these automated machines but euro bills will. Overnight parking (usually 19:00–8:00) is generally reasonable (except in Nice). Curbside metered parking also works (usually free 12:00–14:00 & 19:00–9:00, and all day and night in Aug). Look for a small machine selling time (called *horadateur*, usually one per block), plug in a few coins (€1.50 buys about an hour, varies by city), push the button, get a receipt showing the amount of time you have, and display it inside your windshield.

Theft is a problem throughout southern France. Thieves easily recognize rental cars and assume they are filled with a tourist's gear. Try to make your car look locally owned by hiding the "tourist-owned" rental-company decals and putting a French newspaper in your back window. Be sure all of your valuables are out of sight and locked in the trunk—or, even better, with you or in your room.

APPENDIX

Driving Tips

• Be aware that in city and town centers, traffic merging from the right (even from tiny side streets) normally has the right-of-way *(priorité à droite)*. So even when you're driving on a major road, pay attention to cars merging from the right. In contrast, cars entering the many suburban roundabouts must yield *(cédez le passage)*.

- Be ready for many roundabouts—navigating them is an art. The key is to know your direction and be ready for your turn-off. If you miss it, take another lap.

- When navigating into cities, approach intersections cautiously, stow the map, and follow the signs to *Centre-Ville* (city center). From there, head to the TI *(Office de Tourisme)* or your hotel.

- When leaving or just passing through cities, follow the signs for *Toutes Directions* or *Autres Directions* (meaning "anywhere else") until you see a sign for your specific destination.

- Driving on any roads but autoroutes will take longer than you anticipate, so allow yourself plenty of time for slower traffic. (Tractors, trucks, traffic, and hard-to-follow signs all deserve blame.) First-timers should estimate how long they think a drive will take...then double it. I pretend that kilometers are miles (for distances) and base my time estimates accordingly. While locals are eating lunch (12:00–14:00), many sights (and gas stations) are closed, so you can make great time driving—but keep it slow when passing through villages.

- U-turns are illegal throughout France, and you cannot turn right on red lights.

- Be very careful when driving on smaller roads—many are narrow, flanked by little ditches that can lure inattentive drivers. I've met several readers who "ditched" their cars (and were successfully pulled out by local farmers).

- On autoroutes, keep to the right lanes to let fast drivers by, and be careful when merging into a left lane, as cars can be coming at very high speeds. Cars and trucks commonly keep their left blinker on while in a passing lane, indicating that they plan to get back over to the right.

- Motorcycles will scream between cars in traffic. Be ready—they expect you to make space to let them pass.

- Gas is tricky to find in rural areas on Sunday, so fill up on Saturday. Autoroute filling stations are always open.

- Keep a stash of coins in your ashtray for parking and small autoroute tolls.

Biking

You'll find areas in Provence and the Riviera where public transportation is limited and bicycle touring might be a good idea. For many, biking is a romantic notion whose novelty wears off after the first hill or headwind—realistically evaluate your physical condition and be clear on the limitations bikes present. Start with an easy pedal to a nearby village or through the vineyards, then decide how ambitious you feel. Most find that two hours on a narrow, hard seat is enough. I've listed bike-rental shops where appropriate and suggested a few of my favorite rides. TIs always have addresses for bike-rental places. For a good touring bike, figure about €10 for a half-day and €16 for a full day. You'll pay more for better equipment; generally the best is available through bike shops, not at train stations or other outlets. French bikers often do not wear helmets, though most rental outfits have them (for a small fee).

Cheap Flights

If you're visiting one or more French cities on a longer European trip—or linking up far-flung French cities (such as Paris and Nice)—consider intra-European airlines. And though trains are still the best way to connect most cities in France, a flight can save both time and money on long journeys. When comparing a flight to a train trip, consider the time it takes to get to and through the airport—and how early you'll need to arrive to check in before the flight. Most flights make sense only as an alternate to a train ride of five or more hours in length.

One of the best websites for comparing inexpensive flights is www.skyscanner.net. Other comparison search engines include www.wegolo.com and www.whichbudget.com.

Airlines offering inexpensive flights to Provence and the Riviera include easyJet (www.easyjet.com), Ryanair (www.ryanair .com), and Vueling (www.vueling.com). Airport websites may list small airlines that serve your destination.

Be aware of the potential drawbacks of flying on the cheap: nonrefundable and nonchangeable tickets, minimal or nonexistent customer service, treks to airports far outside town, and pricey baggage fees. If you're traveling with lots of luggage, a cheap flight can quickly become a bad deal. To avoid unpleasant surprises, read the small print—especially baggage policies—before you book.

Resources

Resources from Rick Steves

Books: *Rick Steves' Provence and the French Riviera 2011* is one of many books in my series on European travel, which includes country guidebooks (including France), city guidebooks (Paris, Rome, Florence, London, etc.), Snapshot guides (excerpted chapters from my country guides), Pocket guides (full-color little books on big cities), and my budget-travel skills handbook, *Rick Steves' Europe Through the Back Door.*

My phrase books—for French, Italian, German, Spanish, and Portuguese—are practical and budget-oriented. My other books include *Europe 101* (a crash course on art and history) and *Travel as a Political Act* (a travelogue sprinkled with tips for bringing home a global perspective). For a list of my books, see the inside of the last page of this book.

Video: My public television series, *Rick Steves' Europe*, covers European destinations in 100 shows, with nine episodes on France. To watch episodes, visit www.hulu.com/rick-steves-europe; for scripts and other details, see www.ricksteves.com/tv.

Audio: My weekly public radio show, *Travel with Rick Steves*, features interviews with travel experts from around the world. I've also produced free self-guided audio tours of the top sights and neighborhoods in Paris, Florence, Rome, Venice, and London. All of this audio content is available for free at Rick Steves Audio Europe, an extensive online library organized by destination. Choose whatever interests you, and download it for free to your iPod, smartphone, or computer at www.ricksteves.com or iTunes.

Maps

The black-and-white maps in this book, drawn by David Hoerlein, are concise and simple. The maps are intended to help you locate recommended places and reach TIs, where you'll find more in-depth maps of cities or regions (usually free). Better maps are sold at newsstands and bookstores. Before you buy a map, look at it to be sure it has the level of detail you want.

Michelin maps are available throughout France at bookstores, newsstands, and gas stations (about €5 each, cheaper than in the US). The orange Michelin map #527 (1:275,000 scale) covers this book's destinations with good detail for drivers. Michelin map #332 is good for the Luberon and the Côtes du Rhône, and map #340 is best for the Bouches-du-Rhône (the southern area around Arles). Train travelers will do fine with the maps provided in this book. Drivers going beyond Provence and the Riviera should consider the soft-cover Michelin France atlas (the entire country at 1:200,000, well-organized in a €20 book with an index and maps of major cities). Spend a few minutes learning the Michelin key to get the most sightseeing value out of these maps.

Other Guidebooks

If you're like most travelers, this book is all you need. But if you're heading beyond my recommended destinations, $40 for extra maps and books can be money well spent. If you'll be traveling elsewhere

Begin Your Trip at www.ricksteves.com

At our travel website, you'll find a wealth of free information on European destinations, including fresh monthly news and helpful tips from thousands of fellow travelers. You'll also find my latest guidebook updates (www.ricksteves.com/update) and my travel blog.

Our **online Travel Store** offers travel bags and accessories specially designed by me and my staff to help you travel smarter and lighter. These include my popular carry-on bags (roll-aboard and rucksack versions), money belts, totes, toiletries kits, adapters, other accessories, and a wide selection of guidebooks, planning maps, and DVDs.

Choosing the right **railpass** for your trip—amidst hundreds of options—can drive you nutty. We'll help you choose the best pass for your needs, plus give you a bunch of free extras.

Rick Steves' Europe Through the Back Door travel company offers **tours** with more than three dozen itineraries and more than 400 departures reaching the best destinations in this book...and beyond. Our France tours include Paris and the South of France in 15 days, Paris and the Heart of France in 11 days (focusing on Paris, the Loire, and Normandy), Villages and Vineyards of Eastern France in 14 days, and the one-week Paris city tour. You'll enjoy great guides, a fun bunch of travel partners (with small groups of generally around 28), and plenty of room to spread out in a big, comfy bus. You'll find European adventures to fit every vacation length. For all the details, and to get our Tour Catalog and a free Rick Steves Tour Experience DVD (filmed on location during an actual tour), visit www.ricksteves.com or call us at 425/608-4217.

APPENDIX

in France, consider *Rick Steves' France 2011* or *Rick Steves' Paris 2011*.

Of the several guidebooks on Provence and the Riviera, many are high on facts and low on opinion, guts, or personality. For well-researched (though not annually updated) background information, try the Cadogan guide to Southern France. The colorful Eyewitness series, which focuses mainly on sights, has editions on France, including one for Provence. They're fun for their great graphics and photos, but they're relatively skimpy on content and weigh a ton. The popular, skinny green Michelin guides are dry but informative, especially for drivers. They're known for their city and sightseeing maps, and for their succinct, helpful information on all major sights. English editions, covering most of the regions you'll want to visit, are sold in France for about €14 (or $20 in the US).

Recommended Books and Movies

To learn more about France in general, and specifically for Provence and the French Riviera, check out a few of these books or films.

Nonfiction

For a good introduction to French culture and people, read *French or Foe* (Polly Platt) and *Sixty Million Frenchmen Can't Be Wrong* (Jean-Benoit Nadeau and Julie Barlow). The latter is a must-read for anyone serious about understanding French culture, contemporary politics, and what makes the French tick.

In *A Distant Mirror*, respected historian Barbara Tuchman takes readers back to medieval France. *The Course of French History* (Pierre Goubert) is a concise and readable summary. Ina Caro's *The Road from the Past* is filled with enjoyable essays on her travels through France, with an accent on history. And *The Yellow House* (Martin Gayford) vividly recounts Van Gogh and Gauguin's tumultuous stay in Arles.

Peter Mayle's bestselling memoirs, *A Year in Provence* and *Toujours Provence*, offer an evocative view of life in southern France. The travelogue *Portraits of France* (Robert Daley) includes chapters on Provence. In *At Home in France* (Ann Barry), an American author describes her visits to her country house. *Postcards from France* (Megan McNeill Libby) was written by an observant foreign exchange student. A mix of writers explores French culture in *Travelers' Tales: Provence* (edited by Tara Austen Weaver and James O'Reilly).

A Goose in Toulouse (Mort Rosenblum) provides keen insights on rural France through its focus on cuisine. Foodies may also enjoy *From Here, You Can't See Paris* (Michael S. Sanders), about a local restaurant where foie gras is always on the menu.

Da Vinci Code fans will enjoy reading that book's inspiration, *Holy Blood, Holy Grail* (Michael Baigent, Richard Leigh, and Henry Lincoln), which takes place mostly in southern France. *Labyrinth* (Kate Mosse) is an intriguing tale partly set in medieval southern France during the Cathar crusade.

If you'll be enjoying an extended stay in France, consider *Living Abroad in France* (Terry Link) or *Almost French* (Sarah Turnbull), a funny take on living as a French native. Gourmands appreciate the *Marling Menu-Master for France* (William E. Marling). Travelers seeking green and vegetarian options in France could consider *Traveling Naturally in France* (Dorian Yates).

Fiction

Written in the 1930s, *Joy of Man's Desiring* captures the charm of rural France. (The author, Jean Giono, also wrote the Johnny Appleseed eco-fable set in Provence, *The Man Who Planted Trees*.) *The Fly-Truffler* (Gustaf Sobin) features a character who studies the Provençal dialect. Peter Mayle, whose nonfiction books are recommended above, also writes fiction set in Provence, including *Hotel Pastis* and *A Good Year*. For a list of recommended books for children, see the chapter on Traveling with Children.

Films

To Catch a Thief (1955) features both the French Riviera and crackling performances by Grace Kelly and Cary Grant. In *La Grande Vadrouille* (1966), set during World War II, two French civilians aid the crew of a downed Allied bomber in crossing the demarcation line into southern France. *The Return of Martin Guerre* (1982) takes place during the Middle Ages.

Jean de Florette (1986), a marvelous tale of greed and intolerance, is about a city hunchback who inherits a valuable piece of property in rural France, only to have his efforts thwarted by his villainous neighbor. Its sequel, *Manon des Sources* (1986), continues the story, focusing on the hunchback's beautiful daughter.

Two films based on the memoirs of writer/filmmaker Marcel Pagnol show his early life in Provence: *My Father's Glory* (1991) and *My Mother's Castle* (1991).

Cyrano de Bergerac (1990), about a romantic poet with a large nose, has scenes filmed at the Abbaye de Fontenay. *French Kiss* (1995) includes scenes in the French countryside and Cannes, as well as Paris. *Chocolat* (2000), which was filmed in the Dordogne region, shows Juliette Binoche opening a chocolate shop and stirring up a tiny town. (*The Horseman on the Roof,* from 1995, is also set in southern France and also features the beautiful Binoche.) *The Chorus* (2004), filled with angelic choir music, tells the story of a schoolteacher and the boys he brings together.

Holidays and Festivals

This list includes major festivals in the Provence and French Riviera region, plus national holidays observed throughout France. Many sights close down on national holidays, and weekends around those holidays are often wildly crowded with vacationers (book your hotel room for the entire holiday weekend well in advance). Note that this isn't a complete list; holidays often strike without warning.

Before planning a trip around a festival, make sure that you verify its dates on the festival's website or the France TI (US tel. 514/288-1904, www.franceguide.com, info.us@franceguide.com).

Jan 1	New Year's Day
Jan 6	Epiphany
Late Feb	Carnival (Mardi Gras), parades and fireworks, Nice (www.nicecarnaval.com)
April 24	Easter Sunday
April 25	Easter Monday
May 1	Labor Day
May 8	V-E Day
May 11–22	Cannes Film Festival, Cannes (www.festival-cannes.fr)
May 26–29	Monaco Grand Prix auto race, Monaco (www.yourmonaco.com/grand_prix)
June 2	Ascension
June 12	Pentecost
June 21	Fête de la Musique, free concerts and dancing in the streets throughout France
July	International Music and Opera Festival, Aix-en-Provence (www.festival-aix.com)
July	Avignon Festival, theater, dance, and music, Avignon (www.festival-avignon.com)
July 3–25	Tour de France, national bicycle race culminating on the Champs-Elysées in Paris (www.letour.fr)
July 14	Bastille Day, fireworks, dancing, and revelry
Mid-July	"Jazz à Juan" International Jazz Festival, Antibes/Juan-les-Pins (www.jazzajuan.fr)
Mid-July–early Aug	Chorégies d'Orange, music and opera performed in a Roman theater, Orange (www.choregies.asso.fr)

2011

JANUARY
S	M	T	W	T	F	S
						1
2	3	4	5	6	7	8
9	10	11	12	13	14	15
16	17	18	19	20	21	22
23/30	24/31	25	26	27	28	29

FEBRUARY
S	M	T	W	T	F	S
		1	2	3	4	5
6	7	8	9	10	11	12
13	14	15	16	17	18	19
20	21	22	23	24	25	26
27	28					

MARCH
S	M	T	W	T	F	S
		1	2	3	4	5
6	7	8	9	10	11	12
13	14	15	16	17	18	19
20	21	22	23	24	25	26
27	28	29	30	31		

APRIL
S	M	T	W	T	F	S
					1	2
3	4	5	6	7	8	9
10	11	12	13	14	15	16
17	18	19	20	21	22	23
24	25	26	27	28	29	30

MAY
S	M	T	W	T	F	S
1	2	3	4	5	6	7
8	9	10	11	12	13	14
15	16	17	18	19	20	21
22	23	24	25	26	27	28
29	30	31				

JUNE
S	M	T	W	T	F	S
			1	2	3	4
5	6	7	8	9	10	11
12	13	14	15	16	17	18
19	20	21	22	23	24	25
26	27	28	29	30		

JULY
S	M	T	W	T	F	S
					1	2
3	4	5	6	7	8	9
10	11	12	13	14	15	16
17	18	19	20	21	22	23
24/31	25	26	27	28	29	30

AUGUST
S	M	T	W	T	F	S
	1	2	3	4	5	6
7	8	9	10	11	12	13
14	15	16	17	18	19	20
21	22	23	24	25	26	27
28	29	30	31			

SEPTEMBER
S	M	T	W	T	F	S
				1	2	3
4	5	6	7	8	9	10
11	12	13	14	15	16	17
18	19	20	21	22	23	24
25	26	27	28	29	30	

OCTOBER
S	M	T	W	T	F	S
						1
2	3	4	5	6	7	8
9	10	11	12	13	14	15
16	17	18	19	20	21	22
23/30	24/31	25	26	27	28	29

NOVEMBER
S	M	T	W	T	F	S
		1	2	3	4	5
6	7	8	9	10	11	12
13	14	15	16	17	18	19
20	21	22	23	24	25	26
27	28	29	30			

DECEMBER
S	M	T	W	T	F	S
				1	2	3
4	5	6	7	8	9	10
11	12	13	14	15	16	17
18	19	20	21	22	23	24
25	26	27	28	29	30	31

Late July	Nice Jazz Festival, Nice (www.nicejazz festival.fr)
July–Aug	International Fireworks Festival, Cannes (www.festival-pyrotechnique-cannes .com)
Aug 15	Assumption of Mary
Nov 1	All Saints' Day
Nov 11	Armistice Day
Dec 25	Christmas Day
Dec 31	New Year's Eve

Conversions and Climate

Numbers and Stumblers

- Europeans write a few of their numbers differently than we do. 1 = 𝟣, 4 = 𝟦, 7 = 𝟩.
- In Europe, dates appear as day/month/year, so Christmas is 25/12/11.
- Commas are decimal points and decimals commas. A dollar and a half is 1,50, and there are 5.280 feet in a mile.
- When pointing, use your whole hand, palm down.
- When counting with fingers, start with your thumb. If you hold up your first finger to request one item, you'll probably get two.
- What Americans call the second floor of a building is the first floor in Europe.
- On escalators and moving sidewalks, Europeans keep the left "lane" open for passing. Stay to the right.

Metric Conversions (approximate)

A kilogram is 2.2 pounds, and 1 liter is about a quart, or almost four to a gallon. A kilometer is six-tenths of a mile. I figure kilometers to miles by cutting them in half and adding back 10 percent of the original (120 km: 60 + 12 = 72 miles, 300 km: 150 + 30 = 180 miles).

1 foot = 0.3 meter	1 square yard = 0.8 square meter
1 yard = 0.9 meter	1 square mile = 2.6 square kilometers
1 mile = 1.6 kilometers	1 ounce = 28 grams
1 centimeter = 0.4 inch	1 quart = 0.95 liter
1 meter = 39.4 inches	1 kilogram = 2.2 pounds
1 kilometer = 0.62 mile	32°F = 0°C

Clothing Sizes

When shopping for clothing, use these US-to-European comparisons as general guidelines (but note that no conversion is perfect).

- Women's dresses and blouses: Add 30
  (US size 10 = European size 40)
- Men's suits and jackets: Add 10
  (US size 40 regular = European size 50)
- Men's shirts: Multiply by 2 and add about 8
  (US size 15 collar = European size 38)
- Women's shoes: Add about 30
  (US size 8 = European size 38-39)
- Men's shoes: Add 32–34
  (US size 9 = European size 41; US size 11 = European size 45)

Nice's Climate

First line, average daily high; second line, average daily low; third line, average days without rain. For more detailed weather statistics for destinations in this book (as well as the rest of the world), check www.worldclimate.com.

J	F	M	A	M	J	J	A	S	O	N	D
50°	53°	59°	64°	71°	79°	84°	83°	77°	68°	58°	52°
35°	36°	41°	46°	52°	58°	63°	63°	58°	51°	43°	37°
23	22	24	23	23	26	29	26	24	23	21	21

Temperature Conversion: Fahrenheit and Celsius

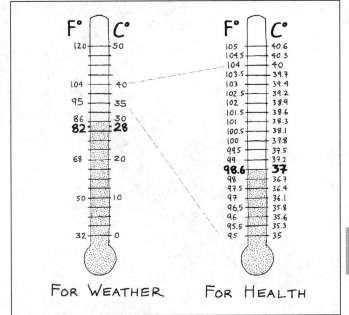

Europe takes its temperature using the Celsius scale, while we opt for Fahrenheit. For a rough conversion from Celsius to Fahrenheit, double the number and add 30. For weather, remember that 28°C is 82°F—perfect. For health, 37°C is just right.

Essential Packing Checklist

Whether you're traveling for five days or five weeks, here's what you'll need to bring. Remember to pack light to enjoy the sweet freedom of true mobility. Happy travels!

- ☐ 5 shirts
- ☐ 1 sweater or lightweight fleece jacket
- ☐ 2 pairs pants
- ☐ 1 pair shorts
- ☐ 1 swimsuit (women only—men can use shorts)
- ☐ 5 pairs underwear and socks
- ☐ 1 pair shoes
- ☐ 1 rain-proof jacket
- ☐ Tie or scarf
- ☐ Money belt
- ☐ Money—your mix of:
    - ☐ Debit card for ATM withdrawals
    - ☐ Credit card
    - ☐ Hard cash in dollars or euros (in $20s or €20s)
- ☐ Documents (and back-up photocopies):
    - ☐ Passport
    - ☐ Printout of airline e-ticket
    - ☐ Driver's license
    - ☐ Student ID and hostel card
    - ☐ Railpass/car rental voucher
    - ☐ Insurance details
- ☐ Daypack
- ☐ Sealable plastic baggies
- ☐ Camera and related gear
- ☐ Empty water bottle
- ☐ Wristwatch and alarm clock
- ☐ Earplugs
- ☐ First-aid kit
- ☐ Medicine (labeled)
- ☐ Extra glasses/contacts and prescriptions
- ☐ Sunscreen and sunglasses
- ☐ Toiletries kit
- ☐ Soap
- ☐ Laundry soap
- ☐ Clothesline
- ☐ Small towel
- ☐ Sewing kit
- ☐ Travel information
- ☐ Necessary map(s)
- ☐ Address list (email and mailing addresses)
- ☐ Postcards and photos from home
- ☐ Notepad and pen
- ☐ Journal

If you plan to carry on your luggage, note that all liquids must be in three-ounce or smaller containers and fit within a single quart-size baggie. For details, see www.tsa.gov/travelers.

APPENDIX

Hotel Reservation

To: _____   _____
          hotel   **email or fax**

From: _____   _____
            name   **email or fax**

Today's date: _____ /_____ /_____
                day   **month**   **year**

Dear Hotel _____ ,
Please make this reservation for me:

Name: _____

Total # of people: _____   # of rooms: _____   # of nights: _____

Arriving: _____ /_____ /_____   My time of arrival (24-hr clock): _____
          day **month** **year**   (I will telephone if I will be late)

Departing: ____ /____ /____
            day **month** **year**

Room(s): Single____   Double ____   Twin ____   Triple ____   Quad____

With: Toilet ____   Shower ____ Bath ____   Sink only____

Special needs: View____ Quiet____ Cheapest ____ Ground Floor____

Please email or fax confirmation of my reservation, along with the type of room reserved and the price. Please also inform me of your cancellation policy. After I hear from you, I will quickly send my credit-card information as a deposit to hold the room. Thank you.

_____
Name

_____
Address

_____
City   **State**   **Zip Code**   **Country**

Before hoteliers can make your reservation, they want to know the information listed above. You can use this form as the basis for your email, or you can photocopy this page, fill in the information, and send it as a fax (also available online at www.ricksteves.com/reservation).

French Survival Phrases

When using the phonetics, try to nasalize the <u>n</u> sound.

Good day.	**Bonjour.**	bohn-zhoor
Mrs. / Mr.	**Madame / Monsieur**	mah-dahm / muhs-yur
Do you speak English?	**Parlez-vous anglais?**	par-lay-voo ah<u>n</u>-glay
Yes. / No.	**Oui. / Non.**	wee / noh<u>n</u>
I understand.	**Je comprends.**	zhuh koh<u>n</u>-prah<u>n</u>
I don't understand.	**Je ne comprends pas.**	zhuh nuh koh<u>n</u>-prah<u>n</u> pah
Please.	**S'il vous plaît.**	see voo play
Thank you.	**Merci.**	mehr-see
I'm sorry.	**Désolé.**	day-zoh-lay
Excuse me.	**Pardon.**	par-doh<u>n</u>
(No) problem.	**(Pas de) problème.**	(pah duh) proh-blehm
It's good.	**C'est bon.**	say boh<u>n</u>
Goodbye.	**Au revoir.**	oh vwahr
one / two	**un / deux**	uh<u>n</u> / duh
three / four	**trois / quatre**	twah / kah-truh
five / six	**cinq / six**	sa<u>n</u>k / sees
seven / eight	**sept / huit**	seht / weet
nine / ten	**neuf / dix**	nuhf / dees
How much is it?	**Combien?**	koh<u>n</u>-bee-a<u>n</u>
Write it?	**Ecrivez?**	ay-kree-vay
Is it free?	**C'est gratuit?**	say grah-twee
Included?	**Inclus?**	a<u>n</u>-klew
Where can I buy / find...?	**Où puis-je acheter / trouver...?**	oo pwee-zhuh ah-shuh-tay / troo-vay
I'd like / We'd like...	**Je voudrais / Nous voudrions...**	zhuh voo-dray / noo voo-dree-oh<u>n</u>
...a room.	**...une chambre.**	ewn shah<u>n</u>-bruh
...a ticket to ___.	**...un billet pour ___.**	uh<u>n</u> bee-yay poor
Is it possible?	**C'est possible?**	say poh-see-bluh
Where is...?	**Où est...?**	oo ay
...the train station	**...la gare**	lah gar
...the bus station	**...la gare routière**	lah gar root-yehr
...tourist information	**...l'office du tourisme**	loh-fees dew too-reez-muh
Where are the toilets?	**Où sont les toilettes?**	oo soh<u>n</u> lay twah-leht
men	**hommes**	ohm
women	**dames**	dahm
left / right	**à gauche / à droite**	ah gohsh / ah dwaht
straight	**tout droit**	too dwah
When does this open / close?	**Ça ouvre / ferme à quelle heure?**	sah oo-vruh / fehrm ah kehl ur
At what time?	**À quelle heure?**	ah kehl ur
Just a moment.	**Un moment.**	uh<u>n</u> moh-mah<u>n</u>
now / soon / later	**maintenant / bientôt / plus tard**	ma<u>n</u>-tuh-nah<u>n</u> / bee-a<u>n</u>-toh / plew tar
today / tomorrow	**aujourd'hui / demain**	oh-zhoor-dwee / duh-ma<u>n</u>

In the Restaurant

English	French	Pronunciation
I'd like / We'd like...	**Je voudrais / Nous voudrions...**	zhuh voo-dray / noo voo-dree-ohn
...to reserve...	**...réserver...**	ray-zehr-vay
...a table for one / two.	**...une table pour un / deux.**	ewn tah-bluh poor uhn / duh
Non-smoking.	**Non fumeur.**	nohn few-mur
Is this seat free?	**C'est libre?**	say lee-bruh
The menu (in English), please.	**La carte (en anglais), s'il vous plaît.**	lah kart (ahn ahn-glay) see voo play
service (not) included	**service (non) compris**	sehr-vees (nohn) kohn-pree
to go	**à emporter**	ah ahn-por-tay
with / without	**avec / sans**	ah-vehk / sahn
and / or	**et / ou**	ay / oo
special of the day	**plat du jour**	plah dew zhoor
specialty of the house	**spécialité de la maison**	spay-see-ah-lee-tay duh lah may-zohn
appetizers	**hors-d'oeuvre**	or-duh-vruh
first course (soup, salad)	**entrée**	ahn-tray
main course (meat, fish)	**plat principal**	plah pran-see-pahl
bread	**pain**	pan
cheese	**fromage**	froh-mahzh
sandwich	**sandwich**	sahnd-weech
soup	**soupe**	soop
salad	**salade**	sah-lahd
meat	**viande**	vee-ahnd
chicken	**poulet**	poo-lay
fish	**poisson**	pwah-sohn
seafood	**fruits de mer**	frwee duh mehr
fruit	**fruit**	frwee
vegetables	**légumes**	lay-gewm
dessert	**dessert**	duh-sehr
mineral water	**eau minérale**	oh mee-nay-rahl
tap water	**l'eau du robinet**	loh dew roh-bee-nay
milk	**lait**	lay
(orange) juice	**jus (d'orange)**	zhew (doh-rahnzh)
coffee	**café**	kah-fay
tea	**thé**	tay
wine	**vin**	van
red / white	**rouge / blanc**	roozh / blahn
glass / bottle	**verre / bouteille**	vehr / boo-teh-ee
beer	**bière**	bee-ehr
Cheers!	**Santé!**	sahn-tay
More. / Another.	**Plus. / Un autre.**	plew / uhn oh-truh
The same.	**La même chose.**	lah mehm shohz
The bill, please.	**L'addition, s'il vous plaît.**	lah-dee-see-ohn see voo play
tip	**pourboire**	poor-bwar
Delicious!	**Délicieux!**	day-lee-see-uh

For more user-friendly French phrases, check out *Rick Steves' French Phrase Book and Dictionary* or *Rick Steves' French, Italian & German Phrase Book*.

INDEX

A

Abbeys: about, 220–221; Montmajour, 74–75, 96; Notre-Dame de Sénanque, 216–217; St. Hilaire, 222

Accommodations: *See* Sleeping; *and specific destinations*

Aigues-Mortes: 107–108

Aiguines: 439; sleeping, 441

Airfares (airlines): 7; carry-on restrictions, 13; cheap flights, 491; telephone numbers, 472

Airports: Marseille, 237–238; Nice, 323–324; telephone numbers, 471–472

Aix-en-Provence: 259–275; eating, 273–275; helpful hints, 261, 264; history of, 265; information, 260; maps, 233, 262–263; sights, 266–271; sleeping, 271–273; tours, 264, 266; transportation, 260–261, 275

Albert 1er Park (Nice): 328

Alpilles Mountains: 74, 88, 89

Amphithéâtre: *See* Arena

Ancient Romans: *See* Roman sites

Angladon-Dubrujeaud Foundation (Avignon): 115, 124

Annonciade Museum (St-Tropez): 418

Annot: sleeping, 306

Antibes: 391–408; eating, 407–408; helpful hints, 396; information, 392; maps, 393, 394–395; sights/activities, 397–404; sleeping, 404–406; transportation, 392–393, 396–397, 408; walking tour, 397–399

Antibes History and Archaeology Museum: 401

Antique Toy and Doll Museum (Isle-sur-la-Sorgue): 200

Apartment rentals: 28–29

Apt: 225

Aquariums: 382, 385–386

Aqueducts: 96–97, 149; Pont du Gard, 149, 152–154

Arab Markets (Marseille): 237, 239, 242

"Arc de Triomphe" (Orange): 164

Archaelological museums: 65–68, 304, 401

Archaeological sites: *See* Roman sites

Ardèche Gorges: 191

Arena (amphithéâtre): Arles, 66, 71; Nîmes, 139, 142–143

Arlaten Folk Museum (Arles): 66, 72

Arles: 60–87; eating, 83–86; events, 64, 77–78; excursion areas, 88–108; helpful hints, 64; information, 61; maps, 62–63, 80–81; sights, 65–77; sleeping, 78–83; transportation, 61, 64–65, 86–87

Arles Ancient History Museum: 65–68

Arles Classical Theater: 66, 70–71

Arles Forum Square: 66, 68–69, 75; eating, 83–84

Art: of the Riviera, 282–283. *See also* Art museums; *and specific artists*

Art museums: Château de Villeneuve (Vence), 427; Fondation Angladon-Dubrujeaud (Avignon), 115, 124; Fondation Maeght (St-Paul-de-Vence), 422, 425; Fondation Van Gogh (Arles), 71–72; La Charité Museum (Marseille), 237, 244; Musée Calvet (Avignon), 115, 124; Musée Chagall (Nice), 298–299, 337–345; Musée d'Art Moderne et d'Art Contemporain (Nice), 296, 302–303; Musée de l'Annonciade (St-Tropez), 418; Musée des Beaux-Arts (Nice), 296, 303; Musée Matisse (Nice),

296, 299–302; Musée Picasso (Antibes), 399–401; Musée Réattu (Arles), 66, 72; Musée Renoir (Cagnes-sur-Mer), 403–404; Musée Yves Brayer (Les Baux), 93

Atelier Cézanne (Aix): 270

ATM machines: 14–16

Attitude, French: 464–465

Audio Europe, Rick Steves: 12, 492

Aux Deux Garçons (Aix): 268

Avenue Jean Médecin (Nice): 330

Avignon: 109–134; eating, 130–133; events, 114; excursion areas, 135–156; helpful hints, 111, 114, 116; information, 109–110; maps, 112–113, 126–127; sights, 115, 116–125; sleeping, 125–130; tours, 116; transportation, 110–111, 133–134; walking tour, 116–124

Avignon Festival: 114

Avignon ramparts: 119

Avignon synagogue: 115, 123

B

Back Door travel philosophy: 40

Baie des Anges: 326–327, 373

Balazuc: 191

Balcon de la Mescla: 438, 440

Ballooning: 210

Bandol: wines, 59, 285

Banking: *See* Money

Barbegal Roman Aqueduct: 96–97

Bardot, Brigitte: 414, 418, 457

Basse Corniche: 358–359, 372–375

Bay of Angels: 326–327, 373

Beaches: Antibes, 397, 402; the Camargue, 105, 107; Cannes, 410; Cap d'Ail, 374; Cap Ferrat, 363, 364–365; Cassis, 251; Menton, 390; Nice, 297–298, 327–328; St-Tropez, 417; Villefranche, 353–354

Beaulieu-sur-Mer: 364, 374

Beaumes de Venise: 57–58, 183–184

Bed & breakfasts (B&Bs): overview, 26–27. *See also specific destinations*

Bedoin: market, 160, 190

Beverages: 37–39. *See also* Wine and vineyards

Biking (bike rentals): 490–491; Antibes, 396; Arles, 64; Avignon, 114; the Camargue, 105, 107; Isle-sur-la-Sorgue, 196, 201–202; Luberon, 194; Nice, 291; Vaison la Romaine, 169, 172; Villefranche, 349

Biot: 404

Bird-watching: 104–105

Boat travel and cruises (boating): Antibes, 396; Avignon, 114, 116; Cannes, 413, 414; Cassis, 247, 254–255; Lac de Ste-Croix, 439; Marseille, 245, 247; Nice, 294, 295; Riviera, 282, 294, 295; St-Tropez, 418, 420; Villefranche, 353. *See also* Canoeing and kayaking

Bonnieux: 219–221; market, 194, 219–220

Books, recommended: 494–495; for children, 444

Bouillon Olive Mill: 218

Boules: 64, 297, 352, 419, 443; about, 208

Brantes: 191

Braque, Georges: 418, 425

Brayer, Yves: 94; Museum (Les Baux), 93

Budgeting: 6–7

Buis-les-Barronies: market, 160

Buis-les-Barronnies: 191

Bullfights: 105; Arles, 77–78

Buoux: 227–228

Buses: 482; best two-week trip, 10–11; Luberon, 193; map, 476–477; Provence, 45–46; Riviera, 281–282, 293–294, 372–375, 421. *See also specific destinations*

Business hours: 13

C

Cabs: 474; tipping, 18. *See also specific destinations*

Cafés (brasseries): overview, 34–36. *See also specific destinations*

Cagnes-sur-Mer: 403–404

Cairanne: 185

Calanque d'En-Vau: 255

Calanque Port-Miou: 255

Calanques: 247, 254–256

Calder, Alexander: 425

Calissons d'Aix: 264, 448

Calvet Museum (Avignon): 115, 124

Camarguais Museum (Stes-Maries): 106

Camargue, the: 104–108; map, 89

Camping (campgrounds): 28

Camus, Albert: 229

Cannes: 408–414

Cannes Film Festival: 281, 307, 411–412

Canoeing and kayaking: Ardèche Gorges, 191; the Calanques, 255–256; Lac de Ste-Croix, 439; Pont du Gard, 151; Sorgue River, 201

Cap Canaille (Cassis): 253, 256

Cap d'Ail: 374

Cap d'Antibes: 399; eating, 408; hiking, 402–403; sleeping, 405

Cap Ferrat: 359–365, 373–374; eating, 365–366; map, 361; sights/activities, 362–365; sleeping, 365

Cardin, Pierre: 222

Car insurance: 484

Car leasing: 472, 485

Carpentras: 193; market, 160, 452

Car rentals: 483–484. *See also specific destinations*

Car travel: 474, 485–490; best two-week trip, 8–9; distance and time, 486–487; Luberon, 193; Provence, 46; Riviera, 282, 421; road signs, 485, 488. *See also specific destinations*

Casinos: Monte Carlo, 382, 387–388; Nice, 328

Cassis: 249–259; eating, 258–259; information, 249–250; maps, 233, 252–253; sights/activities, 251–256; sleeping, 256–258; wines, 59, 251

Castellum (Nîmes): 147

Castle Hill (Nice): 296, 305, 328–329

Cathédrale de la Nouvelle Major (Marseille): 237, 244–245

Cathédrale de Monaco: 382, 385

Cathédrale d'Images (Les Baux): 94

Cathédrale Russe (Nice): 296, 304–305

Cathedral of the Holy Savior (Aix): 271

Cathedrals: *See* Churches and cathedrals

Cavaillon: market, 194

Cavaillon melons: 53, 451

Cave la Romaine (Vaison la Romaine): 172

Cell (mobile) phones: 467, 470

Centre d'Art Présence Vincent Van Gogh (St. Rémy): 101

Centre de la Vieille Charité (Marseille): 237, 244

Cézanne, Paul: 43, 124, 268, 270

Chagall, Marc: 425, 426; biographical sketch, 342; Museum (Nice), 298–299, 337–345; painting style, 340

Changing of the Guard (Monaco): 382, 384

Chapelle Cocteau (Villefranche): 352–353

Chapelle du Rosaire (Vence): 422, 427

Chapelle et Phare de la Garoupe: 402

Chapelle Notre-Dame de Beauvoir (Moustiers-Ste-Marie): 440

Chapelle St. Pierre (Aiguines): 439

Chapel of Penitents (Les Baux): 94

Chapel of St. Pierre (Villefranche): 352–353

Chapel of the Rosary (Vence): 422, 427

Charité Museum (Marseille): 237, 244

Charlemagne: 454, 456

Château de la Canorgue Winery: 219

Château de Lourmarin: 229–230

Château de Villeneuve (Vence): 427

Château d'If (Marseille): 237, 246

Château Eza: 368–369

Château Grimaldi (Antibes): 398–399

Châteauneuf-du-Pape: 57, 165–166
Château Redortier: 58, 182
Cheeses: 33, 34, 53, 123, 132, 156, 317, 443, 453
Chemins de Fer de Provence: 305–306
Children, traveling with: 442–446; packing tips, 444–445; planning tips, 444, 445; top sights and activities, 445–446
Chocolat (movie): 495
Chocolates: 103, 143, 268, 430, 448
Churches and cathedrals: architecture, 455; Cathédrale de la Nouvelle Major (Marseille), 237, 244–245; Church of the Immaculate Conception (Antibes), 398; Eze Church, 369; Monaco Cathedral, 382, 385; Nîmes Cathedral, 144; Notre-Dame d'Alidon Church (Oppède-le-Vieux), 223; Notre-Dame-de-l'Annonciation (Nice), 335; Notre-Dame de Nazareth Cathedral (Vaison), 171; Notre-Dame des Anges (Isle-sur-la-Sorgue), 197–198; Russian Cathedral (Nice), 296, 304–305; St. Laurent Church (Marseille), 245; St. Michael's Church (Villefranche), 353; St. Pierre Church (Avignon), 122; St. Réparate Cathedral (Nice), 336; Saint-Sauveur Cathedral (Aix), 271; St. Trophime Church (Arles), 66, 69–70; St. Vincent Church (Les Baux), 93–94
Church of the Immaculate Conception (Antibes): 398
Cicadas *(cigales):* 183
Citadel (Villefranche): 352
Clelles: sleeping, 306
Climate: 10–12, 499
Clothing: *See* Fashion
Clothing sizes: 498
Cocteau (Jean) Chapel (Villefranche): 352–353
Col de la Chaîne Mountain Pass: 181–182
Col de Vence: 430
Col d'Illioure: 439

Collias: 151
Colline du Château (Nice): 296, 305, 328–329
Colorado Provençal: 225
Confiseries Florian (Pont-du-Loup): 423, 430
Connery, Sean: 373
Consulates: 290, 471
Cooking classes (schools): 473; Aix-en-Provence, 264; Arles, 64; Nice, 297; Vaison la Romaine, 169–170
Corkscrew Museum (Ménerbes): 222
Côteaux d'Aix-en-Provence: wines, 58–59
Côte d'Azur: *See* Riviera
Côtes de Provence: 58
Côtes du Rhône: 157–191; driving tours, 175–191; maps, 158–159, 177; markets, 160; transportation, 158–160; wine and vineyards, 56–58, 165–166, 172, 176–185
Côtes du Rhône Wine Road: 176–185
Count of Monte Cristo (Dumas): 246
Coursegoules: 430
Courses Camarguaises (Arles): 77–78
Cours Mirabeau (Aix): 260, 266–267; eating, 275
Cours Saleya (Nice): 334–335
Cousteau Aquarium (Monaco): 382, 385–386
Coustellet: 218; market, 194
Credit cards: 12, 16–17
Crestet: 172, 180–181; eating, 187–188
Cruises: *See* Boat travel and cruises
Cuisine: of Provence, 51–53; of the Riviera, 283–285. *See also* Eating
Currency and exchange: 14–17
Customs: 19
Cycling: *See* Biking

D
Debit cards: 12, 16–17
De la Gravette (Antibes): 397, 402
Denim: 137, 144, 146

Dentelles de Montmirail: 181–182
Digne-les-Bains: 306
Discounts: 14
Domaine de Cabasse: 186, 188
Domaine de Coyeux: 58, 183–184
Domaine de Durban: 58, 184
Domaine de Mourchon: 180
Domaine des Tilleuls: 186
Driving: *See* Car travel
Drôme Provençale Loop Drive:
    190–191
Ducal Palace (Nice): 334
Dumas, Alexandre: 246, 444

E
Eating: 31–36; budgeting, 7; with
    children, 442–443; restaurant
    phrases, 504; tipping, 18;
    vocabulary terms, 33. *See also*
    Cuisine; Markets; *and specific
    destinations*
Eleanor of Aquitaine: 96, 456, 458
Electricity: 14
Email: 473–474. *See also specific
    destinations*
Embassies: 471
Emergencies: 13, 471
Entrevaux: 306
Espace Van Gogh (Arles): 76
Euro currency: 14–17
Exchange rate: 15
Eze-Bord-de-Mer: 367–370, 374
Eze Church: 369
Eze-le-Village: 367–370

F
Fashion: boutiques, 154, 216, 363,
    403, 439, 452–453; clothing
    sizes, 498; Musée de la Mode
    (Marseille), 237, 242
Fashion Museum (Marseille): 237,
    242
Festival d'Avignon: 114
Festivals: 496–497. *See also specific
    festivals*
Fondation Angladon-Dubrujeaud
    (Avignon): 115, 124
Fondation Maeght (St-Paul-de-
    Vence): 422, 425
Fondation Van Gogh (Arles):
    71–72

Fontaine-de-Vaucluse: 201–202
Fontvieille: sleeping, 82–83
Fontvieille (Monaco): 376, 381,
    384
Food: *See* Cheeses; Chocolates;
    Cuisine; Eating; Markets; Olive
    oils; Tapenade; Truffles
Fort Carré (Antibes): 397, 401–402
Fort de Buoux: 227
Forum Square (Arles): 66, 68–69,
    75; eating, 83–84
Fragonard Perfume (Eze-le-
    Village), 369; (Grasse), 433–434
Fragonard (Jean-Honoré) Villa
    (Grasse): 434
François I: 246, 456
French language: *See* Language
French Riviera: *See* Riviera
Frioul Islands: 247

G
Gallimard (Eze-le-Village): 369
Gambling: *See* Casinos
Gauguin, Paul: 75–76
Gignac: 225
Gigondas: 57, 184–185; eating,
    189; sleeping, 186
Gîtes: 28–29
Glanum (St. Rémy): 97, 100
Glass Museum (Gordes): 218
Gordes: 216, 218; biking, 194;
    market, 194; sleeping, 214–215
Gorges de l'Ardèche: 191
Gorges du Loup: 423, 431
Gorges du Verdon: *See* Grand
    Canyon du Verdon
Goult: 210
Gourdon: 423, 431
Grand Canyon du Verdon:
    435–441; driving tour, 437–440;
    map, 436
Grande Corniche: 358–359, 370–371
Grand Prix of Monaco: 281, 307,
    376, 386
Grasse: 423, 431–434
Great Maritime Port of Marseille:
    245
Grenoble: 306
Gréolières: 430
Gréoux-les-Bains: 440
Grignan: 185

Guidebooks: 492, 494; Rick Steves, 491–492

Gypsies (Roma) of Stes-Maries-de-la-Mer: 107

H

Haribo: 155

Herbes de Provence: 448

High Corniche: 358–359, 370–371

Hiking: Antibes, 402–403; Ardèche Gorges, 191; the Calanques, 255; the Camargue, 105, 107; Cap d'Antibes, 402–403; Cap Ferrat, 360, 362, 363–365; Colorado Provençal, 225; Eze-Bord-de-Mer, 369–370; Gigondas, 184; Grand Canyon du Verdon, 438; Isle-sur-la-Sorgue, 196–197, 200; Joucas, 214; La Turbie, 371; Monaco, 381; St-Tropez, 417, 418; Vaison la Romaine, 172; Villefranche, 353–354, 360

Hill towns: 178–179; of Luberon, 192–231

History: 454–459

Holidays: 27, 496–497

Horseback riding, in the Camargue: 107

Hostels: overview, 27–28, 473. *See also specific destinations*

Hot-air ballooning: 210

Hôtel Carlton (Cannes): 410–411

Hôtel la Mirande (Avignon): 122, 132

Hôtel Negresco (Nice): 306, 312, 322, 326

Hotels: 22–26; chains, 26, 472–473; reservations, 29–31; reservations form, 502. *See also* Sleeping; *and specific destinations*

I

Iles du Frioul: 247

Immigration: 234, 235, 459, 460

Inland Riviera: 421–441; map, 423

International Museum of Perfume (Grasse): 433

Internet access: 473–474. *See also specific destinations*

Isle-sur-la-Sorgue: 194–204; map, 198–199; market, 194, 195, 200

J

Jardin de la Fontaine (Nîmes): 146

Jardin d'Eté (Arles): 75

Jardin du Rochers des Doms (Avignon): 115, 116, 118–119

Jardin Exotique (Monaco): 382, 387

Jardins d'Eze: 369

Joan of Arc: 456, 458

John, Elton: 373

Joucas: 214–215

Juan-les-Pins: 403

K

Kayaking: *See* Canoeing and kayaking

Kids, traveling with: 442–446; packing tips, 444–445; planning tips, 444, 445; top sights and activities, 445–446

L

La Canebière (Marseille): 234, 239, 242–243

La Capelière: 106

Lac de Ste-Croix: 439

La Charité Museum (Marseille): 237, 244

La Ciotat: 255–256

La Citadelle (St-Tropez): 418

La Commune Libre du Safranier (Antibes): 399

Lacoste: 221–222; eating, 222; market, 194

La Côte d'Azur: *See* Riviera

La Croisette (Cannes): 410–411

La Digue de la Mer: 106

La Fare: 182–183

Lagnes: 201

Langlois Drawbridge: 77

Language: 464–465; picnic terms, 33; restaurant phrases, 504; road signs, 485, 488; shopping phrases, 451; survival phrases, 503; wine terms, 54, 57

La Provence Profonde: 224–227

La Rotonde (Aix): 266

La Route des Crêtes: 256

La Trophée des Alpes: 370–371

La Turbie: 370–371

Lavender: 12, 189–190, 303; about, 188; museum (Coustellet), 218

Le Bar-sur-Loup: 422, 423, 431
Le Bassin (Isle-sur-la-Sorgue): 200
Le Chêne: eating, 212, 214
Le Col de la Chaîne Mountain
    Pass: 181–182
Le Colorado Provençal: 225
Le Crestet: 172, 180–181; eating,
    187–188
Léger, Fernand: 404, 425
Le Jardin du Rochers des Doms
    (Avignon): 115, 116, 118–119
Le Mistral: 59, 192
Le Panier District (Marseille):
    234, 243–245
Le Petit Train: *See* Petit Train
Les Alyscamps: 75
Les Arcs-sur-Argens: 58
Les Baux: 89–96; eating, 96; map,
    92; sights, 91–94; sleeping,
    95–96
Les Baux Castle: 91–93
Les Halles (Avignon): 110, 123
Le Suquet (Cannes): 412
Louis XIV: 68, 198, 243, 267, 269,
    303, 326, 334, 369, 370, 384,
    456
Lourmarin: 229–231; market, 194,
    230
Low Corniche: 358–359, 372–375
Luberon hill towns: 192–231;
    map, 196–197; markets, 194;
    transportation, 193–194

M
Maeght Foundation (St-Paul-de-
    Vence): 422, 425
Mail: *See* Post offices
Maison Carrée (Nîmes): 144–145
Malaucène: 181; market, 160, 186;
    sleeping, 186
Manville Mansion City Hall (Les
    Baux): 93
Maps: about, 492. *See also* Map
    Index
Marie Antoinette: 457
Marineland (Biot): 403
Marine Museum (Marseille): 237,
    242
Markets: 449–452; key shopping
    phrases, 451; Aix-en-Provence,
    261, 268–269; Antibes, 398,

401; Arles, 64, 77; Avignon,
    110, 123; Bedoin, 160, 190;
    Bonnieux, 194, 219–220;
    Carpentras, 160, 452; Cassis,
    251; Châteauneuf, 165; Côtes
    du Rhône, 160; Coustellet,
    194; Isle-sur-la-Sorgue, 194,
    195, 200; Lourmarin, 194, 230;
    Luberon, 194; Malaucène, 160,
    186; Marseille, 237, 239, 242;
    Nice, 334–335; Nîmes, 143–144;
    Nyons, 160, 190; Roussillon,
    194; St. Rémy, 97, 103; Sault,
    194; Uzès, 154; Vacqueyras,
    160, 184; Vaison la Romaine,
    169, 171–172; Vence, 426;
    Villefranche, 348–349
Marseille: 232–249; eating,
    248–249; information, 236;
    maps, 233, 240–241; sights, 237,
    239–247; sleeping, 247–248;
    tours, 238–239; transportation,
    236–238, 249
Marseille City Hall: 243–244
Marseille History Museum: 237,
    242–243
Marseille Marine Museum: 237,
    242
Masséna Museum (Nice): 304
Massif de l'Esterel: 410
Massif des Calanques: 254–256
Matisse, Henri: 335, 418;
    biographical sketch, 300–301;
    Chapel of the Rosary (Vence),
    422, 427; Museum (Nice), 296,
    299–302
Mayle, Peter: 192, 204–205, 222,
    228, 229, 494, 495
Mazarin Quarter (Aix): 260,
    267–268; eating, 275
Medical help: 13, 471
Ménerbes: 222
Menton: 390
Metric conversions: 498
Métro (Marseille): 236
Middle Corniche: 358–359
Mistral: 59, 192
Mistral, Frédéric: 68
Mobile phones: 467, 470
Modern and Contemporary Art
    Museum (Nice): 296, 302–303

Molinard Perfume Museum (Nice): 296, 303

Monaco: 376–390; information, 380; layout of, 377, 380; map, 378–379; sights, 383–388; sleeping and eating, 388–389; transportation, 380–383, 389–390; walking tour, 383–387

Monaco Cathedral: 382, 385

Monaco Grand Prix: 281, 307, 376, 386

Monaco Post Office: 382, 384

Monasteries: about, 220–221; St. Paul Monastery and Hospital (St. Rémy), 76–77, 100–101

Monet, Claude: 303, 457

Money: 14–19; budgeting, 6–7

Money-saving tips: 14

Mont Aiguille: 306

Mont-Alban Fort (Villefranche): 354

Monte Carlo: 377, 380, 387–388

Monte Carlo Story (film): 382, 386–387

Montmajour Abbey: 74–75, 96

Mont Rouge: 206, 207

Mont Ventoux: 189–190

Moustiers-Ste-Marie: 439–440; eating, 441; sleeping, 441

Movies, recommended: 495; for children, 444

Moyenne Corniche: 358–359

Murs: 214

Muscats: 183–184

Musée Archéologique (Nice): 304

Musée Arlaten (Arles): 66, 72

Musée Calvet (Avignon): 115, 124

Musée Camarguais (Stes-Maries): 106

Musée d'Art Moderne et d'Art Contemporain (Nice): 296, 302–303

Musée de la Lavande (Coustellet): 218

Musée de la Mode (Marseille): 237, 242

Musée de l'Annonciade (St-Tropez): 418

Musée de l'Arles et de la Provence Antiques: 65–68

Musée de l'Histoire du Verre (Gordes): 218

Musée des Beaux-Arts (Nice): 296, 303

Musée d'Histoire de Marseille: 237, 242–243

Musée d'Histoire et d'Archéologie (Antibes): 401

Musée du Bonbon (Uzès): 155

Musée du Jouet et de la Poupée Ancienne (Isle-sur-la-Sorgue): 200

Musée du Petit Palais (Avignon): 115, 118

Musée du Vin (Châteauneuf): 166

Musée Etienne de St. Jean (Aix): 270

Musée Granet (Aix): 267–268

Musée International de la Parfumerie (Grasse): 433

Musée Masséna (Nice): 304

Musée Matisse (Nice): 296, 299–302

Musée National Marc Chagall (Nice): 298–299, 337–345; map, 339; self-guided tour, 338–345

Musée Océanographique (Monaco): 382, 385–386

Musée Picasso (Antibes): 399–401

Musée Provençal du Costume et du Bijou (Grasse): 434

Musée Réattu (Arles): 66, 72

Musée Renoir (Cagnes-sur-Mer): 403–404

Musée Yves Brayer (Les Baux): 93

Museum of Old Nîmes: 144

Museum of Santons (Les Baux): 94

N

Napoleon Bonaparte: 457, 458

Napoleon Collection (Monaco): 382, 384–385

Newspapers: 14

Nice: 286–345, 373; eating, 316–322; helpful hints, 290–291; information, 287; layout of, 286; maps, 288–289, 308–309, 314–315, 318–319; nightlife, 306–307; sights, 297–306, 325–345; sleeping, 307–316; tours, 295–297; transportation, 287, 290, 291–294, 322–324; walking tours, 325–336. *See also* Old Nice; Promenade des Anglais

Nice Archaeological Museum: 304

Nice Carnival: 281

Nice Fine Arts Museum: 296, 303

Nice Modern and Contemporary
Art Museum: 296, 302–303

Nice Narrow-Gauge Train:
305–306

Nice Opera House: 333–334

Nîmes: 137–149; eating, 148–149;
map, 140–141; sights, 139,
142–147; sleeping, 147–148

Nîmes Arena: 139, 142–143

Nîmes Cathedral: 144

Nîmes Old City: 137, 143–144

North African immigrants
(immigration): 234, 235, 459,
460

Notre-Dame d'Alidon Church
(Oppède-le-Vieux): 223

Notre-Dame de la Garde
(Marseille): 237, 246

Notre-Dame-de-l'Annonciation
(Nice): 335

Notre-Dame de Nazareth
Cathedral (Vaison): 171

Notre-Dame des Anges (Isle-sur-
la-Sorgue): 197–198

Notre-Dame de Sénanque Abbey:
216–217

Nyons: 190; market, 160, 190

O

Ochre Cliffs (Roussillon): 209–210

Ochre Conservatory (Roussillon):
210

Old Grasse: 434

Old Nice: 286, 296, 298; eating,
317, 320; map, 332–334;
walking tour, 330–336

Old Nîmes: 137, 143–144

Old Port (Antibes): 397–398

Old Port (Marseille): 234, 236,
237, 243, 245, 246; eating,
248–249

Olive-Huiles du Monde (St.
Rémy): 103

Olive oils: 103, 218, 320, 332–333,
448

Oppède-le-Vieux: 222–223

Orange: 160–165; map, 162

Ouvèze River: 167, 171, 172, 191

P

Packing tips (checklist): 501; for
children, 444–445

Palace of the Popes (Avignon):
115, 120–121

Palais des Papes (Avignon): 115,
120–121

Palais Lascaris (Nice): 336

Palais Princier (Monaco): 382,
384–385

Panier District (Marseille): 234,
243–245

Paradou: sleeping, 96

Parc de la Mer (Biot): 403

Parc du Rochers des Doms
(Avignon): 115, 116, 118–119

Parc Naturel Régional du Verdon:
See Grand Canyon du Verdon

Passports: 12, 13

Perfume: about, 432; Fragonard
Perfume (Eze-le-Village), 369;
Fragonard Perfume (Grasse),
433–434; International Museum
of Perfume (Grasse), 433;
Molinard Perfume Museum
(Nice), 296, 303

Pétanque: See Boules

Petit Palace Museum (Avignon):
115, 118

Petit Train: Aix, 266; Antibes,
397; Arles, 65; Marseille, 239;
Nice, 305–306; Villefranche,
352

Philip the Fair Tower (Villeneuve):
115, 125

Phones: *See* Telephones

Picasso, Pablo: 72, 124, 404;
Museum (Antibes), 399–401

Picnics: 32–34; glossary of terms,
33. *See also* Markets

Place Audiberti (Antibes): 401

Place aux Herbes (Nîmes): 143–
144, 148

Place Crillon (Avignon): 131

Place d'Albertas (Aix): 268

Place de la République (Arles): 69

Place de l'Horloge (Avignon): 117

Place de l'Hôtel de Ville (Aix):
269–270

Place des Châtaignes (Avignon):
122

Place des Corps-Saints (Avignon): 131

Place du Centenaire (Eze-le-Village): 368

Place du Forum (Arles): 66, 68–69, 75; eating, 83–84

Place du Marché (Nîmes): 143, 148

Place du Palais (Avignon): 117–118

Place du Palais (Monaco): 383–384

Place Lamartine (Arles): 64, 73, 77

Place Masséna (Nice): 331

Place Nationale (Antibes): 401

Place Richelme (Aix): 268–269

Place Rossetti (Nice): 336

Plage de Paloma (Cap Ferrat): 364

Plage de Passable (Cap Ferrat): 363, 364–365

Plage du Bestouan (Cassis): 257–258

Plage le Goéland (Cannes): 410

Politics: 459, 461

Pont d'Arc: 191

Pont d'Artuby: 438

Pont d'Avignon: 115, 119–120

Pont du Gard: 149–154; aqueduct, 149, 152–154; map, 150

Pont du Gard Museum: 152

Pont-du-Loup: 423, 430

Pont St. Bénezet (Avignon): 115, 119–120

Pont St. Julien: 219

Popes Palace (Avignon): 115, 120–121

Port Grimaud: 419

Post offices: 474; Monaco, 382, 384

Pottery: 191, 404, 448

Prince's Palace (Monaco): 382, 384–385

Promenade des Anglais (Nice): 296, 297–298; eating, 321–322; guided walks, 295–296; walking tour, 325–329

Provence: 43–275; cuisine, 51–53; map, 44; planning tips, 43–45; top 10 towns and villages, 47; tours, 46–48; transportation, 45–46; wines, 53–59. See also specific destinations

Puyméras: eating, 187

Q

Quai des Etats-Unis (Nice): 328

R

Railpasses: 476–479, 493

Rasteau: 58

Réattu Museum (Arles): 66, 72

Renoir (Pierre Auguste) Museum (Cagnes-sur-Mer): 403–404

Rental properties: 28–29

Restaurants: See Eating; and specific destinations

Rhône River: 115, 118–120; cruises, 114, 116

Riviera: 278–441; art scene, 282–283; cuisine, 283–285; helpful hints, 280–281; inland, 421–441; maps, 279, 423; planning tips, 279–280; top art sights, 283; tours, 281; transportation, 281–282, 292–295, 421. See also specific destinations

Roman sites (ancient Romans): 454; Aix-en-Provence, 265; Arles, 60, 65–71; Barbegal aqueduct, 96–97; La Trophée des Alpes, 370–371; Nice, 299, 304; Nîmes, 137, 139, 142–143, 144–147; Orange, 160, 161–164; Pont du Gard, 149, 152–154; Pont St. Julien, 219; Provence, 48–51; top 10 sights, 49; St. Rémy, 97, 100; Vaison la Romaine, 170–171

Roma (Gypsies) of Stes-Maries-de-la-Mer: 107

Rosary Chapel (Vence): 422, 427

Roussillon: 205–214; eating, 212, 214; map, 206; market, 194; sights, 207–210; sleeping, 211–212

Route des Crêtes: 256

Rue Biscarra (Nice): 320–321

Rue de la Poissonnerie (Nice): 335

Rue des Teinturiers (Avignon): 123, 131–132

Rue Droite (Nice): 335–336

Rue Obscura (Villefranche): 353

Rue St. François de Paule (Nice): 332–333

Russian Cathedral (Nice): 296, 304–305

Rustrel: 225

RV rentals: 472

S

Sablet: 58, 185
Sade, Marquis de: 221–222
Saignon: 226–227
St. Bénezet Bridge (Avignon): 115, 119–120
Ste. Marguerite Island: 410, 413
Sainte-Cécile-les-Vignes: market, 160
Stes-Maries-de-la-Mer: 105–107
St. Hilaire Abbey: 222
St. Honorat Island: 410, 413
St. Jalles: 190–191
St. Jean-Cap-Ferrat: 363–365, 373–374; eating, 365–366; sleeping, 365
St-Jeannet: 429, 430
St. Julien Bridge: 219
St. Laurent Church (Marseille): 245
St. Marcellin-lès-Vaison: 172
St. Michael's Church (Villefranche): 353
St. Michel Bridge: 191
St-Paul-de-Vence: 422, 424–425
St. Paul Monastery and Hospital (St. Rémy): 76–77, 100–101
St. Pierre Chapel (Villefranche): 352–353
St. Pierre Church (Avignon): 122
St. Rémy-de-Provence: 97–104; eating, 103–104; map, 99; sights, 98, 100–101; sleeping, 101–103
St. Réparate Cathedral (Nice): 336
St-Saturnin-lès-Apt: 224–225; market, 194
Saint-Sauveur Cathedral (Aix): 271
St-Tropez: 414–420; eating, 420; map, 416–417; sights, 415–419; sleeping, 419–420
St. Trophime Church (Arles): 66, 69–70
St. Vincent Church (Les Baux): 93–94
Salin de Giraud: 105–106
Santons: 270, 448; museum (Les Baux), 94
Sarragan Caves: 94
Sault: 190; market, 194
Seasons: 10–12

Séguret: 176, 178–180; eating, 188–189; sleeping, 186
Sentier Touristique Piétonnier de Tirepoil: 402–403
Shopping: 13–14, 447–453; budgeting, 7; Cannes, 412–413; hours, 13; key phrases, 451; VAT refunds, 18–19; what to buy, 447–448. *See also* Fashion; Markets
Sightseeing: best two-week trips, 8–11; budgeting, 7; general tips, 20–21; priorities, 8–9; top kid-friendly sights, 445–446. *See also specific sights and destinations*
Signac, Paul: 414, 418
Sleep code: 25
Sleeping: 21–31; budgeting, 7; with children, 442; reservations, 29–31; reservation form, 502. *See also specific destinations*
Soccer: 238
Sorgue River: 124, 194–195, 198–201; canoeing, 201
Special events: 496–497. *See also specific events*
Sports: *See Boules;* Bullfights; Soccer
Spring of Nemo (Nîmes): 145–146
Stamps, in Monaco: 382, 384
State Department, U.S.: 471
Suzette: 182; eating, 189; sleeping near, 187
Synagogue (Avignon): 115, 123

T

Tapenade: 51, 200, 448
Tavel: 58, 130
Taxes: VAT refunds, 18–19
Taxis: 474; tipping, 18. *See also specific destinations*
Telephone numbers, useful: 470–473
Telephones: 29, 465–470
Temperatures, average monthly: 499
Temple of Diana (Nîmes): 146
TGV: *See* Train travel
Theater (théâtre antique): Arles, 66, 70–71; Orange, 161–164

INDEX

Three Corniches: 358–359, 370–375
Time zones: 13
Tipping: 17–18
Tour guides: tipping, 18. *See also specific destinations*
Tourist information: 463–464. *See also specific destinations*
Tourist Train: *See* Petit Train
Tour Philippe-le-Bel (Villeneuve): 115, 125
Tourrettes-sur-Loup: 422, 430
Tours: Rick Steves, 493. *See also specific destinations*
Tower of Philip the Fair (Villeneuve): 115, 125
Toy and Doll Museum (Isle-sur-la-Sorgue): 200
Train travel: 475–482; best two-week trip, 10–11; general tips, 480–482; Luberon, 193; map, 476–477; Provence, 45–46; Riviera, 281–282, 292–293; seat reservations, 13, 480; terms and abbreviations, 475. *See also specific destinations*
Transportation: 474–491; budgeting, 7; map, 476–477. *See also specific destinations*
Travel advisories: 471
Travel insurance: 12
Travel smarts: 6
Trinquetaille Bridge (Arles): 77
Trophée des Alpes: 370–371
Truffles: 103, 222, 452

U
Uzès: 154–156

V
Vacqueyras: 184; market, 160, 184
Vaison la Romaine: 167–175; eating, 174–175, 187; map, 168; sights, 170–172; sleeping, 172–174, 185–187
Vallauris: 401, 404
Vallon Pont d'Arc: 191
Valréas: 188
Van Gogh, Vincent: 96, 124; in Arles, 68–69, 71–76; in St. Rémy, 76–77, 97, 100–101

VAT refunds: 18–19
Velleron: 201
Vence: 422, 426–429
Vercingétorix: 456
Verdon Gorge: *See* Grand Canyon du Verdon
Veynes: 306
Viens: 226
Villa Ephrussi de Rothschild (Cap Ferrat): 362
Village des Bories: 217–218
Villa Jean-Honoré Fragonard (Grasse): 434
Villa Kérylos: 366
Villedieu: 172, 187; eating, 189
Villefranche-sur-Mer: 346–358, 373; eating, 356–357; map, 350–351; sights, 352–354; sleeping, 354–356; transportation, 348, 357–358
Villeneuve-lès-Avignon: 125
Vineyards: *See* Wine and vineyards
Visitor information: 463–464. *See also specific destinations*
VoIP (Voice over Internet Protocol): 470

W
Waterwheels: 124, 198–199
Weather: 10–12, 499
Wine and vineyards: 37–38; Aix-en-Provence, 264; Cassis, 59, 251; Châteauneuf-du-Pape, 57, 165–166; Côtes du Rhône, 56–58, 165–166, 172, 176–185; key terms, 54, 57; Provence, 53–59; guided tours, 47–48
Wine Museum (Châteauneuf): 166
World War I: 209, 328, 434
World War II: 245, 269, 328, 353, 416

Y
Yves Brayer Museum (Les Baux): 93

Z
Zidane, Zinédine: 238, 457

INDEX

MAP INDEX

COLOR MAPS
Provence & the French Riviera:
  ii-iii

INTRODUCTION
Top Destinations in Provence &
  the French Riviera: viii
Provence & the French Riviera: 2
Best Two-Week Trip by Car: 9

PROVENCE
Provence: 44

ARLES
Arles: 62
Arles Hotels & Restaurants: 80

NEAR ARLES
Near Arles: 89
Les Baux: 92
St. Rémy Area: 99
Restaurants in St. Rémy's Old
  Town: 102

AVIGNON
Avignon: 112
Avignon Hotels & Restaurants:
  126

NEAR AVIGNON
Near Avignon: 136
Nîmes: 140
Pont du Gard: 150

**ORANGE AND THE COTES
  DU RHONE**
The Côtes du Rhône Area: 158
Orange: 162
Vaison la Romaine: 168
Côtes du Rhône Driving Tour: 177

**HILL TOWNS OF THE
  LUBERON**
The Luberon: 196
Isle-sur-la-Sorgue: 198
Roussillon: 206

**MARSEILLE, CASSIS, AND
  AIX-EN-PROVENCE**
Marseille, Cassis & Aix-en-
  Provence: 233
Marseille: 240
Cassis: 252
Aix-en-Provence: 262

THE FRENCH RIVIERA
The French Riviera: 279

NICE
Nice: 288
Nice Hotels: 308
Old Nice Hotels & Restaurants:
  314
Nice Restaurants: 318

OLD NICE WALK
Old Nice Walk: 332

CHAGALL MUSEUM TOUR
Chagall Museum: 339

**VILLEFRANCHE-SUR-MER,
  CAP FERRAT, AND EZE-
  LE-VILLAGE**
Between Nice and Monaco: 347
Villefranche-sur-Mer: 350
Cap Ferrat: 361

MONACO
Monaco: 378

**ANTIBES, CANNES, AND
  ST-TROPEZ**
Antibes Area: 393
Antibes: 394
St-Tropez: 416

INLAND RIVIERA
Inland Riviera: 423
Le Grand Canyon du Verdon: 436

FRANCE: PAST AND PRESENT

Typical Church Architecture: 455

APPENDIX

Public Transportation in Provence
   & the French Riviera: 476
French Railpasses: 478
Driving in Provence & the French
   Riviera: Distance & Time: 486

Free mobile app (and podcast)

With the **Rick Steves Audio Europe** app, your iPhone or smartphone becomes a powerful travel tool.

This exciting app organizes Rick's entire audio library by country—giving you a playlist of all his audio walking tours, radio interviews, and travel tips for wherever you're going in Europe.

Let the experts Rick interviews enrich your understanding. Let Rick's self-guided tours amplify your guidebook. With Rick in your ear, Europe gets even better.

Thanks Facebook fans for submitting photos while on location! From top: John Kuijper in Florence, Brenda Mamer with her mother in Rome, Angel Capobianco in London, and Alyssa Passey with her friend in Paris.

Find out more at ricksteves.com/audioeurope

Join a Rick Steves tour

Enjoy Europe's warmest welcome...

with the flexibility and friendship of a small group

getting to know Rick's favorite places and people.

It all starts with our free tour catalog and DVD.

Great guides, small groups, no grumps.

▸ Plan Your Trip

Browse thousands of articles and a wealth of money-saving tips for planning your dream trip. You'll find up-to-date information on Europe's best destinations, packing smart, getting around, finding rooms, staying healthy, avoiding scams and more.

▸ Eurail Passes

Find out, step-by-step, if a railpass makes sense for your trip—and how to avoid buying more than you need. Get a bunch of free extras!

▸ Graffiti Wall & Travelers' Helpline

Learn, ask, share—our online community of savvy travelers is a great resource for first-time travelers to Europe, as well as seasoned pros.

Rick Steves' Europe Through the Back Door, Inc.

turn your travel dreams into affordable reality

▸ Free Audio Tours & Travel Newsletter

Get your nose out of this guide book and focus on what you'll be seeing with Rick's free audio tours of the greatest sights in Paris, London, Rome, Florence and Venice.

Subscribe to our free Travel News e-newsletter, and get monthly articles from Rick on what's happening in Europe.

▸ Great Gear from Rick's Travel Store

Pack light and right—on a budget—with Rick's custom-designed carry-on bags, roll-aboards, day packs, travel accessories, guidebooks, journals, maps and DVDs of his TV shows.

130 Fourth Avenue North, PO Box 2009 • Edmonds, WA 98020 USA
Phone: (425) 771-8303 • Fax: (425) 771-0833 • www.ricksteves.com

Rick Steves®

www.ricksteves.com

EUROPE GUIDES

Best of Europe
Eastern Europe
Europe Through the Back Door

COUNTRY GUIDES

Croatia & Slovenia
England
France
Germany
Great Britain
Ireland
Italy
Portugal
Scandinavia
Spain
Switzerland

CITY & REGIONAL GUIDES

Amsterdam, Bruges & Brussels
Athens & the Peloponnese
Budapest
Florence & Tuscany
Istanbul
London
Paris
Prague & the Czech Republic
Provence & the French Riviera
Rome
Venice
Vienna, Salzburg & Tirol

SNAPSHOT GUIDES

Barcelona
Berlin
Bruges & Brussels
Copenhagen & the Best of
   Denmark
Dublin
Dubrovnik
Hill Towns of Central Italy
Italy's Cinque Terre
Krakow, Warsaw & Gdansk
Lisbon
Madrid & Toledo
Munich, Bavaria & Salzburg
Naples & the Amalfi Coast
Northern Ireland
Norway
Scotland
Sevilla, Granada & Southern Spain
Stockholm

TRAVEL CULTURE

Europe 101
European Christmas
Postcards from Europe
Travel as a Political Act

Rick Steves guidebooks are published by Avalon Travel,
a member of the Perseus Books Group.

NOW AVAILABLE: eBOOKS, APPS, DVDs, & BLU-RAY

eBOOKS

Most guides available as eBooks from Amazon, Barnes & Noble, Borders, Apple iBook and Sony eReader, beginning January 2011

RICK STEVES' EUROPE DVDs

Austria & the Alps
Eastern Europe, Israel & Egypt
England & Wales
European Travel Skills & Specials
France
Germany, Benelux & More
Greece & Turkey
Iran
Ireland & Scotland
Italy's Cities
Italy's Countryside
Rick Steves' European Christmas
Scandinavia
Spain & Portugal

BLU-RAY

Celtic Charms
Eastern Europe Favorites
European Christmas
Italy Through the Back Door
Surprising Cities of Europe

PHRASE BOOKS & DICTIONARIES

French
French, Italian & German
German
Italian
Portuguese
Spanish

JOURNALS

Rick Steves' Pocket Travel Journal
Rick Steves' Travel Journal

APPS

Rick Steves' Ancient Rome Tour
Rick Steves' Historic Paris Walk
Rick Steves' Louvre Tour
Rick Steves' Orsay Museum Tour
Rick Steves' St. Peter's Basilica Tour
Rick Steves' Versailles

PLANNING MAPS

Britain, Ireland & London
Europe
France & Paris
Germany, Austria & Switzerland
Ireland
Italy
Spain & Portugal

Credits

Contributor
Gene Openshaw

Gene is the co-author of seven Rick Steves books. For this book he wrote material on Europe's art, history, and contemporary culture. When not traveling, Gene enjoys composing music, recovering from his 1973 trip to Europe with Rick, and living everyday life with his daughter.

Rick Steves' Guidebook Series

Country Guides

Rick Steves' Best of Europe
Rick Steves' Croatia & Slovenia
Rick Steves' Eastern Europe
Rick Steves' England
Rick Steves' France
Rick Steves' Germany
Rick Steves' Great Britain
Rick Steves' Ireland
Rick Steves' Italy
Rick Steves' Portugal
Rick Steves' Scandinavia
Rick Steves' Spain
Rick Steves' Switzerland

City and Regional Guides

Rick Steves' Amsterdam, Bruges & Brussels
Rick Steves' Athens & the Peloponnese
Rick Steves' Budapest
Rick Steves' Florence & Tuscany
Rick Steves' Istanbul
Rick Steves' London
Rick Steves' Paris
Rick Steves' Prague & the Czech Republic
Rick Steves' Provence & the French Riviera
Rick Steves' Rome
Rick Steves' Venice
Rick Steves' Vienna, Salzburg & Tirol

Rick Steves' Phrase Books

French
French/Italian/German
German
Italian
Portuguese
Spanish

Snapshot Guides

Excerpted chapters from country guides, such as Rick Steves' Snapshot Barcelona, Rick Steves' Snapshot Scotland, and Rick Steves' Snapshot Hill Towns of Central Italy.

Pocket Guides (new in 2011)

Condensed, pocket-size, full-color guides to Europe's top cities: Paris, London, and Rome.

Other Books

Rick Steves' Europe 101: History and Art for the Traveler
Rick Steves' Europe Through the Back Door
Rick Steves' European Christmas
Rick Steves' Postcards from Europe
Rick Steves' Travel as a Political Act

Avalon Travel
a member of the Perseus Books Group
1700 Fourth Street
Berkeley, CA 94710

Text © 2011, 2010, 2009, 2008, 2007 by Rick Steves
Maps © 2011, 2010, 2009, 2008 by Europe Through the Back Door
Printed in the United States of America by Worzalla
First printing October 2010

Portions of this book were originally published in *Rick Steves' France, Belgium & the Netherlands* © 2002, 2001, 2000, 1999, 1998 by Rick Steves and Steve Smith; and in *Rick Steves' France* © 2010, 2009, 2008, 2007, 2006, 2005, 2004, 2003 by Rick Steves and Steve Smith.

ISBN 978-1-59880-662-5
ISSN 1546-2749

For the latest on Rick's lectures, guidebooks, tours, public radio show, and public-television series, contact Europe Through the Back Door, Box 2009, Edmonds, WA 98020, tel. 425/771-8303, fax 425/771-0833, www.ricksteves.com, rick@ricksteves.com.

Europe Through the Back Door Reviewing Editors: Jennifer Madison Davis, Cameron Hewitt
ETBD Editors: Tom Griffin, Cathy McDonald, Sarah McCormic, Cathy Lu, Gretchen Strauch
ETBD Managing Editor: Risa Laib
Avalon Travel Senior Editor and Series Manager: Madhu Prasher
Avalon Travel Project Editor: Kelly Lydick
Copy Editor: Jennifer Malnick
Proofreader: Patrick Collins
Indexer: Stephen Callahan
Production & Typesetting: McGuire Barber Design
Cover Design: Kimberly Glyder Design
Graphic Content Director: Laura VanDeventer
Maps & Graphics: David C. Hoerlein, Lauren Mills, Laura VanDeventer, Barb Geisler, Mike Morgenfeld, Brice Ticen
Front Cover Photo: Lourmarin © Steve Smith
Front Matter Color Photos: page i Lavender © Dominic Bonuccelli; page iv, Côtes du Rhône Wine Loop © Steve Smith
Photography: Steve Smith, Gene Openshaw, David C. Hoerlein, Rick Steves, Cameron Hewitt, Mike Potter, Robyn Cronin, Dominic Bonuccelli, Dorian Yates, Rich Earl